Crime *and*

Punishment

in Latin

America

Crime *and* Punishment *in* Latin America

Law and Society since Late Colonial Times

Edited by RICARDO D. SALVATORE,

CARLOS AGUIRRE, *and*

GILBERT M. JOSEPH

DUKE UNIVERSITY PRESS

Durham & London

2001

© 2001 DUKE UNIVERSITY PRESS
All rights reserved
Printed in the United States of America
on acid-free paper ∞ Designed by Amy Ruth Buchanan
Typeset in Carter & Cone Galliard by Keystone Typesetting, Inc.
Library of Congress Cataloging-in-Publication Data appear
on the last printed page of this book.

Contents

List of Tables and Figures, *vii*

GILBERT M. JOSEPH   Preface, *ix*

Acknowledgments, *xxiii*

Introduction

CARLOS AGUIRRE and RICARDO D. SALVATORE   Writing the History of Law, Crime, and Punishment in Latin America, *1*

PART I

Legal Mediations: State, Society, and the Conflictive Nature of Law and Justice

CHARLES F. WALKER   Crime in the Time of the Great Fear: Indians and the State in the Peruvian Southern Andes, 1780–1820, *35*

ARLENE J. DÍAZ   Women, Order, and Progress in Guzmán Blanco's Venezuela, 1870–1888, *56*

JUAN MANUEL R. PALACIO   Judges, Lawyers, and Farmers: Uses of Justice and the Circulation of Law in Rural Buenos Aires, 1900–1940, *83*

LUIS A. GONZÁLEZ   Work, Property, and the Negotiation of Rights in the Brazilian Cane Fields: Campos, Rio de Janeiro, 1930–1950, *113*

PART II
The Social and Cultural Construction of Crime

CRISTINA RIVERA-GARZA The Criminalization of the Syphilitic Body: Prostitutes, Health Crimes, and Society in Mexico City, 1867–1930, *147*

DAIN BORGES Healing and Mischief: Witchcraft in Brazilian Law and Literature, 1890–1922 *181*

KRISTIN RUGGIERO Passion, Perversity, and the Pace of Justice in Argentina at the Turn of the Last Century, *211*

PABLO PICCATO *Cuidado con los Rateros*: The Making of Criminals in Modern Mexico City, *233*

PART III
Contested Meanings of Punishment

DIANA PATON The Penalties of Freedom: Punishment in Post-emancipation Jamaica, *275*

RICARDO D. SALVATORE Death and Liberalism: Capital Punishment after the Fall of Rosas, *308*

CARLOS AGUIRRE Disputed Views of Incarceration in Lima, 1890–1930: The Prisoners' Agenda for Prison Reform, *342*

DONNA J. GUY Girls in Prison: The Role of the Buenos Aires Casa Correccional de Mujeres as an Institution for Child Rescue, 1890–1940, *369*

LILA M. CAIMARI Remembering Freedom: Life as Seen From the Prison Cell (Buenos Aires Province, 1930–1950), *391*

Afterword

DOUGLAS HAY Law and Society in Comparative Perspective, *415*

Contributors, *431*

Index, *435*

List of Tables and Figures

Tables

1 Agrarian Structure of Coronel Dorrego, 1895–1947, *86*

2 Coronel Dorrego: Wheat Prices and Number of Claims, 1920–1940, *88*

3 Judicial Cases in the County of Coronel Dorrego According to Type, Plaintiffs, and Outcome (Percentages), *89*

4 Main Sugar-Producing Counties, Brazil, 1929/30–1933/34 (in 60-kilogram bags), *115*

5 Claims by State, 1940–1950, *133*

6 Sentenced and Arrested for Theft, Federal District, 1871–1939, *238*

7 Arrested for Theft, Mexico City, 1885–1895, *239*

8 Arrested for Theft, Mexico City, 1922–1926, *240*

9 Sentenced and Arrested for Theft, Federal District, Average per Period, *241*

10 Sentenced and Arrested for Theft, Federal District per 100,000 Population, Average per Period, *242*

11 Campaign against Rateros, Trades Stated by Suspects, *251*

Figures

1 Inmates, Women's Jail, 1898–1914, *375*

2 Ages of Minor Prisoners, 1889–1903, *376*

3 Inmates, Women's Jail, 1915–1923, *377*

4 Ages of Girls in Prison, 1915–1923, *378*

5 Inmates, Women's Jail, 1923–1929, *386*

Preface

GILBERT M. JOSEPH

For the generation of Latin Americans who witnessed their friends and neighbors arrested without a warrant, tried in military tribunals without benefit of counsel, subjected to torture, and even "disappeared" without a trace, to talk about the contested terrains of law, crime, and punishment in Latin America may seem a bit far-fetched.[1] Yet, if we want to dismiss such an experience as the product of an exceptional historical moment—the "dirty wars" of the late 1960s through the late 1980s—and focus on more "normal times," we still cannot be greatly encouraged by what we see: lawsuits that drag on for years and are so costly that justice becomes the privilege of the rich; polities that daily undermine the laws that supposedly protect the rights of citizens; violent acts committed by the police against common people; and discrimination by the courts against women, homosexuals, prostitutes, people of color, indigenous populations, and the poor and uneducated. Indeed, Latin Americans joke sardonically that the only ones really able to take advantage of neoliberalism's ostensibly reformed legal apparatuses are the drug lords. All of which tempts us to concur with those who have come to regard institutions of law and punishment not as contested ground where different groups seek to assert themselves, but as tools of domination, time-worn expressions of class rule.

Yet, as this rich collection demonstrates, such a dark, instrumentalist view of law and society in Latin America (or any other region, for that matter), though it contains more than a kernel of truth, tells but a portion of the story. It ignores the reality that no system of rule can be excessively egregious or arbitrary for very long; in order to maintain power in liberal democratic societies, ruling groups have to fashion ideologies of legitimation that have a modicum of credibility. In the process, they are constantly obliged to negotiate with diverse social groups and in some measure to accommodate their interests, practices, and meanings — their *legal cultures,* if you will. Of course, the specific dimensions of this process inevitably depend on, first, the nature of the ruling group (including its degree of internal cohesion, the number of contenders that share power, and the constituencies they serve), and second, on the degree of organization, consciousness, and combativeness of a society's subordinate groups. As the historical essays in this volume reveal, it was owing to these interclass and intraclass struggles, themselves intersected by the dynamics of race, ethnicity, gender, and generation, that the law sometimes became a powerful vehicle of emancipation as well as of domination.

The aim of this collection is to evoke the multivalent nature of Latin America's experience with the law in all its complexity and historical nuance. Social theorists like Jürgen Habermas and Michel Foucault have provocatively accounted for the role that law plays in the Enlightenment project of the West, and a new generation of Latin American legal historians has begun to apply their ideas to the region.[2] Thus, Latin America's elite-run states, in their efforts to stake their claim as progressive modernizing societies, expanded the ideological and public sphere, unleashing and empowering social forces they were soon forced to monitor and control if they were to remain in power. That elites developed new fields of medical, anthropological, and legal knowledge to define these unruly popular forces as *criminal* and deviant is not surprising; nor is it that members of these same "dangerous classes" would attempt, in their own ways, to use the legal system to advance claims to the rights of citizenship and the promises of modernity around which they had been mobilized. What is exciting about the contributions in this volume is their capacity to flesh out this scenario in fine-grained detail across a broad range of venues since late colonial times. These *legal contact zones* range well beyond the police station, courtroom and prison to include government regulatory bodies; hospitals and insane asylums; municipal councils and church-run orphanages; slave, working-class, and bourgeois households; and the shifting domains (and multiple identities) of peasant rebels, urban thieves, and small town caciques and pettifoggers, among others.[3] These were sites of political and cultural encounter, where the rules of the game were taught to subordinate groups and social, ethno-racial, and gender hierarchies were underscored, but where subaltern actors might also point up the contradictions of ruling projects, redress grievances, and even challenge aspects of state, class, or patriarchal domination. In almost every case the volume's authors eschew facile, dichotomous notions either of the process of modernization or subaltern resistance to it. In the process they provide a more textured, multistranded account of the uneven advance of liberalism and the medical-legal state in Latin America after independence.

As Ricardo Salvatore and Carlos Aguirre make clear in their introductory essay, studies of the law are nothing new in Latin American historiography. Indeed, a venerable institutional and intellectual history *(historia del derecho)* — particularly the study of colonial-era legislation and legal codes *(derecho indiano)* — dates back to the mid-nineteenth century. The "new legal history" on display here, however, is much more than old wine in new bottles. These excursions into the legal realm not only deepen our understanding of the institutional and ideological dimensions of crime and punishment, but also contribute to newer histories of gender and sexuality, science and disease, ethnicity and race, the labor process, subaltern politics, and agrarian protest. Particularly welcome is the *integrative* nature of the enterprise: at an unsettled intellectual moment when the dismantling of overarching paradigms and master narratives has put hyperpositivist social scientists at loggerheads with poststructuralist cultural historians in a manner that risks polarizing entire fields (witness the recent acrimony among Latin American labor historians), this ensemble of essays suggests that studies of the law may be one arena where practitioners of both academic cultures might coexist nicely.[4] The collection represents a healthy blend of traditional, materially grounded social history (see, for example, the essays by Juan Manuel Palacio and Luis González) and more recent cultural and discursive approaches (see the essays on the cultural construction of crime); indeed, several of the essays deftly integrate both methodological approaches (see the essays in part III, most notably Ricardo Salvatore's, Diana Paton's, and Donna Guy's, and the integration of "legal cultures," "markets," and "personality" in Douglas Hay's afterword). Studying the operation of the law allows us to approach larger relationships, processes, and meanings in history as a whole, as "bundles of relationships," to use Eric Wolf's phrase. In other words, the law is one of those domains that joins the state and society, one that invites the study of connections between broad, structural changes and alterations in the character of political, social, and cultural life.[5] Speaking metaphorically, the law might be seen as a kind of pivot on which broader historical processes and relations between groups turn.[6]

Given the new legal history's integrative potential, it is not surprising that the field has contributed importantly to the wholesome trend of "hemispheric convergence" in the writing of Latin American history that some scholars have begun to celebrate of late.[7] The contributors to this volume represent an even split between Latin American and North American scholars — a healthy balance that is also reflected in the growing community of scholars who have institutionalized themselves in a section of the Latin American Studies Association (LASA) devoted to the "Law and Society." This rich inter-American dialogue around legal matters has been enhanced by the staging of a series of interdisciplinary conferences and research seminars (e.g., in Buenos Aires, New Haven, San Juan, and London) as well as regular sessions at LASA meetings, and the publication of a spate of anthologies and special journal issues. The common denominator in these disparate activities, which are promoting a true "Americanization" of knowledge, is the dynamic leadership role played by my fellow editors, Carlos Aguirre and Ricardo Salvatore.[8]

The new legal history is also integrative in its capacity to examine the "longer waves" that run throughout the Latin American past. Several of the essays oblige us to reflect on broader political, social, and ideological trends that minimize the significance of the watershed separating the region's "colonial" and "national" periods. Let us briefly consider the interrelated themes of liberalism and conservatism, the rise of the positivist state, and the process of modernization in Latin America.

What did liberalism mean on the ground? One of this book's subtexts is the constraining legacy of Spanish imperial legal codes that remained on the books in the generations following independence — sometimes until the end of the nineteenth century. Thus, although progressive intellectuals and representatives of the state often spoke a language of citizenship and individual rights, and eclectically incorporated liberal principles into the architecture of the new penal systems, early national legal establishments consistently undermined the implementation of liberal discourse. Creole state-builders in Argentina, Venezuela, and Peru were reluctant to get rid of colonial legislation right away; to do so would deprive them of malleable judicial instruments they might use selectively. Why did repression often increase precisely as avowedly liberal regimes swept into power? The contributions by Salvatore and Arlene Díaz suggest that with crime on the rise and the social and patriarchal order jeopardized by the elimination of a society of castes and estates, the liberals themselves succumbed to fears of an impending struggle pitting their modernizing urban civilization against a residual rural barbarism. Ultimately, the rights of man, the equality of all before the law, and representative forms of government were superseded by moral and social imperatives that perpetuated laws and procedures bequeathed by an absolutist corporatist state. In terms of the law, there was remarkable continuity across the divide of independence.[9]

What role, then, did liberal precepts really play in nineteenth-century Latin America? To answer this question, we have to range beyond the essays in this volume. To begin with, it is wrongheaded to interpret liberal principles merely as fashionable importations, an expression of Latin America's reflexive cultural dependence on Europe and North America. Diverse social groups stamped their own meanings on liberalism and these constructions could change over time. Liberalism was a hydralike creature with many manifestations: to assess the impact of liberal ideology we have to ask what interests liberal principles served and what limits interest groups imposed on the abstract principles that initially appeared so boundless and universal. As Hay points out, for many of the region's nineteenth-century elites liberalism was a classic economic doctrine that mandated and naturalized the ruthless expansion of markets and the breakup and commodification of communally held lands. By contrast, liberalism took on very different colorations among Latin American artisans and peasants and the "organic intellectuals" that made common cause with them. Radical liberals in the cities often espoused an intense anticlericalism that in some contexts metamorphosed into anticapitalism (witness Mexico's anarcho-syndicalist Magonistas). "Popular" liberalism in the countryside frequently did not reject religion. It did invoke patriotic heroes and traditions; for example, in Mexico it featured Padre Hidalgo and Independence, Benito Juárez and the war against the French. And far from validating the inexorable march of progress and civilization that elites invoked, popular liberals, in one form or another, appealed to a bloody, often bleak, but utterly "moral" struggle over generations to preserve — on the field of battle, if not under cover of law — their freedom and dignity against encroaching forces of oppression.[10]

Emilia da Viotti Costa has reminded us on more than one occasion that for all its fragility, contradictions, and polymorphism on the ground, almost everyone acknowledges the influence of liberalism while seeming to forget the role of conservative thought in the process of state formation and modernization in Latin America. To this extent, it would seem that liberalism has indeed become a hegemonic ideology. Nevertheless, the postindependence survival of colonial codes and laws throughout the region, which can only be explained by the concomitant persistence of colonial-era social and economic structures, the slow pace by which Spain's former colonies became real nations, and the different rhythms whereby diverse regions and social sectors were incorporated into the capitalist world system, argues for a reassessment of the influence of conservative ideas in the making of "modern" Latin America. Indeed, as liberalism carried the day politically in one Latin American country after another, erstwhile conservatives frequently shed their party affiliations, but conservative modes of thought endured. No doubt they were given a boost by the Restoration in France that followed that nation's great Revolution — a period that coincided with the emergence of the modern state in many Latin American countries.[11]

There is good reason to characterize the centralizing, positivist dictatorships, which ruled Latin America at the turn of the next century, exemplars of a hybrid "conservative liberalism." Nonetheless, the eclectic nature of such regimes has prompted some recent scholars of the Latin American state to eschew the traditional liberal-conservative dichotomy as a touchstone for interpreting Latin America's "long nineteenth century."[12] Certainly the essays in this volume bolster such a position: their analyses of the emergence of a "medical-legal state" in Argentina, Brazil, Mexico, and Peru make clear that Latin American state-builders and criminologists were actively engaged in reading and implementing ideas from Europe and North America, and sought to impose them in rather different ways on diverse political, social, and ethno-racial populations. The positivist criminology that fueled this medical-legal state was propounded initially by the Italian Cesare Lombroso and disseminated by his many disciples. In essence, it posited that biology played a determinant role in criminality and that "born criminals" could be identified by atavistic deficiencies of mind and body. Such born criminals were to be dealt with severely; indeed, many positivist criminologists advocated life imprisonment for them, no matter how petty their crimes, even as they supported alternatives to prison (e.g., parole, suspended sentences) for "occasional criminals" led astray by a bad social environment.

Why was Lombroso so attractive to Latin American (and Italian) state-builders even as his ideas were received with less enthusiasm in northern Europe and North America? The essays by Dain Borges and Pablo Piccato suggest that, as in Italy, Latin America's weak states found in Lombroso's concoction of anthropology, biology, medicine, and law a compelling rationale for monitoring, categorizing, disciplining, and centralizing control over their still-fragmented and regionalized populations. It is instructive to note, for example, that in the popular parlance of Mexico's late Porfiriato (around the turn of the century), to *archivar* an individual meant to jail him or her. Moreover, like their Italian counterparts, Latin America's ruling elites sought to *forjar patrias,* to fashion secular national identities. As comparative legal scholar Mary Gibson has observed, in both Italy and Latin America, "positivist criminology offered a modern, 'scientific' school of thought to oppose to Catholic culture in the mission of homogenizing the nation and separating 'normal' [citizens] from those that posed a threat to the new state. Criminal anthropology also had the advantage of encoding a racial hierarchy, so that certain groups could claim superiority to others."[13]

The specific cast of the new positivist criminology varied across time and place. Lombrosian doctrines were never appropriated lock, stock, and barrel, and the essays in parts II and III provide clues why certain aspects of the medical-legal project were embraced by state-builders while others were rejected. Still, basic questions must be answered: To what extent did biological notions of criminality succeed in displacing environmental and cultural explanations, and how did this affect the actual formulation of policy? Did states adopt those Lombrosian measures they could easily afford or that increased the power of central administrators? To what extent did the state's immediate need to undermine or cultivate the support of the church become a factor in the shaping of initiatives? And if, as these essays suggest, Latin American positivists had gained enough power to redefine strategic political problems as solvable only through their peculiar mix of legal and medical policies, how much do we really know about these professions themselves? The essays suggest that they were far from monolithic; comparative research by Gibson and other Europeanists reveals that neither professional group converted entirely to the new doctrines. Even in Lombroso's back yard, dissension was rife among lawyers, many of whom remained faithful to the classic Enlightenment school of liberal criminology, which traced the etiology of crime to the free will of individuals. Less researched are the debates within the medical profession, though many contemporary doctors continued to argue, for example, that medical policy toward prostitutes should be based on consent rather than coercion; that, far from being atavistic throwbacks, prostitutes were society's unfortunates, who could learn to protect themselves from sexually transmitted diseases. Will we find similar trends among Latin American lawyers and doctors?

The essays in this volume leave little doubt, however, that Latin America's turn-of-the-century criminologists viewed themselves as secular missionaries, imbued with a burning morality and called on to solve society's ills through the application of modern "scientific" truths. In this regard, the contributors illuminate the cultural dimension of the political transition from the liberal states of the early nineteenth century to the positivist dictatorships and the populist regimes of the late nineteenth and early twentieth centuries. The essays are particularly rich in their engagement of the role that doctors and social scientists played in the construction of political authority itself and in the articulation of ideologies of national identity. In the papers by Cristina Rivera-Garza and Kristin Ruggiero, for example, we gain special insight into the role that medical providers and criminologists played in the process of state and nation formation and how the individual's body and health became part and parcel of that process in Mexico and Argentina. Both authors graphically portray the manner in which politics entered the hospital or clinic and, in effect, converted these medicalized spaces into courtrooms. Together with the essays on the prison experience by Aguirre, Guy, and Lila Caimari, they document the ways in which male and female bodies were differentially construed by the legal process as youthful bodies, socially productive and reproductive bodies, passionate bodies, diseased bodies, and deviant bodies; and how prisoners and hospital inmates themselves understood their situations and adapted legal and scientific language to contest these identities and create alternative legal and social lives. Rivera-Garza and Ruggiero also show how the language of medicine became useful for describing broader political concerns, such as fears about low fertility rates, the future of young people, and the "degeneration" of the nation itself.[14]

Finally, the essays afford us an opportunity to reflect on the broader, uneven process whereby Latin America became "modern." Recent scholarship on the region has called into question linear notions of modernization as an inexorable and overwhelming historical current; in the process, such work has revealed how people from all walks of life have always shaped its content, pace, and direction.[15] In their explorations of the legal realm, the present contributors advance our understanding of the often paradoxical and contingent nature of modernization from the perspectives of state, elite, and subaltern actors. The endurance of colonial codes well into the age of positivism has already been discussed. Ruggiero's paper provocatively uses state and elite attitudes toward "passion" as a barometer of the "pursuit of progress" in turn-of-the-century Argentina. Thus, although passion was held to foster irrationality and an excessive amount of it threatened the social fabric and needed to be controlled, it was also considered by some elite jurists as an antidote to the kind of unchecked materialism, utilitarianism, and individualism that "were enervating the national spirit" and "destroying national ideals." In similar fashion, Paton's essay on punishment in postemancipation Jamaica demonstrates the pitfalls of maintaining dichotomous distinctions between corporal and carceral regimes and assuming that adoption of the latter marks the transition from "premodern" to "modern" forms of punishment. In fact Paton shows that, owing to the problematic nature of the transition from slave to free labor in Jamaica, particularly the incidence of black flight, elites reintroduced flogging following emancipation and operated both types of punishment side by side, hoping that one would reinforce the other. Her essay — read in conjunction with those of Charles Walker, Díaz, and Aguirre — also demonstrates that although subordinate groups may have attempted to negotiate their own encounter with transforming, "modernizing" processes, and often grounded their challenges to them in earlier or alternative state discourses, their popular and legal cultures were never immune to the ideological inspirations and economic opportunities inherent in these processes.

Salvatore and Aguirre devote a portion of their keynote essay to plotting out meticulously an agenda that prioritizes "big problems" for future research: to wit, the need for more attention to popular conceptions of justice; the mediating role of legal "hingemen" and "lubricators" in bringing law within reach of the poor; the residual impact of corporate privileges (*fueros*) on the justice system after independence; the changing relationship of women to the law; the impact of penal institutions on their populations; the study of forms of representation of criminals and suspects; and so on. But this is only part of the challenge, which is as daunting as it is exciting.

For whereas the legal landscape has been carefully mapped for Europe and the United States, where the historiography is well advanced, such is hardly the case for Latin America. Indeed, for many countries the fundamental contours of the legal system remain to be charted. For example, some nations have had much more experience with jury trials than others; what difference has this made? Basic surveys of police establishments and court systems, of legal codes and the consolidation of family law, of the background and training of lawyers — to name but a few critical topics — remain to be undertaken before we can assess the similarities and differences of these institutions across time and place. In addition to producing such institutional primers, there is also a need, where critical masses of statistical data exist, to quantify general trends in arrests, prosecutions, and punishment. Needless to say, such data need to be handled and interpreted with enormous sensitivity — as the essays in this volume dissecting class, cultural, and gendered forms of bias attest.[16] But it would be useful to know how patterns of murder, theft, destruction of property, and a variety of other crimes correlate with qualitative studies of social and cultural life. What anomalies catch our attention?

If it is to continue to flourish, the new legal history of Latin America must validate a diversity of methodological and interpretive approaches and eschew parochialism. Just as numbers matter, so, too do textual strategies for studying forms of representation. Until quite recently, Latin America was largely absent from the debates that have shaped the field of postcolonial studies — a field that has made tremendous advances in the deconstruction of images and discourses of criminality.[17] Latin American legal historians must therefore read comparatively, not only across the boundaries of Latin American nations with quite diverse histories but also in the more developed legal historiographies of Europe and the United States. The benefits of such a comparative perspective are on display in this volume in the essays of Paton and Hay, which pose questions drawn from other colonial and postcolonial contexts that Latin Americanists would do well to consider.

Notes

1 These observations, intended to puncture the "romance with resistance" afoot in the profession of late, were made by Emilia Viotti da Costa (herself a victim of military repression in early-1970s Brazil) at the conference "Contested Terrains of

Law, Justice, and Repression in Latin American History" held at Yale University in April 1997. I am indebted to Emilia for insights that sharpened a number of the ideas presented here and elsewhere in the volume.

2 For a perceptive discussion of Habermas and Foucault and the dialectical tension their ideas pose for students of Latin American legal history, see Robert Buffington, "Introduction: Conceptualizing Criminality in Latin America," in Carlos Aguirre and Robert Buffington, eds., *Reconstructing Criminality in Latin America* (Wilmington, Del.: Scholarly Resources, 2000), pp. xi–xix.

3 I am adapting the notion of "contact zones" from Mary Luise Pratt, *Imperial Eyes: Travel Writing and Transculturation* (New York: Routledge, 1992). For the concept's recent application in a more expanded Latin American context, see Gilbert M. Joseph, "Close Encounters: Toward a New Cultural History of U.S.-Latin American Relations," in Gilbert M. Joseph, Catherine C. LeGrand, and Ricardo D. Salvatore, eds., *Close Encounters of Empire: Writing the Cultural History of U.S.-Latin American Relations* (Durham and London: Duke University Press, 1998), pp. 3–46.

4 For a window onto the unsettled state of things and the acrimony that has been generated, see the debate in the special issue of the *Hispanic American Historical Review,* "Mexico's New Cultural History: *Una Lucha Libre?*" 79, no. 2 (May 1999). See also John Womack Jr., "Labor History and Work" (paper presented at the symposium "Industrial Relations in Latin America: A New Framework?" at Harvard University, November 5, 1999).

5 Eric R. Wolf, *Europe and the People without History* (Berkeley: University of California Press, 1982), pp. 9, 17, 355; cf. Charles Tilly, *As Sociology Meets History* (New York: Academic Press, 1981), esp. 44; and William Taylor, "Between Global Process and Local Knowledge: An Inquiry into Early Latin American Social History, 1500–1900," in Olivier Zunz, ed., *Reliving the Past: The Worlds of Social History* (Chapel Hill: University of North Carolina Press, 1985), pp. 115–190.

6 Eric Van Young used roughly the same metaphor in connection with the colonial Mexican great estate. Van Young, "Mexican Rural History since Chevalier: The Historiography of the Colonial Hacienda," *Latin American Research Review* 18, no. 3 (1983): 5–61, esp. 25.

7 See, for example, Thomas E. Skidmore, "Studying the History of Latin America: A Case of Hemispheric Convergence," *Latin American Research Review* 33, no 1 (1998): 105–127; and Gilbert M. Joseph, "Reclaiming 'the Political' at the Turn of the Millennium," in Gilbert M. Joseph, ed., *Reclaiming the Political in Latin American History: Essays from the North* (Durham: Duke University Press, 2001).

8 The LASA section was founded by Aguirre, Joseph, and Salvatore in 1997; Aguirre and Salvatore served as co-chairs from 1998 to 2000. For recent publications that embody this "discursive community" of new legal historians, see Aguirre and Buf-

fington, eds., *Reconstructing Criminality;* Eduardo Zimmerman, ed., *Judicial Institutions in Nineteenth-Century Latin America* (London: Institute of Latin American Studies, 1999); and the special issue on "Criminal Justice History in Latin America," edited by Salvatore, in *Crime, History and Societies* 2, no. 2 (1998).

9 In addition to the essays by Díaz and Salvatore in this volume, two other papers presented at the Yale conference illuminate the gap between the rhetoric and performance of liberalism after independence: Sarah Chambers, "Old Laws, New Interpretations: Continuity and Change in the Criminal Justice System in Early Republican Arequipa, Peru," and Osvaldo Barreneche, "Laws vs. Procedures: Judiciary and Criminal Justice in Early Nineteenth-Century Buenos Aires, Argentina."

10 The recent literature on the many faces of elite and popular liberalism during the nineteenth century is quite rich—too voluminous to cite here. In addition to the suggestive contributions in this volume, Charles Hale, Alan Knight, Florencia Mallon, Guy Thomson, and Peter Guardino have made important contributions for Mexico, and Paul Gootenberg and Emilia Viotti da Costa have written pathbreaking studies for Peru and Brazil, respectively.

11 Again, I am drawing upon Viotti da Costa's rich commentary at the Yale conference.

12 See, for example, Erika Pani, "Dreaming of a Mexican Empire: The Political Project of the Imperialistas," *Hispanic American Historical Review* 82, no. 1 (February 2002).

13 Gibson's quotation is from her commentary at the Yale conference, which informs the discussion of Lombrosian criminology here.

14 This discussion draws on insights from Katherine Bliss's rich commentary on "Passion, Honor, Sexuality, and Social Order," at the Yale conference. For a complementary perspective on these themes, see Robert Buffington, "*Los Jotos:* Contested Visions of Homosexuality in Modern Mexico," another paper presented at the same meeting and subsequently published in Daniel Balderston and Donna J. Guy, eds., *Sex and Sexuality in Latin America* (New York: New York University Press, 1997), pp. 118–132.

15 Representative of this work is Paul Vanderwood's excellent monograph *The Power of God against the Guns of Government: Religious Upheaval in Mexico at the Turn of the Nineteenth Century* (Stanford: Stanford University Press, 1998).

16 For additional discussions of the pitfalls that complicate the use of legal documents, see William B. Taylor, *Drinking, Homicide, and Rebellion in Colonial Mexican Villages* (Stanford: Stanford University Press, 1979); Eric Van Young, "To See Someone Not Seeing: Historical Studies of Peasants and Politics in Mexico," *Mexican Studies/Estudios Mexicanos* 6, no. 1 (Winter 1990): 133–159; Gilbert M. Joseph, "On the Trail of Latin American Bandits: A Reexamination of Peasant Resistance," *Latin American Research Review* 25, no. 3 (1990): 7–53; and the forum of commentary and debate that ensued in the same journal, vol. 26, no. 1 (1991): 145–174.

17 For provocative discussions of how Latin Americanists might contribute to ongo-

ing debates about "postcoloniality" and "subaltern studies," see Fernando Coronil, "Foreword," in Joseph, LeGrand, and Salvatore, eds., *Close Encounters;* and Floren-cia E. Mallon, "The Promise and Dilemma of Subaltern Studies: Perspectives from Latin American History," *American Historical Review* 99, no. 5 (December 1994): 1491–1515.

Acknowledgments

Given the far-flung nature of the international collaboration that produced this volume, a number of heartfelt thanks are in order. The conference that launched the project, "The Contested Terrains of Law, Justice, and Repression in Latin American History," was held at Yale University in April 1997. It assembled over thirty specialists from North America, Latin America, and the United Kingdom working on law-related historical problems from a variety of perspectives across disciplines and academic generations. Sponsored by the university's Council on Latin American Studies, the Center for International and Area Studies, and the Latin American Working Group at Yale Law School, the event was generously supported by the Kempf Memorial Fund at Yale. We owe special thanks to Nancy Phillips, then Senior Administrator of the Council on Latin American Studies, and her assistants Sarah Dix, Delia Patricia Mathews, Edward Hanmer, and Albert Ko for skillfully managing the logistics of the conference.

The editors are especially grateful to those colleagues whose ideas and enthusiasm ensured the success of the conference and made this volume possible. In addition to the individuals whose work appears in these pages, we thank the following people who contributed research findings and commentaries in New Haven: Rolena Adorno, Osvaldo Barreneche, Katherine Bliss, Marcos Bretas, Robert Buffington, Robert Burt, Sarah Chambers,

Emilia Viotti da Costa, Mary Gibson, Thomas Holloway, Laura Kalmanowiecki, Josefina Ludmer, David Parker, Pablo Policzer, Charles Tilly, and Víctor Uribe. The participation at the working sessions of Yale graduate students in Latin American history and postdoctoral fellows in the university's Program in Agrarian Studies helped produce a lively encounter.

As the proceedings of the conference evolved into the present volume over the next two and a half years, we incurred other debts. Our editorial work was generously supported by our respective institutions: the Universidad Torcuato Di Tella (Salvatore), the University of Oregon (Aguirre), and Yale University (Joseph). The two anonymous readers for the Duke University Press provided incisive critiques that greatly improved the volume. Yale doctoral candidate J. T. Way ably assisted in the preparation of the final manuscript. Finally, it is a pleasure (once again) to acknowledge the unstinting guidance and support we received at every stage of the project from our marvelous editor at Duke, Valerie Millholland.

Ricardo D. Salvatore, Carlos Aguirre, and Gilbert M. Joseph

Introduction

Writing the History of Law, Crime,

and Punishment in Latin America

CARLOS AGUIRRE *and*

RICARDO D. SALVATORE

Law is not a bounded set of norms, rules, principles, values, or whatever from which jural responses to distilled events can be drawn, but a distinctive manner of imagining the real. — Clifford Geertz

In recent years, the study of law, justice, and related phenomena (crime, prisons, criminology, courts, litigation, and so forth) has received increasing attention by scholars from a variety of disciplines within Latin American studies.[1] Although these efforts come from disparate methodological, theoretical, and disciplinary traditions, they all share the conviction that law and legal phenomena are crucial elements in the formation and functioning of modern societies and thus deserve more attention than they have hitherto received. Previous approaches had essentialized the law as either a purely normative framework that guaranteed social equilibrium through the application of "justice" or as a set of state-produced norms that reflected and reproduced elite power. These views have been challenged by more nuanced and sophisticated approaches that treat law as an ambiguous, malleable, and slippery arena of struggle the limits and parameters of which are themselves the result of contention and negotiation. According to these new perspectives, law produces and reformulates culture (systems of identity, practices, and meaning), and it shapes and is shaped by larger processes of political, social, economic, and cultural change. Disassociating law from a strict and reductionist juridical/legalist approach is probably the single most important contribution of this body of scholarship. And although historians have contributed a good deal to effect this transformation, it has been very much the result of a multi-disciplinary effort in which other disciplines such as legal studies, political philosophy, anthropology, sociology, and cultural studies have made fertile contributions.

Within the field of Latin American history, this transformation has been some time coming. Long the domain of lawyers and amateur historians, and usually confined to the institutional/juridical study of codes, procedures, and institutions, *historia del derecho* (legal history) gradually lost its appeal among new generations of historians, much more interested in social, political, and economic history and, more recently, in the history of culture, representation, and identity formation. The study of law and legal phenomena — very narrowly defined — was left, with few exceptions, to the patriarchs of traditional history, when it was not abandoned altogether.

This trend has been reversed in recent years. In the last decade, the study of law and legal phenomena has come to the forefront in historical studies of Latin American societies, opening up a fascinating area of analysis. This novel territory, resulting from the convergence of multiple subdisciplinary endeavors and perspectives, promises to shed light on an important number of issues: the dynamics of social and cultural change, the nature of the state and its relationship with civil society, the formation of legal cultures, the operation of formal and informal systems of justice, the interaction between Western and indigenous legal systems, the mechanisms that give form and meaning to socially accepted forms of punishment, the role of courts and litigation in the dissemination of notions of rights and citizenship, the dynamics of gender, racial, and generational conflict, and so forth.

In dialogue with contemporary trends in international historiography, as well as with efforts in other disciplines, this renewed interest in law and legal issues has begun to yield a number of important monographs and theses. Scholarly conferences and panels on questions of law, crime, and punishment have consolidated this ongoing interest, producing a critical mass of valuable scholarly work. This volume provides an opportunity to showcase a sample of some of the best scholarship on the history of law and related issues. We expect that this collection will help to define better the contours and concerns of this burgeoning area of studies and to raise a set of questions about the role of law, crime, and punishment in the history of Latin America. We think these concerns and questions could soon play an important role in forging a research agenda for our discipline. The individual contributions to this volume speak for themselves; their foundation on patiently taken archival evidence, their well-specified hypotheses and persuasive argumentation, and their attention to both context and text will be evident to the reader. What this introduction seeks to accomplish, therefore, is to locate these essays — and the research agendas from which they stem — within the frame of recent trends in the historiography of Latin America. In addition, our introduction attempts to offer a programmatic agenda for future work in the areas of law, crime, and punishment. But only by remembering where we have come from, can we understand where we are going. Thus, we ask the reader to tolerate a short detour into the historiography of law in the region, as a way of presenting the basic issues, characterizing the specific problems under scrutiny, and delimiting the contours of scholarly convergence. In the final section, we attempt to identify future avenues of progress.

From Historia del Derecho to the Social History of Law

The process of state consolidation initiated in the Latin American republics after their independence from colonial powers was dependent, to a great extent, on the successful implementation of an effective and universal legal system. Although numerous laws outlived the period of colonial domination (for instance, the *Siete Partidas,* a thirteenth-century text, and the *Recopilación de las Leyes de Indias,* issued in 1680, were still invoked by courts and judges well into the second half of the nineteenth century), there was usually a conscious effort on the part of republican legislators to abandon or at least to modify Spanish law in those aspects regarded as anachronistic, barbarous, unjust, or arbitrary. Spanish law, as we know, was fragmented into various jurisdictions (royal, ecclesiastical, customary, *de gentes,* natural), subject to various and contradictory interpretations, and laden with the intolerable admission of privilege. Not only were Spanish laws not rationally ordered (codified and subject to hierarchies), but they were also resistant to the principle of universality. The importance attributed to custom and the excessive discretion of judges created tremendous uncertainty and heterogeneity. Naturally, this type of law was not conducive to the experiment of modern nation-building. The new republics ascribed in principle to notions of popular sovereignty, equality under the law, and representative government, notions that were inconsistent with the mosaic of legislation inherited from Spain.[2]

Postindependence legislators enacted an array of new laws, codes, and constitutions, but they were generally easier to write than to enforce. Although Spanish legal traditions continued to influence this effort, many legislative pieces were (selectively) cloned from French, British, and other European sources, which were usually considered the *non plus ultra* of juridical science and progress. The prominence of lawyers among the cadres of postindependence policy-makers is further evidence that legislation and codification were considered fundamental to the successful consolidation of the newly independent republics.[3] But success was not immediate. At first "codifiers" found strong resistance among the very political elites whose values they shared. And the early constitutions fell rapidly, replaced by new constitutions or abandoned as instruments of the rival political party. *Caudillo* regimes continued to enact decrees, circulars, and other types of regulations in a manner reminiscent of the colonial *cédulas, ordenanzas,* and *bandos de buen gobierno,* and other similar legal statutes. But even these regimes believed that the new societies and polities could be ordered only under the supremacy of the law.[4] It was only after 1850, as constitutional arrangements began to hold, that there was a new energy again to take up the enterprise of enacting a legislative corpus valid for the whole nation. So, legislators took upon themselves the task of compiling civil, commercial, and penal codes.

By the late nineteenth century, relatively solid legal traditions already existed in many Latin American cities, which materialized in lawyers' guilds, law schools, legal journals, and international exchanges. Lawyers sought (and eventually achieved) state recognition and protection for their corporate privileges.[5] This process of professional consolidation led, almost naturally, to the emergence of an interest in the history of law. The drafting of new codes and constitutions required the collection of legal antecedents and this engaged lawyers and jurists in a search for origins. In Argentina, in the 1850s and 1860s, the specialized publication *El Judicial* (which catered to lawyers) began to collect and publish some rare pieces of colonial legislation. Estanislao Zeballos, one of the prominent members of the Generation of 1880, founded the *Revista de Derecho, Historia y Letras,* responding to an audience that shared an interest in all three disciplines. Courses in legal history began to be taught regularly, and the first books and theses that traced the history of law in Latin American countries began to appear in the 1870s. By the turn of the century, publications on legal history were already gathering momentum.[6] This type of scholarly/legal activity (writing the history of law as a progressive sequence of codes and laws) had a strong political component as well, inasmuch as many of these jurists and amateur historians were also interested in developing solid legal institutions and traditions as part of state efforts to dispense with the anarchy and chaos associated with *caudillismo*. Nevertheless, intermittent political instability, as well as successive waves of enthusiasm and frustration with the application of laws, made it necessary — in the eyes of legislators and jurists — to revise codes and other pieces of legislation constantly. Profusion and confusion were the inevitable result. One of the virtues of these early efforts at writing the historia del derecho was precisely their authors' interest in ordering the information, very much as contemporary historians did with the political histories of their countries.

This approach to legal history continued well into the twentieth century. At this time, most practitioners of history were interested in the study of institutions (such as the church or the army), politics (understood as the contention of forces around and through state institutions), and major military episodes such as foreign wars. Within this historiographical context, legal history occupied an important niche, even if university courses on historia del derecho were generally taught in law-school classrooms and by professional lawyers, not historians. The consolidation of this trend also brought important fields of specialization. For example, the history of penal law was developed by criminologists and penologists whose efforts achieved disciplinary maturity in the 1920s.[7] Also, the emergence of (official and unofficial) *Indigenista* currents in countries such as Peru and Mexico in the 1920s, 1930s, and 1940s brought with it an interest in what was sometimes called indigenous law — more properly, the history of state legislation about Indians.[8] The effort of compilation and systematization was almost always accompanied by proposals to enact specific reforms favoring indigenous populations. The need for tutelary legislation that would putatively protect the Indians as they were assimilated into the national state was a major concern for Indigenistas.[9]

A parallel but somehow distinctive trend was developed since the early 1900s in both Spain and Spanish America: the history of *derecho indiano*, that is, the body of legislation that governed the Spanish American colonies until the early nineteenth century. Ricardo Levene (1885–1959) in Argentina and Rafael Altamira (1866–1951) in Spain are generally recognized as founders of this field of study.[10] Historians took on the task of reviewing, summarizing, and ordering the rather immense Spanish legislative effort in the so-called Indies. Studies on economic, social, labor, racial, and religious colonial legislation became abundant and constituted, especially up to the 1950s and 1960s, an important branch of the historiography of colonial Spanish America. Levene and Altamira had a number of younger disciples in both Spain and Hispanic America: José María Ots y Capdequí and Alfonso García-Gallo in Spain, Ricardo Zorraquín Becú in Argentina, Bernardino Bravo Lira in Chile, Silvio Zavala and Toribio Esquivel Obregón in México, Guillermo Lohmann Villena in Perú. The historia del derecho indiano became a genuine specialty within the historical profession—and even today its practitioners continue to publish important monographs and organize international conferences.[11] Historians of derecho indiano very rarely moved beyond the institutional / juridical framework for studying the history of Spanish law in colonial Spanish America, and very frequently they adopted a sympathetic view of Spanish rule.

During the 1970s and early 1980s, a renewed interest in the study of law and legal phenomena in the region flourished, especially among North American historians. Some efforts focused on key institutions of the state, trying to understand the mechanisms used to ensure authority, legitimacy, and political control. Stuart Schwartz analyzed the Brazilian colonial system of high justice; Woodrow Borah studied the institution of the "Protector of the Indians" in colonial Mexico; Thomas Flory analyzed the formation of the judicial system in nineteenth-century Brazil; and Colin MacLachlan reconstructed the history of the Tribunal de la Acordada, a sui generis penal institution in late colonial Mexico.[12] These were not just traditional histories of judicial institutions, for they posed important questions—quite centrally, about the relationship between state and society mediated by the law. But in all these works, interest continued to center on legal and state institutions; they were not attentive to the questions raised, for example, in the work of British "new social historians" (the so-called Warwick school). Thus, they did not focus on the problem of the law as a theater of power, nor seek to discover in judicial records the voices and tactics of the powerless, those until then abandoned to "the condescension of history." The publication of *Albion's Fatal Tree* in England and of *Roll, Jordan, Roll* in the United States, which had started a minor revolution in the writing of history, had little if any immediate repercussions in the Latin American field.[13]

Interest in investigating crime as a prism of society, as a treasure chest holding clues about class formation and class conflict (as the British new social historians believed) remained exceptional. Seminal works were not followed up and consequently the "social history of crime" did not gather momentum in Latin America. There were some exceptions, though, such as William Taylor's book on homicide and rebellion in colonial Mexico and Paul Vanderwood's study of banditry in nineteenth-century Mexico.[14] The influence of E. P. Thompson and other "bottom-up historians" was felt more powerfully in studies of slavery, peasant rebellions and, especially, labor history. Very few historians ventured, however, into the study of law and legal phenomena, for there was an overwhelming interest in more open forms of conflict and social change such as rebellions, revolutions, workers' strikes, and the like.[15] And when historians did pay attention to law — Steve Stern's study of Indian litigiousness in early colonial Andean Peru is a case in point — they did so within the parameters of a clearly Marxist framework, viewing law as a mask for colonial power and as an inhibitor of more confrontational (and allegedly more effective) ways of contesting colonial power.[16]

About the same time, a less theoretically oriented trend developed among quantitative urban and social historians. They began to study crime in urban societies such as Buenos Aires, Mexico City, or San Juan, with their interest focused on quantifying crimes, perpetrators, arrests, victims, and the like. Following similar efforts in Europe and North America (by historians such as Eric Monkkonen, among others), they offered insights into issues such as modernization, urbanization, and social change. But they were generally limited in their ability to illuminate the complexities of crime in urban societies, inasmuch as they very rarely moved beyond the legal definition of crime and the use of statistics to identify trends in criminality and policing. Once again, many of the important questions being raised by social historians such as Thompson or Hay were not of interest to these historians.[17] True, they borrowed from British "new social historians" the insight that crime and criminal records held the key to examining social conflict, but the latter's reflections on the role of the legal system within the process of class formation were not put under scrutiny.

A more fruitful trend was the study of banditry. Here, the influence of Eric Hobsbawm's seminal work stimulated a short debate about the social or political nature of Latin American banditry. A number of monographs studied banditry in Brazil, Peru, Cuba, Mexico, and other countries, most of them concluding that the "social bandit" model was nonexistent or, at least, very rare. Later, historians began to move beyond the often sterile dichotomy of social bandit versus common bandit, striving to connect banditry with other forms of rural struggle such as peasant rebellions, the development of national politics, and a variety of forms of subaltern agency.[18]

From the Social History of Crime to Poststructuralist Legal Studies

Several theoretical and disciplinary trends that developed since the late 1970s and early 1980s have lately become important sources of renovation within the historiography of law and legal phenomena in Latin America. The social history of crime and criminal justice in Britain; the increasing attention to Gramscian concepts such as hegemony, historical block, and subaltern culture; the Foucauldian emphasis on power, knowledge, and the body; the work of "subaltern studies" in India and elsewhere; developments in legal anthropology; and the growing and renewed interest in cultural history — all began to influence work done on Latin American history in general and in the study of law in particular. The so-called conflict theory of law, for instance, offered an important, though in some ways reductionist, approach to the study of law. Historians such as E. P. Thompson, Eugene Genovese, Peter Linebaugh, and Douglas Hay insisted on the essentially conflictive nature of law, but they generally reduced it to an expression of *class* conflict.[19] These scholars made an interesting and creative use of the Gramscian notion of hegemony,[20] relating it very closely to the use of legal tactics to offer dominated groups the fiction of a system of rule of law through a very well calculated display of mercy and justice. One of the virtues of this approach was its insistence on viewing the operation of the law from below, thus taking into account the perceptions, initiatives, and input of the lower groups not just in the operation, but even the formulation of the law.

Another source of renovation came from the revitalized interest that emerged around the mid-1970s in the operation of the criminal justice system, which offered new angles from which to analyze the impact of law and the state's repressive apparatus on the common folk. A number of European and North American historians revisited the history of institutions of confinement and punishment, searching for clues to understand the nature of past social relations and ideologies. Prisons, in particular, but also other forms of punishment such as public executions, received considerable attention. Authors such as David Rothman, Michael Ignatieff, Pieter Spierenburg, Patricia O'Brien, David Garland, and Peter Linebaugh took on the task of unpacking the several rationales behind the use, abuse, reform, or dismissal of certain forms of punishment.[21] Working with quite different theoretical frameworks these authors nonetheless shared the conviction that punishment is a socially constructed artifact, that is, the product of a variety of social, political, cultural, and legal circumstances.[22] If this is true, the study of punishment could illuminate a number of themes that were of interest to historians: namely, the nature of the state, changes in cultural sensibilities, forms and dimensions of class conflict, the formation of labor markets, and the struggles around social and labor discipline, among others.

Although Michel Foucault's *Discipline and Punish* was translated into Spanish almost immediately after its original publication in France, its impact was, for a while, almost nonexistent among Latin American historians. It was only in the 1990s that Foucault's influence was felt more powerfully and with a much broader scope than merely the history of punishment. Several essays in the volume *The Birth of the Penitentiary in Latin America*, for example, engaged some of the themes that Foucault developed: the constructed nature of crime, the ways in which prisons "fabricated" deviance, the resonance of crime and punishment throughout society, the capillary forms of power effected inside the prisons, and so forth. Critically incorporating Foucault's concepts and themes, Latin American historians have certainly benefited from his agenda for deconstructing the social and cultural logic behind the formation of modern societies.[23]

Simultaneously, a vociferous revolution was taking place in European and North American intellectual circles: the poststructuralist turn. Among the topics debated was the disappearance of the modern and the emergence of the postmodern (condition), the complexity of layers in which social reality is embedded, the death of the author, the opacity and literacy of most texts, the questioning of the written as the only sensorial "reality," and the importance of spectacle in modern life. This renovation brought forth a problematization of the "texts" that historians were reading and a greater interest among historians in the methods of anthropology and literary criticism. The lack of a clear historical dimension in these discussions (despite some valuable exceptions), however, delayed the adoption by historians of these new conceptual and hermeneutic tools.[24] Especially among North

American historians of Latin America, the impact of poststructuralist currents was quite limited and piecemeal.

Three components of this trend have had important consequences for the study of law and related issues. First, there is a growing attention to culture. Using new and old sources, and clearly influenced by the new trends in literary criticism and cultural studies (the so-called New Historicism, American studies, French "new" cultural history, and more recently, cultural, postcolonial and subaltern studies), historians have begun to look at culture as less a "derivation" or "manifestation" of structural factors and more as a domain of generation of social action and concepts—a domain that in itself is a locus of contestation and struggle and both illuminates and problematizes other areas of social life. Whether a "new cultural history" has already come to fruition is subject to discussion.[25] Yet it is possible to argue that today, in Latin American historiography, cultural history has not only reached maturity and legitimacy, but has taken a sort of "imperialist" outlook, to use Eric Van Young's term.[26]

Second, there is a renewed interest in a much more contextualized political history. Studies of the state, for instance, have taken a clear position in viewing it less as a "structure" that exerts its impact on "civil society" than as a field of force, an arena of contestation, in which not only powerful but also marginal, subordinate, and previously neglected groups have a bearing.[27] This contestation, we may add, appears as centrally mediated by the law. Studies on "state formation" that focus on the making of a legal system offer fascinating angles from which to analyze the relationship between state and society in historical perspective.[28] Recent work pays greater attention to the workings of the legal system and the formation (or reshaping) of legal cultures among the lower groups. This is not the only possible outcome of the fruitful confluence of political and legal history, though. The formation of local clusters of power (in which economic, social, and judicial power are intermixed), the legal ramifications of protracted conflict between social groups, and the political resonance of legal rituals (such as public executions, for instance), are all promising areas of research, as some papers in this collection attest.

Third, there is an increasing dialogue between anthropology and history. In the 1980s, anthropologists rediscovered the role of law in community cohesion and conflict and came to view law as a battleground in which different groups and individuals competed against each other around issues of power, control, prestige, and meaning.[29] New work focused on litigation and court procedures as central elements in the formation of legal cultures and the definition of social boundaries. Forms of argumentation and court appearances, for instance, became important areas of anthropological analysis.[30] Legal anthropologists have also long been interested in indigenous customary legal orders and the interaction of Western and non-Western legal systems. More recently, they have revisited the study of the relationship between law and colonialism. In Africa, for instance, studies on the making of "customary law" have emphasized its "invented" nature as a means to assure the cooptation of colonial subjects. These studies have also underlined the Janus-type nature of colonial law: while it brought new forms of oppression and control, it also opened up new arenas of dispute — not just between colonizers and colonized subjects, but within each of these groups as well.[31]

Recent interest in subaltern studies has also proved to be fruitful in rethinking the history of law in Latin America.[32] Like previous, notably Marxist, attempts at writing history from below, scholars belonging to this perspective have sought to uncover the experience of the subordinate, but, unlike such precedents, subaltern studies offers a much more conscious critique of the strategies of representation advanced not only by members of those elites, but also by the scholarly and political communities that pretend to "speak for" the subaltern. Furthermore, practitioners associated with subaltern studies also question the viability of "grand narratives" (including Marxism, structuralism, and nationalism in its various forms) that offer comprehensive agendas for interpreting and acting upon social reality. This recent perspective offers fruitful ways to rethink the relationship between law, domination, and power. First, the very insistence on finding alternative, subaltern narratives about the social, encourages the search for the voice of the weak in legal documents, procedures, and performances.[33] Prominent attention to issues of language, representation, and narrativity, on the other hand, has made historians mindful of the importance that the subtleties and nuances of discursive practices have for exploring conflict, meaning, and power relations. Thus, interest in legal discourses (texts of codes and treatises, the development of criminology, forms of argumentation, and others) is likely to produce fruitful results in the future. Finally, the emphasis on the multidimensionality of processes of identity formation and re-creation translates into the demand for a more attentive look at the forms and content of legal disputes by different sets of actors (slaves, women, peasants, workers, Indians, and the like). An Indian subject, to give but one example, may want to appear as a poor and indigent member of the "Indian race" at one moment, and as a member of the national community who wants to assert his/her rights as citizen at another.

Thus, the historiography of Latin America began to experience interesting changes in the 1980s. There has since been an outburst of historical studies in a myriad of directions: culture and daily life, sexuality, violence, gender issues, discourse and representation, family, and so forth. A few, important studies on prostitution, for example, raised the question of the relationship between the regulatory powers of the state, the medical profession, and the construction of subaltern alterity. Foucault's work on the history of sexuality stimulated fruitful research, engaging historians of gender in questions of social discipline, the hygienic movement, and prostitution.[34] The influence of the third wave of studies of the *Annales* school, concerned with *mentalités,* culture, and daily life, was felt in the work of historians such as Alberto Flores Galindo in Peru and Joao J. Reis in Brazil.[35] To a large extent, the methodological renewal of our discipline has had to do with the growing interest in questions hitherto appropriate to anthropological research: group identity, symbolic exchange, ritual practice, and spirituality. The interaction between history and anthropology generated quite stimulating studies dealing with issues such as indigenous memory and religion, workers' traditions and rituals, the deconstruction of dominant ideologies, and the like.[36] Regrettably, the progress made in legal anthropology has had less impact on historians of Latin America. The pioneering work of Laura Nader has had relatively little diffusion among historians of the region.[37] Works such as the recent books by Charles Cutter and Susan Kellogg have brought back to the field of historiography some of the questions posed by Nader and her colleagues.[38] Indigenous communities seem to prefer justice systems that privilege communal "harmony," and this requires a great deal of judicial discretion and a preference for damage compensation over punishment. Was the colonial judiciary more benevolent and accommodating toward indigenous demands and cultural preferences? This is but one of the important questions raised in the recent scholarly work that has emerged in the convergence between history and anthropology.

The Complexity and Multidimensionality of the Law

The historical study of law, crime, and punishment is currently undergoing a substantial transformation. It has only been in the 1990s that a new and seemingly consistent interest in the history of law and legal phenomena in Latin America has come to fruition. This volume is, in many respects, an initial attempt to map both the achievement and the promise of this field. Among the dimensions of this transformation the most important has been the extension of the concept of "the law" into multiple directions. What does this multidimensionality and complexity entail?

The law is a complex and often confusing arrangement of norms of different hierarchy and origin intended to order social interaction. It assumes basic social agreements, and thus can be viewed as another type of "imagined community." It is a powerful instrument of social control designed to mold the bodies and souls of those subject to its rule. Its enforcement mobilizes an important part of the state apparatus: the police, the judiciary, the army, and an array of penal and welfare institutions. Furthermore, the law contributes "reasons" for state governance, serving perhaps as the fundamental element conveying legitimacy to government. Hence, the legal sphere is a "theater" or forum in which a pedagogic work takes place in a continuous fashion—from here emanate normative messages about illicit behavior, crime, and punishment. As an ideology, the law assumes rhetorical forms of substantive impact on everyday discourse, for the law constitutes the reference system to which people appeal in defense of their rights—the law is not only *ley* but also *derecho*. As we can see, the law is many things at the same time.

In addition to all this, the law is an arena of social contestation. It is a terrain in which individuals and groups with different interests, resources, and quotas of power confront each other and try to "work the system" (Hobsbawm) to their own advantage. Naturally, there is always a previous step: legal norms have to be written and enacted, and this is a process (one that certainly deserves much more attention than it has received by historians) in which elite and state interests are generally preponderant—though by no means omnipotent. The operation of the law, not surprisingly, has generally reflected the continuous power exercised by state officials, members of the upper classes, and professional lawyers and jurists. But to say this is just the beginning of any inquiry, for law has always offered avenues for the subaltern to challenge, circumvent, manipulate, and even profit from the law.[39] Certain areas of legal regulation are, of course, more likely to offer this avenue to the underprivileged. Litigation around slave or family rights, for example, may offer to contending parties more room to maneuver and manipulate the law than penal legislation, where one of the contending sides is usually the state—represented by prose-cutors—and where certain groups or individuals are much more vulnerable to abuse by law-enforcing agents such as the police or the military. But even here, as some of the articles in this collection show, there is usually latitude for the subaltern to challenge the powerful or, at the very least, to attempt to put limits to the exercise of command.

Our interest in the history of law, thus, goes well beyond merely investigating and establishing who won what and how often. Law and legal phenomena offer a unique window from which to explore not just the execution (or violation) of legal precepts, but also the confrontation, appropriation, reshaping, and dissemination of values, concepts, notions, ideas, images, social tactics, and forms of argumentation whose study can offer valuable insights for our understanding of any given society.[40] The concept of "legal cultures" may be used here to encapsulate all these components of the population's relationship with, and attitudes towards, the law. We would like to emphasize the plural in the concept of "legal cultures," for there is usually more than one "distinctive manner" of "imagining the real"—to use again Geertz's phrase—at any point in time and space.

Furthermore, what an individual or group may think about the law is subject to specific forms of appropriation and use, for a certain legal consciousness is far from being essential or immutable. In other words, legal attitudes (and thus, legal actions, arguments, and practices) are changing and malleable: the individual that violates the legal prohibition to drink and drive might ferociously argue about the strict application of the law when his or her rights are being abused. Law thus becomes not just a contested terrain, but also a terrain in which the forms and nature of contestation are subject to change and negotiation, and in which the actors' own perception about rights, justice, and legality may vary accordingly.[41]

The Law in Latin America: Rule, Unrule, or Misrule?

According to standard interpretations, Latin American countries—with only a few partial exceptions—have not been able to establish solid, effective, and universal legal systems. Political turmoil, economic shortages, and authoritarian cultures, this line of reasoning contends, have historically combined to thwart the establishment of cohesive and reliable legal frameworks. According to political scientist Guillermo O'Donnell, a system of "rule of law" can be defined as a system in which (at the very minimum) "law is fairly applied by the relevant state institutions, including, but not exclusively, the judiciary."[42] Such a system, according to this view, has never existed in most countries of the region, and it does not exist even today, when formal democracies have been established and constitutional rule has become the norm. This position maintains that law has usually been, and to a large extent still is, arbitrary, and its effects have customarily been used to consolidate privileges, informal modes of appropriation, power, and authority, and a variety of kindred illegalities. In this scenario, legal rights have been quite difficult to assert, and resistance against arbitrariness (generated by either private or state sources) has been difficult to carry out.

If anything, this perspective maintains, the law in Latin America has been the source of much more injustice than fairness, has been more often manipulated than revered, and has created — in some countries more than others — a scenario of legal fiction that conceals the injustices of the *país real*. Such a situation, furthermore, has affected not just interactions among individuals, but the relationship between them and the state, and has ultimately served as one of the bases for the weakness of the whole constitutional order. The lack of democratic traditions in the region would be very closely linked to this disregarding of the law and its application. As Jeremy Adelman and Miguel Angel Centeno have argued, "the rule of law, to the extent that it exists in Latin America, still faces its foundational challenge: its inability to bear equally upon the rulers and the ruled."[43]

This depiction needs to be elaborated, for it fails to discuss the social bases that have nurtured over the centuries a system of unfairness that, paradoxically, may be the only stable feature amidst a rather unstable social milieu. But, in addition, it insists on testing the Latin American cases against a certain ideal type of situation (total equality before the law) that has never existed and probably never will. Instead of an impossible system of rule of law we would prefer to refer to regimes that achieve (or do not achieve) the hegemony of the law, that is to say, a political or institutional regime in which a substantial portion of the litigants and people under legal processes understand and abide by the procedures and institutions designed by lawmakers and judges. In a more strict sense, we could add a second condition, that people valorize the legal order as a component of their social and civic identity and exercise of rights. Under this definition, the power of the laws to define the social order and people's positions with respect to it prevails over other formal, institutional criteria.

We would suggest that the arbitrary nature of the legal systems in Latin

America has contributed to (and has been shaped by) a type of legal culture that attributes to law more elasticity than it is supposed to have. In this regard, one cannot fail to see some continuity with the colonial justice system. An excessive amount of judicial discretion and an amazing complexity in the legal order facilitates the negotiation of power relations and patronage in the sphere of justice. Moreover, if we are to believe recent scholarly work on the subject, this system enjoyed a great deal of legitimacy among the less privileged, the Indian pueblos, mestizos, and lower classes. We are not suggesting that arbitrariness always helped the underprivileged; quite the contrary. We are simply arguing that by virtue of its very arbitrariness (which includes a good dose of corruption), the legal system in Latin America has generally created a greater sense of optimism regarding the eventual outcome of legal procedures than the poor and underprivileged had reason to expect, given the actual record of the tribunals' and courts' allocation of sentences. Future research on the formation and development of legal cultures in the region will bring us closer to understanding this process.[44]

Our proposal to study law in its multiple dimensions and to view it as a contested terrain, then, becomes all the more critical in the Latin American context, for this contestation takes place in a highly malleable arena, one in which the rules of the game are themselves subject to negotiation, dispute, manipulation, and corruption. This does not turn the situation into a more democratic kind of confrontation, but it does transform it into a contest in which other (informal, illegal, subjective, monetary) means become more central than would have been the case if a system of rule of law were solidly entrenched. In addition, the kind of scenario we have described is much more likely to occur in remote, provincial, and rural areas. Here, as many scholars have observed, the designs of central state authority are even more difficult to enforce. By and large, justices of the peace and other local judicial authorities have been less powerful and (at the very least, in the perception of the litigant) more permeable than their counterparts in the major cities.[45]

The enforcement of laws and the hegemony of the legal systems (as different from the rule of law) has historically varied according to political regime. Some regimes have been more keen than others in disseminating a pedagogy about the law. And some regimes, more than others, have allowed the judiciary to establish its own rules, procedures, and traditions. Hence, subaltern subjects have faced over the course of Latin American history a variety of systems of justice, predicaments about the law, and different degrees of duress in law enforcement. Equally important, law enforcement has been quite directly related to the centralization or decentralization of governmental authority. Over time, the degree of arbitrariness of the judicial system varied considerably: different regimes of governance (caudillismo, elitist liberal constitutionalism, oligarchic liberal regimes, populisms) influenced the procedures and forms of the justice system in ways that historians still need to determine. This degree of arbitrariness and discretion was augmented, rather than diminished, with the consolidation of modern states guided by positivist, medico-legal technologies of social discipline. At this point, only further research can help identify these different situations and trace out the broader trends in the evolution of justice.

Have Latin American countries, then, become disciplinary societies? Yes and no. The formation of a disciplinary society, with its institutional network of prisons, hospitals, asylums, and schools, has achieved in Latin America a notable development. And, judging from the increase in prison populations, there has been a trend toward a greater exposure to this kind of coercive modernity. Yet, at the same time, the region's long experience with republican regimes of government (operating at less than full throttle, if you will) has exposed many in the population to the forces of the state, with its legal arguments and its extralegal mechanisms of persuasion. The legal terrain (as an arena of contestation) has expanded and contracted throughout history, providing a learning experience to subalterns about the contrasts between the promises of legal modernity and the realities of a society divided along class, gender, and ethnic lines. The Habermasian sphere of rights coexists with the Foucauldian disciplinary machinery, producing interactions and subjectivities that are complex, ambivalent, and changing, and that historians are only now beginning to understand.

Toward a New Social and Cultural History of the Law

The study of law and legal phenomena in Latin America is therefore reaching an exciting moment. Numerous publications, panels, and conferences, testify to the field's vigorous development. We tried both to subject to scrutiny and to explore the potential of this new wave of scholarly interest at an international conference organized at Yale University in April 1997. Thirty scholars, mostly historians, gathered for three days to discuss twenty-three papers, a selection of which is included in this volume. The discussions that took place during the conference greatly enriched each of the contributions, which were afterward revised by the authors. The resulting products are offered here, organized around three major themes.

The first section, "Legal Mediations: State, Society, and the Conflictive Nature of Law and Justice," includes four essays that explore law as both a mediator of social conflict and an essential agent of state building. The operation of the legal system appears here as a dynamic, malleable, and conflictive scenario, in which competing forces — the state, elites, interest groups, subalterns — strive to advance their own agendas. Focusing on Indians in eighteenth-century Cuzco contesting state intrusion into local affairs (Walker), cane workers negotiating rights with the Brazilian Estado Novo (González), women in nineteenth-century Caracas facing new state regulations on family and gender rights (Díaz), or farmers disputing rural power in early twentieth-century Buenos Aires province (Palacio), these articles illuminate crucial aspects of the political, cultural, and social history of their regions by looking at the ways in which various actors relate to each other through the legal system. These essays demonstrate the richness and usefulness of legal sources, the attention due to litigation as an important component of the political strategies of quite diverse social actors, and the importance of analyzing the spheres of power surrounding each and every legal battle.

The second section, "The Social and Cultural Construction of Crime," brings together essays that attempt to deconstruct the social and cultural (as opposed to the strictly legal or juridical) nature of crime. Firmly rooted in the most innovative developments in cultural history, these essays explore the intersections, exchanges, resonances, and mutual borrowings occurring between different forms of discourse in order to produce social phenomena that came to be considered as criminal. The essentially multifaceted nature of crime, the conflictive views that shape and are shaped by it, and the creative ways in which those views are both reproduced and challenged, are clearly demonstrated in the essays in this section. Pablo Piccato uses the character of the *ratero* in order to explore competing views about the lower classes in early-twentieth-century Mexico City; Dain Borges tracks the differing images of religious healing in legal, medical, and literary documents in turn-of-the-century Brazil; Cristina Rivera-Garza uses the case of prostitutes in Mexico City to explore state and medical treatment of the body and social hygiene in late-nineteenth-century Mexico City; and Kristin Ruggiero examines how "passion" was played out in the arguments put before criminal courts in turn-of-the-century Buenos Aires. Together, and clearly departing from previous approaches to the study of crime, these essays advance our understanding of the cultural ramifications of social phenomena that, far from being just a legal event, are clearly immersed in complex webs of meaning and both create and irradiate symbols, images, and other cultural forms.

The essays in the third and final section, "Contested Meanings of Punishment," offer valuable insights into the workings of criminal justice systems, in an effort to uncover the cultural, political, and social implications of a variety of forms of punishment. As David Garland, among others, has suggested, punishment is a sort of artifact that needs to be analyzed in its multiple meanings and roles. In accordance with such a conceptual framework, these essays provide us with new angles from which to understand the nature, role, representation, and effects of different forms of punishment. Once again, far from considering punishment as merely a legal phenomenon, or as the inevitable result of the appetite for social control among social and political elites, these essays adopt a much more contextualized perspective that helps us situate punishment within its social, political, and cultural coordinates. Carlos Aguirre and Lila Caimari attempt to recover the voices and views of prisoners about incarceration and freedom, respectively — a perspective usually absent in standard histories of imprisonment. Donna Guy offers a detailed analysis of the rationales behind correctional institutions for minors in Buenos Aires; Diana Paton explores the social and political ingredients of punishment in post-emancipation Jamaica; and Ricardo Salvatore sees the death penalty as a pedagogical tool used by the Argentine state in order to instill an array of social and cultural values among the population.

The concluding remarks by prominent social historian Douglas Hay offer a valuable appraisal of this set of essays from a widely comparative perspective. Hay's comments raise a number of interesting issues, suggest avenues for further research, and highlight the specificities of the Latin American cases and the commonalities they share with those of other regions of the world.

An Agenda for Further Research

The coming to fruition of a new approach to the study of law and legal phenomena in the Latin American context opens up a number of avenues for future research that promise to enrich a variety of ongoing multidisciplinary debates.

With good reason, Douglas Hay notes in his commentary the lack of attention devoted by Latin American legal historians to the question of "popular justice." The construction of a moral order centered on custom, the appropriation and adaptation of state law by popular or subaltern agents, and the understandings derived from a protracted contact with legal authorities appear to have escaped historiographical inquiry, reflection, and debate. This is not only because, as Hay puts it, Latin America belongs to the other side of the great divide separating common law and statutory law traditions. The question of popular legal culture (or cultures), we believe, should be central to the analysis of the social history of law in Latin America. Unfortunately, very few authors have directed their inquiries in this direction. There is some recent work on the ways indigenous peoples used the colonial legal system, but these have remained tied to old discussions regarding the benevolence or wretchedness of Spanish colonialism.

The transition from colony to independence presents us with an interesting dilemma to resolve. The new patriot leadership built a new layer of laws *(derecho patrio)* on top of a legal edifice they did not bother to tear down, the derecho indiano. This created ambiguity, uncertainty, and a great deal of judicial discretionary powers. How did subaltern subjects experience this transition? Did they claim "rights" contemplated in the old legislation? Did they oppose new decrees, ordinances, and laws based upon a knowledge and understanding of colonial laws? How did the abolition of "privilege" and the decline in the military and ecclesiastical *fueros* affect the chances of subaltern subjects to attain justice? Did the distance between "the popular" and "the legal" widen with the consolidation of nation-states? Before we generalize imprudently about how backward and "illegal" popular understandings about justice in the region were, we need to sift through tons of archival materials to really begin to understand the relation between *state* and *popular* legal cultures. Perhaps the overlapping of colonial and postindependence legislation opened up new opportunities for subaltern subjects. Perhaps the contrary was true, as judges acquired increased discretionary powers that ultimately denied rights previously granted to subalterns.

That our collection deals more with *state legal culture* than with popular understandings of the law and its uses cannot be denied. But there is a reason for this. Our comprehension of the procedures, arguments, and understandings used by the judicial system is still terribly inadequate. We have only begun to pose rather basic questions about the formation of this judicial system: for example, its prerequisites and antecedents, the education of lawyers, the tensions between reformers and traditionalists, the role lawyers and judges played in the consolidation of centralized nation-states, and so forth.[46] The importance of the positivist revolution in the legal system (not only in the criminal and penal systems) still needs to be addressed. Before we begin to pose questions about the legal culture of popular or subaltern agents, it is worthwhile to examine what happened to statutory law, how judges interpreted it, and how major processes in Latin American history (e.g., the postindependence fragmentation of political sovereignty, the substitution of *cabildos* by justices of the peace, the loss of autonomy of appellate courts, the struggle for constitutional supremacy, and the dramatic centralization of state authority at the end of the nineteenth century) affected the dynamic relationship between law and society.

Furthermore, we need to separate the activities, tactics, and understandings of subjects seeking justice from the intricacies of the justice system, the discretionary powers of its authorities, and the regularity with which they impose the burden of the law on the powerless and not on the powerful. Both sides of the question need to be addressed separately, even though elite and popular agents interacted. In other words, our understanding of legal cultures has to be connected to and understood in relation to popular agents' interaction with the state in general and with the judicial system in particular. In this regard, a crucial question relates to the pedagogic work of the law. To what extent has law been a predicament, stubbornly beaten upon the heads of the subaltern? Did lawyers' guilds, newspapers, union publications, or other civil associations disseminate legal concepts among the population? Have our courts served as theaters of authority in which the powerful could teach the powerless lessons about the necessity of legal/ moral conduct? How much did popular agents know about the parts of a legal (criminal or civil) legal process? The reception, understanding, dissemination, and refashioning of legal concepts in popular culture is a pending task for Latin American legal historians.

Another problem that needs to be addressed refers to the decline over the postindependence period of corporate fueros. The consolidation of a secular, centralized state authority was predicated upon the dismantling of these corporate privileges, more in tune with the colonial *sociedad estamental*. What was the effect of this crucial reform in the legal system and procedures of the independent nations of Latin America? How did the legal know-how from ecclesiastical, military, and mercantile courts influence the formation of the modern civil and criminal courts?[47] If the period of civil wars was dominated by military politics and strategies, was it also true that military law dominated the procedure and logic of the justice system? If not, how could judicial authorities attain the degree of independence and autonomy needed to enforce important statutes and regulations, against the interest of military authorities? Those who find in present-day Latin America that an independent judiciary still remains an elusive goal have reasons to doubt that such an entity existed in the past. But it is reasonable to hypothesize that in the postindependence period the judiciary gradually acquired a certain autonomy from the three major corporations of the colonial period (the church, the military, and the merchants' guilds).

We should also recall that the actual operation of a given legal system is never circumscribed to a straightforward execution of the legal norm, nor is it limited to the face-to-face encounter of litigants, judges, and lawyers. In the first case, it is important to analyze the myriad ways in which the written law is interpreted, argued, and used, as well as the rhetorical and even theatrical tactics used by the many actors involved. Here, we need to learn more from legal anthropologists who have long realized the importance of looking at courts as "performances." Although a shortage of sources may hinder the historian's efforts to deconstruct these strategies, a more creative and subtle reading of archival records may yield interesting observations. In the second case, we need to look at what Gil Joseph called "legal lubricators," that is, the assortment of legal "experts" (informal attorneys — called *tinterillos* in some countries — community leaders, local power brokers, legal clerks, and the like) that have played (and certainly continue to play) a central role in facilitating the access of important sectors of the population to the legal system.[48] A closer look at these mediating agents will certainly sharpen our understanding of how national legal systems were constructed and how effectively they were implemented throughout Latin America, how different sets of actors (urban lower groups or rural peasants, for instance) got in contact with codes, judges, and tribunals, and how certain aspects of a given legal culture were disseminated.

This connects with the question of accessibility to the courts of law by poor people, which Hay raises in his commentary. In the context of Latin American history, getting at this problem means investigating the difficulties that legal language presented to subalterns and the possible appropriation and use they made of it.[49] We must pay special attention to the practical results that ensued from the employment of a private representative and compare them to the results that were attained by people resorting to the *Defender de Pobres* (defendant of the poor). The rationality of the judicial tactics of subalterns (or the absence of same) depends on the answer we give to this question. Whether "justice" was or became more accessible is related to the actual interventions and results produced by these state legal agents and by the counsel and encouragement provided by tinterillos to people willing to litigate. Another aspect of this question relates to the ability of subaltern witnesses to present testimony to the courts. This crucial issue has not been sufficiently investigated. Were women, people of African origins, slaves, children, or the insane denied the right to present evidence or to give testimony? Did independence and, more generally, the formation of a national state produce major changes in the rights of witnesses?

An issue deserving special attention is the particular situation of women with regard to the law in the different countries of the region, and its evolution over time. Certainly, the enactment of civil codes in the second half of the nineteenth century put women in a situation of strict legal subordination vis-à-vis men. While married, they ceased to be treated as "capable persons" and acquired a legal condition similar to that of children. The same could be said with regard to the criminal codes that were enacted near the end of the nineteenth century. These statutes made women explicitly "irresponsible" for many crimes, because of their "naturally emotional" personality structure. But what happened in the interregnum? What was the legal condition of women during the late colonial and early national periods? How did early postcolonial constitutions deal with the question of women? Were they denied legal "personhood" and legal representation? Did women succeed after independence — as Arlene Díaz suggests — in exploiting the loopholes of disordered legislation to argue for their own economic and social rights within the institution of marriage? Did inheritance laws stemming from the Hispanic legal tradition make it easier for women to acquire and administer property than in countries of the Common Law tradition?[50] This period of transition (1810–1860) — before the advance of codification, positivist criminology, the social hygiene movement, the consolidation of national states, and the project of "progress" — seems to be crucial for understanding the encounter between women and state law and, therefore, should be made a priority in our research agenda.

Another important question relates to the relationship between law and ideology in the nineteenth century. New scholarship, in this collection and elsewhere, affirms the centrality of medical discourse and power in the remaking of legal and state practices in Latin America starting in the 1880s.[51] Medico-legal concepts seem to have had an earlier and more lasting impact on the societies and culture of Latin America than on those of Europe and the United States. Why was this so? Why did liberalism and classic penology fail to dominate legal structures and state practices? Why was the doctrine of "social defense" able to displace notions of individual responsibility, free will, and the contractual nature of human behavior? Much work of a comparative nature needs to be done to "place" Latin America within contemporary trends in legal thought and ideology. We can no longer take a few essays on moral or legal theory and use them to examine the replication and adaptation of liberalism to postindependence Latin America. For the changes in legal cultures that marked the transition between derecho indiano and *derecho patrio* were of gargantuan proportions. In between, there were isolated performances, reforms that did not congeal, untenable constitutions, and a multiplicity of laws and decrees that bore the marks of liberalism. But liberalism was merely an intermezzo—a brief transition between colonial notions of justice and a justice organized around the principle of social defense. The legal arena provides another enticing opportunity to revisit the failure of liberalism as a viable organization of society-state relations.

The study of forms of representation of criminals and their impact on both the formulation of codes and the prosecution of suspects, to mention but one possible course, ought to become a central component in the future development of legal studies in Latin America. The study of images of crime and criminals as presented in literature, media reporting, scientific treatises, testimonies, poems and popular ballads, and other forms of representation will allow us to explore the (sometimes subtle, sometimes quite evident) links between them and specifically legal phenomena.[52] Instances of "moral panic" are another possible avenue to explore the connections between law and popular culture. In such cases, a combination of real events, rumors, media manipulation, and public paranoia, generally in the midst of an otherwise critical situation, may generate stiff state repression as well as popular support of it—which may in turn affect the relationship between the law and those groups affected by the cleanup campaign, generally in the form of criminalization of certain conducts and practices.[53]

Finally, there is the matter of the penal institutions and their impact on the captive populations. Prisons, reformatories, penal colonies and other such institutions continued the work of law in both a legal and illegal manner. They were the territory of extralegal coercion, unobserved internal bylaws, punishments not prescribed in the judicial sentence, and "customary orders" built by inmates, guards, and authorities alike. How did this system of practices relate to the hegemonic discourse about the law (equality and justice)? These institutions operated under principles of obedience to rules and classification; hence, the premium was on difference, not equality. Implicit in the idea of rehabilitation were notions of "fall," "disease," and "vice." How did these institutions combine ancient (religious) and modern (medical) discourses and put them at the service of perverse systems of sociability? These institutions constituted the other face of the law, a sphere where the subaltern subject had almost no possibility of contestation. How and to what extent were these institutions colonized by medico-legal power? Was this process irreversible?

As we can see, there is plenty to do in this attempt to refashion one of the oldest traditions in the historiography of Latin America. This volume, needless to say, does not represent the culmination of this effort, but only a small contribution to its flourishing. We are confident that the reader will find in the pages that follow a confirmation of the potential that this endeavor has for rewriting the social and cultural history of Latin America.

Notes

1 For recent collective efforts see Ricardo D. Salvatore, ed., "Criminal Justice History in Latin America," special issue of *Crime, History & Societies*, no. 2, vol. 2 (1998); Ricardo D. Salvatore and Carlos Aguirre, eds., *The Birth of the Penitentiary in Latin America* (Austin: University of Texas Press, 1996); Carlos Aguirre and Robert Buffington, eds. *Reconstructing Criminality in Latin America* (Wilmington, Del.: Scholarly Resources, 2000); Juan Méndez, Guillermo O'Donnell, and Paulo Sergio Pinheiro, eds., *The (Un)Rule of Law and the Underprivileged in Latin America* (Notre Dame, Ill.: University of Notre Dame Press, 1999).

2 For a discussion about the complexity of colonial legislation, see Víctor Tao Anzoátegui, "Ordenes normativos y prácticas socio-jurídicas: la justicia," in *Nueva Historia de la Nación Argentina*, vol. 2 (Buenos Aires: Planeta, 1999), pp. 283–315.

3 On lawyers in the early independent period, see especially Víctor Uribe, "Kill All the Lawyers! Lawyers and the Independence Movement in New Granada, 1809–1820," *The Americas* 52, no. 2 (Oct. 1995): 175–210.

4 Rosas, for instance, insisted that *paysanos* (country folks) learn the norms of the

land and obey them without exceptions. See Ricardo D. Salvatore, *State Order and Subaltern Experience in Rosas's Buenos Aires Province* (Durham, N.C.: Duke University Press, forthcoming), chap. 4.

5 It would be interesting to study the process by which each republic granted lawyers the exclusive right to represent litigants, thus banning (at least in theory) informal legal practitioners. This process was neither automatic nor swift, and its study may yield important elements for understanding several aspects of the process of state formation.

6 See, for example, Román Alzamora, *Curso de historia del derecho peruano* (Lima: Imprenta del Estado, 1876); Alberto Brenes Cordoba, *Historia del derecho* (San José, Costa Rica: Tip. Lehmann, 1913); Tomás Miguel Arganaraz, *Contribucion al estudio de la historia del derecho* (Córdoba, 1919); Toribio Esquivel Obregón, *Apuntes para la historia del derecho en México* (México: Antigua Librería Robredo, 1900); Carlos Bunge, *Historia del derecho argentino* (Buenos Aires: Facultad de derecho y ciencias sociales, 1912); and Fernando Velez, *Datos para la historia del derecho nacional* (Medellin: Imprenta del departamento, 1891).

7 Spanish penologist Luis Jiménez de Asúa, for example, contributed greatly to developing this field in several Spanish American republics. Among his numerous books, see especially *La legislación penal y la práctica penitenciaria en Suramérica* (Valladolid: Talleres Tipográficos "Cuesta," 1924). See also Miguel Macedo, *Apuntes para la historia del derecho penal mexicano* (México: Editorial Cultura, 1931).

8 Atilio Sivirichi, *Derecho indígena peruano* (Lima: Ediciones Kuntur, 1946).

9 See, for example, José Antonio Encinas, *Contribución a una legislación tutelar indígena* (Lima: C. F. Southwell, 1918). A perceptive analysis of this trend in relation to penal legislation on Indians is Deborah Poole, "Ciencia, peligrosidad y represión en la criminología indigenista peruana," in Carlos Aguirre and Charles Walker, eds., *Bandoleros, abigeos y montoneros: Criminalidad y violencia en el Perú, siglos XVIII–XX* (Lima: Instituto de Apoyo Agrario, 1990), pp. 335–67.

10 See, especially, Rafael Altamira, *Estudios sobre las fuentes de conocimiento del derecho indiano* (Lisboa: Empresa Nacional de Publicidade, 1900); Ricardo Levene, *Introducción a la historia del derecho indiano* (Buenos Aires: V. Abeledo, 1924); Rafael Altamira, *Técnica de investigación en la historia del derecho indiano* (México: J. Porrúa e Hijos, 1939); José María Ots Capdequí, *Manual de historia del derecho espanol en las Indias y del derecho propiamente indiano* (Buenos Aires: Editorial Losada, 1945); Rafael Altamira, *Manual de investigacion de la historia del derecho indiano* (México: Instituto Panamericano de Geografía e Historia, 1948). For a recent synthesis, see Ismael Sánchez Bella, Alberto de la Hera, and Carlos Díaz Rementeria, *Historia del derecho indiano* (Madrid: MAPFRE, 1992).

11 For a recent overview, see Víctor Tau Anzoátegui, *Nuevos horizontes en el estudio histórico del derecho indiano* (Buenos Aires: Instituto de Investigaciones de Historia del Derecho, 1997).

12 Stuart B. Schwartz, *Sovereignty and Society in Colonial Brazil: The High Court of*

Bahia and Its Judges, 1609–1751 (Berkeley: University of California Press, 1973); Thomas Flory, *Judge and Jury in Imperial Brazil, 1808–1871: Social Control and Political Stability in the New State* (Austin: University of Texas Press, 1981); Woodrow Borah, *Justice by Insurance: The General Indian Court of Colonial Mexico and the Legal Aides of the Half-Real* (Berkeley: University of California Press, 1983); Colin Mac-Lachlan, *Criminal Justice in Eighteenth-Century Mexico: A Study of the Tribunal de la Acordada* (Berkeley: University of California Press, 1974).

13 Eugene Genovese, *Roll, Jordan, Roll: The World the Slaves Made* (New York: Vintage, 1976); Douglas Hay et al., *Albion's Fatal Tree: Crime and Society in Eighteenth-Century England* (New York: Pantheon, 1975).

14 William B. Taylor, *Drinking, Homicide, and Rebellion in Colonial Mexican Villages* (Stanford: Stanford University Press, 1979); Paul Vanderwood, *Disorder and Progress: Bandits, Police, and Mexican Development* (Lincoln: University of Nebraska Press, 1981; 2d ed., Wilmington, Del.: Scholarly Resources, 1992).

15 Here we can offer only a sample of the best scholarship in these areas. Work on peasant rebellions and revolts was surveyed in two anthologies: Steve J. Stern, ed., *Rebellion, Resistance, and Consciousness in the Andean Peasant World* (Madison: University of Wisconsin Press, 1987), and Friedrich Katz, ed., *Riot, Rebellion, and Revolution: Rural Social Conflict in Mexico* (Princeton, N.J.: Princeton University Press, 1988). On slavery and slave agency, see Rebecca Scott, *Slave Emancipation in Cuba: The Transition to Free Labor* (Princeton, N.J.: Princeton University Press, 1985); Robert Paquette, *Sugar is Made With Blood* (Middletown, Conn.: Wesleyan University Press, 1988); Joao J. Reis, *Rebelião escrava no Brasil: a história do levante dos malês, 1835* (Sao Paulo: Brasiliense, 1986). Studies on labor history include Daniel James, *Resistance and Integration: Peronism and the Argentine Working Class, 1946–1976* (New York: Cambridge University Press, 1988); Peter Winn, *Weavers of Revolution: The Yarur Workers and Chile's Road to Socialism* (New York: Oxford University Press, 1986); John French, *The Brazilian Workers' ABC: Class Conflict and Alliances in Modern São Paulo* (Chapel Hill: University of North Carolina Press, 1992). An overview in Emilia Viotti da Costa, "Experience versus Structures: New Tendencies in the History of Labor and the Working Class in Latin America: What Do We Gain? What Do We Lose?" *International Labor and Working Class History* 36 (fall 1989): 3–24. More recently, John French has offered an illuminating example of the confluence between labor and legal history. See his "Drowning in Laws but Starving (for Justice?): Brazilian Labor Law and the Workers' Quest to Realize the Imaginary," *Political Power and Social Theory* 12 (1998): 181–218.

16 Steve J. Stern, "The Social Significance of Judicial Institutions in an Exploitative Society: Huamanga, Peru, 1570–1640," in George Collier et al. eds., *The Inca and Aztec States, 1400–1800* (New York: Academic Press, 1982), pp. 289–320.

17 See Lyman Johnson, ed., *The Problem of Order in Changing Societies: Essays on Crime and Policing in Argentina and Uruguay, 1750–1940* (Albuquerque: University of

New Mexico Press, 1990); Blanca Silvestrini, *Violencia y criminalidad en Puerto Rico, 1898–1973: apuntes para un estudio de historia social* (Río Piedras: Universidad de Puerto Rico, Editorial Universitaria, 1980); Boris Fausto, *Crime e Cotidiano: A Criminalidade em Sao Paulo (1880–1924)* (São Paulo: Ed. Brasiliense, 1984).

18 The bibliography on banditry in Latin America is enormous. Key works include Vanderwood, *Disorder and Progress;* Linda Lewin, "The Oligarchical Limitations of Social Banditry in Brazil: The Case of the 'Good' Thief Antonio Silvino," *Past and Present* 82 (Feb. 1979): 116–46; Richard Slatta, ed., *Bandidos: The Varieties of Latin American Banditry* (New York: Greenwood, 1987); Gonzalo Sánchez and Donny Meertens, *Bandoleros, gamonales y campesinos: El caso de la violencia en Colombia* (Bogotá: Ancora, 1984); and Aguirre and Walker, eds. *Bandoleros, abigeos y montoneros.* A suggestive reappraisal of this issue is Gilbert Joseph, "On the Trail of Latin American Bandits: A Reexamination of Peasant Resistance," *Latin American Research Review* 25, no. 3 (1990): 7–53. See also the ensuing debate in *Latin American Research Review* 26/1 (1991).

19 E. P. Thompson, *Whigs and Hunters: The Origins of the Black Act* (New York: Pantheon, 1975), Peter Linebaugh, *The London Hanged: Crime and Civil Society in Eighteenth-Century London* (New York: Cambridge University Press, 1992); Genovese, *Roll, Jordan, Roll;* Douglas Hay, "Property, Authority, and the Criminal Law," in Hay et al. *Albion's Fatal Tree,* pp. 17–63.

20 By *hegemony* the Italian Marxist thinker Antonio Gramsci meant a system of domination in which the ruling groups managed to gain the seemingly voluntary acquiescence of the subordinated. See the introduction to Chantal Mouffe, *Gramsci and Marxist Theory* (London: Routledge & Kegan Paul, 1979).

21 David J. Rothman, *The Discovery of the Asylum: Social Order and Disorder in the New Republic* (Boston: Little, Brown, 1971); Michael Ignatieff, *A Just Measure of Pain: The Penitentiary in the Industrial Revolution* (New York: Pantheon, 1978); Pieter Spierenburg, *The Spectacle of Suffering: Executions and the Evolution of Repression* (New York: Cambridge University Press, 1984); Pieter Spierenburg, *The Prison Experience: Disciplinary Institutions and Their Inmates in Early Modern Europe* (New Brunswick, N.J.: Rutgers University Press, 1991); Patricia O'Brien, *The Promise of Punishment: Prisons in Nineteenth-Century France* (Princeton, N.J.: Princeton University Press, 1980); David Garland, *Punishment and Welfare: A History of Penal Strategies* (Aldershot: Gower, 1985); Peter Linebaugh, *The London Hanged: Crime and Society in the Eighteenth Century* (London: Penguin, 1991).

22 On this, see especially David Garland, *Punishment and Modern Society* (Chicago: University of Chicago Press, 1990).

23 For a valuable effort at identifying Foucault's relevance for historians, see Randall McGowen, "Power and Humanity, or Foucault among Historians," in Colin Jones and Roy Porter, eds., *Reassessing Foucault: Power, Medicine, and the Body* (London and New York: Routledge, 1994), pp. 91–112.

24 These exceptions include Sean Wilentz, *Chants Democratic: New York City and the*

Rise of the American Working Class, 1788–1850 (New York: Oxford University Press, 1984); Patrick Joyce, *Visions of the People: Industrial England and the Question of Class, 1840–1914* (Cambridge: Cambridge University Press, 1990); Keith M. Baker, *Inventing the French Revolution* (Cambridge: Cambridge University Press, 1990); Lynn Hunt, *The Family Romance of the French Revolution* (London: Routledge, 1992); and Robert Darnton, *The Great Cat Massacre* (London: Allen Lane, 1984).

25 See the special issue of *Hispanic American Historical Review* devoted to discussing Mexico's "new" cultural history (vol. 79, No. 2, May 1999).

26 Eric Van Young, "The New Cultural History Comes to Old Mexico," *Hispanic American Historical Review* 79, no. 2 (1999): 211–247.

27 See, for example, Florencia Mallon, *Peasant and Nation: The Making of Post-Colonial Mexico and Peru* (Berkeley: University of California Press, 1995); Peter Guardino, *Peasants, Politics, and the Formation of Mexico's National State: Guerrero, 1800–1857* (Stanford: Stanford University Press, 1996); Charles Walker, *Smoldering Ashes: Cuzco and the Creation of Republican Peru, 1780–1840* (Durham: Duke University Press, 1999); Gilbert Joseph and Daniel Nugent, eds., *Everyday Forms of State Formation: Revolution and the Negotiation of Rule in Modern Mexico* (Durham, N.C.: Duke University Press, 1994); Salvatore, *The Wandering Working Class.*

28 See, for example, Eduardo Zimmermann, "El poder judicial, la construcción del estado, y el federalismo: Argentina, 1860–1880," in Eduardo Posada-Carbó, ed., *In Search of a New Order: Essays on the Politics and Society of Nineteenth-Century Latin America* (London: Institute of Latin American Studies, 1998), pp. 131–52.

29 See the important collection edited by Mindie Lazarus-Black and Susan F. Hirsch, *Contested States: Law, Hegemony and Resistance* (New York: Routledge, 1994).

30 Sally E. Merry, "Courts as Performances: Domestic Violence Hearings in a Hawai'i Family Court," and Susan F. Hirsch, "Kadhi's Courts as Complex Sites of Resistance: The State, Islam, and Gender in Postcolonial Kenya," both in Lazarus-Black and Hirsch, eds., *Contested States.*

31 For a review of these studies, see Sally E. Merry, "Law and Colonialism," *Law and Society Review* 25, no. 4 (1991): 889–922. See also Kristin Mann and Richard Roberts, eds., *Law in Colonial Africa* (Portsmouth, N.H.: Heinemann, 1991).

32 On the usefulness of subaltern studies for Latin American historiography, see especially Florencia Mallon, "The Promise and Dilemma of Subaltern Studies: Perspectives from Latin American History," *American Historical Review* 99, no. 5 (1994): 1491–1515. See also "Subaltern Studies in the Americas," Special Issue of *Dispositio/n* XIX, no. 46 (1994), and John Beverley, *Subalternity and Representation: Arguments in Cultural Theory* (Durham, N.C.: Duke University Press, 1999).

33 See, for an example of this strategy, Ricardo Salvatore, "Stories of Proletarianization in Rural Argentina, 1820–1860," *Dispositio/n* XIX, no. 46 (1994): 197–216.

34 Margaret Rago, *Do cabaré ao lar: A utopia da cidade disciplinar* (Rio de Janeiro: Paz e Terra, 1987); Luis Carlos Soares, *Prostitution in Nineteenth-Century Rio de Janeiro* (London: Institute of Latin American Studies, 1988); Donna J. Guy, *Sex and*

Danger in Buenos Aires (Lincoln: University of Nebraska Press, 1991); Sueann Caulfield, "Getting Into Trouble: Dishonest Women, Modern Girls, and Women-Men in the Conceptual Language of *vida policial, 1925–1927*," in Barbara Laslett et al., eds., *History and Theory: Feminist Research, Debates, Contestations* (Chicago: University of Chicago Press, 1997), pp. 328–58; Sueann Caulfield and Martha de Abreu Esteves, "Fifty Years of Virginity in Rio de Janeiro: Sexual Politics and Gender Roles in Juridical and Popular Discourse, 1890–1940," *Luso-Brazilian Review* 30, no. 1 (summer 1993): 47–73; Magali Engel, *Meretrizes e doutores: saber médico e prostituição no Rio de Janeiro, 1840–1890* (São Paulo: Editora Brasiliense, 1989), Margareth Rago, *Os prazeres da noite: prostituição e códigos da sexualidade feminina em São Paulo, 1890–1930* (Rio de Janeiro: Paz e Terra, 1991).

35 See, for example, Alberto Flores Galindo, *Buscando un Inca: Identidad y utopía en los Andes*, 4th edition (Lima: Editorial Horizonte, 1988); João José Reis, *A morte é uma festa: ritos fúnebres e revolta popular no Brasil do século XIX* (São Paulo: Companhia das Letras, 1991).

36 Joanne Rappaport, *The Politics of Memory: Native Historical Interpretation in the Colombian Andes* (New York: Cambridge University Press, 1990).

37 Laura Nader, ed., *Law in Culture and Society* (Chicago: Aldine, 1969. Reprinted, Berkeley: University of California Press, 1997).

38 Charles Cutter, *The Legal Culture of Northern New Spain, 1700–1810* (Albuquerque: University of New Mexico Press, 1995); Susan Kellogg, *Law and the Transformation of Aztec Culture, 1500–1700* (Norman: University of Oklahoma Press, 1995).

39 In the words of anthropologist John Comaroff, "the law may serve those who contest authority as well as those who wield it." Comaroff, "Foreword," in Lazarus-Black and Hirsch, eds. *Contested States*, pp. ix–xiii.

40 This is precisely the kind of exploration that Allen Wells and Gilbert Joseph attempted in their monograph, *Summer of Discontent, Seasons of Upheaval: Elite Politics and Rural Insurgency in Yucatán, 1876–1915* (Stanford, Calif.: Stanford University Press, 1996).

41 This perspective challenges, in many respects, the view of the law as just an instrument of social control. Certain interpretations grounded in both Marxist and Foucauldian theories continue to view law as, in the first case, a weapon of class domination and, in the second, as one of the most important devices in the creation of modern "disciplinary" societies. Though we will not deny that there is ample support for these views, they nonetheless offer a sort of reductionist rendition of the role of law in modern societies. For an insightful discussion of Marxist views on law, see Philip Corrigan and Derek Sayer, "How the Law Rules: Variations on Some Themes in Karl Marx," in Bob Fryer et al., eds., *Law, State and Society* (London: Croom Helm, 1981), pp. 21–53. An illuminating discussion of Foucault's views on power, government, and the law is Mitchell Dean, *Critical and Effective Histories: Foucault's Methods and Historical Sociology* (New York: Routledge, 1994). Needless to say, the literature on both issues is overwhelming.

42 O'Donnell further explains: "By 'fairly' applied I mean that the administrative application or judicial adjudication of legal rules is consistent across equivalent cases, is made without taking into consideration the class, status, or power differentials of the participants in such processes, and applies procedures that are pre-established and knowable." Guillermo O'Donnell, "Polyarchies and the (Un)Rule of Law in Latin America: A Partial Conclusion," in Méndez et al., eds., *The (Un)Rule of Law*, pp. 307–308.

43 Jeremy Adelman and Miguel Angel Centeno, "Between Liberalism and Neo-Liberalism: Law's Dilemma in Latin America" (unpublished manuscript), p. 12.

44 It is worth emphasizing, though, that a view like this will help overcome notions that always attribute to the victims of legal arbitrariness a sort of stubborn stupidity, for they keep believing that justice will eventually come.

45 There is a critical difference between the amount and nature of power held, for instance, by a magistrate in nineteenth-century Lima or Mexico City, and a local justice of the peace in a remote village in the Andes. Quite different rules would apply in each case. As Joanna Drzewieniecki has suggested for the case of judges in Andean Peruvian villages, "even though they were quite obviously representatives of the system of domination and part of their legitimacy rested on the fact that they had power, judges still had to please peasants to some extent if peasants were to continue to provide them with a source of income and if everyday levels of tension were to be kept within acceptable levels." Joanna Drzewieniecki, "Indigenous Peoples, Law, and Politics in Peru" (paper delivered at the LASA 1995 conference, Washington, D.C.).

46 See the work by Víctor Uribe and Eduardo Zimmerman, previously cited. See also Fernando de Trazegnies, *La idea de derecho en el Perú republicano del siglo XIX* (Lima: Pontificia Universidad Católica del Perú, 1980).

47 As Douglas Hay suggests, we need to do research not only on the workings of the criminal justice system but on the whole machinery of justice, with its various overlapping layers and jurisdictions. It is the very complexity of this multilayered system that generates the ambivalence, the contradictions, and sometimes the bureaucratic cruelty that real actors encounter in their interactions with legal authorities.

48 Joseph's comment came during the discussions at the Yale conference. A fascinating treatment of this issue for China is Melissa Macauley, *Social Power and Legal Culture: Litigation Masters in Late Imperial China* (Stanford, Calif.: Stanford University Press, 1998). See also Carlos Aguirre, "Tinterillos and Leguleyos: Subaltern Subjects and Legal Intermediaries in Modern Peru" (paper presented at the LASA 2000 congress, Miami).

49 Here, again, the figure of the tinterillo as a key translator of legal lexicon for subaltern subjects takes on crucial relevance.

50 Díaz's assertion that Venezuelan middle-class women had incorporated by the mid-nineteenth century the rhetoric of liberalism and were arguing for rights in terms of

ciudadanía (citizenship) should challenge social historians of the period. For if this pattern of behavior and discourse were generalized, it would mean that women in nineteenth-century Latin America were a bit ahead of contemporary advocates for women's rights in Europe and the United States, actually claiming citizenship rights in court.

51 See Ricardo D. Salvatore, "Positivist Criminology and the Emergence of a Medico-Legal State in Argentina," in Peter Becker and Richard Wetzell, eds. *The Criminal and His Scientists* (Cambridge: Cambridge University Press, forthcoming).

52 An exemplary study in this regard is Marie-Christine Leps's examination of the mutual borrowing of images and themes between criminology, literature, and journalism in nineteenth-century Europe, *Apprehending the Criminal: The Production of Deviance in Nineteenth-Century Discourse* (Durham, N.C.: Duke University Press, 1992). For a study of literary representations of Argentine criminals, see Josefina Ludmer, *El cuerpo del delito: un manual* (Buenos Aires: Perfil Libros, 1999).

53 See, for instance, Erich Goode and Nachman Ben-Yehuda, *Moral Panics: The Social Construction of Deviance* (Oxford: Blackwell, 1994).

PART I

Legal Mediations: State, Society, and the

Conflictive Nature of Law and Justice

Crime in the Time of the Great Fear:

Indians and the State in the Peruvian

Southern Andes, 1780–1820

CHARLES F. WALKER

From late 1780 until the middle of 1781, the Tupac Amaru rebellion reverberated throughout the southern Andes of Peru. Led by José Gabriel Condorcanqui, who assumed the name of Tupac Amaru II, rebels imprisoned, humiliated, and executed authorities, destroyed textile mills and haciendas, and planned or dreamed about what to do on overthrowing the colonial state. Although the leaders were executed in 1781, insurgency continued to the south and motivated malcontents throughout South America. The rebels stunned Spaniards and other observers. Yet rebellion was not the only strategy used by the lower classes in this period. In the years preceding and following the uprising, Indians of the Cuzco region, the key social base of the rebellion, also addressed their grievances in the courts. Through the *protector de indios,* the legal representative of the Indians, they filed lawsuits against authorities whom they considered abusive. In these cases, they pledged their support to the King and implicitly and at times explicitly recognized Indians' inferior position in colonial Peru. In this essay, I examine the seeming contradiction between members of the same social group — and at times the very same individuals — taking such dramatically different routes.[1]

The legal system constituted a crucial meeting ground in colonial Spanish America. In the courts, the state inculcated and enforced its notions of hierarchy and social order. Yet, as many analysts have shown, subaltern groups also used the courts to address grievances, point out contradictions, and even challenge aspects of colonial rule. The legal system buttressed social and racial distinctions while also providing the means for groups to soften or question these hierarchies.[2] It constituted a contact zone or "contested terrain" in which the rules of colonialism were imposed yet at the same time contested.

The analysis of crime and society in Cuzco during the decades that bridge the eighteenth and nineteenth centuries, and thus the transition from colony to republic, sheds light on a pair of related questions. What did the massive use of the legal system by Indians mean in terms of Spanish control? In this regard, did the Indians' efforts in the courts strengthen Spanish rule by reinforcing colonial codes of behavior and discourse? Specifically, did this reliance on the courts and its ideology dovetail with the anti-Indian measures and discourse imposed by the state after the defeat of the Tupac Amaru rebels? Second, did this reliance on the courts preempt other forms of political behavior, above all collective action such as rebellions? Late colonial Cuzco represents a particularly rich case for studying the relationship between the use of the legal system and rebellions. The court cases reviewed here are nestled between the massive Tupac Amaru rebellion and the series of uprisings that ultimately made up the War of Independence in the southern Andes.

Indians and the Courts

In the wake of the Tupac Amaru rebellion, authorities punished anyone suspected of supporting the rebels and repressed key elements of indigenous culture. José Gabriel Tupac Amaru, his wife and key military strategist Micaela Bastidas, other family members, and the movement's inner circle were executed in grisly public rituals in April 1781, their body parts displayed for months. In some towns, soldiers forced all adult men into the plaza and killed one out of every five.[3] The Bourbon state removed indigenous authorities, *caciques,* believed to be loyal to Tupac Amaru, himself a cacique. They also banned a central text in eighteenth-century Inca nationalism, Inca Garcilaso de la Vega's *Royal Commentaries of the Incas and General History of Peru,* and prohibited dances, clothing, and artwork associated with the Incas and Indian culture. Authorities lobbied for the "extirpation" of the Indian language Quechua and the Castilianization of the

Andes. The massive uprising had enraged representatives of the state and they were anxious to punish and prevent, efforts supported by non-Indian groups.[4]

In this somber context, "the Great Fear," Indians from communities or *ayllus* employed a host of strategies to defend their political autonomy and economic resources, including horizontal and vertical alliances, threats of violence, passive resistance, and, above all, lawsuits. In hundreds of trials, Indians denounced mistreatment by local authorities, often questioning these individuals' right to hold office. In a period when residents of Cuzco were constantly reminded of the physical, economic, and cultural costs of a failed rebellion, Indians took advantage through the legal system of the state's fear of another uprising and its determination to constrain local officials. Their repeated use of the legal system reflected their belief that it worked.[5] By countering the post–Tupac Amaru Bourbon "reconquest" through lawsuits, Indian peasants not only contested the reforms but reshaped relations among local authorities, the state, and themselves.

I examined more than one thousand trial records, *causas criminales,* from 1783 to 1823: 575 from the Real Audiencia, 389 from the Intendencia, 218 from the Cabildo, and 71 from Intendencia-Provincia. In theory, the Audiencia should have served as an appeals court for cases viewed in the Intendencia (introduced in 1784), the main legal institution, and the Cabildo, which handled nonviolent urban transgressions. Yet many cases proceeded directly to the Audiencia, founded in 1787. In general, it judged the more serious crimes.[6] Cases were found from every *partido* of Cuzco as well as Huamanga, Guayaquil, La Paz, and Arequipa. Almost half the cases tried in the Real Audiencia, the Intendencia, and the Intendencia-Provincia were crimes committed within the city of Cuzco. Other prominent areas were Quispicanchis, Canas y Canchis, Chumbivilcas, and Abancay. Not surprisingly, these were economically important areas with two nuclei of criminal activities: *obrajes* (textile mills) and trade routes. Higher populations, greater economic activity, proximity to the courts, and generally stronger links to the state's operations and discourse explain here as elsewhere the higher percentage of crimes in urban and economic centers. However, as the cases involving remote, predominantly Quechua monolingual communities demonstrate, the legal system, both its redressive and repressive components, reached deeply into Cuzco's rural society in the late colonial period.

The analysis here focuses on roughly 20 percent of the total cases, those involving behavior by authorities considered by the colonial state and/or members of local society to be abusive and inappropriate. This included tax fraud and unjustified imprisonment, but most were described generally as "abuses." Of course, many cases of abuse never reached the courts. Fear of retribution discouraged many from lodging a complaint. Many conflicts were resolved (or dropped) at a local level. Abusive conduct was thus much more extensive than that reported in the trials, but by the same token, the means of recourse for civil society were not limited to lawsuits. In almost all of these trials, a great deal of negotiation and accommodation took place prior to the lawsuit.

Several important limitations of criminal trials as historical sources need to be noted. First, despite the use of the courts by every sector of society, a great deal of criminal behavior was not tried in the formal legal system. Local authorities—caciques, Spanish mayors, and Indian mayors—were authorized to punish petty transgressors without formal trial.[7] Violent, seemingly arbitrary behavior that served to buttress the powerful frequently characterized these efforts at local "law enforcement" and social control. Much criminal behavior was punished without the intervention of the state, local or viceregal. Court records contain numerous references to private jails in haciendas and obrajes.[8] The elite was not alone in taking justice into its own hands. The local population, including the peasantry, dealt quite harshly with thieves and other transgressors. Although some criminals such as infamous rustlers were handed over to colonial authorities, most crimes involving people of the same community were managed directly. The trial records reviewed here thus slight intraclass crimes.[9]

When using trial records as an historical source, the context of the courtroom must be taken into account. In his study of colonial Mexico, William Taylor points out a series of inherent distortions of criminal trials. Colonial employees transcribed, summarized, edited, and, in the case of Peru, often translated the testimonies in the trials. More importantly, the strategies and terminology employed in the courts were shaped by and designed to conform to colonial notions about law and society. Therefore, the explanations provided by the defendants, particularly about their motives, must be interpreted cautiously.[10] The gap between peasant society and official colonial discourse and practice was even greater in Peru than in Mexico. This is evident in the shoddy statistical data found in the Peruvian trials compared to those reviewed by Taylor. Not only was the state seemingly unable to register information on rural society (except for tax rolls) but in the trials it demonstrated little interest. When Indian litigants or witnesses testified, a rough calculation of his or her age was made and often no profession was listed. The predominant notions about Indians as a homogenous social group, and the indolence of state officials, explain this comparative inattention to sociological detail. Although Quechua translators were provided, the courtroom in Cuzco represented a foreign and intimidating site for a highlands peasant. It should be kept in mind, however, that Andean Indians had a centuries-long tradition of court battles and that many of the Indians participated as willing plaintiffs.[11] Coercion against the defendants was apparently infrequent. In colonial criminal trials, a surprising and welcome amount of forthright statements about local society can be found.[12]

Caciques and Politics: Bloods versus Newcomers

Caciques were the primary defendants in the trials in late colonial Cuzco against abusive authorities. In the Real Audiencia, they were accused in 44 percent of the cases (37/84) while subdelegates were accused in 20 percent, *recaudadores* or tax collectors in 20 percent, and mayors in 11 percent. In the Intendencia (including Intendencia-Provincias), caciques were accused in 36 percent of the cases (22/58); mayors in 22 percent; priests, subdelegates, and members of the military in 12 percent each; and recaudadores in 10 percent.[13] These cases reflected the enduring struggles over the cacique office. Throughout the eighteenth century, ethnic caciques faced pressure from above, the demanding Bourbon state, as well as below, as their Indian constituents resisted increasing demands channeled through the caciques and questioned their legitimacy. The Tupac Amaru rebellion accelerated efforts by the state to replace ethnic or hereditary caciques.[14] Unfortunately, it is not always clear whether the accused cacique was hereditary (*de sangre,* "blood") or a newcomer *(interino)*. In eleven of the thirty-seven cases in the Real Audiencia against caciques, explicit mention was made about their status as interinos. These include some of the cases with the most flagrant and systematic abuses. Indians were the plaintiffs in 72 percent of the Real Audiencia cases and 48 percent of those in the Intendencia. The protector de indios lodged these suits, but the indigenous plaintiffs testified in every case. Often they were supported by other authorities such as priests or contending caciques.

Two major types of *abusos* challenged in the courts stand out. The first was systematic exploitation: usurpation of land, tribute fraud, coerced labor, and the forced sale of goods (*reparto,* banned in 1780). The allegations often included reports of wanton violence and "immoral behavior" such as adultery or polygamy. Usually concentrating on a particular authority, the accusations generally mentioned the complicity of others. The second major category was violence or imprisonment by an authority against a commoner. The fact that the beating or imprisonment was often preceded (provoked according to the defendant) by a confrontation over the authority's misbehavior indicates that these two categories were related: exploitative practices were often backed up by violence while economic gain and coercive social control constituted integral elements of local power.

Almost every possible combination of abuses can be found. In fact, it was unusual for a single allegation to be lodged, as these practices were usually related. For example, a subdelegate in Quispicanchis was accused of forcing Indians to work for him at a textile mill and at his house for free, charging exempt Indians the head tax in order to pocket the money, and replacing authorities with his friends and relatives.[15] Another subdelegate reportedly worked with an accountant and a cacique to sell unwanted or overpriced mules, dried potatoes, corn, and coca leaves to Indians. This enterprise allowed him to demand free labor and the use of extensive community lands.[16] The *alcalde mayor-recaudador-cacique* of Ocongate sent Indians to work in coca plantations in the Paucartambo valley, sold mules, iron, and other goods in exchange for the best livestock at "very low prices," and excluded Indians from the tax rolls despite charging them tribute. His father was rumored to have conducted similar operations, "keeping the courts always busy."[17]

In a 1792 case against Don Pedro Villavicencia, cacique interino of Sangarará, Quispicanchis, and his ally, the priest Don Manuel Mariano Alvarez, Indians from six ayllus testified that the cacique would not allow them to work on highland estates to earn their tribute money. He forced them, instead, to labor on his "opulent estate" under much worse conditions. The list of complaints against Villavicencia also included overpriced repartos that had to be paid in cash, forced donations during religious festivals, fines for those who did not dress properly in these festivals, arbitrary taxes during the redistribution of land, imprisonment of debtors when they attended mass, forced donations of potatoes by the heads of the ayllus, whippings, and demands for many free laborers. The defendants saw the hand of a former cacique behind the accusation. In the end, Villavicencia was apparently suspended as cacique.[18] This and other trials depict the close relationship among the different types of exploitation. Authorities used the returns in one of these activities to reinforce another. For example, they channeled profits from tribute collection and fraud into commercial activities, while transforming debts into free or cheap labor. "Power" was not constituted in this period by the control of a single economic resource such as land but rather by combining economic gain through a number of enterprises with efforts to monopolize political dominance.

Despite the oppressive scenarios portrayed in the trials, local power emerges in the records as short-term and fragile. On one hand, many of the malfeasants were outsiders who presumably wanted to gain money, allies, and status and then move on to more lucrative enterprises. They did not attempt to entrench themselves locally. On the other hand, divisions within elite groups and active resistance by the peasantry hindered the accumulation of economic and political power. Even with broad alliances and numerous concessions, a newcomer confronted powerful enemies. For example, local priests often challenged caciques interinos from the beginning of their tenure, while subdelegates faced the opposition of venerable caciques. Despite public displays of power such as indiscriminate whippings, officials feared provoking the commoners. Officials depended on them economically and worried about inciting protests locally or in the courts. In light of the crown's distaste, albeit haphazardly enforced, for wayward authorities, local authorities dreaded the possibility of rumors or accusations about misbehavior reaching Intendancy officials. Therefore, beyond the veneer of local omnipotence, the power of local officials in this period remained brittle.

The alliances depicted in these trials highlight the tangled political alignments in the post–Tupac Amaru era after the creation of the Intendancies and the erosion of the cacique office. Political alliances assumed no standard pattern in this period. The subdelegates needed the support of the locally powerful. They frequently allied with caciques, either those they had placed in office or acquiescent veterans. They could, however, also align with influential economic figures such as hacienda owners, militia leaders, or even priests. Nearly every possible combination of collusion between subdelegates, priests, caciques, and local authorities can be found in the trials. These include a subdelegate-accountant-cacique; priest-cacique; subdelegate-priest; cacique-alcalde mayor; subdelegate-tax agent-cacique-scribe; and so on.[19] I found cases pitting subdelegates against priests, Spanish mayors against priests, priests against caciques, priests against lieutenant colonels, priests against mayor-caciques, and priests against caciques.[20] Certain patterns recurred more often. Above all, priests and representatives of the Bourbon state were increasingly at odds in this period. This was due both to the general effort of the state to gain access to a greater share of the church's income, including that of the priests, and to local disputes over resources, particularly those of the indigenous peasantry.[21]

Cases against an official were usually part of an enduring, behind-the-scenes struggle over local political power. Often, disputes over the *cacicazgo* that had raged for decades played an important part. The post–Tupac Amaru purge, the ambiguity regarding the office, and the resulting political vacuum kindled these struggles. An 1806 document lists thirty-nine requests for the office of cacique, most of them former officeholders.[22] The same document also tallies ninety-three complaints by Indians against "caciques and others," the majority against caciques.[23] The struggles over the cacicazgos often formed part of broader conflicts. For example, in the frequent battles between a subdelegate and a priest, each contender promoted a different nominee for the post of local cacique. Generally, the subdelegate would defend his nominee, a cacique interino, by accusing the other of having supported Tupac Amaru and engaging in subsequent rabble-rousing. The priest or other defenders of the blood cacique would harangue the newcomer for disrupting tradition and endangering local stability, insinuating the possibility of a revolt.

The Indians were more inclined to accuse caciques interinos than hereditary caciques. The newcomers had weaker ties to the community and thus had fewer constraints on their behavior. While an abusive hereditary cacique and his family faced pressure from friends and associates, a newcomer was more concerned with his relationship with his superiors than with local complaints. One should not, however, romanticize the behavior of the hereditary caciques; their misconduct is detailed in numerous cases. Inheriting the position did not automatically confer legitimacy in the eyes of the Indians. Yet each cacique's political survival depended on the maintenance of reciprocal relations with indigenous society. If a cacique's Indians resisted fulfilling the state's demands for tribute and labor, he had to make up the difference. His ability to punish transgressors was limited, as he and his family members faced the daily consequences of losing the respect and confidence of the local population.

The recently named outsider was more interested in assuring a quick profit. Although good relations with local Indians facilitated his work, gaining the capital needed to maintain ties to the members of the political and economic elite was generally a greater priority. Many caciques interinos aspired to higher office. The origins of the interinos varied (some were true outsiders, while others were locals, often mestizos, who used the position to fortify their socioeconomic position), but they were less concerned than the hereditary cacique about maintaining norms of reciprocity and acceptable behavior. It does not take much imagination to realize, for example, that for the cacique in Pucará (Lampa province) after the Tupac Amaru uprising, who did not speak Quechua and therefore had to rely on a translator, the margin for negotiation with monolingual Indians was small.[24] Although the imprecision in the use of the term *cacique* prevents any quantitative comparison between complaints against hereditary caciques versus outsiders (often the difference was not noted and a Spanish last name is not a reliable criterion), the interinos were the objects of the most detailed complaints and their legitimacy was frequently questioned because of their origin.

Francisco Martínez and the Limitations of Power

One cacique interino ran into trouble before officially taking office. In 1785, Francisco Martínez, at this point identified as a sergeant of the dragoon militia, was said to have demanded "as *cacique*" five reales (five-eighths of a peso) of a tribute debt from Narciso Santos Mamani, the former cacique of Marangani, Sicuani. Tensions ran high in the Sicuani area, the center of the Tupac Amaru rebellion. Mamani refused to pay, shouting that "if my monarch knew about these outrages against Indians, nobody would dare to commit them." Martínez and his thugs beat up Mamani. The trial evolved around Mamani's purported support for Tupac Amaru in the recent rebellion and his intemperate, subversive nature.[25] In 1793, Martínez became embroiled in another series of lawsuits that questioned his conduct.

Ventura Aymitumi accused Martínez, cacique interino since 1789 of the Quehuar ayllu ten kilometers northwest of Sicuani and promoted to militia captain, of collecting tribute from exempt Indians, impounding animals, monopolizing water, and imprisoning Aymitumi when he protested. Identified as an Indian, Aymitumi descended from a line of caciques, a position he held until replaced by Martínez. While still a leader of the ayllu, he had seen his prerogatives diminish greatly since the Tupac Amaru rebellion. Above all, he no longer collected taxes or had the right to the use of laborers from the community. In various trials, he described how Martínez forced

Indians to work on his "great estate," providing them with only a bit of coca leaves and boiled wheat while he made enormous profits marketing his goods in Upper Peru. He insisted that Martínez had become rich "on the sweat and fatigue of the ayllus," and claimed that Martínez and his guards not only roughed him up several times, forcing him to hide in the hills, but harassed his extended family.[26] The subdelegate of Canas y Canchis, Don Juan Bautista Altoaguirre, defended Martínez, reprimanding Aymitumi for his lazy, drunken, and subversive spirit: "Occupied by his laziness, he disturbs the tranquility of the other Indians, seducing them in drunken sessions, like those he held in the recent rebellion in which he was a dedicated traitor, to conspire against honorable citizens."[27]

In 1795, Martínez had Aymitumi and other Indians arrested, charging that they resisted paying tribute, and had attacked his hacienda "like in the time of the Rebellion," burned his crops, and killed his foreman. Although Aymitumi had originally called for Indians to thwart Martínez by not paying their head tax, at this point he apparently called for more direct actions. Martínez stressed Aymitumi's putative support for Tupac Amaru, an allegation corroborated by a Spanish resident of Sicuani, Esteban Bustamente. Martínez and his supporters never failed to mention this, a weighty accusation for decades following the uprising.[28] With the aid of a translator, Aymitumi claimed that this trial was retaliation for his lawsuit against Martínez. He argued that he had been forced to fight for the rebels because his father was a cacique, and that he ultimately participated in the campaigns against the rebels in Upper Peru after the death of José Gabriel Tupac Amaru. Aymitumi again condemned Martínez for forcing Indians to work on his hacienda and taking their animals. He also pleaded for a quick trial, noting his urgency to return to Sicuani to harvest his crop. Several Indians such as Pascual Fernández, a fieldworker, seconded his accusations. Aymitumi clearly sought to regain the hereditary cacique position, garnering the support of the ayllu's Indians. In 1795 and again in 1798, Aymitumi took Martínez to court for his vindictive conduct, including the "redistribution" of his land.

In the 1798 case, Martínez was forced to pay the court costs and was warned not to harm Aymitumi.[29] He complained that he was a sick, ruined man, afraid to return to Sicuani where thieves had looted his house. After several more trials involving Aymitumi and Martínez, the latter was removed from the cacicazgo of Quehuar. The Indians' persistence paid off. Martínez ultimately failed to use his position as cacique to become wealthy and rise in the colonial bureaucracy.[30] Aymitumi, however, had spent more than three years in Cuzco pursuing these different cases, much of the time in jail. He did not regain the cacique position. As in many cases, both sides appeared to end up losing.

Indians and Legal Discourse

In the trials, lawyers and witnesses clearly expressed the prevailing official views of Indians and of state policy vis-à-vis the indigenous population in the late colonial period. Although opposing lawyers in cases concerning abusive practices against Indians battled in long, often bitter legal struggles, their arguments reveal shared notions about Indians. Enlightened ideas about the possible rationality of the Indians had not seeped into eighteenth-century legal discourse. The defense of those accused of improper behavior against Indians was forthright. If not compelled by outsiders, Indians would recede into idleness and vice. Without coercion or persuasion, Indians would produce only for subsistence, purchase little, avoid work on estates, and fail to pay tribute. They would turn their back on Christianity, return to pagan rites, and drink too much. The argument that authorities had to use force with the Indians, which had a long tradition in colonial Peru, was used in many trials. In 1793, a subdelegate downplayed the accusations against him for whipping and hitting Indians in the following terms:

> These [accusations] are worthy of scorn because the Indians need it in that if not punished, they get hopelessly presumptuous. I know this by experience, which is why I must alert Your Highness that if Indians are not corrected with whippings, their arrogance, drunkenness, laziness, absence from Doctrine and mass, and failure to pay tribute to the detriment of the caciques will be inevitable.[31]

In almost every case against an official for abusive behavior, the defendant argued that he had always had in mind the best interests of the Indians and the crown and that his endeavors ultimately sought to facilitate the fulfillment of colonial obligations and to prevent subversion. Usually, some choice comments were added about the necessity of occasional violence against Indians and their untrustworthiness in the courts.

The lawyers or protectors de indios employed a similar discourse in the defense of Indians. They argued that if not protected by the state, Indians would fall into the hands of exploitative outsiders. The concomitant inability to fulfill tribute and labor obligations was usually implied. When defending an alleged criminal, the protectors contended that the ignorant or infantile state of the Indian led him toward such behavior. In 1820 a lawyer defended an Indian accused of assassination by noting his race's immaturity and irrationality:

> The Indians' lack of ingenuity, reason, and talent as well as their rusticity do not allow them to discern situations and avoid mischief. This deplorable situation, which excuses them from malice in their actions, derives from their uncivil lives and lack of enlightenment in which they miserably vegetate, making them through privilege a class of minors. All the laws and municipal ordinance treat them leniently . . . even more so than children.[32]

Even in pitched legal battles, prosecutors and the defense shared an understanding of Indians as inferior, irrational beings.

The Decisions

No sentence was found in 67 percent of the cases in the Real Audiencia and 84 percent in the Intendencia. In those with sentences in the Real Audiencia, removal from office (10 percent of the total) and fines (8 percent) constituted the most common forms of punishment. Court costs, jail terms, and acquittal were ordered in three cases each. The outcome of the numerous cases with no decision remains a puzzle.[33] The fact that cases were found in which the defendant was acquitted indicates that no sentence was not the same as a verdict of not guilty. In the cases with decisions, the loss of a position, hefty fines, and the other verdicts constituted unwelcome punishment for the guilty.[34] Despite the high number of cases with no sentences, lawsuits constituted a potent threat. The Indians' repeated use of the courts suggests that they considered it an effective weapon.

Whatever the outcome, confronting a lawsuit as a defendant represented a troublesome burden. Not only was it a costly, time-consuming process, particularly because of the renowned corruption and indolence of the Peruvian courts, but a defendant also lost legitimacy in the eyes of the state and local society. Trials publicized shady dealings and political alliances. The defendant had to organize a defense and confront the charges, which were often bolstered by the testimony of long-standing enemies. A petty charge could thus resurrect decades-old disputes and conflicts. Even if the defendant believed that he had done no wrong and could convince the court, a public reading of the charges against him was unwelcome. As in contemporary Latin America, defending oneself from legal charges of corruption and abuse represented a potential calamity for an official.

Why was the Bourbon state responsive to lawsuits filed by peasants and their representatives in an area that had recently been the site of a massive rural uprising? Primarily because it was concerned about another rebellion and relied on Indian tribute in its dogged efforts to increase fiscal revenues. The post–Tupac Amaru policy thus combined repression with negotiation. Colonial authorities, conscious that exploitative corregidores and other local officials had helped kindle the rebellion and had often obstructed tax collection, supported the punishment of errant officials. Cuzco's heavily indigenous population contained a large percentage of the viceroyalty's tribute payers. In the testimonies against the officials, the plaintiffs generally stressed the defendants' disruptive behavior and their failure to fulfill their colonial obligations. The state took notice. Viceregal officials believed that maintaining control of Cuzco was essential for the defense of Peru. Because of their concern over internal and external threats to security and their search for greater revenues, Bourbon authorities had little sympathy for officials who raised the ire of the indigenous population.

Hegemony and the Courts

The question whether the use of the courtroom increased the legitimacy of the Bourbon state in the eyes of Indians and other plaintiffs needs to be engaged from two related perspectives: whether it augmented their respect for the colonial state and drew them into colonial structures and whether it preempted other forms of mass political actions, namely rebellions. The answer is a guarded no on both accounts. Their triumphs demonstrated to the peasants that the colonial state, or at least certain representatives or echelons, continued to acknowledge their rights to relative political autonomy and to freedom from pernicious interlopers. Yet at the same time their defeats in the courtroom, and the series of complaints that prompted them to sue in the first place, increased their hostility toward the state. It needs to be remembered that Indians did not always win their legal battles. Not only did they lose many cases but, more significantly, many of the trials reviewed here included Indians on opposing sides, both that of the defendant as well as that of the plaintiff. Political divisions in late colonial Cuzco not only pitted Indians versus non-Indians but, in most cases, Indians against other Indians.

Because Indians can be found on both sides of local political divisions, is it an exaggeration to speak of these lawsuits as efforts by Indian communities rather than by mere individuals or small groups of people of similar background? In other words, did figures such as Aymitumi serve as proxies for the Indian population in the Andes? I contend that they did. In these trials, litigants invariably moved beyond their own personal woes — the injustice done by the defendant — and stressed systematic wrongdoing and how it affected their ayllus or beyond. In fact, to present a lawsuit, a risky, time-consuming process, they needed the backing of substantial segments of their community. In the eyes of the state, these individuals represented the communities. The colonial state strove to maintain Indians or the Indian republic as a separate social/fiscal category with its own obligations and rights. Treating them uniquely in the legal system represented a crucial component of this distinction. When Indians were arrested for rustling, stealing, or avoiding taxes, they were almost always cast and treated as a *forastero,* someone living outside of his/her community. In the eighteenth century, this meant that they were moving away from the category of Indian, as embodied in the ayllu or community.[35] In the trials reviewed here over abusive authorities, both the litigants and colonial authorities understood that the cases derived from the community of Indians. This does not mean, of course, that all Indians supported those bringing the lawsuit. It does mean that people such as Aymitumi felt that he had the backing of a significant portion of his ayllu, support that helped his case. In other words, although the lawsuits against obnoxious authorities did not emerge from some sort of unified, even homogenous Indian society, they were masterminded by community leaders who felt that they had broad local backing.

What about the legal discourse that denigrated Indians: did the use of the courts reinforce the ideological codes underlying Indians' subordinate position in colonial society? Certainly the legal system served as a key forum for representatives of the state and members of the elite to express and propagate their disdain for Indians. The anti-Indian spirit of the post–Tupac Amaru "Great Fear" looms large in the trials of the era. The centrality of a legalistic style and vocabulary in colonial literature demonstrates the importance of the courts in Spanish American culture.[36] In terms of the Indians themselves, I would propose a cautious interpretation. Invoking legal terms and strategies which implicitly or explicitly justified Spanish rule and colonial hierarchies does not mean acceptance of these codes. Hegemony is not so simple. On the other hand, subaltern groups should not be credited with crafty resistance every time they used colonial institutions to their advantage. Although they could benefit from their lawsuits (and certainly suffered in the courts as well), we cannot assume that they understood their efforts as subversion (or "resistance") and shunned the ideological and political ramifications of their use of the courts. In the case of Quehuar, for example, Aymitumi and others were not targeting the Bourbon Reforms or the even more abstract concept of Spanish colonial rule. Instead, they were trying to lessen the demands and abuse of an imposed authority and, in the case of Ventura Aymitumi, regain local office.

Litigants in Cuzco emphasized the defendant's (usually an authority) misbehavior, invoking diverse codes of conduct. They most commonly employed a Habsburgian notion of state and society in which authorities were understood to be guardians of Indians, part of a pact between crown and subjects. Litigants would describe the defendant's misconduct, stressing the breach with common practice overseen by His Majesty the King. Indians also questioned the validity of imposing newcomers, whose placement and behavior they contended violated traditional relations between the state and the indigenous peasantry.[37] This venerable "Long Live the King and Death to Bad Government" motif was not merely a retrograde effort to resurrect the colonial past. As the Comunero rebels in New Granada as well as the Tupac Amaru uprising and the War of Independence struggle in the southern Andes indicated, it could be used to delegitimize rulers and even to justify overthrowing the state.[38] It had revolutionary potential. In the Cuzco region, this Habsburgian code constituted the primary language of rebels in the eighteenth and early nineteenth centuries, mixing with calls for the resurrection of the Inca empire as well as strands of Enlightenment thought.[39]

Plaintiffs also used a more directly functionalist approach, pointing out that abusive endeavors by authorities diminished Indians' ability to fulfill their tribute and labor obligations. The plaintiffs echoed the state's avowed goal to root out abusive authorities and networks of political and economic alliances. They played to the Bourbons' desire to thwart corrupt intermediaries, improve tax collection, and prevent unrest prompted by unrestrained authorities. Although defendants would occasionally imply that disreputable conduct by a state official could foster subversion, this was done with great care. In light of the state's concern with the prevention of another uprising, royal authorities were probably quicker to suppress potential rebels than to punish divisive authorities.

This blending of discourses illustrates both the divisions within Indian society as well as the intricacies of the ideological conflicts of the late colonial period. The use of the legal system reflected and perhaps reinforced these divisions, but it in no way caused them. The Indians did not explicitly question in the courts the predominant ideology of Indians as needy inferiors, but this does not mean that they accepted these views. It means that they knew that they could not challenge them in their lawsuits, and that their representatives did not deem this necessary, expedient, or even correct.

In terms of the relationship between the legal system and social movements, events in the early nineteenth century vividly demonstrated that using the courts did not impede more radical behavior. From 1805 to independence in the 1820s, decades after the Tupac Amaru rebellion, Cuzco was the site of numerous revolts, including the misnamed Pumacahua rebellion of 1814–15. The use of the legal system had not prevented the peasantry from taking more direct action. The fact that reliance on the courts from 1787 until 1814 was sandwiched between two massive revolts refutes the argument that "reformist" tactics such as lawsuits impeded more revolutionary activities. In fact, the preparation of a lawsuit could mobilize a community, thus facilitating organized protest if legal remedies failed. Rebels would claim that justice had not been served when their plea had been turned down or a favorable sentence not carried out.[40] A lawsuit against authorities did not prevent the very same people from rising up collectively. In preparing a legal battle, they did not envision these efforts leading to mass insurrection. Instead, if frustrated in their efforts in the courts and if the political context changed, this legal challenge could be a first step toward insurrection. This was the case in many areas of the southern Andes from 1808 until 1815, when demands on the Indian population worsened, redress in the courts and from political reforms failed, and events in Spain changed dramatically.

Yet what did Indians achieve using the legal system? I argue that the contradictions of Bourbon policies, the stagnant economy, and above all the resistance of the indigenous peasantry impeded the implementation of the accelerated reforms plotted out by the revanchist colonial state. Efforts by peasants, primarily in the form of lawsuits, helped stymie the changes envisioned by viceregal authorities. Certainly, while not as catastrophic as it might have been, the period did prompt or heighten changes that continued to mark Andean society well into the republican period. Centrifugal forces gained strength as a variety of figures vied to supplant the waning powers of the cacique. A particularly harsh anti-Indian discourse emerged that persisted during the War of Independence and into the republic. The already formidable schism between the Andes and Lima-based intellectuals widened. Nonetheless, Indians did not stand by as these changes took form. Cuzco's first Intendant, Benito de la Mata Linares, depicted a contentious peasantry. He noted in 1790 that "since the time of the rebellion, Indians display a haughty and bold pride that they did not show before, having lost that terror, that servile fear which used to strike them just hearing the term Spaniard, having learned to use our arms, and having lost their fear."[41] The courts played an important role in Indians' defense of autonomy and economic resources and ultimately in their challenge to Spanish domination.

Notes

1 Portions of this chapter were included in chapter three of *Smoldering Ashes: Cuzco and the Creation of Republican Peru, 1780–1840* (Durham, N.C.: Duke University Press, 1999). I would like to thank Carlos Aguirre, Douglas Hay, Gil Joseph, and Rich Warren for their suggestions for this essay. I also want to acknowledge the participants in the conference held at Yale University for their stimulating comments.

2 On the question of domination and the legal system, see the essays in Mindie Lazarus-Black and Susan F. Hirsch, eds., *Contested States: Law, Hegemony and Resistance* (New York: Routledge, 1994), and, for Latin America, Gilbert M. Joseph, "On the Trail of Latin American Bandits: A Reexamination of Peasant Resistance," *Latin American Research Review* 25, no. 3 (1990): 7–53.

3 This was the case of Santa Rosa, south of Cuzco. See Real Academia de Historia, Madrid, Colección Mata Linares, no. 1994, June 22, 1781, Informe de Don Antonio Martínez al Visitador General D. José Antonio de Areche.

4 For summaries of the repression, see Alberto Flores Galindo, *Buscando un Inca*, 4th ed. (Lima: Editorial Horizonte, 1994), pp. 138–141; Pablo Macera, "Noticias sobre la enseñanza elemental en el Perú durante el siglo xviii," *Trabajos de historia*, vol. 2 (Lima: INC, 1971): 215–301; and Bruce Mannheim, *The Language of the Inka since the European Invasion* (Austin: University of Texas Press, 1991), pp. 74–77.

5 Brooke Larson notes a similar phenomenon in Cochabamba. She argues that "the

strong presence of the state, following the great Indian rebellions, and its renewed effort to intervene in the public domain, probably encouraged some peasants to engage in 'judicial politics' against their immediate overlords, even at a great risk to their own future." Brooke Larson, *Colonialism and Agrarian Transformation in Bolivia: Cochabamba, 1550–1900* (Princeton, N.J.: Princeton University Press, 1988), p. 201. See also David Cahill, "Una visión andina," *Histórica* 12, no. 1 (1988): 138.

6 For summaries of the colonial legal system, see H. A. Cooper, "A Short History of Peruvian Criminal Procedure and Institutions," *Revista de Derecho y Ciencias Políticas* 32 (1968): 215–267, especially 225–239; Colin MacLachlan, *Criminal Justice in Eighteenth-Century Mexico: A Study of the Tribunal of the Acordada* (Berkeley: University of California Press, 1974); Woodrow Wilson Borah, *Justice by Insurance: the General Indian Court of Colonial Mexico and the Legal Aides of the Half-real* (Berkeley: University of California Press, 1983); Sarah Chambers, "'Inundar la República de Sangre?' El desorden y el derecho penal en Arequipa entre la colonia y la republica," *Crónicas de Historia del Derecho* 1 (1994): 7–31; and, specifically on the Audiencia of Cuzco, Carmen Torero Gomero, "Establecimiento de la Audiencia del Cuzco," *Boletín del Instituto Riva Agüero* 8 (1969): 374–522.

7 They did not have authority to try major crimes such as homicide or subversion, and could not sentence criminals to obrajes. Ward Stavig, "Ladrones, cuatreros, y salteadores," in Carlos Aguirre and Charles Walker, eds., *Bandoleros, abigeos, montoneros: Criminalidad y violencia en el Perú, siglos XVIII–XX* (Lima: Instituto de Apoyo Agrario, 1990), pp. 69–103.

8 Because evidence of the local practice of justice appears in the formal legal system only when this behavior was so abusive as to merit a lawsuit, more benevolent practices are neglected. Clearly, the trials reviewed here do not provide a satisfactory portrayal of local justice. In one trial, a reference is made to a jail in the home of one of Cuzco's prestigious families, Doña Marquesa de Rocafuerte. Archivo Departamental del Cusco (hereafter ADC), Real Audiencia, Causas Criminales (hereafter CC), Leg. 125, 1801.

9 For analyses of crime in late colonial Peru, see Ward Stavig, "Violencia cotidiana de los naturales de Quispicanchis y Canas y Canchis en el siglo XVIII," *Revista Andina* 3, no. 2 (1986): 451–468.

10 William Taylor, *Drinking, Homicide and Rebellion in Colonial Mexican Villages* (Stanford: Stanford University Press, 1979), pp. 91–92. Testimonies therefore can illuminate the subject population's notions about the state, what it wanted to hear, and what it accepted. On this question, see Joseph, "On the Trail." Eric Van Young also raises this (and many other) questions in his essay, "To See Someone Not Seeing: Historical Studies of Peasants and Politics in Mexico," *Mexican Studies/ Estudios Mexicanos* 6, no. 1 (1990): 133–159.

11 For analyses of the litigious nature of Andean peasants past and present, see Linda Seligmann, *Between Reform and Revolution: Political Struggles in the Peruvian Andes,*

1969–1991 (Stanford: Stanford University Press, 1995); Steve Stern, *Peru's Indian Peoples and the Challenge of Spanish Conquest, Huamanga to 1640* (Madison: University of Wisconsin Press, 1982); Franklin Pease, "¿Por qué los andinos son acusados de litigiosos?" (unpublished manuscript, 1995); and Eric J. Hobsbawm, "Peasant Land Occupations," *Past and Present* 62 (1974): esp. 120–126.

12 For an interesting critique of historians' decontextualization of trial records, essentially the coercive, foreign environment faced by defendants, see Renato Rosaldo's analysis of Emmanuel Le Roi Ladurie's classic *Montaillou*, "From the Door of His Tent," in James Clifford and George Marcus, eds., *Writing Culture: The Poetics and Politics of Ethnography* (Berkeley: University of California Press, 1986), pp. 77–97.

13 These percentages only consider the category "abuses." In many trials, numerous defendants were named, which explains why the totals surpass 100 percent.

14 Studies on eighteenth-century caciques and the pressures they faced include Karen Spalding, "Kurakas and Commerce: A Chapter in the Evolution of Andean Society," *Hispanic American Historical Review* 54/4 (1973): 581–599, and Brooke Larson, "Caciques, Class Structure and the Colonial State in Bolivia," *Nova Americana* 2 (1979): 197–235. For important recent studies, see Luis Miguel Glave, *Vida símbolos y batallas* (Lima: Fondo de Cultura Económica, 1992), esp. chap. 5; Scarlett O'Phelan Godoy, *Kurakas sin sucesiones: del cacique al alcalde de indios Perú y Bolivia 1750–1835* (Cuzco: Centro Bartolomé de Las Casas, 1997); Nuria Sala i Vila, *Y se armó el tole tole: tributo indígena y movimientos sociales en el virreinato del Perú, 1784–1814* (Lima: IER José María Arguedas, 1996); Mark Thurner, *From Two Republics to One Divided. Contradictions of Postcolonial Nationmaking in Andean Peru* (Durham, N.C.: Duke University Press, 1997).

15 ADC, Real Audiencia, CC, Leg. 142, 1816.

16 ADC, Real Audiencia, CC, Leg. 105, 1790.

17 ADC, Real Audiencia, CC, Leg. 112, 1803.

18 ADC, Real Audiencia, CC, 108, 1792.

19 ADC, Real Audiencia, CC, 105, 1790; Real Audiencia, CC, Leg. 104, 1790; Intendencia, CC, Leg. 104, 1787; Intendencia-Provincias, CC, Leg. 122, 1790; Intendencia, CC, Leg. 109, 1797; Real Audiencia, CC, Leg. 107, 1796.

20 ADC, Intendencia, CC, Leg. 104, 1787; Intendencia, CC, Leg. 107, 1792; Intendencia, CC, Leg. 108, 1794, and Intendencia-Provincias, CC, Leg. 123, 1791; Intendencia, CC, Leg. 111, 1801; Intendencia, CC, Leg. 116, 1817; and Intendencia, CC, Leg. 108, 1794, in which the drunken cacique shouted, "the priest is not necessary for anything."

21 See David Cahill, "Repartos ilícitos y familias principales en el sur andino: 1780–1824," *Revista de Indias* (1988): 182–183; Scarlett O'Phelan Godoy, "El sur andino a fines del siglo XVIII: cacique o corregidor," *Allpanchis* 11 (1978): 17–32; Nuria Sala i Vila, "Gobierno Colonial, Iglesia y poder en Perú, 1784–1814," *Revista Andina,* 11, no. 1 (1993): 133–161, and her "Algunas reflexiones sobre el papel jugado

por la iglesia y el bajo clero en las parroquias de indios en Perú (1784–1812)," in Gabriela Ramos, ed., *La venida del reino* (Cuzco: Centro Bartolomé de Las Casas, 1994), pp. 339–362.

22 ADC, Libros, #244, Libro Matriz de los Inventarios de Autos, Registros, Libros y demás papeles que existen en esta Escribania de causas de la Real Audiencia del Cuzco, 1806, pp. 77–79.

23 Ibid., pp. 97–101.

24 ADC, Real Audiencia, CC, Leg. 103, 1789. For some examples, see Sala i Vila, *Y se armó*, pp. 78–84.

25 ADC, Intendencia-Provincias, CC, Leg. 120, 1785; and Intendencia, CC, Leg. 103, 1784.

26 ADC, Real Audiencia, CC, Leg. 110, 1793. This section of the Cuzco archive has been reorganized and some of these trials are now found in different *legajos* than those listed here.

27 ADC, Real Audiencia, CC, Leg. 110, 1793.

28 The courts showed little ambiguity toward participants in the Tupac Amaru rebellion. For any litigant, loyalty during the Tupac Amaru rebellion benefited his or her case, while any hint of favor toward the rebels had dire consequences. In 1792, a cacique accused of pocketing tribute money defended himself by stressing his royalist efforts during the rebellion. In the same year, in a case against a defendant accused of "seducing and perturbing these idiotic and ignorant peoples," prosecutors emphasized his role in the rebellion more than a decade earlier. ADC, Real Audiencia, CC, Leg. 107, 1792; Leg. 108, 1792.

29 ADC, Real Audiencia, CC, Leg. 111, 1793; Real Audiencia, CC, Leg. 114, 1795; Real Audiencia, CC, Leg. 116, 1795; and Real Audiencia, CC, Leg. 120, 1798. For another case involving Aymitumi, see Intendencia-Provincias, CC, Leg. 120, 1786. Other examples of cases against caciques named after the Tupac Amaru rebellion include ADC, Real Audiencia, CC, Leg. 134, 1897; Real Audiencia, CC, Leg. 113, 1794; Real Audiencia, CC, Leg. 111, 1793; and Intendencia, CC, Leg. 109, 1797.

30 Real Audiencia, CC, Leg. 116, 1795; and Real Audiencia, CC, Leg. 120, 1798. This case is also reviewed in Sala i Vila, *Y se armó*, pp. 135–139.

31 ADC, Real Audiencia, CC, Leg. 111, 1793.

32 ADC, Real Audiencia, CC, Leg. 144, 1820.

33 For an intelligent analysis of the logic of sentencing in colonial Spanish America, see Taylor, *Drinking*, p. 102. See also Ruth Pike, "Penal Servitude in the Spanish Empire: Presidio Labor in the Eighteenth Century," *Hispanic American Historical Review* 58, no. 1 (1978): 21–40; Charles R. Cutter, *The Legal Culture of Northern New Spain, 1700–1810* (Albuquerque: University of New Mexico Press, 1995), pp. 125–146; Ricardo D. Salvatore and Carlos Aguirre, "The Birth of the Penitentiary in Latin America: Toward an Interpretive Social History of Prisons," in Salvatore and Aguirre, eds. *The Birth of the Penitentiary in Latin America: Essays on*

Criminology, Prison Reform, and Social Control, 1830–1940 (Austin: University of Texas Press, 1996), pp. 1–43.

34 Some defendants pushed their loyal lineage even farther back. In a case involving Andahuaylas of the Ayacucho area, references were made to this area's support for the Spanish in the sixteenth century. Intendencia, Gobierno, Leg. 151, 1816–1818.

35 On forasteros, see Ann Wightman, *Indigenous Migration and Social Change: The Forasteros of Cuzco, 1570–1720* (Durham, N.C.: Duke University Press, 1990).

36 Roberto González Echeverría has noted the influence of legal discourse in colonial literature in his *Myth and Archive: A Theory of Latin American Narrative* (Cambridge: Cambridge University Press, 1991). We need to know more about the courts and the dissemination of ideas.

37 Frequently, the plaintiffs strengthened their case by detailing the defendant's disregard for accepted moral practices. For example, Indians accused a cacique in Cotabambas of fraud and battery but also of killing "a daughter," stealing from the church, and living in complete adultery." ADC, Intendencia, CC, Leg. 109, 1797. See also Ward Stavig, " 'Living in Offense of Our Lord': Indigenous Sexual Values and Marital Life in the Colonial Crucible," *Hispanic American Historical Review* 75, no. 4 (1995): 597–622.

38 See John Phelan, *The People and the King: The Comunero Revolution in Colombia, 1781* (Madison: University of Wisconsin Press, 1978), esp. pp. 79–88.

39 I examine this fusion in *Smoldering Ashes.*

40 Golte found that Indian communities' frustrations with the expensive and protracted lawsuits against abusive officials encouraged more radical, direct actions. Jürgen Golte, *Repartos y rebeliones* (Lima: IEP, 1980), p. 134. See also the essay by Sergio Serulnikov, "Su verdad y su justicia: Tomás Catari y la insurrección aymara de Chayanta, 1777–1780," in Charles Walker, ed., *Entre la retórica y la rebelión: las ideas y los movimientos sociales en los Andes, siglo XVIII* (Cuzco: Centro Bartolomé de Las Casas, 1996), pp. 205–243.

41 Real Academia de Historia, Madrid, Spain. Colección Mata Linares, 3427, September 10, 1790.

Women, Order, and Progress in

Guzmán Blanco's Venezuela, 1870–1888

ARLENE J. DÍAZ

G uzmán Blanco's rise to power in 1870 inaugurated the era of "order and progress" in Venezuelan politics. Stressing that a country's progress depended on attaining social and political stability, Guzmán Blanco set out to undo decades of economic havoc, political insecurity, and endemic civil strife. Although historians have aptly researched the new policies devised to boost economic growth and consolidate state power, few scholars have highlighted the key place that women, the family, and the domestic sphere, more generally, occupied in the regime's program for the "moral regeneration" of Venezuela.[1] For the first time in the nineteenth century the Venezuelan government had a coherent political and ideological program, which emphasized notions of gender.

Here I outline the content of Guzmán Blanco's hegemonic project on family and gender relations as elaborated by male intellectuals in the regime's official newspaper, *La Opinión Nacional* (founded in 1868).[2] I examine official discourse on women and family life, and discuss the most important legal reforms introduced in 1873. Complementing that exploration, I also discuss how courts of justice implemented guidelines for women by enforcing the new civil and penal codes of 1873.

Order, Progress, and the Patriarchal Family

The process of moral regeneration faced substantial obstacles. From the promulgation of the first constitution in 1811, all Venezuelans were theoretically equal before the law. Yet under such codes as the *Siete Partidas,* inherited from Spanish rule, women's legal submission to men continued. Equality under the law required redefining men's power to control the family and women. Here was a major challenge that Guzmán Blanco liberals confronted when writing the 1873 civil and penal codes. In writing these codes, governing elites had to balance the promise of individual autonomy with the need for state control. Their handling of public vis-à-vis private affairs of the family discloses the tensions reformers were grappling with and the contradictions of liberalism as an ideology. The debate between patriarchy and equality consumed their energies.

The regime used the rhetoric of equality, but it also stressed the conventional subordination of women and children to the male head of household.[3] Liberals infused the new civil code with deeply embedded Spanish patriarchal ideas. The governing elites widely accepted that maintaining a stable society depended on this tradition. A government seeking effectiveness had to preserve a hierarchical chain of command that began with the president's power and ended with the male head of household, the *padre de familia.*

To create a sense of order, nation, and national belonging the government constructed and circulated a republican discourse based on patriotic male heroes.[4] Its greatest achievement was a cult of independence leader Simón Bolívar as the true father of Venezuela. Through this cult, Guzmán Blanco portrayed himself as heir to Bolivar's feats that brought progress to the republic.[5] Both Bolívar and Guzmán Blanco were models of citizenship to emulate. Public festivities focusing on Bolívar aggressively disseminated this image throughout the country. Consolidating this association in public memory required unveiling statues, publishing official state histories venerating the heroes of Independence, and naming buildings and government entities in Bolívar's honor.

The republic's leaders and rulers constituted a public male sphere of propertied, educated men. Serving the republic was a male duty. This conception of politics as male terrain did not overshadow or weaken a parallel discourse about the duties of women in the domestic sphere. The discourse about the republic had a male and a female foundation. While Guzmán

Blanco portrayed himself as the great patriarch, head of a civilized family and leader of a civilizing project, his wife Ana Teresa Ibarra became the model of female responsibility, teaching morals and patriotism within the family. Hence, women forged much of the republican agenda.[6]

La Opinión Nacional conveyed a cult of womanhood as a venue for regeneration where customs were loose and domestic values scant.[7] The government's concern was to return power to women within the domestic sphere, so at least theoretically women would help transform the "uncivilized habits" of their families. In the positivist agenda, the "Moral Regeneration Plan" made its people's discipline the government's proper work.

Despite the regime's anticlerical leanings, it sought the blessing of the church for its political program. In one of its first issues *La Opinión Nacional* reproduced a sermon by Presbítero Dr. Andrés Manuel Riera Aguinagalde, explaining his philosophy of women's social role. This concept rested clearly on *Marianismo,* the cult of the Virgin Mary.[8] Though church doctrine embedded his message, Riera's thinking dovetailed with the government's desired social reforms.[9]

Father Riera's sermon linked the regime's definition of womanhood with religious commitment. The connection becomes clear if one understands that humanity, the fatherland, and the family were cardinal values for positivists. Drawing on Comte, the reformers saw women as key representatives of altruism: ideal representations of humanity. Accordingly, they valued women for their fertility and as moral teachers of future citizens. Thus positivists easily adopted a trope of the feminine figure. Paramount among these feminine figures was the Virgin Mary, who became for positivism a cognate for the "Virgin Mother," the allegory of humanity.[10] Riera, therefore, provided a religious rationale for the importance of women in marriage and forming families. He argued that woman had to be rehabilitated from Eve, who participated in original sin. Christ's virgin mother represented "the new Eve," the rehabilitated woman. From that time onward, the Holy Spirit blessed women, but this new status as blessed persons entailed responsibilities and sacrifices.[11]

Hence Riera emphasized the centrality of women's submission to men. Being the family's apostles, women had to inspire men and children through their example to become religious, nonviolent, and responsible. Only when women succeeded in their family mission could they claim to have emulated all the virtues that the Virgin had taught women — that is, to quietly sacrifice themselves for the family's sake.[12] Finally, because of their crucial role in the preservation of society, Riera discouraged women from struggling for their rights.[13]

These ideas recurred in other newspaper articles. Some pieces, for instance, encouraged mothers to make their sons useful citizens and respectable heads of households, hence to perpetuate the patriarchal order.[14] Women had the pivotal role of contributing to the nation's progress by "transforming" men into good, disciplined workers.[15] In this way tranquility would reign in the republic's family, creating order and progress.

To achieve peace through the family, women's subordination to men was critical. But it was difficult to justify. When the regime drafted the first liberal civil code (*c.* 1873), it had to resolve — or at least explain away — the contradictions between a republican constitution and the old monarchical codes. The government did not embrace gender equality. Any idea that lessened male family power seemed disruptive to the social order, especially when the government sought tranquility. A means of resolving the problem was to stress the increased importance of women in the family, plus the idea that both genders were equally significant in separate spheres.[16]

While publicly celebrating women's role in the family, the regime reinforced the Spanish patriarchal tradition in the courts. The court rulings analyzed below demonstrate that judicial institutions governed women more rigidly than they had during the colonial era. Hence during the late nineteenth century a glaring contradiction emerged at the core of the liberal agenda. Liberal reforms made the prevailing gender inequality in Venezuela untenable; yet they also strengthened patriarchy under state aegis.[17] Marianismo helped to justify ideologically this contradictory outcome. Since then family law has become a key aspect of Venezuelan government policy.

Discourse in Law and in Practice

Although women gained attention in official discourse during the late nineteenth century, their legal rights remained basically unchanged from the colonial past.[18] In law and in practice we see evidence of this situation in five pivotal areas of legislation directly touching women: *patria potestas* or male authority over females, marriage, breach of promise, divorce, and sex crimes.

Patria Potestas and the Powers of Men and
the Courts over Women and Children

Female submission to males has been a cultural given, reinforced both by law in the new Venezuelan liberal civil code of 1873 and afterward by court practices. As established in articles 173–186 of the 1873 civil code, a married woman had to submit to her husband, following him wherever he established residence. The courts regularly enforced this law.[19]

The age-old Spanish norm — men as heads of household, women's legal representatives, and administrators of their properties — continued in the 1873 code. By 1900 married women still had no juridical identity, unless they were pursuing a claim against their husbands or defending themselves against a criminal charge. Otherwise they could appear in court only when licensed by their husbands. If the husband was unable or unwilling to provide a license, she could get a court license only with a judge's permission. Moreover, when a woman got a license from the court, she had to explain to a judge the nature of any transaction she wanted to make and get the judge's permission before going forward.[20]

The code of 1873 created modest improvements in women's legal status; but mainly they affected single and widowed women.[21] First of all, the age when children had to request parental permission for marriage was lowered, thereby increasing children's autonomy. In 1873 the age of majority was lowered to twenty-one for males and eighteen for females.[22] In this way, the new regulations increased individual freedom and limited parental authority, reflecting the influence of the liberal idea of the autonomous individual.

Second, under the new code, widows could have guardianship of their own children.[23] The law provided for the single mother who had recognized her children to be the tutor, having similar parental rights to those of married men or widows. Husbandless women who behaved virtuously had more legal powers over their children than did married women. But these laws were only enforced in limited ways.

The period's legal changes seemed promising on paper, but the reality was completely different. Despite formal changes in the law, the parental powers of the padre de familia seemed indisputable in the Venezuelan courts. An exemplary case involved Juana Guevara and Manuel Lugo. This lower-class couple lived together between 1864 and 1871, and in 1868 she gave birth to a girl, whom she recognized as her natural daughter in the baptismal record. In 1872 Lugo, the girl's natural father, also recognized her in a public document. However, Guevara defended her rights as the girl's guardian because she had recognized the girl before the father did. Still, the Supreme Court did not approve her claim because she had not questioned Lugo's assertion of paternity. In article 285 the law established that the natural father is the guardian of the child he recognizes; the mother could be the guardian only if the father failed to do so. Thus the court held that in the interest of the minor, the girl could not be "deprived without justified reason of the rights and advantages" that emanated from her father's spontaneous recognition.[24] By basing its decision on the child's interests, the court stressed the importance of maintaining the power of the padre de familia.

We may see these legal changes, as well as others analyzed later in this essay, as part of a new relationship between the family and the state. Jurists tried to accommodate patriarchal family morality to the liberal idea of the state's limited powers. To protect and promote family values, a judge was justified in deciding what was best for the children — a doctrine that U.S. historian Michael Grossberg refers to as "judicial patriarchy."[25] Judges often showed a bias against women whose behavior was not proper, and in favor of men who had recognized their natural children. Since colonial times men were neither obliged to recognize their children by law, nor could their paternity be investigated.[26]

Although modest changes increased the legal liberties and powers of both single and widowed women, the state was more concerned with married women and the promotion of marriage.[27] Newly enacted laws on breach of promise increased the state's involvement in the private matters of courtship and marriage.

Matrimonios a palo, *or "Shotgun" Weddings*

We might mistakenly believe that the 1873 civil code proviso on breach of promise was meant to tackle Caracas's high illegitimacy rate of 53 percent.[28] However, this law had a limited effect on illegitimacy, as it applied to only a few cases of women who proved they met the elite's standards of femininity.

This new law tried to address the false promises of marriage men made to gain sexual access to women, a problem known since colonial times.[29] When pregnancy resulted from a male's seduction of a virtuous female by a promise of marriage, the judge could declare the couple officially married — even if the seducer never appeared in court. This legislation has been referred to as *matrimonio a palos,* since the court declared formal marriage without the couple's consent.[30] If a jury judged the woman both virtuous and pregnant, it could rule, *juris et de jure,* that the man indeed seduced her with an offer of marriage. This jury, composed of elite males, had to decide if the man was indeed the father of the child, and if the woman deserved legal protection because of her good morality.

The jurors had to be married, honorable padres de familia, have four children of different sexes, own property, manage a commercial establishment, or support themselves by a scientific profession.[31] If the man confessed to impregnating the woman, or if the jurors decided unanimously that he had done so, they had to establish a date for celebrating the marriage. But if the couple did not marry by that date, the judge could establish the marriage by legal fiat. If the woman involved was not pregnant, the male could either marry her or pay for the damage to her honor.[32] In such cases the only evidence of a promise of marriage admitted by the court was a proof that banns had appeared at the municipal hall.

The law intended to remedy an old problem by promoting marriages and perhaps legitimizing out-of-wedlock children; but getting such legal protection required women to prove their virginity. This policy assumed that only those behaving in a "civilized" manner deserved this type of legal protection. For only women behaving "honestly" (i.e., chastely) could constitute a legal family.

Cases of this sort occurred quite often in my sample of lawsuits for the late nineteenth century (1875–1880). In those years 21.6 percent of 199 lawsuits dealt with promise of marriage.[33] Of the forty-three cases studied, the court issued a definite opinion only nine times: in six cases, the couple married by judicial fiat, and in three cases the male defendant won because the court did not consider the woman virtuous.[34]

Another pattern is that in four of the six cases with couples married by judicial fiat, the defendants' lack of evidence was taken as further proof of their guilt. Such was the case of Merced Mota and Angel María Acosta.[35] In court the defendant said only that the plaintiff was "unquestionably virtuous," but that he had not told her he was willing to marry. Still, as evidence of his commitment, Merced presented the love letters he sent her. They promised marriage if she would please him sexually. For the jury these letters proved that Acosta had seduced Mota, and that his lack of defense showed his intent.[36] Because Acosta failed to marry Mota in the ten days legally prescribed, the judge married the couple by judicial fiat.

The baker Ricardo Lezama experienced a similar situation. His failure to respond to the claim earned him a matrimonio a palo.[37] In March 1876, Zoila Antonia Mosquera's father filed a suit claiming that Lezama kept delaying marriage to his daughter, although he had completed all the necessary paperwork. The problem was that there was opposition to the marriage. Ricardo's other girlfriend, Candelaria Manzo, filed suit against him as well because he had offered to marry her, and she alleged pregnancy by him. Manzo gave birth to a girl in November 1875.[38] But while Manzo's case was resolved in December 1875, Lezama still did not marry Zoila, who also bore his child in June 1876. In this case, the jury took into account the fact that he did not answer the demand as well as the fact that Mosquera had proven to be virtuous. They declared him the father of Mosquera's son and obliged him to marry her in twenty days. After more than forty days, Mosquera's father complained to the court that Lezama had still not married his daughter. The marriage ensued quickly.[39]

In the other two cases where the defendant responded to the lawsuit and the plaintiff won her suit, there had been both a formal promise of marriage and parental permission to marry.[40] The parental permission was important because the defendants were minors in both cases. Because article 82 of the civil code of 1873 established that males under twenty-one could not marry without parental consent, some defendants used this law to avoid a shotgun marriage. By arguing that they were minors without parental permission to marry, they called on the padre de familia's powers to confront the judges' power. Hence they highlighted a problem created by the state's intrusion into private matters.

In 1879, Juana Bautista Córdova, an educated, honest middle-class pregnant woman filed a claim against Pedro Pérez for breach of promise.[41] Several witnesses testified that Córdova was virtuous; that only Pérez had often visited her parents' home; that many also considered him her boyfriend because of his evident respect for her. Moreover, a credible witness said that Pérez had not denied fathering the pregnancy, and never indicated that Córdova was not a virgin when they first coupled. Finally, another authoritative witness said that Pérez had asked him to find an abortion-inducing medicine.

However, the defendant's lawyer proved that, as a minor, Pérez could not engage in any contract without parental consent. To substantiate his claim, the lawyer used an 1874 case of breach of promise in which the jury accepted this argument. In no other case did a contending party use a verdict from another lawsuit to justify an argument.

In the 1874 case, the defendant's lawyer explained the heart of the problem. He claimed that if the court disregarded article 82's prohibition of minors marrying without parental consent, "the law should discard this article, to avoid mocking paternal authority."[42] The breach of promise law did not contemplate this conflict between paternal and legal power, which created procedural problems. Should the state dictate the forced marriage of an underage son, ignoring paternal power? In the case of Pérez and Córdova, the judge instructed the jurors to limit their opinion to the two points established legally, that is, to determine whether or not they believed that Pérez had fathered the child and to judge whether Córdova was unquestionably honest.[43]

Based on those guidelines, the jury ruled that the couple should marry in fifteen days. The defendant's attorney objected that the judge never gave an opinion on the issue of Pérez's patria potestas and lack of parental permission to marry before the court reached a verdict. The judge then decided to disqualify himself. The court did not marry Pérez and Córdova; the incomplete court document does not say whether a new judge was appointed.

Emancipated adults usually won cases by disclosing the plaintiff's immorality. This strategy freed Juan Antonio Sucre from a forced marriage. In 1879, Luisa López sued him because she was five months pregnant and he would not marry her. Sucre responded that López's immoral behavior had victimized him. He also said that López's mother could not attest to her daughter's honesty when the mother was not legally married. López's mother had a stable concubinage with López's father. Thus, claimed the defendant, the alleged mother exemplified immorality. Responding to these allegations, López's father asked two prominent citizens to certify his and his family's admirable morality. To counteract this evidence, Sucre presented López's previous boyfriends in order to question them about her immoral behavior. But this strategy did not succeed.[44]

Finally the jury held that "since the plaintiff declared that her illicit relationship with Juan Antonio began during the first week of the month of January of 1876 and ended on 26 March 1879, and given that one of the conditions that the law demands to enable a pregnant woman to ask for a marriage [is that she be virtuous], the jury declares unanimously no [i.e., for the defendant]." The jury found López's fidelity irrelevant; women were punishable if they consented to a long relationship without marriage. Love letters and pictures presented as key evidence of men's courting intentions were unimportant if women did not meet the double moral standard legally required.

Indeed, in two of the three cases where the defendant won because the woman was "not virtuous," the couples already had stable concubine relationships, which included children. The court considered this fact evidence against the woman's honesty, even if she behaved as a faithful, virtuous, and committed mother and companion.

This pattern of verdicts in breach of promise cases contrasts with similar legal cases I compiled for the late colonial period (1786–1791). In the late eighteenth century males were punished—sometimes severely—for delaying marriage while living in concubinage with their fiancées.[45] If a man were about to marry, his previous girlfriend also had a chance, at least in church tribunals, to prove he had first proposed to her. Thus, the colonial courts' priority was to formalize unions and, to some degree, to defend women in such circumstances. From this evidence we may conclude that the 1873 civil code and judicial practices at the tribunals worsened the legal situation of women in both breach of promise and other cases.

Those who had alternative conceptions of gender relations and identity reacted against the unrealistic conditions imposed by this law. The law thus created a struggle over understandings and meanings of proper gender roles. The case of Manzo and Lezama discussed earlier exemplifies this problem. Manzo dropped her lawsuit, saying, "Today I am convinced that an imposed marriage with Lezama will not bring me the peace and happiness I seek because we do not share the love and esteem that must constitute the basis of the conjugal union."[46] Manzo contested the breach of promise law's imposition of marriage, for she demanded that the law recognize what she considered crucial: mutual love as a basis for marriage. Manzo thus challenged the court's definition of marriage, which ignored human feelings and thus made marriage a formality without substance.

She settled the suit in exchange for her boyfriend's recognition of their daughter, and his commitment to support the child and satisfy his paternal duties.[47] This outcome seemed optimal for the lower classes. They appreciated the benefits of freedom from marriage, even if they lived at the margins of the law. This lower-class behavior becomes even more meaningful when one considers how difficult it was to get a divorce.

Separation of Bed and Board and Nullity of Marriage

With secular marriage established by the 1873 civil marriage law, the state had to create new divorce procedures.[48] But the legal rationale for granting a divorce did not differ greatly from Spanish colonial law. As in the *Siete Partidas* only death could truly dissolve a marriage, allowing the bereaved spouse to remarry.[49] Nonetheless, some instances permitted a separation of bed and board or divorce. A wife's adultery was acceptable grounds for separation or divorce, regardless of circumstances. A husband's adultery required that the concubine lived in his house or "in a notorious place," and that the situation constituted an insult to his wife.[50] Voluntarily abandoning the home and extreme physical abuse were also valid grounds for divorce. These reasons were the most common ones for filing for divorce.[51] The other two circumstances were new and yet rarely invoked: (1) if the husband prostituted his wife, (2) if he and/or his wife fostered corrupting their sons or prostituting their daughters.

The state's control of marriage, making it a contract rather than a sacrament, also meant that civil courts would handle petitions for nullity of marriage. As under colonial law, a marriage could only be nullified if the partners were minors, close relatives, or if they had not freely consented to the marriage.[52] The 1873 code also included two new situations that could validate a petition for nullity: that either party was bigamous, and that the marriage ceremony failed to meet the legal requirements.[53]

How did the new legislation work in practice? The sample years show only three requests for nullity of marriage, and given the weighty proofs and claims required, the court approved two of them, which dealt with bigamy.[54] In the third, unapproved case, the couple claimed nonconsummation of the marriage and the bride's father forcing her to marry.[55]

Contrasting with rare petitions for nullity of marriage, which ended with a judgment, claims for divorce were numerous, but very few received a formal court sentence. Indeed, the late nineteenth-century sample confirms an increase in divorce cases: 47, or 23.6 percent, out of 199 cases. According to our sample, during the colonial and early republican periods divorce claims were only 6 to 7 percent of civil and ecclesiastical lawsuits.[56] Surprisingly, only five of the forty-seven cases received a verdict; the court approved two divorces and denied three. In the other samples I made for the colonial and early republican periods, a higher percentage was approved: 25 percent of all requests for 1786–90, and 32 percent for 1835–40. Modern courts, it seems, did not treat divorce positively.[57]

In cases of "separation of bed and board," one divorcée was upper-class, and the others were working-class. All three plaintiffs and defendants with rejected claims were working-class. As in the breach of promise cases, the vast majority of settled, inconclusive, or incomplete cases were lower-class litigants (37 of 42). Only three litigants were upper-class, and six were middle-class. Again, these numbers suggest that the elites' use of the courts was slight, while both working- and middle-class litigants often sought legal means of settling their private affairs.[58]

Why did courts approve so few divorces from 1875 to 1880? A close look at the denied verdicts may show the grounds persuasive to judges.

María Teresa Belsinger, who made cigars in the morning and match-boxes at night, sued her husband for abandoning his marital and paternal duties and often abusing her. Juan Bautista Acereto, the defendant, contra-dicted Belsinger's allegations, arguing that as a baker he was poor, unable to provide their eight children with more than his meager earnings. He main-tained that he had always fulfilled his paternal duties. Belsinger's witnesses testified to the many times her husband had insulted, beat, and even threat-ened her with a knife. Acereto testified that all Belsinger's witnesses were retaliating for his past insults to them. Most of these witnesses had lived with the Acereto family, and had experienced their daily struggles. Acereto's witnesses called him a well-behaved, hard-working man.

This lawsuit passed through four courts before receiving a definitive decision. The first court discounted all the plaintiff's witnesses, alleging their prejudice. Thus the court found inconclusive evidence that Acereto had abandoned his family, or that his verbal and physical offenses were excessive enough, as required by law, to grant a divorce. The case exempli-fies causes that threaten a marriage, which a conscientious reconciliation should remedy — at least for the children's benefit — before the situation gains the criteria for granting a divorce.[59]

Belsinger appealed to the Superior Court of Justice, which ruled her witnesses' testimony was valid, as none considered themselves Acereto's enemies. This court also found the testimonies of the defendant's witnesses invalid, as they referred to a period long before the marital problems be-gan. The court revoked the previous judgment, approving divorce on the grounds that due to their frequent discussions, their children and the public order would be affected if they continued to live together. Moreover it was argued that Belsinger had proved her integrity and aptitude for bringing up the children.[60]

The angry Acereto appealed; the Supreme Court revoked the second judgment, reiterating that abuse must be excessive to warrant divorce. Any quarrel or rash behavior would not suffice.[61] Without evidence of life-threatening injuries that made marital life impossible, the court could not grant a divorce. But the court made other points as well. This time the judge claimed that he had not abandoned her.

Moreover, the judge made clear that the failure to support the family was not a cause for divorce. Basing the sentence on articles 174–175, the court established that the husband only had the obligation to satisfy his wife's needs in proportion to his means and condition. In addition, the woman "should contribute to the subsistence of the husband when his means are insufficient."[62] This judgment affirmed equality—in order to defend the husband. Belsinger may give the impression that she wanted support, appealing to the inequality of custom and women's traditional role. But her true motive was to complain that Acereto did not fulfill his marital duties, thus burdening her with all the familial responsibilities.

The Supreme Court verdict insisted that for the well-being of children and of society, ordinary unpleasantries should not lead to a separation. But more importantly, "the duties as a husband and father and the morality and respect that must be instilled in the children's hearts, require the undeniable duty of silencing resentments that are not established on any serious grounds, in order to avoid disputes and scandals that weaken the family ties *and undermine the respect due to the always sacred figure of the father* [emphasis mine]."[63] This last part of the Supreme Court judgment clarifies why divorce may have been so difficult to obtain. First, the need to keep families together was pivotal to children's well-being and social continuity. That is, familial peace brings an orderly state.[64] Secondly, the decision implied that a woman must bow to authority, avoiding confrontations that threaten the family. Most importantly, women had to have a sacred devotion to the padre de familia. Thus divorce lawsuits threatened not only the foundations of society, but also the male rulers of that society. For the well-being of Venezuelan society, women must accept their burdens, just as Father Riera advocated.

Belsinger would not relent. But her appealing to the country's highest court, the Corte de Casación, brought disappointment again.[65] This court also sustained the previous three rejections.[66] Even when a husband sued his wife for adultery, the court reasoned similarly. The verdict in the lawsuit of Luis Felipe Delgado against Teolinda Hernández remarked: "[the] causes of divorce are not only private matters but are also matters of public order and interest, and consequently, the parties can not agree to the separation of the marriage when there is no justified legal cause."[67]

Again, the court refused a separation because of the critical effect that a divorce would have on the private and public interests of the nation. Only familial peace would ultimately create order for the state. Building a modern nation required women's submission to the home, which was the rightful responsibility of the law. Hence the state's duty was to intrude into private life. The judge used the verdict essentially to impose domestic peace. Such judicial efforts succeeded in eight of the forty-seven divorce cases, although the settlements did not require the couple to live together again.

Of the remaining thirty-two inconclusive or incomplete lawsuits, two were dismissed due to the plaintiffs' death. The lack of further information on these cases could indicate an informal settlement or disregard by the parties, the courts' disinterest in pursuing these claims, or lost records. Clearly the courts seldom granted formal separation of bed and board; so how were the two granted divorces unique? First, as when judges in breach of promise cases ruled in the plaintiff's favor, the defendant did not provide evidence.[68] Second, the evidence presented included prior lawsuits and formal complaints against the defendants and, in one case, the defendant's confession of adultery. In these cases, the judge found the evidence too overwhelming to ignore.

One might think that once marriage became a contract controlled by the state and not a religious sacrament, people would have had more freedom to dissolve that marital contract. But a divorce law dissolving marriage and allowing a second marriage among divorcées did not appear until 1904.[69]

Rape and Estupro

To consider all the legislation most affecting women at this time, we must also evaluate sex crimes. If the state regarded chastity as a key element of women's condition, would the penal code and the courts protect victims of rape? Would the tribunals punish men's sexual aggression against women?

Answers to these questions reflect the trends already discussed concerning women's legal identity. Judges in the late nineteenth century had to balance their desire to punish immoral behavior with their need to avoid potential challenges to Venezuelan men's exalted status. Hence in only one of nine cases of *estupro* in the 1875–80 sample was the aggressor punished; in two the defendant was acquitted. In the other cases the defendants were released on bail, as the plaintiffs made no formal accusation and, most importantly, presented no definitive proof of the accused's guilt.

The penal code of 1873 introduced a new legal term — *violación* or rape — to designate what had been known as *estupro con fuerza*.[70] Estupro still applied in cases with no violence accompanying sexual intercourse if, for instance, deceitful seduction had occurred. For the crime to be classified as an estupro, the victim had to be a virgin between ten and eighteen.[71] Rape applied when the crime involved physical violence used on women of any age.

Estupro carried a lighter punishment than rape. For estupro, the sentence could involve a maximum of eight months if the aggressor was a priest, public authority, tutor, teacher, or guardian, and between three to twelve months for an unknown attacker.[72] Anyone guilty of rape could be jailed for two to five years, but if the suspect proved that the victim did not behave as a "*mujer honesta* — a chaste woman," the sentence could be lowered to a maximum of eighteen months' imprisonment.

As in colonial times, the implicit understanding prevailed that women could instigate such crimes. This assumption promoted the idea of woman as a devil who seduced men.[73] If the court found any indication that a woman lacked chastity, then the aggressor did not need to take all blame for the crime. So the issue was not to judge a criminal act, but how the victim conformed to the rules of moral behavior. In this way each verdict sought to defend the dominant norm of conduct.

In my sample it is difficult to differentiate between estupro and rape in practice. All the crimes between 1875 and 1880 were committed against girls between three and sixteen, and use of force and chastity were to be proved at trial. Nevertheless, in six of the nine cases, the person bringing the case to the tribunals claimed that the crime was rape, probably seeking a harsher punishment for the accused.

Indeed, proof is the most problematic aspect of sexual crimes. Judges closely considered the girl's sexual and social behavior, as we see in the case of twelve-year-old María Paula Báez.[74] The court asked about her occupation, and whether she had worked and gone out alone at night. The court also asked why she did not seek help right after the crime, and if she had resisted the aggressor.[75] But Báez's testimony did not help her. She was an orphan in the care of her aunt and godmother, and ran errands and carried water day and night. The rapist, her aunt's brother, threatened to throw her out of their home if she refused intercourse.

By the time a doctor examined Báez — almost two months after the rape — no evidence of a crime remained; she had only contracted syphilis. As in other such cases, the timing of the family's response also played a role. Judges interpreted a delayed complaint as the family's lack of concern. More importantly, the delay might make a physical exam useless if the doctor could no longer determine when the girl had lost her virginity.[76] Following extensive investigations, the court noted that no legally recognized representative had made a formal accusation, legally required in article 46 of the Code of Criminal Procedure. Consequently, it freed the defendant and dismissed the case.

In the same vein, proving that the victim suffered bleeding was critical for both the plaintiff and the judges.[77] Blood was proof that a girl had indeed been deflowered, and hence that a corpus delicti existed. As a judge in another case explained, if physicians examining the victim determined that the hymen membrane was intact, then no crime had occurred, for only that rupture determines the loss of virginity.[78] For that reason, the defendant was acquitted of all blame and charges.

As in the divorce cases discussed above, the court would not find in favor of the plaintiff without positive proof of an impairing injury.[79] In rape cases, if the aggressor used force but did not deflower the girl, this fact counted as a mitigating factor in the sentence.[80] The intent to commit the crime, even if the assailant confessed would not weigh as heavily as physical violence.[81] This practice allowed the court to commend men who controlled their "male instincts." But it could also show that the legal system released men from responsibility for their acts: it was fine to abuse women, as the deed left no hard proof.

Male aggressors were punished after a fashion, sometimes inconsistently and often lightly. In the late nineteenth century most men accused of estupro and causing bodily injuries were released on bail (*fianza de cárcel segura*).[82] Judges granted bail on two grounds: either the injuries were not very serious, and the victim recovered completely; or the crime's punishment was less than two years.[83] I surmise that release on bail meant the accused could return to court if necessary, and prevented men from committing another crime. If a man repeated the offense, the judge could not grant bail again.[84] Release on bail was a subtle way to "punish" the accused without imposing jail time. I have no evidence that judges issued verdicts when they released the accused on bail. Those released on bail also stayed under court surveillance through a bondsman responsible for their possible return to court.[85]

Prison time by convicted offenders varied greatly. The only convicted rapist in my sample spent two years, seven months in jail. In the other cases, the offenders spent between thirteen days and a year in jail while their cases awaited hearing. For the public this sentencing pattern may have looked like lenient sentences.

We may conclude that the state was complicit in preserving males' good reputation in sexual crimes sentences as well. Hence the crime's burden fell on women, who enjoyed no legal protection. The courts' actions in rape cases could imply that women usually provoked these crimes, thereby encouraging justifications for controlling female behavior.

Conclusion

The official discourse cast a new role for women in a "morally regenerated" Venezuela. Still, the regime's legal reforms did not match the rhetoric. The 1873 code did not greatly change women's legal condition. The governing elite's ideology romanticized their domestic power while blocking the social changes that might have resulted when women sought legal protection. My findings suggest that only those women who followed the elite ideal of womanhood — those who proved without reasonable doubt to be virtuous and chaste — received favorable court rulings.

Court decisions served to punish women who did not follow the call for bourgeois domestic morality and progress. The courts made the law both a practice and a discourse. They penalized women who did not embody the state's ideal of femininity and, in contradiction to their liberal agenda, the state intervened in the private sphere by ruling over courtship, marriage, child custody, and divorce. Through law and the practice of the courts the liberal state promoted sexual norms, family organization, and feminine honor. In this way the regime intended to re-create legally its moral regeneration program. This project integrated patriarchy, the new family morality, and the promise of individuality and equality with the liberal ideal of limited state powers, the need for tranquility, and the desire to exclude the lower classes from power.

With a justice system seldom disputing male power, why did women go to court? The late nineteenth century saw fewer and less extensive lawsuits than had the colonial and early republican periods. This fact is intriguing, since the population of Caracas was 24 percent larger than in 1835.[86] Thus, we might infer that the courts heard only a fraction of the city's cases involving crimes and complaints.

However, many of those female litigants challenged, consciously or not, prevailing ideals of womanhood. Women like María Teresa Belsinger — who pursued her divorce in four different courts — concretely addressed the contradictions between the regime's discourse and practice. However, most female litigants did so individually and less consciously, by infusing the prescribed roles for women with different meanings. As I have discussed elsewhere, women appropriated those elements of government discourse that empowered them and rejected those that were useless.[87] My sample showed that many litigants did not desire formal marriage; that living outside the boundaries of legitimacy was no less honorable than formal unions. In the late nineteenth century, both public and hidden lawsuits transcripts expressed this challenge to the state's discourse. Hence it is questionable whether the disciplinary efforts of the government were effective.[88]

Still, for jurists, government efforts to revitalize and pacify the country provided the opportunity to create a better defined, more secular family policy. The modern state was to be organized through a more competent sexual control of women, directly promoted by the courts' decisions and, more subtly, by the diffusion of ideal social roles and images. Sunday masses reproduced this discourse, highlighting the Virgin Mary as a model of behavior for women. The scandal of a lawsuit allowed the courts and the government to convey a public message about the benefits of assuming new roles and responsibilities.

In this way the judiciary became another institution seeking to promote discipline and appropriate social behavior. This strategy would produce precisely the virtuous republican mothers so deeply desired by people like Father Riera and Guzmán Blanco. In this sense, Guzmán Blanco could be better remembered as the restorer of the domestic order than for his achievements in bringing peace and political order in Venezuela.

Notes

This essay is based on archival research carried out with the aid of the American Bar Foundation, the Ford Foundation, the Graduate School and the History Department at the University of Minnesota. I wish to thank Luis A. González, Ricardo D. Salvatore, Muriel Nazzari, Robert McCaa, and Peter Guardino for their comments.

1   For an analysis of politics during the Guzmán Blanco period, see Mary B. Floyd, *Guzmán Blanco: la dinámica de la política del Septenio* (Caracas: Instituto Autónomo Biblioteca Nacional and FUNRES, 1988); María Elena González Deluca, *Negocios y política en tiempos de Guzmán Blanco* (Caracas: Universidad Central de Venezuela, 1991); Robert H. Lavenda, "The First Modernizing Attempt: Modernization and Change in Caracas, 1870–1908" (Ph.D. dissertation, Indiana University, 1977); and John V. Lombardi, *Venezuela: The Search for Order and the Dream of Progress* (New York: Oxford University Press, 1982).

2   Published from 1868 to 1892, this newspaper was the regime's self-proclaimed printed advocate. As such it promoted Guzmán Blanco's political project. Fundación Polar, *Diccionario de historia de Venezuela* (Caracas: Fundación Polar, 1988), s.v. "Guzmán Blanco, Antonio, Gobiernos de."

3   On the "rhetoric of equality," see Arlene J. Díaz, *"Vicenta Ochoa, muchas veces muerta:* Male Arguments and Female Strategies for Searching Political Legitimacy in Early Republican Caracas, Venezuela" (paper presented at the Berkshire Conference on the History of Women, University of Rochester, June 1999). See also Julie Skurski, "The 'Leader' and the 'People': Representing the Nation in Postcolonial Venezuela" (Ph.D. dissertation, University of Chicago, 1993).

4   See Skurski, "The Leader and the 'People.'"

5   Ibid.; Germán Carrera Damas, *El culto a Bolívar: esbozo para un estudio de la historia de las ideas en Venezuela* (Caracas: Universidad Central de Venezuela, 1969).

6   Skurski, "The 'Leader' and the 'People,'" 72–73. On the gendered aspects of republicanism, see Joan B. Landes, *Women and the Public Sphere in the Age of the French Revolution* (Ithaca, N.Y.: Cornell University Press, 1988), and José Murilo de Carvalho, *A formação das almas: o imaginário da república no Brasil* (São Paulo: Companhia das Letras, 1990).

7   According to Carl Sach, who traveled across Venezuela between 1867 and 1877, Guzmán Blanco's title of "Regenerador" or the concept of "Regeneración" refers to the renaissance or pacification in Venezuela during his tenure. See Elías Pino Iturrieta and Pedro Calzadilla, eds., *La mirada del otro: viajeros extranjeros en la Venezuela del siglo XIX* (Caracas: Fundación Bigott, 1993), pp. 263, 258; Floyd, *Guzmán Blanco,* 36. Comtean philosophy also stressed the idea of "moral regeneration." Given Guzmán Blanco's leanings toward positivism, the borrowing of the idea of regeneración is not a coincidence. See Carvalho, *Formação das almas,* 129–130. See also "La idea de lo futuro II: Por dónde debe comenzar la reorganización del país," *La Opinión Nacional,* 21 Nov. 1868, p. 1.

8   "Sermón: sobre la misión cristiana de la mujer," *La Opinión Nacional,* 18 Nov. 1868, p. 2. The sermon was delivered at the Santa Rosalía parish, which, along with Catedral and Santa Teresa were the three most prestigious parishes in Caracas in the late nineteenth century. Lavenda, "First Modernizing Attempt," 302–303. There are similarities in the way in which priests in Michoacán portrayed the Virgin Mary

during the Mexican Revolution and the case of Caracas. See Marjorie Becker, *Setting the Virgin on Fire* (Berkeley: University of California Press, 1995), 13–19.

9 Indeed, although he was a clergyman, Father Riera had always had liberal inclinations. The holder of a doctorate in theology from the University of Caracas, Riera had the reputation of being an accomplished speaker. He was active in the Federal Wars as chaplain of General Ezequiel Zamora's army, which fought on the side of the Liberals led by Antonio Leocadio Guzmán, the father of the future Regenerador. The Venezuelan Congress appointed Presbítero Riera to the bishoprics of Barquisimeto (1864) and Calabozo (1867), but on both occasions the Vatican rejected his candidacy. *Diccionario de historia,* s.v. "Riera Aguinagalde, Andrés Manuel."

10 Carvalho, *Formação das almas,* p. 130. Carvalho provides an authoritative analysis of the political implications of Comtean philosophy in Brazil.

11 Riera set out a distinction between the condition of women in ancient and Christian times, one that resembled the dichotomy of *civilización* and *barbarie* so popular at the time. See, for instance, "Cuestión de urbanidad," *La Opinión Nacional,* 13 May 1869, p. 1; and "Recreaciones del hogar," *La Opinión Nacional,* 5 May 1871, p. 1.

12 Marianismo, in this context, did not, as has been argued by some authors, carry the connotation of a cult that praised female superiority. To the contrary, it stressed the importance of women as submissive, hard-working wives and mothers. See Evelyn Stevens, "Marianismo: The Other Face of Machismo in Latin America," in Ann Pescatello, ed., *Female and Male in Latin America* (Pittsburgh: University of Pittsburgh Press, 1973), pp. 89–102. In the same book, see also Jane Jaquette, "Literary Archetypes and Female Role Alternatives: The Woman and the Novel in Latin America."

13 There are a number of examples in *La Opinión Nacional* in which the fear of women's struggles could be perceived. See, for example, "Derechos de las mujeres en Cuba," *La Opinión Nacional,* 24 Mar. 1870, p. 2.

14 "La madre y el niño," *La Opinión Nacional,* 7 Mar. 1877, p. 1. These ideas mirrored those of Comte who believed that, ideally, the woman who represented humanity was a thirty-year-old woman with a child in her arms. Carvalho, *Formação das almas,* p. 81.

15 The need to discipline workers was not unique to Venezuela. For parallel policies in Brazil, see Sidney Chalhoub, *Trabalho, lar e botequim: o cotidiano dos trabalhadores no Rio de Janeiro da Belle Epoque* (São Paulo: Brasiliense, 1986); Martha de Abreu Esteves, *Meninas perdidas: os populares e o cotidiano do amor no Rio de Janeiro da 'Belle Epoque'* (Rio de Janeiro: Paz e Terra, 1989).

16 On this issue, see Carvalho, *Formação das almas,* p. 130; and Rachel Soihet, *Condição feminina e formas de violência: mulheres pobres e ordem urbana, 1890–1920* (Rio de Janeiro: Forense Universitária, 1989), pp. 111–113.

17 Research on the family in nineteenth-century United States has shown similar patterns. An essential reading is Michael Grossberg, *Governing the Hearth: Law and the Family in Nineteenth-Century America* (Chapel Hill: University of North Carolina Press, 1985), pp. 289–307.

18 Women in Mexico and in the Southern Cone had a similar experience. See Silvia M. Arrom, "Changes in Mexican Family Law in the Nineteenth Century: The Civil Codes of 1870 and 1884," *Journal of Family History* 10, no. 3 (fall 1985): 305–317; and Asunción Lavrin, *Women, Feminism, and Social Change in Argentina, Chile and Uruguay, 1890–1914* (Lincoln: University of Nebraska Press, 1995), pp. 193–226.

19 See: "José Prágedes Nuéz contra su consorte Ana Pérez, para que viva con él consumando [su] matrimonio o por la nulidad de éste," Archivo del Registro Principal del Distrito Federal (hereinafter ARPDF), Civiles, 1876, Letra P, exp. 2; "Copia de la sentencia pronunciada en el juicio seguido por José Prágedes Nuez contra su consorte Ana Pérez para que convenga en la nulidad de su matrimonio," ARPDF, Civiles, 1876, Letra N, exp. 5. "Emilio Roo solicitando que su consorte María de Jesús Mejías le entregue sus hijas Ines, Luisa y Trinidad Roo," ARPDF, Civiles, 1876, Letra R, exp. 18. "Juan Guillermo Castillo contra su consorte Merced María García para que se le obligue a volver a su consorte a llevar sus deberes conyugales," ARPDF, Civiles, 1877, Letra C, exp. 27.

20 1873 Civil Code, article 183. This practice, in which women had to request permission from a judge before doing any transaction, had been common since colonial times. For the late nineteenth century see "María de las Nieves González sobre autorización para administrar sus bienes y los matrimoniales," ARPDF, Civiles, 1878, Letra G, exp. 20, fol. 5v; "María de la Merced Goicoechea de Herrera sobre autorización para administrar bienes," ARPDF, Civiles, 1877, Letra G, exp. 29; "Brígida Isabel Gascón solicitando licencia de su marido para aceptar una donación," ARPDF, Civiles, 1876, Letra G, exp. 1.

21 Arrom has argued similarly for Mexico. See Arrom, "Changes in Mexican Family Law."

22 In 1867 the age of majority was lowered to twenty-three for males and twenty for females (article 54). The ages established in 1873 remained the same in the 1896 code. Unlike Mexico, in subsequent codes Venezuela did not retain the 1862 requirement that women stay at home until age thirty. See 1862 Civil Code, Book 1, title 3, law 2, chap. 2, article 6.; Arrom, *Women of Mexico City,* p. 33; Rogelio Pérez Perdomo and Miriam San Juan, "Iguales Ma Non Troppo: la condición jurídica de la mujer en Venezuela en el siglo XIX," in Ana Lucina García Maldonado, ed. *La mujer en la historia de América: Obra enciclopédica* (Caracas: Asociación Civil la Mujer y el Quinto Centenario de América y Venezuela, 1995), pp. 258–282.

23 1873 Civil Code, articles 232 and 285.

24 1873 Civil Code, articles 231–254. "Juana Guevara contra Manuel Lugo por la

entrega de su menor hija Dolores Guevara," ARPDF, Civiles, 1875, Letra G, exp. 7, fols. 65r–65v.

25 Michael Grossberg, "Who Gets the Child? Custody, Guardianship, and the Rise of a Judicial Patriarchy in Nineteenth-Century America," *Feminist Studies* 9 (summer 1983): 235–260.

26 Article 208 of the 1873 civil code established: "Queda prohibida toda inquisición acerca de la paternidad ilegítima, y ningún tribunal podrá admitir demanda ó gestión sobre ella." A similar law was enacted in the 1862 civil code (Book I, title 5, law 4) and in the 1896 civil code (article 211), although the later code continues a special consideration that appeared in 1873 for cases of elopement or violent estupro. Republican paternity laws were influenced by the Spanish requirement for proof of paternity. Either the father had to recognize the child formally, or there had to be positive proof of his cohabitation with the child's mother. See Joaquín Escriche y Martín, *Diccionario razonado de legislación civil, penal, comercial y forense* (Caracas: Imprenta de Valentín Espinal, 1840), s.v. "paternidad"; and Siete Partidas, Book 7, title 7, Partida 4. In the nineteenth century the only way to verify paternity was by the father's recognition in a public document or by the later marriage of the child's parents.

27 The juridical system excluded modes of family organization other than formal marriage. The 1873 penal code (article 423) made concubinage a crime, especially if the couple lived a licentious life.

28 Articles 60–67, 1873 Civil Code; Lavenda, "First Modernizing Attempt," 302.

29 This was the first time that a republican code allowed breach of promise claims, as the 1862 civil code did not do so (title III, law 1, articles 1–3). See *El Código Civil de Páez* (Caracas: Academia Nacional de la Historia, 1974). However, authorities enforced the 1862 civil code only briefly — from April to August 1863.

30 Pérez Perdomo and San Juan, "Iguales Ma Non Troppo."

31 Luis Sanojo, *Instituciones de derecho civil venezolano,* 4 vols. (Caracas: Imprenta Nacional, 1873), 1:126.

32 Ibid., 1: 120–126. I found no lawsuit in which this situation occurred.

33 I used civil, criminal, and ecclesiastical lawsuits in which women were involved. These cases form part of a larger project in which three samples were compiled every fifty years since the foundation of the Real Audiencia (High Court of Appeals) in 1786 through the inception of liberal and positivist regimes in the late nineteenth century. See Arlene J. Díaz, "*Ciudadanas* and *padres de familia:* Liberal Change, Gender, Law, and the Lower Classes in Caracas, Venezuela, 1786–1888" (Ph.D. dissertation, University of Minnesota, 1997).

34 In two of these nine cases, at least one party was upper- or middle-class. In five cases, the female plaintiffs had legally married parents. The middle class used the law on "breach of promise" successfully, as they valued marriage for keeping or improving their social position. This fact emerges clearly from the other thirty-four

cases: where the female plaintiffs were lower-class and had unmarried parents, adverse decisions usually resulted. "Zoila Antonia Mosquera contra Ricardo Lezama por esponsales," ARPDF, Civiles, 1876, Letra M, exp. 19; "Sofía Díaz contra Miguel Gerónimo Velázquez por esponsales," ARPDF, Civiles, 1875, Letra D, exp. 10; "Sofía Domínguez contra Francisco Aguiar, por esponsales," ARPDF, Civiles, 1877, Letra D, exp. 10; "Ursula Key por su meno hija Susana contra Antolín Iriarte, por esponsales," ARPDF, Civiles, 1877, Letra K, exp. 1; "Tomasa Muñoz contra Ramón Montilla, por esponsales," ARPDF, Civiles, 1877, Letra M, exp. 2; "Augusta Velázquez contra Félix María Bosa, por promesa de matrimonio," ARPDF, Civiles, 1878, Letra V, exp. 14; "Carmen Figuera a nombre de su hija Rosario Díaz demanda a Rafael E. Alvarado por esponsales," ARPDF, Civiles, 1879, Letra F, exp. 16; "Luisa López contra Juan Antonio Sucre, por esponsales," ARPDF, Civiles, 1879, Letra L, exp. 6; "Mercedes Mota contra Angel Acosta, por esponsales," ARPDF, Civiles, 1879, Letra M, exp. 47.

35 "Mercedes Mota."

36 Ibid., fol. 17r.

37 "Zoila Antonia Mosquera."

38 "Candelaria Manzo," fol. 41v.

39 "Zoila Antonia Mosquera," fols. 20r and 21r.

40 "Basilia Domínguez contra Francisco Aguiar, por esponsales," ARPDF, Civiles, 1877, Letra D, exp. 10; "Carmen Figuera a nombre de su hija Rosaura Díaz demanda a Rafael E. Alvarado por esponsales," ARPDF, Civiles, 1879, Letra F, exp. 16.

41 "El General José Nicomedes Ramírez en representación de Juana Bautista Córdova demanda a Pedro Pérez hijo por esponsales," ARPDF, Civiles, 1879, Letra C, exp. 38.

42 In practice, parental consent meant that the father authorized a child's marriage. Only in the father's absence is the mother's permission accepted in court. "El General José Nicomedes Ramírez, fols. 47v–48r.

43 Ibid., fol. 63r.

44 "Luisa López contra Juan Antonio Sucre," fol. 28r.

45 See Díaz, "*Ciudadanas* and *padres de familia*," 113–118.

46 "Candelaria Manzo," fol. 42r. Other examples are discussed in Díaz, "*Ciudadanas* and *padres de familia*," chap. 9.

47 While illegitimacy was common in Venezuela, a child born outside marriage but recognized by the father did not bear the same social stigma experienced by an unacknowledged child. The latter case could imply that the child was a bastard, born of a mother or father unable to marry (i.e., in an adulterous, incestuous, or sacrilegious union), thus suggesting that the woman had an immoral and illegal relationship. We see this situation in a word used in colonial and nineteenth-century Venezuela: *botado,* a throwaway. The term disparages foundlings, who were often born of illegal relationships. Moreover, natural and illegitimate children had different legal rights. Two sources discuss the distinctions: Linda Lewin's

"Natural and Spurious Children in Brazilian Inheritance Law from Colony to Empire: A Methodological Essay," *The Americas* 48, no. 3 (January 1992): 351–396; and *Diccionario razonado,* s.v. "hijo legítimo," "hijo natural," and "hijo espúrio o bastardo."

48 For a discussion on civil marriages see Díaz, *"Ciudadanas* and *padres de familia,"* chap. 8. In terms of the juridical procedure, a divorce lawsuit followed the same steps as an ordinary trial, with the exception that the court was required to promote a conciliation between the parties. After the suit was brought to court, the judge summoned both parties to a first hearing in ten days, where he invited them to reconcile. If that was not possible, a new citation was issued in one hundred days after a reply to the lawsuit was made. If a settlement was impossible in that time, a marriage counselor for the defense was appointed and the trial continued as usual. See *Código de Procedimiento Civil de 1873,* article 37.

49 Partida 4, title IX, law 7.

50 1873 Civil Code, article 152, number 1.

51 Voluntary abandonment of the marital home was not a cause for divorce under Spanish law. In the 1875–80 sample, seventeen cases claimed divorce on grounds of adultery and thirty for abuse and/or abandonment.

52 *Diccionario razonado,* s.v. "disolución de matrimonio," and "divorcio"; Partida 4, title V, Book 1, laws 12, 15, 17; and 1873 civil code, articles 126 and 130.

53 1873 Civil Code, articles 127 and 131. The latter article put an official end to clandestine marriages that were possible under canon law. For a discussion of clandestine marriages in Caracas, see Díaz, *"Ciudadanas* and *padres de familia,"* chap. 3.

54 "Jesús María González Bello contra José de la Presentación Sánchez y Carolina Ragas por la nulidad del matrimonio contraído por éste," ARPDF, Civiles, 1877, Letra G, exp. 44; "Isabel Hernández de Mendivil contra Antonio de Mendivil y Salomé Mendivil por la nulidad de matrimonio contraído por éstos," ARPDF, Civiles, 1878, Letra H, exp. 17.

55 "José Prágedes Nuez contra su consorte."

56 In the colonial sample (1786–91) showed eight divorce cases (of a sample of 139 cases), in which the court granted only two temporal and one perpetual divorce. Two were withdrawn, and three records were incomplete. The early republican sample (1835–40) shows nineteen different claims out of a total of 254. Of these, only nine had a verdict, and only six were approved. See Díaz, *"Ciudadanas* and *padres de familia,"* chaps 2 and 5.

57 The story of the world-acclaimed Venezuelan pianist and composer Teresa Carreño reveals the elite stance toward divorce. In 1886, Guzmán Blanco asked her to organize the opera season in Caracas. Because Teresa Carreño was divorced and had even remarried in Europe, a great scandal for the times, Venezuelan elites shunned her and boycotted her shows and performances, making the season a

complete failure. Because her extraordinary talents were not matched by morally acceptable behavior, Teresa Carreño could not be acceptable to the elite. *Diccionario de historia,* s.v. "Carreño, Teresa."

58 The 1875–80 sample shows strikingly few cases coming from the elites: five percent. When compared with the percentage from the other samples (21 and 15 percent for the 1786–91 and 1835–40 samples respectively) a clear trend emerges: the lower classes gained presence in the courts, and the percentage of elite lawsuits declined. For a discussion of Caracas litigants' social class from the late colonial period to the Guzmán Blanco regime, see Díaz, "*Ciudadanas* and *padres de familia,*" chap. 7. Moreover, wives litigated most of the divorce cases (76 percent), as in the earlier samples. Yet, by the late nineteenth century, more men sued for divorce, all accusing their wives of adultery.

59 "María Teresa Belsinger contra Juan Bautista Acereto por divorcio," ARPDF, Civiles, 1875, Letra B, exp. 5, fols. 32v–33r.

60 Ibid., fol. 39r.

61 Ibid., fols. 51v–52r.

62 Ibid., fols. 52v.

63 Ibid., fols. 52v–53r.

64 Joan W. Scott analyzes the multiple ways in which gender structures the household and broader politics. See *Gender and the Politics of History* (New York: Columbia University Press, 1988), p. 47.

65 This court is roughly equivalent to an appellate court in the United States, although the Venezuelan institution is based on the French model. The term *cassation* derives from the French *casser* (to quash). This refers to the nullification of judicial decisions by lower courts based on erroneous interpretations of the statutes. John Henry Merryman, *The Civil Law Tradition,* 2d ed. (Stanford: Stanford University Press, 1985), pp. 39–41. On the evolution of this judicial organ in Venezuela, see *Diccionario de historia,* s.v. "poder judicial."

66 "Manuela Blandín de López contra su marido Juan Evangelista, por divorcio," ARPDF, Civiles, 1880, Letra B, exp. 33; "Luis Felipe Delgado contra su consorte Teolinda Hernández por divorcio," ARPDF, Civiles, 1879, Letra D, exp. 17.

67 "Luis Felipe Delgado contra su consorte," fol. 36r.

68 "Mercedes García contra Juan Bautista Castillo por divorcio," ARPDF, Civiles, 1878, Letra G, exp. 52; "Serapio Martínez contra su consorte Ramona Delgado por divorcio," ARPDF, Civiles, 1878, Letra M, exp. 3.

69 An exception would be Costa Rica, the first country to have a divorce law in Spanish America in the nineteenth century that allowed both the dissolution of the bond of the union *(divortium quaod vinculum)* and the separation of bed and board *(divortium quaod thorum et cohabitationem)* without interruption since its enactment on 26 April 1876. Another overlooked situation is Haiti, which regulated divorce matters in its civil code of 1825. See Hugo E. Gatti, *La disolución del vínculo matrimonial* (Montevideo: Centro Estudiantes de Derecho, 1967), 52–53, 56.

70 The word *estupro* disappeared in the 1897 penal code and jail sentences for violación became harsher. See 1897 Penal Code, articles 338–346.

71 See articles 428–431 on estupro and articles 423–427 on violación in the 1873 civil code. Although article 428 establishes that estupro is sexual intercourse with a virgin older than twelve years of age, article 423 (number 3) includes under estupro the nonviolent crime against girls who are older than ten.

72 If the aggressor was a close relative, the 1873 code (article 430) specified that a harsher punishment would be considered.

73 See Elías Pino Iturrieta, *Ventaneras y castas, diabólicas y honestas* (Caracas: Planeta, 1993).

74 "Proceso de estupro. Inculpado: Juan Machado," ARPDF, Criminales, 1879, Letra M, exp. 39.

75 This contrasts with the questions asked of the defendant Juan Machado. The tribunal queried him about the victim, if he knew where she worked, who raped her, and why he was arrested. "Proceso de estupro," fols. 6v–7r.

76 This happened, for instance, in the claim against Juan Machado discussed above and in "Criminal contra Felipe Kuey por imputársele el delito de estupro por fuerza," ARPDF, Criminales, 1878, Letra K, exp. 1.

77 See "Criminal contra Vicente Berthier Tompson por violación," ARPDF, Criminales, 1875, Letra B, exp. 2; "Proceso de estupro" discussed above; "Sumario seguido contra Ildefonso León por violación perpetrado en la persona de Trinidad Bigot," ARPDF, Criminales, 1877, Letra L, exp. 2.

78 "Contra Juan Ramón Gómez por violación de la impúber Isabel Hernández," ARPDF, Criminales, 1880, Letra G, exp. 9, fols. 30v–31r.

79 This is clear in the law dealing with bodily injuries in which only serious, handicapping injuries would carry a punishment. Minor injuries would not be punished, including those caused by a padre de familia. See 1873 Civil Code, articles 368–378.

80 On this issue, see "Contra Juan Ramón Gómez"; "Sumario seguido contra Ildefonso León por violación perpetrado en la persona de Trinidad Bigott," ARPDF, Criminales, 1877, Letra L, exp. 2, fold. 28; "Contra Ricardo Ramos por el delito de violación," ARPDF, Criminales, 1876, Letra R, exp. 5, fols. 36–37r.

81 Ildefonso León admitted that he was "embromándola pretendiendo ofenderla, pero no resultó," and Juan Ramón Gómez said that "se abstuvo de hacer lo que se había prometido." "Sumario seguido contra Ildefonso León," fol. 8v; "Contra Juan Ramón Gómez," fol. 2r.

82 The terms *fianza de cárcel segura* or *libertad provisional* do not mean what in English is understood as probation. In Venezuela, someone under libertad provisional in the late nineteenth century was not necessarily convicted of a crime; the person was just accused of committing an offense and a judgment on the guilt of the defendant had not necessarily been issued.

83 1873 Code of Criminal Procedure, article 110. This type of outcome, in which an aggressor was freed on bail because the injuries were not severe, was common in

cases of physical abuse, bodily harm, and injuries. See, for example, "Criminal contra Pedro Pablo Vera por golpes," ARPDF, Criminales, 1878, Libro UV, Letra V, exp. 2; "Lucia Acosta, heridas," ARPDF, Criminales, 1879, Letra A, exp. 2; "Averiguación contra Julián Acosta, por golpes dados a su padre natural Víctor Aguilar," ARPDF, Criminales, 1879, Letra A, exp. 4; "Averiguación sobre unos golpes que dice la Sra. Rafaela Arias de Llaguno le infirió su marido Emiliano Llaguno," ARPDF, Criminales, 1880, Libro LM, Letra LL, exp. 1; "Ynstrucción sumaria sobre una herida inferida a Reyes Madera," ARPDF, Criminales, 1878, Libro HJK, Letra H, exp. 6; "Contra Santos Machado por herida," ARPDF, Criminales, 1878, Letra M, exp. 6; "Averiguación sobre una herida que le fue inferida por Andrés Sánchez a Rosaura González," ARPDF, Criminales, 1880, Letra S, exp. 2.

84 1873 Code of Criminal Procedure, articles 112 and 117.

85 1873 Code of Criminal Procedure, articles 113–114. Males under twenty-one and women were not entitled to be sponsors according to this code.

86 See Díaz, "*Ciudadanas* and *padres de familia,*" chap. 7.

87 Díaz, "*Ciudadanas* and *padres de familia,*" chapter 9. A later and shorter version of that chapter appeared as " 'Because my Sex without Honor Is Good for Nothing' ": Challenging Normative Gender Roles in Guzmán Blanco's Venezuela," *Occasional Paper Series of the Indiana University-University of Michigan Consortium on Latin American and Caribbean Studies* (Bloomington, 1999).

88 Eileen J. Findlay argues similarly for Puerto Rico. During the early years of U.S. rule in the island, the colonial government intended to promote formal marriages among Puerto Ricans by making full divorce possible. See her "Love in the Tropics: Marriage, Divorce, and the Construction of Benevolent Colonialism in Puerto Rico, 1898–1910," in Gilbert M. Joseph, Catherine LeGrand, and Ricardo Donato Salvatore, eds., *Close Encounters of Empire* (Durham, N.C.: Duke University Press, 1998), pp. 139–172.

Judges, Lawyers, and Farmers:

Uses of Justice and the Circulation of Law

in Rural Buenos Aires, 1900–1940

JUAN MANUEL PALACIO

T he agrarian history of the Pampean region in the modern period has been written in terms of large landowners and prosperous tenants. The relative absence of violent social conflicts in Argentine rural history, compared with the rest of Latin America, has reinforced this perspective. In this essay, I seek to revise this model by focusing on the workings of law and justice in a rural district located in the most important wheat-growing area of Argentina, the county of Coronel Dorrego, in Southern Buenos Aires province.

This essay establishes, first, that the precariousness and instability of the conditions of wheat farming in the Pampean region produced multiple everyday conflicts. It also argues that most of these conflicts were contained by the gradual development of a strong "judicial culture" forged by the everyday practices of the region's inhabitants over time. Two elements proved decisive in the evolution of this judicial culture: a clear administration of justice by the *jueces de paz* (judges of the peace) and the key role rural lawyers played in spreading the law and defining judiciary procedures. Mundane disputes over issues like loans, tenancy, and labor contracts were the most common expression of social conflict in the region and were the domain of the judge of the peace. Insofar as the court was able to contain them effectively, the resolution of small-scale litigation helped prevent the development of larger conflicts. The Pampean region rarely exploded in agrarian revolt. On the contrary, social and economic frictions were articulated and defused within the formal parameters of the legal framework mediated by the local courts.

Farmers

In 1937, a committee of prominent citizens of Coronel Dorrego published a volume celebrating the county's fiftieth anniversary. Like similar volumes produced by other towns of the Pampas for similar occasions, this one contained 385 elegant pages in tabloid size and laminated paper, filled with photographs and illustrations, and proudly marked the milestone in the existence of that district of Buenos Aires province. After several historic and statistical articles about the county, the book continued with a series of biographical notes about its inhabitants. Depending on their importance, merchants and *estancieros* (landowners), long settled in the county, as well as recently settled *chacareros* (farmers) with more modest resources, were portrayed in articles, ranging from two complete pages to a quarter of a page, with or without photographs and illustrations. The book included 249 biographies, all following the same format and sharing the same self-congratulatory tone:

> The history of the progress of Coronel Dorrego presents many examples of industry and perseverance, exercised during the most difficult and harshest period of its formation, revealing the strong lineage of some of those first inhabitants who addressed their energy to the land of the region. Miguel Pinnel (died 1936) is one outstanding example: an inexhaustible fighter whose vigorous profile has proved, in a tangible way, how it is possible to scale to the highest economic position from a modest beginning by means of hard work and dynamism.[1]

After this promising introduction, the report of the principal landmarks of Pinnel's economic rise continued on the same hagiographical note. Born in Luxembourg, he arrived in Argentina in 1888 with his family and worked in Benito Juárez county for three years. Then he rented 300 hectares in the neighboring county of Tres Arroyos, and continued to rent increasingly larger areas until he became the owner of 2,300 hectares in Coronel Dorrego in 1910.

Such an optimistic publication had no room for accounts of failure. To appear in the volume, it was necessary to have not only a more or less successful and progressive story to tell, but also the money to pay for both the space in the book and the work of the biographer. Financed in part by a few advertisements of banks, insurance companies, and local merchants, the publication was paid for mainly by the contributions of the people who had their biographies included: a whole page biography, with photograph, cost one hundred pesos, the equivalent to the monthly salary of two field laborers or sixteen days' wages at the time of harvest.[2]

Undoubtedly, this publication portrayed not so much the actual social and economic condition of Coronel Dorrego in 1937, but rather a state of mind and a faith in progress that had long dominated the mood of the Pampean agrarian community. By 1937, however, conditions underlying such optimism were showing clear signs of extinction.[3] By then, an exhausted productive frontier and a prolonged crisis of world wheat prices, worsened by the global economic crisis of 1930, pointed increasingly to the end of the good old days. Yet, the Coronel Dorrego anniversary volume repeated the format and tone of similar publications of other rural villages that had reached their fiftieth anniversary one or two decades earlier, when the agrarian situation gave them more reason to celebrate.

Similarly, a false optimism characterizes the historiography, which later outlined in a more technical and erudite form the history of chacarero agriculture. Transplanting the "farmer model" scholars have likened the Pampean experience to other "open frontiers," such as the American Midwest, the Canadian prairies, and Australia—perhaps influenced by the clearly biased photographs that illustrated Pampean anniversary boosterism.[4]

This evidence needs to be reevaluated. The aforementioned book contained the biographies of 249 farmers and cattlemen from Coronel Dorrego, including 119 landowners and 114 tenants, who had an average plot size of 650 hectares. If we contrast these data with those of the 1937 Agricultural Census, we realize that the people portrayed in the book represent only 20 percent of the county's total producers. According to the census, the county had a total of 1,270 producers, distributed among 286 landowners and 966 tenants—the latter in charge of nearly 80 percent of the crop-producing farms. It is also immediately apparent that the book's sample was biased toward the richest farmers, since according to the census average plot size in the county was less than 300 hectares (see table 1).[5] The lives of the farmers in Coronel Dorrego omitted from the book were very different from those portrayed in the biographies. Every day they endured, with

TABLE I Agrarian Structure of Coronel Dorrego, 1895–1947

	Population	Cultivated area (hectares)	Average plot size (hectares)	Plots 0–300 hs (%)	Number of plots	Number of owners	%	Number of tenants	%
1895	4,914	802	—	—	—	23	47.9	25	52.1
1908	—	130,525	—	—	—	—	—	—	—
1914	11,528	154,009	184	65.6	835	58	10.7	442	81.4
1922	16,955	201,132	—	—	—	—	—	—	—
1937	—	334,698	263	76.0	1,270	286	22.5	966	76.0
1947	20,471	302,412	248	50.0	1,217	338	27.7	980	68.4

Sources: 1895: Segundo censo de la República Argentina: mayo 10 de 1895 (Buenos Aires, 1898); 1908: Argentina, Censo Agropecuario Nacional, La ganadería y la agricultura en 1908 (Buenos Aires, 1909); 1914: Argentina, Tercer censo nacional: año 1914 (Buenos Aires: Rosso y Cía., 1916); 1922: Coronel Dorrego, Provincia de Buenos Aires, Primer censo municipal levantado el 30 de julio de 1922; 1937: Argentina. Ministerio de Agricultura, Censo nacional agropecuario: Año 1937 (Buenos Aires: Guillermo Kraft Ltda., 1939–40); 1947: Argentina, Presidencia de la Nación, IV Censo general de la nación (Buenos Aires, 1947).

varied results, the conditions of wheat production in the Pampas, which were marked by juridical and economic instability, uncertainty and extreme precariousness.

The historical roots of this situation can be traced to the generalized spread of wheat cultivation in the province of Buenos Aires in the 1890s. On the one hand, landowners, traditionally more comfortable with real estate and livestock production than the risky business of agriculture, left cereal production in the tenants' hands, who gladly accepted the invitation. Ironically, tenants' demand increased the value of the land and with it the attractiveness of land speculation, widening the gap separating the average farmer from landownership. On the other hand, the scarcity and high cost of manual labor had given momentum to early mechanization of wheat farming, by the 1910s comparable in Argentina to that of more advanced countries.

These features were especially marked in regions of more recent settlement like Coronel Dorrego, where recently arrived producers had fewer resources, where tenancy levels were higher, and where mechanization had gone further.[6] Created in 1887 as a detachment from the county of Tres Arroyos and as a necessary station on the long route that wheat traveled down to the port of Bahía Blanca, Coronel Dorrego became the south-ernmost wheat district within a few years.[7] A first wave of settlers, arriving in the area during the two first decades of the county's institutional exis-tence, managed to become important farmers either by renting consider-able extensions of land or becoming landowners. Later arrivals had to settle for renting small[8] tracts of land, with which they tried their luck each year.[9]

This land-extensive and mechanized tenant agriculture lacked the most elemental juridical and institutional instruments for this system of produc-tion: official credit and appropriate legislation on tenancy. Let us first look at credit. In Argentina, official agrarian credit had long been limited to the loans granted by the Banco Hipotecario Nacional, which favored the spec-ulative interests of huge landowners and cattlemen, and remained out of reach for small farmers and tenants, that is, for productive purposes.[10] Contrary to what some authors argue, however, loans were neither absent nor insufficient: loans did exist and were within reach of any farmer, at any time. Yet, because of the almost complete absence of channels for cheap, formal long-term loans granted by state institutions, the average Pampean farmer had to resign himself to a perverse, informal and very expensive — though perfectly oiled — credit network, under local control.

The key actors in this network were the rural merchants, owners of *almacenes de ramos generales* (country stores) who offered *cuentas* (credit accounts) to farmers located in their area of influence. In these accounts, farmers accumulated debts during the year to be paid with the proceeds of the harvest. Merchants supplied the seed, basic tools for cultivation such as plows and rakes, and sacks for the harvested crop. Sometimes, when the merchant was also the representative of an importer, he sold on credit more expensive machinery like harvesters. In addition, the country merchant frequently advanced the money for cash rents, usually payable in advance; for the wages of day laborers, both the few contracted for sowing and the more numerous laborers needed for the harvest; or for the rental of thresh-ing machines. Some merchants simply gave farmers periodic cash advances. The farmers' accounts also included credit for basic foodstuffs and clothing for the chacarero and his family during the year. When harvest time arrived, the almacenero had first claim on the product, and the farmers "sold" them their wheat to cancel the debts incurred during the agricultural year.

The informal local credit system had a human face and exacted a high price. For the average farmer of Coronel Dorrego, the country merchant personified the market. Not only did the merchant represent the market of

TABLE 2 Coronel Dorrego: Wheat Prices and Number of Claims, 1920–1940

	Wheat prices ($/100kg)	Number of claims	Number of seizures
1920–24	14.77	73	31
1925–30	11.85	116	51
1930–34	6.52	251	144
1935–40	9.31	149	79

Sources: Prices: 1920–33: *Revista de Economía Argentina* (Buenos Aires) XVIII, pp. 205–206; 1934–39: *Anuario estadístico de la República Argentina* (Buenos Aires, 1948), p. 497; Claims: *JPCD-C*, 1920–1940.

consumption goods, agricultural inputs, and credit during the year, he also represented the wheat market, in which the farmer participated only through the expensive mediation of these merchants. Almaceneros compensated the high risks of operating in this precarious economy with the low price they paid for the crop.[11]

By merely signing some documents, the farmers could obtain loans from other sources, besides the country merchants to be paid at the time of harvest. Insurance companies usually gave farmers insurance premium on credit, but they also gave cash advances. Local representatives of machinery importers sold on credit. Farmers could also turn to the landowners or, more generally, to the lessors who could be, in turn, main tenants; to other farmers; to ordinary people transformed into improvised moneylenders; and to the local branches of state banks.[12] Even the workers and the day laborers worked on credit: when they were not paid through the country merchants, they accepted promissory notes.

The landscape of this informal credit system was an infinite universe of money vouchers, promissory notes, and customer accounts often carrying multiple endorsements, that circulated and were negotiated in the county as a virtual local currency. Everyone involved waited for December and January, when the wheat and oat harvest took place. If the harvest was good and the prices were not excessively low, it was enough for chacareros to cancel all debts and to save some money for the next cycle. If, on the contrary, the harvest was ruined or prices collapsed, not infrequent circumstances, debts became unpayable and the cycle ended in seizures and evictions. Consequently, 85 percent of all legal claims initiated in these years were filed

	Origin of the claims				Participation of lawyers	Outcome		Lawsuits initiated by		
	UPN	US	UR	E		Sentences	Settlements	Lessors	Merchants	Workers
	(1)	(2)	(3)	(4)	(5)	(6)	(7)	(8)	(9)	(10)
1900–9	37.5	32.1	3.6	14.3	62.5	17.9	30.4	23.2	30.4	26.8
1910–19	51.7	10.0	15.0	11.7	46.7	16.7	35.0	30.0	40.0	8.3
1920–24	57.5	4.1	5.5	23.3	37.0	31.5	24.7	38.4	28.8	4.1
1925–29	73.3	12.9	11.2	0.9	33.6	14.7	14.7	15.5	54.3	11.2
1930–34	62.5	13.1	12.0	6.8	39.0	16.7	37.8	14.7	47.4	13.5
1935–39	61.7	10.7	6.7	10.7	22.8	12.1	55.0	16.1	27.5	10.7
Average	60.7	12.9	9.6	9.4	37.0	17.0	35.5	19.6	40.5	12.2

Notes: UPN: Unpaid promissory notes; US: Unpaid salaries; UR: Unpaid rents; E: Eviction trials.
Sources: JPCD-C, 1900–1940.

against farmers, and more than 80 percent of these claims originated in unpaid promissory notes, insurance premiums, country store accounts, and rents (see Table 3).

The other source of instability for the agricultural producer in Dorrego was caused by his precarious juridical relationship with the land. Despite the importance of tenancy in Pampean agriculture, Argentina did not have any tenancy law until 1921, and the contractual relations between landowners and tenants were extremely precarious during the period under study.

This legal void was deeper in regions with a greater proportion of tenants, like Coronel Dorrego. According to the 1922 local census, almost a third of the landowners, classified as "rentiers," rented all of their lands, and many of the rest rented considerable portions of their properties.[13] This agrarian structure was the visible side of a huge and complex real estate business: to the category of landowner we should add the large tenants and merchants who rented land only to sublet it to tenants who, finally, dedicated themselves to wheat cultivation. It was not unusual, moreover, to find people subletting to second or third parties.

In the absence of a specific regulatory norm, this universe of lessors and sublessors maintained a fragile equilibrium. Contracts, when they existed, were overwhelmingly verbal, especially for subletting. Some contracts were annual or biannual, but most were arranged "without term," for a share of the crop or, more frequently, for a fixed rent in cash.

Beside the uncertainties for the tenants, this situation produced a great deal of paperwork and even some confusion in the small bureaucracy of the local courts. The civil code, for example, specified a year's advance notice for evictions. So every year, as a preventive measure, the lessors went to court to notify their tenants that their contracts ended the following year and they should vacate the land. This, in turn, generated a cascade of notifications from tenants to subtenants, from subtenants to their own subtenants, and so on, many times ending in lawsuits. The subtenants were at the bottom of the ladder. Even though they were as numerous as tenants in Dorrego, they had only minimum legal support, since their permanence on the land was subject to the conditions — already unstable — agreed on by the main tenants.

In 1921, the long-awaited law arrived.[14] With the law of rural rents, Argentine legislators expressed a concern they shared with their counterparts throughout Latin America. The production of cheap food for growing urban and industrial populations required a policy that protected farmers, placing economic and social priorities above the speculative interests of the landowners. Greater state intervention to improve the institutional framework for economic development, overcoming obsolete legal structures or, in the Argentine case, nonexistent ones, would achieve that goal.[15] The Argentine leadership of the time was not completely impervious to this debate, despite the relative absence of an urgent "agrarian question" in the Pampas. The violent episodes in Patagonia and, especially, a tenants' revolt in Santa Fe, known as *el Grito de Alcorta,* had already caught the attention of a political class increasingly concerned with social disorders.

This environment of ideas produced a compromise law whose salient characteristic was its inefficacy. The statute sought to attack the evil of tenants' instability on two fronts: the length of the contracts and the protection of the smaller tenant. Thus, the law regulated only the leasing of farms of less than 300 hectares (article 1), and for these it set a minimum term of four years (article 2). These provisions were not, however, a big obstacle for landlords who wanted to avoid their effects. The first they could elude simply by renting, from then on, pieces of land of a minimum size of 301 hectares. The second remained largely ineffective since the law did not explicitly obligate the parties to sign written contracts. The practice of verbal contracts, with all the advantages that their ambiguity and intangibility had for the lessors, became more extensive.[16]

The other tenancy law of this period, enacted in 1932, aimed at correcting those two important shortcomings in the 1921 law.[17] The new law included all rented rural lands, regardless of their size, stipulated a five-year minimum lease (article 2) and, most important of all, required the parties to sign written contracts before a notary public or the Judge of the Peace of each county (article 4). Although the revised law offered important protections, defects arose in its application. As there was no effective state control in remote rural areas, a high percentage of contracts continued to be arranged verbally. According to the 1937 census, almost half of the tenants of Buenos Aires province fell into the "without contract" category, while in Coronel Dorrego, out of 966 existing tenants only some 300 had registered their contracts before the local court.[18]

Thus, the tenancy laws of the period did little to correct the principal problems of the farmers or to change the unpredictable relationship between tenants and the land. Only decisive state intervention, and the imposition of an enforcement bureaucracy in even the remotest corners of the province, could change the state of things. This occurred only after the revolutionary government of June 1943 took office and imposed a resolute interventionism in the countryside.

Judges

Despite the uncertainties of their daily lives, the people of Dorrego had a profound respect for law and justice. This respect did not originate in the fear of the law's repressive power, but in something deeper and more lasting: the acknowledgment of law as the appropriate arena to settle local conflicts and the judge of the peace as the person to sort out and regulate everyday economic relations. Without the judge, the entire universe of vouchers, cuentas, promissory notes with multiple endorsements, verbal promises of payment or tenancy contracts without term, would have had no value. Without other institutional mechanisms, the judge insured all those informal arrangements vital to the functioning of productive activity. Moreover, the court, bolstered by the prestige it enjoyed in local society, channeled and contained within formal parameters the conflicts generated by an unstable economic life. Precarious as they were, the workings of those arrangements defined a certain "Peace of Wheat," with its clear winners and losers, and accommodated the steady and unperturbed development of social and economic life.

The Justice of the Peace was the original institution to accompany the advance of the frontier in the province of Buenos Aires. From 1821, when the position was created, to 1854, when the Municipalities of the Countryside were instituted, the judges wielded almost all of the powers of the former Spanish *cabildos*. During that period, the judge was also chief of police, commander of militias, collector of the state's rents and contributions, and political boss of his county. The judge was a key figure in the centralized control of a province undergoing chronic political turbulence.[19]

But the rapid social and economic development of towns in rural Buenos Aires created the need for a more complex bureaucratic organization. With the creation of the municipalities in 1854, many attributions of these local courts were eliminated, and for the rest of the century, the powers of judges of the peace were increasingly reduced to the strict administration of justice. The Law of Proceedings for the Justice of the Peace of 1887 defined the functions and competences of the position.[20] These judges intervened in all minor conflicts that originated at a local level: in civil and commercial claims up to the sum of one thousand pesos; and in criminal claims whose penalties did not exceed a one-year jail sentence. When the claims exceeded those limits, or when the sentences imposed by the justice of the peace were contested, the cases were remitted to the Courts of Appeals, located in the cities that were designated as seats of the judicial districts into which the province was divided. For Dorrego the district seat was the city of Bahía Blanca, located sixty-five miles away.

During the entire period under study, the office of Justice of the Peace was defined as *lega* (lay), that is, it was held not by professionals of the law, but by mere citizens. The 1887 Proceedings law stipulated only that judges should be propertied county residents over the age of twenty-five, who knew how to read and write. The election procedure offered a list of three candidates proposed by the municipal government to the provincial government, which, finally, elected the man for the position. He held it for one year, but reelections were possible and usually occurred. In Coronel Dorrego, in the forty years analyzed, there were only seven judges, and four of them held the position for thirty-four of these forty years. In every case, these judges had also been *alguaciles* (warrant officers) and secretaries, positions that constituted, along with that of judge, the small bureaucracy of the court.

Little is known about the social and economic origin of these judges. Except for the landowner Manuel Durañona, who was the judge from 1898 to 1908, the other judges belonged to an urban or suburban middle class of small merchants, who might also have been farm owners. In regard to their political affiliation, they were Liberal, Conservative, or Radical; and although the judges' party affiliation usually corresponded to the political color of the municipal government at that moment, in practice the judges held their positions longer than the parties maintained local executive power.

This stability of judges also had a practical purpose, in a specifically professional and institutional sense, that was closely related to the way the judge acquired mastery of his job. Those landowners, farmers, and small merchants, unfamiliar with the more basic procedures of the law, learned to administer justice on the job. To instruct these officers, the government of Buenos Aires province, throughout the nineteenth century, published a series of manuals, decrees, and circulars designed to instruct the judges in procedural and legal questions.[21] Besides these instructions, the judges had to be versed in the essential codes and laws. At the very least, they had to know the civil and criminal codes, the procedural codes, the basic principles of the national and provincial constitutions, and the growing body of jurisprudence. They also had to stay abreast of all new laws that might apply to their jurisdiction and competence, in particular those concerning the rural sphere.

Judges had to study, know, and use all these instruments in a learning process that started when they took office, or even before, when they began to work at the court as *alguaciles* or secretaries. Their practical education was reinforced in the everyday administration of justice, many times by trial and error. Over the years this job experience, forged through an informal judicial career at the local level, could not be easily replaced and was decisive at the time of election, or reelection, of these officers. Longevity on the job also proved crucial for the judges' reputations. It earned them a widespread respect for their institutional and "professional" skills in the countryside, difficult to achieve if the position had changed hands with every political fluctuation.

The administration of justice in Dorrego meant much more than the strict application of the law and issuing of sentences. Mainly, it was a question of applying common sense and good will to solve the differences generated by everyday productive activities. The very law of the justice of the peace recognized this aspect of the position and urged judges to solve the problems fast and, if possible, in a friendly manner. In its article 55, the law stated that once the claims of the parties had been heard, the judge "will try first of all to bring them to friendly terms, proposing the ways of settlement that *his prudence suggests.*" If settlement was not successful, the next article suggested that the judge issue a sentence "in the same act if possible, or within forty-eight hours."[22]

These terms were almost impossible to meet. Often the court's warrant officer had to travel considerable distances to carry out seizures or evictions, or to deliver a simple notification, and the trips usually took most of the day. And when the claims accumulated at certain times of the year, usually in the harvest months, the court was too understaffed to handle the load with dispatch. Nevertheless, the majority of the claims filed in Dorrego between 1900 and 1940 reached a quick resolution; almost 60 percent of the claims were solved in the first two months. Regarding settlements, Dorrego's judges were quite successful: in the whole period, 36 percent of the claims reached an agreement before the judge, and only 17 percent had a sentence (table 3).[23]

If good intentions did not suffice, judges had to rule according to the laws in effect, and this usually took longer. Some suits could last for more than a year before settlement. This happened, for instance, when a lawsuit for an unpaid promissory note ended in the sale at public auction of the debtor's impounded possessions. Such an outcome also required the procedural steps of notification, seizure, and sentence, the appointment of appraisers and an auctioneer, and the publication of edicts. Sometimes, the parties introduced the testimony of many witnesses; then notifying each one and carrying out the hearings demanded an enormous amount of additional time. Finally, when the lawsuits were appealed, the case had to be transferred and retried.

Some lawsuits required complicated sentences. This happened especially with eviction trials, particularly after passage of the 1921 tenancy law. Table 3 shows the considerable increase in the proportion of eviction lawsuits in the five-year period that followed passage of this law; that period saw an increase in the percentage of trials that reached a sentence. This boom of evictions was surely due to the reaction of landowners to this first manifestation of state intervention in their relationships with tenants. For landowners, state intervention disrupted their control of tenancy. For the court, and for the judicial experience of the local society, this was an important test period, when everybody could measure their strength and their legal and procedural abilities.

The decisive test for the justice of the peace in Dorrego during this period, however, was the long global crisis in wheat prices that lasted from 1925 to 1935. This crisis worsened with the effects of the 1929 international financial crash, and was also accompanied by a terrible series of droughts and crop failures in the Pampean region. These circumstances caused a catastrophe in the fragile financial equilibrium of Coronel Dorrego, formed, as we have seen, by an unstable universe of mutual payment obligations. Table 2 shows a clear correspondence between the fall in wheat prices and the increase in the number of claims. As the price of wheat fell, more and more people went to court to cash their promissory notes and cuentas. Many notes were surely long overdue, but the generalized panic made liquidity urgent. In particular, preventive seizures of farmers' holdings increased more than claims, a pattern that reveals the desperation of the creditors to insure their debts in the context of increasingly fewer securable assets.

The long crisis provoked a general collapse of the farmers' payment capacity. The crisis also badly affected the financial reserves of rural merchants, who were used to waiting more than a year before requiring the settlement of consumer accounts in court. In that sense, the increase in the proportion of claims initiated by merchants during the prolonged crisis was a symptom of the generalized state of nervousness (see column 9, table 3).

This deep crisis was ultimately contained by the local court. The judge had to strive to reach the largest possible number of agreements, since it was likely that, with low prices and poor harvests, all the crop produced on the farms of Coronel Dorrego during those years would not suffice to pay all the existing debts. In that sense, the court was quite successful. The number of claims tripled in a few years, but the percentage of sentences maintained its historic level (tables 2 and 3). To achieve this long-term result, the court had to exercise all its power of persuasion and remain sensitive not only to the difficult situation of the farmers, but also to the situation of the majority of creditors, who suffered from the break in the chain of payments. There is no reason not to trust José Bérola, a small merchant of Dorrego who, in a claim against one of his debtors, asked the judge to consider his difficulties:

The judge knows well that we are enduring a moment of intense economic depression, and that wholesale commerce has restricted credits in an alarming way, and that the small merchant must defend himself trying to keep the balance, the selling on credit *(el fiado)* being our worst scourge. If we were in better times, we would not have come to court to use compulsory procedures, but the case is that the state of our finances is precarious and the creditors do not wait.[24]

If all the attempts at mediation failed, the judge could not elude the strict application of the law. In that situation, it fell to the judge to be very meticulous in organizing the dismantling of the properties proposed by the creditors. He had to act carefully, giving precedence to debts that, by law, had privilege over others, such as crop insurance and salaries. The judge had also to be attentive to counteract the strategies of lawyers, who were especially skillful in cashing the money owed to their clients through ingenious procedural stratagems. José Bérola himself, in the above-mentioned case, warned the judge about that risk: "It is very likely that Mr. Bertolozzo, if he has a little bit of good will and does not listen to the advice of *'leguleyos'* (lawyers), who are always interested parties, will bring his payment up to date, the more so if the Judge of the Peace intervenes."[25]

The successful resolution of these critical situations was vital for the reputation of the local court. To maintain the necessary legitimacy, the administration of justice had to be "just" and equitable in the eyes of society and, especially, in the eyes of the parties most damaged by the system. In theory, this was not easy, considering that it was the beneficiaries of the system who used justice more frequently. An analysis of all civil and commercial claims in this period indicates that more than 60 percent were initiated by owners, merchants, and insurance companies (table 3). The defendants, meanwhile, were 85 percent farmers, mainly tenants and subtenants. If we add to these claims the annual eviction notices from landowners and large tenants, it becomes apparent that justice was an especially flexible and useful instrument for the local elite — those who, owing to their social, economic, and cultural standing enjoyed "more law."[26]

Contrary to common judicial situations in other Latin American rural environments — where, for instance, expropriated peasants filed claims to repair an injustice — those who initiated lawsuits in Dorrego, besides being the richest groups, were pursuing just claims. After all, nobody could doubt that farmers' debts existed; the farmers themselves usually recognized them.

But what makes the Pampean case interesting is that, unlike many of their Latin American peers, the Pampean rural elites chose more institutional means to satisfy their claims—even though the law was often slow and troublesome—instead of resorting to direct coercive action. The less favored groups, like subtenants and rural workers, moreover, also trusted the justice of the peace, and confided in him to solve their differences, whether with their employers, their lessors, or among themselves.

This is not to say that the court absorbed all conflicts. There were certainly many private arrangements that never reached the court, especially on large estancias with many tenants and workers, in which patron-client relations worked as an effective means of social control.[27] In addition, tenants and workers had their own organizations to channel their demands and used them to deal with particularly critical situations. In the years following the 1930 crisis, for example, tenants within the local agrarian cooperative organized *comisiones pro-rebaja de arrendamientos,* special ad hoc commissions to negotiate a reduction of rental payments with the landowners of the county. But even in these crucial years, chacareros did not neglect the institutional arena, as they continued to fight their cases in court, even while they tested other strategies.

During these forty years, 12 percent of all claims came from rural workers who had not received their salaries, had been underpaid in their daily wages, or had not received a compensation for a job-related accident. Claims by workers were much more numerous in the first years of the period, when fewer legal protections existed, but claims decreased over time, as workers obtained some rights, and, especially, as the society of Coronel Dorrego settled down and workers gradually ceased to be itinerant and became familiar faces (column 10, table 3).[28]

There are many cases revealing that even rural society's have-nots held the judge and the legal system in respect. In most cases involving claims for wages, for example, workers had only a voucher, written by hand—and not always signed—and sometimes just a verbal promise of payment. Scanty documentation, however, proved no obstacle to workers trusting the good will of the judge to solve claims in their favor. Take the case of day laborer Emilio Garavaglia, who filed a claim for damages against Antonio Rodríguez Alonso. The farmer had not fulfilled his promise to employ Garavaglia during the harvest.[29] In another case, subtenant José Vilariño, sentenced to be evicted, asked only that the judge be present "in person" at his eviction, not that the ruling be reversed.[30]

One further example illustrates that it was not only the manner in which the justice of the peace administered the law, but also what the judge represented for the lower social sectors, that insured their continued respect of and participation in the legal system. On March 21, 1922, the tenant Miguel Rodríguez filed an eviction claim against his subtenant, Félix Bardi, because their verbal contract on the rent of 200 hectares had expired. Bardi showed up in court a few days later and declared that, "protecting himself according to what National Law 11,170 established, he was not going to leave the land, since he had plowed it too."[31] On September 14, the judge accepted this objection and ruled to reject the claim of Rodríguez. The judge based his ruling on the facts that the defendant had not been notified correctly of the termination of his verbal contract; that Bardi was protected by the above-mentioned law; and that, since the tenant had "sowed the land, [the eviction] would cause the ruin of an honest farmer."[32]

Not satisfied with this decision, Rodríguez appealed to the court in Bahía Blanca. In the hearing there, his representative argued to reverse the ruling. Since at the time the two parties made the contract "law 11,170 had not been passed yet, this law does not protect [Bardi] because it does not have a retroactive effect, as is established in its art. 2." With respect to the other aspect of the Justice of the Peace's decision ("the ruin of an honest farmer"), "*I should remind you that the civil law does not admit arguments of a sentimental nature,* and it does not authorize the judges to rule on the intrinsic value or the equity of the law."[33] Bardi's representative countered that interpretation of law 11,170, to which "the distinguished Counselor of the plaintiff wants to give such a limited and restricted effect: this Counselor will not ignore that . . . the Law was issued to remedy whenever possible the afflicted situation of the workers, without distinction, since, lacking the means to obtain their welfare independently, they are subject to and depend on the so-called capitalists or landowners." Finally, in regard to whether or not civil law allowed arguments of sentimental nature, Bardi's representative stated "that is a new error, a new mistake: *judges are real and conscious judges* and it is not possible to declare that the laws do not take into account arguments of sentimental nature . . . because the Law grants prudential time limits, so those who have to leave a property can perform the harvest and have time to solve their future situation."[34] On February 7, 1923, on the grounds that law 11,170 did not have a retroactive effect, the Court of Appeals revoked the decision of the Judge of the Peace, condemning Bardi to leave the land in ten days.

The Bardi case illuminates another side of the legitimacy of local judges in Coronel Dorrego. The residents of the county trusted the very person of the judge. He was a neighbor who knew and shared local problems. In contrast to the anonymous and impersonal court of appeals, the justice of the peace guaranteed a familiarity with the people and their problems which made him more receptive to "arguments of sentimental nature." In that sense, the law of justice of the peace was wise in trusting the terms of conciliations to "what the prudence [of the judge] suggests to him," because that "prudence" was molded by the knowledge of shared experience and made these judges "real and conscious judges." Moreover, the fact that these officers did not have a clear political affiliation or a defined class extraction—or, at least, that those identities were less important to the judges' constituency than their role as judges—contributed to their image of impartiality and to the consolidation of their legitimacy in society.[35]

Lawyers

Between those who offered justice and those who sought it, there was a key character: the rural lawyer. These "lawyers" were not university graduates, nor did the law require certification to represent others before a court of peace. They were ordinary residents of the county who specialized in lawsuits, acting "professionally" in favor of landowners and merchants, on the one hand, and of tenants, subtenants, and workers, on the other. These lay specialists were well-known characters in the county. Although they resided in the county seat, rural people had rapid access to them by word of mouth. They were a small group: no more than two or three at a time attended to the needs of the small legal market of Coronel Dorrego.

Besides representing individuals, many of these rural lawyers were contracted as legal counselors by local institutions. Insurance companies, banks, the municipality, and the agrarian cooperative probably provided most of the lawyers' income.[36] The lawyers also supplemented their income by acting as moneylenders, or by cashing promissory notes. After all, nobody was better trained than they to cash the notes.

Like the justices of the peace, these lawyers learned their trade on the job. Many of them had worked as secretaries of the local court, where they had acquired a knowledge of the proceedings. All of them were associated with a legal firm in Bahía Blanca, with a twofold purpose. In the event that a law suit was appealed, a professional would be needed. These firms also helped them when a complex case in Dorrego required special knowledge of more arcane law or jurisprudence. But for everyone involved, these "lawyers" were considered the people best versed in the law and its proceedings in Coronel Dorrego. Even the judges consulted them off the record before issuing a sentence in difficult cases that required more legal erudition.[37]

Over time, the office became more professional. In the 1930s, the "lawyers" who attended most of the claims of legal representation in Dorrego were university *procuradores,* people holding an intermediate degree obtained after four years at the law schools, and in the 1940s two professional lawyers practiced in town. Many of these lawyers, with or without official credentials, used their contacts and their reputation to launch a political career. Initiated at the local level, as members of the city council or as mayors, some rose to hold seats in the provincial and national congresses.[38]

Who asked for the services of these rural lawyers, and how frequently? In 70 percent of the cases involving legal representation, these lawyers acted in favor of landowners and merchants. This clientele, after all, initiated the majority of claims and had better access to lawyers' services due to their economic standing. But if we examine how frequently plaintiffs of all social statuses went to court with legal representation, we get a more complex picture. People of means, landowners, merchants, and insurance companies had legal representation in only 35 percent of their cases. But subtenants and, in particular, day laborers came to court with representation more frequently than their social superiors; workers litigated through lawyers 60 percent of the time. In other words, it was more common to see a day laborer or a tenant in a lawsuit accompanied by a legal representative than to see a merchant or a landowner in the same situation. Litigants low on the social and economic ladder had proportionally more at stake, prompting them to sacrifice the family savings to engage a lawyer.

This was what Jerónimo Delgado, Arturo Dable, and Otto Sponholz understood. They were monthly workers in the employ of farmer Antonio Sabatini, who had failed to pay their salaries. The workers decided to go to town and file a claim. Lacking the money for transportation, they covered "the distance between the defendant's farm and town on foot, arriving completely exhausted."[39] Once there, the workers confided their problem to the owner of the Hotel El Plata. Not only did the hotel owner lodge them for free, he advised them to seek counsel from "somebody skillful" and, since they knew nobody, recommended "the university *procurador* Primo Storti." Then, "the same hotel owner led us to the house of Mr. Storti who, once he heard all about us, offered to file claim on our behalf with the data we had given him."[40]

Hiring these lawyers was sometimes decisive for the protagonists of the law suits. The local experts knew the loopholes in the law, were skilled in argumentation and discursive tactics, as well as in procedure. They could twist the course of a case and define its outcome through the use of opportune measures, delay strategies and psychological manipulation. For instance, for a creditor, it was fundamental to freeze the debtors' possessions in time if he wanted to get the money before it was distributed to others. If the creditor had a promissory note or any other obligation signed by the debtor, he needed only two witnesses to verify the signature on the document. For this purpose, lawyers always had two people "who worked as witnesses" and, with their dubious testimony, facilitated a speedy procedure.[41] Being first in line for payment was not the only consideration. Freezing assets before or immediately after the harvest secured the notes with the farmers' most valuable possession: the crop, whether in the field or in sacks. For those who wanted to avoid all judicial procedure, they could opt to transfer the obligation — the promissory note and even the cuentas — through an endorsement and at a lesser price to local moneylenders or to the lawyers. After all, it was also likely that a claim would end in a settlement, which often meant that creditors received less than the full amount owed.

Speed and efficiency in these measures were aimed at counteracting the debtors' tactics, which were also orchestrated by lawyers. The most common debtor's strategy was not to recognize the whole debt, or to question the way in which some of the items had been calculated. Customer accounts were ideal for this strategy, because of the diverse categories of the debts contracted throughout a year: cash advances, payments to workers, or to insurance companies, rent, seeds, food, and so on. The variety of debts incurred made it possible to object to more than one item. This kind of objection usually led to the summoning of witnesses, which had the virtue of complicating the trial procedurally and, therefore, delaying it, playing on the impatience of the creditor to reach a favorable agreement — a reduction of the amount of the debt, an extension of the obligation, or a payment plan.

For the debtors who had signed documents, the options were more limited. In this case, it was possible to avoid an inevitable seizure by hiding possessions on neighbors' farms or by denying ownership. Both were short-term tactics. As a last resort, a plaintiff who did not find goods to seize could ask for an *inhibición,* a measure implying that, for a determined period of time, the debtor would violate the law if he disposed of the goods he owned or acquired in the future, without the authorization of the law.[42] Finally, the most audacious debtors could deny the authenticity of the document, the signature or the date. This strategy provoked the naming of experts and a substantial delay in the proceedings, but it also incurred the risk of having to face more expensive judicial costs if the stratagem failed.

In the whole period, a few cases, all involving the advice of a lawyer, used this strategy. In 1939, the farmer Donato Yezzi, represented by Primo Storti, declared that the date of the promissory note he allegedly had to pay had been "evidently falsified." Yezzi asserted that the date was in fact 1931 and not 1939; therefore the debt had expired. In one sense, the strategy failed. Yezzi was forced to pay the debt and the judicial costs on February 3, 1942. In another sense, the tactic was successful: the trial had started in December 1939, and Yezzi was able to delay the proceedings for more than two years.[43] In another case, also from 1939, all of the tenants of the Chapar family estate had been summoned to recognize signatures on a document they had signed years before, in which they agreed to leave the land on February 28, 1939. Duly advised, these farmers went to court and declared that the signatures were just a "coarse imitation," which left the landlords with two options: negotiation or an endless trial. The tenants reached a one-year extension of their contracts to February 28, 1940.[44]

For eviction trials, the strategies were similar. Before the passing of the tenancy laws, landowners who wanted to evict tenants had to notify them within the period stipulated by the civil code. If they had not taken this precaution and still wanted the eviction, however, landlords had other re-sources. They could refuse to receive rent payment. Because the code con-sidered lack of payment a cause of eviction, the lessor could then sue, alleging breach of contract on the part of the tenant. Another tactic was simply to falsify the terms of a verbal contract. The landowner declared that the contract was "without term," which meant, according to the civil code, for one year.

Tenancy laws generated similar strategies. Even though these laws estab-lished minimum leasing terms, they did not actually make them mandatory, but only gave tenants the right to opt for them. For the contract to be effective for those minimum terms, the tenant had to communicate the option to the landowner, in writing, six months prior to the termination of the contract. Landowners could pretend they had not received the notification on time, and then allege that the tenant had not made use of that option.

Against these procedures, tenants acquired the necessary antidotes through time, working hand in hand with lawyers. In the event that the landowner refused to receive payment, the tenant could make a *consignación* (judicial deposit) of the rent, and if he was attentive to the dates, he could efficiently counteract the tactic. He could do the same thing to exercise his option on the minimum term established by the rental laws. In cases where the conditions of verbal contracts were under dispute, tenants had fewer weapons; in the absence of written documents, the argument became somewhat theoretical. If the landowner had declared that the contract was "without term," it was the tenant's responsibility to prove conclusively the falsehood of the allegation by proving the existence of a contract for a determined number of years — no easy task.

Finally, for tenants facing an inevitable eviction, delay was the best strategy. Delaying the trial, if possible, until the next agricultural cycle, brought the tenant under the protections of the civil code for those who had their land tilled, and thereby won one more year. This was the strategy of farmer Bardi, cited earlier. His allegation that his land had already been plowed convinced the justice of the peace, who ruled in favor of Bardi in order to avoid "the ruin of an honest farmer." To delay eviction trials, tenants also disputed the conditions of verbal contracts, which provoked the summons of witnesses.

Primo Storti complained about such tactics when he represented landowner Pedro González in an eviction trial against tenant Juan José Lopetegui. Lopetegui's lawyer had not recognized the contract, alleging that his client was González's partner and not his tenant. As proof, the lawyer offered the testimony of three witnesses. One of them lived in a neighboring county and another in the city of Buenos Aires, which meant that the judge had to grant an extraordinary term to summon people who lived so far away. This move provoked Storti, well versed in the motives behind such tactics, to remind the Judge that "the posing of inappropriate questions in eviction trials, the demand of extraordinary terms to produce evidence that is almost 'abroad' and other trifles like these, are, in general, measures employed to delay the proceedings of the trial, which the Judge should keep in mind when he decides on such groundless demands."[45]

These tricks of the trade earned a reprieve for some but brought ruin on others. With a reputation for opportunism and "evil means," lawyers gained notoriety in the countryside. The village people, among them victims of the toolkit of legal manipulations, called the lawyers *aves negras,* black birds, comparing them to crows, and alluding to their predatory tactics and skill in retaining large amounts of the litigants' money.

Along with their practices and, more generally, their legal advice, the most important role rural lawyers played in the region was to inform, spread, and circulate the law, especially among the illiterate,[46] and others with scant cultural and economic resources. Without lawyers, these sectors would have had little access to legal information. Workers and farmers lived isolated lives. To go to the town of Coronel Dorrego, fifty miles from the farthest points of the county, was a great event and people made the trip rarely, for a civic or religious holiday, the carnival, or a burial. Most people never set foot in Bahía Blanca, and the vast majority died without seeing Buenos Aires, the capital of the country, located 380 miles away from Coronel Dorrego. In that sense, Storti was not exaggerating by much when he described the witness who lived in Buenos Aires as "from abroad." The landscape of social relations of a typical chacarero from Dorrego in those years consisted of the neighboring farms and the weekly trip to the country store in the closest village. The country store not only sold food and clothing supplies, but also provided a place to chat with other locals about the state of the crops, the wheat market, or the latest news that reached them via the country merchants or from some local newspaper, if they knew how to read.[47] Except for these scarce meetings, rural residents had few sources of information.

Through their interaction with the lawyers, simple laborers and poor immigrant producers, many of them illiterate or non-Spanish-speaking, were well informed. They invoked the protection of specific articles of the civil code or, as in the case of the tenant Bardi, of a law that had been enacted only a few months earlier by the National Congress. Their legal sophistication, knowledge of their rights, and of the scope of the law would be inexplicable, without the influence of the lawyers. If the people of Coronel Dorrego during the first half of this century knew the legal framework, used it in court, and pushed it to the limit to obtain a favorable outcome, it was owing to the action of the rural lawyers who, probably unwittingly, had spread legal knowledge.[48] Moreover, for the people of scant means, who — using Black's image — also had "less law," the "black birds" of the Pampas helped to increase their clients' "amount of law," and the lawyers' knowledge was vital to the aspirations of those who confronted more powerful rivals in court.

Besides knowing and spreading the law, rural lawyers also helped with their tactics to define its scope. Once the law was written, the judges were the key characters who interpreted, updated, and rewrote its spirit with their own writing—jurisprudence—in interaction with the environment they observed and in which they were immersed. This quality made judges men of flesh and blood, "real and conscious judges." Therefore, although the letter of the law was written in the National Congress, its spirit was negotiated in the everyday dialectic of the local courts of the countryside by the parties engaged in litigation, and, especially, by the action of rural lawyers. In the process, these lawyers contributed decisively to the consolidation of an established judicial culture in the Pampean region, pushing the judges, plaintiffs, and defendants in the ongoing task of updating and improving their knowledge of the law and its uses.

Conclusion

Toward 1940, a few farmers of Dorrego had become prosperous agricultural entrepreneurs, who combined their productive activity with real estate business or commerce. Some of them had become owners of the land they had begun by working. They were the ones who memorialized their success in the volume celebrating the county's fiftieth anniversary. The majority, however, in 1940 as in 1900, still confronted the uncertain conditions of wheat production in the Pampean region, with varied luck. The increasing technical demands of production, combined with a structurally precarious and unstable relationship to the land, and with the incipient development of credit, condemned chacareros to perverse local market conditions that systematically devalued their crop.

The institutional apparatus that developed and consolidated during those years did not necessarily change this state of things. The few laws enacted in this period did not eradicate the verbal contracts of work and tenancy, or the accounts with the local merchants. Rural society continued to run on verbal agreements and precarious documents such as vouchers and promissory notes that circulated from hand to hand. The justice of the peace, as "administrator" of the existing legal apparatus, was part of the system and helped to maintain the status quo. Nevertheless, the figure of the judge was crucial for this society to develop in that labyrinth of unwritten rules.

In the first place, the justice of the peace acted as guarantor of the rules of the game, somehow compensating for the deficiencies of the system. Disputed promissory notes and the merchants' accounts, workers' vouchers, verbal tenancy contracts, and even words of honor were validated before him, according to the law. The justice of the peace insured that all those precarious arrangements worked out efficiently. Secondly, it was before him that the rural society of Dorrego deployed the strategies to exploit to the utmost the benefits that might be extracted from the letter of the few laws regulating agrarian life.

Most importantly, the judge guaranteed, if not the resolution, at least the adequate institutional, systematic, and peaceful attention to the mundane conflicts generated by productive activity. If we consider that these disputes are the most common manifestation of social conflict,[49] we can perceive the key role played by the justice of the peace in preserving social harmony in the countryside of Buenos Aires. The court provided an escape valve for those little disputes and prevented larger ones from developing.

The court's ability to diffuse conflict rested on the reputation the judges enjoyed in society. Their reputation was nurtured by the respect local society had for the legal and "professional" knowledge of these officers; for their experience accumulated in a judicial career that had developed before everybody's eyes; for the efficiency shown in critical moments; and, above all, for the acknowledgment of the judge as a neighbor, who shared the everyday problems and needs of the inhabitants of the county. In this sense, these judges were crucial in generating and sustaining what I have called here the "Peace of Wheat" that ruled agrarian life at the local level throughout the Pampean countryside during these years.

In the process, the action of the rural lawyers was also decisive. Products of the system, they found their place amid an increasing demand of justice and a scarce "supply" of law, and from these conditions they made their profit. In the bargain, they inadvertently played a decisive role in the spreading of legal, mainly juridical and procedural, information throughout the countryside of Buenos Aires, helping to create, over time, a strong juridical culture that reached to the lower echelons of society.

The spread of legal knowledge and its uses proved decisive in times to come. In the 1940s, the arrival of Peronism brought an end to the "Peace of

Wheat." Although the state had already begun to regulate the everyday life of Pampean farmers in the preceding decade, the 1940s were marked by an increased state intervention that not only touched all social actors but also changed the nature of social negotiation. The creation of mandatory registers of producers; the obligatory freezing of rents and the indefinite extension of contracts; the compulsory suspension of eviction lawsuits for more than a decade; the annual fixing of product prices; the strict and meticulous regulation of rural work; and the creation of a huge bureaucracy to deal with these new regulations — the position of Secretary of Labor; tenancy boards composed of lessors, tenants, and the state; labor courts; and so on — radically changed the rules of the game of agriculture and rural life. The national state, which until then had been a theoretical entity for the inhabitants of Dorrego, arrived suddenly and brutally, bringing discord with it. The local became increasingly national; the private turned public. For the large landowners and successful merchants of Dorrego, the state's invasion of matters they had always considered strictly private was an offense that could not be repaired until Perón's overthrow in 1955. The hand of the state, moreover, had not only reached into the pockets of the landowning class, a recurrent theme in the literature, but had also tampered with the tacit rules of social and economic coexistence that had been established over so many years.

In the period of Peronist discord that followed the "Peace of Wheat," farmers openly confronted landowners, and workers confronted farmers — all fed by a basic mistrust generated by their growing identity as classes that related to and negotiated with the state. During this period, the legal and judicial knowledge of statute laws and rights, and their use in institutional realms which the society of Dorrego had acquired during the previous decades, proved decisive. In particular, familiarity with the law allowed farmers and workers to profit from the new laws, decrees, regulations, and the new bureaucracy created by the Peronist state, in a struggle for stakes that were higher than ever and that took place more than ever in a legal and judicial arena.

Notes

I am grateful to all the participants in the Yale conference on law, justice, and repression in Latin American History, in particular to Gilbert Joseph, for their helpful comments on an earlier version of this essay. Equally useful were comments by

Hilda Sabato, Ricardo Salvatore, Tulio Halperín Donghi, Sergio Serulnikov, María Bjerg, Gerardo Serrano, and all my colleagues at Instituto Ravignani-PEHESA in Buenos Aires. Special thanks to the staff at the Departamento Histórico Judicial, Suprema Corte de Justicia de la Provincia de Buenos Aires, who gave me access to, and guided me through the sources in which this work is based.

1 *Cincuentenario de Coronel Dorrego, 1887, 29 de diciembre,* 1937, p. 39.

2 Raúl Sáenz López, editor and director of the publication, filed a claim to payment against Graciano Duronto, landowner of the county. *Departamento Histórico Judicial, Suprema Corte de Justicia de la Provincia de Buenos Aires, Juzgado de Paz de Coronel Dorrego,* Fuero civil, File #8370, 9/14/40. (Henceforth, JPCD-C, #8370, 9/14/40).

3 Tulio Halperín Donghi, "Canción de otoño en primavera: previsiones sobre la crisis en la agricultura cerealera argentina (1894–1930)," *Desarrollo Económico* 95 (1984): 367–386.

4 This image was originally grounded in economic and sociological macroanalyses, almost exclusively based on quantitative data. See John Fogarty, Ezequiel Gallo, and Héctor Diéguez, *Argentina y Australia* (Buenos Aires: Instituto Di Tella, 1974); Tim Duncan and John Fogarty, *Australia and Argentina: On Parallel Paths* (Melbourne: Melbourne University Press, 1984); and D. C. M. Platt and Guido Di Tella, eds., *Argentina, Australia, and Canada: Studies in Comparative Development, 1870–1965* (New York: St. Martin's Press, 1985). For some good historical approaches in this comparative line see Carl E. Solberg, *The Prairies and the Pampas: Agrarian Policy in Canada and Argentina, 1880–1930* (Stanford: Stanford University Press, 1987); and Jeremy Adelman, *Frontier Development: Land, Labor and Capital on the Wheatlands of Argentina and Canada, 1890–1914* (Oxford: Clarendon Press, 1994). In Argentina, the valuable works by sociologist Jorge Federico Sábato helped to reinforce this optimistic image of Pampean farmers (see especially *La clase dominante en la Argentina moderna* [Buenos Aires: CISEA, 1980]). His work heavily influenced a new generation of rural historians who are recreating this view on new grounds, through local and private sources. For a critical revision of this perspective see Juan Manuel R. Palacio, "Jorge Sábato y la historiografía rural pampeana. El problema del otro," *Entrepasados* 10 (1996): 46–66. Yet, Pampean historiography is still in a desperate need for more seminal works, with only a few case studies available for the modern period.

5 Argentina. Ministerio de Agricultura, *Censo Nacional Agropecuario: Año 1937* (Buenos Aires: Guillermo Kraft Ltda., 1939–40), vol. 3.

6 According to the National Census of 1914, more than 80 percent of the agricultural exploitation of Coronel Dorrego was in the hands of tenants who had less than five hundred hectares, and the agrarian machinery of the county tripled proportionally the value of that of the province. Argentina, *Tercer Censo Nacional: año 1914* (Buenos Aires: Rosso y Cía., 1916), vol. 5.

7 Félix Weinberg (dir.), *Historia del sudoeste bonaerense* (Buenos Aires: Plus Ultra,

1988); Carlos Funes Derieul, *Historia del partido y localidad de Coronel Dorrego en el siglo XIX (1830–1900)* (Bahía Blanca: Talleres Gráficos Panzini Hnos., 1973).

8 It is important to explain the meaning of "small" in a land-extensive agriculture like the Pampean. Many studies by rural sociologists tried to classify the Pampean farmers in intelligible categories. Without further detail, there is an agreement among them to consider small producers those who rented less than 300 hectares or owned less than 150. See Alfredo Pucciarelli, *El capitalismo agrario pampeano, 1880–1930* (Buenos Aires: Hyspamérica, 1986); Javier Balsa, "La conformación de la burguesía rural local en el sur de la pampa argentina, desde finales del siglo XIX hasta la década del treinta: El partido de Tres Arroyos," in Marta Bonaudo and Alfredo R. Pucciarelli, eds., *La problemática agraria: nuevas aproximaciones* (Buenos Aires: CEAL, 1993) vol. 2, pp. 103–31; see also the papers compiled in Osvaldo Barsky, ed., *El desarrollo agropecuario pampeano* (Buenos Aires: Grupo Editor Latinoamericano, 1991).

9 This is patent in the very life stories contained in the book of the fiftieth anniversary. Most biographies refer to inhabitants who arrived to the county between 1895 and 1915; among those who could buy lands, the majority did so before 1920. For the possibility of access to the land in neighboring counties during the same period, see Blanca L. Zeberio, "El estigma de la preservación: familia y reproducción del patrimonio entre los agricultores del sur de Buenos Aires, 1880–1930," in María Mónica Bjerg and Andrea Reguera, eds., *Problemas de la historia agraria: nuevos debates y perspectivas de investigación* (Tandil: IEHS, 1995), pp. 155–181, and by the same author, "La utopía de la tierra en el Nuevo Sud: explotaciones agrícolas, trayectorias y estrategias productivas de los agricultores (1900–1930)," *Anuario IEHS* (Tandil) 6, 1991, pp. 81–112.

10 Joseph S. Tulchin, "El crédito agrario en la Argentina, 1910–1926," *Desarrollo Económico* 71 (1978): 381–409, Jeremy Adelman, "Agricultural Credit in the Province of Buenos Aires, Argentina, 1890–1914," *Journal of Latin American Studies* 22/1 (1990): 69–87.

11 In the few bills that are available because they have been included in judicial files, the price of wheat perceived by the farmers was, on average, 20 to 25 percent less than the price paid on the market of Buenos Aires.

12 Both the local representatives of machinery importers and the banks (especially the Banco de la Nación Argentina and Banco de la Provincia de Buenos Aires) entered the local loan circuit with the Agricultural Surety Law, in 1914 (Ley 9,644, de Prenda Agraria, 11/20/14, *Anales de Legislación Argentina* [henceforth *ALA*], 1889–1919, pp. 920–922). This law, instead of changing the state of things, consolidated this informal loan circuit, with the possibility of securing loans with movable property (machines, tools, barns, and houses), livestock, and crop mortgages. But farmers, especially the smallest ones, refused this kind of loan, which jeopardized their patrimony directly. They preferred the more informal—and a little more expensive—modality, because it seemed less risky than signed documents.

13 Coronel Dorrego, Provincia de Buenos Aires, *Primer censo municipal levantado el 30 de julio de 1922.*

14 Ley 11,170, de Arrendamientos Rurales, 12/26/21, *ALA,* 1920–1940: 80–81.

15 See Catherine Legrand, *Colonización y protesta campesina en Colombia (1850–1950)* (Bogotá: Universidad Nacional de Colombia, 1988), pp. 132–141; for the diagnosis of Chilean leaders during the 1920s, see George Mc Bride, *Chile: Land and Society* (New York: American Geographical Society, 1936); for Peru, see Colin Harding, "Land Reform and Social Conflict in Peru," in Abraham Lowenthal, ed., *The Peruvian Experiment: Continuity and Change under Military Rule* (Princeton, N.J.: Princeton University Press, 1976), pp. 226–227. For Mexico during the Callista reforms of the 1920s, see Nora Hamilton, *México: los límites de la autonomía de estado* (México: ERA, 1983), pp. 72–103; for Costa Rica and the agrarian projects of the Reformist Party in the 1920s, see Lowell Gudmunson, *Costa Rica antes del café: sociedad y economía en vísperas del boom exportador* (San José: Editorial Costa Rica, 1990), pp. 13–42.

16 The law was much more important and efficacious in acknowledging other rights of the tenants. Article 6 recognized the right to compensation, at the end of the contract, for improvements on the farm (house, trees, water supplies), and even more importantly, article 10 established a list of the estate that could not be subject to seizure, such as personal or movable property, clothes, and essential work instruments (machines, tools, and livestock).

17 Ley 11,627, de Arrendamientos Rurales, 10/18/32, *ALA,* 1920–1940: 261–63.

18 *JPCD*-Contratos de arrendamiento, 1933–1970.

19 Benito Díaz, *Juzgados de Paz de Campaña de la Provincia de Buenos Aires (1821–1854)* (La Plata: Universidad Nacional de La Plata, 1959), pp. 7–26.

20 Ley de Procedimientos para la Justicia de Paz, Buenos Aires, 2 de junio de 1887, in *Colección de leyes usuales de la provincia de Buenos Aires* (Buenos Aires: Librería Nacional, 1907), pp. 99–117.

21 The first manual appeared in 1825. *Manual para los Jueces de Paz de Campaña* (Buenos Aires: Imprenta Independencia, 1825). See also Díaz, *Juzgados de Paz,* pp. 12–14.

22 Ley de Procedimientos. Emphasis added.

23 Not all the lawsuits were settled in court. Many times extrajudicial arrangements that were not registered were reached, so files remained incomplete. Considering that the percentage of incomplete files was close to 50 percent of the total, it is likely that the proportion of settlements was even larger.

24 *JPCD*-C, #5393, 4/21/32.

25 Ibid.

26 For the concept of "quantity of law," see Donald Black, *The Behavior of Law* (New York: Academic Press, 1976), and also *Sociological Justice* (Oxford: Oxford University Press, 1989).

27 There were not many large estancias in Coronel Dorrego, however. This county — and, to a large extent, the whole wheat belt of southern Buenos Aires — was mainly made up of small and medium-size, family-run farms. Although these farms may have been rented plots in larger holdings, this did not mean that they belonged to a system of "estancia," in which a mayordomo regulated the whole economic — and even social — life within the estate, as was very often the case in the large cattle estates of the breeding and feeding belts of the Pampean region. See Juan Manuel R. Palacio, "Arrendatarios agrícolas en una estancia ganadera: el caso de 'Cruz de Guerra,' 1927–1938," *Desarrollo Económico* 127 (1992): 381–409.

28 The creation of the National Department of Labor in 1907, and the law of Job Related Accidents in 1915 (Ley 9,688, de Accidentes de Trabajo, 10/21/15, *ALA, 1889–1919*: 949–1020), even though they had a limited effect in rural areas, were important steps to create a social consciousness regarding the rights of workers. For an analysis of these changes in the context of the "liberal reformism" of the beginning of the century in Argentina, see Eduardo A. Zimmermann, *Los liberales reformistas. La cuestión social en la Argentina, 1890–1916* (Buenos Aires: Sudamericana, 1995), especially chaps. 8 and 9. Later on, in the 1930s, some decrees fixing monthly salaries and harvest daily wages appeared (see Departamento del Trabajo de la Provincia de Buenos Aires, *Legislación del Trabajo de la Provincia de Buenos Aires,* La Plata, 1937). Nevertheless, the defenselessness rural workers suffered during the whole period was not solved until the sanction of the "Estatuto del Peón," a decree of the revolutionary government of 1943 that constituted the first legal instrument for rural workers (Decree #28169, 10/17/44, *ALA,* 1944, IV: 574–592).

29 *JPCD-C,* #6897, 3/4/37.

30 *JPCD-C,* #7902, 12/16/39.

31 *JPCD-C,* #4593, 3/21/22.

32 Ibid.

33 Ibid. Emphasis added.

34 Ibid. Emphasis added.

35 It is important to note that this was not apparently the case with judges of the peace in earlier times. Studies of the nineteenth century show that the repression of banditry and crime, and the recruiting of "vagrants" for the army, were the most visible faces of these judges at that time. This made sense in a less settled, more mobile frontier society such as that of early nineteenth century Buenos Aires province, in which judges — in line with the provincial state's need to control effectively a vast countryside — were especially concerned with keeping social order and protecting private property. Thus, it is no surprise that these judges were then more clearly viewed as representatives and executors of the provincial state's centralized policies, than as impartial administrators of justice, especially concerned with local matters. See Ricardo Salvatore, "Reclutamiento militar, disciplinamiento y pro-

letarización en la era de Rosas," *Boletín del Instituto de Historia Argentina Dr. Emilio Ravignani* 5 (1992): 25–47, and also "'El imperio de la ley': delito, estado y sociedad en la era rosista," *Delito y Sociedad* 4–5 (1993–94): 93–118.

36 Between 1900 and 1915, these lawyers were Baldomero Barreiro, who also had the power of attorney for the provincial Revenue Bureau, and Guillermo Douglas, attorney of the Municipality of Coronel Dorrego, who had been the secretary of the court in 1903 and 1904. In the 1920s, they were Douglas, Vicente Barrios, and José Liberatore, the last the attorney of the Agrarian Cooperative of Coronel Dorrego. The 1930s were dominated by Primo Storti, who had also been the secretary of the court in 1931 and 1932.

37 Interviews with lawyer Nírido Santagada; Héctor Soldini, Dorrego's lawyer who was Primo Storti's right hand for thirty years; and Lindolfo Rubén Barrios, secretary of the court between 1948 and 1993. December 1996.

38 That was the case of Primo Storti, provincial senator in 1973 and of Nírido Santaguada, president of the Municipal Legislative Body in 1948, Major in 1956 and National Representative in 1958.

39 JPCD-C, #6240, 7/15/35.

40 Ibid.

41 Quoted interviews with Héctor Soldini and Lindolfo Barrios.

42 In practice, there were always unscrupulous merchants who were ready to acquire those goods at a conveniently low price.

43 JPCD-C, #7900, 12/12/39.

44 JPCD-C, #7742, 7743, 7744, 7745, and 7746, 4/27/39.

45 JPCD-C, #7752, 12/20/37.

46 According to the 1922 local census, the illiteracy rate reached 20 percent of the population of the county in that year. This figure doubled in the case of day laborers, according to the profile of the parties in the criminal cases carried out in the court of the county (JPCD-Fuero Correccional, 1900–1940).

47 Interviews with farmers Nicolás Stanscia, Alfredo Rasmussen, Nicolás Berenger, Vicente Rostoll, and Jaime Ripoll, April 1996.

48 Catherine LeGrand defines this role well for the case of Colombian tinterillos in the 1920s: "Familiar characters in the countryside, the rural lawyers, called 'tinterillos', had the reputation of provoking the law suits which they lived off. . . . Spurred by personal interest, those individuals, however, played an important role when they spread knowledge of the land legislation in the frontier regions" (LeGrand, *Colonización,* p. 100).

49 For a development of this perspective, see James C. Scott, *Weapons of the Weak: Everyday Forms of Peasant Resistance* (New Haven: Yale University Press, 1985).

Work, Property, and the Negotiation of Rights in the Brazilian Cane Fields: Campos, Rio de Janeiro, 1930–1950

LUIS A. GONZÁLEZ

U nderstanding how nonelite agrarian classes have historically engaged the existing political order requires that one look beyond the loud, dramatic, headline-grabbing moments of collective violence and rebellion that routinely preoccupy scholarly research. A welcome corrective has come from moral economists who have persuasively argued that agrarian struggles often unfold through quotidian strategies rather than in open conflict.[1] If this approach has expanded the arena of contention and conflict to include day-to-day, routine actions, it nonetheless leaves out of its purview those frequent instances in which agrarian classes have followed markedly different strategies such as seeking redress against the dominant social and political forces through the state. In this alternative scenario, the mobilized do not resort to subterfuge. Rather, they publicly invoke the law or call for state intervention to redress grievances, challenge certain policies, seek reforms, and ultimately effect societal change.

The mobilization of Campos sugarcane workers and growers under the Getúlio Vargas regime (1930–1945) best fits the latter scenario. In 1930 Getúlio Vargas rose to power as the civilian head of a political movement that toppled the First Republic, founded in 1889. As provisional president, Vargas ruled by decree through 1934, when he was elected by the constitutional assembly to preside over a newly adopted constitution. This brief constitutionalist interlude was interrupted in November 1937 when, on dissolving congress and banning other political institutions, Vargas proclaimed the Estado Novo dictatorship, which prevailed until 1945.

With mobilization and political action through conventional means (political parties, elections, the congress, harvest boycotts, and strikes) no longer feasible under the Estado Novo, both cane growers and rural workers resorted to petitioning and legal action as the leading strategies to demand and shape reforms in the sugar industry. Cane growers and workers from Campos did not eschew state intervention, but actually turned to the state as a powerful mediator in their disputes with sugar mill owners and landlords. Litigation specifically gained widespread acceptance, not just due to political constraints on independent mobilization or because it was sanctioned by the state, but because the new sugar legislation enacted by the Vargas regime spoke to issues related to work and property that mattered deeply to the tillers of the land. Identifying ways the new rights granted to cane growers and workers by the new legislation affected Campistas and ways the Campistas engaged the legislation and the political establishment behind it is the aim of this essay.[2]

Campos dos Goitacases in northern Rio de Janeiro state is the geographical focus of study. Since the late eighteenth century, when sugarcane growing supplanted cattle-raising as the main economic activity there, Campos has been a key player in Brazilian sugar economy. By the mid-1930s, Rio de Janeiro was the second largest sugar producer in the country, while Campos was the single most important sugar-producing county in all of Brazil, responsible for fourteen percent of the national sugar production (see Table 4).

Vargas's Sugar Policy

Throughout the 1930s and 1940s, the Brazilian state implemented measures that directly affected the agricultural sector. Using production controls to regulate supply in order to stabilize prices of agricultural staples during the depression of the 1930s was perhaps the most conspicuous example of state intervention under Vargas. Still, the sugar economy was the focus of wide-ranging, unprecedented policies that became landmarks in the field of Brazilian agrarian legislation.[3] These policies ranged from setting minimum prices to the regulation of contractual relations between the sugar mills (usinas) and the growers that supplied cane to the mills to process into sugar.[4]

TABLE 4 Main Sugar-Producing Counties, Brazil, 1929/30–1933/34
(in 60-kilogram bags)

County	State	Production	Percentage
Campos	Rio de Janeiro	6,590,627	14.3
Catende	Pernambuco	2,030,991	4.4
Escada	Pernambuco	2,008,410	4.4
Santo Amaro	Bahia	1,871,117	4.1
Santa Luzia do Norte	Alagoas	1,455,191	3.2
Cabo	Pernambuco	1,391,117	3.0
Piracicaba	São Paulo	1,301,426	2.8
São José Lage	Alagoas	1,167,699	2.5
São Lourenço	Pernambuco	1,139,188	2.5
Ataláia	Alagoas	1,068,098	2.3
PARTIAL TOTAL		20,023,864	43.5
Other States		25,988,640	56.5
TOTAL		46,012,504	100

Source: IAA, Anuário Açucareiro para 1935, p. 18.

A sui generis division of labor evolved in the modern sugar industry that separated the agricultural (cane growing and harvesting) from the industrial functions of sugar manufacturing. Because of sugarcane's volatility (it is a highly perishable crop that cannot be stored once it is harvested), the sugar mill generally has monopsonistic control over the independent growers, who are unable to withhold the crop to bargain for better prices. In a context marked by the millers' ability to set prices locally and control crop financing, transportation, and land, the sugar mill exerted unbalanced influence over the regional sugar market, placing constraints on the growers of cane. The latter occupy an intermediate social level between field laborers and the sugar mill owners. In the period under study in Campos, the growers remained internally stratified with respect to ownership. The propertied and the non-propertied both were represented within the ranks of the cane growers in the region. The overwhelming majority, though, were small- to medium-scale producers who earned the equivalent of a factory minimum wage for the season, and many did not have title to land. The household provided most of the farm labor, with additional labor recruited as needed for the harvest.

Conversely, large growers invariably relied on sharecroppers, tenants, and seasonal harvest labor to work the cane fields. The flagship of the reforms introduced by Vargas was the Instituto do Açúcar e do Alcool, created in 1933. Better known as the IAA, this was a semiautonomous federal body (*autarquia*) with powers to maintain stable prices and balance the national sugar market. The IAA regulated domestic sugar production by imposing production quotas by region and withdrawing stocks from the market. A portion of excess sugar was transformed into pure anhydrous alcohol, to be mixed with gasoline for fuel, and the remainder would be sold in the world market at bargain prices. The crops would be financed by taxing the production of the sugar mills and facilitating loans through the Bank of Brazil. The production quotas were to be adjusted periodically according to internal demand. These original tasks were broadened to include the authority to oversee the commercial relationships between the millers and the growers, mainly with respect to payment methods, the allocation of cane supply quotas to individual growers, and contracts for cane delivery and lease of land. Anyone who farmed sugarcane for three consecutive years and had contracted to deliver the crop to a particular mill for the same length of time was entitled to a cane supply quota and other benefits granted by law. The IAA dubbed such a producer a *fornecedor*, derived from the Portuguese verb *fornecer*, to supply. A sugar mill was not compelled by law to accept the crop of any grower who did not meet these criteria. These provisions and the powers granted to the IAA are spelled out in two fundamental decrees: Law 178 of 9 January 1936 and Decree-Law N. 3.855 of 21 November 1941, known as the *Estatuto da Lavoura Canavieira* (the Sugarcane Growing Statute). Decree-Law 6.969 of 19 October 1944 supplemented the Estatuto by according protection to tenant growers, known as *colonos*.[5]

The Estatuto established formal grievance procedures. It created a corporatist court system tailored to the needs of the sugarcane industry. Composed of representatives from millers, growers, and the IAA, the tripartite courts were separate from the ordinary judicial system, so that the litigant parties could seek remedy in the civil courts only when the mechanisms anticipated in the law were exhausted. The documentary basis of my research consists largely of the previously untapped claims (*processos*) filed by growers, agricultural workers, and mill owners with the IAA courts.

The Estatuto effected a deep transformation in the prevailing concept of property as absolute individual dominion. This law reinstated into the national juridical and legal framework a long-standing notion that direct tillage of the land secures rights to the cane grower in spite of the rights accruing to the legitimate property owner.[6] This principle found concrete expression in the security of tenure granted to farm tenants in the Estatuto. Tenants were entitled to renew the lease of the plot of land they had been working. The landlord could deny the renewal, but had to pay a compensation. This was an innovation in modern Brazilian civil law.

The reformers who came to power in the aftermath of the 1930 Revolution had the tools that gave juridical validity to their policies. The 1934 constitution, for example, invested property rights with a "social or collective interest" (article 113) that placed limits on the owner's real right of enjoyment. The Estado Novo charter introduced the corporative theory of the state that established government control over the economy (article 135). Both charters empowered policymakers to intervene in private business relations.[7] These constitutional principles were partly informed by international events — the church social doctrine, Germany's Weimar constitution of 1919, the New Deal in the United States, and Portuguese and Italian corporatism.

It is worth noting, however, that Brazilian reformers also tapped into a rich historical tradition dating back to Brazil's colonial past that placed constraints on property rights, ruled as they were by Roman civil law. State regulation of the sugarcane industry had colonial precedents in the principle of *cana obrigada,* by which sugar mills were obliged to process the cane from neighboring planters. Social, economic, and political considerations also prompted policies that banned the attachment of indebted mills.[8] But a conspicuous feature in Brazilian law is the premium it has historically placed on the productive use of the land. One can secure title to a piece of land — whether public or privately owned — through continued occupancy and beneficial use. This notion checks property rights and the use and enjoyment of landed property. Originally present in the law of royal land grants *(sesmarias),* further reaffirmed in the Land Law of 1850, this deep-seated practice has become a key fixture in Brazilian constitutional law since 1934.[9] The sugar legislation promulgated by Vargas encoded into law and enforced similar precepts.[10]

Social Responses to Legal Changes

Because these reforms touched a nerve in Brazilian society — a society juridically and politically organized on the precepts of private property and the freedom of contract — it is worth examining the differing responses that this legislation elicited among cane growers and rural workers.[11] The fact that the social function of property became the leading discourse that informed the struggles staged by cane growers and rural workers warrants further consideration. Whether a sharecropper, a tenant, or a propertied cane supplier fighting a sugar mill, all involved in sugar production viewed the Estatuto da Lavoura Canavieira as the embodiment of their long-standing aspirations. The 1941 law transformed those aspirations into rights that could be defended in court and enforced against transgressors.

Agricultural Workers and Colonos

After eleven years of arduous farming, Malvino Gomes Campista found himself deprived of land and crops. He was a semiliterate, married cultivator who between 1930 and 1941 worked as a colono on a farm belonging to Manoel Gomes de Araújo.[12] The landlord had a personal cane supply quota of eighty-two tons in addition to a joint quota of eighty-six tons with Malvino at Usina Mineiros, a sugar mill in the vicinity. The parties had a conventional sharecropping contract by which Malvino farmed the land, cut the cane, and loaded the carts, obtaining 50 percent of the returns. The landlord supplied the seeds, plowed the fields, and hauled the cane to the mill, and received the other half of the proceeds.

Colono and landlord were at odds over the payment of cane crop for 1941 and over Malvino's tenure on the farm. Malvino argued that in 1941 the landlord withheld part of the proceeds from the crop to which he was legally entitled as a quota holder. He also charged that when he temporarily moved out of the property because of a family emergency, Manoel Gomes de Araújo took hold of the cane fields. The landlord allegedly cut all the standing cane, set the field on fire, and drove the plow over the first-year ratoons, destroying them.[13] The landlord countered that the claimant breached the colonato arrangement by abandoning the farm unilaterally and that his quota was liable to cancellation because of this action, as set down in the Estatuto (article 69). Manoel also disputed Malvino's status as a fornecedor, arguing that the labor input and risks of cultivation were shared by the two of them. Calling the claimant "an opportunist backslider," who only wanted to take advantage of the guarantees granted by the Estatuto, Manoel hoped that the IAA would dismiss the claim "out of respect to the moral good, justice, and the preservation of individual property."[14]

Submitted on 12 January 1942 — less than two months after the Estatuto was enacted (21 November 1941) — this claim encapsulates the uneasy and intricate relationship between labor input and property rights that the sugar legislation sought to regulate. This case also foreshadows the likely responses the new legislation would stir among conflicting parties. The determined attitude with which each party defended its "rights" bespeaks a clash between competing legal concepts of property, between the existing one in retreat and a new one in ascent. As the product of a fledgling capitalist economy, the Brazilian Civil Code of 1916 enshrined private property as the absolute, unrestricted, and exclusive dominion of a person over a thing (article 524). In the 1930s and 1940s, however, as the liberal foundations of capitalism came under attack, an alternative concept of property rights emerged. Although Estado Novo ideologues believed in preserving the individual's right to use and dispose of things (as long as it was lawful), they tried to accommodate these prerogatives to the collective good. In speaking about the social function of property and public interest, jurists and reformers transformed the liberal notion of property as absolute right into the notion of property as both a right and an obligation. In doing so, reformers explicitly safeguarded the potential claims of a party on another's property, and, equally importantly, provided cane growers with new discursive tools to engage the social and economic system, rooted as it was in private property.

In the specific case discussed above, the colono, Malvino Gomes Campista, recognized the prerogatives of the landlord to share in the proceeds but was adamant in defending his own rights to the fruits of labor stemming from his position as the lead farmer. The labor input arises as the key variable here. For the colono, his labor secured tenure on the land. For the landlord, in contrast, the salary link was what mattered most. Malvino demanded back pay for the 1941 crop, a compensation for damages, and contract renewal as established in the 1941 sugar law. The landlord, however, saw his authority as a proprietor compromised by the new legislation, which interfered with his unrestricted and exclusive right to the land. At a crossroads between old legal traditions and new rules, Manoel Gomes de Araújo professed a deeply ingrained belief in his own absolute and sole dominion over the property in total exclusion of his colono's rights.

The investigations conducted by the IAA officials, however, corroborated Malvino's claim. Drawing on reports from the sugar mill, the IAA determined that the colono delivered cane to the mill in 1941, a fact that contra-dicted the landlord's allegation that Malvino had left the farm and abandoned the crop as well.[15] Eventually, the agency rendered a favorable ruling for the colono. The Estatuto did not allow the landlord to dispose of his colono as he would have wished — through eviction with no compensation.

Protest against personal subjugation and subservience to landlords often pervades claims by rural workers and colonos in Campos. In these cases, the underlying concern of plaintiffs is respect for their toil, too. Referring to an exploitative landowner who refused to increase wages and allow days off to his workforce, Antonio João de Faria, president of the Sindicato dos Trabalhadores Agrícolas e Pecuários de Campos (Agricultural Workers' Syndicate of Campos), likened the situation to the experience of bondsmen in slavery in the old days. Slave labor played a key role in Campos agriculture until abolition in 1888. Faria also thought that the arbitrary refusal to grant vacations constituted a blatant disregard for the government's labor policies.[16] Faria drew upon government discourse on labor to seek a legal remedy for agricultural workers, even though he was fully aware that the labor legislation enacted by Vargas was geared chiefly to urban workers.[17] He also knew that the 1943 bill that would have specifically regulated rural labor unraveled under the fierce opposition of the landed oligarchy.[18] Still, he felt reassured by the recent measures implemented by Vargas and the IAA protecting rural labor and colonos planting sugarcane. After promulgating the Estatuto, Vargas passed Decree-Law 6.969 on 19 October 1944, a supplementary law that broadened provisions on colonato on lands controlled by the sugar mills specifically. On May Day 1943 Vargas introduced a minimum wage for rural workers,[19] followed by two degrees touching rural organization issued in November 1944 and October 1945.[20] Whereas very few rural workers' associations ever got official recognition from the Labor Ministry, the organizations of middle- and large-sized landowners affiliated with the Brazilian Rural Confederation thrived throughout the 1940s and 1950s. In the 1950s, the government systematically thwarted the organization of rural workers. Labor Minister Fernando Nóbrega reportedly halted the recognition of forty class associations during his tenure. In response to this situation, the Communist Party launched a program of organizing rural workers. By 1959, only five rural workers' sindicatos had been officially recognized by the government: two in Bahia, one in Pernambuco, one in Santa Catarina, and another one in Rio de Janeiro. The latter organization, the Sindicato dos Empregados Rurais, based in Campos, replaced Faria's sindicato.[21] Moreover, the organization led by Antonio João de Faria became one of only two rural workers' class associations in the whole country officially recognized by the Ministry of Labor during the Estado Novo.[22]

The developments were promising, but agricultural workers were determined to test the true depth and breadth of the rule of law in the country. On 5 June 1944, their organization complained that Usina São José had unjustly fired José Nunes, an illiterate colono who had six small children. Protesting this arbitrary action, Antonio João de Faria contended that all involved parties, whether Brazilian or not, must observe existing rules protecting laborers.[23]

His explicit allusion to the foreign ownership of the mill was not incidental. Usina São José, the largest mill in Rio, the third largest in the country, and one of the most technically advanced mills in all of Brazil, was in fact owned by British capital. Founded in 1884 by local Campista entrepreneurs, the mill changed ownership various times but was always within Brazilian hands until 1938, when it was taken over by a British concern.[24] The introduction of foreign capital into the Campos sugar industry was rather limited and belated, especially since the early 1900s when the British and the French began to pour in investments more heavily.[25] Thus, for the most part, sugarcane growers had not been exposed to the same degree of nationalist antagonism that stormed other sugar regions in the Caribbean, Africa, and Asia. However belated, the foreign presence in Campos increased already existing tensions among the mills, cane growers, and the workforce.

That Antonio João de Faria borrowed this nationalist rhetoric from the government's discourse on Brazilian economic independence attests to his informed yet selective reading of national events. If the government sought to deliver its promises and ensure the welfare of the workers, he thought it must strive as well to tightly enforce its laws on both national and foreign businesses operating in Brazil. Both the Estado Novo Charter of 1937 and the Estatuto legitimized government regulation of private relations between labor and capital. In the specific case of José Nunes, Faria reasoned, his dual condition both as salaried day laborer (*diarista*) and colono made him eligible for protection under the sugar legislation. Faria expected the government to rule against the mill. The labor leader stated that article 7 of the Estatuto granted colonos working for the mills compensation in the event that they were fired without justification. His renewed hope in the rule of law was certainly a carefully pondered assessment of existing policies.

The mill tried to take advantage of José Nunes's dual position as diarista-colono to deny his rights as a fornecedor. But the Estatuto's provisions, especially article 7, recognized the need to compensate the labor input on the farm. The colono's labor in raising a crop increased the property's value. Through his labor, the colono improved the farm, endowing the property with an asset that it lacked originally. Thus, if the salary linkage was but an angle of José Nunes's relation to the mill, he was entitled to receive a rightful compensation as the law demanded. Failure to recognize the claimant's status as a colono constituted a flagrant abuse for, in Faria's view, the colono's labor added value to the property.

The struggles to assert the colonos' rights as fornecedores raised larger questions about political rights that extended far beyond the local social and economic relations that shaped the daily life of the people involved in cane cultivation. A broader political concern underwrote the struggles of grassroots leaders like Antonio João de Faria. Their goals amounted to nothing less than securing a dignified place for sugarcane colonos in the Brazilian polity. For them, social and political welfare went hand in hand. Accordingly, they used the IAA conciliation boards as a vehicle for political expression and openly airing their grievances.

As Brazilian politics became more open in the final days of the Estado Novo, former friends and foes of Vargas reinvented themselves as advocates of democracy. This seems to have been the case of Dr. Olimpio Saturnino da Silva Pinto, a Campista notable. A prominent lawyer and large propertied sugarcane planter, Dr. Pinto enjoyed an aura of respectability in the region. He was the grandson of Antonio Joaquim da Silva Pinto, the late Barão de São Fidélis. An uncle of his, Dr. Manoel Joaquim da Silva Pinto, himself a sugar mill owner, became a leading statesman in nineteenth-century Rio province.[26] In the late 1920s, Dr. Olimpio himself actively participated in the organization of a producers' cooperative, known as the Sociedade Co-operativa Açucareira Fluminense (1928), with powers to control production output in order to curb market speculation with the crop.[27]

Dr. Pinto must have been taken aback by the accusations filed against him by the rural workers' sindicato just four days before the overthrow of Vargas on 29 October 1945. The sindicato alleged Dr. Pinto neither granted vacations nor increased wages for his workforce and that he routinely harassed his employees at Fazenda Santa Maria in São João da Barra. The sindicato complained that he fired José Machado Henrique after the worker demanded a raise. Machado had worked on the farm for many years and partially lost his sight in a work-related accident on the farm. Now he faced the uncertainty of a layoff.

The buildup of tension in the region in that week must have been unprecedented. On the threshold of a new political era without Getúlio Vargas in command, the sindicato's president took this opportunity to publicly question Dr. Pinto's political convictions. Antonio João de Faria challenged the influential planter from Campos to stand up to his beliefs by vehemently charging: "For a long while [Dr. Pinto] has been talking about democracy . . . now I want to know whether he is *democrata* or not."[28]

A routine labor dispute soon acquired political overtones, probably because for rural workers democracy was not an abstraction but a concrete, tangible concept inextricably linked to their day-to-day existence. For agricultural workers and tenants, democracy comprised both political liberties and social welfare. The sindicato leader's statement conveys the notion that a worker who did not enjoy a fair existence could not be said to live in a democracy. Hence, those who championed the transition to a democratic polity had to reckon first and foremost with the defense of labor rights. Talking about political freedoms in the abstract did not suffice for grassroots leaders like Antonio João de Faria, himself a colono of humble origins, and the rural workers he represented. Linked to Usina Santo Antonio, Faria held a meager quota, amounting only to forty-six tons of cane.[29] For Faria, Dr. Pinto's neglect of the welfare of his workers simply did not match his talk about the virtues of democracy. Faria expected a more comprehensive commitment to a democratic society, one in which both the political and social demands of the people were fully met. In sum, democracy was to be practiced in everyday life through fair and dignified working conditions.[30]

As their mobilization took place in a fluid political world, one might expect that their language varied accordingly. Still, Antonio João de Faria's use of a democratic rhetoric was neither a transient aspect of the struggle nor an opportunistic tactic in a transitional period. On the contrary, the rural workers' leader continued to brandish aggressively the "democracy" argument in the post-Estado Novo period.

In April 1946, in a case involving an evicted colono, Faria chastised landlords and employers as reactionary capitalists that publicly portrayed themselves as "friends of the Fatherland" but privately looked out only for their own narrow individualistic interests. He did not spare strong words for the newly elected government of Commodore Eurico Gaspar Dutra either, as he demanded tighter enforcement of the sugar legislation to prevent cases like this one concerning Dr. Pinto's from happening again.[31]

Testing whether the Dutra democratic government would deliver on its promise of "defending the *povo* and the nation's sovereignty," Faria called on the state "to help out all democratic Brazilians that strive to lead Brazil into a democracy that respects the rights of workers." Failure to do so, he asserted, "would render us subject to utter penury and the reactionary forces." Arguing, as Faria did, that democracy was equivalent to the defense of workers' rights suggests that, for agricultural fieldhands and colonos like him, labor — and the fruits of labor — lay at the basis of society. Everything else was built upon this exploitative relation. Labor applied to the land generated wealth that was ostensibly appropriated by the landlords. Contrasting labor and capital, Faria eloquently declared: "workers and colonos are the true great patriots, because they contribute both to the greatness of the Fatherland and to the abundance *(fartura)* of the employers."[32] Fartura and *penúria* (poverty), then, constituted two faces of the same coin and defined each camp's social and political boundaries. Capitalists thrived by appropriating the fruits of labor. For Faria, the state and legal institutions had the means to correct existing iniquities. In this endeavor, rural workers looked to the state as a powerful ally against capital. This tactical collaboration, however, did not entail compromising workers' rights.

The enactment of the sugar legislation had immediate, far-reaching implications even among rural laborers and growers who were not as outspoken as Antonio João de Faria. In highlighting the value of labor, the Estatuto heightened antagonisms between employers and employees. The new language of rights — and the existence of institutions that backed up its claims — unfolded in the particular social and economic milieu of a predominantly agrarian society. Work relations were imbedded in social and cultural understandings that emphasized certain assumptions, practices, and actions over others. This was especially true in agrarian societies where the bonds linking *patrão* (boss) and laborer were informed by notions of deference, reciprocity, and obligation. Variable and selective codes of morality operated simultaneously among landlords and tenants alike in Campos. In requests for termination of colono contracts, landlords often alleged they could not deal any longer with lazy, recalcitrant, or intractable tenants. That someone would invoke the law to claim rights was tantamount to defiance of and contempt for the landlord's authority.

On a hot late afternoon in March of 1946 Leopoldino de Souza Gomes, an illiterate colono, showed up at the IAA regional office in Campos to file a complaint against Vicente Gomes de Almeida, his landlord and brother-in-law. Leopoldino was married to a sister of Vicente's.[33] The claimant had been working for Vicente as a colono since 1913 and delivered the sugarcane crop to Usina Mineiros under the latter's name. In December 1945, he plowed and prepared the cane field. When he thought he was ready to begin planting, Vicente, his patrão, held him off alleging that the plot needed a second plowing first. But noticing that the area he used to tend was already planted and that his brother-in-law refused to reason, Leopoldino sought IAA mediation.

Vicente answered the accusation immediately. He argued that Leopoldino could not invoke the Estatuto because legally speaking he was not a fornecedor. The defendant believed a fornecedor was someone who actually cultivated the land, which was not the case since it was he and not Leopoldino who ran all farm operations. He did acknowledge that in 1944 he arranged for his brother-in-law to help him with the weeding and gathering of the crop only as a special favor to his in-law. But he noted that Leopoldino never lived on the premises nor contributed to the cleaning of the farm after he moved to downtown Campos. Consequently, the farm output decreased considerably, from forty to fifteen cartloads of cane per crop year.[34] Vicente pointed out that Leopoldino also worked for another farmer and owned a small farm in Paus Amarelos in District 2. For him, these two activities kept Leopoldino busy and explained his wanton neglect of the farm and other responsibilities.[35] But the defendant also offered a more profoundly moralistic reading of Leopoldino's allegedly reckless behavior. In essence, Vicente claimed, the problem with his brother-in-law was that since he had moved to downtown Campos he was so absorbed with the amenities of urban life, such as going to movie theatres, that he simply neglected the demands of farming. He thought this was an unfortunate occurrence precisely at a time when the world demand for sugar was up due to war-related devastation in the European sugarbeet industry.[36]

For Vicente, these kinds of actions by cane growers who failed to comply with their commitments undermined the concerted effort needed to bolster economic recovery at a juncture when markets were heating up. He twice chastised his colono kinsman for failing to cooperate with him and with the nation. Vicente was seemingly distressed by the flow of colonos and farm laborers to the cities, a trend that threatened to damage further the sugarcane industry.[37] Placing his particular predicament in the broader context of national and world economics, the defendant, Vicente Gomes de Almeida, tried to bring home the inequity of his brother-in-law's conduct. Summing up the rebuttal, the defendant's attorney contended that neither the Estatuto nor Decree-Law 6.969 were applicable because Leopoldino worked under the direct control of the landlord.[38]

In litigation, disputes over the moral character of the contending parties usually become grist for one's mill. That is presumably the course of action Vicente's attorney tried to pursue. However shrewd, the argument did not fly. After studying the allegations and the answer offered by the defense, and reviewing all the supportive evidence (witnesses, cane supply records, and farm inspections), the IAA regional attorney ruled in favor of the claimant. By carefully examining the mill records, IAA officials determined that Vicente Gomes de Almeida had eighteen separate quotas at Usina Mineiros, seventeen of which were shared with colonos, one of whom was the claimant himself. This quota, officially recognized by the mill and amounting to thirty-five tons of cane, was proof positive that the claimant was, legally speaking, a fornecedor.[39] Accordingly, Leopoldino de Souza Gomes was entitled to request contract renewal or a compensation if the renewal were denied. The Executive Commission, the IAA's ruling board in Rio, confirmed the regional decision. Leopoldino did not get his contract renewed, but received a cash compensation instead, as the law provided.[40]

Lessees and Lessors

Respect for labor, as materialized in the increased value of the property resulting from crops and other improvements, was an equally central concern of lessees. Landlords, however, viewed the new rights granted to tenants by the new laws as a threat to their prerogatives as proprietors. Hence, differing concepts of property rights and of the place of labor in securing both tenure and quota rights became manifest in these claims.

That labor input secured tenure on the land and quota rights was an idea firmly defended by lessees. This is precisely what Francisco Pessanha de Oliveira asserted in a claim against his landlords Hugo Ribeiro Dias and Hermano Antonio Dias, in May 1946. Oliveira wished to renew the lease on a farm belonging to the Dias brothers. Arguing that the labor he expended on the farm added extra value to the property, he demanded renewal of the lease under the same terms and conditions set in a contract he and his brother José Pessanha Nunes signed with the two landlords in 1940.[41]

Francisco Pessanha de Oliveira had a 181-metric-ton cane supply quota at Usina Paraíso. His relationship with the farm known as "Mato do Chiqueiro," located in Campos's District 2, spanned almost two decades. In the 1920s his parents used to lease the property. Following their death, Oliveira and his brother José began operating the farm on their own. Their first lease went back to 1930. In 1935 the two brothers renewed the lease for another five years, and again in 1940 for seven years. The landlords, Hugo Ribeiro Dias and Hermano Antonio Dias, inherited the farm from their mother.[42]

Oliveira and his brother worked the farm in a sui generis division of labor: each one was responsible for a specific area on the property but the two brothers were responsible for honoring the terms and conditions stipulated in the lease, such as keeping the whole property in good repair and condition, and making the annual rent payment of Rs. 2:650$000, the equivalent of $159 in 1940 U.S. dollars. However, in June 1944, almost three years before the end of the lease, José Pessanha Nunes assigned his rights on the farm to one of the owners, Hugo Ribeiro Dias. Francisco Pessanha de Oliveira and Hugo Ribeiro Dias then agreed to honor the earlier arrangement by which each party took care of a specific piece of the property. Later in 1945, Hugo in turn transferred his rights to Hermano, his brother.[43]

As a result of these transactions, Francisco Pessanha de Oliveira and Hermano Antonio Dias became the only two parties legally bound by the lease on Mato do Chiqueiro—Francisco as the single tenant and Hermano as single proprietor and landlord. These transactions lay at the core of the controversy. The claimant was interested only in renewing the lease on the section of the property presently under his direct control. He was in command of an area of approximately five alqueires, of which three were planted in cane. In addition he raised bananas, oranges, and some lavouras brancas (food crops), such as manioc, pumpkin, corn, and rice for his own consumption.[44] The defendant, however, objected to the renewal because the lease originally encompassed the whole farm, not just a parcel of land. In the course of the proceedings, the parties exposed their contrasting views on rights, obligations, and financial security. Francisco Pessanha de Oliveira reiterated his position that he had contributed to increase the property's value through his labor. He grew sugarcane and vegetable crops on the farm and developed a supply quota, all of which had increased the farm's value. His attorney pointed out that the deed of assignment by which José Pessanha Nunes transferred his rights on the farm to Hugo Ribeiro Dias stipulated that Ribeiro Dias and Oliveira would observe the prevailing division of labor on the farm. They agreed that Oliveira would keep the same plot of land he had been working on, while Hugo Ribeiro Dias would farm the other tract. By the act of transfer, Oliveira obtained effective possession of a portion of the farm. The assignment modified the original contract; consequently, Oliveira could demand renewal of the area directly controlled by him. Moreover, Oliveira's official supply quota granted him the right to demand renewal of the lease.[45] The defendant acknowledged that when he rented out the farm to Oliveira and his brother, it had neither cane crops nor any improvements on it.[46]

Hermano Antonio Dias's admission was a tacit recognition of the asset added to the property by his tenant. But he was reluctant to yield to Oliveira's petition because of his concern with soaring property values in Campos. Hermano himself raised cane on a leased farm of about five alqueires, for which he paid the staggering sum of Cr$10.000,00 per year in rent.[47] That was considerably higher than the annual rent he demanded from the tenants of his larger property in 1940. The landlord's concerns with land values were well founded. He was convinced that renting out the whole property would fetch him a larger rent than just a parcel of land. His position reflects the impact of government policies on the real estate market. Due to government intervention in the sugar market, sugar prices became stable. As the sugar industry recovered and gained importance as a prospective endeavor, the value of landed property devoted to cane farming increased noticeably in Campos. A cursory look at the lease terms of Hermano Antonio Dias's own property, Mato do Chiqueiro, illustrates the increasing value of land in the region. The annual rent increased fourfold in ten years. In the first contract, drafted in 1930, before the creation of the IAA, the Dias brothers fixed the rent at Rs. 650$000 per year. In 1935 they adjusted it to Rs. 800$000. By 1940 the annual rent on the farm ran for as much as Rs. 2:650$000. The policies regulating the sugar economy were in full gear, and their impact reverberated in the real estate market, pushing land prices up. Still, this amount was far below the rent Hermano paid for a leased farm. He believed his tenant was getting the bargain of a lifetime. Nominally, Hermano's reluctance to deal with Oliveira was grounded on financial concerns. He did not complain that Oliveira was a bad tenant, a "backslider" or simply a difficult person to deal with, but rather that the rent was too low. The sugar legislation undermined his freedom of contract and his power to do as he pleased with his property.

Cane Growers and Sugar Mills

The disputes over the cane growers' rights were hardly confined to the terse dictates of the legal path. Plaintiffs and defendants raised broader issues about the place of cane growers in Getúlio Vargas's political projects. Cane growers were determined to probe whether the *estadonovista* ideology of social harmony and of the defense of the small producer — as a buffer against the evils of capitalism — was a hollow pronouncement or a genuine commitment by Vargas and his reform-minded staff at the IAA.

A suit filed by the Aguiar family sheds further light on the interplay between cane growers and the Vargas regime. In August 1941, a few months before the passing of the Estatuto, Genésio Maurício de Aguiar wrote directly to President Getúlio Vargas asking for his mediation to solve a dispute that his old and illiterate father had with Usina Laranjeiras.[48] According to Genésio, his father, Antonio Maurício de Aguiar, had made an oral contract to supply cane to the mill in 1936. Everything had run smoothly until the 1941 harvest season, when the mill notified Aguiar Sr. that it would no longer receive his crop. Genésio Maurício de Aguiar decried the actions of millers who, by squeezing independent cane growers, were undermining the ideals of the government with respect to the welfare of the nation. Aguiar complained that the mills did everything possible to make the growers' life more difficult and miserable. For instance, either the usinas did not provide wagons to haul the cane to the mill or they levied onerous surcharges for providing that service. If the grower himself hauled the cane to the mill, then the mill first unloaded its own wagons before those of the cane suppliers. This was a critical issue. The harvested cane had to be crushed within twenty-four hours or the liquid substance in it would dry or become sour. Any damaged cane was bought at a lower rate. Aguiar held that in 1940 the usina treated him with the same arbitrariness with which it had treated his own father. The mill owner refused to pay him according to stipulated prices, using instead the lower scale for canes bound for alcohol manufacture.

The petitioner made much of his broad experience as farmer, businessman, and public figure in Itaocára, a neighboring town. He considered himself a hard worker who loved agriculture and was committed to working for the welfare of the rural poor. He pointed out that he had been a deputy police sheriff and was once affiliated with several political parties in the region. He had even written for the press defending agricultural interests. But, disappointed with politics, he had moved to Campos, where he devoted himself to more "constructive and productive" tasks such as commerce and agriculture. Even so, he had not detached himself completely from his efforts for the welfare of the collectivity, building schools and undertaking sanitation works on lands subject to flooding and infectious diseases such as malaria.

Aguiar prepared a well-rounded and appealing letter to petition Vargas on behalf of his father. He felt that he had the moral stature to assess the strengths and weaknesses of the state's sugar policy due to his dual background as an agricultural entrepreneur and a benefactor of the region's poor. Aguiar charged that the owners of the mill were conspiring against the government by violating the provisions of the IAA-backed legislation. His disappointment or exasperation with politics was notable, for he shared the official stance of Estado Novo ideologues for whom politics was synonymous with demagoguery.[49] This disappointment motivated him to leave aside politics for other endeavors that would allow him to make a better contribution to society. After displaying the credentials that made him a legitimate spokesman for his father, Genésio Maurício de Aguiar closed his letter in a deferential tone, expressing his longing that justice be done:

> It is a presumption on my part to petition you like this, but as I admire the performance of Your Excellency in the Government of the Country, I armed myself with courage to send to you this long and overwhelming letter, which I know will consume your valuable time. But I would be pleased if my uncouth words served to bring relief to a class that suffers so many obstacles, sweating profusely every day, and even seeing their children leave grade school to till the land instead.[50]

The Secretariat of the Presidency routed the petition to the IAA's headquarters in Rio, which then ordered the regional branch in Campos to investigate quickly. An adjunct of the executive branch, the Secretariat handled the official correspondence directed to Vargas by state governments and federal agencies. Nonetheless, the Secretariat was flooded with petitions, requests, and complaints from the citizenry. This office became an effective link between the government and various social groupings. Individuals from all corners of Brazil brought to Vargas's attention a broad range of issues: from requests for employment to complaints against police harassment and employer noncompliance with labor regulations. The Secretariat took action, finding out from the appropriate authorities the most suitable solution to a given problem and then reported back to the interested party the result of its investigations, whether favorable or not. Through effective follow-up and sometimes by providing concrete solutions to the preoccupations of the citizenry, the Secretariat contributed to make the state accessible to ordinary people.[51]

After receiving orders from the Rio headquarters, IAA officials in Campos began to draw up an indictment by asking the defendant, Usina Laranjeiras, to respond to the grower's complaint. The mill manager, Pericles Correa da Rocha, denied the accusation, alleging that Antonio Maurício de Aguiar had no rights because he was not a legal fornecedor. He declared that Antonio Aguiar was a cattle raiser who planted sugarcane as an accessory activity primarily for making spirits at a local still. In 1936, when the still broke down and discontinued operations, Antonio asked Laranjeiras's management to buy the crop because otherwise he risked losing the fruit of his labor. What was meant to be a temporary arrangement extended into a commercial relationship for several years. Despite the mill's opposition, Antonio expanded cane cultivation, increasing cane deliveries to the disadvantage of the mill's older fornecedores. Therefore, when the mill manager corroborated that the still had been reactivated, he notified Antonio to stop supplying cane to the mill. Finally, Rocha suggested that Genésio Maurício de Aguiar had induced his father to press the claim against Usina Laranjeiras.[52]

The IAA regional branch summoned the parties to testify at a hearing. As for the reasons that prompted him to do business with Usina Laranjeiras, Antonio Maurício de Aguiar stated that he took this action after an embarrassing incident between another son and the still owner. Antonio also denied categorically that Genésio was acting behind the scenes. He sought his eldest son's help because the mill management had been reluctant to negotiate with him.[53] While the proceedings were underway, the IAA's Juridical Division in Rio ordered the mill to continue processing Antonio's cane in an amount equivalent to the average of the deliveries from 1936 until 1938, as required by article 41 of the Estatuto.[54] This novel legal provision assured cane growers that they would not be deprived of an income during the length of the trial. The regional office also dispatched an inspector to examine Antonio's property to assess potential damage to the crop if it were not crushed on time. The inspector determined that the crop had been standing on the fields for the last two years. It was dry and showed signs of damage, but the field could still yield as much as 1,800 metric tons of cane in the 1943 harvest season.[55]

It is quite understandable that Antonio Maurício de Aguiar would covet a supply quota at Usina Laranjeiras. He had a sizable crop and had met the legal requirement of delivering cane to a single mill for three consecutive crop years. The suit, however, took an unexpected twist. In a seemingly contradictory move, Antonio suddenly dropped his claim, arguing that he was satisfied with the way the IAA had led the investigation. He added further that his only purpose was to prove that he was right, and having accomplished just that, he had no further interest in pursuing the suit.[56] The panel of higher instance in Rio that reviewed the case yielded to his request after learning that he had reached an agreement with the mill.[57] The transcript does not tell the exact details of the out-of-court settlement, yet it is highly likely that the IAA would have upheld the grower's right to a quota if he had not dropped the claim. Whether or not the mill manager acted in good faith when accepting Antonio's supplies, the IAA enforced the Estatuto stipulation that any grower who supplied cane to a single mill for at least three consecutive harvests earned the right to become a fornecedor linked to the mill. Undoubtedly, this propelled Usina Laranjeiras to negotiate a deal with the claimant.

The mill owners from Rio scorned changes in the sugar legislation that curtailed their former power and leverage with the federal agency.[58] As a social force, they were strong opponents of the Estatuto, fearing excessive state intervention in the sugar sector.[59] Cane growers from Campos, however, responded assertively to the new official policies. Knowing that they had stronger leverage with the IAA, the growers flooded the regional branch with complaints against landlords and the mills (see Table 5). They concentrated their efforts on fighting at the IAA level where they thought they could better press their demands.[60]

The experience of the Aguiar family was hardly an isolated one. A distinct litigation pattern emerges from the analysis of the 399 lawsuits filed with the IAA in Rio state throughout the 1940s. An overwhelming 70 percent of the complaints were brought by the cane growers and rural workers against the mills; 26 percent had to do with disputes between tenants and landowners; and only in 4 percent were the mills the plaintiffs.

TABLE 5 Claims by State, 1940–1950

State	% Claims
Rio de Janeiro	48.0
São Paulo	24.7
Pernambuco	6.5
Alagoas	6.0
Bahia	3.5
Minas Gerais	3.3
Espírito Santo	3.1
Sergipe	3.0
Paraná	1.5
Rio Grande do Norte	0.3
	N = 1027

Source: IAA Processos.

With regard to the decisions, the IAA almost invariably favored growers over the mills. The IAA ruled in favor of growers in 46 percent (n = 278) of the claims filed against the mills. The latter were only favored in 2 percent of the cases, while in still another 20 percent of the claims the parties reached settlement. Refusal to hear cases due to lack of jurisdictional authority, dismissal based on the merits of the claim, and the dropping of an action by the litigant account for the outcome in the remaining cases (32 percent).[61]

In terms of the social background of the litigants, the data show that all types of growers—whether small or large, propertied or nonpropertied—had access to IAA conciliation boards. More than a third of the claimants had no title to landed property, and from 43 to 46 percent were legally entitled to supply up to 100 metric tons of sugarcane for the season.[62] This quota figure (100 metric tons) serves as the cutoff for identifying small growers. To have an idea (albeit crude) of the income level of a grower in this category, suffice it to say that in 1943 a grower would have received $250 in returns for the season. This represents total gross income, without taking any deductions for expenses, such as tools and supplies. Compare this with the annual minimum wage paid to factory workers in Rio, which in 1943 was $232.[63] As these figures convey, anyone whose main source of income hinged on cane growing lived in precarious conditions.

Subsequent vigorous enforcement of the sugar legislation lent credibility to state intervention in the sugar sector during the Vargas era. Consequently, this experience helped facilitate the consent of the growers toward the regime.

Conclusions

This essay has examined how litigation through the IAA special courts became the predominant form of mobilization used by sugarcane growers and rural workers in Campos during the Vargas period. Why did legal action gain such prominence? To be sure, the political constraints imposed by Getúlio Vargas as his regime banned and shut down the customary means of political participation and mobilization, such as parties, congress, and strikes, partially explains the choice of this form of mobilization. The Vargas regime, however, implemented unprecedented reforms that called into question key fixtures of the Brazilian legal system, most notably property rights and the freedom of contract. As these policies opened up whole new arenas of legal, ideological, and political struggles, cane growers and workers increasingly appropriated the new language of rights — giving it new meanings — and effectively engaged state institutions to promote their demands. New strategies emerged under the changing legal and political structures of the Vargas regime.[64]

The Estatuto da Lavoura Canavieira promulgated in 1941 was not mere rhetoric. It embodied some of the long-standing aspirations of cane growers. This law granted protection to the direct tiller of the land, recognizing that labor expended on raising a crop creates value that ought to be adequately compensated. Security of tenure and cane supply quotas were two of the instruments through which IAA reformers sought to protect cane growers from the power wielded by landlords and mills. The Estatuto effectively transformed those aspirations into rights that were defendable and enforceable through the IAA.[65]

In choosing peaceful mobilization over violent protest and skillfully channeling their grievances through the institutional and legal means established by the regime, cane growers and workers ended up endorsing and legitimizing the foundations of the Vargas state. They became actors in the consolidation of Vargas's power. How this hegemonic process unfolded could not have been more expedient. As an agency solely accountable to the president, the IAA devised policies with a certain degree of autonomy from regional oligarchies and large mill owners. The agency was staffed by competent, reform-minded officials like Dr. A. J. Barbosa Lima Sobrinho and Dr. Vicente Chermont de Miranda, the president and the chief legal counsel of the IAA, respectively, who were deeply committed to seeking better conditions for the tillers of the land. By insuring that grievances were resolved through litigation in its own conciliation boards, the IAA paved the way for the institutionalization of class struggle in the sugar sector. It laid out the rules governing the sugar economy and the legal remedies to any infringement of them. As disputing parties recognized the IAA's authority, this further cemented the claims of the agency as the legitimate forum in which to adjudicate disputes in a routine, orderly, and bureaucratic fashion. One must remember, however, that cane growers had a significant input in the formulation of these reforms, as they pushed the government agency through lobbying and petitions to adopt more comprehensive measures.

All of this leads me to argue that Vargas consolidated power not only through repressive means but also through such mechanisms as the legal system. The creation of the IAA gave the Vargas regime a semblance of professionalism, legality, and, above all, legitimacy, a feature that set it apart from preceding governments. As cane growers skillfully channeled their grievances through the institutional and legal means established by the regime, law and its operation became critical elements in furthering hegemony.[66] This strategy played into the hands of a new political leadership intent on incorporating cane growers into the state. But one must acknowledge that the installation of a bureaucratic apparatus that seemed to be impartial and that tried through concrete means to improve the welfare of sugarcane producers was most unusual for many of those devoted to tilling the land.

After the fall of the Estado Novo in 1945, many of the agencies created by Vargas were abolished, among them the federal agency that regulated the coffee economy. The IAA fared better. Despite unremitting pressure from Paulista usineiros intent on eliminating the IAA, it survived the crisis of the Vargas regime, due, to a large extent, to the ferocious defense mounted by lawmakers from Rio and Pernambuco.[67] The IAA underwent profound transformations over the years until its definitive abolition in 1990. Furthermore, the mobilization of cane growers in Campos had a profound impact on national politics in forthcoming decades. Campos became the Partido Social Democrático's great electoral bastion in Rio, a development attesting to the strong bonds between the political leadership inspired by Getúlio Vargas and the agricultural producers of the region, an outgrowth of a relationship that had crystallized during the first Vargas government.

Notes

Research and writing support came from the Ford Foundation, the American Bar Association, the University of Minnesota Graduate School, and the Indiana University Minority Faculty Fellowship Program. For their helpful comments on earlier versions, I would like to thank Arlene J. Kíz, Ricardo Salvatore, Gilbert Joseph, and the anonymous reviewer. All errors are my own.

1 This approach has been systematically developed over the years by James C. Scott in *The Moral Economy of the Peasant: Rebellion and Subsistence in Southeast Asia* (New Haven: Yale University Press, 1976), *Weapons of the Weak: Everyday Forms of Peasant Resistance* (New Haven: Yale University Press, 1985), and *Domination and the Arts of Resistance: Hidden Transcripts* (New Haven: Yale University Press, 1990).

2 Conscious of the interplay between the intention of the law and the meaning which people attribute to it, legal anthropology has drawn attention to the ways local communities have historically and culturally understood and interpreted official decrees, proclamations, and the law. A perceptive example of this approach is George A. Collier, *Socialists of Rural Andalusia: Unacknowledged Revolutionaries of the Second Republic* (Stanford: Stanford University Press, 1987). For the Latin American context, see Daniel Nugent and Ana María Alonso, "Multiple Selective Traditions in Agrarian Reform and Agrarian Struggle: Popular Culture and State Formation in the 'Ejido' of Namiquipa, Chihuahua," in Gilbert M. Joseph and Daniel Nugent, eds., *Everyday Forms of State Formation: Revolution and the Negotiation of Rule in Modern Mexico* (Durham, N.C.: Duke University Press, 1994), pp. 221–239.

3 For assessments of these laws from a legal perspective, see Vicente Chermont de Miranda, *O Estatuto da Lavoura Canavieira e sua interpretação* (Rio de Janeiro: Instituto do Açúcar e do Alcool, 1943); Barbosa Lima Sobrinho, "A experiência de uma reforma agrária setorial," *Jurídica* 27, no. 78 (June–December 1962): 203–212.

4 Two key works on the topic of state regulation of the Brazilian sugar industry are Fiona Gordon-Ashworth, "International and National Commodity Control, 1930–1945: Sugar and the Brazilian Case" (Ph.D. dissertation, University of Southampton, 1978); and Tamás Szmrecsányi, *O planejamento da agroindústria canavieira no Brasil (1930–1975)* (São Paulo: Editora Hucitec, 1979).

5 Broadly defined, the *colonato* is a sharecropping system. It must not be confused

with the labor regime, also called colonato, that developed in western São Paulo's coffee region in the late nineteenth century. Here it was more of a piecework system, where laborers received separate payments for cultivation and harvesting coffee. Consequently, the risks were divided, not shared between landowner and worker. For the evolution of the coffee colonato, see Thomas H. Holloway, *Immigrants of the Land: Coffee and Society in São Paulo, 1886–1934* (Chapel Hill: University of North Carolina Press, 1980), pp. 71–79. The actual text of these three sugar laws appears in Instituto do Açúcar e do Alcool, *Legislação* (Rio de Janeiro: IAA, 1964).

6　Francisco da Rosa Oiticica, "A função social da terra na valorização do homem," *Revista de Direito Agrário* (Rio) 1, no. 1 (1942): 41–42.

7　The following works provide useful commentary on these two charters: Fábio Lucas, *Conteúdo social nas constituções brasileiras* (Belo Horizonte: Universidade de Minas Gerais, 1959), pp. 65–76; Oscar Tenório, "Regime da propriedade," *O Observador Econômico e Financeiro* no. 71 (Dec. 1941): 85–87; *Dicionário histórico-biográfico brasileiro, 1930–1983,* coord. Israel Beloch and Alzira Alves de Abreu, 4 vols. (Rio de Janeiro: Editora Forense-Universitária/FINEP, 1984), s.v. "Constituição de 1934" and "Constituição de 1937"; and Sônia Helena Novaes Guimarães Moraes, "A questão da propriedade da terra: conceitos e princípios incorporados ao direito agrário latino-americano e a necessidade de uma evolução," *Revista de Direito Agrário e Meio Ambiente* (Curitiba) 2, no. 2 (August 1987): 58–59.

8　For evidence of these and other measures, see Barbosa Lima Sobrinho, *Problemas econômicos e sociais da lavoura canavieira: exposição de motivos e texto do Estatuto da Lavoura Canavieira* (Rio de Janeiro: IAA, 1941), pp. 144–145, and his "Industriais e plantadores de cana no periodo colonial," *Revista de Direito Agrário* 1, no. 1 (1942): 3–10. On the privileges granted to indebted sugar planters in colonial Bahia, see Stuart B. Schwartz, *Sugar Plantations in the Formation of Brazilian Society, Bahia, 1550–1835* (Cambridge: Cambridge University Press, 1985), pp. 195–197.

9　On the rules governing public lands and the regime of landed property in Brazil, see Emília Viotti da Costa, *The Brazilian Empire: Myths and Histories* (Chicago: University of Chicago Press, 1985), pp. 78–93; Warren Dean, "Latifundia and Land Policy in Nineteenth-Century Brazil," *Hispanic American Historical Review* 51, no. 4 (November 1971): 606–625; Eulália Maria Lahmayer Lobo, *História político-administrativa da agricultura brasileira* (Brasília, 1980), pp. 118–124; and Joe Foweraker, *The Struggle for Land: A Political Economy of the Pioneer Frontier in Brazil from 1930 to the Present Day* (Cambridge: Cambridge University Press, 1981), pp. 83–106. For specific case studies of the law's impact on land tenure in the state of Rio de Janeiro, see Sheila Siqueira de Castro Faria, "Terra e Trabalho em Campos dos Goitacases, 1850–1920" (M.A. thesis, Universidade Federal Fluminense, 1986) and Márcia Maria Menendes Motta, *Nas fronteiras do poder: conflito e direito à terra no Brasil do século XIX* (Rio de Janeiro: Arquivo Público do Estado do Rio de Janeiro; Vício de Leitura, 1998). Interestingly, colonial-era Spanish jurists elaborated very similar ideas about the so-called "social function of property," whereby effective exploitation of a plot of land by a tenant or squatter supersedes the proprietor's rights. Even in the national period, these ideas still nourished land legislation in Colombia, for instance. For an engaging analysis of how these conflicting concepts played out in Colombia during the late 1920s to early 1930s, see Catherine LeGrand, *Frontier Expansion and Peasant Protest in Colombia, 1830–1936* (Albuquerque: University of New Mexico Press, 1986), pp. 118–119, 142, 151.

10 This subject is addressed in chap. 3 of my Ph.D. dissertation, "Law, Hegemony, and the Politics of Sugarcane Growers under Getúlio Vargas: Campos, Rio de Janeiro, Brazil, 1930–1950" (University of Minnesota, 1998).

11 A broader discussion of how cane growers mobilized to press for reforms in the sugar sector and how the Vargas state incorporated some of those demands is undertaken in chapter 4 of my dissertation.

12 Arquivo Geral do Instituto do Açúcar e do Alcool (Rio), Fundo Processos, Processo N. 248/45, fols. 13r–15r, 18r. (Hereinafter, AGIAA and processo number.)

13 Ibid., fols. 2r, 28r.

14 Ibid., fols. 5r, 36r, 41r.

15 Ibid., fols. 65r–66r.

16 AGIAA, Processo N. 220/46. Other cases protesting working conditions are Processo N. 18/47 and Processo N. 104/48.

17 In 1943, besides raising the minimum wage for urban labor, Vargas introduced the Consolidation of Labor Laws, which systematized labor relations in Brazil. The code did contain important provisions on rural labor, but these went largely unenforced. On this labor code, see *Dicionário histórico-biográfico brasileiro,* s.v. "Consolidação das Leis do Trabalho (CLT)." The Consolidations' provisions on rural labor are addressed by Clifford A. Welch, "Rural Labor and the Brazilian Revolution in São Paulo, 1930–1964" (Ph.D. dissertation, Duke University, 1990), pp. 32–35. Welch also discusses Vargas's position on adopting reforms benefitting rural workers (pp. 19–30). A revised, enlarged version of this important work was published after I completed this essay and could not be incorporated into my analysis. See *The Seed Was Planted: The São Paulo Roots of Brazil's Rural Labor Movement, 1924–1964* (University Park: Pennsylvania State University Press, 1999).

18 On the Código Rural Brasileiro, see *Repertório enciclopédico do direito brasileiro,* ed. J. M. de Carvalho Santos (Rio de Janeiro: Borsoi, 1947), s.v. "Direito rural"; and Welch, "Rural Labor and the Brazilian Revolution," pp. 36–37.

19 On this measure, see Richard Bourne, *Getúlio Vargas of Brazil, 1883–1954: Sphinx of the Pampas* (London: Charles Knight, 1974), p. 155; and Welch, "Rural Labor and the Brazilian Revolution," pp. 30–31.

20 Welch, "Rural Labor and the Brazilian Revolution," pp. 37–47.

21 See Mário Grynszpan, "Mobilização camponesa no Rio de Janeiro" (M.A. thesis, Universidade Federal Fluminense, 1987), pp. 111–112; AGIAA, Processo N. 295/46, fol. 61v; Processo N. 91/47; Processo N. 124/50, fol. 2r. On rural organizing by the Communists in the post–Estado Novo era, see José de Souza Martins, "El

campesinado en el Brasil," in Pablo González Casanova, ed., *Los campesinos en América Latina,* vol. 4 (México: Siglo XXI, 1985), pp. 49–70; and Welch, "Rural Labor and the Brazilian Revolution," pp. 194–195.

22 Grynszpan, "Mobilização camponesa," 110–115; AGIAA, Processo N. 295/46, fol. 61v; and Processo N. 136/49. On Faria's travails organizing rural workers in Campos, see Waldir P. Carvalho, *Campos depois do centenário* (Campos: Damadá Artes Gráficas, 1991), pp. 58–59; and Arquivo Nacional, Secretaria da Presidência da República, Correspondência, Entidades Representativas de Classe, Lata 171, 1940, Telegram, Sindicato dos Trabalhadores Agrícolas e Pecuários de Campos to President Vargas, 24 July 1940.

23 AGIAA, Processo N. 17/45, fol. 8r.

24 Usina São José ranked third in the country, after Usina Catende and Usina Serra Grande in Pernambuco and Alagoas, respectively. Besides Usina São José, the same British investors bought Usina Santa Cruz, originally founded in 1884. For the convoluted ownership of Usina São José, see Alberto Lamego, *A Terra Goytacá à luz de documentos inéditos,* 8 vols. (Bruxelles: L'Edition d'art; Niterói: Diário Oficial, 1913–1947), 6: 256–260; 8: 122; AGIAA, Processo N. 155/45, fol. 5r; and Processo N. 569/45; *Folha do Commercio* (Campos), 28 Mar. 1935; 30 Apr. 1935, p. 1; 10 July 1937, p. 25; *O Radical* (Rio) 3 Aug. 1936, p. 5.

25 On the turnover of mill property, see Faria, "Terra e trabalho em Campos," pp. 250–251; and González, "Law, Hegemony," pp. 95–102.

26 Dr. Pinto held a large cane supply quota amounting to 2,054 metric tons at Usina Barcelos. See Brasil, *Diário Oficial,* "Mapa de fornecedores do Rio de Janeiro" (Suplemento ao no. 89), 16 April 1943. He also figured among the wealthiest landowners in the region with two properties in São João da Barra, measuring 110 and 40 alqueires, respectively. See Rio de Janeiro (state), Directoria de Agricultura, Serviço de Estatística, *Propriedades agrícolas,* vol. 1, *1925–1927* (Rio de Janeiro: Typ. Marques Araújo, 1927). A unit for measuring area, the Campista alqueire is the equivalent of 4,84 hectares, or 11.95 acres. On the Silva Pinto clan, see Lamego, *Terra goytacá,* 8, pp. 178, 288–289, 349.

27 Rio de Janeiro (state), Instituto de Fomento e Economia Agrícola do Estado do Rio de Janeiro, *Relatório* (Niterói, 1928), pp. 130–131.

28 AGIAA, Processo N. 18/47, fol. 2r.

29 AGIAA, Processo N. 296/45, fol. 7r. Another claim (Processo N. 92/48) deals with the partition of the quota of Faria's father among his mother and other siblings.

30 For works that explore the ideological meaning of democracy, social justice, and citizenship for urban labor in Brazil during the Estado Novo, see Angela de Castro Gomes, *A invenção do trabalhismo* (Rio de Janeiro: IUPERJ/Vértice, 1988); and Jorge Luiz Ferreira, "A cultura política dos trabalhadores no primeiro Governo Vargas," *Estudos Históricos* 3, no. 6 (1990): 180–195. For popular notions of democracy and social justice among urban workers and peasantries in other Latin American latitudes, see Daniel James, *Resistance and Integration: Peronism and the Argen-*

tine Working Class, 1946–1976 (Cambridge: Cambridge University Press, 1988), pp. 15–18; Jeffrey L. Gould, *To Lead as Equals: Rural Protest and Political Consciousness in Chinandega, Nicaragua, 1912–1979* (Chapel Hill: University of North Carolina Press, 1990), pp. 101–104. Notwithstanding the differences across time and place, these ideas seem to have had a valid historical claim worldwide. Barrington Moore argued that for French and Russian peasantries of the late eighteenth and nineteenth centuries, political and economic freedoms were closely intertwined. See *Social Origins of Democracy and Dictatorship: Lord and Peasant in the Making of the Modern World* (Boston: Beacon Press, 1967), pp. 500–503.

31 AGIAA, Processo N. 205/46, fol. 29r.

32 Ibid., fol. 29r for all quotations used in the text.

33 AGIAA, Processo N. 115/48, fols. 3r, 7r.

34 Ibid., fols. 6r–8r.

35 Ibid., fol. 29r.

36 Ibid., fols. 31r–32r.

37 Although intense rural-urban migration did not take hold until the 1950s, it gained impetus in the mid-1940s. See "Notas editoriais," *O Observador Econômico e Financeiro* no. 70 (November 1941): 4–5; and Werner Baer, *The Brazilian Economy: Growth And Development,* 3d ed. (New York: Praeger, 1989), p. 71.

38 Processo N. 115/48, fol. 34r.

39 Ibid., fol. 39r.

40 Ibid., fols. 40r, 45r, 50r.

41 AGIAA, Processo N. 52/49, fol. 2r.

42 Ibid., fols. 7r–8r, 47r–48v, 50r–51v, 53r–53v and 72r–72v.

43 Ibid., fols. 9r–11r, 12r–13r.

44 Ibid., fol. 73r.

45 Ibid., fols. 128r–129v.

46 Ibid., fol. 74r.

47 Ibid., fols. 74r, 140r–141r. In 1942 the Brazilian government introduced a new currency, the cruzeiro, which replaced the milréis. For equivalence purposes, one milréis (1$000) equaled one cruzeiro, written $1.00. At the time, one *conto* (1:000$000) represented one thousand cruzeiros. See Robert M. Levine, *The Vargas Regime: The Critical Years, 1934–1938* (New York: Columbia University Press, 1970), appendix D.

48 AGIAA, Processo N. 474/45, Anexo Processo N. 574/45, fols. 3r–4r.

49 For stimulating studies on the ideological postulates of the Estado Novo, see Gomes, *A invenção do trabalhismo;* Silvana Goulart, *Sob a verdade oficial: ideologia, propaganda e censura no Estado Novo* (São Paulo: Editora Marco Zero, 1990); and Lúcia Lippi de Oliveira, Mônica Pimenta Velloso, and Angela Maria de Castro Gomes, *Estado Novo: ideologia e poder* (Rio de Janeiro: Zahar Editores, 1982).

50 Anexo Processo N. 574/45, fol. 3r.

51 Created by Vargas, this institution declined after his overthrow in 1945, and did

not attain the same importance during his second presidency between 1950 and 1954. On the political role of the Secretariat under Vargas, see Jorge Luiz Ferreira, "Os trabalhadores do Brasil: a cultura popular no primeiro Governo Vargas" (M.A. thesis, Universidade Federal Fluminense, 1989); and Joel Wolfe, *Working Women, Working Men: São Paulo and the Rise of Brazil's Industrial Working Class, 1900–1950* (Durham: Duke University Press, 1993), pp. 109–117.

52 Processo N. 474/45, fols. 14r–15r, 48r.

53 Ibid., fols. 69r, 79r.

54 Ibid., fols. 27r, 45r.

55 Ibid., fol. 82r.

56 Ibid., fol. 84r.

57 Ibid., fol. 90r, 92r.

58 A dissident voice was Bartolomeu Lisandro de Albernaz, a former Campista alderman and sugar merchant who came to own two usinas, São João (1941) and Poço Gordo (1949), in the region. By 1948 Albernaz was serving as the millers' representative on the IAA Executive Commission, and throughout the 1950s represented Rio state in the federal congress as member of the Partido Social Democrático (PSD), a new political party founded by pro-Vargas forces in 1945. On Albernaz's political and business background, see *Dicionário histórico-biográfico brasileiro,* s.v. "Albernaz, Bartolomeu Lisandro de"; and Carvalho, *Campos depois do centenário,* pp. 97, 368–369, 376, 379. On the PSD, see *Dicionário histórico-biográfico brasileiro,* s.v. "Partido Social Democrático."

59 On the mill owners' opposition to the Estatuto, see Barbosa Lima Sobrinho, *Conferência canavieira de 1941* (Rio de Janeiro: IAA, 1943); *O Estado de São Paulo,* 18 July 1941, p. 5; *Jornal do Commercio,* 16 July 1941, p. 8; and 24 Aug. 1941, p. 7; *Pareceres sobre a reforma da Lei no. 178* (Rio de Janeiro: IAA, 1941); "Legislação canavieira," *O Observador Econômico e Financeiro* 67 (August 1941): 101–113.

60 Incidentally, under Vargas, São Paulo urban workers also increasingly sought institutionalized solutions to their grievances through the use of the labor legislation and the labor court system created by Vargas. See John D. French, *The Brazilian Workers' ABC: Class Conflict and Alliances in Modern São Paulo* (Chapel Hill: University of North Carolina Press, 1992), pp. 96–97, 171–172. After the creation in 1957 of a regional labor court in Ribeirão Preto, São Paulo's old coffee region, rural workers there turned to litigation to settle grievances with coffee and sugar planters over issues such as residency and vacation pay. See Welch, "Rural Labor and the Brazilian Revolution," pp. 189–214. The experience of rural workers in Pernambuco's sugar region under the military dictatorship that ruled Brazil from 1964 to 1985 is also representative of this mode of mobilization. Seeking to deflect rural unrest, the military introduced social welfare policies (health services) in the countryside. These measures, however, had the unforeseen effect of propelling rural unionization. Throughout the 1970s, rural labor organizers drew on the availability of these bureaucratized resources to demand the same kinds of civil and

political rights denied by the military. However reformist in outlook, the rural unionization movement incrementally generated pressure for political change. See Anthony W. Pereira, *The End of the Peasantry: The Rural Labor Movement in Northeast Brazil, 1961–1988* (Pittsburgh: University of Pittsburgh Press, 1997), pp. 57–60.

61 For comparison with the labor courts, created in 1939, see Wolfe, *Working Women, Working Men,* pp. 89–90, 121, 145; and French, *Brazilian Workers' ABC,* pp. 86–88, 309, 310 n.63.

62 A massive computer name database of cane growers and litigants was created with data from the 1920 agricultural census, the 1927 rural property tax roll for the state of Rio, the IAA processos, and the 1943 list of quota-holding cane growers, compiled by the IAA and published in the *Diário Oficial,* that shows quota volume and mill affiliation for each individual cane supplier in Campos.

63 Cane price figures for Campos were drawn from data in the IAA claims. Wage figures for Rio were calculated from Eulália Maria Lahmeyer Lobo, coord., *Rio de Janeiro operário: natureza do Estado, cojuntura econômica, condições de vida e consciência de classe* (Rio de Janeiro: Access Editora, 1992), pp. 108–123. For Brazilian currency equivalents in 1943 U.S. dollars, see American International Investment Corp., *World Currency Charts,* 8th ed. (Zurich, 1977).

64 Theorizing that social actors who lack the means to mobilize effectively overcome their structural weakness under specific political conjunctures, Sidney Tarrow writes: "Triggered by the incentive created by political opportunity, combining conventional and challenging forms of action and building on social networks and cultural frames is how movements overcome the obstacles to collective action and sustain their interactions with opponents and with the state." *Power in Movement: Social Movements, Collective Action, and Politics* (Cambridge: Cambridge University Press, 1995), p. 1.

65 It goes without saying that, as with most legislation, the Estatuto had unintended consequences, among which the disappearance of colonos looms large. Because of the rights accorded to tenant farmers and colonos, landowners in Campos grew increasingly hostile to colonato agreements, which began to decline by the mid-1950s. See Processo N. 687/45. For the situation of sugar colonos in São Paulo, see Welch, "Rural Labor and the Brazilian Revolution," pp. 227–228. Holloway reports a similar outcome in São Paulo coffee region in the 1950s as minimum wage regulations and social welfare programs led coffee planters to replace colonos with non-resident day laborers (*Immigrants on the Land,* p. 110). In 1936 Colombian authorities passed a law that accorded possession of land to tenants and sharecroppers. But as LeGrand argues, this measure lead to economic dislocation and the emergence of a rural working class from within the ranks of tenants and sharecroppers (*Frontier Expansion,* pp. 159–161).

66 The paradoxical qualities of law in building hegemony and fueling resistance is aptly analyzed by E. P. Thompson, *Whigs and Hunters: The Origins of the Black Act* (New York: Pantheon, 1975); Douglas Hay et al., *Albion's Fatal Tree: Crime*

and Society in Eighteenth-Century England (New York: Pantheon, 1975); Mindie Lazarus-Black and Susan F. Hirsch, eds., *Contested States: Law, Hegemony, and Resistance* (New York: Routledge, 1994); Susan Kellogg, *Law and the Transformation of Aztec Culture, 1500–1700* (Norman: University of Oklahoma Press, 1995); and Allen Wells and Gilbert M. Joseph, *Summer of Discontent, Seasons of Upheaval: Elite Politics and Rural Insurgency in Yucatán, 1876–1915* (Stanford: Stanford University Press, 1996).

67 In 1952, during Vargas's return to the presidency, the coffee autarquia was reinstituted. On the opposition of coffee interests to Vargas policies, see Alberto Venâncio Filho, *A intervenção do estado no domínio econômico* (Rio de Janeiro: Fundação Getúlio Vargas, 1968), p. 89. On the debates in connection with the abolition of the IAA, see Szmrecsányi, *O planejamento da agro-indústria canavieira*, p. 213; Sônia Draibe, *Rumos e metamorfoses: um estudo sobre a constituição do Estado e as alternativas da industrialização no Brasil, 1930–1960* (Rio de Janeiro: Paz e Terra, 1985), pp. 281–282; *Monitor Campista*, 11 Aug. 1946, p. 1.

PART II

The Social and Cultural Construction of Crime

The Criminalization of the Syphilitic Body:

Prostitutes, Health Crimes, and Society

in Mexico City, 1867–1930

CRISTINA RIVERA-GARZA

O n July 3, 1918, a committee formed by physicians Angel Gaviño
and Joaquín Huici and lawyer Fernando Breña Alvarez drafted
a plan designed to prevent the spread of syphilis in Mexico.
Largely based on precepts of public health from the 1917 Mexican constitution and German laws that declared syphilis to be a health crime, the "Prophilaxis of Syphilis in the Department of Public Health" proposed novel
measures to protect society from sexually transmitted diseases.[1] First, it
required physicians to file official reports of any syphilitic patient under
their care. In addition, official health certificates issued by the Council of
Public Health became mandatory for marriage purposes. A critical reply
appeared quickly on July 9. After painstaking and vocal debates, doctors
Manuel Cañas and Edmundo G. Aragón argued that the plan worked
against the professional confidentiality of doctors and the freedom of the
individual. Instead, they proposed to control syphilis through health education, the propagation of hygienic information in state dispensaries, and
intensified surveillance of prostitution. Although the debate continued
through the fall, the committee reached a compromise by the end of the
year. While doctors agreed to prepare monthly reports on their syphilitic
patients, the Department of Public Health allowed them to omit names and
other identifying references. At a more fundamental level, however, the

committee posed unsettling questions: Were syphilitic patients criminals? If so, did they deserve punishment? After a decade of continuous debates, Mexican law answered with a resounding "yes" when, in 1929, a reformed penal code prescribed punishments for infected individuals that spread the disease.[2] Although short-lived, criminalization was a clear victory of post-revolutionary social medicine.[3]

This essay examines the medical and social terrain in which the syphilitic body became a criminal construct, namely public health and sex. This terrain, just like disease itself, was not only a biological reality but also a dense network of social relations.[4] In following the thread of disease, this analysis brings onto the scene a cast of eccentric characters: doctors, prostitutes, police agents, and public health bureaucrats in an unstable context: the murky waters of state formation. It was in their jolting contacts and mirrorlike encounters that syphilis became a health crime of sexual nature, a *delito de contagio sexual y nutricio,* also known as a *delito de contaminación intersexual.*[5]

Medical concerns about syphilis were not new in postrevolutionary Mexico. In fact, Mexican doctors had used the biological and moral dangers associated with this condition both to support and to oppose the first legislation to regulate prostitution in 1867. However, throughout the late nineteenth century doctors regarded syphilis as a dangerous disease, a moral defect, even an epidemic, but seldom considered it to be a crime. This situation changed drastically after the 1917 Mexican constitution provided an administrative framework to intervene in the personal lives of its citizens. As the state became the promoter and ultimate protector of public health, state-sponsored health institutions gained an unprecedented regulatory access to the bodies, behaviors, and social relations of the population.[6] A complex administrative structure — including the creation of the Department of Public Health and the transformation of the Superior Sanitation Council into a national institution — it served as grounds for the development of an apparatus of social medicine which was as much a "juridical, technical and administrative branch of the federal government" as it was a medical one.[7] Thus, unlike Porfirian physicians, postrevolutionary doctors claiming to defend the lives of innocent victims came to favor and were able to establish penal punishments for bearers of social diseases: not only syphilis, but also alcoholism and, eventually, drug addiction.[8]

The medical debate around the treatment of syphilis is historically relevant because it brings the domain of the body into the analysis of nation-building processes in Mexico. As physicians evaluated programs to protect society from contagion, they discussed the responsibilities of the state in matters of public health. Like no other illness, syphilis also provided doctors with scientific tools to delineate accepted sexual behaviors in society. In addition, although medical data attributed the spread of syphilis to both men and women, emphasis on prostitutes as agents of disease contributed to the demarcation of gender lines in modernizing Mexico. Yet, the fragile character of this process must be stressed.[9] Although state-sponsored health campaigns contributed to the control and eventual eradication of epidemic diseases such as smallpox and yellow fever, success in the battle against syphilis did not come easily. Antisyphilitic campaigns not only involved health authorities and physicians, but also, and more importantly, prostitutes, the alleged source of biological and moral infection. Armed with distinctive languages and experiences, these actors forcefully negotiated their ideas about the control of syphilis in a "common material and meaningful framework" they helped shape.[10]

The criminalization of the syphilitic body was a conflict-ridden phenomenon in Mexico. Attempts to regulate prostitution during the late nineteenth century as well as the sharp increase in the production of sexual knowledge in the field of medicine combined to create the scientific and administrative basis to identify, control, and eventually punish sexual behaviors deemed as deviant. Yet, syphilis was hardly a "secret disease" silenced by repressive measures.[11] On the contrary, syphilis became a popular topic of discussion among physicians and health authorities; the parameters of their discussions of deviant sexual behavior became the enunciative boundaries of other, dissident voices in Mexico.[12] The bodies of prostitutes played a fundamental role in this articulation. On the one hand, as forced patients at state hospitals, prostitutes became the basis for the emergence of Mexican sexual science. On the other hand, prostitutes' varied strategies of resistance against both the regulatory system and state hospitals shed light on the tense dialogue that syphilis and its criminalization entailed.

In attempting to capture the various strategies of power at play in the reformulation of syphilis as a health crime of sexual nature, this study explores three interrelated areas which combined gave birth to modern discourses of sexuality in Mexico: first, the regulations of prostitution, the normative structure which, by the late nineteenth century, inscribed bodies into the law; second, the workings of the Morelos hospital, the institutional apparatus which, as medical branch of the Sanitary Police, provided medical care to syphilitic prostitutes; third, the underpinnings of sexual science in Mexico, the medical discourse developed in and around the bodies of women, notably prostitutes enrolled in welfare institutions. In an effort to capture actors and scenes in actual motion, as though a state of emergency is not the exception but the norm in society, these areas are not presented in a linear way.[13] Instead, they are brought together as "moments of danger," which were woven indeed, but through precarious, tense threads.[14] Legitimized by the scientific impulse of the doctors and under the approval of the state, each one of these areas generated contested relationships, which in turn, created an unstable, highly dynamic, context. I have called this context the murky waters of state formation. In decrepit, humid colonial buildings, doctors and women faced each other, becoming each other's twisted mirror. They proposed and eventually shaped a code of sexual behavior in permanent contestation. This was not the case of two discourses that, already formed, opposed each other, but the slippery case of the deployment of local strategies of power in the very immediacy of contact. Antagonism, ambivalence, and negotiation characterized this process; in short, struggle and paradox. Keep in mind that, as the incorporation of syphilis-related health crimes into penal codes was ephemeral, this is above all the contorted story of a state failure.

Regulating Deviant Bodies

The first Reglamento de Prostitución en México was issued in 1867 in the midst of vehement debate.[15] Written by physician Manuel Alfaro under the administration of José Baez, it attempted to prevent the spread of syphilis and other venereal diseases by demanding that prostitutes enroll in a public registry, pay monthly fees to exercise their trade in a legal manner, and undergo weekly medical examinations. To ensure efficiency, the authorities concomitantly established the Sanitary Police and, a year later, they turned the Morelos hospital into an institution solely devoted to the care of syphilitic women.[16] Together, the Reglamento, the Sanitary Police, and the Morelos hospital constituted the basis of an emerging regulatory system in Mexico.[17] Shortly thereafter, prostitutes' disregard for the law provoked even greater legislation. In 1871, illegal prostitution gave rise to a new regulation. Significantly, it accompanied a rapid succession of ordinances designed to bring order to public life in Mexico City.[18] Legislators further modified the regulation in 1898, 1913, 1914, and again in 1926, when red-

(handwritten margin note: closer to Buenos Aires's reglamento than PR's)

light districts became legally condoned.[19] In 1935, however, Mexico opted *almost the same time as Argentina* for an abolitionist policy and declared prostitution officially illegal.

As in Argentina, public health concerns played a pivotal role in the issuing of the regulation of prostitution.[20] Critics of the regulatory system claimed that official toleration of prostitution could only increase the already alarming growth of syphilis and other venereal diseases among the Mexican population. Like many other nineteenth-century doctors, they believed syphilis to be a biological condition as well as a bodily sign of a moral weakness.[21] This moral defect came to be associated with the overt display of sexuality by prostitutes. Instead of regulation, therefore, they favored prosecution of prostitutes. Prostitution, in their opinion, was a crime against public health.[22] Supporters of the regulation, nevertheless, used similar claims to promote social tolerance of prostitution. Voicing sanitary concerns, physicians and lawyers successfully urged the state to protect the good elements of society from health and moral contagion by creating a stringent system of bureaucratic vigilance to supervise the diseased bodies of the prostitutes.[23] Both parties, however, shared the hygienists' eugenic view that syphilis was a major factor in the degeneration of the race, and hence a direct threat not just to public health but, by extension, to progress and national development — an idea that infused public health policies with a sense of true urgency.[24]

Dr. Manuel Alfaro, a recognized surgeon and the intellectual father of the regulation, soon became a major moral crusader against prostitution and its pernicious effects. He brought not only his medical knowledge to the field but also an insistence on creating an objective analytical system to study, and thus combat, this social problem. Combining statistical data, firsthand interviews with public women, and numerous international studies on the topic, he set up the basis for the creation of prostitution as a social category, a fixed identity in the realm of sexuality in Mexico. Thus, under Alfaro's influence, the 1867 regulation divided prostitutes into two categories: *putas públicas,* who lived in a house of prostitution or bordello; and *putas aisladas,* who used a hotel or lodging house *(casa de paso)* to perform their trade. Further ranking included the classification of prostitutes according to the status of their clientele, the geographic location of their workplaces, and the fees they charged. The *matrona* or woman in charge of the bordello paid monthly fees for each pupil: eight, five, and three pesos for prostitutes of first, second, and third class, respectively. The isolated ones paid enrollment fees of ten, five, and two pesos, depending on their corresponding class. The regulatory system rested, thus, on the prostitutes' earning power.

The most important enforcement agent of the regulatory system was the Inspección de Sanidad, a novel medical and administrative public health organization initially under the direct responsibility of the government of the Federal District and, since 1872, under the auspices of the Superior Sanitary Council. As a medical institution, it was associated with state dispensaries and the Morelos hospital itself, where licensed physicians performed physical examinations of prostitutes. In the administrative office, police agents were in charge of enrolling prostitutes, issuing licenses to bordellos and lodging houses, and managing the financial aspects of prostitution. Thus, by the late nineteenth century, both physicians and police agents emerged as powerful players in examining, identifying, and controlling sexual commerce in the capital city.

According to the regulation, the making of a prostitute began at the registration office where she showed up voluntarily, underwent a medical examination, and, if found in good health, received a *libreta* (booklet) containing her picture, name, medical certification, enrollment fee, and official number. When ill, she was transferred to the facilities of the Morelos hospital as a *detenida* (sequestered person), as public health officials termed it, until she recovered. Thereafter, all prostitutes were expected to undergo weekly medical examinations in state establishments. This rosy description of the regulatory system, however, was hardly the norm. Statistical information showed that, contrary to official expectations, prostitute enrollment did not increase after 1867.[25] Whereas 311 women enrolled in that year, only 203 did the same by the end of 1872. The ominous decay of the regulatory system was even clearer in the rapidly decreasing number of women sequestered at the Morelos hospital. For example, 12,496 prostitutes received forced medical attention in 1871; two years later only 63 women received medical care at the institution.

Authors have explained the failure of the regulatory system in terms of its foreign origins, alleging that such system did not correspond to the national reality of the country, but little attention has been paid to the role of prostitutes themselves in the breakdown of the system.[26] A closer look at local conditions, intertwined with the willingness to accept prostitutes' social agency, reveals a much more contested reality. The regulation itself reflected this fact. The 1871 regulation of prostitution incorporated a concept heretofore unknown: the *insometida*. A term bearing strong connotations of power, the "nonsubmissive" woman was described in article 31 as a prostitute who eluded the vigilance of the police and was not enrolled in the registry books.[27] Although it was clear that the illegal prostitute did not submit to the dictates of the law, her power did not lie in open opposition but on her capacity of elusion. Betraying increasing frustration, officials insistently spoke of the insometida's "indefinite position" and "enigmatic situation" in the regulatory system. Beyond the legal sphere, the insometida's ambiguity proved difficult at a more practical level. For example, as police agents were forced to trust their "practical eye" to identify prostitutes, the insometida's talent for disguise often fooled the representatives of the law. Furthermore, confusion too led to the imprisonment of housewives or decent women in more than one occasion, unleashing public outcry against the Sanitary Police.[28] An uneasy element in the regulatory scheme, the illegal prostitute challenged the law enforcement agency's methods. In fact, prostitutes' escalating refusal to enroll in the offices of public health successfully undercut the very foundation of the regulatory system. By 1873, lack of revenues forced employees to go five consecutive months without pay.[29] The insometida thus became a crucial piece in a complex underground reality that also involved unlicensed bordellos, physicians performing medical examinations in public houses, police agents condoning streetwalkers through bribes, and constant rivalry between Federal District authorities and members of the Superior Sanitation Council. As a physician put it in 1882, vice was indeed regulated in Mexico, but in a distinctive Mexican style in which "unfortunately everything has been total anarchy up to this time."[30]

Shifting images of prostitutes also proved to be an obstacle for social and gender classification in modernizing Mexico. Indeed, debates around the regulation of prostitution contributed to identify and fix negative aspects of womanhood. Concomitantly, the Porfirian cult of female domesticity grew into a full body of accepted ideas.[31] Yet, well-defined profiles of "good" and "wicked" women constructed by health bureaucrats, doctors, and intellectuals did not reflect reality. Instead, plagued by anxiety in a rapidly changing environment, they attempted to author it. For one thing, images of prostitutes were less rigid and more diverse than members of the Porfirian elite were able or willing to acknowledge. The dominant ideology represented prostitutes as corrupted, lazy, and diseased. Yet, romantic and modernist poets combined rejection, compassion, and desire to exalt their sexuality and beauty, magnify their honesty in the midst of a hypocritical environment, and lament their destinies.[32] These ambivalent views of prostitution permeated the novel *Santa* — the first Mexican best-seller, in which the author, Federico Gamboa, used equal doses of horror and sympathy to describe the fall of a young girl to prostitution.[33] Although Santa was punished for her behavior at the end of the novel, the prostitute nevertheless remained holy, at least in name. In contrast, painter José Ruelas depicted a cruel and powerful prostitute whipping a pig in his painting *La Domadora*.[34] Sculptor José Contreras, to whom Gamboa dedicated *Santa*, marbled bodies of women in chains and other elaborated sadomasochistic postures. The *malgré-tout* won him an international award at the 1900 Paris exhibit.[35] Working-class publications, on the other hand, did away with the pretense of desire, denouncing prostitutes as greedy consumers.[36] Representations of prostitutes kept on multiplying, yet as the Sanitary Police created laws to regulate prostitution in Mexico, bureaucrats made greater efforts to confine their ever-expanding images. In fact, official reports of the late nineteenth century increasingly portrayed prostitutes as working women constrained by lack of education and skills.[37] This change in perspective did not result from more lenient views of prostitutes but from collection of data as well as careful analysis of statistical information. Public health doctors played a fundamental role in this process.

Whereas artists and editors approached the topic of prostitution through idealism or downright hostility, medical doctors sought to understand public women of Mexico City through scientific means. Based on a close analysis of five hundred files of Mexican prostitutes between 1868 and 1872, Manuel Alfaro established that most public women were young single individuals lacking family support. The ages of prostitutes ranged from twelve to forty-nine. Most (358) claimed to be orphans, while only 104 had one or both parents, whether alive or not. Almost all (457) were single and childless. The report also showed that, as supporters of female domesticity feared, most prostitutes had been active workers performing a variety of low-paid jobs in the city.[38] When it came to women, wage labor and vice were synonyms in Porfirian Mexico.[39] Yet, although poverty-related issues surfaced as causes of prostitution in almost half of the files, the rest used the concept of "proclivity" to explain the selection of this profession.[40] Furthermore, Alfaro confirmed that prostitutes were likely to suffer from sexual diseases, yet he also denounced former statistics as inaccurate at best. In his opinion, only 8 out of 86 infected prostitutes suffered from real syphilis in 1868. By 1872, only 31 out of 203 were recorded as truly syphilitics. Alfaro was careful in differentiating between signs of "real" syphilis and "noncontagious local lesions."[41] In the secular rendition of the prostitute, she was, above all, the victim of society. As the weakest of weak, the prostitute became dangerous indeed, and in need of correction.

Institutional reports, official statistics, art, literature, and newspaper articles of late nineteenth-century Mexico all but multiplied the images of the bodies of prostitutes in the mirror of society. Diseased indeed, defiant but also victimized, aggressive and alluring, the prostitute emerged again and again wrapped in contrasting meanings. It is clear that as physicians and police agents struggled to inscribe their bodies into the law, they invariably met the challenge of a slippery reality, which escaped, if not directly confronted, their well-defined profiles. As a normative structure, the regulations of prostitution in Mexico did not face, as in England, the opposition of organized sectors of society.[42] Yet, Mexican prostitutes' disregard for the law ultimately limited the effectiveness of the regulatory system. The puzzle lacked the most important piece: a regulation of prostitution without the consent of prostitutes did not make social or financial sense. Soon *clandestinaje* became the rule of an underground economy of sexual commerce. Legal initiatives, however, constituted just one of the various strategies modernizers used to fix prostitution as a stable identity and to control its practice. The professionalization of gynecology and the emergence of an incipient sexual science provided further legitimate tools to dissect and regulate female bodies.

The Informers: Creating a Sexual Science

"As incredible as it may appear," wrote an anonymous editor of the magazine *La Escuela de Medicina* in 1892, "it is a fact that there are no real data on the moral and physical conditions of the female constitution."[43] By the late nineteenth century, however, Mexican doctors' use and discussion of findings of European sexual science indicated increasing interest in the production of scientific knowledge of the female sex.[44] This was hardly an irrelevant task. Doctors considered that the health and beauty of women, the preservation of the family, the development of the country, and the survival of the Mexican nation depended on the scientific and moral knowledge of sex. In their minds, examining bodies and providing recommendations for their rightful use constituted the basis for the construction of a moral and modern Mexican society. First, however, medicine reclaimed the bodies of women as its own. Doctors, likewise, legitimized their role as bearers of a new field of expertise. The process included the slow decline of *parteras* (midwives) in the field of obstetrics, the ascending role of male gynecologists in the care of women's health, and the establishment of state institutions in which doctors had access to women's bodies.

Before the nineteenth century, obstetrics monopolized the production of knowledge of the female body.[45] Obstetrics, however, did not constitute a science, but rather an art in which traditional expertise and direct hands-on experience of women without formal training combined to secure the reproduction of the human species. Although it covered a wide variety of health-related topics — fertility, menstruation, the health of children — its locus was reproduction, not sex. Usually older women, often widows of Indian or mestizo origins, Mexican midwives amassed a complex knowledge of techniques, home remedies, and folk cures to maintain the well-being of both mother and child. Although the role of parteras remained unrivaled well into the nineteenth century, public health regulations challenged their position as early as 1750 when the Real Tribunal del Protomedicato issued rules and prescribed examinations to define the medical role of the midwife.[46] The ascending role of male obstetricians reinforced this process. In 1833, doctors began teaching classes on obstetrics at the Institute of Medical Sciences and, later, in 1842, the School of Medicine formally included courses on this topic in its general curricula.[47] By the late 1870s, doctor José María Rodríguez, a full-time professor at the School of Medicine and the father of Mexican obstetrics, was able to claim that unlike other medical fields, Mexican obstetrics had nothing to envy of European science.[48] Academic obstetricians of the late nineteenth century, however, lacked the practical expertise and the clientele parteras enjoyed. To counter this situation, the School of Medicine established a close connection with the *Hospital de Maternidad e Infancia,* a health institution under the auspices of the Public Welfare System especially devoted to the care of poor women in childbirth and abandoned children.[49] Under the direction of José María Rodríguez, this novel didactic practice proved relevant for the experimentation with new techniques as well as for the legitimization of obstetrics in the medical establishment. Physicians not only welcomed and prized scientific merits of these practices, but also elaborated on the valuable assistance they offered to women of the lower classes otherwise left to the dubious devices of parteras. Yet, public opinion was not as favorable:

> The purpose of the House of Maternity is to offer shelter to women about to become mothers . . . the wife of the wretched artisan . . . the young unwed woman who comes here looking for a place to hide her shame . . . the honest housewife. All of them are now the object of study and the victims of examinations that science might perhaps justify but that women's modesty forbids even in thought. What right does the municipal government have to humiliate these women who are only looking for assistance?[50]

Although the intervention of male doctors in women's bodies met criticism, articles and academic theses on female sexuality grew steadily. Doctors interested in elucidating the physical and moral conditions of the female constitution, however, had to find alternative venues of exploration. The bodies of prostitutes sequestered at the Morelos hospital proved fertile ground for the development of the medicine of women and modern technologies of sex in Mexico. Prostitutes became informers.

On July 12, 1868, a municipal ordinance transformed the San Juan de Dios hospital into an institution devoted solely to the care of indigent women, mostly prostitutes, infected with venereal disease and syphilis. Still under the supervision of a religious order until 1874, the staff lacked medical training, treatments were empirical and, as the creation of a Department of Reformation showed, emphasis was placed on the moral correction of women deemed as sexually deviant. In 1875, nevertheless, physicians took over the administrative and medical control of the establishment now under a secular name: the Morelos Hospital. Under the auspices of the Public Welfare System and as a medical branch of the Sanitary Police, this institution welcomed female syphilitic patients who, as late as 1868, had been assisted at the San Andrés hospital. Public health authorities considered that the "character and habits" of these particular female patients required both medical treatment and disciplinary measures in an all-female environment.[51] To ensure rapid and efficient communication between doctors and police agents, the offices of the Sanitary Police were installed in the same building. In fact, the relationship between the Sanitary Police and the Morelos hospital was "so intimate" that, according to the superintendent of the hospital, they constituted a single institution whose activities paralleled those of "a judge who rules and consigns the offender, and the jail to which the offender is consigned."[52] When riots erupted in 1870, the municipal government provided the institution with police surveillance.[53] The Morelos hospital was indeed as much a jail as a hospital. Both medicine and policing marked the origins of the institution.

The rules governing the Morelos hospital clearly specified the administrative procedures and the codes of behavior expected in its midst.[54] Emphasis on the obedience, cleanliness, and decency of the patients served as basis for the authority of both doctors and health authorities. Freedom of movement within the hospital was restricted. Visits among patients, walks in the hallways, and the possibility of performing work for the hospital required official permits signed by physicians. Neither destitute patients nor prostitutes were allowed to leave the hospital without the previous written consent of a doctor. Punishments for disorderly behavior included isolation and expulsion, depending on the offense. As sequestered patients, however, prostitutes could not be expelled.

Public health doctors discarded empirical methods of cure at the Morelos hospital. They implemented therapeutic techniques used in Europe, such as the administration of mercury shots. Although neither a definite cure nor effective treatments for syphilis or venereal disease existed at the end of the nineteenth century, the Morelos hospital underwent important administrative and medical reforms during this period. Under the leadership of Amaro Gazano, greater emphasis on cleanliness, discipline, and order led to the creation of four isolation rooms especially designed for unruly women. Using newly allocated funds, Dr. Gazano also created an operating room. Meanwhile, outstanding physicians practiced at the Morelos hospital and, accordingly, ties with the Faculty of Medicine grew stronger. Dr. Manuel Carmona, for example, was at once a regular practitioner at the hospital and the president of the school. Nicolás San Juan and Manuel Gutiérrez, both gynecologists of widespread reputation, practiced there on a regular basis. The medical reputation of the Morelos hospital further increased under the administration of Ramón Macías from 1879 to 1911. First, the introduction of surgical gynecology transformed the treatment of diseased women and attracted the attention of various specialists. Second, because Dr. Macías used the hospital facilities to teach surgery, the educational character of the institution was reinforced. By 1879, doctors claimed that, although the Morelos hospital was formally devoted to the care of syphilis and venereal disease, it was now a modern full-service hospital of gynecology. As surgical therapy grew increasingly popular among physicians working at this institution, claims of its gynecological nature were upheld. During 1898–1899, doctors performed 59 major surgeries resulting in 49 cures and 10 deaths. Doctors also performed 212 minor surgeries, 206 with successful results. The high rate of success fostered the optimistic outlook of gynecologists of the era.[55]

By 1912, under the leadership of Dr. Carlos Zavala, the hospital developed new programs even in the midst of profound social mobilizations linked to the 1910 Mexican revolution. Zavala ordered the staff to uproot trees that obstructed sunlight and caused humidity. He also improved the operating room, introduced the use of Salvarsan to cure syphilis, and established a new maternity room where professors of the Faculty of Medicine taught classes on obstetrics. Isolation rooms became sewing workshops in an effort to reform the morals of the patients by providing training and financial support. For the common people of late nineteenth-century Mexico, however, most of the advancements in the field of gynecology achieved at the Morelos hospital went unnoticed. In fact, public opinion grew increasingly critical of the medical treatments and the prevailing conditions of life at the Morelos hospital. Rumors of disorder and immorality slipped through broken windows and feeble fences. Dangers lurked inside the institution and reached the public through the newspapers.

Perceiving female syphilitics only as objects of study, Mexican doctors failed to portray the tense environment in which they worked. As health authorities carried out regular inspections, official reports indicated that the seeming peace of the Morelos hospital was altogether fictional. Sequestered women seldom applauded the scientific enterprise taking place in their bodies and, instead, rebelled against the medical and disciplinary rules that governed the institution. Riots erupted.[56] Prostitutes called them *pronunciamientos,* which literally translated as declarations of war. Indeed, an ongoing state of siege, a state of permanent emergency, characterized the daily routine of the hospital, an intimate war. In addition to violent outbreaks, women at Morelos hospital resisted through massive escapes. Members of the Mexican press, sensing fertile ground for sensational news, promptly showed up.[57] They reported that the patients' loose morals in conjunction with forced confinement were but an explosion waiting to happen. In terms of the magnitude of the conflict, they were right.

Critical views of the Morelos hospital not only originated from within. Conservative sectors of Mexican society deeply resented the fact that prostitutes benefited from the support of the welfare system when they were not indigent citizens in a strict sense.[58] In 1914, Querido Moheno demanded in the House of Representatives the abolition of funds devoted to both the Sanitary Police and the Morelos hospital.[59] He claimed that the regulatory system was a complete failure and that the medical examinations performed at the hospital involved a violation to the inherent modesty of women. He cried out that the regulation was "a *carabina de Ambrosio*," meaning that it was useless and senseless. His demand was unanimously granted. Facing mounting threats from within and without, the hospital reverted to control by a Catholic organization during the revolutionary upheaval. Shortly thereafter, the hospital grounds were used to take care of those wounded in battle. In 1915, new legislation enabled the hospital to reopen with its original program, and so it remained until 1925.

Backed up by academic degrees and invested with the highest moral roles in society, physicians gained increasing access into the heretofore veiled world of female sexuality through institutions of public health administered by the state. Not only gynecologists but also hygienist doctors involved in legal medicine displayed greater concern for the female genitalia and their repercussions in society at large. In fact, the topic was so popular among students of the School of Medicine that a growing number devoted their theses to women's hygiene. In 1903, Manuel Guillén defended a thesis titled "Some reflections about the hygiene of the woman during her puberty" before a committee of the Faculty of Medicine — a text that largely reflected the concerns with female sexuality that characterized the Porfirian era.[60] Further narrowing the scope of his research, Guillén maintained that his study focused on

> women's genital organs, for in them take place the capital phenomena of the female life, which in turn have great influence on their health. Female nervous predispositions are intimately linked to their genital life. In it we can find satisfactory explanations for the numerous pathological, physical and psychological phenomena we observe in women.[61]

Linking the female genitalia to a well-prescribed reproductive destiny was hardly a new proposition at the turn of the century. Establishing a clear connection between the genital life of women and their "pathological, physical and psychological phenomena" represented, however, a further twist in an interpretative scheme fundamentally introducing the category of sex. When Guillén stated that "the ovary and the uterus are centers of actions that reflect [women's] brains, which determine fearsome illnesses and passions heretofore unknown," the female genitalia had become an altogether modern cultural locus: it became sex.[62]

Authors of these studies freely appropriated theoretical and factual information found in European medical magazines, yet Mexican doctors also tried to gather data in local bodies. Prostitutes, again, proved instrumental in the production and dissemination of sexual knowledge in Mexico. Perhaps the most systematic attempt in this regard was a statistical analysis of hymens of Mexican women, a study presented as an achievement of science at the International Fair of Paris.[63] Further literature on the female constitution included analyses of the pollutions of women, which became the subject of various articles in a medical magazine throughout 1889.[64] Physicians examined women of diverse ages whose symptoms included abundant discharges provoked by erotic dreams. The complaints of young girls and widows, but especially the generous information of prostitutes, led doctors to believe that such phenomena were not only common but also natural experiences among women. Meanwhile, in the facilities of mental health institutions, the San Hipólito and Divino Salvador hospitals until 1910 and the General Insane Asylum afterward, psychiatrists often diagnosed women of alleged loose morals with "moral insanity," a mental disorder they believed to be fundamentally linked to abnormal sexual behaviors.[65] Noted criminologists, such as Carlos Roumagnac, also placed emphasis on the sexual roots of deviant behavior.[66] Julio Guerrero's analysis of crime in Mexico, which he called a study in social psychiatry, also highlighted diverse forms of class-related sexual patterns.[67] Hardly surprisingly, he allocated greater degrees of sexual constraint to the upper classes. Among the very poor, women were especially prone to promiscuity and, consequently, to abortions.

Porfirian sexual knowledge was not limited to the academy. In 1889, acting as consultants in the case of a woman who accused her husband of sexual abuse in the form of forced anal sex, physicians F. Pulido and I. Fernández Ortigosa developed a classification of normal and, by extension, abnormal sexual acts at the request of the judge.[68] In what was a blueprint for a cartography of perversity in Mexico, they defined normal copulation as a sexual act taking place between two individuals of different sex, using the organs created by nature to propagate the species. A chart of unnatural acts included pederasty, defined as anal copulation performed by individuals regardless of their sex; sodomy, understood as copulation with irrational beings, namely animals, and also including the use of condoms; and oral sex performed on men, allegedly widespread in Mexico. Additional abnormal acts included oral sex performed on women, masturbation, and lesbianism. After careful physical examination and legal deliberation on the case that brought about the above description, physicians and lawyers alike decided that the wounds found on the plaintiff's body were not life-threatening and, since the alleged sexual abuse had taken place within the home and without witnesses, the husband was left unpunished — a decision that affirmed husband's rights over the interest to censure the "abnormal." As judges evoked the expertise of doctors practicing legal medicine in cases of crimes against decency, statutory rape, and elopement, medical sexual knowledge transcended the realm of scientific inquiry to become a legitimate and powerful tool in defining normality in matters of sexual behavior. By the late nineteenth century, Mexican doctors had achieved growing ascendance in both the private and public spheres of human sexuality.

The production of sexual knowledge in Mexico, however, was not obstacle-free. On the one hand, claims of the inherent modesty of the female constitution limited the practice of obstetricians and gynecologists among mainstream women. On the other hand, doctors practicing at the facilities of the Morelos hospital frequently met with internal resistance — what prostitutes called pronunciamientos and health authorities termed as mutinies, insurrections, strikes, and escapes. The terminology, far more appropriate for war than medicine, strikingly reflected the tension that permeated the grounds of the hospital. Even better, this language illuminated the dynamics of power relations at play between physicians and prostitutes. In the midst of social dislocation and growing discontent in the Mexican countryside, the Morelos hospital came to be the site of a more veiled but equally intense social war. Sequestered female syphilitic patients successfully appropriated the language of insurrection. Doctors and health authorities clearly understood it. As members of a "common material and meaningful framework" they used fathomable tools, albeit for different purposes.

Because stays at the hospital were usually lengthy, opportunities for unrest and rebellion abounded. Spontaneous or organized, rebellious acts hindered the good reputations of the institution, disturbed medical procedures, and affected the finances of the hospital.[69] Riots erupted for a variety of reasons, yet shortages of food and unwarranted changes in hospital routine stand out as major causes.[70] Equally relevant were prostitutes' complaints against forced separation from their children while in confinement.[71] Although authorities often stated that reckless behavior responded to bad examples, specifically the making of a handful of subversive patients, they also noticed that women promptly reacted to restricted access to milk or rigid enforcement of disciplinary measures. Faulty diets had been customary at the hospital, but during the early twentieth century prostitutes took this as rightful grounds for protest. Superintendents, however, called it a pretext. The 1910 Mexican revolution indeed affected the normal life of Mexico City and the regular functioning of the Morelos hospital. Although the cessation of funding in 1914 accounted for the lack of records for this period, documents from 1915 onward registered ascending unrest among sequestered prostitutes.[72]

Public defiance of government policies by women followed a regular pattern. After the customary destruction of medical equipment and furniture, women engaged in collective fights with nurses, clerks, and policemen alike. Then they jumped out of windows, taking with them sheets, blankets, and any other potentially useful garments. Meanwhile, prostitutes used profanities generously—a feat that further marked them as indecent women. Authorities did not remain inert. Measures taken to discipline subversive patients included long periods of isolation and restricted diet. Also, unruly prostitutes were deprived of their clothes and left naked on their beds for days at a time. This procedure was called *encamar* (literally, to put in bed). The most effective measure consisted of cutting off their hair.[73] More often than not, organized riots were followed by massive escapes, which constituted, by far, prostitutes' most common form of defiance. Although attempts to escape had been numerous since the onset of the hospital in 1868, reports from the early twentieth century indicate that the number of successful escapes and accompanying violence had increased. In 1919 alone, two major breakouts totaling 94 prostitutes, and several minor escapes involving 11, rendered 103 prostitutes free from forced sequestration.[74] In the midst of constant disorder, hospital authorities requested the installation of iron bars on the windows of the building, the construction of an iron fence at the entrance of the institution, and increased police surveillance.[75] The Morelos hospital thus resembled a prison more than ever.

Policies of public health encouraged and legitimized scientific research and experimentation on the bodies of prostitutes in order to detect, prevent, and control the spread of venereal disease and syphilis. Significantly, as prostitutes reacted by staging declarations of war, it was clear that both physicians and diseased women were involved in a contested relationship as they collectively, even violently, defined the territory of the modern body, the modern spectrum of sexuality. It was precisely in this territory that the health crime took shape.

Crime, Disease, and the Nation-State

The sexual nature of syphilis left imprints of shame and sin on the bodies of men and women. Popularity known as *avería,* and generally identified as a secret disease, syphilis became nonetheless a popular topic of analysis in medical journals and newspapers in Porfirian Mexico. As early as 1879, international studies indicated that rates of syphilis were especially high in Mexico among European and indigenous peoples alike.[76] Likewise, in 1903, Mexican experts identified syphilis along with tuberculosis, typhus, hepatitis, alcoholism, and pneumonia as the seven most fatal conditions affecting the poor inhabitants of Mexico City.[77] Yet, data gathered by Alberto Pani regarding the causes of death in Mexico during the period 1904–1912 indicated that tuberculosis, pneumonia, typhus, cholera, smallpox, and even alcoholism triggered far more deaths than syphilis itself.[78] Despite this statistical information, however, medical and moral concerns about syphilis grew in the Porfirian era. Fundamentally associated with the diseased body of the prostitute, discussions concerning syphilis provided the state an opportunity to scrutinize, identify, and eventually regulate human bodies.

Discussion of state-funded programs to prevent the spread of syphilis at a national level did not start until 1918. Protected by the 1917 Mexican constitution, which incorporated the right to health, the Department of Public Health acquired unprecedented powers in case of epidemics. Just as had happened among the members of the committee who wrote the draft for the 1918 "Prophilaxis of syphilis," conflicting interpretations regarding the right of the individual vis-à-vis the right of the state in matters of public health stalled the implementation of national programs. Questions abounded. "Should physicians violate their professional right to confidentiality in the name of the right of the community? Would that imply a violation of the constitutional rights granted to all individuals?"[79] Furthermore, "Could technical measures involved in the control of contagious diseases become principles of the law? Could an administrative unit act in a compulsory manner to impose a prophylactic system upon the population?"[80] The answers to these questions came about slowly. Medical research and further discussion on the regulation of prostitution in postrevolutionary Mexico played instrumental roles in the transformation of syphilis from a moral, private defect into a health crime of national proportions.

Public health doctors skillfully used medical statistics to legitimize the implementation of state-led campaigns to prevent the spread of syphilis. According to doctor Bernardo Gastélum, the percentage of syphilis-related deaths rose from less than one percent in 1916 to almost two percent of all deaths in 1925.[81] Simultaneously, alarming news from the revolutionary fronts seemed to confirm that, like prostitutes in the city, *soldaderas* participating in the popular armies were major propagators of disease.[82] From the perspective of social medicine and the rights of the community, this growth justified the prosecution and eventual punishment of the syphilitic body. Note that, as with biological concepts of disease, therapeutic methods often mystify social relations. National crusades against syphilis appeared natural, but they were hardly so. After all, widespread use of penicillin had led to the manufacture of Salvarsan, a cure that had been introduced in Mexican state dispensaries as early as 1914, often with successful results.[83] Nevertheless, health authorities and doctors purposefully fostered the sense of inevitability around the dictates of social medicine. Although it is true that state-led health campaigns allowed doctors to play powerful roles in postrevolutionary Mexico, it is equally relevant that such roles came wrapped in significant meanings: benevolence, human concern and, in short, justice. As explorers of sexuality, as reshapers of human conduct, doctors presented themselves as secular saints. They needed to make a strong case of their own. They did. Yet, as sound as these arguments might have been from the medical perspective, they could not have made syphilis into a crime without further reforms of the regulatory system of prostitution in Mexico.

Growing public outcry against the Sanitary Police led to considerable reforms of the regulation of prostitution in 1898, 1913, 1914, and, finally, 1926. During these years, the discourse on prostitution became increasingly intertwined with public health concerns and questions of social order. Although moral terminologies continued to be present, they were slightly displaced. Better said, they no longer were limited to private but also reached public behavior. The nation was at stake. In fact, reformed regulations openly acknowledged that, as a state institution, the goal of the Sanitary Police was not to tolerate or even regulate prostitution per se but, more importantly, to control those diseases associated with the sexual commerce of prostitutes.

Public health concerns, likewise, led to the reform of the Sanitary Police, the enforcing agent of the regulation of prostitution. Physicians and health authorities alike maintained that examining and supervising the bodies of prostitutes provided the basis for the construction of a healthy society. Furthermore, if prostitutes were to participate in that society, they could not dispose of their bodies at will. According to the head of the Sanitary Police,

> Individuals have no right to live in society unless they are useful, or at least non-threatening to the community. If diseased individuals, dangerous for the public health, do not willingly segregate themselves from social life, then it is the duty of the authority to isolate them. The health of the homeland and humankind alike is far more important than the freedom of a handful of individuals.[84]

Accepting charges of immorality and misconduct, the head of the Sanitary Police proceeded to hire new personnel and scrutinized the moral background of potential police agents. In addition, he installed a new dispensary furnished with modern equipment, adding rooms and bathrooms especially designed for syphilitic prostitutes. In order to promote genital hygiene among public women, he also inaugurated a "beautiful" wax museum where doctors gave didactic talks on hygiene.[85] Yet, wrongdoings associated with the Sanitary Police kept on leaking to the press. In what amounted to be "yet another typical little scandal," a journalist reported the violent apprehension of an honest housewife, whom a police agent mistook for a runaway prostitute.[86] Although the head of the Sanitary Police promptly sent a letter to the newspaper to clarify the facts — the woman in question was, according to official records, a prostitute — his note was not published. The headline was illustrative enough: *acusan de secuestro a un inspector de sanidad* (health inspector accused of kidnapping). Stronger public health measures ensued.

Responding to both the isolationist perspectives of public health authorities and legal prostitutes' demand for a safe area in which to exercise their trade, the 1926 regulation of prostitution introduced the basis for the formation of *zonas de tolerancia* (red-light districts) in Mexico City.[87] All parties involved — authorities, physicians, police agents, bordello owners, and even prostitutes themselves—initially greeted this project with approval, albeit for different reasons. Health authorities presented this initiative as an effective means to combat growing disorder on the streets as well as harmful dissemination of moral and biological viruses throughout society. Police agents favored the geographic concentration of bordellos and lodging houses because it facilitated their work. Doctors supported the formation of red-light districts because they allowed greater control of syphilis and venereal diseases. Bordello owners, in open competition with illegal prostitution, embraced this measure in an effort to protect their profits. Lastly, legal prostitutes, for whom streets had become increasingly unsafe, also welcomed this project. In fact, in letters sent directly to the president, they repeatedly demanded the creation of red-light districts, which they perceived as a means to safeguard their trade and fight the competition of illegal prostitution.[88] By placing themselves under the protection of the law, they demanded respect for rights accorded to all Mexican citizens. However, although evidence of consensus abounded, the implementation of red-light districts was an altogether different story. By 1929, in spite of ongoing general agreement, the parties involved were unable to reach a compromise as to where and how to establish the zonas de tolerancia.

The 1926 regulation clearly specified that the red-light district was to be located as far as possible from residential areas, preferably on the outskirts of the city. Prostitution, however, already occupied vast sectors of downtown Mexico City. Entire neighborhoods around the historical district, such as the Cuauhtemotzin and Santa María la Redonda, were known for their booming prostitution business. Attempts to relocate de facto red-light districts met with widespread and vehement opposition. On one hand, prostitutes alleged that any removal would affect them economically, for customers were already acquainted with prevailing areas of sexual commerce. On the other hand, residents of potential sites for official red-light districts resented the damaging moral consequences of sharing their urban space with prostitutes. Facing mounting protests, the committee in charge had no alternative but to accept existing zonas de tolerancia, adding only stronger measures such as blocking traffic in specific streets and requiring specialized police surveillance.[89] In fact, in a frankly defensive move, they suggested the relocation of schools out of existing red-light districts, adding a critical comment here and there about unwitting urban planners. The sound defeat of public health authorities was all too evident. The debate, however, continued.

Especially vocal in this regard was a civil association of the Cuauhtemotzin district, an organization including factory and property owners as well as workers. In a temperate letter addressed to the head of the Department of Public Health, they denounced the material and moral effects of prostitution in the area, demanding its immediate relocation. "Our proposal is intimately linked to the ever-so-important effort to improve the city, which is an integral goal of the committee to promote tourism."[90] By 1929, it had become increasingly clear that health authorities were in no position to fulfill their demand. Significant sections of the Cuauhtemotzin and the Santa María la Ribera districts became officially condoned as red-light districts.[91] In this way, rather than impose isolationist measures, the state was forced to adapt existing demarcations established by the prostitutes themselves.

In evaluating the project for the 1926 regulation of prostitution, furthermore, official observers noted that measures of control had only triggered illegal prostitution. For this reason, they proposed a greater *liberalidad,* understood as the creation of an environment of "more reserve, less formality, and less pressure."[92] The recommendations included the establishment of centers of hygienic care especially devoted to women who either exclusively or partially lived off sexual commerce; the substitution of male police agents by female ones in areas of prostitution; and granting all women the right to seek medical assistance in private hospitals and institutions other than the Morelos hospital. In financial terms, and questioning the morality of a regulatory system that overtly disapproved of prostitution while economically benefiting from it, they also supported the abolition of membership fees and fines for prostitutes, bordellos, and lodgings. The very foundation of the regulatory system was under siege.

In trying to detect what could be realistically done in terms of regulation, critical observers evaluating the 1926 document also questioned and attempted to redefine the social identity of the prostitute. Former regulations described the prostitute as a "woman who had sexual intercourse with more than one man, either for lucrative purposes or to satisfy a vice." This interpretation, the head of the Sanitary Police argued in 1928, ostensibly interfered with the private sexuality of women, an area better left to the judgment of the individual and not to the state. The regulation could indeed elaborate on moral matters, but only when behaviors affected the well-being of the community. A more refined version thus read: "A prostitute is a woman who engages in sexual intercourse with various men for lucrative purposes. A woman who, even without lucrative purposes in mind, engages in sexual intercourse with various men will also be considered a prostitute only if her overt and frequent behavior constitutes a danger for public health and public morality."[93]

Faced with continuous and relentless pressure, the regulations of prostitution, even when reformed, stood on shaky ground. By the late 1920s, authorities previously confident in the regulatory system's ability to control prostitutes increasingly found "liberal" perspectives more appealing. Ongoing battles for the definition of urban space in conjunction with mounting critical views of the Sanitary Police in national newspapers opened the door for groups supporting an abolitionist policy.[94] It was at this precise moment, on this tense ground, that projects of syphilis prevention became powerful markers in public health policies. As the regulatory impulse crumbled before frustrated eyes, representatives of the state attempted to reassemble the fallen pieces. In trying to gain the upper hand in this process, public health doctors designed national campaigns against syphilis. Rather than objective state initiatives, these health crusades came as a response to growing displays of local power in which prostitutes played active roles.

During the 1920s public health concerns were rearticulated within the larger ideological framework of the Mexican revolution. Based on the right to health included in the 1917 constitution, public health authorities strategically combined notions of economic development with programs of social justice to legitimize the emergence of state-led campaigns to prevent epidemics, notably syphilis. The ascendance of the medicine of sex and the institutional infrastructure of the public welfare system proved instrumental in this process. The introduction of the *delitos de contagio sexual y nutricio* or *delitos de contaminación intersexual* in the 1929 penal code was, without a doubt, a sound victory for public health doctors and postrevolutionary social medicine. Punishment for those who knowingly infected human beings included one to six years in prison, and a fine of forty workdays. Those who unknowingly transmitted the disease paid fines of three to ten workdays. They were also responsible for treatment and additional damages inflicted on innocent victims. Physicians who did not warn their patients of the contagious nature of syphilis received, according to the law, fines of five to twenty work days for the first offense, and a double amount for the second. A third offense caused the suspension of their medical licenses for a year.

Although the overt goal of this penal code was to punish syphilitic bodies regardless of their sex, prostitutes promptly became the main target. During the early 1930s, letters from men all over the country arrived at the Department of Public Health publicly denouncing prostitutes for infecting them.[95] In the midst of a medical milieu that associated syphilis with unrestricted female sexuality, this twist did not come as a surprise. Of even more relevance was the fact that, through public accusations, the names, nicknames, geographic locations, and specific addresses of prostitutes became readily available to authorities willing to take legal action against them. In other words, empowered by penal legislation, men fulfilled roles previously played by agents of the Sanitary Police. And at no cost. The criminalization of the syphilitic body proved to be an alternative strategy to control the same prostitutes who had evaded the regulatory system. Among men, only infected soldiers received similar attention.[96] Authorities advised compulsory medical examinations in army barracks and imprisonment for infected soldiers. Concomitantly, physicians elaborated health guidelines for young men, which fundamentally included sexual abstinence and monogamous sexual relations within the sacred institution of marriage.

Although public health authorities and physicians presented sexual crimes and antisyphilitic campaigns as natural and irrevocable measures to protect society, they nevertheless constituted a well-selected strategy of power to deal with disease. For one thing, ever since the late nineteenth century medical science had demonstrated that venereal disease and syphilis were two distinctive conditions with varying degrees of mortality. Even Manuel Alfaro, the architect of the regulation of prostitution, differentiated between "real" syphilis and "noncontagious local infections." Postrevolutionary doctors in charge of prophylactic programs hardly mentioned this fact. Even when they did, they failed to discriminate and rank the associated health dangers. This silence was political. There was also the problem of Salvarsan. Mexican doctors were aware of its existence. For example, state dispensaries recommended the use of this medication and, on more than one occasion, infected men sent letters to the Department of Public Health asking for the miraculous cure. Public health authorities, however, opted for a more massive, interventionist undertaking. Again, this option came into being as the regulatory system fell to pieces. State concerns with public health legitimized increasing intervention of health authorities in the realm of sexuality. Better said, the exhaustive medical and social intervention in syphilitic bodies, which first emerged in the late nineteenth century, gave life to the realm of modern sexuality in postrevolutionary Mexico. Public health doctors strenuously fought to establish sexual normality and, likewise, to identify its pathologies. Through the bodies of prostitutes, doctors gave themselves titles of expertise in such areas as gynecology and obstetrics, which they later used to support codes of sexual behavior tailored to the needs of the modern nuclear family. To be clear, public health recommendations in sexual matters primarily included sexual abstinence before marriage, and strict monogamy afterward. The scientific status of their professions and the ideological reach of social medicine contributed artifice, to concealing contested social relations, by presenting sexual guidelines as natural creations. When sixty-eight years of regulatory impulse came to an end in 1935, national programs to prevent syphilis replaced it. The "abolition" of prostitution triumphed. After all, as Dr. Bernardo Gastélum succinctly put it, in a world without syphilis, prostitutes would become workers and, more importantly, what they "previously did for money, would then do for love."[97]

The Sexual Subject: Power and Fragility

The syphilitic body became a criminal construct in 1929 when the domain of sexuality was inscribed in the larger framework of public health. As it had been during the Porfirian era, syphilis became a fertile avenue for the analysis and identification of sexual behaviors. Social spaces medically designed for sexual normalcy and sexual deviancy came into existence. In the postrevolutionary era, furthermore, the findings of the medicine of sex and the extensive legislative and administrative structure of hospitals and state dispensaries proved instrumental in the enactment of the construct "crimes of sexual contamination." Social constructs of sexual normality and sexual deviancy were now incorporated into normalizing legal and medical practices and institutions. Strategies of power transversing the syphilitic body thus resulted in the emergence of a new, specifically modern domain of sexuality in which sexual identities grew increasingly fixed. In this domain took place the feminization of syphilis. In this domain also took place the feminization of the sexual subject.[98]

The dangerous bodies of prostitutes became bodies of knowledge in the field of sexual science in Mexico. During the late nineteenth century, scientific research about sex began as an inquiry into the "female question." Physicians fought a relentless war to have access to women's bodies in order to become gynecologists, obstetricians, and experts in sexual matters. They achieved this goal in public welfare institutions, notably the Morelos hospital, in which indigent women and prostitutes affected by syphilis received medical care. Thus public women's ailments and symptoms gave rise to a new scientific field. From its very origins, then, the field of sexuality in Mexico was unequivocally the field of feminine sexuality. The social effects of this scheme were twofold. On one hand, the production of knowledge of female sexuality facilitated the deployment of well-defined social identities through which the female experience was at once fixed and constrained. Thereby the hegemonic figure of the domestic angel, the good woman; and her wicked, perverse twin sister, the prostitute. On the other hand, however, disciplines, legislation, and institutions produced a sexual *subject,* which was also female par excellence. Feared because it was active; dangerous because it could transmit disease; in need of control because, if unsupervised, it could cause the destruction of the family and the entire nation. The power ascribed to this sexual subject was, without doubt, enormous. Was it a pretense designed to facilitate the exercise of the vertical power of the state? Was it perhaps real?

Prostitutes seemed to have understood the potential uses of this scheme when, in 1926, the League of Defense of Fallen Women wrote a letter to President Calles demanding justice.[99] The incident that triggered the prostitutes' protest was common enough. They resented that their children were not allowed to stay with them at the facilities of the Morelos hospital while receiving forced medical treatment. In a two-page document, prostitutes paradoxically portrayed themselves as mute women whose "delicate position in life prevented them from speaking out and demanding justice." They also identified themselves with unfortunate creatures forced by strenuous circumstances to sell their "used flesh" in order "to get the miserable metal coins which rule our society and, through which, all happiness is achieved."[100] Assuming common depictions as unworthy, despicable and low, they nonetheless asserted they constituted the only protection left to Mexican families whose male members continuously took risks by engaging in illicit sexual activities. "We want to let you and society know that we are the only *garantía* of Mexican homes."[101] In the prostitutes' view, then, the sexual subject, the dangerous element in need of control and supervision was unequivocally male. As in a twisted mirror, public women threw their socially constructed image back on their creators. This document, nevertheless, was designed to reach the compassion of a powerful man, the president himself, whom they described as honest and fair in his decision-making.

What remains significant in this text is not only the strategic displacement of the sexual subject, but prostitutes' very use of it. Under specific conditions, in specific practices, the sexual subject, which was female, engaged in reversal. It showed its true face. Furthermore, before signing as members of an organization called the Women Without Homes, they made sure to "invoke the principles of the Revolution and respect for the freedom granted to individuals."[102] The theme of the nation, those murky waters of state formation, surfaced once again. Prostitutes reclaimed rights they deserved as rightful citizens of the country.

A year later, a group of prostitutes who called themselves the *irredentas,* the daughters of misfortune, bitterly complained against various instances of misconduct by members of the Sanitary Police. They especially criticized police agents' leniency toward illegal prostitutes, especially foreign ones. "Is this a matter of nationalism or betrayal, Mr. President?" they directly asked.[103] Their list of charges was long. Although prostitutes paid for Salvarsan shots and other medications on their own, the regulatory system increased fees and fines. Also, when they labored at the workshops of the Morelos hospital, they did not receive wages. Even worse, when in jail, authorities denied them access to food. "Does it mean that we are outside the realm of law?" they questioned. "Do not blame us. We used to be factory workers and rural laborers, but factories have closed and activities in the field have stalled. We believed that 70% of us were forced to lead this life out of necessity, and only 30% chose it because of personal proclivity to vice."[104] Gender-aware, these nationalist daughters of misfortune combined strategic uses of concepts of victimization to denounce growing immorality in male members of the Sanitary Police. "Is this moral?" additional pupils asked when referring to violent mistreatment suffered at the hands of the Sanitary Police.[105] In an even more paradoxical example of reversal, a woman used her status as a legal prostitute to ask health authorities for help.[106] Writing from a state dispensary, she requested treatment at the Morelos hospital because she suffered from venereal disease. When access to the hospital was denied, she uncovered the true reason behind her request. She had left the *mala vida* to live with a man in the neighborhood of Tacuba, but the man turned out to be an alcoholic who locked her up at home. "This man is rotten. I want you to take me out of this house to continue with my life. . . . I will be grateful if you take me."[107] She signed as the queen-devil, *la Diablesa.*

It is not a gratuitous coincidence that this essay, which began with allusions to male-authored portraits of prostitutes as saints, ends now with a self-described devilish female figure. As Michael Taussig elaborated on Jean Genet and the maleficium of state fetishism, there is something at once disconcerting and "wonderfully instructive" in this twist.[108] La Diablesa did not reject, but rather assumed long-lasting depictions of evil and vice associated with prostitutes. In the case of Jean Genet, Michael Taussig spoke of a "fetish" who spoke back and "thus perturbed what was said on the fetish's behalf. In this sense he can be said to be an agent of defetishization."[109] Reversing and unreversing herself, the queen-devil's missive brought news of power (after all, she was resorting to public health authorities), but also news of the fragility of that power (after all, she attempted to use public health authorities in her behalf). The making of a discourse, Michel Foucault once sustained, "transmits and produces power; it reinforces it, but it also undermines and exposes it, renders it fragile and makes it possible to thwart it."[110] The modern sexual subject emerged precisely in the knots of power and fragility in which the postrevolutionary reconstruction of the Mexican state took place.

Notes

I wish to thank Andrew Wiese, Betsy Colwill, Roger Cunniff, and Ricardo Salvatore for their comments.

1 "Profiláxis de la sífilis," in José Alvarez Amézquita et al., *Historia de la Salubridad y de la Asistencia en México* (México: Secretaría de Salubridad y Asistencia, 1960), pp. 111–137.

2 *Código Penal para el Distrito y Territorios Federales* (México: Talleres Gráficos de la Nación, 1929).

3 It was short-lived because the penal code of 1931 no longer included prescriptions against syphilis-related health crimes.

4 See Michael Taussig, "Reification and the Consciousness of the Patient," in *The Nervous System* (New York: Routledge, 1992), pp. 83–109.

5 Studies on this issue began as early as 1927. See "Relativo a las reformas del Código Penal, 1927," Archivo Histórico de la Secretaría de Salubridad y Asistencia. Fondo: Salubridad Pública; Sección: Jurídica; Caja: 5; Expediente: 12. Hereafter referred to as AHSSA. F:SP; S:SJ; C:5; Exp:12.

6 For a detailed description, see Anthony J. Mazzaferi, "Public Health and Social Revolution in Mexico, 1870–1930" (Ph.D. dissertation, Kent State University, 1968).

7 Amézquita et al., *Historia de la salubridad y la asistencia en México,* p. 72.

8 For information on the criminalization of drug consumption, abortion, and alcoholism, see ibid., 11, 145, 153.

9 See William Roseberry, "Hegemony and the Language of Contention," in Gilbert M. Joseph and Daniel Nugent, eds., *Everyday of State Formation: Revolution and the Negotiation of Rule in Modern Mexico* (Durham, N.C.: Duke University Press, 1994), pp. 355–366.

10 Ibid., p. 364.

11 In Mexico, syphilis was usually referred to as "enfermedad secreta."

12 Michel Foucault's critical reflection about the "repressive hypothesis" is useful on this point. See *History of Sexuality: An Introduction* (New York: Vintage, 1978), pp. 10–13. Also relevant are "The History of Sexuality" and "The Confession of the Flesh," in *Power/Knowledge: Selective Interviews and Other Writings, 1972–1977* (New York: Pantheon, 1977), pp. 183–228.

13 Walter Benjamin stated: "The tradition of the oppressed teaches us that 'the state of emergency' in which we live is not the exception but the rule." See Walter Benjamin, "Theses on the Philosophy of History," in *Illuminations,* ed. Hannah Arendt (New York: Harcourt, Brace & World, 1969), pp. 253–264.

14 Walter Benjamin stated: "To articulate the past historically does not mean to recognize it 'the way it really was' . . . It means to seize hold of a memory as it flashes up at the moment of danger." See ibid., p. 257.

15 AHSSA. F:SP; S:IAV; C:1; Exp: 1. For information on earlier attempts at regulating prostitution in Mexico, see Julia Tuñón, *El album de la mujer: antología ilustrada de las mexicanas: volúmen III/El Siglo XIX (1821–1880)* (México: Instituto Nacional de Antropología e Historia, 1991), p. 98. For a detailed description of late nineteenth-century regulations of prostitution in Mexico, see Ixchel Jordá "Prostitución, sífilis y moralidad sexual en la ciudad de México a fines del siglo XIX" (M.A. thesis, Escuela Nacional de Antropología, 1993), pp. 43–81. For historical analyses of efforts tending to regulate sexuality in Europe, see Catherine Gallagher and Thomas Laqueur, eds., *The Making of the Modern Body: Sexuality and Society in the Nineteenth Century* (Berkeley: University of California Press, 1987); John C. Fout, ed., *Forbidden History: The State, Society, and the Regulation of Sexuality in Modern Europe* (Chicago: University of Chicago Press, 1992).

16 Adrián Quiroz Rediles, *El hospital Morelos* (México: Departamento de Salubridad, 1933), pp. 67–72; "El hospital Morelos," *La Escuela de Medicina* I/16 (1880): 1.

17 The regulatory system in Mexico followed guidelines established by Parent-Duchâtelet in France. See Parent-Duchâtelet, *De la prostitution dans le Ville de Paris* (Paris: J. B. Bailliere et fils, 1857).

18 See José María del Castillo Velasco, *Colección de leyes, suprema órdenes, bandos, disposiciones de policía y reglamentos de administración del Distrito Federal* (México: Castillo Velasco e Hijos, 1874). For an analysis of prostitution and the rise of the modern city, see Judith Walkowitz, *City of Dreadful Delight: Narratives of Sexual Danger in Late Victorian London* (Chicago: University of Chicago Press, 1992).

19 "Reglamentos," AHEACM, Consejo Superior de Salubridad, 643. See also Javier Morales Meneses "Los reglamentos para el ejercicio de la prostitución el México," *Fem* 16(116):12–16; Guadalupe Ríos de la Torre and Marcela Suárez Escobar, "Reglamentarismo, historia, prostitutas," in *Constelaciones de Modernidad* (México: UNAM, 1990), pp. 129–149.

20 See Donna J. Guy, *Sex and Danger in Buenos Aires: Prostitutes, Family and the Nation in Argentina* (Lincoln: University of Nebraska Press, 1991). See also David Mc-Creery, " 'This Life of Misery and Shame': Female Prostitution in Guatemala City, 1880–1920," *Journal of Latin American Studies* 18, no. 2 (1986): 333–353.

21 See Laura Engelstein, "Morality and the Wooden Spoon: Russian Doctors View Syphilis, Social Class, and Sexual Behavior, 1890–1905," in Gallagher and Laqueur, eds., *The Making of the Modern Body,* pp. 169–208.

22 Pedro Escobedo, "La reglamentarización de la prostitución," *La Escuela de Medicina* X (1889): 405–407.

23 AHSSA. F:SP; S:IAV; C:1; Exp: 3, 9.

24 For an analysis of the eugenic movement in Latin America, see Nancy Leys Stepan, *The Hour of Eugenics: Race, Gender, and Nation in Latin America* (Ithaca, N.Y.: Cornell University Press, 1991).

25 "Informe del C. Médico Jefe de la Sección Sanitaria," AHSSA. F:SP, S:IAV; C:1; Exp: 15.

26 See Ixchel Delgado Jordá, "Prostitución, sífilis y moralidad sexual." Also, Javier Morales Meneses, "Los reglamentos para el ejercicio de la prostitución en México."

27 AHSSA. F:BP; S:IAV; C:1; Exp:1.

28 Lacking technological equipment, members of the Sanitary Police often resorted to what they called their "practical eye" to identify prostitutes. Incidents involving the failure of police agents' "practical eye" are reported in Ramón Félix del Valle, "La situación del obrero en México," *El Obrero Mexicano* I/9 (1894): 1. Also, "Gacetilla," *El Obrero Mexicano* I/16 (1894): 4. Failure continued over time, see "Abominables excesos de miembros de la policía," *El Sol* (October 12, 1927), p. 1.

29 "Informe," AHSSA. F:BP; S:IAV; C:1; Exp:15.

30 *La Independencia Médica* II/54 (1882): 2.

31 See William E. French, "Prostitutes and Guardian Angels: Women, Work and the Family in Porfirian Mexico," *Hispanic American Historical Review* 72/4 (1992): 529–533. See also Carmen Ramos Escandón, "Señoritas porfirianas: mujer e ideología en el México progresista, 1880–1910," in Carmen Ramos Escandón et al., eds., *Presencia y transparencia: la mujer en la historia de México* (México: El Colegio de México, 1987). Especially illustrative in this regard is the collection of primary sources included in Ana Lau and Carmen Ramos Escandón, eds., *Mujeres y revolución, 1900–1910* (México: INERM, 1993), pp. 69–270. Also, see Verena Radkau, *"Por la debilidad de nuestro ser": mujeres de pueblo en la paz porfiriana* (México: SEP /Ediciones de la Casa Chata, 1989).

32 See analysis of Manuel Acuña, Juan Valle, and Hilarión Frías in Ixchel Delgado Jordá, "Prostitución, sífilis y moralidad sexual," pp. 29, 102–103.

33 Federico Gamboa, *Santa* (México: Utopía, 1903). For an analysis of the uses of the body in *Santa*, see Margo Glantz, *La lengua en la mano* (México: Premiá, 1983), pp. 37–52.

34 For an analysis of erotic art in Mexico, see Margo Glantz "Arte erótico de México," *Arte, Ideología y Sociedad* 4 (1977–1978): 31–39.

35 See Mauricio Tenorio, *Mexico at the World Fairs: Crafting the Modern Nation* (Berkeley: University of California Press, 1996), p. 111.

36 "Prostitución clandestina," *La Convención Radical Obrera* 2 (1887), in Martha Eva Rocha, *El album de la mujer: volumen IV/el porfiriato y la revolución* (México: Instituto Nacional de Antropología e Historia, 1991), p. 110.

37 "Memoria de la prostitución," AHSSA. F:SP; S:IAV; C:1; Exp:4.

38 In the table "Jobs and trades of prostitutes 1868–1872," Manuel Alfaro showed that among prostitutes there were 146 domestic servants, 84 seamstresses, 62 laundresses, 61 unemployed, 35 peddlers, 23 shoemakers, 17 embroiderers, 13 grinders, 8 hatmakers, 5 textile workers, 4 silk workers, 4 market vendors, 2 hairdressers, 2 matchbox makers, 1 upholsterer, and 1 wax sculptor; 32 did not answer. See "Memoria de la prostitución."

39 See Radkau, "*Por la debilidad de nuestro ser,*" pp. 28–34.

40 In the table "Causes of prostitution 1868–1872," Manuel Alfaro classified the answers from 326 prostitutes as follows: 169 proclivity for the profession, 125 poverty, 12 forced by their parents, 8 escaping family mistreatment, 5 jealousy, 4 forced by their lovers, 2 expulsion from home. See "Memoria de la prostitución."

41 "Memoria de la prostitución," AHSSA. F:BP; S:IAV; C:1; Exp: 3, 4.

42 For an analysis of the English middle-class nonconformists, feminists, and radical workingmen who successfully challenged the Contagious Disease Acts in 1870, see Judith R. Walkowitz, *Prostitution and Victorian Society: Women, Class, and the State* (Cambridge: Cambridge University Press, 1980).

43 "Insensibilidad física de la mujer," *La Escuela de Medicina* XI, no. 33 (1892): 631–634.

44 For an analysis of the emergence of sexual science in Europe, see Cynthia Eagle Russet, *Sexual Science: The Victorian Construction of Womanhood* (Cambridge, Mass.: Harvard University Press, 1989).

45 See Nicolás Martínez, *La obstetricia en México: notas bibliográficas, étnicas, históricas, documentarias y críticas de los orígenes históricos hasta el año 1910* (México: Tipografía de la Vda. De F. Díaz de León, 1910).

46 For a detailed description of the regulations of the Real Tribunal del Protomedicato, see ibid., p. 201.

47 Silvestre Romero Roja, "Hojeada histórica sobre obstetricia en México," *Pasteur* IV, no. 1 (1931): 280.

48 "Clínica de obstetricia," *La Escuela de Medicina* I, no. 5 (1879): 3.

49 Margarito Crispín Castellanos, "Hospital de maternidad e infancia. Perspectiva histórica de un centro de beneficencia pública de finales del siglo XIX," in *La atención materno-infantial: apuntes para su historia* (México: Secretaría de Salubridad y Asistencia, 1993), pp. 95–115.

50 Ibid., p. 108.

51 "Informe del hospital Morelos, 1898–1899," AHSSA. F:BP; S:EH; Se:HM; Lg:4; Exp: 9, 17.

52 Ibid., Exp: 9, 18.

53 Quiroz Rodiles, *Breve historia del hospital Morelos,* p. 74.

54 "Reglamento del hospital Morelos, 1900," AHSSA. F:BP; S:EH; Se:HM; Lg:2; Exp:34, 12–14.

55 "Informe del hospital Morelos, 1898–1899," AHSSA. F:BP; S:EH; Se:HM; Lg:4; Exp: 9, 21.

56 "Reporte del hospital Morelos, 1891," AHSSA. F:BP; S:EH; Se:HM; Lg:2; Exp:18. See also "Reportes del hospital Morelos, 1914, 1916, 1919, 1920," AHSSA. F:BP; S:EH; Se:HM; Lg:10, 11, 14, 18; Exp: 3, 7, 15, 18, 19, 20.

57 "Escándalos en el San Juan de Dios: las pupilas llegan a las vía del hecho," *El Popular* (Marzo 13, 1902), p. 1.

58 "Hospital Morelos," *La Escuela de Medicina* I, no. 16 (1880): 1.

59 Felix F. Palavancini, *Los Diputados* (México: Imprenta Francesa, 1915).

60 Manuel Guillén, "Algunas reflexiones sobre la higiene de la mujer durante su pubertad" (thesis, Facultad de Medicina, 1903).

61 Ibid., pp. 2–3.

62 For a discussion on the concept of cultural genitals, see Harold Garnfinkel, *Studies in Ethnomethodology* (Englewood Cliffs, N.J.: Prentice-Hall, 1967).

63 Francisco de Asís Flores y Troncoso, *El hímen en México* (México: Oficina de la Secretaría de Fomento, 1885).

64 "Las poluciones de la mujer," *La escuela de Medicina* I, no. 10 (1889): 1.

65 See Cristina Rivera-Garza, "Mad Narratives: Inmates and Psychiatrists Debate Gender, Class and the Nation at the General Insane Asylum, Mexico 1910–1930" (unpublished manuscript).

66 Carlos Roumagnac, *Los criminales en México: ensayo de psicología criminal* (México: Tipografía El Fenix, 1904).

67 Julio Guerrero, *La génesis del crímen en México: estudio de psiquiatría social* (México: Librería de la viuda de Ch. Bouret, 1901).

68 "Medicina legal: Dictamen pericial en un caso de delito de atentados contra el pudor," *La Escuela de Medicina* I, no. 10 (1889): 4.

69 "Reporte del hospital Morelos, 1891," AHSSA. F:BP; S:EH; Se:HM; Lg:2; Exp:18, 3.

70 "Aclaración, 1902," AHSSA. F:BP; S:EH; Se:HM; Lg:4, Exp: 25.

71 "Al C. Presidente de la República, 1926," AHSSA. F:SP; S:IAV; C:3; Exp:4.

72 "Reportes del hospital Morelos, 1914, 1916, 1919, 1920," AHSSA. F:BP; S:EH; Se:HM; Lg:10, 11, 14, 18; Exp: 3, 7, 15, 18, 19, 20.

73 "Reporte del hospital Morelos, 1916," AHSSA. F:BP; S:EH; Se:HM; Lg:10; Exp:7.

74 "Reporte del hospital Morelos, 1919," AHSSA. F:BP; S:EH; Se:HM; Lg:10; Exp:18.

75 "Informe de Inspección, 1916," AHSSA. F:BP; S:D; Se:DG; Lg:18; Exp: 21, 194.

76 Louis Julien, *Traité pratique des maladies vénériennes* (Paris: J. B. Bailliére, 1879), p. 496.

77 Gonzalo Méndez Luque, "La ciudad de México a los ojos de la higiene" (thesis, Escuela Nacional de Medicina, 1903), p. 66.

78 Alberto J. Pani, *Hygiene in Mexico: A Study of Sanitary and Educational Problems* (New York: G. P. Putnam's Sons, 1917), p. 34.

79 "Profilaxis de la sífilis," *Historia de la Salubridad y la Asistencia en México,* pp. 111–137.

80 Ibid., p. 135.

81 Bernardo Gastélum, "La persecución de la sífilis desde el punto de vista de la garantía social," AHSSA. F:BP; S:AS; Se:DAES; L:1; Exp: 11, 7.

82 Ignacio Sánchez Neira, "Higiene militar," in *Memoria del VII Congreso Médico Nacional* II (México: Secretaría de Educación Pública, 1923), pp. 401–408.

83 "Reporte del hospital Morelos, 1914," AHSSA. F:BP; S:EH; Se:HM; Lg:8; Exp:43. Especially: "Se pusieron 33 inyecciones de salvarsán 606."

84 "Informe que presenta el médico Jefe de la Inspección de Sanidad, 1923," AHSSA. F:BP; S:IAV; C:2; Exp: 34, 1.

85 Ibid., 3.

86 "Acusan de secuestro a un inspector de sanidad," *Excélsior* (February 4, 1929), p. 3. AHSSA. F:SP; S:SJ; C:16; Exp:17.

87 "Observaciones relativas al reglamento para el ejercicio de la prostitución, 1926," AHSSA. F:SP; S:SJ; C:17; Exp:19.

88 "Al C. Presidente de la república, 1929," AHSSA. F:BP; S:SJ; C:13; Exp: 2.

89 "A los CC. Jefe de Departamento de Salubridad Pública y Jefe del Departamento del Distrito Federal," AHSSA. F:SP; S:IAV; C:3; Exp: 10.

90 "Junta de Obreros, Industriales, propietarios y vecinos de las calles de Cuauhtemotzin y adyacentes," AHSSA. F:SP; S:SJ; C:17; Exp:19.

91 "Las zonas de tolerancia en el Distrito Federal, 1929," AHSSA. F:SP; S:IAV; C:3; Exp: 11.

92 "Observaciones relativas al reglamento de prostitución del 12 febrero de 1927," AHSSA. F:SP; S:SJ; C:17; Exp:19.

93 "Observaciones al proyecto del reglamento federal para el ejercicio de la prostitución, 1928," AHSSA. F:SP; S:SJ; C:13; Exp: 2.

94 "Reglamento contra las enfermedades venéreas, reformas al código penal, 1935–1936," AHSSA. F:SP; S:IAV; C:4; Exp:12. The abolitionist system "consisted of

not recognizing the existence of prostitution because it is an *absolute* social fact. . . . [It also involved] a systematic and implacable prosecution of the causes of prostitution." See "Prostitución en las poblaciones fronterizas," AHSSA. F:SSA; S:SubSyA; C:27; Exp:5, 1. This system was used in Brazil; see Sueann Caulfield, "The Birth of Mangue: Race, Nation, and Politics of Prostitution in Rio de Janeiro, 1850–1942," in Donna J. Guy and Daniel Balderston, eds. *Sex and Sexuality in Latin America* (New York: New York University Press, 1997), pp. 86–100.

95 "Actas levantadas contra prostitutas, 1930–1933," AHSSA. F:SP; S:IAV; C:4, Exp: 10.

96 Horacio Rubio, "Proyecto de campaña contra enfermedades venéreas en la República Mexicana. Importancia en nuestro pais del llamado proyecto norteamericano," in *Memoria del VII Congreso Médico Nacional,* pp. 566–576. Emphasis on soldiers related to social concerns about their "abnormal" status. Peter Beattie noted that in Brazil "prior to 1916, the barracks functioned as the male equivalent of the bordello: both attempted to isolate dangerous men and women from honorable households." See Peter Beattie, "Conflicting Penile Codes: Modern Masculinity and Sodomy in the Brazilian Military, 1860–1916," in Guy and Balderston, eds., *Sex and Sexuality in Latin America,* p. 69.

97 Bernardo Gastélum, *La persecución de la sífilis,* 13.

98 Although Robert Buffington pointed out criminologists' interest on male sexualities at the turn of the century, the medical establishment, however, emphasized otherwise. For example, Carlos Roumagnac's attention to female sexual "perversity" was not an exception, but the norm. Also, while massive examination of women's bodies led to the normalization of terminologies (a prostitute became a prostitute in a modern sense), the same did not happen with homosexuality until well in the 1930s. See Robert Buffington, "Los Jotos: Contested Visions of Homosexuality in Mexico," in Guy and Balderston, eds., *Sex and Sexuality in Latin America,* pp. 118–132.

99 "Las mujeres sin hogar, 1926," AHSSA. F:SP; S:IAV; C:3; Exp:4.

100 Ibid., 1.

101 Ibid., 2.

102 Ibid., 2.

103 "Al C. Presidente de la República, 1927," AHSSA. F:BP; S:SJ; C:13; Exp:2.

104 Ibid., 2.

105 "Al C. Presidente de la República, 1927," AHSSA. F:SP; S:IAV; C:3; Exp:2, 2.

106 "Al C. Médico Jefe de la Inspección de Sanidad, 1930," AHSSA. F:SP; S:IAV; C:3; Exp: 23.

107 Ibid., 1.

108 Taussig, "Maleficium: State Fetishism," in *The Nervous System,* pp. 11–140.

109 Ibid., p. 140.

110 Foucault, *History of Sexuality,* p. 101.

Healing and Mischief:

Witchcraft in Brazilian Law and

Literature, 1890–1922

DAIN BORGES

―――――

After sixty years without laws forbidding witchcraft, Brazil's new republican government decreed the Penal Code of 1890, which criminalized spirit possession, love magic, and herbal folk healing as forms of the illegal practice of medicine:

— Article 156: "To practice any of the branches of medicine, dentistry or pharmacy; to practice homeopathy, dosimetry, hypnotism or animal magnetism, without being duly licensed . . ."
— Article 157: "To practice spiritism, or magic and its conjurations, or use talismans and cartomancy, in order to arouse sentiments of hate or love, to insinuate the cure of a curable or incurable disease, in sum, to fascinate and dominate the credulity of the public."
— Article 158: "To administer . . . a substance from any of the kingdoms of Nature, thus performing or exercising the profession of folk healer [*curandeiro*]."[1]

It seems paradoxical that an enlightened, secularizing state would feel the need to revive the repression of witchcraft. Exploring this apparent paradox reveals deep divisions and honest confusion among Brazilian intellectuals — among lawyers, public health reformers, psychiatrists, Catholic priests, and occultists — about the meanings of witchcraft. Images of witchcraft and religious healing were shaped by the reforming drives of the professions, always in some relation to the judicial system. These images inspired reflections on social relations by Brazilian thinkers in the early twentieth century, particularly in the cities of Salvador da Bahia and Rio de Janeiro.

Resort to witchcraft or *feitiçaria*—the loose, derogatory term for all unorthodox magical and religious practices ranging from folk medicine to Afro-Brazilian cults such as *candomblé* and new religions such as spiritism— had long precedent in Portugal, Africa, and Brazil. By 1700, Brazilian sufferers had access to a market of cures that blended Indian, African, and Portuguese folk healing and witchcraft. Many Brazilians, and not only those of African descent, sought healing and spiritual power from creolized African religions—candomblé, macumba, calundu, xangô—that held impressive ceremonies of spirit possession. In one of the best-documented transfers of religious institutions from Africa to the New World, Yorubas brought in through the early-nineteenth-century slave trade established candomblé houses in Salvador that have lasted until the present. All of these heterodox religions performed healing, and the Catholic church classified most of it as witchcraft. But the church also encouraged Africans to form their own Catholic brotherhoods and sometimes tolerated popular devotions that paired Christian saints with African divinities, such as the famous washing of the chapel of Our Lord of Bomfim in Bahia. Some folk healers, such as "blessers" *(benzedeiros),* healed through Christian prayers. Not every religious practice involved healing, and not all healing invoked supernatural causes, but the overlap was great enough that healing and religion were inextricable.

Feitiçaria had always been illegal or on the verge of criminalization. In medieval Europe, even before the discovery of Brazil, civil and church law identified witches principally as those heretics who cultivated a pact with the Devil and participated in witches' sabbaths, but it could also define apparently trivial superstitions as witchcraft practices. In Brazil and Portugal during the colonial period, civil courts, ecclesiastical courts, and the tribunal of the Inquisition all prosecuted feitiçaria; jurisdiction usually fell to the Inquisition.[2] Between 1591 and 1786, at least 119 cases of witchcraft were prosecuted by visiting inquisitors in Brazil or were sent by Brazilian bishops to the Lisbon Inquisition. Witch-hunts elsewhere in Europe peaked in the seventeenth century, but Portuguese witchcraft trials peaked in the early eighteenth century. The clumsily drafted articles forbidding witchcraft in the 1890 code resemble an abbreviated version of the long list of illegal witchcraft practices in the Portuguese Philippine Code, which governed Brazilian criminal law from 1603 through 1830.[3] The Philippine Code defined witchcraft in three tiers: a death penalty for witchcraft involving eucharistic objects stolen from churches, invocation of demons, or use of potions; whipping and banishment for divination and love magic; whipping and a light fine for "rustic superstitions" such as keeping a mandrake root or claiming visions of the future. This civil law detailed many more practices, and particularly more healing practices, than Inquisition regulations, which concentrated on sacrilegious acts and pacts with the Devil. And it never went through anything like the enlightened 1774 reform of Inquisition regulations, which denied the reality of the demonic pact, and redefined sorcerers, *feiticeiros,* as frauds whose crime consisted in believing their pact and powers were real.[4]

The Portuguese Inquisition was abolished in 1821; independent Brazil's 1824 constitution proclaimed toleration of discreetly practiced non-Catholic religions; and the articles criminalizing witchcraft were omitted from Brazil's Criminal Code of 1830. Thus, during most of the Brazilian empire (1824–1889), there was no national criminal law against "witchcraft." However, provincial curfew laws requiring a passport for Africans and freedmen abroad after dark, or laws against disturbing the peace with drum parties (*batuques*), gave police chiefs a pretext to raid candomblés. Most prisoners were jailed briefly, but a few African feiticeiros were deported.[5] Slave owners exercised their discretionary powers to punish suspected witches and poisoners and to tolerate or suppress slave frolics on plantations.[6] In the 1830s and 1840s, towns and provinces passed laws banning candomblé, drum parties, sale of "poisons," and slave carnivals, often in a package of measures concerning "tranquility and public morality": gambling, begging, and bathing in public fountains.[7] Prosecutors occasionally held show trials in which they charged feiticeiros with committing fraud upon clients: in 1871, a judge sentenced Juca Rosa, a flamboyantly successful Rio de Janeiro cult leader with many white clients, to six years in prison for fraud.[8]

There was no clearly stated reason why witchcraft laws were revived in the year 1890. Police chiefs had long discussed African religions as a dangerous element of slave rebellions. The jurist Cândido Mendes de Almeida, in his 1870 edition of the *Código Philippino,* called for stronger laws, arguing that "these superstitions, these ignoble practices, should be reprehended on all sides, even though they might be, as many suppose, harmless, which they are not." In the late 1880s, Rio de Janeiro physicians campaigned vigorously in newspapers against dangerous charlatans and curandeiros, and they demanded forceful action against the illegal practice of medicine. But no urgent public debate focusing on witchcraft preceded the code.[9] 1890 was the first year of republican dictatorship and a moment of enthusiastic, indiscriminate reform. The stalemate that had inhibited legal reform during the empire broke, and very diverse reform measures passed by decree with little debate or consideration. Probably the cascade of pent-up constitutional, economic, and legal reforms simply swept in the penal code.[10]

Thus, despite the conspicuous coincidence between the abolition of slavery in 1888 and the recriminalization of witchcraft in 1890, there was no direct statement that concern about social control of Afro-Brazilians after abolition motivated the reform. However, the witchcraft law did fit trends toward "civilizing" reforms. One such trend was the set of government measures for social control of the lower classes. Another was the set of new medical practices in family medicine and public health that appropriated facets of the social mission of the Catholic church.

Republican Secular Citizenship

Early republican legislation was repressive more than permissive, exclusionary more than inclusive. Brazilian historiography tends to focus on the reforms needed to consolidate capitalism, and to attribute repressive turn-of-the-century reforms to a ruling-class strategy to form a disciplined proletarian working class after the abolition of slavery.[11] However, the liberal political culture of republicanism itself excluded people in the way it implemented citizenship and consolidated secularization. Liberal but antidemocratic, the Brazilian republic broadened the disenfranchising electoral reforms begun in the late empire by limiting the vote to literate males. And in practice, republican political machines rigged elections shamelessly in city and country alike. José Murilo de Carvalho has argued that, recognizing their exclusion from institutions, their "bestialization," the people of Rio de Janeiro became cynical about republican citizenship and nostalgic for the monarchy. Another exclusionary form that republican liberalism took was interference with popular Catholicism. The Catholic church itself had been romanizing throughout the nineteenth century, discouraging the popular Catholicism of shrines and festivals and emphasizing liturgy and catechism. But the first republican government went much farther. It separated church and state, reinforced the guarantee of freedom of religion in the 1891 constitution, and instituted civil marriage—a move particularly resented by country people. Rather than react against priests, people tended to blame the government and secularization.[12]

Republican social reforms intended to "regenerate" Brazilian society fell particularly hard on Afro-Brazilians, who made up about half of the population. In Salvador and Rio, the curbing of popular Catholicism intertwined with new policies of urban social control. Some policies reacted against postabolition assertions of autonomy. Salvador had always been one of the most "African" corners of Brazil, but after 1889 "African" costumes and club themes became more prominent in Bahian carnival, some Afro-Brazilians declined Catholic marriage in favor of civil marriage, and candomblé centers emerged from clandestinity and began drumming in the outskirts. The state and city government, when not protecting the sects in return for political support, sent the police to break up gatherings and arrest sorcerers for the illegal practice of medicine.[13] New republican administrations, nervous about uprisings in southern Brazil, could not ignore an event such as the 1893 pilgrimage of thousands to the shrine of Santo Antonio da Barra at Salvador's outskirts, in response to rumors that only propitiatory offerings of candles to the saint would avert another cholera epidemic.[14] In Rio de Janeiro, some policies that began during the late empire, such as the breakup of *capoeira* gangs and the clearing of unsanitary tenement rows, were pushed harder under the republic.[15] The government's measures culminated in the massive urban renewal of 1903–1906, which razed popular neighborhoods near the center and the docks.[16]

Medicine and Religions

The call in the 1880s to criminalize folk healing and, by extension, witchcraft came mainly from the medical profession. In a sense, popular healers became the involuntary third party to the tensions within the medical profession (as doctors accused one another of charlatanism) and between religious and medical professional elites. From the mid-nineteenth century on, Brazilian physicians claimed increasing authority to regulate both private and public life. This drive displaced authority of the Catholic church over healing, counseling on private behavior, and the manner of death. In many fields, doctors and priests worked together and shared a paternalistic mission of duty toward their patients and parishioners. Some issues, such as urban sanitation, vaccination, shipboard quarantines, and the administration of insane asylums and hospitals, only rarely provoked conflicts between priests and doctors (who were often employees of church agencies).[17] Other issues related to healing raised tensions. A Central Board of Public Hygiene was given authority to certify medical diplomas and punish the illegal practice of medicine with fines, beginning in 1851.[18] And when the Brazilian government gave physicians "sanitary authority" over public health, it opened arenas of competition. For example, laws requiring burial in public cemeteries rather than under the floor of churches were a point of conflict.[19] Upper- and middle-class households were the most disputed arena of conflict between priests and doctors: who should be admitted to the deathbed, the doctor or the priest? who counsels families about sex, marriage, and childrearing? Where doctors and priests could agree was in condemning the influence of superstitions on families.

The introduction of Allan Kardec's branch of middle-class spiritism from France in the 1860s catalyzed both professional medicine and the church to react more aggressively against spirit-possession religions and folk healing practices. Kardecist spiritism, by appealing to middle-class families that tried séances in their parlors, by publishing books and newspapers, by proselytizing, appeared to be establishing a counter-church. Although there was in fact no single Kardecist "church," in the 1880s certain centers and associations, such as the Brazilian Spiritist Federation (FEB) and their newspaper, *O Reformador,* emerged as spokesmen for spiritists. The message of Kardecist "philosophy" directly challenged Catholic dogma: it claimed the existence of multiple worlds, the ascent of spirits through various incarnations from material dark planets to ethereal light planets, reincarnations according to a law of karma, the routine daily interference of disincarnate spirits in our well-being, and so forth. Kardecist writers directly disputed the Catholic doctrines of original sin and final judgment. Catholic bishops and journalists condemned (and satirized) Kardecism vigorously; doctors followed suit, less vigorously but no less dogmatically.[20]

Kardecist spiritist centers often healed in a style that resembled or parodied medical clinics, and they supported heterodox medical systems such as homeopathy and mesmerism. A spiritist "prescribing medium" would incorporate the spirit of a great doctor or benevolent philosopher. The spirit then dictated or wrote out a prescription for spectators in the room, almost always prescribing homeopathic remedies. Some centers ran a free homeopathic pharmacy on the premises. Spiritist "healing mediums" drew on the medical tradition of animal magnetism; they healed by making passes over the bodies of the afflicted, transmitting invisible healing "fluid" given by their spirits. The clients at spiritist centers sobbed quietly, shook in convulsions from fluidic energy, and sometimes became possessed by spirits themselves. Many felt, or were told in diagnosis, that they were suffering from the persecution of "obsessing" malevolent spirits, and sought the centers for relief.[21] The church initiated the opposition to spiritism, but by the 1880s physicians in Rio de Janeiro had begun to call on the public health board to supervise unorthodox medical practice more vigorously.[22]

The 1890 Penal Code

The best statement of the intentions of Baptista Pereira, the drafter of the penal code, appeared in a debate immediately following publication of the code on October 10, 1890. No candomblé house or small-town herbalist protested the new laws. But the spiritist leaders in Rio de Janeiro immediately petitioned the government protesting the criminalization of spiritism, which they considered a violation of constitutional freedom of religion. On December 19, spiritists published their petition to the president. Half of it claimed that spiritism is a new science, emerging from magic just as chemistry had emerged from alchemy, and therefore should not be repressed by a modern state. The second half of the petition argued that, if spiritism is *not* a science, then it must be a religion, and its practice protected under the constitution. They asked the government to suspend the laws and appoint a scientific commission to settle the issue of whether spiritism was a legitimate science.[23]

Two weeks later, Baptista Pereira began a series of articles explaining novelties in the code, such as the labor laws and the laws regarding illegal practice of medicine. He used this series to respond to the spiritists' petition. He ridiculed their claim that spiritism is science, devoting an entire column to the notorious case of fraudulent spirit photography by Kardec's followers in France. He echoed long-standing arguments against hypnotism and spiritism that were current among doctors as well as the church, saying that spiritism caused mental illness and "endangered the health, the life and perhaps the honor" of its practitioners.[24] Baptista Pereira claimed that he had considered leaving spiritism to the laws against fraud, as it had been during the empire, but had decided to put it in the section of the code on "crimes against public health" because he considered the danger to persons greater than the danger to property. He argued that the law did not forbid spiritist research, but only the "practical" or clinical use of spiritism. Baptista Pereira's articles were not binding opinion on the significance of the law, but they foreshadowed the ambivalence or confusion about what, exactly, could and should be illegal that would trouble jurists thenceforth.[25]

The spiritist leader who replied, Adolfo Bezerra de Menezes, yielded a great deal of ground, and seemed almost as hesitant as the jurist, at one point saying that he would accept a prohibition against curing disease by spiritism, as long as spirit mediumship were permitted as experimentation.[26] He concentrated his efforts on defending the claims that spiritism was indeed a science, and if not a science, enough of a religion to be protected by the constitution. Possibly, Bezerra de Menezes equivocated because he wanted to avoid committing his federation to a position on the issue. The question of whether spiritism was a religion or a science divided Kardecists at the turn of the century, and several times split spiritist federations and centers.[27] In the face of the law, it was safer to claim exemption as a religion.

Representations of Witchcraft in Cases

The early enforcement of the laws did not clarify their scope, either. In fact, it demonstrated that Brazilian judges, prosecutors, and lawyers could not agree on the meaning or utility of the laws. No scholar has obtained a complete count of arrests under the laws. Cases began with an arrest, led to an inquiry under a police delegate, and rarely moved to the stage of a trial where witnesses would be reexamined, and lawyers might submit written arguments to a judge. Yvonne Maggie and Emerson Giumbelli located thirty-five complete or well-recorded cases in Rio de Janeiro between 1890 and 1910. Of nineteen cases opened in the first decade of the law, most were dismissed after the stage of a police inquiry, and only two resulted in convictions. Although the law allowed prison sentences of up to six years if grave harm resulted to a patient, those convicted had usually already served the normal sentence, one to six months, while waiting for trial. The accused ranged from traditional folk healers dispensing herbs and unidentified liquids, to unlicensed miracle doctors, to spirit mediums belonging to the FEB and running large free clinics offering homeopathic remedies.[28] Most were men — which runs against patterns of witchcraft accusation in Africa and

Europe. Accusations originated from persons who thought they were being bewitched, from annoyed neighbors of curandeiros, and from public health inspectors. In those cases which can be characterized as test cases, lawyers associated with the FEB defended mediums by claiming that they did not exercise the "profession" of medicine because they took no payment or had other jobs, by proposing that a medium in trance was not consciously and voluntarily giving medical advice, and by insisting that in any case, spirit possession was a religious rite protected under the constitution. A "curing-medium" was not himself the healer, but merely one "whose activity is the simple invocation of superior spirits for the cure of the sick by grace of God."[29]

If any judge epitomized the ambivalent reaction of police and jurists to the danger defined in the law, it was the prominent jurist José Francisco Viveiros de Castro, who published opinions in several cases. Viveiros de Castro argued that the articles of the penal code condemning spiritism were unconstitutional; no matter how absurd, a religion could not be a crime, given the constitutional guarantee of freedom of religion. Thus, a prosecutor should use the laws against fraud or personal injury. And the prosecutor must prove fraud or injury according to the full standards of the penal code for those crimes. Spiritism, per se, was irrelevant or insufficient proof of fraud. Yvonne Maggie characterizes Viveiros de Castro's position as liberal; Emerson Giumbelli interprets it as a "soft positivism," combining liberal defense of freedom of religion, positivist indifference to religious beliefs of a fetishist stage that should inevitably wither away, and progressive impulses to suppress harmful superstitious practices.[30] Yet Viveiros de Castro's rulings and opinions were not definitive. Other judges were willing to make spiritism itself the basis of a crime. In 1898, appeals court judges overruled Viveiros de Castro and convicted one spiritist for a criminal act that they found in the "abusive misuse of the doctrines of spiritism, a practice that not seldom produces mental illnesses."[31]

A second round of test cases in Rio de Janeiro came in 1904, when the government gave public health agencies extraordinary judicial power, a virtual "sanitary dictatorship," to enforce public health codes during the 1903–1906 reconstruction of Rio de Janeiro and campaigns of compulsory smallpox vaccination, rat control, and mosquito control. The special public health tribunal devoted most of its attention to sanitary and building code violations, but sanitary inspectors did initiate cases against leading spiritists in 1904 and 1905.[32] These cases failed, and police and public health authorities in Rio reluctantly arrived at coexistence with the booming clinics affiliated with the Brazilian Spiritist Federation.

The final major round of witchcraft prosecutions came in the 1920s and 1930s. These seem to have been inspired by a new generation of crusading journalists, public health officers, and police inspectors eager to crack down on the urban underworld. In Rio de Janeiro, Yvonne Maggie found records suggesting that there were only handfuls of cases before the 1920s, but dozens of prosecutions each year in the 1920s and 1930s, and then very few after 1945. Studies of other cities suggest a similar pattern of prosecutions.[33] Police inspectors all over Brazil opened campaigns against spiritist centers, often at the prodding of journalists and forensic psychiatrists such as Leonídio Ribeiro, who renewed the accusation that spiritism was a danger to mental health. Enforcement of the laws was assigned to vice squads in 1934. Although they did try a few prosecutions of Kardecist spiritists, they focused their raids on the yards of Afro-Brazilian cults and on un-affiliated spiritist healers. Inspector Pedro Gordilho entered popular legend as a fierce persecutor of Salvador's candomblé from 1920 through 1926.[34]

Two strategies of defending religious centers emerged. In the northern cities of Recife and Salvador, avant-garde psychiatrists and anthropologists argued that respectably traditional, "pure African" religions such as candomblé should be distinguished from dangerously eclectic, improvised cults. Starting around 1935–37, they negotiated with governors and police chiefs to form boards of cult leaders and doctors that would certify traditional centers as authentic folkloric religions, exempting them from the persecution.[35] In Rio de Janeiro, leaders of the FEB confederated the Kardecist centers. They gained many affiliations from centers that hoped membership in the "high" spiritist federation would secure them immunity from police harassment.[36] Yvonne Maggie has read these and other cases to conclude that it became vital for heterodox practitioners to define themselves as dignified "high spiritism," rather than sleazy "low spiritism." Giumbelli argues that the persecution twice forced the hand of Kardecist spiritists, first coercing them to define spiritism as a "religion" rather than a scientific "philosophy" in the 1890s, then encouraging them to shape their identity around their "charity" in contrast to low spiritism's dangerous "exploitation" in the 1920s.[37] Although witchcraft laws remain on the books, the modus vivendi between the state and heterodox religions stabilized around

1945. Accusations now come less from the police than from evangelical churches that perform exorcisms on persons supposedly victimized by spiritist witchcraft.

Police persecution did not stop the growth of heterodox religious healing. Between 1904 and 1920, the Brazilian Spiritist Federation reported giving 100,000 to 300,000 consultations a year in Rio—which could mean they served as much as a fifth of the city's population.[38] Oral traditions of the Salvador candomblé houses complain of the 1920–1945 persecution, but the houses survived nonetheless; sixty-seven of them met and formed an association in 1937. Since the police raids targeted healers and centers more than their clients, at most they seem to have forced a move into semiclandestinity. It is possible that persecution reinforced tendencies of religious development in both north and south: in the north, encouraging legitimation via African "purity" and tradition; in the south, encouraging claims of esoteric high erudition and disinterested "charity." The new religion of Umbanda, which formed between 1922 and 1945 in Rio de Janeiro, combined Afro-Brazilian and Indian spirits in a cosmology heavily influenced by "high spiritist" Kardecist doctrine.

Representations of Magic in Fringe Science

Magic became an object of scientific research and knowledge just about the time that the state decided to criminalize it. One group of researchers at the frontier of medical science became more "open" and attentive to spirit possession practices in the late 1880s, just as the public health laws to protect medical authority were becoming more closed, dismissive, and repressive. The arrival of the new French psychology, particularly the new explanations and practices of hypnotism, encouraged psychical research into uncanny phenomena such as spirit mediumship.[39] In Rio, some physicians interested in hypnotism became psychical researchers. Between 1887 and 1889, a group of professors and students at the Rio medical school experimented enthusiastically with hypnotic therapies for a wide range of ailments, and some of them observed inexplicable psychic phenomena.[40] However, the Imperial Academy of Medicine, Brazil's most prestigious medical association, refused to convene a commission to evaluate their hypnotic cures. The debates verged on accusations of medical charlatanism. The leader of the hypnotists, Dr. Erico Coelho, plunged into republican politics, and the students dispersed after graduation. Although the group did not stay together, their explanation of healing and other phenomena of magical rituals as effects of "suggestion" became the most common rationalization of supernatural powers in Brazilian journalism and literature.

Though most of the experimenters with hypnotism went no farther than marveling at the powers they uncovered, one prominent physician not part of that group became a spiritist leader — and is today one of the healing spirits most often consulted through mediums. The 1886 conversion to spiritism of the political boss and physician Adolfo Bezerra de Menezes (1831–1900) scandalized Rio. After his conversion, Bezerra de Menezes mostly wrote doctrinal tracts and polemics, including the response to Baptista Pereira's defense of the 1890 code. But he also published a medical treatise, *A loucura sob novo prisma* (*Madness Through a New Prism*, 1897), defending the spiritist "disobsession" therapy for madness. In it, he sketches a model of psychiatric practice that overlaps with orthodox psychiatry. He ascribes many mental illnesses to physical brain damage, but claims that others are the result of obsessing spirits who carry a karmic grudge from a past-life encounter with the spirit of the patient. A moral slip by the patient allows the obsessor to lodge at the intersection between the spirit and the brain, "dragging down" the mind. Spiritist psychiatrists can heal this type of madness by incorporating the obsessing spirit in a medium (usually in the absence of the patient), and counseling it to abandon its vengeance. In an interesting twist on doctors' accusations that mediums caused mischief, Bezerra de Menezes projects rascality onto "ignorant spirits," and argues that mediums are healers moved by charity.[41]

Nina Rodrigues

However, the richest medical investigation into the spirits in popular religious healing was undertaken by Raimundo Nina Rodrigues (1862–1906), a pioneer in psychiatry and forensic medicine at the Bahia Medical School. Nina Rodrigues was the leading propagandist of Lombrosian criminal anthropology in Brazil. He proposed anthropometric-psychiatric evaluations to determine appropriate sentencing at all criminal trials (1894), the reorganization of insane asylums, hiring of forensic experts by the police, and many other reforms of the medical-legal system. While visiting the Rio de Janeiro medical school in 1887, he had been at the edges of the circle of hypnotists; after returning to Bahia, he worked with physicians practicing hypnotism, such as Alfredo Britto. Nina Rodrigues was probably the most effective scientific writer of his generation, a remarkably direct popularizer of new psychiatric and anthropological representations of religion.

His research on Afro-Brazilian candomblé initially approached its exotic phenomena from a criminological, social control perspective. He believed that in Bahia, at least, the hold of the state—or the official "civilization"—over the population was weak. In essays on politics and social psychology he chastised the Bahian elite for denying the extent of African beliefs and healing practices. As he once reminded them, during a smallpox epidemic, "no matter how unobservant one's spirit, no matter how much the garbage that covers the streets may conceal, it [was] impossible to traverse the city without noting the singular presence on every corner of popcorn mixed with red palm oil," fetish offerings to the African divinities of smallpox.[42] Nina thought that such signs demonstrated that the Portuguese masters had never Christianized their African slaves, converting them to monotheistic abstractions. On the contrary, Africans had fetishized Bahian Catholicism, adapting it to their "rudimentary animism." Like European colonials in Africa, "in Bahia all classes, even the so-called superior class, are apt to *turn black.*"[43] Energetic measures would be needed to put civilization back in control.

In *O animismo fetichista dos negros bahianos* (*The Fetishist Animism of Bahian Blacks,* 1896), which he published in biweekly installments in Brazil's leading journal of opinion, Nina Rodrigues attempts to explain candomblé's mysteries. Along with fears of poisonous sorcery, much of the prestige of candomblé derived from the ecstatic and majestic demeanor of those possessed by the *orixás,* African "saints." Nina Rodrigues would not dismiss possession trance as fraudulent fakery, what French psychiatrists called "simulation"; he accepts the sincerity of a humble woman who had no memory of having swung from trees in a fury while possessed by her orixá. But he needs no supernatural explanation. The *estado de santo* trance, he argues, is simply a state of temporary alienation, "induced somnambulism with splitting and substitution of personality."[44] He adopts Pierre Janet's theory of dissociation of streams of consciousness and splitting off of mutually amnesiac personalities to explain how the learned personality of an orixá can substitute for the initiate's workaday personality during trance. Ritual dancing and drumming, "like the tam-tam at Salpêtrière" for Charcot's hysteric patients, efficiently suggests to initiates that they enter the hypnotic trance phase of somnambulism. With the help of Alfredo Britto, Nina Rodrigues himself was able to hypnotize a candomblé novice into an estado de santo in his office.

Despite his interest in strengthening the legal system, Nina Rodrigues did not support criminalizing candomblé. Once he had mastered the spirits scientifically, and as he developed a working relationship with sophisticated informants inside candomblé such as Martiniano do Bomfim, he turned more benevolent toward Afro-Brazilian religion. In *O animismo fetichista*, he argues that animistic candomblé beliefs should be countered by a new "catechism" of rational education (in a form appropriate to the limited capacity of racially-degenerate hysterics, of course). In articles collected posthumously as *Os africanos no Brasil* (*Africans in Brazil,* 1939), he defends the right of candomblé to religious freedom. He explicitly criticizes police raids on candomblé as a kind of civilized savagery. The police repression seems to him to be a symptom of a state too weak, in resources or in will, to assume its paternalistic, civilizing responsibility. Ultimately his descriptions of candomblé's subversive idioms of power may have influenced writers who were less committed to the forcible medical regeneration of society.

Spirit Healing in Literature

Brazilian writers used themes of spiritism, witchcraft, and magical healing and harm to reflect on social relations and political power, some of them much more critically than any lawyer or physician. Writers had much more varied careers and no centralizing professional associations, like those physicians had, to coordinate their ideology. Those who entered journalism came closest to forming authoritative centers and consensus, to falling into a mode of campaigns for social reform. But during the 1890s, most Brazilian writers of fiction became less bohemian and more identified with the government's conservative modernizing project of regenerating society.[45] If there was any characteristic stance of writers during the Belle Epoque of 1898 to 1922, it was naturalism, in a sense the literary equivalent of positivist social philosophy. Like positivism, the Brazilian naturalist movement began in the 1870s. It remained important through the 1920s as a realist esthetic oriented by scientific determinism, particularly the biological determinism of medical science. Naturalist literature incorporated medical knowledge and legal discourse about religion and magic.

Generally, writers influenced by naturalism enlisted themselves in the movement for progress and stigmatized popular healing and religion as a menace. Most naturalist literature adopted the Catholic church's and the medical profession's hostile critiques of spiritism, occultism, and popular religion.[46] Coelho Netto's *Turbilhão* (*Whirlwind*, 1906), for example, includes a credible documentary episode in which the central character, Dona Júlia, is encouraged by her black cook Felícia to visit a spiritist center to inquire about her wayward daughter. Her visit is one more step in the moral decline of a middle-class family, and of Rio de Janeiro: when Dona Júlia signs the register at the center, she is number 2,811. The session, described in detail, is by turns homely, sad, and mysterious. Many people testify to cures. But when a young woman falls into convulsions, Dona Júlia reconsiders and leaves suddenly, citing the position of the Catholic church and invoking legal repression as the remedy: "I believe in God, I believe in His power and his mercy. . . . No one is more of a believer than I am, but I can't accept these things. It's because of these and other things like it that so many people go mad. . . . This should be forbidden. It must be that the police don't know." Felícia stays with spiritism and eventually goes mad, conversing with the invisible spirit of her son.[47]

Even when it was not aggressively hostile to popular religion, calling for police intervention, journalism was almost always sensationalistic. João do Rio's *As religiões no Rio* (*Religions in Rio,* 1906), a clever collection of feature stories on the gamut of sects in Rio de Janeiro, covers Afro-Brazilian sects with snide sympathy. But it emphasizes the spine-tingling decadence of pathological practices, such as a satanists' black mass he claims to have attended. João do Rio concedes that the Kardecist spiritists are "sincere," if not very sensible. But most centers he considers "exploitative," using language from the 1890 law: "Beyond a few groups that conduct themselves with relative honesty, the agents of spiritism are shameless rascals. The mediums exploit credulity, the sessions are a cover for depraved acts, and madness sprouts and hysteria rises from each of these incubators of fetishism."[48] His division of Rio spiritism into "sincere" and "exploitative" centers in this influential exposé reflects categories already developing in legal prosecutions and police practice.[49] The final vignette of his series on spiritism describes a scene where parents go to a session with a cynically manipulative healer, seeking help for their sick child: "Suddenly, a voice broke in from below, through gusts of wind, 'Mamma! Mamma! Come quick! Joãozinho's dying, Joãozinho's dead!'"[50]

Two authors, Xavier Marques and Lima Barreto, partly broke from this mold and used the theme of witchcraft to reflect on, and criticize, social and political power. Xavier Marques (1861–1942) was a white Bahian journalist who worked with the state's political machine during the republic and once served as a congressman in Rio. Like Coelho Netto, he was a traditionalist Catholic intellectual, best known for picturesque novels set among Bahian fishermen. Afonso Henriques Lima Barreto (1881–1922) was the most radical writer of Brazil's Belle Epoque. Lima Barreto, a mulatto, is best known for his blunt criticism of racism and positivist race science. He had studied briefly at the Rio engineering school, and derived from it a post-positivist view of "science as hypothesis" that gave him leverage to question the "positive facts" of race science. He worked on newspapers and became sufficiently acquainted with police methods and the clichés of sensationalist crime reporting to ridicule them in satires. Lima Barreto was boycotted by the literary establishment for most of his career; he lived as a petty clerk and a disreputable bohemian. Their literary careers contrasted sharply, but both Marques and Lima Barreto made use of witchcraft beliefs to construct fictional situations that offer insights into Brazilian social relations.

"Going Native" in Xavier Marques's Salvador

It is a Brazilian commonplace to claim that individuals of all classes supplicate spirit-possession religions for supernatural aid or simple favors. The rumor that the police would not arrest feiticeiros because the highest politicians were clients of candomblé circulated widely in the 1890s. Nina Rodrigues's assertion that "in Bahia all classes, even the so-called superior class, are apt to *turn black*," furnishes the premise of Xavier Marques's perceptive novel of Bahian regional customs, *O feiticeiro* (*The Witch Doctor*, 1897; revised 1922).[51]

The plot of *O feiticeiro* (set in 1878, before the witchcraft law) centers on two respectable, white families who unwittingly enlist the same African feiticeiro, not for healing but to curse each other, so that their daughters can win the hand of the hero, Amâncio. Simultaneously, the Bahian chief of police has commissioned the feiticeiro, Elesbão, to hex Amâncio, leader of the subversive Republicans. This coincidence puts the fate of decent families and the maintenance of public order in the hands of Elesbão. He satisfies the good family by placing a spell on the mother of the bad family; he satisfies the chief of police by manipulating Amâncio to resign from the Republican club in order to get his father's permission to marry. Only a few of the characters appreciate the irony of their being "puppets on strings" or in the "spider's web" of the sorcerer's manipulations. But Elesbão's rascally, illicit power becomes Marques's leading example of the general softness of Bahian civilization, permeable to influences from its African underside. Unlike Nina Rodrigues, Marques proposes no measures for social defense; only Elesbão's death from old age releases the families from his hold over them.[52]

It is likely that Xavier Marques, who wrote at the same time that Nina Rodrigues was publishing *O animismo fetichista,* drew on the same stock of gossip. It is even possible that he drew on one of Nina's case histories. As evidence of the effect of hypnosis on trance, Nina Rodrigues relates the case of a young white woman, hysterical and for some time in hypnotherapy, who met her husband's old lover, a black woman, on the street. She felt a pain in her foot, and when she got home, had a hysterical attack. The girl's mother, "who is hysterical and degenerated and lives surrounded by black women who are influential in candomblés," imagined there was witchcraft, and called in an African "uncle" to exorcise her daughter. A male relative called in Nina Rodrigues, who noticed that the uncle's mumbled recitations made the attacks worse. Nina sent away the sorcerer and immediately gave the girl "suggestive injunctions" calming her fears and ending the attacks.[53] Nina Rodrigues's case study resembles the situation in Marques's novel, which details the clientelistic relations between women of good family and the sorcerers of candomblés.

Marques wrote two versions of the novel, each with different emphases. In the first, 1897 edition, *Boto & Cia.,* he focuses on the superstition, "hypochondria," and "nervousness" of Eulália, the spinster who is yearning for Amâncio.[54] The most lurid visions of barbarous witchcraft occur in her dreams. But in his second, 1922 edition, *O feiticeiro,* he tightens the plot in order to implicate the men in spells. He also introduces more psychiatric theory in order to rationally explain the powerful effects of witchcraft as "autosuggestion." For example, the good father, Paulo Boto, reacts in disgust to a fetish plate left outside his door:

> Whatever the efficacy or inefficacy of their spells, the harmful intent, the thought of doing him and his family wrong, was a positive fact. Furthermore, although he kept it quiet, he couldn't entirely avoid instinctive terror at the *coisa feita* ["preparation," or witchcraft fetish]. Autosuggestion of failure, of decline, of misfortune due to the *gris-gris,* worked on him spontaneously.

Paradoxically, the hypnotic, or suggestive, rationalization of candomblé healing and harm seems to have enabled Xavier Marques to move closer to candomblé in the second version of the novel, to use an Afro-Brazilian witchcraft concept for political analysis.

"Switching Head" and Politics

One interesting feature of *O feiticeiro,* perhaps unique in Brazilian literature, is that it exploits the Afro-Brazilian concept of *troca de cabeça,* "switching heads," as a key to its commentary on competition within a paternalistic, patronal system. Early in the novel, the widow Antonia and her dependent Josefa discuss the bad luck of young Salustiano, the suitor of Josefa's daughter:

> [Josefa:] "And on whom does it depend . . . his moving up?"
>
> [Antonia:] "It must be the President of the Province, or the chief of his division. You need to arrange some strong pull. The best pull is a woman's pull. The President is married; maybe through the head-mistress of your school . . ."
>
> "Yes, ma'am," replied the housekeeper, distracted, remembering cases in which persons without luck or with "bad head" had managed to get the wheel of fortune to turn in their favor from one day to the next.
>
> She did not want to and never did disclose that trick to the widow Antonia, even though she had already taken measures of that sort to ensure her daughter's happiness.
>
> "My son-in-law [Boto], for his part, will do what he can. He is a good friend of Salustiano. But I repeat, there is nothing like a woman's protection."
>
> "That's the way of the world," Josefa reflected out loud. "Near here, on Ajuda Street, there lives a rich man who has been a widower for many years, with an only son. He never bothered to take another wife, though there are so many poor girls. He lives with a black woman. He may not care to marry; but those who wish to marry cannot, they lack the means . . ."
>
> "God gives chestnuts to those without teeth."
>
> "To each his head," added the housekeeper, more irritated inside by these iniquities of fortune and already planning to appeal to the one

who could correct them. The thing was simple in her way of looking at it: a "switching of head" [*troca de cabeça*]. The luck of the shacked-up moneybags would pass to the poor and honorable Salustiano; Salustiano's troubles would pass to the other. If the world always had to be made up of the happy and the misfortunate, let the good be happy and save the misfortune for the bad ones.[55]

In this passage, Marques represents fortune not only through the classical and European trope of the Wheel of Fortune, but also in terms of the Yoruba-Brazilian concept of "head."

Yoruba traditional religions of the twentieth century understand the "head," or *ori,* as both the physical head and the person's personality and destiny. Divine predestination seals ori before a person comes into the world; guardian spirits watch over it during life. It is an inescapable lot in life: "A bad ori cannot be washed out with soap." But a person must match his ori with force of character. Laziness or pride can spoil a fine destiny. If guided by divine knowledge, determined action can avert a bad destiny. And the mischief of malevolent witches can divert one's destiny.[56]

In Bahian creole religions, the identification of "head" (cabeça, ori) with one's guardian spirit, or ori-xá, is almost certainly an extension of Yoruba beliefs. Studies of candomblé from the 1890s through the 1960s have documented witchcraft beliefs centering on troca de cabeça.[57] In Bahian troca de cabeça, the witch or the person who employs the witch often prepares a fetish bundle or plate and places it where the person whose head is to be taken will step, pass, or glance. On contact with the fetish, that undeserving person's "good head" exchanges for one's own "bad head."[58] The ritual of troca de cabeça, for someone who actually undertakes it, may symbolize in a concrete way the nature of self-advancement in a universe of limited good.[59] And an accusation that another person has employed troca de cabeça may project the fears and anxieties that a system of favoritism engenders. An ethic of reciprocity entails returning good for food; but it is also an ethic of revenge, retaliation, and balance through returning evil for imagined evil.

How does this amount to a vision of politics? Marques used head-switching as a metaphorical key to patronage and political stagnation in Bahia. Ideally, a system of patronage grounds itself in an ethic of reciprocity, in which each client gets from a patron in protection and beneficence, what they render to him in obedience and deference. Continuing small and large exchanges, like a ball thrown back and forth, keep the relationship alive. But Marques demonstrates that at many points the system generates, as one Bahian patron put it, "conflicting and incompatible" demands.[60] Good will and paternalism cannot satisfy every wish. Indeed, some theorists have argued that there must be scarcity in a patronage system in order for patrons to have something worth bestowing.[61] When clients' ambitions focus on a limited number of offices, as in nineteenth-century Brazil, someone must be postponed for every one who advances. At some point, one man's gain is another man's loss. *O feiticeiro* presents several such conflicts: both Eulália and Antonieta seek supernatural aid in winning Amâncio's love; Salustiano maneuvers against other clerks for a promotion in his government office; the Liberal and Conservative parties vie for the emperor's decisive favor in the all-or-nothing 1878 election. In each of these competitions, the outcome is out of the hands of the interested parties. They must supplicate a higher power, begging it to choose them over the other person. And the higher power — Elesbão or Amâncio's father; the government; the emperor; even God — faces the task of choosing between entangling commitments to both parties.

Xavier Marques uses the witchcraft concept of troca de cabeça to comment on the action of the novel and on Brazilian political life. "Switching head" nicely symbolizes the arbitrary oscillations of favor within a system of patronage, an arbitrariness that extends to the police chief who is supposed to embody the law but instead works through pacts with the underworld.

Healers and Doctors in Lima Barreto's Rio

Lima Barreto, like Xavier Marques, saw Brazilians' magical practices and witchcraft accusations as their commentary on social power. He argued that the resort to magic and religious healing was the result of a human drive to find "Hope" in a hostile world.[62] His radical critique of the Republic shows best in his use of folk healing and witchcraft to structure the subplot of *Triste fim de Policarpo Quaresma* (*The Patriot*, 1915). Written on the model of *Don Quixote*, *Triste fim* chronicles the destruction of Major Policarpo Quaresma, a middle-aged civil servant in the War Department, who is possessed by the illusion of the Patria. Quaresma reads chauvinist books about Brazilian natural resources that feed his hopes for a grand Brazil. In the first stage of his quest, he collects folklore, and he proposes legislation restoring indigenous Tupi as the official language. But the folklore he can find is fragments and nonsense, and his Tupi project meets ridicule that drives him mad. He winds up in a Rio asylum. When he recovers, in the second stage of his quest, he retires to a farm in Curuzu, on the outskirts of Rio, where he tries to cultivate the good Brazilian soil. But ants, the apathy of the country folk, and the mean factionalism of local politics frustrate him. In the third stage, Quaresma volunteers enthusiastically for the Patriotic Battalions called up to defend Floriano Peixoto's republican dictatorship against the monarchist naval revolt of 1893. "Have energy; I follow!" reads his telegram to Floriano. But the brutality of combat and Floriano's indifference to his memorandum proposing national reforms discourage him. When he writes Floriano to protest the illegal execution of prisoners, he himself is executed as a traitor.

Quaresma never makes accusations of witchcraft, even when he is insane. The malice that surrounds him is the concrete enmity of envious conservatives who fear patriotism and reform. But his quest intertwines with the parallel subplot of Ismênia, daughter of his family friend General Albernaz. The illusion that deludes Quaresma is patriotism; that which deludes Ismênia is marriage—the only aspiration taught to petit-bourgeois girls. The Albernaz family supports Ismênia's fiancé through dental school, but as soon as he graduates, he disappears. At first, Ismênia is consoled by the noise of Carnival, which serves to "repress the grief inside her, muffled, compressed, contained, that needed an explosion of screams for which she lacked enough force." In the quiet afterward, she becomes apathetic, then insane, then ill. Her parents try all sorts of doctors, finally turning to homeopathic spiritists and African witch doctors:

> "Was it a spell someone set on my daughter?" asked the lady.
> "Yassum, sure was."
> "Who?"
> "Saint don' wan' tell."

The narrator reflects that "it was a singular situation, that old African black, who certainly hardly forgot the pains of his long enslavement, making use of the residues of his ingenuous tribal beliefs . . . and using them to console those who in another time had been his masters." Ismênia is impressed by such powerful men, "who had immaterial beings, existences beyond and above ours, at their command." However, she does not recover. Unlike the Boto family in *O feiticeiro*, the Albernazes do not prosper from occult forces. Like Quaresma, Ismênia sacrifices her life to an illusion.[63]

Lima Barreto is less interested in contemplating the ironies of reversible social power than Xavier Marques. Like a crusading naturalist, he wants to protest, to expose the impotence of the populace and the lower middle class against malicious sovereign powers that they themselves elevate: the government, political "idols" such as Floriano Peixoto, expert "*doutores*" with a diploma, and above all the police. Unwilling to acknowledge their true enemies, Brazilians invent occult antagonists, evil spirits. But unlike most naturalists, Lima Barreto does not idealize science; scientific explanation of magic is not the answer. "Official science," rather than helping people, is just another form of mystification, inventing scapegoats such as "racial degenerates" and legitimating oppression. In order to provoke critical reflection, *Triste fim* levels witchcraft and science, feiticeiros and doutores, for example by portraying the physician and the curandeira in the town of Curuzu as mirror images of one another.

Witchcraft accusations may even be the only way most Brazilians can recognize and protest their oppression. In Lima Barreto's semiautobiographical first novel, *Recordações do escrivão Isaías Caminha* (*Recollections of the Clerk Isaías Caminha*, 1909), listening to witchcraft accusations gives his naive hero, Isaías, a vital insight into the state. Isaías, come to study in Rio de Janeiro, has just been accused of stealing a watch at his boarding house. In the police station, he sees two poor women, brought into the station for fighting. Bullied by the policemen, one cries, and her words, "full of some great pain," accuse her neighbor of enticing a hen to lay eggs over in her house. The neighbor replies that when she saw the first egg laid in her house, "she thought it was 'hoodoo' [*mandinga*], she thought it was a 'preparation' [*cousa feita*]." This pathetic scene awakens some identification that lets Isaías assert his own protest. The police inspector who questions him won't believe a mulatto can be a student: "The hell you are!" Isaías, at first intimidated and numbed by the unaccustomed racist insults, finally is able to vocalize. "Injustices, sufferings, humiliations, miseries, joined together inside me, rose to the level of consciousness, passed before my eyes, and then I spat it out, syllable by syllable: 'Imbecile!'." Thrown back into jail, "my tears ran and I thought to myself, 'The Nation!'"[64] The police are essential elements to Lima Barreto's explanation of Brazilian witchcraft beliefs: "The struggle against misfortune, against uncertainty about the next day, stemming from the conviction that our luck is insecure and that we are surrounded by superior entities who are no great friends of our happiness and comfort, this leads us to the most curious and unusual domestic superstitions."[65]

Conclusion: An Almost Magical Liberty

The Brazilian critic Antonio Candido, in "The Dialectic of Malandroism," argues that a novel may be "profoundly social, . . . not by being documentary, but by being constructed according to the general rhythm of the society." He suggests that Brazilian characters may interact more realistically in a world of folktale coincidences, of "almost magical liberty of the fictional space," than they do in moralizing, serious Romantic novels.[66] My exploration of representations of witchcraft in law and literature between 1890 and 1922 has asked how institutions and intellectuals responded to Brazilian mentalities and practices heavily imbued with fantasy and wish fulfillment: beliefs that powerful spirits of the dead watch over us, that we can call on them for help, that sorcerers can manipulate their powers, speak with their voice, turn leaves into healing potions, defend us against the malice of our enemies. Practices based on this worldview flourished in Brazilian cities at the turn of the century, as they still do today.[67] The emergence of spiritism, a movement within the literate classes with an elaborate intellectual rationalization, posed a special challenge to the medical profession and the Catholic church, and probably was the critical catalyst of the 1890 restoration of witchcraft laws.

The elaborate fictional worlds constructed by novelists may illuminate the latent motivations of the authorities who persecuted certain Brazilian religious healing as "witchcraft." Both the legal establishment that upheld the 1890 penal code and the medical establishment that mandated smallpox vaccinations in 1903 wished to reform "the general rhythm" of Brazilian society. They aspired to regenerate a sick nation in many ways, one being to purge it of superstitious healing rituals which not coincidentally furnished alternative representations of social power. They approached popular religious ideologies and practices from outside and above, in order to eradicate or neutralize them. The law criminalized those who claimed to control exchanges with the spirits, and interpreted witchcraft in the narrow context of decisions to convict or acquit, to tolerate "religion" but to punish "fraud." The dialogues among defenders, prosecutors, judges, and jurists produced tortuous and ambivalent statements on the place of the supernatural in Brazilian society. Between 1910 and 1940, they settled for an awkward compromise recognizing certain spiritual healing rituals as "charity" and others as criminal mischief. Their actions, like many social interventions of republican reformers, made a traditional idiom of patronage exchange illegal, and labeled sectors of the population as deviants and outcasts. Medical science tried to find a truthful psychological explanation of magical experiences. But it gravitated toward a clichéd diagnosis of spirit possession as mental illness. Even its best works, such as Nina Rodrigues's subtle and ironic investigations of the relations between candomblé magic and social control in Bahia, pathologized popular healing.

It is not that elites were too far removed from the people for comprehension of popular culture. Some literary intellectuals, perhaps because they were less engaged in nation-building institutions such as the courts or the public health services, felt freer to try on the perspectives of popular ideologies of supernatural healing. By treating magic ambiguously either as truly marvelous power or as a real psychological effect of suggestion, writers such as Xavier Marques and Lima Barreto were able to use it to criticize the smugness of official ideology. The conservative Marques played with the "almost magical liberty" of reversible powers and magical solutions to conflicts. The radical Lima Barreto looked down on superstition, but he also hoped that popular symbolism of oppression and evil as witchcraft might enable the Brazilian people to find their indignation at illegitimate authority and eventually to protest their exclusion. He appreciated the compensatory leveling impulse in witchcraft accusations, but saw the magical imagination as a short circuit, a futile circle without happy endings or healing. Both authors saw that witchcraft could reveal a rhythm of social exchanges, ignored by the republic's official institutions, that was one dimension of Brazilian community.

Notes

1 Dec. 847 of Oct. 10, 1890, articles 156–158, my translation. Cited in Emerson Giumbelli, *O cuidado dos mortos: Uma história da condenação e legitimação do espiritismo* (Rio de Janeiro: Arquivo Nacional, 1997), pp. 79–80.

2 Francisco Bethencourt, *O imaginário da magia: Feiticeiras, saludadores e nigromantes no século XVI* (Lisboa: Centro de Estudos de História e Cultura Portuguesa and Projecto Universidade Aberta, 1987), and José Pedro Paiva, *Bruxaria e superstição num país sem "caça às bruxas," 1600–1774* (Lisboa: Notícias, 1997), esp. 189–207, discuss mixed jurisdiction over feitiçaria in Portugal; Paiva concludes that there were probably many civil prosecutions not recorded in surviving documents.

3 *Código Philippino ou Ordenações e leis do Reino do Portugal,* ed. Cândido Mendes de Almeida, 14th ed. (Rio de Janeiro: Typografia do Instituto Philomathico, 1870), Livro V, título 3, para. 1, 2, 3; Laura de Mello e Souza, *O Diabo e a Terra de Santa*

Cruz: Feitiçaria e religiosidade popular no Brasil colonial (São Paulo: Companhia das Letras, 1989).

4 *O último Regimento da Inquisição Portuguesa,* ed. and rev. Raul Rêgo (Lisbon: Excelsior, 1971), original title, *Regimento do Santo Officio da Inquisição . . . pelo . . . Cardeal da Cunha* [1774], Livro III, tit. XI, pp. 179–190, esp. cap. 2, p. 187. Curiously, in cases discussed in Mello e Souza, *O Diabo,* Portuguese and Brazilian authorities seem not to have identified Afro-Brazilian calundu dances as the imaginary witches' sabbath so anxiously sought by seventeenth-century European witch-hunts.

5 Kim Butler, *Freedoms Given, Freedoms Won: Afro-Brazilians in Post-Abolition São Paulo and Salvador* (New Brunswick, N.J.: Rutgers University Press, 1998), p. 192; Rachel E. Harding, *A Refuge in Thunder: Candomblé and Alternative Spaces of Blackness* (Bloomington: Indiana University Press, 2000), pp. 135–138; Dale T. Graden, "Abolition and Freedom in Brazil: Bahia, 1835–1900," ms., 1997.

6 João José Reis, "Nas malhas do poder escravista: A invasão do Candomblé do Accú," in João José Reis and Eduardo Silva, *Negociação e conflito: A resistência negra no Brasil escravista* (São Paulo: Companhia das Letras, 1989), esp. pp. 124–130.

7 Robert Conrad, *Children of God's Fire: A Documentary History of Black Slavery in Brazil* (Princeton, N.J.: Princeton University Press, 1983), pp. 254–267.

8 Gabriela dos Reis Sampaio, "A história do feiticeiro Juca Rosa: Cultura e relações sociais no Rio de Janeiro Imperial" (Ph.D. thesis, Universidade Estadual de Campinas, 2000), and "O caso Juca Rosa" (unpublished manuscript); Rosa was convicted under the Criminal Code of 1830, article 264, para. 4, although prosecutors mentioned the obsolete Philippine Code witchcraft laws. Giumbelli, *Cuidado,* p. 106, mentions another prosecution for fraud in 1881.

9 *Código Philippino,* vol. 5, p. 932; Gabriela dos Reis Sampaio, "Nas trincheras da cura: As diferentes medicinas no Rio de Janeiro imperial" (M.A. thesis, UNICAMP, 1995); Lília Moritz Schwarcz, *Retrato em branco e negro: Jornais, escravos e cidadãos em São Paulo no final do século XIX* (São Paulo: Companhia das Letras, 1987), pp. 232, 236–239.

10 It was by no means inevitable that criminal code reform should have passed. The good luck of criminal code reform in 1890 can be compared to the bad luck of the long-pending civil code reform project. Legislative inertia soon set in, and a civil code was enacted only in 1916, after years of grueling negotiation over its grammar and punctuation.

11 For an excellent analysis centered on formation of a working class, see Sidney Chalhoub, *Trabalho, lar e botequim: O cotidiano dos trabalhadores no Rio de Janeiro da Belle Epoque* (São Paulo: Brasiliense, 1986).

12 José Murilo de Carvalho, *Os bestializados: O Rio de Janeiro e a República que não foi* (São Paulo: Companhia das Letras, 1987); Ralph Della Cava, "Catholicism and Society in Twentieth Century Brazil," *Latin American Research Review* 11, no. 2 (1976): 7–50; C. F. G. de Groot, *Brazilian Catholicism and the Ultramontane Reform, 1850–1930* (Amsterdam: CEDLA, 1996).

13 Peter Fry, Sérgio Carrara, and Ana Luiza Martins-Costa, "Negros e brancos no Carnaval da Velha República," in João José Reis, ed., *Escravidão e invenção da liberdade: Estudos sobre o negro no Brasil* (São Paulo: Brasiliense, 1988), pp. 232–263; Beatriz Gois Dantas, *Vovó nagô e papai branco: Usos e abusos da África no Brasil* (Rio de Janeiro: Graal, 1988); Yvonne Maggie, *Medo do feitiço: Relações entre magia e poder no Brasil* (Rio de Janeiro: Arquivo Nacional, 1992); Butler, *Freedoms Given.*

14 Raimundo Nina Rodrigues, *O animismo fetichista dos negros bahianos,* 1st ed. 1896 (Rio de Janeiro: Civilização Brasileira, 1935), p. 187.

15 Thomas Holloway, *Policing Rio de Janeiro: Repression and Resistance in the 19th-Century City* (Stanford: Stanford University Press, 1993); Sidney Chalhoub, *Cidade febril: Cortiços e epidemias na Corte imperial* (São Paulo: Companhia das Letras, 1996).

16 Eduardo Silva's *Prince of the People: The Life and Times of a Brazilian Man of Colour* (London: Verso, 1993), a case study of the eccentric Prince Obá II d'Africa, suggests that a style of paternalistic accommodation of Afro-Brazilian culture in the empire (epitomized by Pedro II's weekly open audiences in which he conversed with Obá) gave way to a more closed republican system. Jeffrey Needell, "The *Revolta Contra Vacina* of 1904: The Revolt against 'Modernization' in *Belle-Epoque* Rio de Janeiro," *Hispanic American Historical Review* 67/2 (May 1987): 233–269.

17 Beatriz Teixeira Weber, *As artes de curar: Medicina, religião, magia e positivismo na República rio-grandense, 1889–1928* (Santa Maria: Editora UFSM; Baurú: EDUSC, 1999).

18 Roberto Machado, et al., *Danação da norma: Medicina social e constituição da psiquiatria no Brasil* (Rio de Janeiro: Graal, 1978), p. 212. The Sept. 29, 1851, regulation was amended in Jan. 19, 1882, and Feb. 13, 1886; the Board changed its name to Inspectorate-General of Hygiene in 1886.

19 João José Reis, *A morte é uma festa: Ritos fúnebres e revolta popular no Brasil do século XIX* (São Paulo: Companhia das Letras, 1991).

20 For histories of early spiritism, see Giumbelli, *Cuidado dos mortos;* David J. Hess, *Spirits and Scientists: Ideology, Spiritism, and Brazilian Culture* (University Park: Pennsylvania State University Press, 1991); Ubiratan Machado, *Os intelectuais e o espiritismo: De Castro Alves a Machado de Assis* (Rio de Janeiro: Antares, 1983); Marion Aubrée and François Laplantine, *La table, le livre et les esprits: Naissance, évolution et actualité du mouvement social spirite entre France et Brésil* (Paris: Jean-Claude Lattès, 1990).

21 Tito Lívio de Castro, *Das allucinações e illusões* (Rio de Janeiro: Imprensa Mont'Alverne, 1889), pp. 55–59; Donald Warren, "A terapia espírita no Rio de Janeiro por volta de 1900," *Religião e Sociedade* 13, no. 2 (Dec. 1984): 56–83.

22 Sampaio, "Nas trincheras da cura."

23 Adolpho Bezerra de Menezes et al., "O novo codigo penal," *Jornal do Commercio,* Dec. 25, 1890.

24 On the church campaign against spiritism, see Machado, *Os intelectuais,* and crit-

icism equating spiritism and hypnotism as "immoral and dangerous" in the Catholic press, e.g., "O hypnotismo," *O Apostolo* Mar. 20, 23, Apr. 1, 1887. On the church, animal magnetism, and spiritism, see also Alan Gauld, *A History of Hypnotism* (Cambridge: Cambridge University Press, 1992), and Henri F. Ellenberger, *The Discovery of the Unconscious: The History and Evolution of Dynamic Psychiatry* (New York: Basic Books, 1970).

25 Baptista Pereira, "O novo codigo: O novo codigo penal e o spiritismo," *Jornal do Commercio,* Dec. 23, 24, 25, 30, 1890.

26 Max [pseud. Bezerra de Menezes], "O novo codigo penal e o spiritismo" (*Jornal do Commercio,* Dec. 24, 25, 26, 27, 28, 29, 30, 31, 1890.

27 Hess, *Spirits;* Giumbelli, *Cuidado.*

28 Giumbelli, *Cuidado,* pp. 290–294.

29 Joaquim Borges Carneiro, lawyer for the accused, José Ferraz, in Arquivo Nacional, 6a Vara Criminal, caixa 2002, no. 571, 1898, p. 72. Ferraz was tried and acquitted again in 1904; Maggie, *Medo,* pp. 72–73, 90–101, 107.

30 Giumbelli, *Cuidado,* pp. 143–149. He points out that Viveiros de Castro was considered a criminological positivist on other issues and argues that Maggie, *Medo,* is too hasty to describe judicial reasoning whose outcome is tolerance as liberal. Cf. Ricardo D. Salvatore, "Penitentiaries, Visions of Class, and Export Economies: Brazil and Argentina Compared," in Ricardo D. Salvatore and Carlos Aguirre, eds. *The Birth of the Penitentiary in Latin America: Essays on Criminology, Prison Reform, and Social Control, 1830–1940* (Austin: University of Texas Press and Institute of Latin American Studies, 1996), pp. 194–223, on positivist criminology and penology in Brazil.

31 Cited in Giumbelli, *Cuidado,* p. 148.

32 The prescribing medium Domingos Filgueiras was acquitted of using "spiritism and homeopathy," and Leopoldo Cirne of treating smallpox, in 1905 and 1904 (Giumbelli, *Cuidado,* pp. 174–180; Donald Warren, "The Healing Art in the Urban Setting, 1880–1930" (paper at the Symposium on Popular Dimensions of Brazil, University of California at Los Angeles, February 1–2, 1979). There were prosecutions of the Centro Redentor clinic of Rio de Janeiro in 1914, 1921, 1929 and 1932 (Hess, *Spirits,* pp. 96–97; Maggie, *Medo,* pp. 205–222).

33 Maggie, *Medo,* pp. 66–69, located records of 581 arrests in Rio in scattered years 1912–1945. Studies in Salvador using newspaper accounts mention police raids in the 1890s (Rodrigues, *Africanos*), and a cluster during the 1920s: Angela Luhning, "Acabe com este santo, Pedrito vem aí: Mito e realidade da perseguição policial ao candomblé baiano entre 1920 e 1942," *Revista USP* 28 (Dec. 1995–Jan./Feb. 1996): 194–220; Júlio Braga, *Na gamela do feitiço: Repressão e resistência nos candomblés da Bahia* (Salvador: EDUFBa, 1995). Martha Knisely Huggins, *From Slavery to Vagrancy in Brazil: Crime and Social Control in the Third World* (New Brunswick, N.J.: Rutgers University Press, 1985), p. 82, 147–148, found thirty-three arrests in Recife for "catimbauzeiro" (sorcerer) in police records sampled over the three

years 1900, 1910, and 1920. Lísias Nogueira Negrão found 29 stories in São Paulo newspapers about police repression of feitiçaria and folk healing from 1891 to 1928 and 79 from 1929 to 1940. See Lísias Nogueira Negrão, *Entre a cruz e a encruzilhada: Formação do campo umbandista em São Paulo* (São Paulo: Editora da Universidade de São Paulo, 1996), pp. 43–54 and 71–75.

34 Luhning, "Acabe com este santo."

35 Dantas, *Vovó nagô;* Butler, *Freedoms,* pp. 202–209; *Cartas de Édison Carneiro a Artur Ramos: De 4 de janeiro de 1936 a 6 de dezembro de 1938,* ed. Waldir Freitas Oliveira and Vivaldo da Costa Lima (São Paulo: Corrupio, 1987), pp. 152–155.

36 Diana D. Brown, *Umbanda: Religion and Politics in Urban Brazil* (New York: Columbia University Press, 1994), pp. 145–150; the new Umbanda centers founded their own federation in 1939.

37 Maggie, *Medo;* Giumbelli, *Cuidado.*

38 Giumbelli, *Cuidado,* pp. 181, 295–297; of course, clients would have attended multiple consultations, so their proportion of the city's population must be less than a fifth.

39 French debates of the 1880s over hypnotism saw it either as one extreme of a continuum stretching to normal suggestion in daily life, or else as a pathological hysterical state; Gauld, *History,* 279–336.

40 Francisco Fajardo, *Tratado de hipnotismo,* 2d ed. (Rio de Janeiro and São Paulo: Laemmert, 1896).

41 Adolfo Bezerra de Menezes, *A loucura sob novo prisma: Estudo psychico-physiologico* (Rio de Janeiro: Typ. Bohemia, 1926); Hess, *Spirits,* pp. 81–98; Castro, *Allucinações;* Warren, "A terapia espírita."

42 Raimundo Nina Rodrigues, "A loucura epidêmica de Canudos: Antonio Conselheiro e os jagunços," *As collectividades anormaes* (Rio de Janeiro: Civilização Brasileira, 1939), pp. 50–77.

43 Rodrigues, *Animismo fetichista,* echoing E. B. Tylor on Europeans in Africa "going native."

44 Rodrigues, *Animismo,* p. 109; cf. Fajardo, *Hypnotismo,* pp. 251–255. See also Hess, *Spirits.*

45 The new conformism extended to founding an Academy of Literature in 1897; see Needell, *A Tropical Belle Epoque: Elite Culture and Society in Turn-of-the-Century Rio de Janeiro* (Cambridge: Cambridge University Press, 1987); Nicolau Sevcenko, *Literatura como missão: Tensões sociais e criação literária na Primeira República* (São Paulo: Brasiliense, 1983).

46 Machado, *Os intelectuais,* chronicles a softening of Brazilian writers toward spiritism around 1890; Sampaio, "História do feiticeiro," pp. 163–182 and, throughout, discusses the relations between pre-naturalist representations of feiticeiros in literature and the representations of Juca Rosa during his 1871 trial.

47 [Henrique Maximiliano] Coelho Netto, *Turbilhão* (Rio de Janeiro: Edições de Ouro, n.d. [1906]), p. 159.

48 João do Rio [pseud. Paulo Barreto], *As religiões no Rio* (Rio de Janeiro: Organização Simões, 1951 [1906]), p. 200.

49 João do Rio, *Religiões;* Maggie, *Medo.*

50 João do Rio, *Religiões,* p. 206.

51 Xavier Marques originally published the novel as *Boto & Cia.* (Bahia: Empreza Editora, 1897); he rewrote it in 1910 and retitled it *O feiticeiro* in 1922; quotes are from the 3d edition (São Paulo: GRD, 1975).

52 Although there is no record of a chief of police consulting feiticeiros, imperial officials did accuse one another of protecting candomblés; Harding, *Refuge,* pp. 142–143.

53 Rodrigues, *Animismo,* 122–123; cf. Marques, *Boto & Cia.,* pp. 132ff.

54 On *nervoso,* see Luis Fernando D. Duarte, *Da vida nervosa nas classes trabalhadoras urbanas* (Rio de Janeiro: Zahar, 1986), and Nancy Scheper-Hughes, *Death Without Weeping: The Violence of Everyday Life in Brazil* (Berkeley: University of California Press, 1992). In *Boto & Cia.,* Eulalia suffers an attack of "nervoso" while waiting for Amâncio.

55 Marques, *Feiticeiro,* pp. 15–16.

56 E. Bolaji Idowu, *Olódùmarè: God in Yoruba Belief* (London: Longmans, 1962), p. 172; see Robert Farriss Thompson, *Flash of the Spirit: African and Afro-American Art and Philosophy* (New York: Random House, 1983), pp. 9–12, for an interpretation of Yoruba aesthetics emphasizing the relation of character (*iwa*) to head. Interplay of destiny and character may be seen in contemporary Afro-Brazilian tales such as Mestre Didi [Deoscóredes Maximiliano dos Santos], "Conto da mulher que tinha uma filha fabricante de azeite-de-dendê," *Contos de Mestre Didi* (Rio de Janeiro: Codecri, 1981).

57 Nina Rodrigues, *Animismo fetichista,* pp. 87–89; Manuel Querino, *A raça africana e os seus costumes* (Salvador: Livraria Progresso, 1955 [1918]), p. 77. Such practices probably existed well before the late nineteenth century; nineteenth-century sources speak of "luck-fixing houses," *casas de dar fortuna.*

57 It seems likely that as Yoruba religion moved from Africa to Bahia in the nineteenth century, the idea of "switching head" and witchcraft may have moved to the foreground of popular expression of the ori concept. This changing emphasis could have been a consequence of the collective experience of uprooting through enslavement and a widespread conviction among Bahian Africans that their masters were witches who had unjustly stolen from them their destinies. See Monica Schuler, "Afro-American Slave Culture," in Michael Craton, ed., *Roots and Branches: Current Directions in Slave Studies* (Toronto: Pergamon Press, 1979), pp. 121–155. The prominence of head-switching beliefs and accusations in Bahia might have been one way in which Africans modified traditional religious symbols to represent their situation in a New World that was organized to cause them suffering. Xavier Marques's use of head-switching symbolism is quite compatible with this historical interpretation. *O feiticeiro* contains references to the sufferings of slavery and to the

emancipation movement. It also portrays Salvador as a city filled with gossip and malicious envy—fundamentally, the character that Yoruba society attributes to witches or "children of the world." Idowu, *Olódùmaré*.

59 Peter Fry, "Two Religious Movements: Protestantism and Umbanda," in John Wirth and Robert Jones, eds., *Manchester and São Paulo: Problems of Rapid Urban Growth* (Stanford: Stanford University Press, 1978), pp. 177–202; cf. George M. Foster, *Tzintzuntzan: Mexican Peasants in a Changing World* (Boston: Little, Brown, 1967) on limited good and Michael Taussig, *Shamanism, Colonialism, and the Wild Man: A Study in Terror and Healing* (Chicago: University of Chicago Press, 1987), on envy in other contexts.

60 João Maurício Wanderley, Baron of Cotegipe, in Arquivo do Instituto Histórico e Geográfico Brasileiro, Coleção Araujo Pinho, 548/75, letter [n.d.], Cotegipe to João Ferreira de Araujo Pinho. For analysis of the political system, stressing its flexibility rather than its stalemates, see Richard Graham, *Patronage and Politics in Nineteenth-Century Brazil* (Stanford: Stanford University Press, 1990); for a vision of winner-take-all elections, see Judy Bieber, *Power, Patronage, and Political Violence: State Building on a Brazilian Frontier, 1822–1889* (Lincoln: University of Nebraska Press, 1999).

61 James C. Scott, "Patron-Client Politics and Political Change in Southeast Asia," in Steffen W. Schmidt et al., eds., *Friends, Followers, and Factions: A Reader in Political Clientelism* (Berkeley: University of California Press, 1977), pp. 123–146.

62 Lima Barreto, *Coisas do Reino de Jambon,* vol. 8, *Obras de Lima Barreto* (Rio de Janeiro: Brasiliense, 1961), p. 297.

63 *Triste fim de Policarpo Quaresma,* vol. 2, *Obras,* pp. 109, 244–245, 258, 285.

64 *Recordações do escrivão Isaías Caminha,* vol. 1, *Obras,* pp. 115, 117–118. Most of the novel is dedicated to demonstrating that the malevolent occult power of the city, the power whose name, invoked unawares, liberates Isaías from the police station, is the press; and the press irresponsibly incites the Vaccine Riot of 1904.

65 *Coisas do Reino,* p. 282.

66 Antonio Candido, "Dialectic of Malandroism," in *On Literature and Society* (Princeton, N.J.: Princeton University Press, 1995), pp. 79–103.

67 Fry, "Two Religious Movements."

Passion, Perversity, and the

Pace of Justice in Argentina at the

Turn of the Last Century

KRISTIN RUGGIERO

T he concept of passion, as with other concepts such as gender and race that are represented in this volume, contributed to the contested terrain of law, justice, and repression in Argentina at the turn of the last century. Passion was considered to be a medical condition, which in turn made it an extenuating circumstance in criminal cases. This made passion part of both the production of deviance, through its effect on the mind and body, and the mitigation of punishment for that deviance, through its undermining of the human will. The criminal cases used in this essay to examine passion fall between the years 1870 and 1904. During this period and later, most of the treatises on the Argentine penal code and its reforms addressed the issue of passion. In addition, the Argentine doctor Lucas Ayarragaray (1861–1944), who was on the staff of the state mental hospital and the National Department of Hygiene and studied the racial origins of degenerative characteristics, wrote a thesis on the imagination and the passions as causes of diseases in 1887. The Argentine criminologist Eusebio Gómez, who had directed a number of studies of penology and been director of the National Penitentiary, also wrote a treatise on passion, as it was connected with crime, which was published in 1917, although his ideas on this subject were influential before this time. Testimonies and legal arguments in criminal cases necessarily had to confront the issue of passion. Finally, people read about the passions in home medical manuals.

Passion entered criminal cases as a legitimate medical condition, almost as if passion were "tangible," like a disease. It "attacked" the body, exhibited symptoms and crisis points, and had cures. It was considered to be both a normal condition, that is, common to most people, and also a pathology. Medical treatises and the medical-legal reports from criminal cases tracked the path of damage that an attack of passion could inflict on the body. The internal damage began, according to some doctors, in the brain, spinal cord, and nervous system. According to other doctors, the damage could begin anywhere inasmuch as the passions were distributed throughout the whole body, although a "nervous elaboration" had to occur for an act to pass from the virtual to the factual. The damage began when a passion awakened a strong reaction in the nervous system as it tried to adapt. In attempting to remain in harmony with the nervous system, the body's organs reacted. As the organs deviated from their normal physiological state, they caused changes to occur in the body's temperature, blood circulation, and heart rhythm, basically sending the body on a skittish path from excitation to exhaustion.

We find descriptions of the wreckage left by this medical condition in such disparate sources as home medical manuals and scholarly medical treatises meant for professionals. Among the more common symptoms for such passions as anger, fear, melancholy, and hypochondria were apoplexy, aneurysm, and congestions for anger, madness and liver and heart disease for fear; delirium and insanity for melancholy; and palpitations and stomach, liver, and heart disease for hypochondria. In women, the passions could cause suppression of menstruation, menorrhagia, and the nervous disorder called chorea. The generic home remedies for passion included cold baths, salt baths, vomitives, purgatives, and relaxants, and removal of the object that had caused the passion.[1]

The scholarly treatments of passion were elaborations on the theme that passion was a true disease. For example, the Spanish jurist Joaquín Francisco Pacheco (1808–1865), who was frequently cited by Argentine medical and legal authorities, argued that to doubt that passion was a true illness was "ridiculous." The paroxysm of passion figured in the same category, he wrote, as monomania and partial madness. The French forensic doctor M. J. B. Orfila (1787–1853) also argued that it was scandalous to convict a person who had suffered an attack of passion. The French doctor J. B. F. Descuret (1795–1872), in his treatise on the medicine of the passions, which was based on a substantial amount of statistical work that he did in Paris, pointed out that by passion's very etymology, it indicated a suffering that made the body and spirit ill. As Ayarragaray explained in his medical treatise, an enormous amount of nervous energy was needed to sustain a person who was passional, and as a result, the person's organs tired, the nervous system was disturbed, and the person's constitution weakened — exactly as in a sick person with a long illness. In sum, too many intense stimuli perverted or annihilated the body's functions.[2]

With the emphasis of positivist criminology and forensic medicine on the mental state of the delinquent, such a violent assault on the body as passion produced intersected with the justice system in a very real way because it could be used to attenuate or to remove completely personal responsibility for criminal acts. The articles referring to uncontrollable emotions in the law code edited by the Argentine jurist and diplomat Carlos Tejedor (1817–1903) became more explicit in Argentine's first national penal code of 1886, which was based on the Tejedor code. This new code contained four slightly differently worded articles that applied to passion according to the law. The first three had to do with exemptions. First, a state of "madness, somnambulism, absolute imbecility, or complete and involuntary drunkenness" could *exempt* a delinquent from punishment, and in general when the act had been "determined and consummated in any perturbation of the senses or intelligence, not imputable to the agent, and during which he [had] not been conscious of the act or its criminality." A second group of delinquents could be *exempted* if they had acted "impelled by irresistible force, physical or moral." A third group were spouses who had been "surprised by his or her consort in the flagrant crime of adultery," and had suffered "just pain," who were *exempted* if they had "[wounded] or [killed] both or one of the guilty parties." The fourth article had to do with the *reduction* of a person's responsibility for a crime when he or she was in a state of "irritation or rage (*furor*)" that was not his fault, but that did not make him "lose total consciousness of what he was doing."[3] To summarize, when criminals committed crimes in a state of madness and related conditions including drunkenness, disturbance of the senses, irresistible force, and in flagrant adultery, they could be exempted from punishment, and a criminal committing a crime in a state of "irritation and rage" had reduced responsibility. Passion could and did enter into all these states. As Pacheco explained, passion created an "aberration of intelligence, as powerful as any physical and material force." Passion was moral violence and involuntary blindness that forced a man's will, like physical violence forced his hand. "What converts us without our fault into an instrument, [also] cleanses us and exempts us at the same time of any stain, of all responsibility, as human and moral agents. The man who, without liberty, commits a homicide, does not have any more blame than the sword itself, the instrument with which he caused the wound." In such situations, there was neither imputability nor, consequently, a crime. Orfila called the effect of passion a "moral numbness" that paralyzed a person's will and erased his moral responsibility. Passionate crime, most of the experts argued, was characterized by the delinquent's disinterest, violence, and remorse after the crime, indicating that basically there was a fund of positive sentiment toward passion in the medical and criminological fields and in the 1886 penal code.[4]

Passion was not an easy concept to argue, in spite of its general acceptance as an element in crime. First, passion intersected with the controversy over the validity of the concept of free will. The basic premise of a penal system for jurists of the classical school had been that free will had to exist in order for a justice system to confer punishment on an individual. The positivist attack on free will in the second half of the nineteenth century challenged this notion. Positivists, such as the Italian Cesare Lombroso (1835–1909), viewed free will as an illusion; crime as merely an antisocial act in which the presence or absence of free will was not important; and justification for punishment of criminals as based not on the presence of free will, but on the need for "social defense." Empirical evidence showed that passion did not always have the same effect on free will in all cases. The problem was that, to be used by courts, passion either had to annul free will in all cases or leave free will intact. Lawyers could sometimes avoid this pitfall by arguing that the problem lay in the concept of free will, rather than in the concept of passion. Second, a passionate attack did not always lead to a crime, for not everyone sought vengeance in times of passion. Thus, one could not really say that passion "caused" crime. Third, passions often had two sides, which made them difficult to evaluate. The passion of love, for example, was argued by Gómez to be noble and social, yet exalted love could become dangerous. The passion of hatred was ignoble and antisocial, yet hatred of a common enemy was honorable. The passion of honor, sometimes held to be the most "respectable" passion, often led to infamy. Political passion, which was considered morally healthy for a state and was needed to offset utilitarianism, could divide nations and cause human destruction. In other words, the same passion had the power to lead people to both "heroism and villainy."[5]

With all these complexities, which added to the contested terrain of justice, we have to ask what the real impact of passion was on the juridical and medical discourse, including sentencing, in court cases. First, lawyers resorted to passion as an explanation of human behavior frequently enough that the logical assumption would be that they thought it would bring results. In well over half of the cases of physical assault and/or homicide examined from the Argentine National Archives, one or more of the clauses, such as "disturbance," "irresistible force," and "irritation or rage," were used to judge and sentence the delinquent. Much less frequent were the attenuating circumstances of drunkenness, epilepsy, and madness. The clauses of "irresistible force" and so on were apparently used so much, in fact, that there were exaggerated warnings that absolving delinquents on the basis of passion was becoming so common that it could mean the end of the justice system. In his treatise on passion and crime, the criminologist Gómez, for example, criticized lawyers for abusing the excuse of passion and introducing a "false dramaticity" into cases to make the defense of their clients easier. He argued that judges, uninformed about criminal anthropology, too often accepted this dramaticity, and that the public too had become more indulgent of passionate crime, "perhaps fearing their turn would come soon."[6] This last observation of Gómez seems to be a confirmation of the belief that passion could afflict anyone at any time. The cases that have been chosen for this essay to explicate further the function of passion in people's criminal lives show some specific trends. Most importantly, they show that this was a moment where judicial discourse intersected with judicial practice. The cases also show that, although judges accommodated the medical and legal arguments about the influence of passion and often attenuated crimes, they stopped short of exempting delinquents totally from punishment, even though the law allowed them to do so. Finally, they show that although there was a growing medicalization of criminal behavior, and neuroses, epilepsy, hysteria, and so on were introduced to explain violent acts, passion did not lose its place in criminal cases, perhaps because of the language of the 1886 penal code.

Passion and Honor

Adultery, the classic crime of passion, allowed judges to actually exempt the criminal from punishment if a person were overcome by a "blind rage" or an "irresistible force," as the law called it, at the sight of his or her spouse's flagrant infidelity.[7] Victimized spouses were described by the experts, though not in the penal code of 1886, as being justified in an act of violence against the offending spouse and/or consort because of the "just pain" they had suffered. Interestingly, the violence did not have to be the result of the wounded spouse's excessive love for the victim; all that was necessary was that the offended spouse had suffered "just pain." That is, "just pain" did not necessarily presume love.

For a husband, explained the noted Spanish jurist Joaquín Escriche (1784–1847) who was frequently cited in Argentine criminal cases, "just pain" meant seeing with his own eyes the staining of his honor — "that particular honor that husbands acquire the day of their marriage and that a very special judgment makes them lose when their wife dishonors them." Similar to love, the adultery did not actually have to be proven, however; it could just be presumed from circumstances. A husband's honor was definitely wounded by his wife's adultery, but it could also be wounded by her insults to and scorn of his marital authority. The choices in sentencing in these cases were capital punishment, which had been retained in the 1886 penal code for the killing of family members; the maximum prison sentence of twenty years; or a lesser prison sentence, depending on how passion was taken into account.[8] If it was proved that the crime had been an act of passion, then the death penalty was not invoked. The fact of "surprise" was enough to excuse the homicide, which "gave the legal right to kill, even though the act was not done to preserve the husband's or another's life."[9]

Both husbands and wives could be overcome by rage provoked by jealousy, but wives had less access to the excuse of passion because it was commonly accepted that a husband's adultery was less serious than a wife's, and thus her passion was less justified. In the very few cases of wives' violence against their husbands, the trend can be noted that even when a wife's crime seemed to fit the legal and medical model of a passional crime, she was likely to be diagnosed with some disorder such as hysteria. Whereas a husband's passionate response to a situation of anger, jealousy, and just pain was readily understood and taken pretty much at face value, a wife's passionate response was judged as a medical condition.[10] It seems that women's passion might have been believable, that is, not simulated, only when it was expressed in certain ways. For example, a wife's use of passion and sentiment, tears and sweet words to correct her husband's behavior was seen as good, while her use of the court system to reprove her husband was not.

By the early twentieth century, there was a strong movement in Argentina to abolish "surprised in flagrant adultery" from the penal code as an attenuating circumstance from punishment for wounding or killing a spouse and his or her consort, as had been occurring in Europe. The clause created too many cases of injustice, it was argued, because the law allowed a husband to premeditate coldly the death of his adulterous wife, even though he had tacitly consented to her conduct, and then claim "just pain." The problem that Gómez noted was that the law did not examine the nature or quality of the passion of jealousy; it took into account only its intensity. Even people who supported a reform of the law, though, were reluctant to restrict the right that "every man, especially of a certain social class [had], to be protected from responsibility when he [had] acted because of the excitation that his wife's adultery had produced in him."[11] The law had to remain that judges in these cases had the right to exempt the husband suffering from "just pain" from punishment.

In a case from 1870, a customs employee in Buenos Aires, Pascual, experiencing this "just pain," killed his wife.[12] Disagreements between Pascual and his wife Eusebia had reached an intolerable level in their twenty-year marriage, and they had obtained a separation of six months from the Ecclesiastical Court. Pascual took the prescribed measures to control his passion, and had Eusebia confined—put "on deposit," as it was called—which was his marital right.[13] This was a deliciously capitalistic term in that a "deposited" Eusebia was Pascual's investment in his honor. He put her in a rented room, figuring that he would be able to keep an eye on her this way. This saved his wife from possible harm from the irritations of conjugal life, and himself from committing a possible crime against her and landing himself in jail. Eusebia, too, was supposed to curb her passion while on deposit. That is, she was advised to learn to accommodate her husband's wishes, to acquiesce to his authority, and to respect his position as head of the family. Pascual visited Eusebia several times a day, and at night returned in disguise to stand outside her apartment building and spy on her. At times, he thought he saw a man's shadow in his wife's room. His suspicions grew and he decided to move her, but she roundly refused to go. He enlisted the help of the ecclesiastical court and got a summons, but then he could not find her to deliver it. He was desperate. When he did find her — a couple of drinks later — he stormed: "Eusebia, stop and listen: since you haven't come back to me, I'm going to make you drink to the last drop of blood." He grabbed her by the waist, threw her down on the ground, jerked her head back, and slit her throat. She died instantly.

As Pascual's lawyer interpreted his client's act for the court, Pascual had been a victim of a sudden violent passion, an irresistible fit of jealousy. He had not acted out of hatred, sordid interest, an ignoble spirit of vengeance, or an innate tendency toward crime, but rather from the inexplicable relationship of love and jealousy, egged on by his propensity for alcohol. Moreover, the lawyer entered the interesting argument that a corrupt government and society had to expect that people like Pascual would surface. It was not a surprise, he said, that Pascual committed this murder "when cultured men who should be setting an example for people like Pascual put a dagger in his hand and ply him with wine and food to gain his vote and let him commit illegal acts with impunity." The lawyer's argument that had more authority, however, was that Pascual had been provoked to violence by his wife, who had been repudiating him, denying his authority as a husband and his conjugal rights, and inciting his children against him. She had intentionally provoked jealousy in her husband by going to the house of a man whom her husband had forbidden her to see. All her acts were intended to irritate the passionate character of her husband.

The judge in Pascual's case, however, did not accept the defense lawyer's arguments and handed down the death penalty. In contrast, many other cases exist in which wives were judged to have provoked their own deaths and their husbands were given jail sentences rather than death.[14] But here the judge did not allow passion to be a factor in exempting or attenuating the crime, and he meted out a particularly harsh, exemplary sentence. It was to be "death by firing squad in the public plaza of Lorea, to be published in the newspapers and posted on the most visible walls in Buenos Aires, towns, and districts of this Judicial Department."[15] The judge's reasons for imposing this extreme and anachronistic punishment and disallowing passion were interesting. Pascual committed his crime in public and during the day, in cold blood and with premeditation and in the presence of his daughter; he used a knife fit only for the "worst Neapolitans"; and, because he had finished one year of medical school, he had increased his obligations to society and to his victim, making him even more culpable.

The judge's verdict was controversial. By choosing the death penalty, the judge, many people believed, had shown more violent passion than had Pascual. Capital punishment was under attack by 1870, and many Argentines and others considered it inappropriate, nearly defunct anyway, and an outrageous expression of the state's "passion." The gallows had already been abolished, and the commutation of the death penalty to prison for up to twenty years had been established as a possibility.[16] But the law remained in the penal code of 1886 and capital punishment continued to be solicited by prosecutors and judges for atrocious crimes, as in Pascual's case.

Not surprisingly, the defense lawyer appealed Pascual's sentence, but the superior court upheld the judge's death sentence; the vote of the *vocales* (members of the tribunal) was unanimous. There was a great public outcry at this point and a request for commutation of the sentence, which was accompanied by thirty pages of signatures. And in the end, the executive power commuted the sentence to twenty years in the presidio.[17]

There were two glosses on such penalties. The first stems from jurist Escriche's definition of "punishment" as an "evil of passion," that is, as the state's evil committed against an individual's evil.[18] Thus, harsh penalties such as capital punishment dishonored Argentina and, in any case, were ineffective in containing the "flood of human passions." "Such penalties were nothing more than barbarous and bloody spectacles that provoked the gathering of the masses, as if it were a fiesta, to witness the agony and contortions of the condemned." As Pascual's lawyer argued, "death is an irrational way to deal with passions . . . and reveals society's impotence to reform criminals." "Our discredit abroad, if it exists, doesn't come from criminal acts which are committed everywhere, but from the lack of principles and institutions that avoid their frequent repetition."

Exactly opposed was the judge's gloss that *only* an exemplary punishment could restrain passions. For people who attacked honor, laws, and the most intimate sentiments of man, it was felt, only the punishment of death was sufficient. In the judge's view, the death penalty was "terrible, but necessary in shuddering cases like parricide, a crime that it is not possible to pardon." It was indispensable, he maintained, "that the repairing action of the law was vigorously felt in the defense of institutions and of individual guarantees that were threatened and deeply offended, with the multiplication of crimes that dishonored and undermined the credit of Argentina abroad."

The death sentence, he wrote, was beneficial and effective for such "frenetic and unnatural assassins" like Pascual, thus accepting that the "passion" of the state could be legitimately applied here.

What won out in this case, though, was an eleventh-hour reduced sentence based on passion, the only attenuating circumstance in this case. Later generations took up this "enlightened" position and adapted it to scientific criminology. As a defense lawyer explained in a case from 1904, "passion" was what "today's scientific vocabulary" called the internal force that was invoked when an external moral force occurred, and this exempted a person from responsibility or punishment.[19]

Passion and Fixation

Enrique Campanelli had spent several years of his young adulthood in the early 1890s in deep suffering for his unrequited love for Agustina Barat.[20] Recalling here Descuret's association of passion and suffering helps to explain the denouement of Enrique's mental fixation of Agustina, or monomania. He was all set to marry Agustina, as soon as he received a character reference from Italy. When it arrived, in 1894, Enrique found that Agustina had chosen to escape from his entreaties—we are not informed exactly why—by entering a convent. He went there, removed her bodily from the convent, and drove off with her in a carriage. He was then arrested by the police for abduction. The case was dissolved, but Agustina's family no longer supported the marriage. With his one idea of marrying Agustina clouding his reason, Enrique returned to his lover's house one night with two revolvers and shot Agustina's family while they were seated together eating dinner. Agustina's eight-year-old brother later recalled that he had been eating potatoes when he was shot by his sister's boyfriend; he suffered a wound to his left lung. Agustina's father had two gunshot wounds and contusions on his head and face where Enrique had beat him with the butt of the revolver; the mother had a chest wound. Agustina's married sister had forehead and shoulder wounds, and a younger sister had a shoulder wound. The family members were treated by doctors at a nearby pharmacy. Though Enrique had managed to do a fair amount of damage, none of the wounds were serious enough to keep the victims incapacitated for more than thirty days.

In jail, Enrique's medical examination began. The new science viewed delinquents such as Enrique either as demented, literally "lovesick," unfortunates who were not responsible for their actions, or as calculating simulators, perverse and hypocritical, who had intentionally fueled their bad passions, premeditated a crime, and caused damage to society. Enrique's case provided an excellent context in which to examine passion's effect on criminal responsibility and was later used by criminologist Gómez in his analysis of passion and crime. The official forensic medical examiners found that Enrique was "dominated by a pathological amorous passion, a fixed idea," and that "he always satisfied his limited aspirations within [the boundaries of] his romantic character." In addition, the doctors concluded that, judging from conversations with Enrique and an examination of his intellectual, moral, and affective condition, his brain had "some signs of weakness, few acquired notions, and a weak will." Although he did not show signs of mental alienation, they concluded, it was probably in his background. The report was inconclusive, however. The doctors were not prepared to claim that science could prove that Enrique had definitely been affected by disturbances that could have caused him to lose his reason. Nor were they ready to judge if he was dangerous to society. The most they would venture was that Enrique was a monomaniac, but not a madman, a *loco*.

One of Buenos Aires's most prominent lawyers, who did not usually take on a case of this type, did not hesitate to defend Enrique. The law would be unjust, he said, if it did not look into the psychology and analysis of passion for the explanation of Enrique's act. Unfortunate and helpless he was, a man "whose thoughts of Agustina made his eyes lose themselves in the void and whose voice acquired inflections of monotonous singing that were up to the level of those of Sarah Bernhardt's in 'Phèdre,' with pardon for the artistic heresy." (Sarah Bernhardt was in the lawyer's mind perhaps because she had been on tour in South America in the early 1890s and had been portraying violent passion in Racine's play.) When Enrique was so overcome, he became completely demented. "Listening to him," said the lawyer, still in the mode of dramatic references, "I saw resurge the image of some adventurous Tuscan troubadour of long ago . . . this man with 'flesh [*carne*] of passion'; he was warmed by an imagination without brake or limit." The lawyer eulogized Enrique's passion, putting it in the "same mold as Faust's vacillation at the threshold of Margarita." "If things had gone differently," he said, "there would have been one less nun and two more happy people" in the world. Perhaps if Enrique had married, he said, his violent passions would have been tempered by the tranquil love of the home. Instead, the court had to realize that it was dealing with a "confused man, in the middle of our life of regulated [harnessed] passions."[21]

The judge argued that, as violent as a passion was, people had the duty of repressing it, and that rather than trying to dominate the passion when it was possible to do so, many people actually fueled their passions. Such people could not then claim an *absolute* lack of responsibility. However, in the case of Enrique, passion had clearly been a factor and the judge gave him the relatively short sentence of five years of presidio, instead of unlimited imprisonment as the prosecutor had requested. Enrique's sentence also included civil interdiction for an equal time; disqualification from public jobs and the exercise of political rights for seven and a half years; subjection to vigilance by the authorities for three years more after fulfilling his sentence; and indemnification of damages and payment of costs.

What were the arguments that the judge considered that drew him to support the plea of passion? On one side were the theories of criminologists such as Pacheco. A passionate man, he held, should be treated the same as a madman in terms of excusing or attenuating a crime. An unleashed passion and a delirium should be handled the same way: neither required that a person be kept in a cell. Enrique had not shown premeditation and treachery; he had never confessed an intent to kill; he wounded without intention, and the wounds he caused did not incapacitate his victims for work for more than thirty days, which should have made his sentence not more than one year of arrest. On the other side was the judicial logic that if the simple affirmation of the criminal was enough to prove his state of madness, which had been Enrique's claim, all criminals would be assured of impunity for the most atrocious crimes. The fact that Enrique had fled after shooting at members of Agustina's family seemed to indicate that he had been in his right mind and aware that he had committed a crime, nor did the medical report show any form of mental alienation. Moreover, if this had truly been passional love that had confused Enrique's mind, then how, medically speaking, had it occurred, given that Agustina had not even been present on the night of the shootings?[22]

The judge viewed the category of "passional crimes" as much abused, and argued that the presence of passion, by itself, did not constitute grounds for exemption from punishment. However, Enrique's passion did convince him to reduce substantially Enrique's prison sentence to five years. As violent as a passion was, the judge said, all men had the duty of repressing it. If a passion became extreme, a paroxysm, a person had to stop it. If a passion became superior to a person's will — as the medical professionals maintained in the case of Enrique — the person was still responsible because, rather than trying to dominate the passion when it was possible to do so, he had used his will to cherish it and fuel it. Thus, people like Enrique could not claim an absolute lack of responsibility as a consequence of their own lack of energy and foresight.[23]

Passion and Nervous Disorders

Even high state officials were not immune to being overwhelmed by passion, and being held to the same standards of examination and scrutiny as young lovers and customs employees. One day in 1896 at the National Department of Hygiene, the head of the Office of Administrative Control, Francisco N. Viñas, was seated in his office, reading his newspaper.[24] The doctor, Luis Agote, approached him. He was angry about Viñas's accusations against the department and against himself, published in the newspaper the day before. Dr. Agote was head of the Lazareto (quarantine hospital) of Martín García, and many of Viñas's accusations implied corruption in his administration. In his letter to the newspaper in April 1896, Viñas referred to abuses, mistakes, and criminal operations. "The Hygiene Department," he wrote, "shows a perversion in its business and an intolerable disorder." Agote's worst offenses, according to Viñas, included giving the department's business contracts to people who charged more than the going rate; charging his personal trips to the department; using the department's ship to take families to the lazareto instead of to transport coal; allowing doctors to practice medicine without a license and manage pharmacies; using the telegraph for his personal business; tolerating *curanderos* (folk healers); inventing jobs in order to hire friends; and allowing department employees to engage in the illicit sale of disinfectants to ships.

In an aggressive voice, Agote addressed Viñas: "I'm going to give you some advice. Don't touch my family in your accusations because, if you do, shit on you! I'm not [even] going to ask you for an explanation for your behavior since it would be like asking a servant for an explanation. Shitty Gallego, swine!" Viñas answered back: "Go to the Big Mother Whore who gave birth to you." By this point, the situation was out of control. Agote drew his revolver and shot at Viñas.

In Agote's opinion, he had asked Viñas in a kindly way to desist in his accusations, and it was Viñas who had been the aggressor, with Agote only pulling out his gun to defend himself. Viñas claimed that Agote had shot first. Agote, who explained that he carried a gun for self-defense because he often traveled to Martín García and Brazil, said that he had had no intention of injuring Viñas. And here is where passion figures: Agote said that the shot was a spontaneous act, and even more, the result of a nervous fit.

The judge then asked for a medical-legal examination of Agote. The court doctors found that Agote was a flatulent dyspeptic and suffered from nervous exhaustion; that he had a burst blood vessel in the left retina and was nearsighted; that he had liver attacks; that he was an insomniac and was hypersensitive and had heightened reflexes; and that his father and siblings had had nervous attacks.

The report was a warning to intellectuals and professionals, and it reflected the concern doctors and others had for the causal relationship between mental work and illness.[25] The report stated that Agote's dedication to intellectual labor had demanded too much mental effort and tension, and that this had harmed him. He had become thin and pallid with a depressed digestive system; stooped, with a vacant look, without vivacity; with migraine, aloof, indifferent, hypochondriacal. Finally, he suffered from an organic depression that affected his nervous system. "When this depression is prolonged," said the doctors, "the vigor of the nervous cells diminishes and they become sensitive to the slightest disturbances." The conclusion was that Agote was so dominated by his nervous system that he had made an impulsive movement, resulting in a contraction of his muscles and an unintentional firing of his gun. And as Agote's lawyer explained, in people whose nervous system predominates, impulsive movements were frequent, even pathogenic, and were always movements of defense, not aggression. In such people, if they were provoked by pain or fear, for example, their nervous systems produced brusque, disordered contractions of their muscles, in which the intensity could be so great that it could even cause bone fractures.[26]

Agote's explanation of how his intellectual illness had generated a passion is interesting. He said that Viñas's words were "so violent, atrocious, and indecent that they would have made the most intimate and delicate cords of the heart vibrate with indignation." "Viñas hurled his words against my face like a slap. These words produced a spirit of irritation and rage in me." As the Siete Partidas, which Agote quoted in his own defense, stated: "When a man fears for his body, he loses his head; he changes color; he moves the continent."[27]

The prosecutor pressed for a harsh sentence, labeling the case attempted homicide, and argued that if Viñas had not moved he would have been shot in the heart. The defense lawyer pressed for a lesser sentence based on the discharging of arms, and argued that Agote had only been following the orders of his superior, Dr. José María Ramos Mejía. The judge opted to drop the case due to lack of evidence against Agote and perhaps also because Viñas had been previously prosecuted in La Plata in 1883. But Viñas appealed the case, especially because he had been fired from the National Department of Hygiene and had lost a year and a half of his salary. In the end, however, Agote was absolved, perhaps because of his status as a well-known physician and government official.

Nonpassion, Perversion, and Degeneration

Only in its "perversion" did experts consider passion an unmitigated evil — and then only reluctantly. When passion took on the characteristics of being "exaggerated," "negative," or "simulated," it was considered to be a menace. The "born criminal" of the Lombrosian school, who had these characteristics and moreover was "ugly, degenerate, cruel, and lethargic," made a stark contrast to passionate man, who was described as "appealing and attractive, fiery, nervous, and sensitive," and free from any physical or moral degenerative or pathological abnormalities.[28] In contrast to the actions of passionate man, the perverse acts of the born criminal, the degenerate, were considered a dire forecast of the evils of what was considered to be the rapidly encroaching age of utilitarianism and materialism.

Many crimes were described as perverse, but the one featured in late nineteenth-century Argentina as perversity par excellence was Pedro Castro Rodríguez's murder of his wife and daughter in Olavarría in 1888.[29] The murder was perverse because first, it was atrocious, and second, because Pedro showed no remorse for having done it. Pedro, who was to become widely known through the press and professional journals as the "assassin of Olavarría," began his life in Buenos Aires as a priest, which may have added to the horror of his crime. Pedro had a confrontational relationship with the church, beginning in Spain and continuing in Argentina, perhaps because, in spite of having studied medicine for two years, he was forced into the priesthood by his father. Interestingly for the medical history of the family, Pedro's sister, who had been forced to become a nun, was described as "always hysterical, with a slight hysteroid color." Pedro had immigrated to Argentina after an armed argument with a cleric in Spain. In Buenos Aires, he also had incidents. Pedro was openly hostile to the archbishop, and his shocking conduct at a boys' school he had established in Barracas al Sud moved the archbishop to forbid Pedro to say mass or wear priest's garb. Not surprisingly, Pedro eventually apostatized, married Rufina Padín in the Methodist church and had a daughter by her, and joined the "reformed Argentine Church." Later, he returned to Catholicism, "simulated repentance," and accepted an appointment as parish priest of the town of Olavarría, but apparently continued the relationship with his wife and daughter.

As the police learned from Pedro's correspondence and private papers, one day, because he believed his wife guilty of adultery and/or wanted her money, Pedro, on finding Rufina somewhat agitated from her asthma, gave her a strong dose of atropine camouflaged with licorice and served on a piece of bread. She began to vomit and to have heart palpitations. In her painful delirium, Rufina tried to flee. Pedro grabbed her by the neck and began hitting her head with a hammer. Terrorized, their daughter ran to his arms, but he took her brutally in his hands, anchored her between his legs, violently forced poison down her throat, and watched her struggle with death for the next six hours.

After pulling the cadavers of his wife and daughter into the parish church, Pedro stuffed them into a single wide coffin, squashing them down so that the cover would close. He wrote out a burial certificate for a single body, "a very fat woman who had been sent to him from the campo," had "the body" buried, and continued to say mass as usual for several months.

There were several reasons why the examining doctors, Agustín J. Drago and J. M. Ramos Mejía, found Pedro, who at first sight seemed merely "common and of low origin," an example of a "late stage of degeneration." First, the features of his head indicated advanced degeneration. It was a head covered with abundant and coarse skin, "which in some movements [made] coarse folds in his neck, recalling the excessive skin of certain animals"; a narrow forehead; prominent eyebrows "like the celebrated Neanderthal cranium with its multiplicity of simian characteristics"; and a wide, flat face with visible asymmetry. He had a thin mouth and lips; a long, curved nose; fleshy and asymmetrical ears; small eyes; and large and asymmetrical teeth. The doctors' examination of Pedro's hands, which were considered the most useful organ to the progress of the species after the brain, revealed flat and thick fingertips and an index finger with a narrow opposability. The examination of Pedro's degree of sensibility included his fingers, the tip of his tongue and nose, the nape of his neck, the end of his metacarpal, the ball of his thumb, and his lower forearm. Recognizing that these measurements could sometimes vary a great deal, the doctors took into account Pedro's age and social condition, the delicacy of his skin, its anemia or hyperemia, and the temperature of his body and the examining room. The results were that Pedro had reduced general tactile sensation of volume, form, direction, and consistency of objects; reduced local and topographical sensation; and a reduced sense of hearing, taste, and smell. Pedro's dullness, concluded the doctors, came from the contextual poverty of his nervous system.

In spite of the doctors' previous experience with criminals like Pedro Castro, they remained appalled by the "frightening" moral insensitivity of his repeated remark to the doctors and the media: "[My wife] didn't stop looking ridiculous for a moment [when he was dragging her body to the church]. She was my fat wife and since I was dragging her by the feet, her dress wrapped around her head so that I had to laugh at her grotesque figure." Chagrined, the doctors reported that Pedro expressed not a word of remorse for having killed his wife and daughter and was a perfect example of the puerile vanity of criminals. He was relatively enlightened, in that he had studied medicine, literature, theology, natural history, and chemistry; but his intelligence was less than average. The doctors decided that Pedro's nervous system had been affected by his father's gout, and that Pedro was an example of the final stages of degeneration; that is, he was a born criminal. As such, Pedro's photograph was added to Francisco P. Moreno's collection of anthropological specimens at the La Plata museum.

To limit or negate Pedro's responsibility, the doctors had to be able to find him mentally disturbed, mad, or passional. They eliminated the first condition of acute mania and imbecility. Regarding madness, the most likely types of *locura* in a case like this, the doctors said, came from a delirium of persecution, an alcoholic delirium, or larval epilepsy. They eliminated the possibility of a delirium of persecution because there was no evidence that something had clouded Pedro's reason, and he was expansive and a charlatan, unlike people who believed they were being persecuted. The doctors also eliminated delirium from alcohol because Pedro was never a drunk and there was no trace of the dementia that followed drunkenness.

And he had not suffered epilepsy because he remembered everything that had happened. Finally, they eliminated the condition of passion, because the long death scene was inconsistent with the nature of passional impulses, which were described as "brutal, alive and violent transformations of all the living forces of the organism in a movement of irresistible expansion." Moreover, a passional person was afterward immediately contrite, and Pedro's coldness and lack of piety, charity, and repentance were just not consistent with passion. In fact, the ignorance of these sentiments formed the basis of natural criminality. Further, Pedro did not have the appeal and attractiveness of the passional person. Rather, he was, in stark contrast, totally unappealing and had physical degenerative abnormalities not unlike the "born criminal." Having eliminated all possible extenuating circumstances, the doctors concluded that Pedro was totally responsible for his acts. His case was, instead, clearly one of perversity due to degeneration.

Conclusion

Thanks to Pascual's jealousy, Enrique's fixation, Luis's nervous twitch, and Pedro's perversity, we have more of an idea of how the judicial system accommodated passion in the late nineteenth and early twentieth centuries. These cases focus on single individuals' passions, but they also speak, it might be argued, to the larger issue of national identity. While the justice system and the medical profession were analyzing passion and struggling to accommodate it, statesmen and political essayists, who were often also the members of the legal and medical professions, were analyzing passion in terms of the broader debate on national identity. In neither case, individual or national, was there agreement about the role of passion, but it is a confirmation of the importance of passion that the discourse on national identity was often focused around it. An examination of how the issue of passion was incorporated into this discourse will round out the picture of passion provided in the court cases.

For bad and for good, passion was a part of Argentine identity. It is not difficult to find remarks by Argentine statesmen and others that excess passion was a defect in Latin character which the Argentines had inherited from the Spanish, who had inherited it from the Celts.[30] This was especially true in political life, where a positive national character was seen as particularly important for Argentina's acceptance and success in the international sphere. These cultural arguments were important, and it was not a stretch for two of the most famous Argentine jurists and statesmen of the period, Estanislao Severo Zeballos (1854–1923) and Carlos Octavio Bunge (1875–1918), to say that the national character meant all the difference in Argentina's being able to imitate successfully and adapt European political and administrative institutions that would secure the republic a place in the modern world. Of course, rationality, which was usually put in opposition to passion, was a major desirable component in national character. If the two were out of balance, argued Zeballos, it would explain to "future historians the causes of Argentine disorders, deficiencies, and anomalies."[31] This view put the issue of development in a unique light. As one lawyer noted, Argentina's incapacity for progress in terms of political stability was *not* a question of its lack of development, but rather of its *modo de ser,* which included passion.[32]

Yet if passion may have fostered irrationality, it was also considered to be an antidote to some of the less desirable offspring of the pursuit of progress, such as utilitarianism, materialism, individualism, and simulation. These trends were "enervating the national spirit," and "destroying Argentine ideals."[33] As important as scientific reason was, an excess of it would degenerate into utilitarianism if it was not balanced with sensitivity. This is why some of the same people who warned about excessive passion, such as Zeballos, seemed at the same time to show an appreciation for it.[34] Passion, after all, it was concluded, was an important part of Argentine identity, a part not to be undermined, apparently, as criminal cases demonstrate, even in the judging and sentencing of criminals.

Notes

1 D. J. G. d J. Perez, *Nueva medicina doméstica, o sea arte de conservar la salud, de conocer las enfermedades, sus remedios y aplicación, al alcance de todos* (Buenos Aires: Revista, 1854), pp. 26–30. See the discussion of passions as "obscure and dangerous forces" in Hugo Vezzetti, *La locura en la Argentina* (Buenos Aires: Folios Ediciones, 1983), p. 92. For this period's anxiety about the need to isolate potentially disruptive elements such as passions, see Jorge Salessi, *Médicos, maleantes y maricas* (Rosario: Beatriz Viterbo, 1995), pp. 52–57. For the debate on the social question in Argentina and its relationship to "deviant" behavior, see Juan Suriano, ed., *La cuestión social en Argentina, 1870–1943* (Buenos Aires: La Colmena, 2000).

2 Mathieu Joseph Bonaventure Orfila, *Medicina legal*, 4th ed., vol. 1 (Paris: Renouard, 1848), p. 336; Joaquín Francisco Pacheco, *Código penal*, 2d ed., vol. 1 (Madrid: Perinat, 1856), p. 131; Jean Baptiste Felix Descuret, *La Medicina de las*

pasiones, ó las pasiones consideradas con respecto á las enfermedades, las leyes y la religión (Barcelona: Oliveres, 1849), p. 1; Lucas Ayarragaray, *La imaginación y las pasiones como causas de enfermedades* (thesis, 1887), pp. 11–24.

3 Argentine Penal Code, 1886, Book I, Section II, Title 3, Article 81, Incisos 1, 5, 12; and Article 83, Inciso 6.

4 Pacheco, *Código penal*, p. 171; Orfila, *Medicina legal*, p. 336.

5 Eusebio Gómez, *Pasión y delito* (Buenos Aires: J. Roldán, 1917), pp. 45–51.

6 Ibid., p. 166.

7 Argentine Penal Code, 1886, Book I, Section II, Title 3, Article 81, Inciso 12.

8 Joaquín Escriche, *Diccionario razonado de legislación y jurisprudencia*, 4 vols. (Madrid: Cuesta, 1874–76), vol. 1 (1874), *voce* "Adulterio." The death penalty applied to "the person who knowingly killed his father, mother, or child (legitimate or natural), or any other immediate relative, or his spouse, unless there were extenuating circumstances" (Argentine Penal Code, 1886, Book I, Section II, Title 6, Article 94, Inciso 1).

9 Rodolfo Juan Nemesio Rivarola, *Derecho penal argentino* (Madrid: Reus, 1910), p. 450. Two cases in which the judge explained this well are Archivo General de la Nación (Buenos Aires, Argentina), Tribunal Criminal [hereafter referred to as AGN, TC], 2, B, 9, 1877, against James Barret for the homicide of his wife Brígida Barret; and AGN, TC, 2 A, 13, 1886, against Daniel Alzerano for the homicide of his wife María Canforterio.

10 See the example of AGN, TC, 2, D, 53, 1898, against María Cristina D'Ambrosio for the homicide of her husband Antonio Bobe.

11 Gómez, *Pasión y delito*, pp. 221–222.

12 AGN, TC, 2, C, 1, 1870, against Pascual Castro Echeverría for homicide of his wife Eusebia Arrascaete. Ricardo Salvatore points out that this crime was a knife execution, a *degüello*, which, because of its association with the Rosas period in Argentine history, was a particularly dastardly form of committing homicide. See Salvatore's essay in this volume, "Death and Liberalism: Capital Punishment after the Fall of Rosas."

13 The house of deposit institutionalized and concretized the control of passion in a way that infringed on a woman's ability to exercise her legal rights either to defend herself or to prosecute a case against her husband. On the system of "depositing," see Kristin Ruggiero, "Wives on 'Deposit': Internment and the Preservation of Husbands' Honor in Late Nineteenth-Century Buenos Aires," *Journal of Family History* 17, no. 3 (1992): 253–270.

14 The following is a sample of cases from different time periods in which the victim-wives were judged to have provoked their husbands' violence: AGN, TC, 2, A, 1, 1875, against José Alberti for wounds to his wife Catalina Escola; AGN, TC, 2, C, 22, 1881, against José Cayolla for suspected homicide of his wife Filomena Conti; AGN, TC, 2, B, 43, 1890, against Siro Boso for attempted homicide of his wife Margarita Dalio; AGN, TC, 2, D, 63, 1900, against Bautista Daguero for homicide

of his wife María Grattone; and AGN, TC, 2, B, 91, against Gaudencio Borgna for attempted homicide of his wife Dominga Pancro.

15 The use of "cleansing" punishments was true for women too, even though the death sentence was rarely requested for women. In 1860, however, a Córdoba court sentenced a woman to be garroted for the crime of infanticide with suspension of her cadaver for six hours for public viewing, though this was later commuted to nine years' reclusion. (Archivo Histórico de la Provincia de Córdoba, Tribunal Criminal [hereafter referred to as CC], 1860, 268, 4, against Ramona Vergara for infanticide).

16 Death by hanging was abolished in 1859, and the provision for commuting the death penalty went into effect in 1868.

17 The petition was dated August 22, 1870, and the court commuted the sentence on September 15, 1870.

18 Escriche, *Diccionario razonado*, vol. 4 (1876), *voce* "Pena," pp. 523–553.

19 AGN, TC, 2, A, 58, 1904, against Agustín Acre for homicide of his wife Cristina Malagrini.

20 AGN, TC, 2, C, 84, 1894, against Enrique Campanelli for attempted homicide of Juan, María, Margarita, Victoria, and Pedro Barat.

21 The lawyer was Juan Antonio Argerich (1840–1905), who was from an old Argentine patrician family.

22 It was also argued, however, that the act of reprisal did not have to follow immediately the act of witnessed adultery. See as an example AGN, 1904, Agustín Acre case; defense lawyer.

23 AGN, 1894, Enrique Campanelli case; judge quoting a Belgian jurist.

24 AGN, TC, 2, A, 42, 1898, against Luis Agote for firing a weapon at D. Francisco N. Viñas. Luis Agote (1868–1954) graduated from the Faculty of Medicine at the University of Buenos Aires in 1893 and became director of the Department of Hygiene in 1894. A hospital and street in Buenos Aires have been named for him. See Eduardo A. Zimmermann, *Los liberales reformistas: la cuestión social en la Argentina 1890–1916* (Buenos Aires: Sudamericana and Universidad de San Andrés, 1995), p. 161, on Agote's professional view of the death penalty.

25 Ayarragaray's analysis was that, "The devastating influences [of modern society] are above all in the high social classes, in people who are persecuted by calumny, ambition, or who are preoccupied with the realization of a high ideal. People who are given to intellectual work, literary composition, or who are in violent political struggles seldom have flourishing health" (*Imaginación y pasiones*, p. 11).

26 AGN, 1898, Luis Agote case; defense lawyer quoting a treatise on bone fractures.

27 The Siete Partidas date from the period of the Spanish King Alfonso X. Published in 1265, they were in effect in colonial Latin America until independence and in Spain itself until 1831. In using this language, Agote may have been thinking of setting up a duel. (Thanks go to David Parker for this observation.)

28 Gómez, *Pasión y delito*, pp. 69–70. Also Joëlle Guillais, *Crimes of Passion: Dramas of*

Private Life in Nineteenth-Century France (New York: Routledge, 1991), p. 183. For a discussion of simulation in Argentina, especially by José Ingenieros, see Rafael Huertas García-Alejo, *El delincuente y su patología: medicina, crimen y sociedad en el positivismo argentino* (Madrid: Consejo Superior de Investigaciones Científicas, 1991).

29 Material on this case is found in José María Ramos Mejía, Florentino Ortega, Marcelino Aravena, "El asesino de Olavarría: su estado mental al cometer el crimen y despues de él: responsibilidad: interesante estudio médico legal," *Revista Jurídica* 5 (1888): 428–452. See also Cornelio Moyano Gacitúa, *Curso de ciencia criminal y derecho penal argentino* (Buenos Aires: Lajouane, 1899), p. 259, where he reports that Pedro was executed by the *horca;* "Siguen los crimenes," *Revista Jurídica 5* (1888): 386–388; Luis María Drago, *Los hombres de presa* (Buenos Aires: Cultura Argentina, 1921), pp. 162–176. The actual case, if it has survived, is in a section of this archival series that is not yet open for consultation.

30 Miguel Romero, "Política interna: estudio psicológico," *Revista Jurídica* 20 (1901): 217–233.

31 Estanislao Severo Zeballos, "Analecta," *Revista de Derecho, Historia y Literatura* 3, no. 9 (1901): 151, 3/8 (1901): 479; and Carlos Octavio Bunge, "El carácter nacional y la educación," *Revista Jurídica* 19 (1900–1901): 75–76.

32 AGN, TC, 2, C, 64, 1891 and AGN, TC, 2, C, 68, 1891, against Juan Lucio Cascallares Paz and Susana Breuil de Conderc for abortion.

33 "Nuestros propósitos," *Revista Jurídica* 8 (1891): 5–8; review of Uladislao F. Padilla's law thesis, *Revista Jurídica* 19 (1900–1901): 71–72.

34 Zeballos, "Analecta," p. 7.

Cuidado con los Rateros:

The Making of Criminals in

Modern Mexico City

PABLO PICCATO

he collective identity of criminals was a central question for the understanding of society in late-nineteenth-century Mexico City. Scientists and public officials sought to establish clear rules to classify the capital's population. The urban petty thief, popularly called *ratero,* was the unwitting aide for this purpose. The category of ratero was appropriated by criminologists and became an essential tool of social policies against criminality, as it purported to describe a clearly defined trade. Mexican criminologists studied rateros: the law established specific penalties for them; and the city government set out to "eradicate" them from the capital. The unintended consequence of these repressive actions was a transformation of criminality itself. Some criminals did indeed become professional, but their victims and the public in general associated them with violence and police complicity—elements that were absent from the original popular notion of ratero.

By tracing the changing meanings of ratero and *raterismo,* this essay reconstructs the complex forces molding the identity of criminals as a social group (not only in public perceptions of them but also in the characteristics they shared). The hypothesis is that perceptions of crime and criminal practices constitute a unitary subject. Theft and criminality in general ought to be understood as cultural constructions in which multiple actors and social factors intervened. The criminological discourse delved into popular perceptions of crime to identify criminals; but the policies thus established changed those perceptions and the practice of illegalities. An ancillary hypothesis involves the role of criminology as one of the causes of crime itself. The Mexican case is useful to test John Braithwaite's contention that criminology should be considered one of the factors of criminality in the twentieth century, as it has justified taking the responsibility of crime prevention away from civil society, making it the exclusive realm of "deviance specialists."[1]

In order to preserve the diversity of images of theft, the following pages are divided in three sections that follow a loose chronological order. The first section discusses popular perceptions of rateros and the reactions of urban communities to theft. The second describes the criminological definition of rateros and the policies formulated thereof. I focus on the new penalty of transportation to penal colonies and the role of the police in defining rateros. One consequence of those policies is examined in the third section, dealing with the "modern" criminals who emerged after the revolution. The tensions and interactions among perceptions, practices, and reactions against theft bind these themes together.

Thieves in the City

In the beginning, the category of ratero was a useful instrument to make sense of the dramatic transformations experienced by Mexico City's society at the end of the nineteenth century. The expansion of communications and the economic growth associated with Porfirio Díaz's regime (1876–1911) brought a large number of propertyless immigrants to the city. Not all the newly arrived were peasants: many had experienced urban life and all sought to blend into a society with a relatively high literacy rate.[2] Thus, the categories of *lépero* (literally, coarse) or simply *indio* (Indian), traditionally used in the past to refer to the less "civilized," did not suffice to distinguish the recently arrived from those who were neighbors from some time ago.[3]

The haphazard way in which the new immigrants settled in new suburban colonias and old barrios created additional conflicts that could not be easily articulated in terms of traditional social hierarchies. Whereas middle- and upper-class residential developments and downtown avenues enjoyed all the material privileges available in developed nations (such as running water, sewage, electricity, and paved streets), lower-class neighborhoods were neglected by city authorities. Unhealthy conditions (particularly in the lower eastern neighborhoods closer to Lake Texcoco), lack of safety, and a sense of economic uncertainty made life in these areas of the city something quite different from the European models that inspired city authorities and developers. To make things more complex, many inhabitants of the "marginal" city crossed daily into the "civilized" city in order to work, trade, or simply have a good time in one of the hundreds of cantinas or *pulquerías* (shops selling pulque, a fermented beverage) surrounding the downtown area.[4] Growing crime was another consequence of this process of urban expansion. Despite the class-biased concerns of the police, most victims, as well as offenders, belonged to the marginal city. Crime, however, crossed social divides to create a sense, among all groups, of a permanently contested urban space.

The complexity of this landscape demanded some adaptations in the vocabulary used to distinguish social groups. For the majority of the urban population, the category of ratero helped to articulate the growing insecurity accompanying progress. The word *ratero* had long been part of the Spanish language. It connotes moral lowliness and is often related to *rata* or *ratón* (rat, mouse) and the adjective *rastrero* (crawling, but also vile, despicable).[5] In its most direct sense, people used *ratero* as a synonym for thief, applied to strangers in the circumstance of a larceny. The word simply stated a fact based on immediate evidence: "He is a ratero because he is running with my belongings." Depositions of victims and witnesses in judicial proceedings contain examples of this use.[6]

Additionally, and with greater frequency from the 1890s on, *ratero* was also used by the daily press to signify membership in a trade. This appears clearly in the daily and popular press. *Nueva Era* and *La Voz de México* referred to petty thieves as "rats" who arrived in "plagues," "waves," or "invasions."[7] *El Universal* printed on its first page pictures of alleged rateros, including several beggars and a destitute mother with her children. The text warned that many beggars and peddlers were in reality rateros and swindlers.[8] These perceptions had an echo in the Mexican derivations of the word *ratero,* which included *raterismo* or the adjective *rateril* to refer to the group or trade of thieves.[9]

Rateros plied a trade comparable to other artisanal crafts. Since the middle of the nineteenth century at least, artisans saw the weakening of their associations and the disappearance of the support that the law had provided them. Rateros never had the protection of the law that bakers or others did, but by the end of the century they were perceived to form the same kind of loose fraternity. Rather than an institutional structure, what united rateros was the knowledge of a craft, that is, a set of techniques transmitted from master to apprentice. Rateros were the men characterized by their ability to pick pockets or break into homes, and by their knack of evading the action of the law. In 1929, *Excélsior* reported on an individual who used a "magician's box" to steal shoes from stores.[10] The newspapers talked about rateros in terms that stressed their coordination and unified techniques. In 1897, the liberal *El Hijo del Ahuizote* opined that "rateros not only pick pockets, but they also attack their victims with knifes, and can even slap policemen."[11] Rateros could pass as "decent" citizens and fool the unaware, and they could also avoid punishment by fabricating lies and hiding their identity.

These perceptions attributed to raterismo a considerable degree of institutionalization. In 1929, *Excélsior* reported that the police had discovered "a true thieves' school" and arrested students and professors. The report described the school as having classrooms, complete regulations and even a graduation ceremony. Graduates joined a band of rateros that worked in coordination with the school. To be admitted to the band, the report stated, applicants could avoid having to attend classes by proving that they were *rateros conocidos* (well-known thieves).[12] *Excélsior*'s report is not supported by additional evidence about such a school, but the belief in the existence of a close-knit community of thieves did reach a wide sector of public opinion.

Like other artisans, rateros had to sell the product of their work. Thus, people identified rateros with areas of the city regarded as places of danger and intense commerce. The barrio of Tepito and the nearby Lagunilla market were the most famous among these neighborhoods. The Baratillo market was known as the "thieves market," where stolen and second-hand goods were commonly bought and sold.[13] Located near Tepito, colonia La Bolsa was also considered a center for thieves and all sorts of criminals. An 1895 guide of the city (eloquently subtitled *"Cuidado con los rateros"*) warned visitors about La Merced market, which "is famous for the number of rateros who work there."[14] In the view of many victims of theft, rateros belonged in places of vagrants and criminals. In October 1925, several individuals robbed José Sorribas, taking his hat and money. The following day, Sorribas told the police, he went to Tepito to buy a new hat, and he saw one of his attackers, Rafael Téllez, in the gardens where "many vagrants lie in the morning to take the sun."[15]

Associated with street commerce, rateros were adept at the widespread practice of pawning. Pawnshops, the official Monte de Piedad, and street markets bought and sold all sorts of items; many merchants, particularly at pulquerías, accepted clothes and other items in exchange for the products.[16] Questions were rarely asked about the origin of the objects. Pawning, after all, was part of the domestic economy of most families, particularly when work and cash were scarce. The economic expansion of the late Porfiriato made wage relations and commercial exchange the source of income for a rapidly increasing percentage of the population. Wages were replacing other traditional extramonetary arrangements that had characterized artisanal workshops. The cost was greater instability for workers. A large portion of the population also survived through street vending, buying and selling products in small quantities every day. Pawnshops were essential in both cases, as one could pawn and later recover properties just to get by for a day. Having cash at hand was imperative, not only to buy food, clothes, and pulque, or the merchandise that would be peddled during the day, but also to pay for lodging—which many did on a weekly or daily basis.[17] In 1906, for example, Pablo Severiano was arrested because Salvador Jaime saw him wearing a vest that had been stolen from Jaime's house the previous night. Severiano told the police that he had bought the vest at a pulquería from Manuel González. Severiano was released after some days in jail, but González was sentenced to six years in prison.[18]

Theft, whether committed by rateros or not, was after all the result of economic pressures. Available statistics suggest that increases in theft coincided with periods of economic strain in the city. Tables 6–8 provide the total number of those arrested and sentenced for theft between 1871 and 1938. The trend is one of growth during the last years of the Porfiriato until the mid-1920s and decrease thereafter. The average number of sentences per year fell sevenfold from 1895–1909 to 1927–1938 (see table 9). The number of sentences and arrests per 100,000 inhabitants also shows a decrease after the revolution (see table 10).[19]

Shorter variations in theft rates, such as the increases after 1903, 1907 and 1928, coincide with periods in which lower-class living conditions were negatively affected by the economy. Data for 1916–1920 render a lower average of sentences per year than the previous cycle, but evidence from qualitative sources suggests that in 1915 there was another peak in thefts, coinciding with hard times for the capital's population because of the civil war that started in 1910. Although the national economy was still in sham-

TABLE 6 Sentenced and Arrested for Theft: Federal District, 1871–1939

Year	Sentenced	Arrested	Year	Sentenced	Arrested
1871	1,006		1905	2,222	
1872	1,032		1906	2,675	
1873	1,223				
1874	1,197		1908	4,055	
1875	804		1909	3,229	
1876	753				
1877	1,584		1916	1,395	
1878	1,566		1917	1,330	
1879	1,789		1918	1,578	
1880	2,202		1919	813	
1881	1,312		1920	422	
1882	923				
1883	646		1927		941
1884	386		1928		1,777
1885	463		1929		1,687
1895		2,636	1930		2,241
			1931		2,567
1897	1,230	2,343	1932		2,078
			1933		2,480
1900	1,083	3,404	1934		1,562
1901	1,178	4,420	1935		1,382
1902		2,025	1936		1,347
1903		1,893	1937	586	1,324
1904	2,145	2,164	1938	581	1,615
			1939	536	1,347

Sources: Dirección General de Estadística, *Estadística del ramo criminal en la República Mexicana que comprende un periodo de quince años, de 1871 a 1885* (México: Secretaría de Fomento, 1890); Ministerio Público del Distrito y Territorios Federales, *Cuadros estadísticos e informe del Procurador de Justicia concernientes a la criminalidad en el Distrito Federal y territorios, 1900–6, 1908–9* (México: La Europea, 1900–6, 1908–9); Procuraduría General de Justicia del Distrito y Territorios Federales, Sección de Estadística, *Estadística de la penalidad habida en los juzgados del fuero común del Distrito y territorios federales durante los años de 1916 a 1920* (México: Talleres Gráficos de la Nación, 1923); Alfonso Quiróz, *Tendencia y ritmo de la criminalidad en México* (México: Instituto de Investigaciones Estadísticas, 1939); Secretaría de Economía, Dirección General de Estadística, *Anuario estadístico 1938* (México: Talleres Gráficos de la Nación, 1939); *Anuario estadístico 1940* (México: Talleres Gráficos de la Nación, 1941).

TABLE 7 Arrested for Theft: Mexico City, 1885–1895

Year	Arrested
1885	459
1886	484
1887	592
1888	778
1889	977
1890	1,046
1891	1,493
1892	1,758
1893	1,773
1894	1,935
1895	2,123

Source: Anuario estadístico de la República Mexicana 1895 (México: Secretaría de Fomento, 1896).

bles in the 1920s, reconstruction was well under way in Mexico City by the second half of the decade. Depression hit after 1929, contributing to an increase in thefts from 1930 on.[20] Except for the mid-1910s period, the statistical data are supported by qualitative sources in pointing to periods when the incidence of thefts increased. Despite the new modalities of crime to be examined in the third section of this chapter, petty theft remained a common occurrence of everyday life.[21]

The economic reasons behind theft became apparent to the people of Mexico City by the fact that suspects and victims were often related. Most of the cases of theft I have analyzed involved victims and offenders who resided close to one another, were related by ties of family or friendship, or simply lived in the same building or neighborhood. Judicial records also suggest that many offenders were as poor as their victims, neighbors, acquaintances and coworkers. Approximately half of the cases of theft in the database of judicial archives involve victims and offenders who resided close to each other or were related by kinship, friendship, or work.[22]

This context is necessary in order to understand popular perceptions of raterismo. The response of the urban communities was the key element of social reactions to theft. Even if people perceived rateros as specialists in crime, their reactions were influenced by a common experience about the

TABLE 8 Arrested for Theft: Mexico City, 1922–1926

Year	Arrested
1922	4,473
1923	4,465
1924	4,416
1925	4,523
1926	2,500

Source: Estadística Nacional 347 (15 Jan. 1927): 10–11.

motives behind petty crime. As opposed to state and elite reactions, which I will discuss in the next section, everyday responses to theft relied on direct and informal strategies. Victims who managed to catch thieves tried to settle the issue by following two basic rules, which applied to suspects who were known by the community but also to strangers. First, judicial intervention had to be avoided or limited to a few days of incarceration for the suspect. The reason for this reluctance was the corruption and delays that characterized criminal courts. If the thief was indicted, the trial would drag for months, while the stolen property was definitively lost and the suspect remained isolated from his or her community. After all, the offender usually lived next door, or was known to the victim. Victim Sara Prado, for example, declared that she only wanted suspect María Vargas to return the purse she had taken, but "she wants nothing else against the accused."[23]

The second rule was a consequence of the first: the victim and his or her neighbors tried to negotiate a satisfactory solution with the suspect in order to recover the stolen property before violence had to be used or anyone had to go to jail. When Dimas Barba accused José Vázquez of stealing a bundle of his wife's clothes, Vázquez promised to pay for the cost of the stolen clothes. Indeed, the file contains a paper signed by one Raymundo Vázquez in which he promises to pay the victim fifty pesos if the charges against José Vázquez are dropped.[24] These negotiations prevented violence, as most thefts did not involve the use of force and victims rarely resorted to physical confrontations in order to achieve a negotiation. In a common situation, *vecindad* (tenement) concierges often stopped the suspect, and a policeman was called to make the arrest and take the suspect to the station. The negotiations took place on the way there, sometimes in front of the policeman or

TABLE 9 Sentenced and Arrested for Theft: Federal District, Average per Period

Period	Sentenced	Arrested
1871–1885	1,032.00	
1885–1895		1,046.00
1895–1909	2,183.50	2,343.00
1916–1920	1,330.00	
1922–1926		4,075.40
1927–1938	581.00	1,651.00

Note: 1927–1938 average of sentenced from *Tendencia y Ritmo,* 1927–1936. Data for 1885–1895 and 1922–1926 correspond to Mexico City.
Sources: Tables 6 to 8. In 1895, Mexico City had 70 percent of the Federal District's population. In 1921, the percentage was 68 percent.

the clerk who wrote down the first depositions. Teodora Rodríguez, for example, offered to give some money to her accusers at the police station. A police officer escorted her to her house, but she could not find her husband or produce the money, so she was officially arrested.[25] Most negotiations, as in this case, were only recorded in judicial proceedings when they failed to solve the problem. They suggest that the street-corner gendarme was little more than another member of the community, who often knew those involved and was not particularly keen on incarcerating suspects.[26]

In this regard, gendarmes complemented the role of urban communities, particularly vecindades, in protecting neighbors' property. Judicial records reveal that members of these communities shared information and protection with their neighbors. This was largely the result of the newly arrived population's need to reconstruct networks of support in the adverse environment of modern Mexico City. Instead of the anomie usually linked with urbanization, theft cases show the strong social life of urban communities organized around old barrios (like Tlatelolco or Tepito), new lower-class colonias (Guerrero, Obrera) and, on a smaller scale but with the strongest links, the vecindad.[27] Key to the success of these networks of protection were *porteras* (concierges). Usually female, porteras sought to protect vecindad neighbors from intruders. They suspected everyone, but concentrated their fear on unknown rateros. In doing so, and in trying to maintain crime prevention under their control, porteras and neighbors reinforced the cohesion of their communities. These reactions explain why,

TABLE 10 Sentenced and Arrested for Theft: Federal District per 100,000 Population, Average per Period

Period	Sentenced	Arrested
1871–1885	355.60	
1885–1895		220.28
1895–1909	403.22	432.67
1916–1920	146.79	
1922–1926		662.31
1927–1938	47.25	134.27

Sources: Table 9; 1885 population from Ariel Rodríguez Kuri, *La experiencia olvidada: el ayuntamiento de México, política y administración, 1876–1912* (México: El Colegio de México, 1996); population for 1895, 1900, 1921, and 1930 from *Estadísticas históricas de México* (México: INEGI, 1984), based on figures of national censuses. Data for 1885–1895 and 1922–1926 correspond to Mexico City.

in contrast with other contemporaneous cities, petty larceny was reported less frequently than crimes against persons. In the latter offenses, the police did not wait for the victim to press charges, whereas in cases of theft police usually only acted at the victim's request.[28] Assuming that the urban poor dealt with most occurrences of theft without the authorities' intervention, it is possible to argue that the intervention of urban communities played a larger role than official punishment in the treatment of the problem of theft.

The notion of ratero served to distinguish the thief who was a stranger from the petty thief, who could be dealt with without the intervention of authorities. By calling someone a ratero, lower-class victims and their communities were also exercising their ability to shame transgressors. Shaming could be an effective preventive measure because it warned transgressors of the consequences of exclusion from the community. Being called a thief and going to jail could turn suspects into rateros, and thus exclude them from communal networks of support—a costly proposition. Witness Belem inmate Consuelo Hernández's letter to President Francisco I. Madero, in which she asked for a pardon, arguing that need had forced her to commit a "shaming fault"—stealing a shawl to pawn it and buy food for her children. The effect of the loss of reputation and informal support derived from her situation was clear: "Believe me, sir, that I felt like dying, not for me but for my children who were left abandoned. I have no family and they are orphaned. . . . I have been here for a year of bitterness, consumed in thinking about my little children, now living with the strangers who helped me by taking them in but, as you know, the hanger-on soon bores."[29]

Imagined Rateros

Official views of thieves reflected little sympathy for Consuelo's pains. In his book *Las colonias de rateros,* published in 1895, Antonio Medina y Ormaechea argued that thieves disrupted "modern society" by "introducing fear inside homes; disturbing peace in the streets; planting mistrust among social classes; and undermining the authority of the government."[30] Medina y Ormaechea suggested that thieves, whom he and other writers also called rateros, be banished from the cities and sent to forced labor colonies. Other opinions were stronger. In 1897, Miguel Macedo proposed the use of flogging against thieves.[31]

The state and the dominant classes of early twentieth-century Mexico City adopted a radical stance toward the problem of theft. First, in order to eradicate urban petty thieves systematically, observers had to construct them as a collectivity. Classifying the population in general had been one of the goals of Mexican criminologists — a goal they eagerly borrowed from the positivist founders of the scientific discipline of criminology. The idea of the "born criminal" formulated by Cesare Lombroso became part of the vocabulary of Mexican debates about crime, yet it was not easily translated into penological practice. The best-known model was devised by Macedo himself, who in 1897 maintained that Mexicans could be distinguished in three categories: individuals wearing plain shirts were the lowest class, followed by those who wore jackets and, at the top of the scale, the group that used frock coats.[32]

More precise than these vague classifications, the ideas about rateros allowed writers and officials to reconcile scientific knowledge, public policies, and class prejudice. The category was useful because, unlike other notions from criminology, it flexibly combined the elite discourse about crime with the experience and vocabulary of city dwellers. Pure biological reasoning, dear to the orthodox sources of the discipline, was too strict and difficult to found empirically to make it functional for public policy.

Criminological descriptions of rateros oscillated between hereditary explanations and empirical observations — an ambivalence consistent with the eclecticism of Mexican criminology and with received ideas about the causes of crime. Scientists and journalists referred to the genetic origins of rateros' "decadence." Trinidad Sánchez Santos listed rateros among the kinds of degenerated offspring of alcoholic parents.[33] Criminologist Julio Guerrero called raterismo an "endemic" phenomenon of the capital.[34] Rateros were a clearly-defined lower-class social group, identifiable by their criminal skills and their presence in certain areas of the city. Beyond the biological vocabulary, writers discussed rateros based on direct observations of life in the streets of the capital. In *Las colonias de rateros,* Medina y Ormaechea defined rateros as those thieves who stole less than a thousand pesos and did not use violence. He wrote, "Those little tricksters, those untidy women, those shirtless [*descamisados*] who wander in the city streets until they find the most favorable opportunity to dispossess pedestrians of any objects they might be carrying, those burglars . . . are almost all minors, have no family ties, education, or work."[35]

Elite observers established a close relationship between the lack of social attachments and the proliferation of rateros, thus implying that the "plague" was a consequence of recent migrations to the capital. In this perspective, rateros naturally thrived in the cities but were not born there. They were "the rubbish from other towns" who came to the capital to profit from anonymity.[36] According to *El Imparcial,* while the "non-ratero men" were willing to emigrate to places of harder climate to get jobs and feed their families, rateros tried to stay in places with nice weather and avoided work.[37]

Regardless of the explanation, public officials and legislators believed that the problem of raterismo demanded the state's action against suspected thieves as a group. Such action, if it was to be systematic and proportionate to the problem, required the reform of existing legislation about theft, to adapt it to the notion that rateros were a special kind of criminal. The 1871 penal code defined theft according to the classical tenets of criminal law, by centering on the action to be punished rather than on the person who committed the crime. *Robo* was the physical appropriation of an object "without right or without the consent of its legitimate owner."[38] Punishment for theft without violence ranged from three days to five years in prison, according to the value of the stolen property. Circumstances, such as committing the theft at the workplace, could add to the prison term imposed by the judge.[39] For influential writers and officials of the Porfiriato, however, the existing penalties were not satisfactory. They blamed the repeated "waves of crime" on the leniency and legalism of the criminal code, and even the Ministry of Justice determined that longer sentences were not enough to deter thieves.[40]

Implicit in these criticisms was the idea that thieves required special forms of punishment, even if that went against the code's premise that only free individual actions could be punished, and that all citizens were equal in front of the law. In taking this position, Mexican penologists echoed Italian criminology's critique of the judicial system. In this regard, the notion of ratero summoned a rare agreement between criminologists and jurists in prerevolutionary Mexico.[41] In 1897, *El Imparcial* proposed that different penalties be established for different social groups: "against the ratero, it is hard to admit it, cruelty is necessary, if defending the interests of honest people can be called cruelty. [They should face] swift trials and punishments that would inspire greater fear than [the forced labor colony of] Valle Nacional."[42] I noted earlier Macedo's modest proposal of returning to the use of whipping, which *El Imparcial* also supported.[43] The San Lázaro penitentiary (inaugurated in 1900) did not solve the problem of rateros because the building housed fewer than seven hundred male inmates deemed "incorrigibles of bad behavior." Inspired by modern penal ideas, the penitentiary was not intended to inflict humiliating and cruel punishment. By contrast, raterismo demanded a large-scale solution without the enormous expense and delays involved in the construction of the San Lázaro building.[44]

The purported solution to the problem of the inadequacy of punishment for raterismo was banishment by transportation to penal colonies. Advocates of transportation depicted it as a social policy with progressive consequences for the cities.[45] In *Las colonias de rateros,* Medina y Ormaechea introduced Mexican readers to the new ideas about transportation discussed among international penologists. He proposed the use of penal colonies against "the audacious and cynical rateros." Transportation, noted Medina y Ormaechea, was more rational than whipping, which was a "barbaric" method tainted by its use by foreign invaders against Mexicans and expressly preempted by article 22 of the constitution. The comparison between transportation and whipping was valid, however, because both practices stigmatized rateros and offered public examples of the state's strong hand against theft.

Medina y Ormaechea also defended the attractive economic possibilities of transportation, describing it as an extension of colonization policies, in which lands and islands belonging to the nation would be put to use to regenerate criminals through labor. Prisoners' work, he suggested, could also be productively used in the construction and maintenance of highways and railroads.[46] The benefits of forced labor, already exploited by planters, would trickle back to the cities. According to Julio Guerrero in 1900, the deportation of rateros had already increased wage levels in the capital. Coupled with industrialization, this improvement was creating the "people for democracy," in which income differences were not substantive, and the true equality of citizens was possible.[47] Thus, it was claimed, transportation would have a beneficial impact on the progress of urban society as a whole.

Following these ideas, several legislative reforms established specific penalties and facilities for convicted thieves, and gave political authorities greater intervention in the execution of sanctions. In 1894, a reform to the penal code authorized the executive power to designate the "places and work" to be served by theft convicts. According to the Ministry of Justice, the amendment's goal was to "repress theft and cease the alarm caused by the frequency and daring with which it is committed." Lawyers called it "the law against rateros," as it explicitly targeted "rateros" and others guilty of theft.[48] The 1894 reform's goal was to formalize time-honored methods to banish criminals from the cities. During colonial times, sentences for crimes such as vagrancy, disorderly conduct, gambling, and desertion often involved the chain gang to Havana, or to labor in fortifications at Perote or Veracruz.[49] After independence, forced recruitment in the army became common and, at least since 1867, political authorities of the Federal District sent prisoners to forced work camps.[50] After the 1894 law, the police arrested scores of rateros and sent them to camps in Valle Nacional or Yucatán. Many suspects died in the camps due to harsh working conditions. According to American journalist John Kenneth Turner, this traffic (which he equated with slavery) benefited police officers throughout the country, including Mexico City's police chief Félix Díaz, who received ten pesos for each man sent to Valle Nacional.[51]

The final formulation of penal ideas about raterismo came in June 20, 1908, when a new law established the penalty of transportation to penal colonies (*relegación*), to be used against rateros, counterfeiters, vagrants, and other "habitual criminals." Convicts would serve double the time of their prison sentences, for at least two years, in the recently acquired colony of Islas Marías, in the Pacific Ocean.[52] According to its sponsors, transportation targeted "habitual criminals, who constitute the veteran section of the army of crime, who commit the largest number of crimes . . . keep police constantly busy and form the nucleus of the prison population."[53] The reform and the inauguration of the Islas Marías colony received the support of the press but, like the 1894 reform, it did not attract the great public attention generated by the penitentiary in 1900.[54] The abuses associated with convict labor explain the government's willingness to present relegación simply as a penitentiary improvement.

The fight against rateros was not free of tensions. Police campaigns against thieves, which were based on collective and often indiscriminate arrests, imposed on thousands of people the consequences of police zeal, even if they were not suspects of any specific crime. And, in the wake of the reforms that increased the executive power's authority over the execution of sentences, city administrative officials overlooked judicial procedures in order to send rateros to penal colonies.[55] In 1910, 2,238 people were sentenced to transportation to the islands, most of them for theft.[56]

Police campaigns were based on the premise that, thanks to their daily experience of street life, the police could easily distinguish rateros from the rest of the population. In 1897, El Imparcial reported that as part of the present "war against this social plague" the government had authorized "intelligence agents [who] know all rateros, the places where they can be found and even their addresses," to round up subjects.[57] In 1906, the Gaceta de Policía declared triumphantly that these actions had prompted many rateros to leave for other cities, because they had more troubles than before to escape the police and because they feared the penitentiary.[58] The Gaceta also published police portraits of suspects, listing their name, alias, and modus operandi. The information, the editors claimed, was useful for police officers, travelers, and storekeepers.[59] Although such optimism might be questioned (the police department, headed by Félix Díaz, helped in the publication of the Gaceta), the idea of linking the police's effectiveness with the number of thieves on the streets reveals the key function of that institution in defining and creating raterismo.[60]

Officials and newspapers maintained that police action need not be encumbered with an excessive respect for the law — even if the police already enjoyed considerable leeway to use violence.[61] Claiming to fight rateros, the police could arrest "suspects" without accusing them of any specific crime and referring to them as "well-known rateros." This label was flexible enough to actually create criminals out of the urban population. Policemen would later explain that the accused had been surprised in unspecified "suspicious activities" or found with objects whose origin he or she was not able to explain satisfactorily — regardless of their low value. Manuel González, for example, was arrested in March 1918 "because he was found with clothes whose ownership he cannot demonstrate, although nobody has claimed them as stolen." He was placed under the city council's authority, probably to be later transported to the Islas Marías. The clothes he was carrying, however, were so dirty that the authority ordered them thrown away.[62]

Campaigns against rateros continued with enthusiasm after the revolution. In 1916, *El Universal* approvingly reported that the police chief was rounding up "an infinite number of rateros" and sending them to Yucatán and other distant places.[63] In his message to Congress in April 1917, Venustiano Carranza announced that the government had taken steps to "repress with great severity the plague of raterismo that had developed in the city."[64] In that year, Mexico City authorities officially reestablished the use of transportation and undertook a systematic campaign of arrests. Suspects by the hundreds were detained and warned by the police to abandon the streets or be banished.[65] The campaign was based on a seldom-used section of the 1871 penal code, which dealt with "Vagrancy and Begging" within the chapter about "Crimes against public order." Article 854 established that *vagos* [vagrants] were those who, "lacking property and rents, do not exercise an honest industry, art or trade for a living, without having a legitimate impediment [to do so]." Rateros were included in this definition, as they lacked an "honest" trade. Thus, the governor of the Federal District instructed the Inspector General de Policía to arrest and admonish all suspects to get a job in ten days, as the first step before their formal arrest.[66] City council archives contain hundreds of records of arrests for reasons ranging from being a "sleeping drunkard" or urinating in the street to insulting the governor of the Federal District. Officers described many of those arrested as "well-known *rateros*" or "pernicious rateros."[67] If detained a second time, they could be transported to the islands. Just as the police defined the status of "well-known ratero," the decision to send suspects to the islands was largely discretionary. In December 1916, for example, governor of the Federal District César López de Lara personally selected approximately one hundred rateros at the penitentiary to be sent to the islands in the next shipment. Another hundred suspects were released in the same act.[68]

The 1917 campaign relied on policemen's eyes to detect rateros, but it also began to compile systematic information about criminals. After the arrest, the police gathered personal data about the suspect: place of birth, trade, age, address, and a physical description. In order to establish the suspect's status, personal files also included letters of recommendation signed by acquaintances, employers, or relatives.[69] The information about individual suspects compiled in these campaigns supported more generalizations about rateros as a clearly defined and large social group. In 1920, for example, the police chief painted an alarming image of the confrontation between policemen and rateros. The police, he claimed, had been reduced after the revolution from seven thousand to two thousand "men without weapons." Of these, only seven hundred were in the streets at any given time, yet they had to face ten thousand rateros.[70] After the fall of Carranza in 1920, the Federal District's government carried out an "administrative action" against rateros that built on the foundations of the 1917 campaign. Officials interviewed rateros and compiled personal files about them. The goal was to reach "a moral judgement about the arrested," and the result could be transportation to the Islas Marías (by authority of the Secretaría de Gobernación) or simply a periodical evaluation of the suspect's behavior.[71]

Police campaigns and "administrative actions" against rateros began to lose their uncontested force in the 1920s. Witness the public confrontation between governor of the Federal District Celestino Gasca and Inspector General de Policía Jesús Almada regarding the ability of the police chief to deal with rateros independently of the governor and the judiciary.[72] Campaigns against rateros also generated a strong opposition from the legal profession, whose intervention in the judicial and penal process was curtailed by the extrajudicial acts of administrative authorities. In 1911, legal scholar Antonio Ramos Pedrueza asserted that the 1894 law against rateros and the 1908 penalty of transportation had not reduced the number of thefts. He directed at penal colonies the same criticism usually reserved for jails, namely, that they created career criminals by placing first-time offenders together with recidivists.[73] Aware of the harshness of the new penalties, some judges avoided imposing the full extent of the law on theft offenders, explaining their sentences with references to the economic conditions of the lower classes. These criticisms emerged from judicial attitudes toward property crimes marked by the revolutionary experience, and by a renewed skepticism from lawyers toward positivist criminology — trends that would lead to the swift abrogation of the 1929 penal code (an example of positivist penology) in 1931.[74] Prisoners used available legal resources to avoid transportation, and higher courts granted their appeals against their sentences, thus delaying their implementation.[75] The *cuerda* (as the chain-gang to the islands was called) generated protests because it usually meant cutting short suspect's appeals. In June 1930, several prisoners and their families complained in criminal courts that city authorities were overruling a judge's decreed suspension of the cuerda. Despite several appeals granted by judges, the police forcefully took several suspects from their hospital beds to the train station.[76] Against the best opinion of judges and suspects, the departure of cuerdas remained a routine event that included convicts and political prisoners in the 1930s.[77]

Campaigns against rateros left lasting legacies in Mexico City dwellers' understanding of crime and punishment. The first was to demonstrate in practice that rateros were a collectivity, even if the police had a key role in defining them as such. The cuerdas, separating numerous suspects from their city and their families, only reinforced the isolation of those offenders. Another legacy of transportation survives to this date in the belief that the police can effectively detect and act against criminals without the burden of the law. In both ways, the notion that criminology is one of the factors of crime, suggested by Braithwaite, is supported by the Mexican experience. The scientific discourse produced by Mexican criminologists gave the police and legislators the technical authority to identify those belonging to "the criminal population." The next section discusses one of the consequences of these policies.

Modern Crime

Criminological discourse and official campaigns against thieves fed the widespread belief that rateros were a distinct trade. Was there any reality behind this claim? The data from judicial records and from the 1917 campaign suggest that those labeled as rateros were no different from the rest of theft suspects: around four-fifths of them were male and single; about half of them could not read. They resembled most of the city's population in that half of them were born there. A comparison of the data about ratero suspects in this campaign and the information about suspects in a sample of judicial cases for 1900–1931 yields suggestive differences. The police seem to have defined rateros as those suspects who were particularly visible in public spaces. Although women constituted a fifth of the suspects in trials, only 7 percent of the arrested in the 1917 campaign were female. Merchants, artisans, construction workers, and cart drivers, many of whom

TABLE 11 Campaign against Rateros, Trades Stated by Suspects

Trade	No.	Percentage
Artisan	220	25.46
Merchant	164	18.98
Assistant	38	4.40
Cart driver	38	4.40
Shoemaker	36	4.17
Construction worker	25	2.89
Delivery	20	2.31
Journeyman	19	2.20
Apprentice	17	1.97
Industrial worker	16	1.85
Coach driver	15	1.74
Shoeshiner	15	1.74
Car driver	13	1.50
Domestic worker	13	1.50
Unemployed	2	0.23
Other	72	8.33
No data	141	16.32
Total	864	100.00

Source: AHA, Vagos y rateros, 4157 to 4160.

peddled their services in the streets, increased their percentage among rateros, relative to their role as suspects in judicial records. Journeymen and domestic workers, by contrast, had a lower profile in the ratero campaign (see table 11). More "respectable" trades were largely absent from the number of rateros: policemen and military men went from 6 percent in the judicial files to less than half a percent in the 1917 campaign. Ratero suspects were young. Their median age was twenty, five years less than that of judicial suspects, and only 12 percent of them were married—against 21 percent of judicial suspects. In sum, the arrested in campaigns against rateros resembled more the criminological and police image of criminals, rather than those who were suspects of actual crimes.[78]

Recidivism, a defining trait of rateros, is difficult to document in judicial records, although testimonial evidence suggests it was common. Previous incarcerations of a suspect were established during trial based on a report produced by the archivist of Belem jail, but the procedure was unreliable, given that experienced suspects often changed their names.[79] Some offenders, like Victoriano Jaramillo and Mariana Hernández, who were arrested in 1912 for fighting each other, could be very active and yet avoid long-term punishment. Since 1910, Jaramillo had been arrested for theft nine times and once for battery, and had been released each time for lack of evidence. Since 1901, Hernández had four arrests for battery (from which she was released once for lack of evidence), and eight for theft (she was released for lack of evidence on three occasions).[80]

There was indeed a relatively small group of offenders who personified the ideas about rateros as a skillful and evasive trade. The best remaining evidence of such "criminal" knowledge is the specialized language documented by the *Dictionary of Crime* compiled by criminologist Carlos Roumagnac on the basis of interviews with Mexico City inmates and his own experience working for the police and the newspapers. The dictionary included specific words such as *el retorcijón* for stealing a clock by breaking its chain, or *descabezar,* to indicate the same act but by breaking the ring. Roumagnac reconstructed entire phrases in this incomprehensible jargon: *Oye, gorri, rúpale a tesco el mondovero* meant, "Hey, pal, steal the clock from this guy."[81] Other authors found a similarly specialized language. *Dar chicharrón* meant to steal from homes by breaking a lock; *chicharronero,* therefore, was the kind of thief who broke locks.[82] This vocabulary, however, should not be construed as proof that petty thieves embraced the identity of rateros. To do so would go against their basic need to evade the police. It is significant, in this regard, that these vocabularies do not include the word ratero and its derivations.[83]

But the identity of "modern" rateros (as opposed to the petty thieves traditionally encompassed by the term) was not so much centered around a technique, as it was focused on their relationship with penal institutions and the police. After 1900, and more clearly after the revolution, modern professional rateros acquired a closer relationship with authorities, and were more likely to use violence and a complex organization in their activities. This caused a transformation in public perceptions of crime: from the "invasion" of petty thieves feared by Porfirian elites to the professionalization of violence and corruption felt by the same lower-class victims of petty theft. Evidence about these new rateros' lives is scarce, but we know that they were frequent guests of jail, where they learned the ways in which the police and courts functioned, and that they were better prepared to use guns. This knowledge and those connections with public officials enabled rateros not only to better avoid punishment but also to carry out major crimes.[84]

Incarceration for long periods or several short terms was the first factor to build modern rateros' collective identity. Inmates' learning of certain knowledge inside prisons was a well-known fact, recorded in 1871 by Antonio Martínez de Castro. He described prisons as true schools of crime, where "the ratero thief and the bandit; the one convicted of fighting and the murderer . . . the guilty and the one under trial" live together in idleness, sharing stories and projects about past and future crimes.[85] Such was the case, for example, of Carlos Pineda and David Rojas, founders of a car-stealing ring in the late 1920s. They declared to the judge that the origin of their association was in the penitentiary.[86] The original members of the notorious Banda del Automóvil Gris [Gray Automobile Gang] met in Belem jail and escaped together during the 1913 Decena Trágica.[87] Prison life was characterized by strong hierarchies enforced with violence, and the authorities' complete lack of control over the social life of inmates. The associations thus established translated into a common experience about the workings of the police and the judicial system, because inmates' concerns revolved around the always uncertain pace and result of their trials. It was no coincidence then, that on their way out of Belem, the escapees of 1913 burned the prison's archives.[88]

A defining trait of successful rateros was the ability to avoid long incarcerations. Antonio Martínez (known as *El Enterrador,* the grave-digger) offers the best example of the connections and abilities that could be acquired during incarceration. Martínez knew the workings of the judicial system and tried to make the best from the connections established in prison. In 1923, Martínez and Luz González were convicted of murdering and burying the corpse of their wealthy friend Ignacio Oliver, in a famous case that came to be known as "The crime of the Desierto de los Leones."[89] Martínez was released in 1929, thanks to a presidential amnesty. He then approached the judge who had sentenced him, asking for a job. The judge assisted Martínez, and he "worked during several months arranging pardons for several inmates of the penitentiary." In 1930 Martínez entered the gang organized by Pineda and Rojas at the penitentiary.[90] Soon incarcerated, his active involvement in prison life did not cease. In 1931, he and other inmates of the penitentiary signed a letter to President Pascual Ortiz

Rubio supporting the firing of a police officer who, they reported, was corrupt and "had been a member of the well-known ratero gang called Los de la Gorra Prieta (The Black Cap gang)." The letter referred to criminal archives to substantiate its accusation.[91]

Knowledge of the system gave rateros the means to cope with police persecution. Suspects like Martínez knew the police's reliance on confessions to obtain guilty verdicts. Thus, after his second arrest, Martínez refused to confess and accused the police of torturing him and forcing other suspects into declaring against him. He realized that there was no advantage in yielding to investigators' pressure to admit one's guilt because, despite the mandates of the legislation, judges never considered confessions as mitigating circumstances.[92] Confession was all the more important for prosecutors because the impact of witnesses' testimonies was often diluted in cross examination, inasmuch as victims' descriptions were usually vague, or after witnesses failed to appear in later hearings.[93] To counter accusations, suspects like Rafael Téllez appealed to the belief that criminals were clearly different from "decent people." Téllez, who was identified by a victim in the barrio of Tepito and accused of robbery, claimed that he was an "honest" person whose relation with the rateros who were with him at the time of his arrest was only incidental and argued that in his work, selling lottery tickets, "he usually had in his hands bills for one or two hundred pesos . . . which demonstrates that people trust him." He was released after the victim failed to reappear in court.[94]

The strategies used by suspects to avoid conviction were often nothing more than the use of rights granted by the law. Although available to any citizen, these resources were in fact seldom used by suspects, and could increase suspicion against those who did. Enemies of rateros depicted the exercise of the right of appeal, or the use of several defense lawyers, as a perversion of the law, intended to delay the trial, the testimony of witnesses, and transportation. The premise of these claims was that defendants knew about those resources only because they had been in prison before. Thieves with a close contact with authorities owing to multiple incarcerations could be labeled "well-known rateros" and become the target of unmotivated arrests. Thus, ratero suspects were further stigmatized when they dared to use their experience of the law and their knowledge of the operation of the judicial system.[95]

The official onslaught against rateros and the resulting experience of inmates led to a transformation in public perceptions of crime and professional criminals. The use of force was not a common feature of urban criminality in the early years of the century, but violent robbery became the central element of public fears of crime since the 1910s. Modern raterismo became associated with the use of violence — something lacking in the early Porfirian definitions of the trade.[96] According to Judge David Fernández Jáuregui, in 1920 criminality was increasing and changing its methods: "It is not any more the pickpocket who is satisfied with stealing a clock, but now we are dealing with rateros who use their knife or their gun to rob their victims."[97]

Organized gangs of criminals (which combined the use of guns, a higher degree of planning, and some degree of official complicity) became a visible symptom of the modernization of criminality in the capital.[98] Thus, even if modern professional rateros were a minority among those accused of theft, the pervading sense of insecurity in the streets at night seemed to demonstrate the existence of a trade of criminals.

Modern criminal gangs were surrounded by an aura of elegance and technical prowess that resembled images brought by movies and literature from Europe and the United States. In 1897 an article titled "La evolución del robo" (the evolution of theft), signed by one Cestas el Roto, described the increasing refinement of theft since antiquity. Old raterías seemed dull and backward when compared to the practices of contemporary swindlers.[99] In 1914, members of a gang specializing in opening safe boxes were arrested. They confessed to have imitated the Black Glove Gang, from Nick Carter movies.[100] In 1920, Gobernación minister Manuel Aguirre Berlanga defended censorship arguing that the movie *Los misterios de Nueva York* had taught Mexican thieves to perform "high class robberies" formerly ignored in Mexico.[101] Automobiles were also part of the image of danger and modernity associated with these gangs.[102] The noticeable change regarding the methods and skills of thieves was portrayed in a 1925 editorial in *El Universal* entitled "La criminalidad triunfante" (Triumphant Criminality). Recent robberies, noted the newspaper, could be classified, after Thomas de Quincey, as "works of art." They demonstrated "the technical advance of criminals" and "the same ways that Mexico City is no longer a provincial city, pleasant and welcoming, and has become a cosmopolitan center, criminality, which used to wear diapers, has now grown and matured."[103]

The famous case of the Banda del Automóvil Gris illustrates the new patterns of organized theft that arrived in Mexico City with the revolution. The gang became a focus of public attention and a symbol of modernization and danger in the capital. Its members usually targeted upper-class victims, rode around in elegant cars, and liked to spend their share of the take in elegant restaurants and cantinas.[104] Their operations began under Zapatista rule and continued during the Constitutionalist (i.e., Carrancista) occupation of the city. The structure of the gang was intricate: several groups, unknown to one another, performed special tasks, while the "brain" of the system, Higinio Granda, coordinated them and received information and support from revolutionary officials. This criminal sophistication took inspiration from the style of popular foreign criminal bands. Before his execution, another member of the Banda del Automóvil Gris declared with pride that the robberies of the gang would be the envy of thieves throughout the world.[105] The gang used different devices to enter houses, gathering information from official sources in order to find attractive victims and escape police intervention. When breaking into their victims' homes, they wore uniforms and showed search warrants signed by police commanders.[106] The warrants were apparently obtained through a network that involved a secret policeman (Major José Palomar) who worked for General Pablo González.[107] The manner in which Constitutionalist officers dismantled the band further supported suspicions about the involvement of officers. Several of its members were executed by orders of González before they could be interrogated by civilian authorities.[108] Higinio Granda was released from prison in 1920, with the support of González, and worked afterward as a clerk in criminal courts and later as a land speculator.[109]

Accusations against Pablo González regarding his involvement with the Banda del Automóvil Gris became part of presidential politics in 1919, because he was one of the likely successors of Carranza.[110] In an effort to clean his image before a frustrated bid for the official candidacy, González supported the production of the 1919 movie *El automóvil gris,* in which the truth about the case would be exposed. Although the movie was a success, it did not improve González's image.[111] The "dirt" in the higher ranks of government had been a frequent criticism against the Porfirian regime; the image of Victoriano Huerta was associated with alcohol and dishonesty; but the Carrancistas were, by far, the favorite target of popular scorn. The term *carrancear,* meaning "to steal," was coined in these days.[112]

In the popular mind, therefore, the modern features of organized urban crime translated into an increasingly tenuous separation between authorities and criminals. Since the 1910s, thieves could wear uniforms or badges. This was a result of the confusion of uniforms and insignia brought about by the multiple armies that entered the capital during the mid-1910s. In 1914, for example, a bread seller had to give his money to a uniformed man, who claimed to be a Constitutionalist captain.[113]

The case of the *coronela* Celia Hernández, one of the few instances in which officers were arrested and tried by civilians, portrays the confusion and the reactions generated by these abuses. Hernández commanded a group of Zapatista soldiers who entered a house in broad daylight in May 1915. She and other officers claimed to be looking for Carrancistas, but they seized money and other valuables. The victim of the robbery, Juana Ayala, pressed charges against her, declaring that Hernández was in fact a prostitute. The police arrested Hernández, probably because her age and sex made her claim to a high military rank less legitimate. Nevertheless, the Zapatistas released her from Belem in July before abandoning the city to the Constitutionalists.[114] The Banda del Automóvil Gris may have been more systematic, but Hernández's impunity provided similar evidence of the mixed interests of authorities and criminals.

The development of police institutions contributed to this complicity, as the capital's police force, like professional criminals, acquired a complex structure and increased its use of guns and cars in the first decades of the twentieth century. Porfirio Díaz's regime reorganized and reinforced the city's police as an instrument to maintain external order in public spaces. Yet, rumors of corruption and abuse of violence characterized the last years of the regime.[115] During the revolution, gendarmes were often no more than witnesses of the disorders created by troops. Since 1920, the police department acquired even greater autonomy from city authorities, as demonstrated by Governor Gasca attempts to reign in Inspector Almada. Presidents Alvaro Obregón and Plutarco Elías Calles (1921–1928) made a point of providing policemen with cars, better guns, and militarized uniforms and organization. At the same time, the activities of plain-clothes judicial and private police bodies acquired a greater role in the investigation of crimes. Rather than signal better public safety, the latter development often meant that the police's actions escaped public scrutiny.[116] In addition to this increased ability to use force, the police's "power of definition" became essential to establishing criminals' collective identity, as the earlier discussion of transportation suggests. Although the postrevolutionary police remains to be studied in depth, its role in the modernization of Mexico City's criminality is clear.

Conclusions

Postrevolutionary organized robbery never became as frequent as petty larceny, and certainly did not displace it, but it acquired greater public resonance. Modern criminals were a worrisome symptom of the cultural and political changes occurring in Mexico City. Members of gangs such as the Banda del Automóvil Gris saw themselves as part of a cosmopolitan world of cars, guns, movies and night clubs. On the other hand, public opinion (including poor and better-off victims) suspected gangs of acting in cahoots with politicians and the police. Urban robbers, it should be clear by now, never became a variation of rural social bandits. The rich were not necessarily their targets, and they left no evidence of any intention to redistribute their profits. With their sumptuary consumption and their associations with high officials, these new rateros proved to the inhabitants of the city that criminal tendencies did not mark the difference between classes. They did confirm, however, the official double standard toward suspects: excessive penalties against petty rateros, but corrupt collaboration with big thieves.

The polarities of elites versus subordinate groups and of popular attitudes in opposition to social control obscure more than they explain. A frequent derivation of these views is the contention that crime is caused by the labeling imposed by the institutions of control on the poor. The preceding pages do show the isolating consequences of suspicion and incarceration. But they also show that victims, their communities, and Mexico City's fragmented public opinion reacted against those who violated property rights, regardless of the amount of the booty involved.

Explanations centered on the "subculture" of crime have a similar obscuring effect. In this view, criminals reinforce their own values in an enclosed world of transgression, foreign to the rest of the population. The history of professional gangs, however, proves that the desires of criminals did not differ from those of the law-abiding. More importantly, the multiple uses of the notion of ratero show that the attitudes and practices that separated the "decent" from the criminal were a matter of public contention.

The disputed perceptions of criminals in early twentieth-century Mexico

City support the hypothesis that crime should be studied as a cultural construct. The preceding pages discussed three incarnations of that Lombrosian construct, "the criminal." First, the ratero as an artisan, defined long before the Porfiriato but becoming a key for the understanding of social change at the end of the nineteenth century. Then, the ratero as a part of a plague, a notion formulated by contemporary criminologists, and embraced by policy-makers and policemen, on the premise that criminals were clearly different from the rest of the population. Finally, the modern ratero: professional, dangerous, and probably connected with authorities. These three versions coexisted during the period, and the first and third survive in contemporary perceptions of crime. But it was during the early decades of the twentieth century that the interaction of contrasting views of crime shaped public policies in ways that thousands of inhabitants of Mexico City found dangerous and unfair.

Notes

1 John Braithwaite, *Crime, Shame and Reintegration* (New York: Cambridge University Press, 1989), p. 5. It is not possible in the space of this chapter, however, to probe fully into the action of communities against crime — an important element of Braithwaite's thesis. For a discussion of this aspect see Pablo Piccato, *City of Suspects: Crime in Mexico City, 1900–1931* (Duke University Press, forthcoming). I am indebted to Carlos Aguirre, José Luis Barrios, Ted Beatty, Jonathan C. Brown, Donna Guy, Xóchitl Medina, Ricardo Salvatore, and Gil Joseph for their comments on previous versions of this essay, and to the University of Texas at Austin, the Center for U.S.-Mexican Studies of the University of California, San Diego, the Consejo Nacional para la Ciencia y la Tecnología, and the Instituto Nacional de Estudios Históricos de la Revolución Mexicana, for their material support.

2 In 1900, more than half of Mexico City's inhabitants were born in other states. *Estadísticas sociales del porfiriato, 1877–1910* (México: Dirección General de Estadística, 1956), p. 73; Keith A. Davies, "Tendencias demográficas urbanas durante el siglo XIX en México," *Historia Mexicana* 5, no. 4 (1972): 505. In 1900 the nation's literacy rate was 18 percent, but in the Federal District it was 45 percent. *Estadísticas históricas de México* (México: INEGI, 1984).

3 According to Miguel Macedo, *lépero* was becoming less common by the turn of the century. Macedo, *La criminalidad en México: medios de combatirla* (México: Secretaría de Fomento, 1897), p. 12. But the term continued to be used in descriptions of disreputable and bawdy characters in the city. *El Universal*, 16 Feb. 1917, p. 1; *Excélsior*, 29 Oct. 1929, 2d sec., p. 1.

4 For the growing literature stressing class divisions of Mexico City space, see John

Lear, "Mexico City: Space and Class in the Porfirian Capital, 1884–1910," *Journal of Urban History* 22, no. 4 (May 1996): 444–492; María Dolores Morales, "La expansión de la ciudad de México en el siglo XIX: el caso de los fraccionamientos" in Alejandra Moreno Toscano, ed., *Investigaciones sobre la historia de la ciudad de México* (México: INAH, 1974), pp. 189–200; Jorge H. Jiménez Muñoz, *La traza del poder: historia de la política y los negocios urbanos en el Distrito Federal desde sus orígenes a la desaparición del Ayuntamiento (1824–1928)* (México: Codex, 1993), p. 9; Pablo Piccato, *"Urbanistas, Ambulantes,* and *Mendigos:* The Dispute for Urban Space in Mexico City, 1890–1930," *Anuario de espacios urbanos* (1997): 75–113.

5 The 1737 Spanish *Diccionario de autoridades* defines *ratero* as *"el ladrón que hurta cosas de poco valor, o de las faltriqueras"* (the thief who steals things of little value, or pocket items). The origin of the word, according to the same *Diccionario,* is found in the *germanía* (thieves' jargon), where *rata* means *faltriquera* (pocket). The contemporary *Diccionario de la lengua española* defines *ratero* as an adjective for the thief who "steals things of little value with skill and caution" (*hurta con maña y cautela cosas de poco valor*). Although I find no evidence linking the origin of the term *ratero* with *rata* or *ratón,* the association was commonly made in Mexico. The *Diccionario de autoridades* also defines *ratero* as *lo que va arrastrando por la tierra* (that which crawls on the ground), as *rastrero,* and adds the metaphorical meaning of *bajo en sus pensamientos o acciones o cosa vil o despreciable* (low in thoughts or actions; a vile or despicable thing). Real Academia Española, *Diccionario de autoridades* (Madrid: Gredos, 1963 [1737]); Real Academia Española, *Diccionario de la lengua española,* 21st ed. (Madrid: Real Academia Española, 1992). This echoes the Brazilian use of *gatuno* for *ratero,* linked to *andar de gatinha* (to crawl on all fours).

6 See Archivo del Tribunal Superior de Justicia del Distrito Federal, Reclusorio Sur (hereafter AJ, RS), 18493, Theft, 1922; AJ, RS, 1074705, Theft, 1915, p. 4.

7 *Nueva Era* 1, no. 20 (21 Aug. 1911): 3; *La Voz de México,* 29 Jan. 1890, p. 2.

8 *El Universal,* 21 Dec. 1916, p. 1; ibid., 23 Dec. 1916, p. 1.

9 Santamarina's *Diccionario de mexicanismos* defines *rateril* as *relativo al ratero* (relating to the ratero) and *raterismo* as *hábito de ser ratero; arte del ratero* (the habit of being a ratero; the ratero's art), thus emphasizing the use of the word to refer to a collectivity. This usage also appears in other Latin American countries. Francisco J. Santamaría, *Diccionario General de Americanismos* (México: Pedro Robredo, 1942), vol. 3, p. 16. The word gained access to the standard Spanish of lawyers. "Ratería" is defined as a small theft conducted with caution. Rafael de Pina and Rafael de Pina Vara, *Diccionario de derecho,* 12th ed. (México: Porrúa, 1983), p. 413.

10 *Excélsior,* 4 Oct. 1929, 2d. sec., p. 1.

11 *El Hijo del Ahuizote,* 17 Jan. 1897, p. 39.

12 The police arrested more than forty suspects, and twenty-four remained in jail after the first investigations. *Excélsior,* 11 Oct. 1929, 2d sec., p. 1.

13 For viceroyal attempts to close the Baratillo market, see Gabriel J. Haslip, "Crime and the administration of justice in colonial Mexico City, 1696–1810" (Ph.D.

dissertation, Columbia University, 1980), p. 82. Smith mentions a "thieves' market." Eaton Smith, *Flying Visits to the City of Mexico and the Pacific Coast* (Liverpool: Henry Young and Sons, 1903), pp. 72–73.

14 *México y sus alrededores: Guía para los viajeros escrita por un mexicano: Cuidado con los rateros* (México: Tip. Luis B. Casa, 1895), p. 15.

15 AJ, RS, 19368, Theft, 1925. Inhabitants of La Merced resisted the notion that theirs was a thieves' neighborhood. Rodney D. Anderson, *Outcasts in Their Own Land: Mexican Industrial Workers, 1906–1911* (DeKalb: Northern Illinois University Press, 1976), p. 46. Antonio Martínez and David Rojas, members of a car-theft gang broken up in 1930, met in the Tepito plaza. AJ, RS, 23196, Criminal association and robbery, 1930.

16 See for example, AJ, RS, 705331, Theft, 1911. On the Monte de Piedad, *Memoria del ayuntamiento de 1901* 2, pp. 39–41; Marie Eileen Francois, "When Pawnshops Talk: Popular Credit and Material Culture in Mexico City, 1775–1916" (Ph.D. dissertation, University of Arizona, 1998).

17 On the growth of the wage-earning population, see Stephen Haber, *Industria y subdesarrollo: la industrialización de México, 1890–1940* (México: Alianza Editorial, 1992), pp. 43–45. On the intensity of commerce and existence of money in Mexico City, see Fernando Rosenzweig, "El desarrollo económico de México de 1877 a 1911," *Secuencia* 12 (Sept.–Dec., 1988), pp. 160, 167; *Anuario estadístico de la República Mexicana* (México: Secretaría de Fomento, 1902), pp. 246–47. On conditions during the late Porfiriato, see John H. Coatsworth, "Producción de alimentos durante el Porfiriato," in *Los orígenes del atraso: nueve ensayos de historia económica de México en los siglos XVIII y XIX* (México: Alianza Editorial, 1990), p. 177; Anderson, *Outcasts in Their Own Land,* p. 68. María Magdalena Gutiérrez, for example, made about a peso a day in 1931, buying vegetables in La Merced market early in the morning and selling them downtown. Archivo Histórico de la Secretaría de Salud, Beneficencia Pública, Sección Asistencial, Serie Asilados y Mendigos, f. 7. On the loss of paternalistic ties in artisanal shops, see Carlos Illades, *Hacia la república del trabajo: la organización artesanal en la ciudad de México, 1853–1876* (México: El Colegio de Mexico-Universidad Autónoma Metropolitana, 1996).

18 AJ, RS, 705331, Theft, 1911.

19 Mexican statistics of crime share the inaccuracies observed in other cases. See V. A. C. Gatrell, "The Decline of Theft and Violence in Victorian and Edwardian England," in *Crime and the Law: The Social History of Crime in Western Europe since 1500* (London: Europa Publications, 1980), pp. 243–351; Carlos Roumagnac, *La estadística criminal en México* (México: García Cubas, 1907), pp. 19, 10–14. Mexican statistics, critics claimed, failed to account for recidivism and the delay of the processes. Ignacio Fernandez Ortigoza, *Identificación científica de los reos* (Mexico City: Sagrado Corazón de Jesús, 1892), p. 8. Yet, the general trend of increase before the revolution and decrease thereafter, up to the 1980s, has been underscored by studies. See Rafael Ruiz Harrell, *Criminalidad y mal gobierno* (México:

Sansores y Aljure, 1998), p. 18, and Ira Beltrán and Pablo Piccato, "Crimen en el siglo XX: Fragmentos de análisis sobre la evidencia cuantitativa," in Ariel Rodríguez Kuri and Sergio Tamayo, eds., *Ciudad de México: Los últimos cien años, los próximos cien años* (México: UAM, 2001).

20 Data from tables 6 to 8 and Alfonso Quiroz Q., *Tendencia y ritmo de la criminalidad en México* (México: Instituto de Investigaciones Estadísticas, 1939); for an increase of theft in the years before the Revolution based on police data, see Laurence John Rohlfes, "Police and Penal Correction in Mexico City, 1876–1911: A Study of Order and Progress in Porfirian Mexico" (Ph.D. diss., Tulane University, 1983), pp. 168, 245; James W. Wilkie, *The Mexican Revolution: Federal Expenditure and Social Change since 1910* (Berkeley: University of California Press, 1967), p. 38.

21 Theft constituted a fifth of all sentences and arrests between 1895 and 1938 — second only to battery. Between 1916 and 1920, for example, theft made an average of 22.67 percent of those sentenced each year in the Federal District, Procuraduría General de Justicia del Distrito y Territorios Federales, Sección de Estadística, *Estadística de la penalidad habida en los juzgados del fuero común del Distrito y Territorios Federales durante los años de 1916 a 1920* (México: Talleres Gráficos de la Nación, 1923). For perceptions of an increase before the revolution, see *La Voz de México,* 18 Jan. 1890, p. 2; *Gaceta de Policía* 1, no. 2 (19 Oct. 1905): 3; Carlos Roumagnac, *Los criminales de México: ensayo de psicología criminal: seguido de dos casos de hermafrodismo observado por los señores doctores Ricardo Egea . . . Ignacio Ocampo* (México: Tipografía El Fénix, 1912), p. 373. For examples in the press referring to the *plagas de rateros,* see *El Hijo del Ahuizote,* 17 Jan. 1897, p. 39; *El Imparcial,* 4 Jan. 1897, p. 2, c. 2; *La Voz de México,* 29 Jan. 1890, p. 2; Macedo, *La criminalidad en México,* pp. 23 and 4. For perceptions of increase during the revolutionary decade, see Venustiano Carranza, address to Congress, *Diario de los Debates de la Cámara de Diputados* XXVII, 1, no. 9 (15 Apr. 1917): 13. *El Demócrata,* 12 Oct. 1914, p. 1. Francisco Ramírez Plancarte, *La ciudad de México durante la revolución constitucionalista* (México: Botas, 1941), chaps. 12 to 20. After 1920, commentators asserted that criminality had not decreased so much as the statistics suggested, but neither was it booming as the press claimed. Manuel I. Fierro, "Algunas consideraciones . . ." in *Estadística de la penalidad,* 3; Casimiro Cueto, "Consideraciones generales y apuntes para la crítica, estadística de la criminalidad habida en el Distrito Federal durante el año de 1922," *Boletín de la Sociedad Mexicana de Geografía y Estadística* 5, no. 12 (1928): 38. The space devoted by the daily press to police news decreased noticeably during the early 1920s, but the tendency changed again toward the end of the decade. See, for example, *El Universal,* 10 June 1924; ibid., 3 Oct. 1924; ibid., 1 and 13 Sept. 1926; *Excélsior,* Sept. 1925.

22 In nineteen of the fifty-two cases of theft where address information is available, one or more of the accused lived no more than a few blocks away from the victim. Twenty-six of ninety-seven theft suspects lived in the zone where the theft took place. In several others, victims and offenders were otherwise related. For further

discussion on the database compiled from judicial archives, see Piccato, *City of Suspects,* intro. to part 2.

23   AJ, RS, 781370, Theft, 1913.

24   AJ, RS, 10746893, Theft, 1915.

25   AJ, RS, 705334, Theft, 1912.

26   On the tendency of gendarmes to drink with pulquería patrons, see "Porqué son borrachos los gendarmes," *Don Cucufate* v. 1, no. 4 (20 Aug. 1906), p. 2; Archivo Histórico del Antiguo Ayuntamiento, Mexico City (hereafter AHA), Justicia Comisarías, 2717, 14.

27   On vecindades, see Julio Sesto, *El México de Porfirio Díaz (hombres y cosas): estudios sobre el desenvolvimiento general de la República Mexicana: observaciones hechas en el terreno oficial y en el particular,* 2d ed. (Valencia: Sempere y Cia, 1910), p. 245; Ramírez Plancarte, *La ciudad de México durante la revolución constitutionalista,* pp. 426–427. Within the area of older buildings near downtown, vecindades were the result of subdividing large upper-class homes, and during the nineteenth century they housed tenants from different economic backgrounds. The construction of tenements for the express purpose of renting apartments was more common in newly developed areas or in demolished downtown lots. See Lear, "Mexico City," p. 476. For the multiple social strata among vecindad tenants in the early nineteenth century, see Jaime Rodríguez Piña, "Las *vecindades* en 1811: tipología" in Alejandra Moreno Toscano et al., *Investigaciones sobre la historia de la ciudad de México (II)* (México: INAH, 1976), pp. 68–82. On the contemporary role of urban communities and extended families, see Larissa A. de Lomnitz, *Cómo sobreviven los marginados* (México: Siglo Veintiuno, 1975).

28   For an example of vecindad concierges acting against thieves or other suspects, see AJ, RS, 1074694, Theft, 1915; AJ, RS, 434207, Battery, 1903; AHA, Presos penitenciaría, 3665, 10. For a victim refusing to call the police because the families of the offenders promised to give one of them "a good whipping," see AJ, RS, 281, 596570, Theft, 1909. Articles 17, 21, and 103 of the 1917 constitution established that prosecution could be pursued only by the judiciary. This theoretically prevented victims from actively intervening in judicial proceedings. Instituto de Investigaciones Jurídicas, *Diccionario jurídico mexicano* (México: Porrúa-UNAM, 1987) I, p. 39. In contemporaneous Buenos Aires, by contrast, property crimes were more common than crimes against persons. Lyman L. Johnson, "Changing Arrest Patterns in Three Argentine Cities: Buenos Aires, Santa Fe, and Tucumán, 1900–1930," in Lyman L. Johnson, ed., *The Problem of Order in Changing Societies: Essays on Crime and Policing in Argentina and Uruguay, 1750–1940* (Albuquerque: University of New Mexico Press, 1990), p. 129. The same can be said about German cities. Eric Johnson, "Urban and Rural Crime in Germany, 1871–1914," in Eric A. Johnson and Eric H. Monkkonen, eds., *The Civilization of Crime: Violence in Town and Country since the Middle Ages* (Urbana: University of Illinois Press, 1996), p. 227.

29   AGN, Fondo Francisco I. Madero 70. For a discussion of the preventive impact of

shame, see John Braithwaite, "Shame and Modernity," *The British Journal of Criminology* 33, no. 1 (winter 1993): 2; and in Mexico City communities, Lomnitz, *Cómo sobreviven los marginados,* pp. 212–215.

30 Antonio Medina y Ormaechea, *Las colonias de rateros* (México: Imprenta del Gobierno en el Ex-Arzobispado, 1895), pp. 30–31.

31 *El Imparcial,* 1 July 1897, p. 1; Macedo, *La criminalidad en México,* pp. 35–36.

32 Macedo, *La criminalidad en México,* pp. 7–8, 16, 19; ibid., "Discurso pronunciado en la ceremonia inaugural de la Penitenciaría de México" [1900], in Archivo General de la Nación, *Boletín del Archivo General de La Nación: La Penitenciaría de México* 18 (1981–1982): 12. Macedo's classification was adopted in prison regulations. Manuel González de Cosío, *Memoria que presenta al Congreso de la Unión et General . . . Secretario de Estado y del Despacho de Gobernación* (México: Imprenta del Gobierno Federal, 1900), p. 855. For a classification of the Mexican population based on their sexual mores, see Julio Guerrero, *La génesis del crimen en México: estudio de psiquiatría social* (Paris: Vda. de Ch. Bouret, 1901); on the influence of positivism, see Pablo Piccato, "La construcción de una perspectiva científica: Miradas porfirianas a la criminalidad," *Historia Mexicana* 185 (1997): 131–81; in France, Tarde developed the idea of a "professional criminal." Marie-Christine Leps, *Apprehending the Criminal: The Production of Deviance in Nineteenth-Century Discourse* (Durham, N.C.: Duke University Press, 1992), p. 33.

33 Trinidad Sánchez Santos, *El alcoholismo en la república mexicana: discurso pronunciado en la sesión solemne que celebraron las sociedades científicas y literarias de la nación, el día 5 de junio de 1896 y en el salón de sesiones de la Cámara de Diputados* (México: Imprenta del Sagrado Corazón de Jesús, 1897), p. 28.

34 Guerrero, *La génesis del crimen,* p. 137.

35 Medina y Ormaechea, *Las colonias de rateros,* pp. 30–31.

36 Junta General del Ramo de Pulques, *Dictámen que presenta la comisión nombrada por la . . . al señor Gobernador del Distrito: Impugnando el vulgar error de que el consumo de esta bebida nacional es causa de la criminalidad en México, y en el que se exponen las razones legales con que se combaten las medidas restrictivas que atacan la libertad de este comercio* (México: Tipografía Artística, 1896), pp. 14–15; *El Imparcial,* 1 Apr. 1897, p. 2.

37 *El Imparcial,* 10 Jan. 1897, p. 1.

38 CP 1871, 368. The offense was consummated *al momento en que el ladrón tiene en sus manos la cosa robada; aun cuando lo desapoderen de ella antes de que la lleve a otra parte, o la abandone* (at the moment the thief has a stolen object in his hands, even if it is taken back from him before he carries it elsewhere or abandons it), CP 1871, 370.

39 *Código penal para el Distrito Federal y Territorio de la Baja-California sobre delitos del fuero común y para toda la República Mexicana sobre delitos contra la Federación. Edición correcta, sacada de la oficial, precedida de la Exposición de motivos dirigida al Supremo Gobierno por el C. Lic. Antonio Martínez de Castro, Presidente de la comisión*

encargada de formar el Código (Veracruz y Puebla: La Ilustración, 1891 [1871], hereafter cited as CP 1871), 376, 388, 400, 404.

40 A 1900 internal memorandum acknowledged that, in spite of the recent reforms to the penitentiary system "it can be noted that the crime of nonviolent robbery has not diminished as much as has been hoped". The solution, added the memorandum, was to force judges to adhere strictly to guidelines regarding punishment of recidivism. AGN, SJ, 372, 364.

41 See Enrico Ferri, *La sociologie criminelle,* 3d ed. (Paris: Arthur Rousseau, 1893), chap. 2. See also David Garland, "Of Crimes and Criminals: The Development of Criminology in Britain," in Mike Maguire, Rod Morgan, and Robert Reiner, eds., *The Oxford Handbook of Criminology* (New York: Oxford University Press, 1994), pp. 17–68. On the reluctance of Mexican jurists to embrace the penological ideas of positivist criminology, see Piccato, "La construcción de una mirada científica"; José Angel Ceniceros, *El nuevo código penal de 1931, en relación con los de 1871 y 1929* (México: Botas, 1931).

42 *El Imparcial,* 7 Jan. 1897, p. 1.

43 Macedo, *La criminalidad en México,* pp. 35–36; *El Imparcial,* 1 Jul. 1897, p. 1.

44 Manuel González de Cosío, *Memoria que presenta,* p. 891. "Sobre el número y clase de presos que debe alojar la Penitenciaría de México," *Boletín del Archivo General de la Nación: La Penitenciaría de México* 5, no. 4 (1981–1982): 36.

45 For a good synthesis of the discussions and projects of transportation, see Rohlfes, "Police and Penal Correction," chap. 6. The development of transportation as an alternative to the prison was embraced by the British government in the late eighteenth century, although it faced the opposition of Jeremy Bentham. John Hirst, "The Australian Experience: The Convict Colony," in Norval Morris and David J. Rothman, eds., *The Oxford History of the Prison: The Practice of Punishment in Western Society* (New York: Oxford University Press, 1995), p. 264.

46 The Sociedad Agrícola, noted the author, was currently studying the use of prisoner labor in these colonies. Medina y Ormaechea, *Las colonias de rateros,* p. 1. These proposals were not divorced from the author's interests. In 1881, Antonio and Carlos Medina y Ormaechea had proposed the establishment of a penitentiary system based on the building of penitentiaries underwritten by their Compañía Constructora de Penitenciarías en la República Mexicana. Antonio A. de Medina y Ormaechea and Carlos A. de Medina y Ormaechea, *Proyecto para el establecimiento del régimen penitenciario en la República Mexicana* (México: Imprenta del Gobierno, en Palacio, 1881), p. 23. See also *Gaceta de Policía* 126 (6 May 1906): 9.

47 Guerrero, *La génesis del crimen,* p. 155.

48 The same wording was used in article 8 of the Reglamento General de Establecimientos Penales del Distrito Federal, decreed in September 14, 1900. González de Cosío, *Memoria que presenta,* p. 843; Medina y Ormaechea, *Las colonias de rateros,* pp. 30–31. Antonio Ramos Pedrueza, *La ley penal en México de 1810 a 1910* (México:

Díaz de León, 1911), p. 17. Another decree of the same month simplified the procedures for sentencing theft without violence. In December 1903, a new reform to the code increased the sentences for theft without violence, from four to nine years. AGN, SJ, 372, 364. For the 1903 reform, CP, 1871, 376.

49 See Teresa Lozano Armendares, *La criminalidad en la ciudad de México: 1800–1821* (México: Universidad Nacional Autónoma de México, 1987), pp. 98–99; for a personal example of transportation, and its negligible effects, see "Causa formada de oficio de la Real Justicia á Don Santiago Balvas por vago y mal entretenido," Puebla, 1817. Edmundo O'Gorman Collection, Benson Latin American Collection, University of Texas at Austin. See also Colin MacLachlan, *La justicia criminal del siglo XVIII en México: un estudio sobre el Tribunal de la Acordada* (México: SepSetentas, 1976), p. 131. For service in the army, see Christon I. Archer, "To Serve the King: Military Recruitment in Late Colonial Mexico," *Hispanic American Historical Review* 5 (1975): 239; ibid., *El ejército en el México: borbónico, 1760–1810* (México: Fondo de Cultura Económica, 1983), p. 288.

50 José Angel Ceniceros at the Primer Congreso Criminológico y Penitenciario, *El Universal,* 18 Oct. 1923, p. 1. During the Porfiriato, convicted thieves were transferred to the Secretaría de Guerra's authority, which turned them over to the military commanders. Government of the Federal District to Secretaría de Justicia, 11 June 1904, AGN, SJ, 468, 406. After 1911, enlistment offered prisoners a good prospect for a sentence abbreviated by desertion. For enlistment of inmates, see Vicente Fuentes to President Huerta, Cárcel General, 14 Mar. 1914, AGN, SJ, 894, 4554. On the *leva* during Madero's government, see Alan Knight, *The Mexican Revolution* (Lincoln: University of Nebraska Press, 1990), vol. 1, p. 457; on Huerta, ibid., vol. 2, pp. 78–79.

51 John Kenneth Turner, *Barbarous Mexico* (Chicago: Charles H. Kerr, 1910), pp. 75, 107. See Rohlfes, "Police and Penal Correction," p. 155.

52 Ramos Pedrueza, *La ley penal,* pp. 12, 17.

53 Secretaría de Justicia. Comisión Revisora del Código Penal, *Trabajos de revisión del código penal: proyecto de reformas y exposición de motivos* (México: Tip. de la Oficina Impresora de Estampillas, 1912), vol. 4, pp. 414–415, 428.

54 *Trabajos de revisión del Código Penal,* vol. 4, pp. 414–415; *El Imparcial,* 31 July 1908, p. 1.

55 See *El Universal,* 27 June 1930, p. 1, for a case of a confrontation between a judge's order and the forceful transportation of prisoners to the Islas Marías penal colony. The postrevolutionary press interpreted these conflicts as the excessive concern of judicial authorities for the rights of individuals who threatened society, *El Universal,* 30 June 1930, p. 3. For the illegal detention of prisoners, see also Rohlfes, "Police and Penal Correction," p. 280.

56 *Trabajos de revisión del Código Penal,* vol. 4, p. 428.

57 *El Imparcial,* 12 Oct. 1897, p. 2.

58 *Gaceta de Policía* 1, no. 19 (4 Mar. 1906): 2. See also *La Nación,* 28 July 1912, p. 6.

59 *Gaceta de Policía* 1, no. 9 (17 Dec. 1905): 9; ibid., 1, no. 10 (24 Dec. 1905): 2.

60 For the implications of the police's "power of definition," see Alf Lüdtke, *Police and State in Prussia, 1815–1850* (Cambridge: Cambridge University Press, 1989).

61 Beatings to obtain confessions were commonplace during the Porfiriato. Revolutionary forces in the capital captured a former policeman known as El Matarratas (the ratkiller) who had been accused of killing several rateros (hence his nickname) during Félix Díaz's tenure as police chief, and political opponents of Huerta after 1913. *El Demócrata,* 25 Sept. 1914, p. 1. Several of the accused in the case of the car-theft band arrested in September 1930 claimed that their confessions had been obtained through torture. AJ, RS, 23196, Criminal Association and Robbery, 1930, p. 17.

62 AHA, Policía Presos Penitenciaría, 3664, 3. AJ, RS, 781373, Theft, 1914.

63 *El Universal,* 21 Dec. 1916, p. 1.

64 *Diario de los Debates de la Cámara de Diputados* XXVII Legislature 19 (15 Apr. 1917): 13.

65 *El Universal,* 25 Jan. 1918, p. 1; AHA, Policía Presos Penitenciaría, 3664, 1. For the campaign records see AHA, Vagos y rateros, 4140, 14.

66 The penalty against vagrants was up to eleven months of arrest and a fine of up to five hundred pesos. CP 1871, 855. Alberto Jiménez to President of the City Council, 30 Nov. 1917, AHA, Vagos y rateros, 4140, 14; AHA, Vagos y rateros, 4157, 1.

67 AHA, Policía Presos Penitenciaría, 3664 and 3665.

68 *El Universal,* 14 Dec. 1916, p. 3. In the mid-nineteenth century, the governor of the Federal District had the authority to *calificar* suspects, deciding punishment for minor offenses. Salvador Rueda Smithers, *El diablo de semana santa: el discurso político y el orden social en la ciudad de México: en 1850* (México: INAH, 1991), p. 72.

69 AHA, Vagos y rateros, 4157 to 4160.

70 *El Universal,* 14 Oct. 1920, p. 9.

71 Ceniceros, *El nuevo código penal de 1931,* pp. 32–33. For the continuity of these methods, this time against beggars, see Beneficencia Pública del Distrito Federal, *La mendicidad en México* (México: Departamento de Acción Educativa Eficiencia y Catastros Sociales, 1931); AHA, Sección Asistencial, Serie Asilados y Mendigos.

72 *El Universal,* 1 Oct. 1920, p. 1; ibid., 14 Oct. 1920, p. 9; ibid., 14 Oct. 1920, p. 3; ibid., 12 Oct. 1920, p. 12; ibid., 13 Oct. 1920, p. 1.

73 Ramos Pedrueza, *La ley penal,* p. 17. For an identical argument expressed in 1948, see Luis Garrido, "La utopía de las islas," in *Ensayos penales* (México: Botas, 1952), p. 87.

74 Sentence by Julio Montes de Oca on 1915, AJ, RS, 1074681, Theft, 1915; AHA, Justicia Juzgados Correccionales, 2759, 1; *El Foro,* 30 Sept. 1897, p. 4. Judge Francisco Flores, for example, decided in 1914 that he would not apply article 387 of the penal code against Juan Tavera. The article established five years for theft in an inhabited building, and Tavera had stolen 4.50 pesos worth of tools from a house in which he had entered through a window. In the sentence, Flores quoted Demetrio Sodi, who denounced article 387 for "confusing thefts of different seriousness."

Flores decided that the house was not yet inhabited and sentenced Tavera to six months in prison. AGN, SJ, 894, 4610.

75 *El Foro,* 23 Oct. 1897, p. 3; *El Imparcial,* 10 Dec. 1897, p. 2; *El Universal,* 27 June 1930, p. 1. The trip itself was very hard, and life in the islands particularly difficult. See the first-hand experience of José Revueltas, *Los muros de agua* (México: Ediciones Era, 1978).

76 *Excélsior,* 27 June 1929, p. 1.

77 In August 1929, for example, a group of 133 "rateros and degenerates" was sent to the Islas Marías penal colony. *El Universal,* 3 Aug. 1929, 2d sec., p. 1. For the transportation of political prisoners in 1931, see Archivo Histórico de la Secretaría de Salud, Fondo Salubridad Pública, Sección Salubridad del Distrito Federal 29, 7; Revueltas, *Los muros de agua.* For the success of appeals against banishment, see *El Universal,* 28 June 1930, p. 1.

78 The sample number analyzed from the 1917–1919 campaign is 864 individuals. The sample from judicial archives includes 282 suspects from 209 cases.

79 Ramos Pedrueza, *La ley penal,* p. 14; Moisés González Navarro, *Historia moderna de México: el porfiriato, la vida social* (México: Hermes, 1957), p. 427. According to the press, rateros and cruzadoras avoided the use of photography for identification purposes by changing their facial expression at the moment of being portrayed. *Gaceta de Policía* 1, no. 17 (18 Feb. 1906): 2. In 1905, the Ministry of Justice asked judges to request information from police chiefs to find out about the recidivism of theft suspects, AGN, SJ, 515, 603; also AGN, SJ, 680, A. On criticisms of available statistics, see Roumagnac, *La estadística criminal,* p. 14; *El Universal,* 30 June 1930, p. 3; Macedo, *La criminalidad en México,* p. 23; Fernandez Ortigoza, *Identificación científica de los reos.*

80 This time, Jaramillo was sentenced to two years and six months and Hernández to thirty days of arrest. AJ, RS, 705332, Battery, 1912. Some extreme examples of recidivism prompted lawyers to demand reforms eliminating short prison sentences. *El Imparcial* reported that Anselmo Cejudo, "specialist in stealing curtains from windows," had forty-three entrances in Belem jail, and had been sent twice to the Valle Nacional penal colony. *El Imparcial,* 4 Jan. 1900, p. 1. Legislators proposed that short prison terms be used less frequently, in order to prevent rateros from "teaching" their skills to first-time petty offenders. The 1923 Criminological Congress approved the proposal. The idea of suspending the execution of prison sentences, formulated by Miguel Macedo's committee for the reform of the penal code, was adopted by the 1931 code. *El Universal,* 16 Oct. 1923, p. 1; ibid., 18 Oct. 1923, p. 9. See also *Código penal para el Distrito y Territorios Federales y para toda la República en Materia de Fuero Federal* [1931] (México: Botas, 1938), art. 90. José Angel Ceniceros, *Tres estudios de criminología* (México: Cuadernos Criminalia, 1941), pp. 116–117.

81 Roumagnac, *Los criminales en México,* p. 26.

82 Guillermo Colín Sánchez, *Así habla la delincuencia y otros más . . .* (México: Porrúa, 1991), p. 52. See also Francisco Méndez Oteo, *Diccionario de caló: el lenguaje del hampa en México* (México: Chabat, 1956); Arnulfo Trejo, *Diccionario etimológico latinoamericano del léxico de la delincuencia* (México: UTEHA, 1968).

83 According to Roumagnac, the words for "thief" and "ratero" were *rupante* and *riño,* respectively. Roumagnac, *Los criminales en México,* p. 126. According to Trejo, *rata* and *ratón* are preferred to *ratero* in the slang of Mexican delinquency, among other words like *cacle, caco, carrancista* or *carranclán, rupa* or *rupante,* and *talón.* Arnulfo Trejo, *Diccionario,* p. 18. A 1987 dictionary of crime did not include the word *ratero,* but listed *rata, ratón,* and *ratoncito* with the meaning of thief or ratero. Guillermo Colín Sánchez, *Así habla la delincuencia,* p. 172.

84 As in Victorian England, these "professional criminals" were a minority, but they had a large impact on public perceptions of crime and the police's social function. Clive Emsley, *Crime and Society in England, 1750–1900* 2d ed. (London: Longman, 1996), p. 175. In modern England and United States professional criminals are defined as felons engaged in organized activities. Dick Hobbs notes the shared culture of market and workplace activities, entrepreneurship, geographical concentration in cities, and a taste for conspicuous consumption. Dick Hobbs, "Professional and Organized Crime in Britain" in *Oxford Handbook of Criminology,* pp. 441–468, esp. 447–449. According to Hobbs, "To establish and maintain a niche in the contemporary marketplace, violence is a key resource." Ibid., p. 460. The following analysis departs from Hobbs's model in my emphasis on the role of punishment, police, and judicial institutions in creating the professional identity of rateros.

85 Antonio Martínez de Castro, *Código penal para el Distrito Federal y Territorio de la Baja-California sobre delitos del fuero común y para toda la República Mexicana sobre delitos contra la Federación: Edición correcta, sacada de la oficial, precedida de la Exposición de motivos dirigida al Supremo Gobierno por el C. Lic. . . . Presidente de la comisión encargada de formar el Código* (Veracruz and Puebla: La Ilustración, 1891), p. 34. The same words are used in Medina y Ormaechea, *Proyecto para el establecimiento,* p. 12. Several of Carlos Roumagnac's interviewees narrated their learning in jail. Roumagnac, *Los criminales en México,* pp. 310–311. Martínez de Castro noted that minors and first-time offenders were housed together with recidivists. Juvenile offenders lived along adult offenders in Belem prison, and the correctional facilities and orphanages of the period where dominated by violence and the influence of older inmates. González de Cosío, *Memoria que presenta,* pp. 82–83. The problem was common to other prisons besides Belem. Dr. Alberto Lozano Garza, "El problema de los niños dentro de las prisiones" in *Memoria del primer congreso nacional penitenciario celebrado e la ciudad de México del 24 de noviembre al 3 de diciembre de 1932, convocado por la dirección antialcohólica* (México: Talleres Gráficos de la Nación, 1935), p. 263.

86   AJ, RS, 23196, Criminal association and robbery, 1930.

87   Juan Mérigo, *La banda del automóvil gris y yo!* (México: n.p., 1959), p. 11.

88   Mérigo, *La banda del automóvil gris,* p. 1. For prison life, see Piccato, *City of Suspects,* chap. 8.

89   *El Universal,* 2 Oct. 1923, 2d sec., p. 1.

90   AJ, RS, 23796, Criminal Association and Robbery, 1930.

91   AGN, Presidente 1931 / 2, 2245.

92   See for example, AJ, RS, 18517, Theft, 1926.

93   For the vague and often contradictory descriptions of suspects by witnesses and victims, see AJ, RS, 1074699, Theft, 1915. See also AJ, RS, 18483, Battery, 1921; AJ, RS, 10746893, Theft, 1915. In a 1919 case, two suspects provided diverging descriptions of the man who was trying to sell some stolen pieces of leather. One described him as "short, lean, wearing yellow shoes, grey suit, narrow pockmarked face." The other described him as being "regular constitution, short, white, beardless, wearing a white shirt and trousers, black hat, brown shoes, and no signs of smallpox scars on his face." Another witness described him as "short, strong, white, wearing no vest, a light suit, yellow shoes, without remembering additional details." Not surprisingly, no arrest was made based on these descriptions. AJ, RS, 1067900, Theft, 1919.

94   AJ, RS, 19368, Theft, 1925. See also AJ, RS, 1074681, Theft, 1915.

95   *El Imparcial,* 12 Oct. 1897, p. 2; *La Nación,* 20 Jul. 1912, p. 2. For the case of a thief arrested by a policeman who was also his friend, see Roumagnac, *Los criminales en México,* pp. 324–325. For the use of *ratero conocido* label as justification of arrest, AHA, Policía Presos Penitenciaría, 3664, 1; AHA, Vagos y rateros, 4157, 1.

96   See list of weapons and objects seized from suspects in 1919, AHA, Gobernación, 1112, 123. See also Rohlfes, "Police and Penal Correction," p. 245. Statistics suggest that before the revolution theft was decreasingly violent in the capital. In the 1871–1885 period, 7.94 per cent of sentences for theft in the Federal District were for theft with violence; in 1900, the percentage was 2.27. Dirección General de Estadística, *Estadística del ramo criminal en la República Mexicana que comprende un periodo de quince años, de 1871 a 1885* (México: Secretaría de Fomento, 1890); *Cuadros estadísticos e informe del Procurador de Justicia concernientes a la criminalidad en el Distrito Federal y territorios* (México: Ministerio Público del Distrito y Territorios Federales, 1900). Between 1922 and 1926, 6.24 percent of all reported thefts involved violence, with a peak of 11.16 percent in 1923. *Estadística Nacional* 3, no. 47 (15 Jan. 1927): 10–11.

97   *El Universal,* 17 Oct. 1920, 2d sec., p. 1.

98   For a comparable development in Brazil, see Boris Fausto, *Crime e cotidiano: a criminalidade em Sao Paulo, 1880–1924* (São Paulo: Brasiliense, 1984), pp. 127, 134–135. On contemporary "career" criminals, see Neal Shover, *Great Pretenders: Pursuits and Careers of Persistent Thieves* (Boulder: Westview, 1996).

99   *El Imparcial,* 7 Sept. 1897, p. 3.

100 Ibid., 7 May 14, p. 1.

101 Alvaro Matute, "Salud, familia y moral social (1917–1920)" *Históricas* 31 (1991): 34. According to *El Demócrata,* the way in which the Banda del Automóvil Gris operated resembled the famous "Apaches" of Paris. *El Demócrata,* 13 Dec. 1915, p. 1; ibid., 20 Dec. 1915, p. 1.

102 The number of cars in those years increased rapidly. In 1924, 32,537 automobiles were registered in the country; by 1930, the number rose to 63,073. *Estadísticas históricas de México* (México: INEGI, 1984), p. 694. Cars were associated with the new risks of walking in the streets. Between 1933 and 1936, 2,257 persons died in the country as a consequence of traffic accidents. Dirección General de Estadística, *Anuario estadístico 1938* (México: Talleres Gráficos de la Nación, 1939). For the use of a car in a rape, see *El Universal,* 10 July 1931, 2d sec., p. 1. Car-theft rings involved a relatively large and complex organization. *El Universal,* 13 May 1925, 2d sec., p. 1; see also *La Nación,* 30 July 1912, p. 6.

103 *El Universal,* 9 May 1925, p. 3.

104 See Constancio Bernaldo de Quiros, *El bandolerismo en España y en México* (México: Editorial Jurídica Mexicana, 1959), p. 391; Mérigo, *La banda del automóvil gris.*

105 *El Demócrata,* 20 Dec. 1915, pp. 2, 6. Granda was Spanish, but the driver of the car was said to be Japanese. Fausto notes that in São Paulo most theft offenders were foreigners (*Crime e cotidiano,* p. 154). In Mexico City, however, foreigners only made for a very small fraction of the population, and the presence of two of them in the band only gave it a more cosmopolitan air.

106 *El Demócrata,* 20 Dec. 1915, p. 6; ibid., 13 Dec. 1915, p. 1.

107 This information, recorded by Alfonso Taracena and later by Juan Mérigo, circulated by word of mouth, but no newspaper reported it. Taracena, *La verdadera revolución mexicana,* vol. 4, pp. 55, 64; Mérigo, *La banda del automóvil gris,* p. 6. But see *El Demócrata,* 20 Dec. 1915, p. 6. Federico González Garza had issued, back in January 1915, a prohibition of unauthorized military searches in private houses. But the practice remained common during the occupations of the capital by revolutionary armies. *La Convención,* 20 Jan. 1915, p. 4.

108 Bernaldo de Quiros, *El bandolerismo,* p. 292, 395; Taracena, *La verdadera revolución mexicana,* vol. 4, pp. 77, 97, 109–110, 118; vol. 5, pp. 65–82; *El Demócrata,* 13 Dec. 1915, p. 1; ibid., 20 Dec. 1915, p. 1.

109 Mérigo, *La banda del automóvil gris,* pp. 175–176.

110 Martín Luis Guzmán, *Obras completas* (México: FCE, 1984), vol. 2, pp. 568–574; John Womack Jr., *Zapata and the Mexican Revolution* (New York: Vintage, 1970), pp. 322–326.

111 Aurelio de los Reyes, *Medio siglo de cine mexicano: 1896–1847* (México: Trillas, 1988), p. 80.

112 Guzmán, *El aguila y la serpiente,* in *Obras completas,* vol. 1, p. 380. The Constitutionalists were also called *Con sus uñas listas* (with their claws ready) in "En-

tusiasta despedida a los ladrones Carranza, Nerón y sus fariseos," leaflet, n.d., and "La Cucaracha (Canción dedicada al Iscariote barbón)," leaflet, n.d., Mexican Political Parties Propaganda, Benson Latin American Collection, University of Texas at Austin (hereafter MPP). For other examples, see Ramírez Plancarte, *La ciudad de México,* 223–224, 245; "Los dos bandoleros (Parodia de una fábula conocida)," leaflet, n.d., MPP. Against Porfirian corruption see *El Ahuizotito* 1, no. 3 (26 Apr. 1906): 2. The suspicions about high-ranking revolutionary officials were rarely substantiated in court. Mérigo, apparently the only high-ranking revolutionary formally accused in connection with the gang, claims that González had the case's records disappeared. Mérigo, *La banda del automóvil gris,* p. 169. For a defense of González's reputation, see Pablo González, *Centinela fiel del constitucionalismo* (Saltillo: Textos de Cultura Historiográfica, 1971).

113 *El Demócrata,* 23 Sept. 1914, p. 1; several rateros were also apprehended in these days, some of them wearing fine police uniforms. Ibid., 25 Sept. 1914, p. 1.

114 AJ, RS, 1024566, Theft, 1915.

115 Rohlfes, "Police and Penal Correction," chaps. 1 and 2. For the gendarmes' duties regarding public behavior, see "Reglamento de las obligaciones del gendarme" [1897], article 57 in González de Cosío, *Memoria que presenta,* p. 765. A confusing episode in which a suspect of attempting against Porfirio Díaz's life was killed by a mob caused the arrest of several police officers and the suicide of the Police Chief. *Hijo del Ahuizote,* 26 Sept. 1897; ibid., 28 Nov. 1897, p. 758; see also *Nueva Era,* 15 Aug. 1911, pp. 1–2.

116 For the need to reorganize the police, see *El Universal,* 14 Oct. 1920, p. 9. One of Obregon's first actions as President was to fire all members of the Policía Reservada in Archivo General de la Nación, Presidentes Obregón–Calles (hereafter AGN, POC), 104-S-5; a purge of the police in 1921 in AGN, POC, 122-D2-P-4; and in 1922, AGN, POC, 122-D2-P-13; on militarization, see AGN, POC, 122-D2-P-6. For increased resources assigned to the capital's police under Obregón, see AGN, POC, 121-D5-D-1; AGN, POC, 121-D5-P-8; AGN, POC, 122-D2-P-2; AGN, POC, 121-D5-G-22; on the establishment of mounted police, see AGN, POC, 121-D5-G-22; AGN, POC, 121-W-D-2; on the distribution of new guns, see *Excélsior,* 22 Nov. 1921, 2d sec., p. 1. For an exposé of police corruption, see *Excélsior,* 24 Nov. 1921, 2d sec., p. 1; AGN, POC, 307-P-12. For the "secret budget" for the Judicial Police between 1923 and 1928, see AGN, POC, 121-P4-G-1; AGN, POC, 121-P4-P-12; AGN, POC, 121-G-I-3. For the establishment of new detective agencies and private police, see *El Universal,* 8 May 1925, 2d sec., p. 5; and in the early 1930s, Archivo General de la Nación, Dirección General de Gobierno, 2.014(29)22, c.2, exp. 15.

PART III

Contested Meanings of Punishment

The Penalties of Freedom:

Punishment in Postemancipation Jamaica

DIANA PATON

When the British parliament passed an act abolishing slavery in Britain's colonies in 1833, one of the first instructions sent to colonial governors was that they plan for substantial changes to state institutions of penality: policing, the judiciary, and the mechanisms of punishment.[1] It was clear to officials in the Colonial Office that the abolition of slavery, which by definition removed the private right to punish from the hands of planters, would require a reconstruction and elaboration of state responses to acts defined as criminal. Less clear was how these state institutions should be reconstructed. Should West Indian penal regimes be modeled on those of Britain, which were themselves undergoing substantial modification in the 1830s? Or did the specific circumstances of colonial society require that penal policy follow a different path to that in the metropolis?

These questions were the subject of considerable debate among those who wrote and spoke about political matters in Jamaica in the postemancipation period, as well as among those in Britain who took an active interest in colonial policy. In the early postemancipation period, those arguing for a Jamaican policy mirroring that of Britain won out, and a program of prison construction and reform was adopted, with stated goals of the "rehabilitation" of prisoners and the "reformation" of their characters. By the mid-1850s, however, this program was widely understood to have failed. This sense of failure is not especially surprising: in the history of punishment there is nothing more common than the perception that a previous generation's reforms have achieved nothing. Indeed, a similar onset of pessimism took place in Britain in this period as well. However, whereas there the utopian effort to "reform" was replaced with closer surveillance and differentiation of the "criminal class" from the "respectable" working class, in Jamaica the population as a whole came to be constructed as criminal. Imprisonment continued to be the mainstay of the penal system, but flogging was reintroduced, and private individuals were enabled to control and profit from the labor of prisoners.

Throughout this period, gender distinction was a fundamental, if sometimes unspoken, criterion for determining penal policy. In the period of rehabilitation, part of the goal of imprisonment was to accustom prisoners to acting in appropriately gendered ways. Later, the laws reintroducing corporal punishment specified that only men could be whipped, although this fact was rarely commented on at the time. No single narrative can thus describe change over time during this period, for men's and women's encounters with the judicial and penal systems differed considerably.

The debates around punishment served as a location where members of the colonial elite elaborated different positions about the nature of the Jamaican population. In some ways, the debates were more significant for what they tell us about constructions of "race" in this period than they are for what they tell us about penal policy. Much of what was expressed on both sides was never fully implemented. All of the people involved in the debate around punishment saw black Jamaicans as different from and inferior to white people, but the reasons for and appropriate response to this supposed inferiority changed over time. The program of rehabilitative imprisonment assumed that all people responded in the same way to the same environment, and posited an idealized disciplined, responsible, and respectable worker as the goal to be achieved. This ideal stood in opposition to the stereotype of the feckless, irresponsible, and demoralized slave. The argument for whipping and private use of prison labor relied on a more dehumanizing form of racism, in which black people were presented as permanently unable to reach the idealized standard. It was the latter construction of racial difference that came to dominate debates around penality by the 1850s.

After Slavery: Restructuring and Rehabilitation

The full abolition of slavery in 1838 led to considerable change in the function of prisons, as was the case wherever a dominant slave system was dismantled. During slavery, prisons served mainly to supplement the autonomous disciplinary system of the plantations. In 1834 more than three-quarters of the slaves serving sentences in the island's twenty-plus jails and houses of correction were undergoing punishment for running away.[2] Prisons also held slaves committed without trial on the authority of their masters, runaway slaves who had been apprehended and committed to prison while the authorities waited for their masters to claim them, and, occasionally, slaves incarcerated in order to protect them from their owners.[3] With the end of slavery, prisons ceased to be used to punish breaches of slave discipline. Masters lost the power to commit their slaves to prison without trial in 1834, at the start of the transitional period known as "apprenticeship." The governor, Lionel Smith, ordered that 176 slaves serving prison sentences for a variety of offences be released on August 1, 1838, the first day of full freedom.[4] By 1840, while the prison population had expanded dramatically, all prisoners (with the exception of debtors) were held under the criminal law, which now made no overt distinctions between people by race or former slave/free status.[5]

Prior to 1838, the local government in each Jamaican parish had control over the prisons in that parish, and no islandwide coordination went into their management. In that year, however, the British parliament passed the West India Prisons Act, giving the governors of Britain's Caribbean colonies direct power to make regulations governing prisons and to appoint prison inspectors and officers.[6] Jamaican planters, who dominated the parochial vestries and magistracy, at first objected to this change, but eventually reconciled themselves to the act when the British government made clear that it would not seriously intervene in the elected assembly's legislative and fiscal decisions.[7] In the period of relative political calm that followed, successive governors and assemblies followed a program of prison reform largely modeled on dominant practice in Britain and the United States. As in those countries, the stated goal of imprisonment was to reform inmates through labor and religious reflection.[8] This process took place under the management of John Daughtrey, who was the Jamaican General Inspector of Prisons from 1841 to 1861. A passionate believer in the advantages of free labor, Daughtrey saw his role as building a modern penal system to replace what he saw as the corrupt, brutal, and—perhaps most significantly—ineffective institutions that had existed during slavery. Like many of his counterparts in Europe and Latin America, Daughtrey visited North American prisons and was very impressed by the new penitentiaries, especially the one in Philadelphia, which kept prisoners in almost total isolation under what was known as the "separate system."[9] He attempted to apply the lessons he took from the United States to the penal institutions under his jurisdiction. He had plans for the new Jamaican penitentiary building, construction of which began in 1845, drawn up in the United States on the "radiating principle, so advantageous for inspection and supervision," invoking the panoptic model that dominated penal thought at the time.[10]

The most dramatic changes made by Daughtrey were to the organization of the islandwide system of prisons. In the early 1840s many prisoners were transferred between the various existing institutions, in order to achieve a fundamental principle of penal reform: the classification of prisoners so that those deemed similar to one another were kept in the same institution. The Kingston house of correction was rebuilt as the (male-only) General Penitentiary, and male prisoners convicted of felonies throughout the island were transferred there. A separate female penitentiary was established, several houses of correction were closed, and twelve others became single-sex "district prisons," reserved for convicts serving sentences of two months or longer. With "serious" criminals thus removed and concentrated in a smaller number of prisons, the remaining jails and houses of correction now confined only debtors, untried prisoners, and those serving short sentences.[11] Whereas thirty-one prisons had held inmates in 1838, only eighteen existed in 1843.[12]

Within the prisons, the most fundamental principle of good management was gender segregation. Critics of the slavery-era prisons condemned them repeatedly for their failure to separate male and female prisoners from one another.[13] In the new prisons, if it was physically possible to separate prisoners into no more than two groups within a prison, that division was to be according to gender. New regulations specified that male prison wardens should not come into contact with female prisoners.[14] By separating prisoners (and staff) along gendered lines, the potential for heterosexual expression within the space of the prison was removed, thus emphasizing the institution's separation from the world outside.[15] This was especially important given that most Jamaican prison sentences were relatively brief.

In the new gender-segregated prisons, prisoners were required to enact their gender in particular ways. Religious teaching emphasized the particular attributes of manliness and femininity thought to be appropriate for a newly free population. Work assignments were allocated according to gender: women washed clothes, cooked, and cleaned the prison buildings, while men repaired roads, broke stones, or did agricultural work. Despite the fact that women routinely performed agricultural labor in the developing peasant economy of postemancipation Jamaica, prison inspectors considered such work to be "inappropriate." Samuel Pryce, the prison inspector for St Thomas in the East, recommended in his 1841 report that the prisoners in Manchioneal women's prison be employed washing clothes for hire. "At present I am not prepared to suggest to his Excellency, any other mode of labour adapted to females," he noted, rejecting other possible types of work. "Our creole women have never been accustomed to [such labour] and do not understand it, for which reason I consider it quite impossible, being more properly the work adapted to the male sex."[16] By 1841 it was illegal for women prisoners to work outside the prison, while men continued to do so in many of the district prisons.[17] Women thus experienced a more thoroughgoing version of the rehabilitative prison's principle of seclusion from the world outside than did men.

Having concentrated the serious criminals in a relatively small number of prisons, Daughtrey focused his attention on the institutions' internal regimes. By the mid-1840s he was satisfied with the improvements he had made. In his 1844 and 1845 reports on the penitentiary he described these advances. Prisoners were now separated into groups so that those convicted of serious offences did not come into contact with inmates awaiting trial or serving short sentences. Rather than being chained to prevent escape, prisoners were restrained by a wall twenty feet high, with guardtowers at each corner. They worked silently in open-air workshops within the prison walls, which had themselves been rebuilt using convict labor. Daughtrey's 1844 report on the penitentiary emphasized the value of both the work and the silence, claiming the latter as one of his "greatest achievements." "No voices are heard now but those of the officers of the establishment," he boasted. "No sounds but of the hammer, the axe or the saw."[18] Instead of receiving money to buy food, prisoners received a strictly measured daily ration. Infractions of prison discipline were no longer punished by flogging; instead, prisoners were subjected to solitary confinement.[19] An Anglican clergyman preached a sermon each Sunday and provided other means of religious instruction. Inmates no longer worked as guards. Daughtrey believed that these modifications had created an environment in which prisoners could successfully be reformed. "The prison has been certainly made to many a school of order and obedience," he claimed in 1844. "Those who had before been subject to no restraining, many have here been compelled to submission. They have been mastered and subdued." According to Daughtrey's statistics, the Jamaican recidivism rate now stood below that of England and the United States, proof of the penitentiary's success.[20]

Daughtrey's penal policy was based on his assumption that in Jamaica he dealt with a population racially distinct from, and inferior to, that of Britain and the United States. Reports from his time as a stipendiary magistrate, before his appointment as General Inspector of Prisons, indicate his belief that black people lacked self-control, ambition, and responsibility and were generally childish. He described the language of apprentice protest as "violent jabber" that "excited" other apprentices, and pointed out that Africans were "a race proverbially talkative."[21] In sum, he subscribed to the stereotype of "Quashee" or "Sambo" that historians have recognized as a common view of enslaved people in many slave societies.[22] In Daughtrey's interpretation, this childlike passivity was primarily induced by slavery, rather than biology, and thus would be replaced by responsibility given enough experience of freedom. Thus, in contrast to later colonial penal theorists who would argue that the racial inferiority of the population meant that metropolitan penal theories could not be applied in colonial situations, Daughtrey advocated the thoroughgoing adoption of European and North American penal ideologies, rather than their rejection. Imprisonment in a reforming prison was supposed to "raise" the prisoner up to the standards of European civilization. Daughtrey considered the Jamaican population to be "mere adult children."[23] Nevertheless, his approach to penality could not, as later penal policies would, deny the possibility that Afro-Jamaicans could be full human beings. Although the systems of penal discipline advocated by European and North American penal reformers were never fully implemented in Jamaica, Daughtrey understood this to be the result of a regrettable lack of resources. He never argued that black inmates responded to penal treatment differently than did whites.

Daughtrey's vision of the rehabilitated freedman who was "mastered and subdued" and whose "moral feelings" were reawakened was part of a much broader imaginative reconstruction of postslavery society. His view of the future was allied to that of missionaries and Colonial Office officials who believed that, if the correct environment could be provided, former slaves would learn to behave appropriately to their "station" as workers, as men and women, and as Christians. Such a vision was exemplified in a speech to former slaves made by the "coloured" magistrate, Richard Chamberlaine. "Freedom brings with it no exemption from labour; it rather increases your cares and anxieties," Chamberlaine warned his audience. "Remember that you are henceforth to buy your own clothes, your own salt food, your own medicines, your own nourishment. . . . Your wives and daughters will require their fine clothes for their chapels, churches, and holidays. . . . In order to obtain these, the comforts and necessaries of civilized life, you will have to labour industriously." Chamberlaine aimed to stimulate the pride of free men, rather than retrain those who had committed crimes. Nevertheless, his imagined future Jamaica was projected against an anxiety that freed people would not, in fact, participate fully in wage labor. "And if you can support your selves for a week by two days' labour," he asked, somewhat defensively, "must you not continue to work the other four days to supply the increased wants of your improved condition to make provision for the rainy day?"[24] Chamberlaine's exhortation emphasized his audience's ability to choose their own future; but skirted the question of what would happen should freed people not agree that they "must" continue to work as wage laborers to supply their "increased wants." The penitentiary provided a partial answer. It would teach labor, appropriately gendered behaviour, and Christianity to those freed people who rejected advice such as Chamberlaine's.

Thus, in the mid-1840s the Jamaican penal regime shared the goals of modern penal systems as they have been described in the standard "revisionist" histories of punishment.[25] Jamaican prisons aimed to discipline their inmates through routine and tried to reconstruct their subjects. Daughtrey claimed that "[t]he severity of a well regulated prison consists in a steady pressure of the discipline on mind and body," which anticipates Foucault's analysis of the "capillary" and "productive" nature of modern power. To be sure, much remained of the unreformed prison system, especially in the minor prisons, but this was hardly a peculiarity of Jamaica.[26] If anything, the changes in Jamaican penality were more dramatic than those in the metropolis. Prison administration was centralized in Jamaica to a degree that would not be reached in Britain until the 1877 Prisons Act centralized control of all prisons under the Prison Commission. In 1845 Jamaican law actually permitted less corporal punishment than did British. Flogging had been abolished as a punishment for crime in 1840.[27] In the same year it was abandoned as a punishment for infractions against prison discipline, except in rare cases.[28] The treadmill, which had been introduced as a rationalizing move but had come to be seen as an instrument of corporal punishment inflicting pain, was removed from all Jamaican prisons in 1840 but continued to be used in British prisons throughout the nineteenth century.[29] By several of the penal reformers' measures, and in their own gendered metaphor, the colonial "daughter" had outgrown her "mother" country.[30]

The Return of the Repressive

However, the development toward a "disciplinary society" was not long-lasting. Rehabilitative imprisonment did not progress along the lines that its advocates had hoped for. Daughtrey's confidence notwithstanding, problems were evident almost from the beginning. The construction of the new penitentiary building was slow: the foundation stone was not laid until 1845, and in 1856 the building remained incomplete.[31] The principle of classification of prisoners began breaking down almost immediately after it was established. In 1844 an act was passed setting aside a section of the penitentiary for a house of correction to receive those awaiting trial and convicted of minor crimes in the city of Kingston, thus bringing the categories of prisoner disaggregated from one another in 1840 — serious criminal, minor offenders, and the untried — back into the same institution.[32] The female penitentiary, created to receive serious female offenders in 1842, was combined with the male (the "General Penitentiary") in 1853.[33] Extensive discussions of the relative merits of the "separate" and "silent" systems of prison discipline ended with the full adoption of neither. In the district prisons throughout the island, male prisoners still worked in full public view.[34]

As confidence in rehabilitation waned, a growing campaign developed in favor of those methods of punishment that had recently been abandoned. Several historians have noted that whipping as a punishment for crime and as a method of controlling prisoners reentered the judicial and penal systems in the 1850s and 1860s. They have usually focused on the act passed in early 1865 known as the "Whipping Bill," which made second and subsequent convictions for larceny — the most commonly prosecuted crime — punishable by up to fifty lashes for those over sixteen, and twenty-five lashes for juveniles.[35] The focus on larceny implies a relatively straightforward class interpretation: property owners used the law to protect themselves against the propertyless. Such an interpretation seems justified by statements like that of the Colonial Office official who argued in 1864 that "when thieving reaches a point at which it interferes with production, it certainly seems to me time to whip, and to whip well."[36] It is also supported by the fact that rising levels of theft of food crops were associated with the widespread drought of 1863–1865, which was exacerbated by the scarcity of wage work available to peasants whose crops had failed. The 1865 Whipping Bill was presented by its advocates as a response to this rise in theft.[37]

While rising theft was clearly significant, it cannot account for the shift toward whipping. For one thing, even if this was the reason for the implementation of a punishment felt to be harsh, it still remains to be explained why the punishment chosen at that time should have been whipping. In fact, by 1865 there was a substantial postemancipation set of precedents for the use of flogging as a judicial punishment, and flogging thus seemed a "natural" choice. Although larceny came to be seen as the defining aspect of the "crime problem" in the 1860s, the reintroduction of flogging into the penal system began in 1850, in a period when the argument in favour of flogging was made on an eclectic variety of grounds, and did not focus primarily on property crime. Pro-flogging arguments were made by a wide variety of people within the political elite: when the 1850 bill was brought before the assembly, it passed with almost no opposition.[38] Charles Grey, the governor, reported to the Colonial Office that although he did not support the change, "the feeling that something of the kind was required was too strong for me to oppose the bill."[39] That 1850 act enumerated a long list of crimes for which up to 117 lashes could be inflicted, 39 lashes at a time: rape, assault with intent to commit rape, sodomy; assault with intent to commit sodomy, bestiality, attempt to commit bestiality, carnally knowing children "of tender years" or attempt to commit, and arson.[40] Thus, with the exception of arson, the named crimes involved sexuality. Property crime could lead to corporal punishment because of a provision that flogging could be used to punish an individual convicted of a felony if he had previously been convicted of a felony, but lack of systematic recordkeeping meant that in practice this provision was difficult to apply. Thus, of the twenty-nine cases I have found in which the lash was used in the thirty months of flogging's relegalization, seventeen were for crimes involving sexuality (bestiality, rape, attempted rape, and "unnatural" assaults), while eight were for thefts (of the remaining four cases, three were for arson, one for assault with intent to murder).[41]

In the period between 1850 and 1865, a series of laws was passed providing for flogging, most of which augmented the categories of crime that could be punished corporally. By 1860 the crimes of burglary, obeah, and maliciously cutting, maiming, or destroying cattle or sheep had been added to the previously named offences as punishable by a flogging, in addition to a prison sentence, when committed by men.[42] Debate over penality in the 1850s tended to focus on which types of crimes should be punished by flogging, with most contributions advocating the addition of crimes to the list. Discussion of how prisons should be organized was mostly displaced by arguments assuming the failure of the reforming prison and advocating flogging in its stead.

Flogging was proposed as an appropriate response to almost any kind of crime in this period. A major focus, however, was with crimes of sexuality (often coded as crimes of "the passions"). Especially in the early part of the 1850s, these crimes, which I categorize as a single group because that was how they were discussed at the time, received more attention than did property crime, even though petty theft was, as in almost all criminal justice systems, the most widely prosecuted crime. Justice McDougall, one of Jamaica's most senior judges, praised the 1850 act for its likely effect in preventing "crimes of this disgusting and dangerous character."[43] The *Falmouth Post* argued that since the abolition of slavery the population had shown "a greater indulgence in the corrupt passions" than previously; the "depraved" individuals who committed such crimes would be moved only by "the most degrading punishment to which a human being can be subjected."[44] In 1852 a judge singled out rape, sodomy, and assault, as well as larceny, as "besetting crimes of the people," a characterization that led the *Falmouth Post* to call once more for the flogging of "the depraved beings, who are the slaves of unruly passions."[45] In October 1854 the judge sentencing James Miles to flogging and imprisonment for bestiality declared that he did so as a response to a crime that was "disgracing this country from East to West."[46] A major impetus for the revival of flogging seems to have been the desire to use corporal punishment as a response to crimes that intimately involved the body of the criminal. The convicts' illicit — and sometimes coercive — corporeal pleasure was to be met with the infliction of bodily pain.

As some of these quotations already indicate, arguments in favor of flogging often invoked a harshly racist language about the nature of the people who would be subjected to the punishment. One of the earliest calls for the reintroduction of flogging, made in 1842, described a black convict as "possess[ing] no other feelings than the physical sensations of the beast"; individuals of this "kith and kind," the article continued, "ought to be dealt with as brutes are, and flogged into tameness and submission."[47] Ten years later the *Falmouth Post*'s call for flogging of those who were "slaves of unruly passions" argued that it was necessary because the prevalence of sexual and violent crimes demonstrated that "Afric's sons and daughters, are in a fair way of relapsing into their 'original state of barbarism.'"[48] These two arguments invoked subtly different racist discourses, the one comparing black people to animals, the other arguing that, on a linear measure of degrees of "civilization" in which Europeans or Britons stood at the top, Jamaican blacks were moving backward. Both used supposed racial difference to argue for a divergence in Jamaica's penal policy from the British and North American "norm" that Daughtrey advocated. This dehumanizing racism fit easily with the idea that Jamaicans were especially prone to crimes against the sexual order. The ability to control one's sexual urges was assumed to be a mark of a high level of civilization. Thus, Jamaicans' apparent failure to control their "passions" demonstrated that their bodies were not properly subject to control by their minds, and therefore that punishment should be addressed to the body rather than the mind. Rather than aim to raise criminals "up" to European standards, these arguments implied the permanent, unchangeable inferiority of black people.

Commentary on flogging often invested it with an almost magical power to change the pattern of crime. Unlike the advocates of rehabilitative imprisonment, people who argued for flogging did not feel the need to provide logical arguments for how flogging was supposed to work. A letter to the editor published in the *Falmouth Post* in 1850 argued that if the courts were able to flog offenders they "will soon find the numbers of criminals decreased."[49] Similarly, in 1865 H. B. Shaw, the General Inspector of Prisons, who replaced John Daughtrey, advocated flogging for larceny, arguing that "once it is known such a bill has become law, and a few examples have been made in the different districts of the island, there will be little heard of thefts of provisions in the rural districts."[50] Flogging was assumed to be a more effective deterrent than was imprisonment, but the reasons for this were rarely articulated. Shaw and those who shared his point of view believed the lash to have symbolic power that outweighed its actual use.

Almost entirely undiscussed in the process of introduction of these new laws was the fact that they applied only to men. Although the initial 1850 law did not make a distinction between men and women, this seems to have been an oversight. When that law was renewed the following year, it specified that "male" offenders could be flogged.[51] Almost no debate took place about this exclusion of women. I have found only one reference to it, an aside in an editorial in the *Falmouth Post*. Arguing for the extension of corporal punishment to the crimes of obeah, myalism, assault on children "of tender age," and arson, the editorialist argues that "corporal chastisement, from which, of course, females should be exempt," is essential to the "suppression" of these "evils."[52] Despite alarmist arguments about the necessity for corporal punishment, no anxiety was expressed that this new form of punishment could not be applied to women. Even the editorial, quoted above, arguing for flogging as a response to the reversion to barbarism of "Afric's sons and daughters," did not appear to notice that the "daughters" were in fact excluded from this new punishment. A dramatic shift in elite attitudes had clearly taken place since the 1830s, when the claim was frequently made that women were more disorderly than men.[53] It seems that, by the 1850s, the archetypal criminal was so firmly male that no alternative harsh punishment for women was thought to be necessary to parallel the flogging of men. The reasons for this shift require further investigation. However, the exclusive concern with men reinforces the point that the reintroduction of flogging was connected more with anxiety about sexuality than with anxiety about property crime. The crimes of bestiality, sodomy, and rape, for which flogging was most commonly used, were crimes that, by custom or legal definition, were strongly associated with men.

Eventually, attention with regard to flogging did shift toward property crime, especially "praedial larceny" (the theft of still-growing crops), which came to be seen as the problem in Jamaican criminal justice. In 1866, in the wake of the Morant Bay rebellion, the Jamaican Assembly abolished itself, and Jamaica became a crown colony, ruled by a governor appointed in London.[54] Although Jamaican government policy was in some ways more concerned with popular welfare, this change did not disrupt the trend toward corporal punishment. In 1872, district courts gained the right to pass sentences of flogging, which had previously been reserved to higher courts. In 1877 the punishment of flogging was extended once more: it could now be added to sentences for first offences of praedial larceny, of whatever value.[55] Flogging was maintained as a punishment for crime well into the twentieth century.[56]

The reintroduction of flogging should not be understood as a return to the days before penal reform. Rather, corporal punishment was integrated into a modernized penal system. Imprisonment continued to be the main punishment received by men, and the only one received by women. Floggings were to take place in addition to, rather than instead of, imprisonment. Convicts sentenced to flogging usually received relatively long sentences as well as the corporal punishment. Imprisonment was no longer accompanied by such high hopes of reconstructing the personality of the inmate, but the basic pattern of life within the prison was not much changed from the 1840s. Meanwhile, the same attention to uniformity, centralized control and precise ordering was applied to corporal punishment that had earlier been used in reforming the prisons. The floggings of the 1850s and 1860s differed from those of the slavery period in several ways. Most obviously, they were inflicted on the authority of the state, rather than the master. But they also differed from the floggings handed down as punishments by slave courts. Their execution was intended to be orderly and controlled. Judges were instructed to specify precisely the number of lashes to be inflicted and the amount of time that was to pass between their infliction, and had to restrict themselves to limits set by law. A series of specified people, including medical doctors and constables, had to be present to observe the punishment. Floggings were not to be carried out by fellow convicts, as they often had been before 1839. In 1865 the penitentiary acquired a "model cat [of nine tails]" to be used for all whippings that took place within its walls. H. B. Shaw reported that this whip weighed 9 ounces, with the handle weighing 6.75 ounces and the tails 2.25 ounces. Its nine cord tails, on each of which were three knots, were 33 inches long, while the handle measured 19.75 inches.[57]

The specificity of such rules and descriptions implies a concern to overcome what Jeremy Bentham had identified as the major problem with flogging as a means of discipline: its lack of uniformity. Lashes, Bentham pointed out, inflicted a highly variable degree of pain, depending on the disposition and strength of the person inflicting them.[58] And yet flogging was still, as it had always been, the infliction of physical violence and pain by one human being on another. Jamaican legislators and policy-makers now disregarded the other aspects of the penal reformers' critique of flogging: that it was inherently indecent; that it degraded the individual who suffered it (and also those who inflicted it and observed it); and that for these and other reasons it failed to reform criminals. This disregard is not surprising, since by this time those in power had given up on the effort to reform criminals. Deterrence, rather than reform, had become the goal of punishment, and it was argued that the racial nature of the Jamaican population meant that the prospect of imprisonment could not deter them from crime, but that of flogging would.

The Privatization of Punishment

Around the same time that flogging was reintroduced, several experiments took place that allocated direct authority over significant numbers of convicts, along with the product of their labor, to private individuals. Like flogging, these experiments marked a shift away from the goal of transforming prisoners. In 1854 a "Penal Servitude Act" was passed, allowing the governor to grant a license for the release of convicts who had served more than half of their sentences. Those so licensed were bound to serve as agricultural laborers for three-quarters of their remaining sentences, during which time they would work for six days a week and receive nine pence per day, plus lodging, medical attendance, and a suit of clothes. They had no choice over where they were sent, or to whom they were bound. The license could be revoked at any time, including on the demand of the employer.[59]

Where work in the penitentiary was supposedly designed to accustom prisoners to regular work as a moral lesson, the penal servitude system more directly used prisoners' labor for its productive capacity. The system in many ways anticipated the convict lease system that existed in the American South from the Civil War until around World War I. As with Jamaican convict leasing, employers gained direct control over the labor of prisoners. States contracted to supply convicts to employers, who paid a fee per convict per year to the state, and were supposed to provide convicts with food, clothing, housing, and medical attention—although supplies provided were rudimentary at best. U.S. convict lessors did not pay wages to their convicts. Despite structural similarities, the American system was far more extensive than the Jamaican, because the South underwent an economic resurgence in the late nineteenth century, creating a wide range of industries in search of cheap and flexible labor. Convicts played a significant role in the rebuilding and industrialization of the South after the devastation of the Civil War. They were employed in different industries depending on the state, with the most significant being railroad construction, mining, and cotton and sugar plantation work.[60]

In the first year of its operation 159 convicts were released under the Jamaican penal servitude act to fourteen different employers, who took between two and twenty men at a time.[61] Between them these employers, who were drawn overwhelmingly from the island's political elite, acquired more than 27,000 days of cheaper-than-usual labor.[62] Probably more important to them than the cost of this labor was its reliability. Jamaican planters had complained since the end of slavery about the unreliability of the labor supply. Particularly galling was the workers' refusal to subordinate the labor needs of their own land to those of the estates and plantations, and their consequent practice of undertaking wage labor for intermittent periods. John Daughtrey reported that planters found convict workers to be "the most useful people on the estate and an example of industry and civility to all the rest." He attributed this to the beneficial influence of their experience in the penitentiary, but it is more realistic to understand the planters' comments (assuming that Daughtrey accurately reflected planter opinion) as a reflection of the relative compliance of forced compared to free workers.[63] The ticket-of-leave system thus functioned similarly to the state-subsidized immigration of indentured workers from India and Africa that was prevalent in the same period.[64]

Young offenders were especially likely to be turned over to the authority of private individuals. Reformatories for boys and girls were established in 1858 and 1857 respectively. In 1864 the St George's Home and Reformatory for Boys accommodated an average of 169 inmates, roughly half of whom had been convicted of crimes, the other half being described as orphans or destitute. The reformatory was a privately managed institution, although most of its income came from the government, through fees paid to support each inmate sentenced to its custody. Despite its name, the reformatory was primarily concerned with using the boys' labor for immediate profit than with reforming them so that they would be effective wage laborers on release. In 1864 Governor Eyre reported that of several experiments in cotton cultivation, the only one he expected to succeed would utilize the labor of the boys at the reformatory.[65] The next year the assembly passed an act allowing magistrates to apprentice for up to five years children under sixteen who were convicted of stealing, or destroying and damaging with intent to steal, property worth less than ten shillings, so long as they were proven "to be leading an idle and vagrant life, not attending any school or being sufficiently under the control of their parents."[66] This law was eventually disallowed by the Colonial Office, but not until it had been in force for over a year.[67] The management committee of the Boys' Reformatory noted in its 1865 report that forty-eight boys had been apprenticed under its terms. Two of the people to whom they were apprenticed took twenty and eighteen boys respectively, indicating that "apprenticeship" in the sense of learning a trade was as much a misnomer here as it had been during the 1834–1838 "apprenticeship" period.[68]

The Kingston and St Andrews Girls' Reformatory had been established one year before the boys' institution, with many of the same stated goals. Its practice with regard to the new apprenticeship law illustrates another aspect of the growing divergence between penal treatment of males and females. In contrast to its brother reformatory, the Girls' Reformatory does not seem to have apprenticed any of its inmates under the 1865 act, probably because employers wanted male rather than female labor. The Girls' Reformatory accommodated seventeen girls in its first year of operation and had expanded to eighty-seven inmates by 1863.[69] Rather than use its inmates for agricultural work, it aimed to train the girls in the work skills required for domestic service. However, the Ladies' Reformatory Association found it difficult to find enough outlets for the labor they had available. Their 1860 report noted that "the want of suitable employment for the female youth of Kingston has been long keenly felt and bitterly deplored," and argued that this was a major cause of the "vice and crime in our midst."[70] The gendered structure of the labor market both made it harder for young women to find suitable employment and made it harder for those involved in attempting to reform them to profit by their labor.

Punishment and "Race"

Thus by 1865 the reformatory ideal had been largely replaced. Efforts at reforming criminals persisted with regard to particular groups of the population, most notably young women, but at the symbolic level the ideal punishment was a flogging inflicted on a male criminal. The island's prisons continued to contain large, and growing, numbers of prisoners, but nobody whose comments were recorded expected them to emerge reformed. Earlier penal ideals that aimed indirectly to benefit employers by teaching criminals the positive value of work were superseded by mechanisms that directly supplied the planters with labor, while serious offenders received punishment through bodily pain.

The reasons for the alleged failure of rehabilitative imprisonment were much debated, with two major arguments put forward. First, the prisons were said to provide living conditions that were too comfortable to pose real hardship. An editorial in the *Falmouth Post* asked rhetorically, "What does the experienced thief care about being sent to hard labour in the house of Correction for two or three weeks? He knows that during the time he remains there, he will be well housed, well clothed, and well fed, and with this knowledge he takes the chance of detection."[71] A year later the same paper repeated this argument, claiming that the "worthless, abandoned wretches" within the prisons "boast . . . they are better fed, better housed, and better clothed, than on the estates where employment is offered to them for the cultivation and manufacture of the products of the soil."[72] Another newspaper, the *Colonial Standard,* connected the supposedly comfortable living conditions in the penitentiary directly to the "nature" of the Jamaican population:

> A mere term of imprisonment in the General Penitentiary, excellent as is the system there carried out, and terrible as it would be to the educated, or man of refined mind, is, in sober truth, rather a temptation to commit crime than a punishment to the debased and brutal minded wretches with which alas! our community is thronged, and who compose the mass of the felons of our isle! — Within the walls of the General Penitentiary they are better cared for than they are, or can hope to be, when at liberty.[73]

Jamaicans in general — the community is "thronged" with them — are thus "debased and brutal minded," in contrast to the "man of refined mind" who appears to live elsewhere. This argument referred ultimately to the problem known as that of "less eligibility": a penal institution must provide its inmates with a standard of living worse than they would get in the world outside, or else it would act as an incentive to crime.[74] The lower the standard of living outside, the more difficult it was to create an institution that fell below them without injuring the health of its inmates. Those who made this argument effectively admitted that Jamaicans were too poor for rehabilitative imprisonment. At first sight this may seem somewhat ironic, given that a commonly made racist argument of the time was that Jamaicans were "idle" because the bountiful and fertile land in which they lived meant that they did not need to work.[75] In fact, the two arguments could reinforce the racist conclusions drawn from each: Jamaicans had a low standard of living because they were idle, rather than because of the social relations in which they found themselves living. Therefore, the fact that it was difficult to produce a penal institution that provided an inferior standard of living led to the condemnation of the people's supposed lack of a work and consumer ethic, rather than to a critique of these social relations.

The second argument relied even more explicitly on ideas about race. Commentators on penality repeatedly claimed that the desire to separate oneself from convicted criminals was a mark of civilization. Jamaicans, they argued, were not civilized enough to realize that they should stigmatize criminals. This point was held in common by advocates of rehabilitation and of flogging. John Daughtrey integrated this view into his argument for rehabilitative imprisonment, claiming that Jamaica's low recidivism rate could be accounted for by the lack of stigma encountered by ex-prisoners. Because they were easily able to find employment and reintegrate themselves into their communities, they were less likely to reoffend, he argued, contradictorily labeling this an indication of a low level of civilization: "The readiness with which a [released convict], not notoriously and habitually vicious, obtains his usual employment and admission again to something like his former status among his fellows, is probably one cause of the smaller number of reconvictions in this country," he argued.[76] Daughtrey was unusual in putting forward such a positive view. Thus, an editorial in the *Falmouth Post* claimed that Jamaican criminals "care nothing about the temporary deprivation of liberty" because "when discharged from a district prison or the penitentiary, they are regarded as 'martyr,' and received with open arms by their former associates, who are not yet so civilized as to shun companionship with such depraved characters."[77] Similarly, according to a letter to the editor of the same newspaper, "When the ignorant, half-civilized negro is convicted of a too free indulgence in one of his besetting sins, then his sympathizers exclaim—'ah, my brudder, I wish you well through your trial.'"[78] The "half-civilization" of the "negro" is demonstrated here not only by "his indulgence" in crime (note the implication in the term "indulgence" that the problem is a lack of self-control), but also by his peers' refusal to condemn him. Because of such refusal, it was claimed, imprisonment did not serve as the "terror to evil-doers" that it should. It functioned only as a passing phase in the life of an inmate, rather than a long-standing marker of difference. This argument was then used to condemn the entire Jamaican population, rather than merely those who committed crime.

Ever since emancipation, commentators on the Jamaican penal system had noted the failure of the population as a whole to stigmatize those who committed crimes or were subject to punishment. For instance, in 1840, stipendiary magistrate W. A. Bell decried the lack of "moral courage" among the peasantry in his area, evidenced by their refusal to report suspicions about who had perpetrated crimes to the authorities.[79] Similarly, another magistrate commented that Jamaican communities would welcome back a member who had been imprisoned, "more as a martyr than a criminal."[80] The claim that criminals were perceived as "martyrs" was made frequently, as in the *Falmouth Post* editorial cited in the previous paragraph. Perhaps the epitome of this view was expressed by H. B. Shaw in 1865:

> A thief or any other criminal does not lose caste from having been in the penitentiary. On his discharge, he is as well received by his relatives, comrades and friends, as if he had merely returned from a long journey. He does not feel the bitter disgrace that criminals in other countries do on being let out of prison; consequently, the terror or irksome feeling that his confinement in the penitentiary may have caused soon wears off, and he is ready, on the least temptation, to commit crime again.[81]

Shaw concluded from this that penitentiary punishment could not work in Jamaica. The obvious replacement was whipping.

The argument over the merits of rehabilitative imprisonment and of flogging and privatized convict labor expressed different understandings of both the purpose of punishment and the meaning of "race." Rehabilitative imprisonment was primarily aimed at reconstructing the individuals who passed through the prison, and thus was concerned primarily with perfecting the institution's internal regime. In the new logic, the reform of prisoners was at once utopian and unnecessary. What was important was that the population as a whole was deterred from committing crime through fear. Up until this point of the argument, Jamaican commentators made many points that echoed those in British discussions of penal policy. Commentators in Britain grew cynical in the 1850s and 1860s of the potential effectiveness of rehabilitation. Discussions of penality in the two islands parted company over the question of how deterrence would work. Throughout their discussions of Jamaicans' failure to stigmatize criminals, commentators worked with a conceptual opposition between the Jamaican population on the one hand and an imagined "civilized" (implicitly, British) group with a much deeper respect for the law on the other, as is demonstrated by the characterization of Jamaicans as "half-civilized" or "uncivilized" cited earlier. The opposition revolved around the idea of shame. In civilized societies, according to this argument, the mere fact of having been in prison was shameful, and the fear of being shamed by being marked out as a former prisoner (that is, a criminal), rather than the fear of what will happen in prison per se, was what deterred most people from committing crime. Thus, as Shaw had put it, Jamaicans did not feel the "disgrace" felt by criminals in "other countries." In Jamaica (and, by extension, other uncivilized and/or colonial places) going to prison was not shameful, because the population in general did not understand having been sent to prison as a sign of wrongdoing, but rather as signifying resistance (or "martyrdom"). To quote again from the *Falmouth Post:* "In a country like this, where the lower classes are not yet sufficiently intellectual or moral to repudiate an association with parties who have legally expiated their crimes within the walls of a Penitentiary or District Prison, the knowledge that imprisonment for five or six months has no terrors which need be dreaded, has a most pernicious effect."[82] In such a society, however harsh the experience of imprisonment, it did not deter people from committing crime, inasmuch as fear of the penitentiary itself was not sufficient to deter. The "terrors which need to be dreaded" could only be established through fear for the body.

That the rehabilitative penitentiary project "failed" in Jamaica should not surprise us; rejection of their premisses is probably the most frequent fate of penal programs. Indeed, Jamaican opinion was congruent with a general trend in European and North American thought about crime and penality in this period. By the early 1860s reformatory prisons were under severe attack in Britain, and a series of acts between 1862 and 1864 legislated for physically harsh prison regimes including extensive treadmill labor and restricted diets. The effort to break down and rebuild the character of the criminal was replaced by a stress on making the experience of imprisonment one of physical hardship.[83] In 1863, following a moral panic around violent robbery, termed "garroting," a so-called Garrotter's Act introduced whipping as a punishment for this crime. However, this did not establish a trend toward the reintroduction of corporal punishment in Britain, although it did feed into the discourse that facilitated the tightening of prison regimes.[84]

What is interesting about the "failure" of rehabilitative imprisonment in Jamaica is the way in which it was mobilized to "prove" the racial inferiority of the entire population. Jamaica's penal system could not have changed as it did without the change in British ideas on penality. The Colonial Office of 1838 would not have allowed a piece of legislation such as the 1865 Corporal Punishment Act (the "Whipping Bill") to take effect. But what happened in Jamaica was not just a more extreme version of a reactionary trend in Britain; the difference was qualitative as well as quantitative. In Britain, the harsh penal measures prescribed in the 1860s were understood to be a way of dealing with a hardened criminal minority of the population, the "dangerous classes," or "residuum."[85] Thus, during the 1862 "garroting panic" an article in the *Observer* contrasted the honest workers of Lancashire with London's morally degenerate garrotters:

> If we look at the distressed artisans of Lancashire who are starving, and have poor weeping wives and hungry children looking up to them for bread, which would almost justify a man helping himself to what does not belong to him, we find crime has greatly diminished. It is not hunger that drives a man to crimes like these; it is more probably caused by a life of idleness and debauchery. Thieves from childhood, with the prison stamp branded on their souls, they are lost to shame and self-respect, and look to jail as a contingency which is not a bad one, after all, to put up with.[86]

Although such "thieves from childhood" were to be scorned and feared, they nevertheless existed in opposition to the "respectable" working class. The respectable formed the majority of the population, and their male household heads could be trusted enough to be given the vote in 1867.[87]

In contrast, in Jamaica the whole population, including the peasant proprietors who in classic liberal theory were seen as having "independence" and a real property-holding stake in society, came to be seen as criminal and irreformable. This is the real difference between the failure of the rehabilitative prison project in Britain and Jamaica. In discussions of the need for flogging, the Jamaican population as a whole filled the conceptual space of the "residuum" in Britain, as "other" to the respectable. In Britain comparisons were made between different groups of the population; in Jamaica the criminal was made to stand in for the population as a whole, which was then compared to an idealized outside group. Governor Eyre's answer to a memorial from peasants in the parish of St George's, which complained of badly maintained roads, unemployment, and destruction of the petitioners' crops by livestock trespass and theft, clearly demonstrates this. Eyre argued that the problem was due to a low level of morality and "civilization" among the petitioners. He failed to recognize their claim to respectability, implying that they themselves produced the "idle thieves" of whom they complained:

> I wish to see them [small settlers] make larger and better dwellings, distribute their families in separate sleeping rooms at night, make provision for medical attendance, pay more attention to their ordinary daily dress . . . devote more time to the care and instruction of their children, train them up to habits of industry and honesty. . . .
>
> You justly complain of the insecurity of property, and that whilst the honest labourer plants, the idle thief reaps; but the remedy is chiefly with yourselves. It is the rising generation, the young, and the strong, and the healthy of both sexes, who fill our Gaols, and such must continue to be the case unless the small settlers and other residents in the country districts, improve in civilization.[88]

After touring the island and receiving many memorials of distress similar to that from St George, Eyre concluded that harsher laws against larceny, including punishment by flogging, were needed. Although similar comments were directed at the British "dangerous classes" in this period, what is notable here is the direction of such moralizing rhetoric at the entirety of the Jamaican population, including the most "respectable" property-holding group. Unlike in Britain, where the franchise was being extended, Jamaicans were soon to be denied any input into their government, as direct rule from London replaced representative government in the wake of the Morant Bay rebellion.[89]

These ideological developments in Jamaica, while differing significantly from the British experience, have close parallels in several other colonial and postcolonial societies where changing penal regimes have been studied. In Peru and Puerto Rico, as in Jamaica, the "failure" of rehabilitative imprisonment confirmed in the mind of the dominant class that the population as a whole was racially other, inferior, and barbarous.[90] As Kelvin Santiago-Valles comments with regard to Puerto Rico, the propertied classes used the penal system "to ideologically represent the majority of the population in the island—particularly the poor peasantry—as being both lazy and depraved."[91] Such similarities suggest a pattern of similarity in colonial societies, structured as they are by racial as well as class domination. In Jamaica, the idealized reference point against which popular behavior was measured was not internal to the island, as it was in Britain, but external.

Michel Foucault argues that the purpose of penitentiary punishment is not to reform prisoners but to create a category of "delinquents" whose existence will both divide the popular classes and lead to their acceptance of state regulation.[92] Although he does not consider the situation of places where the penitentiary was not the dominant form of modern punishment (at least at the level of representations), this point provides a clue to what was happening in Jamaica. In Jamaica there was no real desire on the part of elites to create the opposition delinquent/ordinary worker; rather, the penal regime emphasized the oppositions colonizer/colonized; white/black; Briton/Jamaican. Discussions of punishment consigned the whole population to the category of "delinquent." This contrast, incidentally, provides support for Foucault's point with regard to penitentiary punishment in Europe and North America. The need to spell out just how the penitentiary program had failed led penal authorities in Jamaica to explicitly state the argument that Foucault attributes to them, but that was rarely articulated in Europe — that what mattered about the penitentiary was its branding of the prisoner as a criminal.

Popular Attitudes to Law and Punishment

To what extent were Daughtrey's, Shaw's, and Bell's observations about Afro-Jamaicans' responses to the penal system based in reality? Was it true that Jamaicans in general did not respect judicial decisions, did not stigmatize those who were sent to prison? It is tempting to take the racist claims that Jamaicans were "uncivilized" or "half-civilized" and invert them, arguing that such claims reveal a profound popular alienation from the judicial system, a sense of class and race solidarity in which the "people" rejected the state's efforts to claim legitimacy for its decisions. In fact, however, this does not seem to have been the case. Popular attitudes are extremely difficult to judge, not only because of lack of evidence but also because opinion is in any society more likely to be divided than unitary. Historians of crime and punishment in England, for instance, have reached very different conclusions from similar evidence on this type of issue.[93] The evidence from Jamaica leads me to believe that the situation there was more complex than simply one of popular rejection of the state's definitions of criminality. Jamaicans did not welcome any "criminal" back into their communities as a "martyr." Rather, most Jamaicans had strong views on what was acceptable and what was not acceptable behavior, views that only partially coincided with those codified by the state's legal system, and that were not uniformly held. Insofar as popular attitudes can be categorized, they were instrumental: when the state legal system acted to punish those who the community held to have done wrong, people were happy enough with this; when it failed to do so, or when it punished someone for an action which was not considered wrong, they protested.

One incident that took place in 1856 illustrates these dynamics well. Fifteen men were tried at the Cornwall Circuit Court for "riot and assault." The evidence presented in court indicated that the "riot" had been an act of vigilantism, in which the group attacked a man named Henry Gordon because they believed him to have been responsible for the death of Ann Lewis, a local woman. Gordon, who had a reputation as an obeah man, was reported to have threatened Lewis, who afterward died. The "rioters" had broken into Gordon's house, carried him away, and beaten him about the head. All fifteen were found guilty and sentenced to six months' imprisonment, a decision that reportedly went against the wishes of the many spectators in court.[94]

This event illustrates a complex set of attitudes toward the law and the penal system. On one hand, the group's decision to use direct violence against Gordon suggests their lack of confidence in the state's processes of justice. These fifteen men, and the audience in court that supported them, did not believe that a satisfactory result could be obtained by going through legal channels. No evidence is given as to whether or not they had made any efforts to have Gordon prosecuted in court, but given that, according to the press report of the case, the group was unable to provide evidence that Gordon had caused Lewis's death, they presumably would not have been successful had they done so. Whatever evidence had convinced them that Gordon had used obeah to kill Lewis, it would not convince the court, whose assumptions and standards of proof derived from a different epistemological system to that held by the vast majority of Jamaicans who believed in the power of obeah. The group was therefore correct to believe that, in this case, they could not achieve what they saw as justice through the formal mechanisms of the state. In this case it seems likely that the fifteen convicts were indeed welcomed back into their communities as "martyrs" when they returned from their prison sentences. To an extent, then, elite complaints that Jamaicans failed to stigmatize criminals referred to a real difference between popular attitudes in Jamaica and those in England. In England, although many people probably remained skeptical of the fairness of the law, no alternative system for evaluating responsibility challenged legal discourse as obeah did in Jamaica.[95]

On the other hand, the case clearly does not indicate that members of this community did not stigmatize "criminals." If Henry Gordon had received a prison sentence for obeah it seems likely that at least one faction of the community involved would have been very pleased. It is hard to imagine his receiving an unconditional welcome back into the village at the end of his sentence. The claims that Afro-Jamaicans rejected the decisions of the courts generated a racist stereotype out of a partial truth. Further evidence could be presented on both sides of the argument: defendants in court sometimes claimed that the system was stacked against black people; crowds protesting about other matters sometimes attacked prisons and courthouses and released prisoners; the commissioners sent to inquire into the Morant Bay rebellion of 1865 concluded that lack of popular confidence in the judicial system was a major cause of the rebellion.[96] Evidence of popular support for the judicial system is by its nature harder to find, but there were occasions when communities turned in escaped prisoners, and when groups of peasants reportedly called for convicts to be flogged.[97] Common popular complaints about the irregular frequency of court proceedings indicate a frustration with the state's failure to provide a service to the people, but not a rejection of the decisions that the courts would make.[98] Likewise, the large audiences reported at many trials indicate a strong sense of investment in the proceedings, although not an uncritical acceptance of their outcomes.[99] It is probably true that, in the 1860s, fewer Jamaicans than Britons accepted the state's claim to be the only arbiter of justice and resolver of disputes. But, overall, Jamaican people appear to have had strong beliefs about what kind of behavior was unacceptable and required punishment, beliefs that often did coincide with the state's definitions of "crime."

The *Falmouth Post* supported the sentence in the Gordon case, claiming that "in a colony like this, where the ignorant masses have been accustomed since their emancipation from degraded bondage, to the enjoyment of a licentious liberty, it is essentially necessary that offences of an aggravated nature should be visited by exemplary punishment."[100] Such a claim indicates a great divergence between elite and popular understandings of the meaning and effects of judicial decisions. The attack on Gordon surely did not arise out of "licentious liberty," but rather out of the transgression by one individual of a particular set of strictly held standards of conduct. Far from acting out of "ignorance," the defendants seem to have been trying to enforce order. But because their efforts did not act to reinforce the power of state institutions of law and penalty, they were used to add to the image of Jamaicans as existing outside the law.

Conclusion

Penal developments in Jamaica did not follow the path we might expect given the many accounts of the history of punishment in Europe and North America. Whereas in those places a shift took place from punishment focused on inflicting bodily pain to punishment aiming to control the prisoner's mind, in Jamaica this was not the case. Elements that are usually identified as defining modern punishment, such as the shift away from corporal punishment and the state's exclusive power over the prisoner, were in Jamaica much less clearly the dominant trend. After a brief period in which penal reform along the same lines as took place in Britain was dominant, new forms of corporal punishment and privately run punishment were integrated into the penal system.

This is not simply because Jamaica and other colonial societies were "backward." We should not imagine Jamaica as following the same road as Britain but going more slowly; as I have shown, during the era of rehabilitative imprisonment, Jamaica was if anything ahead. Although their paths later diverged, the goals and preoccupations of Jamaica's administrators of justice were as modern as Britain's. But Jamaica's was a more violent, more coercive modernity. We should avoid presenting a dichotomous distinction between corporal and carceral punishment as the essential difference between modern and premodern punishment. Both types of punishment in fact operated side by side in Jamaica in the postemancipation period.

Arguments about penality did more than advocate particular policy options. They also postulated different positions about the nature of the Jamaican population, positions which constructed competing understandings of "race." Rehabilitative imprisonment, as a goal, could only make sense on the understanding that individuals, including black Jamaicans, would respond in the same way to a given environment. This view could quite happily encompass the idea that Jamaicans were by nature or training passive and subservient, inasmuch as those were the qualities that such imprisonment was designed to create. But such a view had to return to the claim that the people it focused attention on were human. The arguments for flogging and privatized punishment entailed the construction of a more overtly violent and dehumanizing racial discourse, in which black people were marked out not just by their passivity but by their brutality and lack of civilization. These arguments were significant not just for the implications they had for penal policy, but perhaps more significantly because they prepared the way for the indiscriminate violent repression that followed the 1865 Morant Bay rebellion. To *The Times* of London the rebellion demonstrated that it was "impossible to eradicate the original savageness of the African blood."[101] In the course of the rebellion's suppression, 439 people were killed, 600 flogged, and over 1,000 homes burnt.[102] Such violence could be easily resorted to because the Jamaican population had been put firmly beyond the boundaries of the human community. Discussions about punishment and crime had played a significant role in locating Afro-Jamaicans beyond those boundaries.

Notes

Abbreviations used in the notes:
    CO   Public Record Office, Kew, Colonial Office papers
    JA   Jamaica Archives, Spanish Town, Jamaica
    PP   British Parliamentary Papers

1 Stanley to Governors of Legislative Colonies Despatch E, 19 Oct. 1833, PP 1835 (177) L.

2 That is, 380 of 490 convicts. Calculated from enclosures in Sligo to Stanley no. 24, 31 May 1834, CO 137/192. This includes a few slaves whose offense is listed as running away in addition to another offense.

3 For more detailed discussion of the function of prisons during slavery, see chapter 2 of my Ph.D. dissertation, "No Bond But the Law: Punishment and Justice in Emancipation-Era Jamaica, 1780–1870" (Yale University, 2000), and Michael Craton, *Searching for the Invisible Man: Slaves and Plantation Life in Jamaica* (Cambridge, Mass.: Harvard University Press, 1978), chap. 10.

4 Encs. in Smith to Glenelg no. 149, 13 August 1838, CO 137/231.

5 On Michaelmas 1840, 1170 prisoners were held in jails and houses of correction. Calculated from Return of the Gaols and Houses of Correction in Jamaican Blue

Book of Statistics for 1840, CO 142/54. (There are extensive arithmetical errors in this table — I have recalculated the figures.)

6 "An Act for the Better Government of Prisons in the West Indies," 1 and 2 Vict. c. 67. CO 318/136.

7 The Jamaican House of Assembly, elected on a male-only property-limited franchise, originated all legislation, but the British government could veto the assembly's decisions in the name of the crown. For an excellent discussion of Anglo-Jamaican politics in this period, see Thomas C. Holt, *The Problem of Freedom: Race, Labor, and Politics in Jamaica and Britain, 1832–1938* (Baltimore: Johns Hopkins University Press, 1992), pp. 105–112. See also Swithin Wilmot, "Political Developments in Jamaica in the Post Emancipation Period, 1838–1854" (D.Phil. thesis, Oxford University, 1977), pp. 47–50.

8 For discussion of British and North American penal practice in this period, see Michael Ignatieff, *A Just Measure of Pain: The Penitentiary in the Industrial Revolution, 1750–1850* (London: Macmillan, 1978); Robin Evans, *The Fabrication of Virtue: English Prison Architecture 1750–1840* (Cambridge: Cambridge University Press, 1982); David J. Rothman, *The Discovery of the Asylum: Social Order and Disorder in the New Republic* (Boston: Little, Brown, 1971).

9 Elgin to Stanley no. 81, 28 June 1843, CO 137/279.

10 John Daughtrey, "Inspectors Report of the General Penitentiary," 1 Oct. 1845, enc. in Elgin to Stanley no. 104, 17 Dec. 1845, CO 137/285 (hereafter Daughtrey Report 1845).

11 Metcalfe to Russell no. 210, April 10 1840, CO 137/258.

12 Report of Captain J. W. Pringle on Prisons in the West Indies. Part I Jamaica. PP 1837–38 (596) XL (hereafter Pringle Report) gives figures for 1838; CO 142/57 gives them for 1843.

13 See for instance Edward Long, *History of Jamaica* II, p. 214, quoted in Adolph Edwards, "The Development of Criminal Law in Jamaica up to 1900" (Ph.D. thesis, University of London, 1968), p. 122; First Report (Second Series) of Commissioner on Criminal and Civil Justice in the West Indies: Jamaica, PP 1826–27 (559) XXIV; Pringle Report.

14 See the rules and regulations for several prisons enc. in Smith to Glenelg no. 50, 28 March 1838, CO 142/50.

15 I have found no anxiety about the possibility of homosexual behavior.

16 S. Pryce to Higginson, 1 Jan. 1841, in Metcalfe to Russell no. 210, CO 137/258.

17 Metcalfe to Russell no. 212, 30 April 1841, CO 137/255.

18 John Daughtrey, "Brief Review and Report of the General Penitentiary" 26 Feb. 1844, enc. in Elgin to Stanley no. 57, 6 April 1844, CO 137/279 (hereafter Daughtrey Report 1844).

19 Governor Metcalfe had instructed prison superintendents discontinue flogging as punishment for breaches of prison discipline in 1840. Higginson to all Custodes no. 501, in Metcalfe to Russell no. 210, 29 April 1840, CO 137/258.

20 Daughtrey Report 1844; Daughtrey Report 1845. The claim with regard to recidivism is in the 1845 report.

21 John Daughtrey, Stipendiary Magistrate's report on St Elizabeths, 30 June 1835, enc. in Sligo to Glenelg no. 48, 7 July 1835, CO 137/200 ("violent jabber"); Daughtrey Report 1844 ("proverbially talkative").

22 Orlando Patterson, *Slavery and Social Death: A Comparative Study* (Cambridge, Mass.: Harvard University Press, 1982), p. 338.

23 Daughtrey Report 1845.

24 Speech by Chamberlaine at Manchioneal Wesleyan Chapel, reported in *Morning Journal*, 17 August 1838, enc. in R. Chamberlaine to Normanby no. 8, 27 June 1839, PP 1839 (523) XXXVI.

25 For example Michel Foucault, *Discipline and Punish: The Birth of the Prison*, trans. Alan Sheridan (London: Vintage Books, 1977); Ignatieff, *Just Measure of Pain*; Rothman, *Discovery of the Asylum.*

26 Margaret DeLacy, *Prison Reform in Lancashire, 1700–1850: A Study in Local Administration* (Stanford: Stanford University Press, 1986), and Seán McConville, *A History of English Prison Administration,* vol. One, *1750–1877* (London: Routledge & Kegan Paul, 1981), pp. 365–374, show that penal reform in English local prisons lagged far behind national policy.

27 "An Act to amend the laws relating to offences against the person," 4 Vict. c. 45. See also Higginson to all Custodes no. 501, in Metcalfe to Russell no. 210, 29 April 1840, CO 137/258.

28 The circular also recommended the abandonment of flogging as a punishment within penal institutions.

29 Higginson to all Custodes no. 1211, in Metcalfe to Russell no. 210, 4 May 1840, CO 137/258. Ignatieff, *Just Measure of Pain,* p. 177.

30 In 1850 the Colonial Office Secretary, James Stephen, compared Jamaica to the white settlement colonies: "We emancipate our grown-up sons, but keep our unmarried daughters . . . in domestic bonds." Quoted in Holt, *Problem of Freedom,* p. 235.

31 Daughtrey Report 1845; Bell to Labouchere no. 62, 10 Dec. 1856, CO 137/332.

32 7 Vict. c. 63.

33 16 Vict. c. 23.

34 See for instance St Thomas in the Vale Vestry Minutes JA 2/1/2.

35 28 Vict. c. 18. The Colonial Office refused to assent to this act unless the maximum number of lashes was reduced to thirty-six. Cardwell to Eyre no. 213, 1 June 1865, CO 137/388.

36 Minute by "C. F.," on Eyre to Cardwell no. 256, 10 Sept. 1864, CO 137/384.

37 Wilmot, "Political Developments," p. 261; Holt, *Problem of Freedom,* 286–287.

38 *Falmouth Post,* 29 Jan. 1850.

39 Grey to Grey no. 30, 23 March 1850, CO 137/306.

40 13 Vict c. 36 no. 3847.

41 Official court records do not survive for this period. These cases were taken from the court reports in the newspapers the *Falmouth Post* and *Morning Journal* for the period. The papers did not report every criminal trial, but when they did report a court session they seem to have reported all cases that were tried at that session.

42 The following acts allowed for flogging for various crimes: 13 Vict c. 36 (1850), 14 Vict. c. 24 (1851), 16 Vict c. 17 (1853), 19 Vict. c. 28 (1856), 19 Vict. c. 30 (1856), 24 Vict c. 18 (1861). Several of these are reenactments of expiring or recently expired legislation.

43 Address to Grand Jury of Supreme Court, reported in *Falmouth Post*, 26 Feb. 1850.

44 *Falmouth Post*, 19 Mar. 1850.

45 *Falmouth Post*, 26 Oct. 1852.

46 *Morning Journal*, 21 Oct. 1854.

47 *Jamaica Standard and Royal Gazette* 24 Aug. 1842.

48 *Falmouth Post*, 26 Oct. 1852. The editorial places the phrase "original state of barberism" in quotation marks to indicate that it is quoting from a judge's statement to a grand jury.

49 Letter from "Civis," *Falmouth Post*, 5 Feb. 1850.

50 Governor Eyre, address on the prorogation of the house of assembly, enc. in Eyre to Cardwell no. 37, 21 Feb. 1865, CO 137/388; Shaw, "Report" 1865.

51 14 Vict. c. 24.

52 *Falmouth Post*, 18 Feb. 1851. Myalism is a specifically Jamaican form of ritual religious practice, designed to counter the power of obeah.

53 For example Sligo to Spring Rice no. 110, 25 Dec. 1834, CO 137/194; report of S. M. Arthur Welch enc. in Sligo to Aberdeen no. 60, 27 March 1835, CO 137/198; report of S. M. Samuel Pryce enc. in Sligo to Glenelg no. 401, 2 April 1836, CO 137/210.

54 A major rebellion of Jamaican peasants and other rural people took place in 1865, centered on the town of Morant Bay in eastern Jamaica. It took place after a sustained period of economic hardship on the island, and was sparked by conflict over the administration of justice and over land. The rebellion was harshly suppressed. For further discussion, see Mimi Sheller, *Democracy After Slavery: Black Publics and Peasant Radicalism in Haiti and Jamaica* (London: MacMillan, 2000); Gad Heuman, *"The Killing Time": The Morant Bay Rebellion in Jamaica* (London: MacMillan, 1994); and Holt, *Problem of Freedom*, chaps. 8 and 9.

55 Law 4 of 1872 and Law 6 of 1877.

56 For instance, flogging remained a legal punishment for obeah in the 1950s. Edwards, *Development of Criminal Law*, p. 487.

57 Shaw, Information on the General Penitentiary, enc. in Eyre to Cardwell no. 48, 16 March 1865, CO 137/388.

58 Ignatieff, *Just Measure of Pain*, p. 75.

59 18 Vict. c. 22. The daily wage for agricultural labor at this time was about one shilling.

60 For a summary of the uses of convicts in different states, see David M. Oshinsky, *"Worse than Slavery": Parchman Farm and the Ordeal of Jim Crow Justice* (New York: Free Press, 1996), pp. 57–82. See also Alex Lichtenstein, *Twice the Work of Free Labor: The Political Economy of Convict Labor in the New South* (London: Verso, 1996).

61 Enc. in Barkly to Labouchere no. 27, 20 Feb. 1856, CO 137/330. None of the convicts had identifiably female names, and very few names were ambiguous with regards to gender. It is unclear whether the demands of planters or the availability of convicts accounts for this gender bias — probably a combination of both.

62 Ibid.

63 John Daughtrey, "Remarks on the Penal Servitude Act," enc. in Barkly to Labouchere no. 27, 20 Feb. 1856, CO 137/330.

64 William A. Green, *British Slave Emancipation: The Sugar Colonies and the Great Experiment* (Oxford: Clarendon Press, 1976), pp. 261–292; Verene A. Shepherd, *Transients to Settlers: The Experience of Indians in Jamaica 1845–1950* (Leeds: Peepal Tree Books, 1994); Douglas Hall, *Free Jamaica 1838–1865: An Economic History* (New Haven: Yale University Press, 1959), pp. 53–59.

65 Eyre to Cardwell no. 256, 10 Sept. 1864, CO 137/384. In this period the American Civil War had interrupted supplies to Britain's textile processing industries.

66 28 Vict. c. 19.

67 Cardwell to Storks no. 47, 29 Jan. 1866, CO 137/388.

68 "Annual Report of the Committee of Management of the Boys Reformatory of Kingston," enc. in Eyre to Cardwell no. 57, 22 Mar. 1865, CO 137/388.

69 "First Annual Report of the Ladies' Industrial and Reformatory Association," enc. in Darling to Lytton no. 22, 31 Jan. 1859, CO 137/343; Eyre to Cardwell no. 237, 12 Aug. 1864, CO 137/384.

70 "Second Annual Report of the Kingston and St Andrew's Girls' Reformatory," enc. in Darling to Newcastle no. 28, 28 Jan. 1860, CO 137/348.

71 *Falmouth Post,* 18 Jan. 1850.

72 *Falmouth Post,* 18 Feb. 1851. See also *Falmouth Post* editorial of 17 Aug. 1850, which makes a very similar point.

73 *Colonial Standard,* reprinted in *Falmouth Post,* 1 June 1852.

74 On the concept of "less eligibility" see David Garland, *Punishment and Welfare: A History of Penal Strategies* (Aldershot: Gower, 1985), chap. 2.

75 This was a fundamental argument of Thomas Carlyle's influential "Discourse on the Nigger Question," for discussion of which see Holt, *Problem of Freedom,* pp. 280–286.

76 Daughtrey Report, 1845.

77 *Falmouth Post,* 18 Feb. 1851.

78 Letter from "Civis" in *Falmouth Post,* 5 Feb. 1850.

79 W. A. Bell, report on St Dorothy, 1 Sept. 1840 enc. in Metcalfe to Russell no. 51, 30 Nov. 1840, PP 1841 (344) III.

80 T. A. Dillon report, 12 Jan. 1854, enc. in Barkly to Newcastle no. 1, 21 Feb. 1854, PP 1854 [1848] XLIII.

81 H. B. Shaw, "Report of the Inspector of Prisons" in Eyre to Cardwell no. 69, 30 March 1865, CO 137/388.

82 *Falmouth Post,* 22 June 1852.

83 William James Forsythe, *The Reform of Prisoners 1830–1900* (London: Croom Helm, 1987), chap. 6.

84 Jennifer Davis, "The London Garotting Panic of 1862: A Moral Panic and the Creation of a Criminal Class in Mid-Victorian England," in V. A. C. Gatrell, Bruce Lenman, and Geoffrey Parker, eds., *Crime and the Law: The Social History of Crime in Western Europe since 1500* (London: Europa, 1980), pp. 190–213.

85 Gareth Stedman Jones, *Outcast London: A Study in the Relation between Classes in Victorian Society* (London: Pantheon, 1984 [1971]).

86 Quoted in Davis, "London Garroting Panic," p. 201.

87 The 1867 Reform Act codified the concept of respectability by enfranchising male household heads who had been renting accommodation for twelve months or more.

88 Eyre to Cardwell no. 234, 23 July 1864, CO 137/384.

89 Catherine Hall, "Rethinking Imperial Histories: The Reform Act of 1867," *New Left Review* 208 (1994): 3–29.

90 Carlos Aguirre, "The Lima Penitentiary and the Modernization of Criminal Justice in Nineteenth-Century Peru," and Kelvin A. Santiago-Valles, " 'Forcing them to Work and Punishing Whoever Resisted': Servile Labor and Penal Servitude under Colonialism in Nineteenth-Century Puerto Rico," both in Ricardo D. Salvatore and Carlos Aguirre, eds., *The Birth of the Penitentiary in Latin America: Essays on Criminology, Prison Reform, and Social Control, 1830–1940* (Austin: University of Texas Press, 1996), pp. 44–77 and 123–168.

91 Santiago-Valles, "Forcing them to Work," p. 131.

92 Foucault, *Discipline and Punish,* pp. 271–292.

93 Compare, for instance, the argument of David Philips, *Crime and Authority in Victorian England: the Black Country, 1835–1860* (London: Croom Helm, 1977) with those presented in the essays by Hay and Snyder, Hay, and Davis in Douglas Hay and Francis Snyder, eds., *Policing and Prosecution in Britain 1750–1850* (Oxford: Clarendon Press, 1989).

94 Details of the case are given in *Falmouth Post,* 5 Dec. 1856.

95 I explore the meaning of obeah as an alternative framework of justice in the final chapter of my dissertation, "No Bond But the Law."

96 For defendants' claims that Jamaican courts offered "no justice" to black people see the report of Trelawney Quarter Sessions in Falmouth Post, 19 Aug. 1845; rioters in Falmouth in 1859 attacked the prison and the court house, and released all the prisoners; the details are reported in Darling to Newcastle no. 103 9 Aug. 1859, CO 137/345; the claim with regard to the rebellion at Morant Bay is one of the conclu-

sions in Report of the Jamaica Royal Commission, 1866. Part I: Report, PP 1866 [3683] XXX.

97 For a report of popular cooperation with attempts to recapture escaped prisoners see *Falmouth Post,* 2 Feb. 1842; for calls for flogging by "respectable" peasants see letter to the editor from "An Observer" in *Falmouth Post,* 11 July 1848, also Eyre to Cardwell no. 256, 10 Sept. 1864, CO 137/384; Eyre to Cardwell no. 59 Mar. 22 1865, CO 137/388.

98 For such complaints see Evidence of Hinton Spalding, 24 June 1842, Select Committee on West India Colonies PP 1842 (479) XIII; *Falmouth Post,* 12 Jan. 1842, 4 Oct. 1859, 4 July 1862.

99 Such reports were very common. A few examples include *Falmouth Post,* 12 May 1846 (Hanover Quarter Sessions), 28 Apr. 1848 (St. James Quarter Sessions), 15 Aug. 1851 (Trelawney Quarter Session), 17 Jan. 1854 (St Anns Quarter Sessions), 7 Nov. 1862 (St. Catherine Circuit Court).

100 *Falmouth Post,* 5 Dec. 1856.

101 *The Times,* 13 Nov. 1865, quoted in Christine Bolt, *Victorian Attitudes to Race* (London: Routledge & Kegan Paul, 1971), p. 76.

102 Catherine Hall, "Competing Masculinities: Thomas Carlyle, John Stuart Mill, and the Case of Governor Eyre," in *White, Male and Middle Class: Explorations in Feminism and History* (Cambridge: Polity Press, 1992), p. 254.

Death and Liberalism:

Capital Punishment after the Fall of Rosas

RICARDO D. SALVATORE

In 1852 the firm of Baring Brothers sent an agent to Buenos Aires to persuade the government to reopen negotiations on the question of the 1824 loan, still unpaid. The agent, according to H. S. Ferns, brought with him a rifle and pair of pistols to regale General Justo J. de Urquiza, the new governor of Buenos Aires. Soon after his arrival, the agent witnessed a turnaround in the political situation — the revolution of September 11, 1852. He changed his mind and sold the intended gift. Weapons seemed to have become an inappropriate present in the new political climate. "In this country," the Baring Brothers agent wrote in his diary, "conditions have changed in extreme . . . all the dignitaries and officers I dealt with are enlightened doctors in law and peaceful civilians. Thank God, the *era of caudillos is over* [my emphasis]."[1]

In a sense the British agent was not mistaken. New sensibilities and practices of sociability brought by the liberal leadership to the political arena heralded a time of peace and prosperity and, consequently, the end of an era of civil wars, caudillo politics, and brutality. Contemporaries experienced 1852 and the years that followed as a period of historical discontinuity. Reminded daily of the atrocities committed by the past dictatorship (the Rosas regime), they came to view the *tiranía* as a unique experience, never again to be repeated. Though the process of institutional reform was just beginning, the fall of the dictator opened up space for the enhancement of individual liberties. The reemergence of a free press would consolidate public opinion and reduce the arbitrariness of the rulers. A more independent judiciary, the creation of municipalities, and the new provincial constitution (1854) created a sense that basic individual rights would be guaranteed. In particular, people expected that the new regime would protect the property and life of citizens. If this were so, firearms would cease to be a necessity.

Far from an irreversible trend, the process of institution-building that followed Rosa's defeat at Caseros encountered many obstacles. The debate about key issues for the future of the province (government finances, banks and money, taxation, and recruitment) added instability and uncertainty to the lives of *porteños*. Whereas the launching of the first railroad project and the free transportation of the rivers created favorable expectations about economic growth, peace was not yet a firm conquest. After September 1852, various violent episodes assailed the tranquility of porteños: the siege of the city by General Lagos, the landings of Urquicista troops on the coast, Indian invasions on the western frontier, and insurrections in the Littoral provinces. In addition, in the mid-1850s, the population of Buenos Aires was assaulted by a quite modern fear: a crime panic. Middle- and upper-class urbanites experienced this transition as a time of individual and collective insecurity. The promises of the liberal leadership not withstanding, porteños had still many reasons to keep their firearms at hand.

If the Baring Brothers agent had stayed long enough, he would have also noticed some important elements of continuity undermining his early assessment. He would have seen in the capital, or perhaps in country towns, the spectacle of public executions being conducted for the sake of the new liberal order. Some forty of these spectacles were carried out between 1852 and 1864. If he were an assiduous reader of local newspapers, the British agent would have concluded that Buenos Aires was not as safe as he had thought: enlightened "doctors" were busy passing death sentences for murderers while "peaceful civilians" lived under the menace of crime. The past dictatorship did not seem so distant after all. The executions were little different from those conducted during the Rosas administration and, what is more important, those who presented capital punishment as necessary for the preservation of social order used arguments reminiscent of those used by the "Restorer of the Laws."

Despite important differences between Rosismo and the liberal administrations, judges continued to believe in the efficacy of exemplary punishment. Executions, in particular, were deemed essential to the legal and political apprenticeship of lower-class people. Whether the regime was a tyranny or a democracy did not make much difference, for the lower-classes remained "uncivilized" and lawless. Among subaltern subjects, judges thought, the sight of hanged bodies produced enough fear to keep them from committing crimes. The confidence liberals deposited on the new institutions (elementary schools, immigration laws, and civic militias) did nothing to undermine this basic belief. On the contrary, the experience of Rosismo reinforced the view that a resilient rural culture, still prone to violence, could only be taught "democracy" and "progress" with a pedagogy of terror.

This chapter investigates the role of capital punishment in the construction of a social and political order after Caseros. The suggestion that there is a relationship of necessity between death and democracy points to the continuity of penal policy between Rosismo and the liberal regimes that followed. Representing a preliminary stage of a longer research project, this essay tries to map the contours of a problem ignored by Argentine historiography: the sentencing to death of common criminals during the decade following the fall of Rosas.

How could the same pedagogy of terror serve two distinct social and political experiments? What sustained the necessity of public executions after Caseros? Why did common murderers become such a public threat? Was there a parallel continuity in public sensibilities about executions? These are some of the questions that stimulate my inquiry. Traditional explanations of the abolition of the death penalty in Argentina have overlooked this important moment of transition. Political histories, guided by the same enthusiasm and partisanship as that which motivated the British agent, have overestimated the changes between the Rosas and the subsequent liberal periods. It is a good time to review the conventional wisdom, and there is nothing better than the hanging pole to fix our attention.

The Death Penalty: Continuity and Change

During the postindependence period, the death penalty was abundantly used to sustain the social and political order of the new republic. The first revolutionary junta (1810) sentenced to death conspirators against the new government. The first triumvirate (1811) punished the privateers acting in the name of the Spanish crown with hanging. The 1813 assembly, known for its decision to abolish privileges of nobility and instruments of torture, and for having freed the slaves' children, established capital punishment for desertion. Later, directors Posadas and Alvear (1814–15) used the death penalty against duelists, traitors, and deserters.[2] The Rosas regime continued with this tradition, using executions to punish a variety of crimes. The regime executed recidivist deserters, political adversaries, and common criminals. It was particularly severe with assassins and thieves.

Executions, it could be argued, were part of the political culture of the civil war period, a time when conflicts of authority or sovereignty were resolved through armed confrontations. In military campaigns, both *federales* and *unitarios* resorted to shootings or *degüellos* (beheading with a knife) as the culmination of a favorable battle. Engaged in a confrontation aimed at the total elimination of the enemy, both forces believed that the execution of prisoners was a practical necessity of the war, justified by logistical arguments. For the state that governed in peacetime, the justification of executions was different. Exemplary punishment served to restore the social and political order. As a sort of balm that helped to pacify the exalted passions of the times, spectacles of death formed part of a governmental pedagogy. Rosas was not alone in this regard. Other statesmen, before and after his administration, shared Rosas's arguments about the political necessity of public executions.

The liberal leadership that assumed governance of the province after September 1852, although committed to building a different sort of republican government, still found it convenient to maintain this practice. Nor were there legal impediments to do so. The constitution of 1853 (enacted by the congress of Santa Fé and not ratified by the province of Buenos Aires until 1860) abolished capital punishment for political cases only.[3] The death penalty for common crimes remained, the only change being that the condemned would be shot (and then hanged) instead of knifed. Without significant reforms in criminal legislation, judges in Buenos Aires and in other provinces continued to pass sentences according to Spanish colonial laws. These prescribed the death penalty for a variety of crimes (murder, theft, treason, rebellion, and so on).

During the liberal transition, three factors contributed to make capital punishment politically important: the consolidation of an enlightened public opinion; the need to reactivate the memory of the past dictatorship; and the public's perception of growing personal insecurity. Magnified by the press, a few judicial cases reviewing the atrocities committed during the Rosas era gained public notoriety. Soon public attention shifted to the common murderers. Responding to public feeling in the face of a rise in violent crimes, judges imposed stiff sentences against criminals. Those accused of "treacherous crimes" (*crímenes aleves*) commonly received the death penalty. The exemplary trials against the *mazorqueros* (members of the Mazorca, or Sociedad Popular Restauradora) and the press's invention of a crime panic were two sides of the same coin: the difficult construction of order under the liberal-republican regime.

Judged by contemporary standards, the number of actual public executions remained low during the entire 1852–1864 period. This indicator rose significantly in the years 1854 and 1855, reaching a peak of eleven executions per year. After this period, the number of annual executions declined until 1864, when they practically ceased to exist.[4] After 1864, executions continued but were circumscribed within institutional or enclosed environments (the army, the prison) and, more often than not, were related to special circumstances such as rebellions or political assassinations. The rise and fall in the use of capital sentences during a period of institutional experimentation is full of significant connotations.

The same factors that had facilitated the resurgence of the death penalty in 1854–55 contributed to its decline after 1856. Newspapers created the propitious climate for reinstating capital punishment. They urged the public to witness and condemn the political murders of the past regime. They alerted the public about the potential invasion of rural violence into the citadel of "civilization." In short, they helped fashion a public opinion that legitimated the use of state violence. Curiously, after 1856 the involvement of public opinion worked in the opposite direction. That year, the public reaction to the death sentence of a female assassin (Clorinda Sarracán) forced the judiciary to reconsider the morality and necessity of capital punishment.

Suddenly, a public policy that seemed so integral to the machinery of government was disarmed by the very public opinion created by liberal publicists. From then on, liberal institutions raised increasing obstacles against the death sentence, obstacles that amounted to a de facto abolition of capital punishment. In September 1857 the legislature passed a bill authorizing the governor to commute death sentences for "treacherous crimes." The same year, the chamber decreed the suspension of the practice of hanging the dead bodies of the executed. In 1858 the chamber made compulsory the consultation of death sentences with superior courts. Surrendering to this mounting pressure, in 1859 the Superior Tribunal of Justice decreed that all death sentences should be confirmed by the superior court by a unanimous decision.[5]

This short cycle of public executions (with its two phases of enthusiasm and rejection) coincided with the experiment led by liberals to establish a new institutional order. Because part of this new order was predicated on the notion of greater citizen participation and the enhancement of civil liberties we have called this ideal regime "liberal republicanism" or, simply, "liberalism." The services that capital punishment could provide to this political project depended on the state of public opinion and on the supposed menaces facing society and the state. These were constructed states, emerging at the conjuncture of a dynamic relationship articulating magistrates, the press, and the public. These states of opinion and fear presented politicians and judges with the ingredients to reinforce or deactivate the machinery of the scaffold. In what follows, I discuss this dynamic, examining in turn the executions, the construction of a "moral panic" and the arguments that sustained both. The essay concludes with an examination of the political uses of death in a liberal-republican order.

The Executions: Judicial Reasons

During 1852 and 1853, death sentences were used to punish aberrant political crimes committed during the Rosas dictatorship. Figures such as Badía, Troncoso, and Cuitiño were executed as a means of reassuring porteño residents that the new regime, in spite of its troubles, could at least do justice to the assassins of the massacres of 1840 and 1842. Though much was done in these trials to implicate Rosas as ultimately responsible for this type of violence, the new authorities postponed accusing the ex-governor directly until 1857.[6] By all accounts, the executions of *mazorqueros* failed to satisfy the desire for justice generated among the upper and middle classes. By 1856, those who expected that these trials would open the way for reconsidering the vast amount of governmental abuse during the Rosas era had reasons for disappointment.

After 1854, there was a shift in the direction of penal policy. The judiciary ceased to consider cases involving political crimes associated with the past regime and instead favored the resolution of common crimes. This is reflected in the statistics of public executions. All death sentences passed between 1855 and 1864 involved cases of aggravated murder, sometimes in combination with assault and robbery. No longer was any functionary of the past regime sent before the firing squad. This shift in policy (its practices and rationale) was generated within the judiciary. After 1854 judges became lenient with regard to political crimes committed during the Rosas administration, absolving all but a few infamous members of the regime. Even Antonio Reyes, Rosas's faithful secretary for many years, was absolved of all wrongdoing in 1855, after having been sentenced to death a year earlier.

Judges justified these absolutions with two different arguments. One was the *doctrine of uncontrollable fear,* according to which members of the regime were said to have acted, not only following orders from Rosas (directly or indirectly), but also on the knowledge that, if they did not comply with these orders, their lives would be in danger. Like a state of mental disorder or emotional distress, fear made the accused irresponsible for their crimes. The other was the *doctrine of generalized savagery,* according to which soldiers, officers, policemen, and other auxiliaries of the Rosas regime were said to have acted with a cruelty and violence that was characteristic of the period. The dictatorship had impregnated social relations with such a high level of violence that the latter became "natural" among lower-class subjects, particularly among peasants. Therefore, merely belonging to this class or the fact of having lived through the experience of Rosismo was considered a mitigating circumstance for murder.

In March 1848, Manuel G. López, an *alcalde* during the Rosas administration, had ordered the shooting of a Basque prisoner put in his custody. When the case was tried in November 1855, the prosecution asked the death penalty for López. The judge, instead, sentenced López to five years in prison (the Cámara later confirmed this sentence). To ground this verdict, the judge invoked the doctrine of "generalized savagery." The condition of the accused (lower class) and his political sympathies (federalist) in the particular context of the Rosas dictatorship served to explain and excuse his criminal behavior.[7] A complementary argument used by the defense, that the accused must have felt "compelled" to commit this crime to protect himself from any punishment from the governor, was also accepted by the court as reasonable. Given Rosas's unbounded and arbitrary power, it was normal to assume that fear should dominate the behavior of a local policeman.[8]

In 1869, another crime committed under the dictatorship was pardoned under a similar argument. Mariano F. Espiñeira, arrested in 1848 by Justice of Peace Calixto Calderón, spent fourteen months at the prison of Santos Lugares just for saying that federalist soldiers were mercenaries.[9] His arrest came from a suggestion (not even an order) made by General Pacheco to the justice of peace. After Caseros, Espiñeira sued Calderón for unjustified imprisonment, not suspecting that his case would drag along in the courts for eighteen years. In 1869, when the final decision came, he was shocked. The Cámara pardoned Calderón (who was dead) based on the doctrine of uncontrollable fear: the justice of peace, the judges stated, was unable to defy a single order of Rosas's generals without risking his own life. The "fear to provoke the Tyrant's ire" was sufficient reason to justify Calderón's conduct; under a regime of terror, this servant could have done nothing else but satisfied Rosas's desires. In fact, argued the chamber, not Pacheco but Rosas was ultimately responsible for Espiñeira's arrest.

In this way, the judges eliminated the penal responsibility of the agents of state violence, concentrating all the blame in a few political actors. Devoid of legal arguments to prosecute other authors of criminal excesses during the previous regime, lawyers ceased presenting this type of case. As a result, many state violations against the lives and property of citizens were never fully investigated, much less tried in a court of law. The murders for which the "assassins of 1840" were tried represented a small proportion of all the political assassinations allegedly committed during the Rosas administration. Despite the press's insistence on reactivating the public's memory about the excesses of the past regime, the judiciary chose to put an end to the issue.[10] This explains why, after 1853, the hanging pole was reserved almost exclusively for the punishment of common criminals.

Our reconstruction of public executions for the period 1855–1864 places the number of executions in the neighborhood of thirty-six to forty, almost all of them in cases of aggravated murder.[11] Other executions, chiefly those carried out within army barracks, might have escaped registration. Though not impressive, in comparison with the numbers of executions carried out contemporaneously in the United States and Europe, this estimate suggests that liberals were as willing to resort to capital punishment as the hated dictator. The main criterion used by judges for extending death sentences was that the crime had been committed with some degree of premeditation and treachery. Hanging, in particular, was reserved for cases considered *crímenes aleves*.

What constituted a treacherous crime can be measured by the sentences judges meted out. Usually, the murderers had used a disproportionate amount of violence against their victims and had carried out their crimes with treachery. Pedro Alcántara García, for example, had killed Lucas González with a pole, striking the head of the victim many times while González was sleeping. Juan José Acosta, sentenced to death in 1855, had killed Teresa Martínez with a knife after raping her. Tomás Ordoñez, also executed in 1855, was said to have knifed Agustín Aguero while the victim was sitting at a dance (*baile*), the murder being committed in the absence of any dispute or exchange of words (judges interpreted that the assassin simply killed for the fun of it [*de gusto*]). Or the case of Raymundo Reyes, who killed a fellow peon with a burning log, disfiguring his face. These were crimes that shocked the sensibilities of the population.

Moreover, the brutality of these crimes reminded judges of the violence of the past Dictatorship. Judge Federico Olmo, trying to convey in his sentence the treacherous nature of the crime committed by Santiago Molina and Loreto Heredia in 1856, compared the murder to the slaughter of animals.[12] Lassoed and dragged through the dirt like a calf, the victim was later knifed across the neck, as peons would do in the slaughterhouse. This method of killing was the one preferred by the Mazorca (Rosas's secret police) to dispense with Rosas's political opponents. The association between the slaughterhouse and the terror of the Rosas period (a compelling motif in Sarmiento's *Facundo*, in Ascasubi's *La Refalosa*, and many travel narratives) was a signal of ominous developments. The conclusion was obvious. The countryside, still dominated by the political culture of Rosismo, was accustomed to killing people like animals. Hence, the need for the continuity of exemplary punishment.

The characteristics of some victims (female, very young, elderly, Indian, foreign, etc.) must have added notoriety to the crime, but it was the heinous nature of the killings that led judges to opt for the capital punishment. Of the thirty-three murder victims recorded, twenty-seven of them were male and six female. Generally, the victims were relatives, lovers, or coworkers of the murderers, or they were unknown persons killed in the environment of anonymity and confusion of a barroom or dance. Passion, economic gains, or simple revenge were the most current motives declared at the trials. There were cases in which felons seem to have killed for no apparent reason. The numbers of foreigners and native-born among the victims were almost the same. Among the victims were an *indio* (Indian), a *pardo* (similar to mulatto), and a *moreno* (Black); the rest must have been of white or *trigueño* (sunburned mestizo) complexion. We know little about the occupations of the victims: among the male victims we find *pulperos,* ranchers, artists, peons, bakers, peasants, and policemen; the occupation of the female victims was not recorded.

Most executions took place near the site where the murder was committed. Of thirty-four sentences recorded, twenty-three corresponded to middle-size rural towns such as Salto, Arrecifes, Tandil, Dolores, and Azul.[13] Death sentences in Buenos Aires were less frequent (11 out of 34). Generally, the executions were carried out in the central square of these towns. The town's neighbors were invited to attend through signs posted on poles. The pedagogy of death, however, was intended for a wider audience, namely, the peasants of the surrounding district. Considered a territory where the legacy of the Rosas period was still strong, the countryside was also seen as the repository of rebellious traditions and of a culture hostile to progress. Horrible rural crimes, as interpreted by judges, represented an enactment of the "barbarism" left by an epoch of terror and violence.

In the form they were carried out, these executions were no different from those of the Rosas era. After a priest delivered his sermon, the condemned was placed on a stool or bench *(banquillo)* and shot by a firing squadron. Usually, he was offered the alternative of being blindfolded during the execution. After the shooting, the dead body was hanged from a pole or placed on an elevated wooden structure (*patíbulo*). Here it remained exposed to the public gaze for between four and eight hours. Only those sentenced for crimenes aleves were subject to the hanging and exhibition of the dead bodies; the rest were sentenced to death by shooting but not exposed afterward.[14] Another carry-over from the Rosas period was the system of "lottery." In the cases where more than one felon was sentenced to death, a lottery decided which one would be executed. The rest generally had their lives spared (their sentences were commuted) but were compelled to watch the execution. To add suspense and drama to the spectacle, the lucky ones turned into privileged observers of exemplary justice.

One of the main objectives of the hangings was their public nature. Executions were public spectacles in which the liberal state communicated to its citizenry important lessons of governance. In the district where the condemned was to be hanged, judges ordered that sufficient notice of the execution be posted. The local public, particularly propertied residents, were encouraged to witness the ceremony. The judges who sentenced Santiago Molina and Loreto Cejas, for example, wanted the whole *vecindario* (neighborhood) of Dolores and its surroundings to observe the event and ordered, consequently, the distribution of execution notices in all towns of the department. Though broadly distributed, the invitation excluded people who were not *vecinos* (neighbors), mainly transients and travelers.[15] No doubt judges were trying to prevent the formation of riotous crowds, or the attendance of relatives and friends of the condemned.

The short time the bodies were exposed was related to the memory of earlier hangings, during the Rosas era, in which the crowds either desecrated the bodies of the executed or showed sympathy for the felons' plight.[16] The degradation or abuse of bodily parts evoked the cruelty, profanity, and excesses of the civil war, aspects of a history liberals wanted to leave in the past. Under the reign of freedom, the bodies of the executed had to be whole and untouched. They had to separate these visions from those associated with the previous regime: decapitated bodies rotting on the sidewalks and heads exposed on pikes. In addition, short exposures reflected the "parsimony of violence" that liberals associated with democratic regimes. A liberal regime had to avoid inflicting a punishment considered disproportionate with the felon's crime. The exhibition of bodies served the purpose of establishing the law in the eyes of the public, but a prolonged exhibition would have projected the wrong image.

The way in which the executions were carried out was the same as during the Rosas period, except in two respects: the time the bodies were exposed, and the publicity given to the event. During the Rosas period, the bodies of the executed were exhibited for at least half a day, generally more. The victims were generally shot in the morning, and their bodies remained exposed to the public view until sundown. Also during the Rosas administration, the public nature of the executions depended on the nature of the crime committed. If the crime was desertion, the execution was carried out within the quarters of a garrison, and the public was not allowed to witness it (except for those who "won" the lottery). In cases of murder, theft, kidnapping, and other grave crimes, Rosas ordered the death sentence, but this did not always result in a public execution.

Considering the number of executions in the two periods, the differences were not very significant. According to the most reliable figures, the number of official public executions ordered by Governor Rosas (not including the shooting of *unitario* military officers or the killing of indigenous peoples) reached fifty-two.[17] Of these, twenty-four were military deserters executed within regiments or frontier garrisons (hence, events not open to the public). The rest (28) were individuals accused of a variety of crimes (9 for homicide, 8 for robbery, 3 for assault resulting in wounds, 3 for political reasons, 2 for fleeing prison, 1 for vagrancy, and 2 for various felonies).[18]

More importantly, Rosas and the post-Caseros leadership shared the same belief on the necessity and efficacy of capital punishment — no matter how different things were in terms of political assassinations, confiscation, and banishment, or in the use of the justice system for recruiting purposes. To be sure, they applied this principle to different criminals: Rosas used it to scare deserters, unitarios, thieves, and other law offenders; the post-Caseros leadership reserved capital punishment for the mazorqueros of the past regime and for common murderers.

The Making of a Moral Panic

The judicial experiment with capital punishment found in the liberal press one of its major supporters.[19] The liberal press explicitly applauded the execution of the mazorqueros as a form of legitimate public reparation for the crimes committed by the past dictatorship. Indirectly, it contributed to the creation of an environment of fear, a situation bordering on a moral panic in which capital punishment appeared as necessary for the restoration of social order.[20] Liberal publicists accompanied the transition between executions of political murderers and executions of common murderers, providing the necessary connections between the new "crime wave" and the legacies of the past regime. Informing the public about horrible and aberrant crimes, reminding the public about the violence of the Rosas era and, maintaining public confidence in the new justice system, the liberal press processed and shaped the public interest in support of exemplary punishment.

The siege of Buenos Aires by General Lagos (December 1852–March 1853) reactivated the fears of a resurgence of Rosismo. The countryside, carrying the old federalist banners, was attacking the city in retaliation for the policies of the new liberal government. Urban publicists, to support the liberal cause, portrayed the besieging army as a phantom of the past, an assembly of federalist brutes, given to depravity and cruelty.[21] *El Nacional,* for example, reported acts of incredible savagery committed by Lagos' troops: shootings, degüellos, and castrations, among other atrocities. *La Tribuna* carried the story of an elderly woman being stripped and whipped in front of soldiers on Urquiza's orders. The instrument used, assured the newspaper, was not a regular whip (*chicote*) but a knout (*verga*) used by the Mazorca in Rosista times.[22]

The depiction of the cruelties of *federales* prepared public opinion for future trials against the Rosista leadership. As soon as the siege was lifted, liberal publicists started to demand the trial and punishment of the "assassins of 1840" and the confiscation of all of Rosas's assets.[23] The demand for justice, in view of the recent events, was necessarily limited. Instead of requiring that all the functionaries of the past regime be put on trial, liberals urged the sentencing of the most conspicuous members of the Mazorca: Reyes, Cuitiño, Troncoso, and Badía, among others. It would later become clear that these trials were the linchpin on which liberals would reconstitute public memories in support of their political project.

The capture and trial of the "assassins of 1840" proceeded swiftly — between August and November, the justice system tried the main authors of the killings of 1840 and 1842. Of the nine persons accused of these crimes, five were sentenced to death. During this time, newspapers encouraged the public to engage in the trials, denouncing the cruelties committed by the accused against the victims' families or the losses of property suffered as a consequence of their actions.[24] The newspapers also reported the condition and state of mind of the accused, celebrating their death in advance.[25] The readers responded with enthusiasm to the news: according to historian Sáenz Quesada, "[T]he people massed in front of the newspaper offices to buy the special editions which detailed the vicious assassinations of the Mazorca."[26]

Soon, the public knew about the death sentences of Badía, Troncoso, Suárez, Cuitiño, and Alén. The liberal press backed these decisions with enthusiasm. *La Tribuna* warned its readers neither to forget the crimes of the Mazorca nor to pardon the assassins, and urged the public to support the death penalty as the only instrument available to contain popular violence.[27] In October 1853 *El Nacional* published the full sentence condemning the mazorqueros, underlining the importance of the judicial decision. According to this decree, the execution of Badía and Troncoso taught a lesson to the lower classes, a lesson that could prevent in the future the repetition of "tyranny."[28] *Los Debates* celebrated the execution of mazorqueros as a popular, democratic achievement, phrasing the events in words similar to those used by the judiciary.[29] The public executions of political criminals would serve as a chastisement and warning to common criminals.

The satirical periodical *El Diablo* put the news of the executions in harsher terms: Rosas's assassins had been given a "passport to hell" where the Devil was eagerly waiting for them.[30]

From October to December, porteños witnessed two executions each month, in a climate described by the liberal press as the vindication of republican principles.[31] In November, Floro Vázquez, an officer of the rebel forces, was tried and sentenced for the brutal death of two young officers of the National Guard. *El Nacional,* which had followed the case, published the death sentence against Vázquez and reported his execution on November 24, 1853. The writer remarked on the cold-bloodedness and serenity of the accused in the face of death: how he asked to address the public, how he threw his jacket into the crowd, and how he blindfolded himself and laughed before the shooting.[32] The newspaper did not comment how rapid the whole process had been, the execution being staged only three days after the sentence was passed. In late December, the executions of Ciriaco Cuitiño and Leandro Alén followed; these were the last offenders executed for political crimes. Henceforth, the scaffold would be used to teach the public about the excesses and treachery of common criminals.

Gradually, the press prepared the public to accept the notion that personal violence was on the rise, even though the province was on the road to political pacification. Newspapers, which had started dealing mostly with political and institutional issues, soon added a column about crime. Some murder cases, considered extreme in their cruelty and cold-bloodedness, were singled out as news and reported in gruesome detail. The killing of an entire family, the murder of a pregnant woman, or the coldbloodedness of an assassin produced an outburst of public condemnation which soon turned the particular case into a cause célèbre.

To establish the new public danger, newspapers resorted to impressionistic accounts of life in the countryside.[33] For example, *La Reforma Pacífica* described the situation in Quilmes in 1856:

> *A las 12 del día se asesina un hombre o se le dá puñaladas, y los malhechores se burlan de la justicia, porque no se les persigue, porque no se les castiga. Al entrarse el sol, ya no se puede tener abierta una casa de familia por los escándalos y riñas que tienen esos vagabundos, sin más ocupación que la del cuchillo en una mano y el naipe en la otra.*

At noon, a man is murdered or stabbed and wrongdoers scoff at the justice (system), because nobody prosecutes them. At dusk, a family house can no longer remain open, due to the scandals and quarrels provoked by vagrants, those who have no other occupation than (holding) the knife in one hand and the cards in the other.[34]

The new insecurity to citizens' persons and property coincided with massive Indian attacks on the frontier. Liberal newspapers, nonetheless, chose to focus on the rise of personal crimes among lower-class *cristianos*. Their main strategy was to bring to the light—to put before the eyes of the citizenry—the dark side of rural popular culture. To this effect, nothing produced a greater effect than reporting *crímenes aleves*.

The murder of the *estanciero* (landowner) Planes, his wife, two daughters, and a peon in the district of Ranchos in November 1855 caught the public's attention. The knowledge that a whole family was "executed" by peons of the same ranch and that a young peon was killed while sleeping attracted public curiosity, not only because the crimes were brutal and cold-blooded, but also because they were difficult to comprehend. The motivation of this multiple murder and theft did not square with the brutality of its execution.[35] And, more importantly for urban residents, the event showed the enormous potential for violence hidden in an apparently peaceful countryside.[36]

The celebrity of a crime, explained *El Judicial,* was due to "the ferocity of killers, to the victims' defenseless condition, and to the bloody details of the execution."[37] The case of Raymundo Reyes, who killed a fellow peon with a burning log, disfiguring his face, or the case of Juan Sosa, who assassinated his lover's husband in front of the latter's wife and children, provoked horror and repulsion among readers. Certain spaces, such as the ranch, the farm, and the pulpería, appeared as repositories of potential violence. Among crimes considered aberrant, none were more intriguing and repulsive than those committed against women. The killing of pregnant women, the rape and kidnapping of young girls, and passionate crimes involving jealous husbands immediately caught the attention of the public.

Crime enigmas were particularly suitable news. When the body of a young lady (Doña Edelvira Iriarte y Rivadavia) was found on the banks of the river, the public found in the case a fertile terrain to cultivate all kinds of stories.[38] The press, stimulated by "public interest," tried to solve the mystery, providing information to complement the picture produced by gossip and rumor. The cooperation between the public voice and the press alerted the justice system to the case and kept interest high.[39] Public excitement was such that the Chamber of Justice made its employees work during Easter in order to prepare the case.[40]

Although Buenos Aires was still closer to a *gran aldea* (large village) than to a metropolis, publicists found in the city a brutality and perversion more appropriate to a London, Paris, or other major European city. The origin of such violence was, of course, the penetration of rural culture into the city. Not by coincidence, the panic about crime grew immediately after the rebel forces ended the siege of Buenos Aires. The second half of 1853 inaugurated a golden age for criminals, according to M. Sáenz Quesada. By 1854, the moral panic was already established. Incredible stories ran across the city, spreading fear among residents. These stories spoke of gangs of children assaulting jewelry stores, of delinquents who undressed their victims in the street, of rings of professional robbers (such as that of Domingo Parodi, the hunchback), of immigrant horticulturalists brutally attacked on their way to the market. In this context of fear, publicists demanded the restoration of hangings and lashes for common robbers — punishments that were at odds with the new liberal sensibilities and contrary to judicial practice.[41] By 1855 porteños were demanding greater controls on brothels, black dancing academies, and produce markets as a means of curtailing the perceived crime epidemic. Besieged by the dark forces of rural culture, the city — the refuge of civilized democracy — seemed unable to offer security of property and life to its citizens.

Why this new interest of liberals in crime? The question had a political importance. The lack of protection in the face of barbarous attacks was a major weakness of the new democratic regime, for it meant that the property of families and of businesses (the two basic supports of a political regime based on possessive individualism) could not be safeguarded. This defenseless condition was particularly threatening when native delinquents discharged their vengeance on immigrants. That is why *Los Debates,* a political newspaper, called the attention of its readership to the "Crime of San Vicente." An immigrant businessman, Sr. Ponzatti, lost all his capital when two masked individuals had entered his property, barbarously beaten his black maid, and burned his store to the ground.[42] Crime could potentially stop immigration, one of the pillars of the liberal project for reconstructing the nation.

To an extent, then, the press was undermining the liberal project, painting a picture of growing personal insecurity just when the liberal leadership was claiming some progress in the reconstruction of republican institutions. Some publicists, aware of this contradiction, tried to find some answers. The solution to this riddle was to locate the danger outside, that is, in the countryside, and secondly, to blame the past dictatorship for the resurgence of personal violence. The thesis of the Rosas legacy, used to execute the mazorqueros, could be now employed in explaining the rise in criminality. Whereas the new republican institutions (including the new National Guard) were able to contain the resurgence of federalists as a political threat, the cultural heritage of Rosismo was still intact.[43] This meant, among other things, a propensity for brutality and violence in rural areas that was hard to control.

El Judicial found that several factors were responsible for the rise in criminality, among them: the habits formed during the dictatorship, the increased number of rural taverns (places of a wild sociability, beyond the reach of the state), the generalized use of the knife to solve personal differences, and the lack of religious and civil education among the lower classes.[44] Among these factors, the heritage of Rosismo was given a prominent place in the liberal press.

Making the connection between horrible crimes and the past dictatorship was, in some cases quite natural. The murder of a pregnant woman and his two children in Chapaleufú in 1856 brought back the memory of Camila O'Gorman, a pregnant upper-class woman executed by Rosas's orders in 1848. Without mentioning the case, *El Judicial*, could blame the murder on the Rosas legacy by simply activating collective memories:

> *Es deplorable, desconsuela ver reaparecer en tan corto tiempo delitos que por su crueldad y barbarie, parecen agenos a la época de moralidad y progreso, de que tanto nos ufanamos. Sólo en tiempo de la dictadura se vieron crímenes parecidos a éstos, los que aún duermen velados por el misterio, y se atribuyeron entonces a la política sanguinaria del dictador.*

> It is deplorable, it is afflictive to see in so short a time felonies reappear that, due to their cruelty and barbarism, seem alien to the age of morality and progress that we take so much pride in. Only in the times of the dictatorship have we witnessed similar crimes, those that still sleep under the veil of mystery and were then attributed to the sanguinary policy of the dictator.[45]

To the editor of *El Judicial*, even minor crimes were taken as signs that the monster of anarchy was awakening. In April 1855, the newspaper reported various incidents involving soldiers that disturbed the tranquility of the town of San Nicolás.[46] A soldier shooting an officer, a fight between two soldiers in a wedding, soldiers' threatening and killing immigrants during carnival night — all pointed to a situation of tolerated illegality resembling the years of the Mazorca.

To the liberal elite, the connection between the past regime and the current wave of violent crimes was clear. To the rest of the population, this was not self-evident: because most of the population was attuned to local news, transmitted via rumor, violent crimes committed elsewhere had a minor impact on the life of each locality. More importantly, peasants tended to associate the fall of Rosas with a decline in number of requisitions and forced recruitment, that is, with a time of pacification. To convince them that these were indeed violent times must have required an important effort. Over the course of the five years that followed Caseros, liberals spent rivers of ink to establish in the popular consciousness the connection between the past dictatorship and the current rise in criminality.

A renewal of the book industry served to make available an increasing number of titles dealing with the past regime. The same year Sarmiento's *Campaña en el Ejército Grande* was made available through the newspapers (1853), *El Nacional* published Ascasubi's poem *La Refalosa,* probably the most enduring condemnation of the violence of Rosismo.[47] Also in 1853 the Imprenta de Mayo advertised the publication of the works of Rivera Indarte, one of the most prolific and consistent critics of Rosas.[48] Other publications such as *Rosas y su hija en la Quinta de Olivos* (1852), *Episodios Sangrientos del año 40* (1856), *El prisionero de Santos Lugares* (1857), or *Los mártires de Buenos Aires* (1857) contributed to the enterprise of reactualizing the memories of the dictatorship. In addition to printed materials, liberals made available visual images of Rosista leaders as a means of focusing popular indignation on concrete persons. In the Fussone brothers' warehouse, where a large portrait of Antonino Reyes was exhibited, the public went to see one of the most powerful men of the past regime.[49] Associating portraits with crimes, liberals hoped to sharpen the public's memory of the "villains" being discussed in the news.

Once established, the "Rosista legacy of violence" could serve two purposes. It could help people distinguish clearly between a democratic present and a dictatorial past, and it could assist the public in understanding the present rise in crime as a sign of the unfinished project of civilizing the pampas. The scaffold served these political objectives well. A visible demonstration of the effectiveness of the state in the punishment of crime, the executions gave legitimacy to the reformed justice system. Moreover, the violence displayed was public, institutionally sanctioned, and bounded. This differentiated the new regime from the past dictatorship. Because most of the criminals were from rural origins, urbanites could also contemplate on the hanging poles the remnants of a culture still uncivilized, brutal and violent. As a containment of the barbarity of rural life and as the exorcism of a tyrannical past, executions provided an important service to the liberal project of reconstruction.

The Politics of Death

For the liberal leadership that controlled the politics of the city after 1852, capital punishment was a necessary instrument for political stabilization but also a medicine to be used carefully and in small doses. When in 1853 *La Tribuna* demanded the death of the "assassins of 1840" as a precondition for the forging of a new political union, many liberals took as self-evident the connection between capital punishment and a liberal-republican regime. Institutional and symbolic reasons cemented this connection. The pedagogy of death promised to contain popular excesses and, therefore, diminished the risk of institutional instability (the possibility of the "people" overthrowing elected governments). The vanishing of leading figures of the Mazorca also separated the ideal liberal regime from the past experience of Rosismo.[50] Establishing that distance—putting an end to the era of caudillos and civil wars—was crucial for the success of the experiment of refounding the republic along liberal principles.

Buenos Aires, claimed the liberals, was leading a political regeneration that required denouncing the violent culture of the past, establishing the legitimacy of the justice system, and reestablishing the public's trust in political institutions. Capital punishment assisted in the attainment of all of these objectives. Deactivating the old antinomies (unitarios vs. federales) required the staging of public dramas that marked the end of an era and healed the wounds of the political community. Watching the mazorqueros hang from poles, citizens would realize that the time of civil wars, the period of polarization of opinion was over and would start building the social and political "fusion" necessary to the functioning of a republican democracy.[51] The refoundation of a republican order demanded first the reconstitution of a moral community, lacerated and divided by eighteen years of dictatorship. The return of public morale would create a climate of cooperation in which it would be possible to pass institutional reforms leading to enhanced citizen control of government.

Like the period of anarchy which led to the formation of the Pax Rosista (1820–1835), this was a time of transition, a period in which it was necessary to calm the passions in order to institute a stable system of governance. Like Governor Rosas, post-Caseros liberals had to reconstitute "order" as a precondition for the establishment of political and legal authority.[52] Hence, it is not remarkable that both Rosas and the liberals considered public executions as a guarantee of the stability of government. But Rosista and liberal conceptions of the political utility of the scaffold were different.[53] For Rosas, the nation was engaged in a holy war whose ultimate goal was the extermination of unitarios. In a republic threatened by domestic agitators and foreign forces, state-induced violence was a condition for the restoration of order.[54] The war was total, and so was the violence. The post-Caseros porteño leadership, on the other hand, had a more parsimonious view of violence. State violence could produce the new social and political amalgam required for establishing the "republic of freedom" only if used in limited doses. Under a liberal model, the building of new institutions (electoral methods, communications, municipalities, schools, national militias, tax-collection systems) necessitated a degree of consent from the citizenry. Stretched between the demands of authority and the imperatives of freedom, liberals conceived of state violence as selective, contained, and exemplary.

In a liberal republic, state violence could never be extreme. It had to remain within bounds, in the same way that the power of the executive was bounded. It was only a means for directing public attention to the double dangers of a past always ready to reemerge (caudillo politics) and of a culture still uncivilized and violent (rural culture). This explains the parsimony of violence exercised by liberals.[55] Although liberals wanted to tell a political message through the bodies of the executed, they felt uncomfortable about large numbers of rustic spectators. What mattered was the other type of publicity, the dissemination of news through the newspaper, a publicity targeted mainly to urban inhabitants with reading skills. This was the audience liberals wanted to instruct. A plethora of publications about crime (and about the Rosista era) revealed the nature of the democracy imagined by liberals: a regime reserved for the participation of an informed and civilized citizenry, preferably urban, proud of its struggles against dictatorship, and scornful of everything relating to rural culture.

The judges who ordered capital sentences did not wish the public to associate liberal governments with an unbounded authority to inflict damage. They preferred sanitized executions, devoid of cruelty and as little exposed to people's reactions (festive or riotous) as possible. In particular, they wanted to prevent bodies from being mocked, touched, profaned by the crowds. In a representative democracy, political sovereignty was entrusted to government and could not be directly exercised by the people. People's interaction with the bodies of the executed (hanging vegetables on them, damaging organs, spitting on them) was not only uncivilized and brutal but also conveyed a dangerous proximity between political sovereignty and authority. This proximity was a sign of the inarticulate democracy of the Rosas period, a symptom of a regime that had exploited popular excesses in exchange for adulation and loyalty.

Whereas the terror of the Rosas era consistently targeted unitarios, army deserters, and common delinquents, the public violence of the new regime shifted its target quite suddenly from political assassins to common murderers. Though the trial and execution of the "assassins of 1840" seemed at the time as epoch-making events, in the long run the executions of common murderers surpassed those of political criminals in a proportion close to 7:1. Why was this so? Why this shift in criminal policy? Why did the execution of common murders become so important for the political legitimacy of the regime? Was there a change in the liberal perception of social and political threats?

The different treatment the courts accorded to common and political criminals are comprehensible in the context of a profound public debate about the legacies of Rosismo. After 1854 judges began to exonerate political criminals from all guilt. Once the murders of 1840 and 1842 had been apparently elucidated, judges moved to reject new charges brought against other functionaries of the past regime.[56] In a political environment charged with mutual accusations and suspicions—many of them based on alleged participation in the past dictatorship—judges considered that it was best to put the issue to rest.[57] Except for a minority of doctrinaire unitarios, the rest of the population was suspect of having assisted the Rosas regime in one way or another, and this was dangerous to the stability of the political system. If everybody was (or could have been) a *rosín* (a Rosista sympathizer), then nobody was endowed with the public virtues required for elective positions. To calm these muddy waters, judges found a simple and clever solution: Rosas was to be blamed for all the violence of the past, so that all other authorities or employees might be excused for their crimes.

This solution was consistent with the "truth" liberals wanted to affirm about the past dictatorship: a sort of political absolutism, in which policemen, bureaucrats, and local justices had unwillingly followed irrational and criminal orders. In a way, all reverted back to the center of the political model: to Rosas himself. This view of the past privileged a cultural perspective that bestowed the "federalist plebe" with all the attributes of barbarism. On this point, judges and liberal publicists coincided. The Rosista legacy consisted of two contradictory elements: passivity in the face of tyrannical authority and a natural propensity for violence. Borrowing from a model that had previously explained the limits and possibilities of the republic (Sarmiento's *Facundo*), liberals arranged their arguments so that the ultimate explanation was always the same: barbarism.[58]

This discourse of the legacy of Rosismo — a discourse centering on irredeemable subaltern political subjects — impregnated liberal political debate. The memories of the Dictatorship were always part of the arguments, coloring all explanations and discussions. It was Rosas's fault, argued *El Judicial,* that the popular classes were left without the benefits of education and religious instruction. To fabricate republican virtue out of this raw material — a rural culture untouched by any civilizing mission — was close to impossible.[59] A similar argument, frequently deployed, stated that rural subalterns were accustomed to violence. They had made their livelihood always in contact with knives and blood. They had killed unitarios and Indians with passion and brutality. Violence was already ingrained in habits and mental attitudes.[60]

A violent popular culture was an obstacle to the construction of a democratic polity. Violent crimes could inhibit immigration, spread insecurity among property owners, and interfere with military recruitment. Naturally, an increase in interpersonal violence undermined the association between peace and progress that was at the root of liberal ideology. Worse still, a violent peasantry might demand a greater participation in the making of democracy, reinstating caudillos more in tune with their lifestyles and conceptions of governance. How could these would-be citizens of the republic respect a neighbor's rights and the laws of the nation if they could not control their own passions?

That is why the attention of publicists concentrated on violent rural crimes. Here were the clues to understanding the past dictatorship, that combination of terror and popularity that was so difficult to comprehend and whose understanding was so crucial for any viable project of institutional reform. Popular passivity in the face of strong leadership and rural violence were difficult to eradicate. Popular rural culture, interpreted within the contours of the Rosista legacy, seemed to provide innumerable examples of a lack of self-control and a propensity for rebellious politics. Owing to its unbounded nature, rural culture was a menace to the whole edifice of stable and elective government.

Prisons, Memory, Governability, and Gender

To be sure, there were other arguments used for sustaining the necessity of capital punishment during this period of transition. One that was frequently used asserted that, despite the best intentions of magistrates, the lack of modern prisons made it impossible to substitute the death penalty for more humane forms of punishment. This was the argument used by the Superior Tribunal of Justice in 1855, on the occasion of its annual report to the provincial assembly.[61] Before the construction of a modern penitentiary in 1876 (the Penitenciaría de Buenos Aires), it was very unlikely that prisoners would complete long sentences: they either died of disease or escaped. Besides, no prison before this time had the facilities required for cellular isolation, the modern method of seclusion.

The question of prisons — the need to ensure the humane treatment of prisoners — played on liberal sensibilities and was intimately connected with the question of capital punishment. During the 1850s, the government made various attempts to improve the condition of existing prisons. Though little progress was made, at least the issue received greater attention than before. In part, this was motivated by the public's renewed concern for the fate of prisoners. Judges started to visit prisons more regularly; religious services were introduced in the Cárcel Pública; and charities and the public were invited to interact more frequently with inmates.[62] These interactions, in the end, would result in greater sympathy with prisoners and work against the strict logic of capital punishment. Even so, the lack of modern prisons worked against the possibility of abolishing the death penalty.

This practical reason worked in tandem with the pedagogical one, the need to provide a useful object lesson to lower-class actors. Thus, the new penal consensus—reflected in the policy of executing certain criminals while ensuring clean prisons and good treatment to the rest—was not the result of expert opinion or penal theories. It emerged, rather, as a distillation of anxieties and desires derived from the experience of the dictatorship. Both the judges who extended death sentences to common murderers and the publicists who contributed to create the crime panic shared the view that they were living in a postdictatorial period. They endeavored to understand the past in order not to repeat it. Thus, judges were particularly sensible to similarities between the crímenes aleves of the present and the state violence of the past.

The comparison Judge Olmos made between the murder committed by Molina and Heredia in 1856 with the central scene of El Matadero, the public slaughterhouse, exemplifies this almost compulsive connection with recovering public memory. The liberal elite, in its search for a new order, found any trace of the old regime threatening: a whip used by the hated Mazorca, the red ribbon in a soldier's jacket, a peasant shouting "Viva Rosas," policemen threatening degüello to foreigners. Death sentences were grounded in deep-rooted anxieties about the incorporation of lower-class members of society to the enterprise of democracy and progress. These anxieties were part of the Rosas legacy and therefore constituted an integral element in the reconstruction of memory carried out by the post-Caseros leadership.

Public executions revealed serious weaknesses and contradictions in the liberal project of state building. To posit death as a precondition of political institutionalization entailed the recognition of grave problems of governability. We need only recall that, at the peak of public executions (1855–56), pampa Indians launched massive invasions against frontier towns. The provincial state was unable to generate enough military muscle to repress them. Also, contemporary conflicts with the government of the Confederation (over questions of custom revenues, river navigation, and sovereignty) could easily lead to new military confrontations. The Lagos rebellion had demonstrated how vulnerable the city was to the concerted attacks of its own countryside. The National Guard detachments proved motivated enough to fend off Lagos's rural militias but were useless in a fight against other provincial forces or indigenous tribes. How could the province be governable if the old polarities and confrontations (hence, the menace of civil war) still persisted? How could a weak state, with reduced military capabilities, guarantee the right to life and property for its citizens? The death penalty was the temporary solution to this lack of state capacity — it was a show of strength that covered up the weakness of the new administration.

Furthermore, the doctrines invented by the courts to exorcise the Rosista past ("generalized savagery" and "uncontrollable fear") stood in tension with the new republic imagined by liberals. The construction of a more democratic political system required an effective and credible system of justice, one that did not leave aberrant crimes in impunity.[63] The handful of show trials of the mazorqueros revealed the weakness of the new state to deal effectively with the past. This weakness was a major drawback for a regime interested in granting security to property and life. Absolving without a trial those presumed of political crimes left the impression among the public that they were living among dangerous criminals. This impression had unforeseeable consequences for the political system. With their pasts left unmolested, old rosines could return to the political arena with a vengeance. Conversely, any liberal candidate could be suspected of having an involvement with the past dictatorship. In an environment of generalized distrust and suspicion, in which libel and defamation became effective political weapons, public trust in the representative system was bound to decline.

If the justice system was unable to distinguish the adepts of tyranny from freedom-loving citizens, the indictment of post-Caseros liberals of the political culture of the Rosas era appeared to be mere rhetoric. In order to make independent and informed political choices, electors needed to know who had committed what crimes during the Dictatorship. Accusations of rural barbarism (heaped upon Rosistas) juxtaposed with claims of distinction and civilization (accorded to porteño liberals) were not enough. The fear of a resurgence of Rosismo still characterized the politics of Buenos Aires. The Lagos rebellion was still too near to dispel the belief that porteño liberals were an urban minority surrounded by a majority of rural federalists.

Finally, there was the gender question, the crucial aspect that turned upside-down the existing consensus about the death penalty. The case of female murderer Clorinda Sarracán initiated a process of gradual but effective decline in the use of the death penalty as punishment for murderers. Sarracán, a woman accused of the brutal murder of her husband in complicity with his lover, had been sentenced to death. As rumors circulated that she was pregnant, the public turned against the scheduled execution. A petition signed by seven thousand residents forced the Buenos Aires legislature to suspend the execution. The Superior Tribunal of Justice, considering that the legislature had overstepped its own jurisdiction, refused to review other cases contemplating the death penalty. Thus, the suspension of Sarracán's execution prevented the completion of other cases, preparing the terrain for a congressional debate on the abolition of the death penalty. The public opinion laboriously built by liberal publicists finally turned against its creators.

The public's solidarity with the female murderer surprised the liberals, and took away many of the arguments they had used to sustain the need for capital punishment. Suddenly, the death penalty appeared to offend "other" liberal sensibilities. Moreover, the case brought a new element into the discussion about the death penalty: the voices of immigrants defending their culture in the public sphere. The argument put forward by *L'Emigration,* an immigrants' newspaper, that "it was not democratic to kill a woman" added a new dimension to the problem. The immigrants who had participated actively in the defense of Buenos Aires now wanted to be heard on an issue they considered of vital import: the power of the state to inflict damage on women. For them, this was an issue related to the promises of the liberal state vis-à-vis property and propriety. The state, they argued, was reaching too far beyond its own sphere when it wanted to punish women publicly. This was, most certainly, a right reserved to men in the private domain.[64] The liberal state, according to male immigrants, ought to respect families in the same way it respected private property. To violate the bodies of women was an inadmissible intrusion of the state in the male private domain.

To an extent, liberals had prepared the ground for this masculine reaction. The assertion that the Rosista state had violated the privacy of the home was an important indictment used by liberals against the past dictatorship. Rosas's agents had arrested unitarios in their private residences, had killed them in view of their families, and many times, in order to further the humiliation, had raped, kidnapped, or killed the female members of the family.[65] For liberals, the home was the most sacred place; and it was the gravest sin of the dictatorship to have profaned this sanctuary.[66] Implicit in this motif of liberal discourse was the promise that a liberal state would never do that, that it would respect the sanctity of home and the sovereignty of male heads of household over their daughters and wives. Thus, when the immigrant press demanded the concession of this right, liberals had no other choice but to concede.

The execution of a woman, if not prevented, might produce a heady, dangerous mixture in the popular imagination. The situation of Clorinda Sarracán reminded the public of the tribulations and violent death of Camila O'Gorman, one of the martyrs of Rosismo, executed in 1848. The comparison acted as a symbolic detonator of public sensibilities. The memory of Camila endangered the ideological edifice that liberals had built between themselves and the recent past. Rosas's violence had not stopped at the womb of a pregnant woman. Would the liberal government do the same? Liberals in the end were not prepared to go that far for the sake of the preservation of order. They needed to avoid any association with a violent past that they had helped to establish (through public executions and the press) in public memory. Faced with new constituencies and aware of changing public sensibilities to the executions, liberal judges gradually rid the state of the burden of the spectacles of the scaffold. They suspended the hanging of bodies, prolonged the stay of execution period, raised the conditions for death sentences, and in the end, abolished the whole category of crímenes aleves.

Notes

1 H. S. Ferns, *Gran Bretaña y Argentina en el siglo XIX* (Buenos Aires: Solar-Hachette, 1968), p. 287.

2 "Las ejecuciones en la historia argentina," *Qué Sucedió en Siete Días,* 88 (June 19, 1956): 6–7.

3 For the porteño authorities, limitations contained in a constitution they had not signed were of no significance.

4 The number of death sentences for crímenes aleves were: eleven in 1855, eight in 1856, four in 1857, three in 1858, one in 1859, two in 1860, two in 1861, none in 1862, four in 1863, and one in 1864. Information taken from *El Judicial,* 1855–1864.

5 Abelardo Levaggi, *Historia del derecho penal argentino* (Buenos Aires: Perrot, 1978), pp. 135–136.

6 Early on, we must remember, the new government confiscated Rosas's assets. The confrontation between liberal porteños and the Urquicistas concentrated on the question of the legal or illegal means by which Rosas's fortune was obtained. His responsibility in the assassinations, torture, and other forms of violence exercised by his administration were considered several years later.

7 *"Que no habiéndose probado a López otro crimen, ó hecho que demuestre perversidad de*

alma en una época en que la crueldad y la violencia eran la disposición habitual de los hombres de su condición y principios políticos, debe darse a las circunstancias que le desfavorecen una interpretación más benigna." "Not having proven any other felony against Lopez, or any action revealing the perversity of his soul at a time in which cruelty and violence were the habitual dispositions of men of his condition and political principles, a more benign interpretation should be granted to the circumstances that are against him." *El Judicial,* May 29, 1855. Translation by the author.

8 "*Que siendo López un empleado que custodiaba a Curuchete y debía presentarlo vivo o muerto, no está en el riguroso deber de probar su excepción, cuando después de un acontecimiento como el que motiva este proceso, pasado sin testigos, asegura que se vió necesitado a ejecutar el hecho para salvar su responsabilidad, que en la época de Rosas no tenía límites en semejantes casos; y tiene derecho por consiguiente e que toda duda a este respecto se resuelva en su favor.*" "Being that Lopez was an employee who guarded Curuchete and had to deliver him dead or alive, he is not under the strict obligation to prove his exemption, when after an event such as the one which motives this process, without witnesses, he assures us that he found himself in the necessity to execute that action to save his responsibility, which in Rosas's time had no limit in such cases; hence, he has the right that every doubt in this regard be resolved in his favor." Ibid. Translation by author.

9 "Pleito que, ya, lleva 18 años," *El Judicial,* October 20, 1869.

10 Ironically, the same liberal leadership, which seemed so interested in unveiling the crimes of the past dictatorship, was reluctant to prosecute all the authors of political assassinations during the Rosas era. Valentín Alsina, president of the lawyers' association and member of the Cámara de Justicia was also a publicist, directly involved in the recreation of the memory of the crimes of Rosas.

11 According to the information provided by *El Judicial,* the number of death sentences passed between 1855 and 1864 amounted to thirty-six. This figure probably contains an underestimation of the order of 10 to 20 percent. As some judges failed to pass the information to the editor of *El Judicial,* the newspaper was not confident that the death sentences published were all that took place. For the crucial period 1852–54, we do not have a reliable figure of the number of times the judges used capital punishment.

12 ". . . y aún la forma misma del asesinato, en la que, equiparándose la víctima a un irracional, fue llevado a la rastra al matadero." ". . . and even the very form of the murder, in which the victim, treated as an animal, was dragged along to the slaughterhouse." *El Judicial,* June 27, 1856.

13 It seems as if only the *pueblos* (medium-size towns) could hold this type of spectacle. When Raymundo Reyes was shot and hanged, his body was exposed in the square of Dolores because the place where he committed the murder, Tuyú, was still not a town. *El Judicial,* February 23, 1856. The same happened when Santiago Molina and Loreto Cejas were executed; the event was scheduled in Dolores because Pila was not yet a town.

14 Victoriano Pacheco, sentenced to death for murder and assault in 1855, was shot in Independence Square and then buried. His body was not exposed to the public gaze.

15 In other cases, execution notices were distributed to the justices of other districts but were not posted, so as to avoid unwelcome visitors. The order of execution of Tomás Ordoñez prescribed: "The chief of police [of Tandil] should print enough copies, and order them to be posted in public sites, and have them circulated with equal effect to the justices of peace of the countryside the same day of the execution or afterward . . ." *El Judicial*, July 11, 1855.

16 A fictionalized narrative of how crowds desecrated the bodies of the Reynafé brothers, the assassins of Gen. Facundo Quiroga, can be found in Eduardo Gutiérrez, *Juan Manuel de Rosas: los dramas del terror* (Buenos Aires: Harpón, 1944).

17 In May 1865 *El Judicial* published a summary of the punishments inflicted by Rosas, taken from the sentences of the trials. According to this source, 315 were sentenced to death, 1,411 to forced service in the army, 176 went to prison, 93 received whippings, 93 were declared subject to persecution, elimination, and pillage (the *unitarios*), one was sentenced to banishment, and one to forced labor. In total, there were 2,090 registered victims of the past tyranny. Among those sentenced to death the newspaper included: 124 Indians shot by the military in a public square in 1836, eleven unitario military officers shot in San Nicolás 1831 and Arroyo del Medio 1839, as well as many murders committed by the Mazorca at night and without any written order. A greatly exaggerated account of Rosista violence was Rivera Indarte's *Tablas de Sangre:* the author claimed that Rosas had killed by degüello 1,765 persons, had shot 1,393, had assassinated 722, and had poisoned four. In addition, there were 14,920 who were killed in combat. Ernesto Quiroga Micheo, "Los Mazorqueros ¿Gente decente o asesinos?" *Todo es Historia* 308 (March 1993): 47.

18 "Sentencia contra Rosas," *El Judicial*, March 5, 1865.

19 I refer to newspapers like Sarmiento's *El Nacional*, Mitre's *Los Debates*, Calvo's *La Reforma Pacífica*, and *La Tribuna*.

20 For the concept of moral panic, see Stanley Cohen, *Folk Devils and Moral Panics* (New York: St. Martin's Press, 1980).

21 The guardsmen defending the city, instead, were portrayed as self-controlled and disciplined citizens-in-arms fighting for "freedom."

22 *La Tribuna*, August 25, 1853.

23 The editorial of *La Tribuna* of August 9, 1853, read: "*El pueblo de Buenos Aires pide a voces el castigo de los asesinos del año 40, en desagravio a la moral pública ultrajada y como único medio de establecer sobre bases seguras la fusión política que el mismo Urquiza ha proclamado . . .*" "The people of Buenos Aires demand in high voice due punishment for the assassins of the year 40, as a vindication of the offended public moral and as the only means for establishing under safe bases the political union proclaimed by Urqiza." Translation by author.

24 *"Llamamos la atención sobre los Edictos Judiciales que se registran en nuestras columnas, citando a todos los que tengan que acusar a esos célebres bandidos, a todos los que tengan que llorar la pérdida de un padre, un hijo, un esposo, una persona querida arrebatada por la alevosía de un puñal asesino, a todos los que se vean privados de sus fortunas adquiridas legalmente, y que hayan sido infamemente despojados por la arbitrariedad y la fuerza bruta. ¡Ciertos estamos que no serán pocas las acusaciones que fulminen contra los bandidos de los años 40 y 42!"* "We call your attention about the Judicial Edicts published in the columns of our newspaper. They summon all those who have something to declare against these infamous bandits, all those who cry the loss of a father, a son, a husband, or a loved one taken away by the traitorous and murderous dagger, all those who were deprived of their legally acquired fortunes and robbed by the arbitrariness of brute force. We are sure that the accusations against the bandits of the years 1840 and 1842 will not be few." *La Tribuna,* August 13, 1853. While Antonino Reyes was in prison, a portrait of him was shown in a merchant's warehouse, so as to familiarize the public with one of the leading figures of the past regime.

25 Under arrest, these "ferocious murderers" seemed tamed, commented *El Nacional,* as if accepting in advance that their time had passed. "La Mazorca," *El Nacional,* March 15, 1853.

26 María Sáenz Quesada, "Crimenes después de Caseros," *Todo es Historia* 85 (June 1974): 36.

27 *"Si no aplicásemos inmediatamente la última pena a esos verdugos, abriríamos para lo futuro las puertas a un mal que difícilmente podríamos contener más tarde; haríamos comprender a los reos que la flojedad, que siempre nos ha perdido, es el Juez que los arrebataría ahora de las manos de la Justicia, y entonces ¿qué habríamos adelantado?"* "If we do not immediately apply the death penalty to these executioners, in the future we would open the doors to an evil that will be difficult to control later; we will be telling those felons that cowardice, the vice which has always made us fall, is the Judge that will rescue them from justice's hands, and then what would we have gained?" *La Tribuna,* August 11, 1853. Translation by author.

28 *"En este sentido, la sentencia de los asesinos Badía y Troncoso, va a contribuir a derramar en el pueblo las sanas doctrinas, que descendiendo hasta las últimas clases de la sociedad acompañadas del ejemplo, harán imposible toda tiranía entre nosotros. Tales son [las doctrinas], que el asesinato no se prescribe jamás, y que hay siempre una mano justiciera que persigue al criminal hasta entregarle atado de pies bajo la cuchilla y que nadie debe obediencia a sus superiores para violar las leyes divinas y humanas, sino para hacer aquello que sea lícito . . ."* "In this sense, the sentence of murderers Badía and Troncoso will contribute to spill over the people the healthy doctrines which, reaching down to all classes in society and supported by example, will make impossible another tyranny among us. Such as the doctrines that assassinations never prescribe and that there is always the hand of justice that persecutes the criminal until he is delivered hand-tied and on his knees, and that nobody owes obedience to his

superiors in order to violate the laws of god and man, but only to do what is illicit . . ." *El Nacional,* October 18, 1853. Translation by author.

29 "*Los diez mil hombres se disiparon en un día como el humo, y Troncoso, Badía, Cuitiño y los degolladores que habían ensangrentado en otro tiempo las calles de Buenos Aires gritando '¡Mueran los Salvages unitarios!', subieron al patíbulo para escarmiento de los criminales.*" "The ten thousand men vanished like smoke in one day, and Troncoso, Badía, Cuitiño, and the beheaders, who in the past had bloodied the streets of Buenos Aires shouting 'Death to the savage Unitarians,' climbed up the scaffold as a lesson to all criminals." *Los Debates,* November 11, 1857. Translation by author.

30 *El Nacional,* in its issue of November 14, 1853, reproduced with enthusiasm this article of *El Diablo.*

31 Ibid., pp. 36–38.

32 *El Nacional,* November 22 and 24, 1853.

33 Crime statistics were few, but those in existence were used to create the same sense of public danger. Homicides were rising to a "terrifying figure," observed *El Judicial* in May 1855, after reviewing the current arrest figures. Of the 113 prisoners in the state jail, 101 were accused of murder.

34 *La Reforma Pacífica,* December 6, 1856. Translation by author.

35 *El Judicial* carried the news of this crime in its issues of November 17 and 29, and December 11, 1855.

36 Locally, the resonance of the case was important. The justice of peace had no trouble in gathering fifty vecinos to chase the alleged murderers, some of them reaching the province of Santa Fe and arresting the accused. But in Buenos Aires, the event would have passed unnoticed, unless reported by the newspapers. *El Judicial* complained that between November 2, when the crime was reported by *Crónica,* porteños were unaware of the existence of such a violent crime.

37 *El Judicial,* November 29, 1855.

38 "*Mil conjeturas se hacen sacadas de diversos hechos que se dicen concocidos y la prensa insta por su esclarecimiento.*" "People make all sorts of conjectures about the different felonies that are said to be known and that the press tries to elucidate." *El Judicial,* December 11, 1855. Translation by the author.

39 "*El Tribunal ha sido instruído por los diarios de esta capital y por la voz pública, que el viernes de la semana anterior fue encontrado el cadáver de una joven en la ribera del río en el bajo del Socorro.*" "The Tribunal has learned from the newspapers of this capital and by the public voice that last Friday, the corpse of a young lady was found on the banks of the river in *the bajo del Socorro.*" Ibid. Translation by the author.

40 *El Judicial,* December 17, 1855.

41 See M. Sáenz Quesada, "Crímenes después de Caseros."

42 "Crimen de San Vicente," *Los Debates,* January 3, 1858.

43 On the political culture of Rosismo, see my "Fiestas federales: representaciones de la República en el Buenos rosista," *Entrepasados* V, no. 11 (1996).

44 *El Judicial,* May 1, 1855.

45 *El Judicial*, July 11, 1856. Translation by the author.

46 *El Judicial*, April 1, 1855.

47 Also in 1853, appeared the compilation of Ascasubi's poems entitled *Trovos de Paulino Lucero*, a book exalted by Sarmiento as the best effort to pull the gaucho from his lethargic past.

48 "A los Guardias Nacionales," *La Tribuna*, August 18, 1853.

49 *"Exhibición pública — En la calle del Perú no. 62, en el almacén naval de los Señores Fussone Hermanos, se halla de exposición el Retrato del primer cómplice de las maldades de Rosas titulalo Teniente Coronel Antonino Reyes, condecorado con la Gran Cruz de la Mazorca. Invitamos al público a que pase a conocer a éste famoso discípulo de Caco, cuyo retrato tiene bastante semejanza con el original."* *La Tribuna*, August 18, 1853.

50 This is not the place to deal with the political and social project of the liberals. The institutional structures recommended by Sarmiento and Alberdi (the limitations on the authority of the executive, the electoral system and the legislatures, the municipal regime, the distinction between civil and political liberties, the condition of the immigrant, etc.) are brilliantly discussed in N. Botana, *La tradición republicana* (Buenos Aires: Sudamericana, 1984), cap. 7.

51 "Fusion" was the word used, referring to a sort of armistice between ex-unitarios and ex-federales necessary for the working of the new political institutions. See Alberto R. Lettieri, *La república de la opinión* (Buenos Aires: Biblos, 1999).

52 Liberals' depiction of the Rosista regime as a time without law is incorrect. Rosas legitimized most of their decisions in the mandate he received to establish an effective legal order and was quite successful in establishing this order. Similarly, in the provinces, other caudillos acted on the basis of an authority granted by laws and legal political institutions. See Ricardo Salvatore, " 'El Imperio de la Ley': Delito, estado y sociedad en la era Rosista," *Delito y Sociedad* 3, nos. 4–5 (1993–94): 93–118; and N. Goldman, "Legalidad y legitimidad en el caudillismo: Juan Facundo Quiroga y La Rioja en el interior rioplatense (1810–1835)," *Boletín del Instituto de Historia Argentina y Americana Dr. Emilio Ravignani*, 3d series, no. 7 (1993): 31–58.

53 The argument that distinguishes the Rosas regime as a "state of terror" and the liberal regime as a moderate regime respectful of individual liberties is not convincing. Public executions (whether used by Rosas or by his liberal successors) were a form of terror conceived by state functionaries as a means of terrifying the population into obedience of the law or of the federalist system. To be sure, compared with the authority of the liberals, that invested in Rosas was certainly vast, almost without limits. The liberal state might also have produced in the end a lesser number of deaths than Rosas regime (though we are not at all yet certain that this was so). But both regimes used terror: the execution of criminals, the shooting of deserters and political rebels, the repressive incursions into Indian territory.

54 For the meaning of the republic displayed in public events during the Rosas period, see R. Salvatore, "Fiestas Federales."

55 Alberdi's distinction between unlimited *civil* liberties and limited *political* liberties clearly exemplifies the fear liberals had of extending democracy to the masses.

56 In fact, the trial of Rosas (started in 1857), closed all other proceedings against political murderers. For a discussion of the ideological bias and formal errors of the Rosas trial, see Vicente Zito Lema, "La condena judicial de Rosas," *Todo es Historia*, 34 (February 1970): 42–52.

57 The Rosista terror, claimed *La Reforma Pacífica* in 1856, was replaced by the fear of being publicly calumniated. Every politician was calling the other mazorquero or rosin as a means to win elections. "El Terror," *La Reforma Pacífica*, December 2, 1856.

58 "La barbarie, siempre el fantasma de la barbarie" (Barbarism, always the phantom of barbarism), remarked N. Botana, *La Tradición Republicana*, p. 347.

59 This reflection came from a visit that judges made to the Buenos Aires prison in 1855. *"Abandonados los presos a sí mismos, privados de toda ocupación como de toda distracción, sumidos por consiguiente en el ocio, fuente de tantos vicios, y perteneciente por lo general a una clase que, gracias a la desastrosa dictadura, ha vivido durante veinte años en total abstracción o lejanía de las nociones morales, era indispensable irlos introduciendo paulatinamente en la región, para ellos desconocida, de las ideas religiosas."* "Abandoned to themselves, deprived of all occupation and distraction—hence, subsumed into idleness, the source of so many vices, and commonly belonging to a class that, thanks to the disastrous dictatorship, has lived during twenty years in the total absence of moral notions, it is indispensable that we introduce the prisoners to the unknown region of religious ideas." *El Judicial*, July 11, 1855. Translation by the author.

60 Not by chance, the main disagreement between liberals Sarmiento and Alberdi centered on this question: whether the rural inhabitants of the pampas were redeemable through elementary education or if, on the contrary, they needed to be replaced by European immigrants, already acculturated into hard work, free commerce, and legal government.

61 *". . . como carecemos de presidios y prisiones adecuadas, resulta que para los delitos graves, no existe propiamente pena alguna aplicable, a no ser la capital: todas las demás son irrealizables."* ". . . as we lack adequate prisons, it happens that, for grave felonies there is no penalty we can apply, except for the capital penalty: all the rest are unpractical." Informe del Superior Tribunal de Justicia a la Asamblea General, May 1, 1855, *El Judicial*, May 29, 1855. Translation by the author.

62 This interaction between the public and the prisoners might have conditioned later public responses to executions, in the direction of a rejection of corporal punishment.

63 The question of the institution of a *national* system of justice was, of course, not relevant to this period, mostly because this issue only appeared after the constitutional agreement of 1860. The obstacles which this process faced are discussed in Eduardo Zimmermann, "Los abogados, las instituciones judiciales y la construc-

ción del estado nacional: Argentina, 1860–1880" (paper presented to the Coloquio Internacional de Historia del Delito y la Justicia en América Latina, Universidad Torcuato Di Tella, Buenos Aires, October 1996).

64 Immigrants had a more proprietary view of families than creoles. Women and children were considered *their* property—indeed, their most valuable assets—and, as such, not subject to the interventions of the state.

65 Mitre's words in *Los Debates* about this issue (*"la tiranía feroz que azotó y afrentó a nuestras madres, a nuestras hermanas y a nuestras hijas en los templos, y hasta en el santuario del hogar doméstico"*) was replicated in many different texts. *Los Debates,* November 11, 1857.

66 According to liberals, the terror of the Rosista state was unbounded and gender-blind; it reached into the privacy of the homes of *gente decente* (high-class people) and it killed women with the same regularity and pleasure as men.

Disputed Views of Incarceration in Lima, 1890–1930: The Prisoners' Agenda for Prison Reform

CARLOS AGUIRRE

n the early nineteenth century, prisons throughout Latin America and elsewhere began to be designed as instruments to transform inmates into docile, industrious, and obedient subjects, ready to be incorporated into the labor market, the army of consumers, and the community of law-abiding citizens. In order to accomplish that multifarious goal, prisons were supposed to effect a routine of regulated and closely monitored daily activities (work, instruction, hygiene, praying, recreation), a strict regimen of rewards and penalties, and a brainwashing campaign that would eventually help convince inmates of the worthiness of good and proper behavior. According to the ideology of prison reform, the goal was no longer to punish the body of the criminal, but to conquer his or her soul and mind.[1] The difficulties reformers and prison officials must have had in actually reaching into the prisoners' souls and minds are matched only by the obstacles historians have faced in deciphering the inmates' worldview. As several historians have emphasized, however, writing the history of prisons without incorporating the experiences, views, and agency of the inmate population would leave out an essential aspect of the history of imprisonment, not only because of the importance of registering the views of the subaltern, but also because that would give us a hint as to the effects and results of the prison reform package. How to "read" prisoners' own views about life in general and their incarceration in particular is not an easy matter. Lack of sources, first, and then all the difficulties of comprehending texts produced under highly oppressive circumstances, complicate the historian's task. And yet, it only seems necessary that we try to accomplish this goal, for recovering the prisoners' voice would help us understand the actual imprint of imprisonment on its subjects.[2]

Among the different types of texts produced by inmates are, of course, letters. Writing (and often times, smuggling) letters is a tactic used by prisoners everywhere. Prisoners have always tried to reach the outside world (and, occasionally, other fellow inmates) in search of help, understanding, love, and support. Prisoners have always used the written word for voicing complaints, accusations, demands, and requests. Illiterate prisoners realize — maybe for the first time — the importance of the written word, and they seek assistance in conveying their feelings through paper and ink. In the case of Lima prisons, and especially during the 1920s, inmates wrote numerous letters to political and judicial authorities requesting or demanding attention to their situation. These letters constitute a fascinating — though by no means unproblematic — source for approaching the prisoners' own perception about the realities of prison life and their strategies for coping with the harshness of prison. A review of the content and nature of those letters will allow us to grasp something of the prisoners' own mental and cultural world, and it will reveal the connections between the world of the prison and broader changes affecting Peruvian society as a whole. Despite the ambiguities they reveal, on which I will comment later, a clear trend emerges from the study of this set of letters found in the archive of the Ministry of Justice: by the late 1920s, their nature and content began to reflect recently acquired political and doctrinal tenets that marked a double shift. First, there was a shift from a strictly individualistic to a collective approach in the pursuit of prisoners' goals. By the late 1920s, numerous letters signed by large groups of inmates began to reach authorities and other outsiders, which clearly reveals both a new awareness about the importance of collective action and the emergence of new mechanisms for putting that action in motion. Second, there was a change from a subservient and deferential tone to a more assertive and denunciatory style that, in addition, reveals the appropriation by inmates of some of the rhetorical tools and devices used by criminologists and prison experts in their bid for the implementation of "modern" prison disciplinary regimes.[3]

In explaining this double shift, we need to take into account at least two concurrent factors. First, there was a proliferation of organizations and individuals (philanthropists, professionals, criminologists, physicians, penologists, and journalists) that, since the 1890s, had begun to disseminate, among other ideas, the principles of prison reform outside and inside the prison walls. Although the presence of these outsiders was not intended to enlighten the inmates about their rights but to convince them of the worthiness of hard work and obedience, they nonetheless seem to have alerted the prison population about the potentially subversive nature of the rhetoric of prison reform, especially when contrasted with the nasty realities of Lima's prisons. Second, the shifts that we are describing demonstrate that broader changes in Peruvian society also resonated inside the prison walls. At a time when growing sectors of the population began to organize in political parties, labor unions, and other civil organizations, inmates at Lima's prisons also began to organize themselves and to assert their demands in collective rather than individual ways. The presence of large numbers of political prisoners in Lima's prisons during the latter period of the Leguía administration (1919–1930) must have further helped the inmates' efforts at organization and collective action.

In the first section of this essay, I review the various forms of outside intervention in the lives of the inmates that were effected in Lima's prisons during the period from 1890 to 1930. I show both the limitations of those interventions and the potential they had for fostering the prisoners' own proactive forms of contestation. In the second section I analyze the changing nature and content of prisoners' letters and identify the factors that help understand those shifts.[4] My concluding remarks point to the significance of these changes, as they reveal the limitations of prison reform efforts (in both their material and ideological levels), as well as the creative ways in which prisoners were able to contest the regime of oppression that was enforced upon them.

Outside Looking In

By the 1890s, and following the introduction to Peruvian soil of positivist criminology, prisons became, to a degree unknown in earlier periods, the focus of attention by different groups of outsiders. Criminologists, penologists, and physicians began to tour Lima's prisons in search of clues that would help them understand the nature of crime and the characteristics of the criminal population. Journalists began to explore and report on the conditions of living inside the prisons and the peculiarities of the prison population. Philanthropists gave birth to patronage and humanitarian societies and began to visit Lima's prisons offering consolation and relief to their inmates. The most traditional (and seemingly ineffectual) of all these interventions, however, was the customary *visita de cárcel* (jail visit) that public authorities had to perform every week in order to check the conditions of the prisons and make sure that prisoners were treated according to legal mandates.

The visita de cárcel was a legacy of the colonial period. Spanish law mandated it as a way of checking the conditions of prisons and inmates but, more importantly, as a means of displaying the alleged compassion and protection that the crown awarded its subjects. Inmates used the occasion to verbalize their complaints against jailkeepers, but the whole ritual was in fact little more than a formality. Visitas de cárcel were also performed on special occasions, such as the proclamation of the Spanish constitution in September 1820, which happened to be the last visita conducted by a Spanish viceroy.[5] This practice was maintained by Peruvian independent regimes throughout the nineteenth century. Shortly after Peru achieved formal political independence from Spain in 1821, for instance, liberator José de San Martín visited Lima's jails, verified the wretched conditions of prisons and prisoners, and issued a few decrees attempting to end the horror and abuses he had witnessed. Lima's jails offered inhumane conditions of living, subjected the prisoners to torture and abuse, and lacked any meaningful disciplinary regime. San Martín wanted the new independent government to pay attention to this issue, for, according to him, fair justice and the humane treatment of convicts ought to be landmarks of the republican order and thus would establish a radical difference with the way Spanish colonialism had abused its subjects.[6] In 1822, San Martín's successor, the marquis of Torre Tagle, issued the first prison bylaws (Reglamento de Cárceles) for independent Peru. Most rules were mere administrative regulations, and the best they did for prisoners was to grant them one hour in the morning and one in the afternoon for leaving the cells and getting some sunshine and fresh air, and to mandate the separation of prisoners by sex and age. Both measures were rather difficult to implement, and in most Peruvian prisons they were never really enforced. Neither was the elimination, also ordered by Torre Tagle, of the *derecho de carcelaje,* a fee that inmates had to pay at their release and that had become an instrument for perpetuating abuses against the generally poor occupants of Peruvian prisons.[7]

In 1854, the Reglamento de Tribunales y Juzgados established new rules for the visita. Not only judicial authorities, but also the inmates' counselors and anyone interested in the prisoners' welfare were invited to participate in the prison tour, which was meant to be a public event. Twice a year, during Christmas and Palm Sunday, the visita de cárceles in Lima was to be led by the president of the republic himself.[8] Very scant documentation about these visitas has survived, so their actual effects are hard to measure. Sketchy information would indicate that despite its ineffectiveness, the visita nonetheless allowed the display of conflicting views about the prison and the conditions of incarceration and was used by prisoners to enunciate their complaints. In November 1891, for example, *El Diario Judicial* — whose director, Paulino Fuentes Castro, was one of the most enthusiastic Lombrosian criminologists — criticized the practice for its "disorderly" character and for allowing the prisoners to establish a sort of familiarity with judicial authorities, "which undermines the prestige of the magistrates and the respect prisoners must have for their judges."[9] *El Comercio* described the visita performed by President Morales Bermudez and other authorities in January 1894. The president faced a military formation of the inmates and listened to their complaints. *"Almost all these miserable men talked to him. Your Excellency listened to them patiently, offered them phrases of consolation, and told them that he could not give them freedom."* One inmate, "almost dead, bleeding by the mouth," asked for compassion. He was later pardoned.[10]

The visita de cárcel was little more than a routine formality, one more of the many state-mandated ceremonies that yielded very few practical results.[11] It was used to display the allegedly majestic nature of the Peruvian legal system, to give inmates and their relatives an opportunity to be "heard," and occasionally, in flagrant cases, to demonstrate humanitarian sentiments. For the judicial and political authorities actually taking part in those visits, it was probably experienced as a boring and even repellent kind of duty. For prisoners and their relatives, it was an opportunity to voice grievances and/or supplications that, in most cases, did not produce the expected results. The visita was finally discontinued in the mid-1910s.[12]

Private individuals also began to conduct intermittent visits to Lima's prisons after 1890.[13] They were members of the first "patronage societies" that, emulating similar European institutions, were formed in the early 1890s. They followed doctrines of prison reform that emphasized the need for such civil organizations for the protection of the prisoner against abuse inside the prison and, once released, against those negative influences—vice, corruption, unemployment, and poverty—that would lead him or her to recidivism. Those associations promised to assist prisoners in their basic needs, help them "readapt" to society after their release, and oversee that the law was observed in all matters related to the application of justice. Like their counterparts in Europe, they were generally formed by members of the intellectual and social elite moved by what they considered humanitarian compassion toward prisoners and ex-convicts.

The first Sociedad de Patronato (patronage society) was founded in Lima in the early 1890s by University of San Marcos law professor Ricardo Heredia and his students. During the next few years, the Sociedad was very active visiting the prisoners, listening to their complaints, making sure that they were paid for their work, and assisting them at the end of their prison terms. The first action of the Sociedad took place in November 1892: a young Indian man that had completed his prison sentence was placed in a shoe factory by the Sociedad and was given shelter in Heredia's own house.[14] In January 1893, to mention another such action, penitentiary inmates were given new uniforms after the Sociedad interceded with prison authorities.[15] Ricardo Heredia invested a good deal of energies in this campaign, which also included writing articles and letters in newspapers demanding that authorities comply with the bylaws.[16] He even assisted inmates with cash from his own pocket, while a group of upper-class ladies collected money on behalf of the Sociedad to be distributed among the inmates.[17] As the years passed, however, the Sociedad became inactive. Heredia did not succeed in driving public attention (and funds) to this purpose, and after his death in 1899 the Sociedad languished.[18]

It was only in the 1910s and 1920s that the issue was revisited by new generations of criminologists. A thesis written in 1919 insisted on the importance of such organizations as the only means to prevent recidivism.[19] In 1923, the Asociación Humanitaria del Perú (Humanitarian Association of Peru) was created in Lima with the goal of "protecting every defenseless being against abuse and cruelty, regardless of their race, religion, class, or nationality." The "defenseless" they wanted to protect included prisoners, children, and animals.[20] The 1924 penal code mandated the creation of a Consejo Local del Patronato (Local patronage council) in every jurisdiction in which a Correctional Tribunal operated. In Lima, it began to function as early as October of that year.[21] The Consejo had, among its duties, the administration of the indemnification fund for the victims of crimes, the promotion of private patronage societies, the surveillance and protection of both inmates and paroled convicts, and the processing of applications for pardon. There is scattered evidence about this institution, whose main duty seems to have been the evaluation of prisoners who were seeking pardon and the overseeing of those who actually received it.[22] With some regularity, members of the Consejo toured Lima's prisons and energetically demanded urgent reforms. For example, in January 1926, they criticized the "repugnant liquid" that inmates at the penitentiary received as soup, or the miserable wages that inmates were paid for their work in the penitentiary workshops.[23] A few months later, the president of the Consejo, Dr. Mata, issued a report demanding, among other things, an improvement in food, clothing, and infrastructure. Moreover, he insisted on the need for a new penitentiary. He even suggested that inmates were used as "slaves" in the service of the penitentiary's economy.[24]

A similar role was played by other private institutions and individuals that in the late 1920s began to offer assistance and relief for the prisoners. The *Sociedad los Amigos del Preso,* formed in 1929 under the direction of Mrs. Ada H. Dulanto, was committed to the "material relief and moral improvement" of all prisoners and to help them straighten their financial and moral condition once they were released,[25] while *Acción Social de la Juventud* was authorized in 1930 to carry on "humanitarian actions" inside the penitentiary.[26] An Indigenista group, the "Comité Central Pro-Indígena Tahuantinsuyo," began helping indigenous inmates released from prison to get funds to pay their travel expenses to go back home.[27] Finally, a vigorous campaign was conducted on behalf of Lima's inmates in the late 1920s by activist and writer Angela Ramos, who instituted celebrations such as the "Prisoner's Christmas" (*Navidad del preso*) in all Lima's prisons and effected many other initiatives to assist the prisoners.[28]

As in the case of the official visitas de cárcel, philanthropic initiatives embodied a typically paternalistic and hierarchical relationship between outsiders and prisoners. The fulfillment of prisoners' expectations depended basically on the good will, time, money, or sincerity of the individuals involved. The effects of philanthropic activities on the well-being of prisoners may have been rather marginal, but their campaigns — in particular those of Ricardo Heredia in the 1890s and Angela Ramos in the late 1920s — contributed to raise fundamental questions regarding the way the state treated incarcerated men and women. In addition, and probably most importantly, those campaigns helped disseminate among the convicts the notion that their legal and humanitarian rights could find support in at least certain social and political circles, and thus, that their actions and initiatives might well lead to changes in their situation.

Angela Ramos's campaign was particularly effective in this regard. She wrote articles, organized festivities, collected money, lobbied the government for legislative changes, and, in general, tried to turn public attention to an issue—the welfare of the prisoners—that had received very scant attention in the past. She was very energetic in denouncing the miserable conditions of Lima's prisons and demanding a more humane treatment for prisoners. She brought to the authorities' attention specific cases of torture and abuse, and lobbied the government to take action in concrete cases, such as the release of "Palito," an indigenous prisoner who was agonizing from tuberculosis in Guadalupe. She was also a loud advocate of those being apprehended, convicted, and exploited as "vagrants" in the El Frontón penal island, in the streets of Lima, or in remote locations such as the Perené river, in the Amazon region, where they were used to build roads.[29] Angela Ramos did all this without directly challenging the government's overall policies but, instead, by invoking President Leguía's alleged commitment to the welfare of the people, the stability and modernization of the country, and the implementation of scientific methods of government.[30] The implicit contradiction between discourse and practice in Leguía's penal policies that Angela Ramos's campaign revealed had a tremendous impact in the ways prisoners addressed the issues surrounding their incarceration, as we will see.

State authorities and philanthropists were not the only ones who visited the prisons and talked to inmates. In the late nineteenth century, criminologists and penal experts began to pay attention to prisons and prison populations as subjects of study and research. The introduction of positivist criminology in Peru stimulated a growing interest on the part of students of law and medicine to conduct research about crime and criminals and, following similar trends in Europe and North America, they found that prison populations offered a readily-available "sample" of the criminal population from which they could draw conclusions based on allegedly scientific investigation.[31] A number of university theses were written by future lawyers and physicians on various aspects of prison population and life such as sexuality, hygiene, tattooing, criminal slang, and the anthropometric and psychological profile of the inmate population.[32] During the 1920s, a more interventionist attitude on the part of these experts began to be effected in Lima's prisons. During the Leguía administration, and especially in the second half of the 1920s, an intense — though not always successful — effort was made to reform Peruvian prisons, to implement "scientific" methods of punishment and rehabilitation, and to effect the mandates of the penal code (individualization of the penalty, criminological/medical study of the inmate population, the creation of an Institute of Criminology, and many others). Some of the most notable physicians and lawyers of this period contributed to this effort: Bernardino León y León, Carlos Bambarén, Victor M. Villavicencio, among others. The Direction General of Prisons, created in 1921, became quite active enacting profuse regulations, organizing public events, and publishing a valuable *Boletín de Criminología*.[33]

Within this context, no longer just a subject of study but also the target for ideological "brainwashing," prison populations began to be bombarded with lectures on topics such as hygiene, sexuality, industriousness, education, and patriotism. Inmates had the opportunity to learn about a variety of penal issues and to familiarize themselves with ongoing debates regarding prison regimes. Although experts, of course, wanted the prisoners to internalize the rules of appropriate behavior (obedience, hard work, sexual abstinence, and the like), inmates seem to have paid some attention to the potentially subversive nature of some of the tenets of the ideologies of prison reform: humane treatment, healthy environment, and elimination of corporal punishment.[34] They not only listened to those experts; because many of their publications were printed by inmates working at the penitentiary's printing and binding workshop, some of them also had an opportunity to read and disseminate those ideas. Although we have no means of assessing the real dimensions of the prisoners' awareness about ongoing debates between penal experts, it is clear, from the analysis of the prisoners' letters, that they indeed appropriated some of the doctrinal tenets of prison experts and used them to foster their own endeavors.

Journalistic interest in prisons also became fashionable in Lima by the turn of the twentieth century. Crime reporting had been, of course, a familiar feature of Peruvian newspapers throughout the nineteenth century, but only occasionally did daily newspapers report on prison conditions. By the late nineteenth century, interest in criminal affairs intensified; to a certain extent, this was also an imitation of similar developments in Europe. Crime stories began to be published, sensational crimes received spacious coverage, and "biographies" of famous criminals also began to appear, first in specialized legal magazines, and then in the daily press.[35] Criminal and prison statistics also started to appear regularly in the daily press. Almost naturally, journalists took the next step and began to tour Lima's prisons, seeking to unveil the "mysteries" of life behind the prison walls.[36] The chance of meeting some of the notorious criminals about whom the press had extensively reported further stimulated the reporters' voyeurism — and that of their readers.[37] Inmates, of course, realized what this was all about: they talked to journalists and probably read the stories in the papers; not surprisingly, they also wrote letters to them, some of which actually got published.[38] Although media interest in prison life per se had probably very little impact on the inmates' living conditions, it helped to overcome the barriers separating prisons from the outside world, in terms of both outside awareness about the conditions of prisons and the inmates' realization that they did matter for some people, even if it was only in a voyeuristic kind of way.

Finally, another group of "outsiders" interacting with inmates was the growing numbers of "political and social prisoners," as they began to be called. The Leguía government displayed an increasingly repressive face, especially after 1923. At different times, dozens, maybe hundreds, of labor activists and members of opposition parties and groups were sent to different prisons.[39] Some of them spent a few days in confinement, others several years. Historian Jorge Basadre emphasizes the fact that political opponents from all sectors of life were imprisoned by Leguía, "the great *señores* of the highest economic aristocracy as well as young students and modest workers."[40] The political climate existing during the *oncenio* — as the eleven-year Leguía regime is usually called — reverberated inside the prison thanks, to a large extent, to the presence of these political prisoners. They usually occupied a separate area from "common" criminals, but the opportunities for interaction between the two groups of inmates were many. It is to be expected that conversations between them should have helped "common" criminals to develop or consolidate a certain degree of political consciousness. In fact, a riot that erupted at the penitentiary on August 25, 1930, brought together political and common prisoners and had to be put down with the help of external armed forces.[41] Several sources about the post-Leguía period reveal that considerable contact took place between common criminals and political inmates, from which both groups ultimately benefited: the former acquired or reinforced notions of rights and certain strategies for demanding them, whereas the latter received help in smuggling letters, books, and other items inside the prisons. On November 12, 1932, for example, it was reported that Aprista inmates at the Cárcel Central de Varones were "inculcating subversive doctrines among the prison population" and that, somehow, using a method that had not been yet identified, they were getting communications from their leader, Haya de la Torre, who was detained at the adjoining penitentiary.[42] Although the relationship between "common" and "political" prisoners was not always smooth and collaborative, the mere presence of the latter brought to daily life inside the prison certain features that could not have gone without consequences: political prisoners were generally well organized, their situation received much more press coverage than that of the rest of the prison population, and their presence usually heightened the levels of confrontation between prison administrators and the inmate population.

All these interventions had inevitable effects on the prison population, which are reflected in the content and nature of the letters I analyze below. The mere circulation of people inside the prison (criminologists, philanthropists, journalists, authorities, and political prisoners) made the "isolation" of prisoners almost impossible, even at the Lima penitentiary, the only prison of its time with the architectural and reglamentary bases for enforcing such isolation. Prisoners were able to inform themselves about political developments outside the prisons and about notions of prison reform and penological treatment that were being aired in academic and other circles, which they internalized and used in their attempts to ameliorate their conditions.

Inside reaching out

Writing letters to outside individuals is not of course an uncommon practice for prisoners anywhere. The archive of the General Direction of Prisons, the centralized bureau created by the Leguía government in 1921, contains a number of letters sent by prisoners to various authorities in the late 1920s. Despite their small number, they allow us to grasp the shifting perceptions among prisoners of their own condition, as well as their changing strategies to get the attention of the outside world and foster their own goals.

Most letters, especially those sent by individual inmates, appealed to the compassion and humanitarian sentiments of authorities by depicting the inmate's miserable existence, the submissive attitude with which he was dealing with his incarceration, and his promise of future rehabilitation and repentance. A good example is the letter written by inmate Manuel Cáceres to Colonel César Landásuri, Director General of Prisons, in 1924: "I am, my good Sir, one of those unfortunate individuals that, far from being malevolent, but rather a victim of the fatal force of destiny, committed an error for which I am sincerely repented. . . . For twelve years and eleven months I have been crying due to a mistake that I made because of my lack of experience, bearing the rigors of prison." He had been sentenced to twenty years of seclusion at the Lima penitentiary. The judge, he said, did not take into account his young age, good antecedents, and state of inebriation at the time of the crime. He asked Landásuri "with sincere tears" to solicit from his friends in the government his pardon on the occasion of the anniversary of the Battle of Ayacucho (the final military action of the Peruvian independence campaign against the Spaniards in 1824). "My gratitude for you will be eternal, and my personal services will be at your order, if I can not correspond in a more dignified way." Manuel was told, shortly after, that he was indeed included in the list of pardoned inmates, but, after several months and various letters, he realized that nine other inmates had already left the penitentiary while he was still waiting. He wrote another letter, which he signed, "A man buried alive, who foresees his resurrection, salutes you, and blesses you."[43]

This tone was pervasive in numerous individual letters addressed to state authorities. Another inmate that requested a transfer from El Frontón to the penitentiary[44] depicted himself as a "disgraced man," "victim of misfortune," "submerged in this valley of tears." If his transfer were granted, he said, he would patiently wait at the penitentiary "without major moral sufferings that make my life even more bitter, until my long-awaited freedom is effected."[45] Another inmate wrote in 1930 to his "godfather," Minister of Justice José Angel Escalante: "I look forward to your goodness and your support for leaving this unjust incarceration. You well know, my dear and respected godfather, that I have not committed any crime, and that I am the victim of a woman of bad antecedents, with the complicity of a police sergeant." In this case, he asked the minister to intercede with the judge and a friendly lawyer to have his case revised.[46]

Indigenous inmates used their ethnic background to reinforce the same tone of deference and suffering that was thought to be an effective way of reaching out for help. Matías Suma, an indigenous prisoner, wrote to the

Director General of Prisons requesting parole: "Your indisputable superiority would facilitate a solid support for us, the unfortunate indigenous inmates of this prison, many of whom, perhaps, are here due to strange or unjust causes."[47] Another Indian, Mariano Condori, who had just been released from prison but lacked the money needed to return to his home town in Azángaro, Puno, wrote a letter to the archbishop of Lima depicting himself as "a humble indigenous vagrant" and explaining how "my indigenous condition and the bad situation that I confront, force me to ask your high authority to take care of a poor man that is not culpable of his current situation." He had not mastered the Spanish language, he revealed, which made his situation even more difficult.[48] These and other similar letters reveal the degree to which a common trope of the Indigenista rhetoric was also used by Indians themselves in order to foster their requests: that of the "miserable Indian race," which, victim of abuse and exploitation by landlords, authorities, priests, and other non-Indian groups, was needy of protection and guidance.[49] During the 1920s, in fact, Indigenismo received official endorsement from the Leguía government and became a common rhetorical device in the state's relationship with the Indian population.[50] An official Patronato de la Raza Indígena (Patronage of the Indigenous Race) was created in 1922, and Leguía promised in 1924 that he would "rehabilitate the Indian to a legal and cultural life, for time has come to put an end to his slavery, which is an insult to the Republic and an intolerable crime for Justice."[51] Indigenous inmates, sometimes following advice from intermediaries,[52] tried thus to capitalize from the "official indigenismo" of the Leguía regime.

Other inmates chose to stress their honesty and industriousness in order to convey a positive image to the authorities. This strategy implied a desire on the part of some inmates to detach themselves from "the world of crime." Many individuals who, technically speaking, had committed a crime, believed that their social, cultural, and employment condition made them very different from the actual "criminal" population. Thus, being treated as or mixed with common criminals was a terrible source of shame and discredit. Abel León, for instance, was an inmate who, despite admitting the commission of a sexual crime, claimed that "I am neither a murderer nor a vulgar criminal. . . . I am an honest artisan, industrious, who used to support my tender children with my daily work." He requested a pardon, but it was denied.[53] Another inmate, Isaac Mayta y Castillo, actually mixed the honest-and-industrious self-portrait with the more pervasive discourse of resignation and submissiveness. He wrote a letter to President Leguía requesting a pardon. He had been sentenced to twelve years at the penitentiary for homicide — which he claimed he did not commit — and for three years had been suffering "with Christian resignation . . . as a national artisan, a respectable, honest, and vice-free worker." In addition, his letter brings yet another component of the prisoners' strategies: the appeal to political clientelism as a way of addressing state authorities. Besides stressing that he was a "national artisan, a tailor," Mayta y Castillo wanted to make sure that the president knew that he was a member of a Leguísta political club. He promised to be an "exemplary artisan," but also that he would be "intimately united to your very noble and patriotic action." He "implored" a pardon from Leguía's "well-known benevolence and philanthropy."[54]

There are strong resonances among all these various ways of addressing public authorities. Inmates clearly preferred to appear as resigned victims rather than as whiners; and instead of asserting rights, they chose to request mercy. They also stressed loyalty, whether it was personal loyalty to a political leader or the more impersonal allegiance to the principles of industriousness, obedience, and lawfulness that, prisoners certainly knew, authorities expected them to adhere to. Because these letters were written to request what inmates depicted (and authorities certainly considered) as "favors" or "rewards," it would have been probably unwise on their part to use more aggressive and seditious language. In reading these letters, we might recall that they usually reveal what James Scott refers to as the "public transcript," which the subordinate uses to convey messages "in close conformity with how the dominant group would wish to have things appear."[55]

The case of Mayta y Castillo was not exceptional in the appeal to political loyalties that prisoners made in order to receive certain mercies. More and more frequently, however, this tactic was used in collective instead of individual letters. In the context of the Peruvian political culture of this period, of course, this is not surprising. The paternalistic and clientelistic nature of Peruvian political culture has been emphasized by numerous historians. Leguía's second regime (1919–1930), with its highly personalistic methods and the overwhelming presence of adulation as an avenue for social and political climbing, strengthened these features of Peruvian political culture.[56] Paternalism and vertical political and social relationships were in fact pervasive in a multitude of social forms of interaction and organization: political parties, trade unions, labor relations in factories and haciendas, education, family structure, and many others. A few examples will illustrate the way prisoners sought to take advantage of this. A letter signed by ninety inmates was sent to President Leguía in June 1929, congratulating him for the solution he had reached in the ongoing dispute with Chile regarding the territories of Tacna and Arica. After the congratulation prisoners expressed "our most fervent hopes that Divine Providence will prolong indefinitely your priceless existence, so that the Fatherland can benefit from your initiatives in favor of true progress and national prosperity."[57] Another collective letter, signed by 140 inmates of the Lima penitentiary and sent to the president in May 1930, offered him their solidarity after he had survived an assassination attempt. "We pledge our most fervent desire for your continual command of the state, and we also express our most loyal adherence to your person."[58] Once Leguía was removed from power in August 1930 (and was, indeed, sent to San Lorenzo Penal Island first, and then to the penitentiary as a political prisoner) similar letters began to reach the new governmental authorities. Inmates at the Cárcel de Varones wrote a letter to the new Minister of Government: they were pleased for "the recovery of civil liberties [*libertades ciudadanas*] after eleven years of oppression." They blamed the Leguía regime both for their convictions — which were charged to corruption among judges — and their plight inside the prison — where they were victims of abuses, injustices, and generalized corruption. They demanded the formation of a commission to review their cases.[59] Shortly thereafter, a collective letter with more than one hundred signatures was sent to President Sánchez Cerro, asking for a reassessment of their sentences. They protested that their confessions had been extracted under torture, but they also made sure to proclaim that they were remorseful for their offenses.[60] Another group of prisoners wrote to the Minister of Justice: "Why in this hour of social emancipation, thanks to the brave crusade of the fearless military man Luis M. Sanches [*sic*] Cerro, have you not thought to send back to their desolated homes a good number of parents incarcerated for minor crimes, whom the old regime had sentenced almost in perpetuity?" The old regime, they added, had subtracted "a good number of citizens ready to collaborate, either with the plow or with the hammer — the ferrous symbol of the worker — for the betterment of the fatherland." They asked to be allowed to unite with all Peruvians in the "cry for freedom" promoted by President Sánchez Cerro.[61]

Whether state authorities were moved by these letters is unclear. Given the lack of meaningful initiative on the part of state authorities to improve the overall state of prisons and the living conditions of prisoners, we can probably infer that this strategy was not really successful. After all, what would state authorities or political leaders receive in exchange, other than gratitude, from the prisoners? It is very dubious, in the political and cultural scenario of Peruvian society during this period, that paternalistic attitudes toward prisoners would have represented major assets in the political capital of military or civil leaders. According to Angela Ramos, many people refrained from intervening in favor of inmates because they considered that there was "nothing to gain" from such actions.[62] Thus, in spite of efforts by individuals such as Ramos herself, "public opinion" was not moved to act upon the situation of prisons and prisoners. An authoritarian society such as Peru, where the political, social, and racial exclusion of the majority of the population was being reinforced during the period of modernization steered by Leguía, was not a very propitious site for the development of widespread support for prisoners and, thus, political rulers did not feel compelled to respond to the prisoners' demands.

But more aggressively accusatory letters were also written, without the submissive or clientelistic posture of those reviewed above. In April 1929, for instance, three inmates wrote a letter to Director General of Prisons Bernardino León y León denouncing the torture of prisoners in the penitentiary.[63] Another letter to León y León was signed by a greater number of inmates from the Cárcel de Varones. "We obey the rules of discipline, but the employees, besides punishing us with underground seclusion, have begun to whip us, in an arbitrary and abusive manner." One inmate, they added, was tied naked by his hands and feet and whipped with a stick. "We are certain that the cries of that *compañero* must have been heard even outside the prison," they asserted. The letter demanded sanctions for the abusive employees. León y León read the letter, went to the prison, and verified the signs of torture. He was given an "explanation": the inmate had seriously offended a guard. No further action, apparently, was taken.[64]

As we have seen, the continuous visits and activities organized inside Lima's prisons by both private individuals and state officials, in which frequent discussion took place regarding the reform of the prison system, gradually made more evident to inmates the flagrant contradictions between discourse and reality where their treatment was concerned. These contradictions were then underlined in their communications with authorities such as the Director General of Prisons or the Minister of Justice. As a result, the subservient and clientelistic inflection was no longer the only way of negotiating with higher authorities the living conditions inside the prisons. Prisoners began to appropriate some of the fundamental tenets of prison reformers in order to foster their own goals. This appropriation was, inevitably, quite selective. As in other cases of subaltern subversion of hegemonic and oppressive discourses, inmates turned the rhetoric of prison reform on its head and began to convey the notion that, if prison reformers and authorities were more consequential with their own preaching, the working and living conditions inside the prisons would be quite different—more humanitarian, indeed.

A few examples will illustrate this process. In a collective letter signed by numerous penitentiary inmates on January 3, 1926, and addressed to the Director General of Prisons, and after the almost inevitable confession of resignation, prisoners denounced that "*discipline,* in the noble sense of the word," did not exist at the penitentiary. What prevailed was malevolence. "We live amidst confrontation between authorities, employees, and inmates. To enjoy tranquillity and certain benefits and privileges, it is necessary to be part of the criminal group of *soplones* [squealers]." Prisoners demanded of the new authorities the eradication of all evils "from their roots," for, if not, "every *modern system* that you would like to implement, will be corrupted by the weeds."[65] Another collective letter from El Frontón inmates to President Leguía conveyed their gratitude for an initiative outlining new rules for conditional freedom: such a bill, they said, "will change the impenetrable look of the misfortune in which we are submerged, and will make us resurface in a climate of *readaptation,* bringing us closer to the *social milieu* from which our ill fortune removed us."[66] In one of the numerous collective letters written after the triumph of Sánchez Cerro, prisoners complained about the inhumane treatment they received in the prison which, they argued, "far from helping us in our *readaptation to the social milieu,* from which we should have never departed, only brings bitterness and hatred to our hearts."[67] Terms such as "discipline," "modern system," "readaptation," and "social milieu" were prominent within the ideology of prison reform, in Peru and elsewhere. Their use in the prisoners' letters reveals the extent to which they were aware of those developments; more importantly, it was done in such a way that instead of challenging the whole package—which, after all, was thought of as a means to subdue criminal behavior and impose effective surveillance and control over the inmate population—they highlighted the contradictions in the reformers' and authorities' actions.

Prisoners, therefore, made it very clear that the way they were being treated not only affected them as individuals and made them suffer, but also belied the whole enterprise on which the government had embarked, namely, the implementation of "modern" and "scientific" prison regimes that would consummate the transformation or readaptation of criminals into honest and industrious citizens. It was clear for inmates that there was an abyss separating rhetoric from reality, but they selectively chose those aspects of the reform program that were congruent with their own agenda. The reformers' emphasis on readaptation through humane treatment, adequate infrastructure, and, especially, the eradication of physical abuse and torture was particularly appealing for the prisoners.

As a result, prisoners came up with their own "prison reform" program. By this I mean the formulation—not always explicit or systematic—of a comprehensive design of how prisons should operate, something that had always been the exclusive prerogative of penal experts. This was, indeed, a big leap for inmates: they (or at least some of them) overcame both the subservient inflection traditionally used in their requests and the clientelistic appeals to political loyalty as means of achieving their goals, and moved on to articulate their own platform of prison reform. This "program" appeared in fragmentary form in numerous letters, but it finally took shape in a collective letter signed in December 1931, which, significantly, also demanded, among other things, the removal from his position as director of the penitentiary school of one of the most prominent penal experts of his time, Víctor M. Villavicencio. It was as if Villavicencio had come to embody the incongruities of the official rhetoric of prison reform and, thus, inmates wanted to get rid of him while, at the same time, they outlined their own, different, agenda for prison reform.[68] The platform presented in this letter was quite extensive. It demanded fairness in the calculation of prisoners' wages, an issue that had been raised over and over again by penologists since at least the 1860s; the elimination of all restrictions on visitors; the regulation of parole procedures, especially regarding which infractions and penalties should be counted in the Tribunal's evaluation; the provision of appropriate food, clothing, and medicines; the allowance of greater freedom to work on their own, as sort of "free" workers, so as to be able to feed their families; the release of all restrictions on the sale of goods manufactured by them; and the hiring of female employees for performing the inspection of female visitors.[69]

Some of these proposals affected one of the most crucial aspects of the organization of prison life — in particular, at the Lima penitentiary — namely, the organization of prison work. Wages for prisoners was always a delicate issue and at times generated extensive debates between administrators, penologists, state authorities, and private entrepreneurs. The demand for fairness in the allocation of those wages, together with the proposal for more freedom to work on their own and the unrestricted sale of the products of such work — shoes, furniture, handcrafts — were meant to offer inmates a greater degree of control over their own time, work, and money, undermining the exploitation they usually suffered from private contractors and prison administrators. The other items in the agenda point to basic "humanitarian" demands that would have dramatically improved their conditions of living: appropriate food, clothing, and medicines, conspicuously and consistently poor in Lima's prisons. This was the most ambitious plan for "prison reform" ever proposed by the prison population itself, and it was almost as exhaustive as those designed by penologists and criminologists in the late 1920s. Although, not surprisingly, the prisoners did not get what they asked for, such a comprehensive platform was both the culmination of a period of increased awareness and organizational and ideological maturity, and the foundation for future collective action.

Conclusion

As we have seen, the nature and content of prisoners' letters were varied and multifaceted. Many individual inmates used a tone of resignation and subservience in their requests for mercy. They generally emphasized the miseries and torments of prison life, trying to generate compassion and sympathy among authorities; others stressed their repentance and regret for the crimes they had committed. Even in cases when other criteria were used — pointing to their status as Indians, good workers, innocent victims, or members of the ruling-party political club — these assets were phrased within a discourse dominated by an attitude of subservience. It would be wrong to interpret these strategies as simply revealing of the prisoners' submission and lack of resources. As many students of subaltern groups and ideologies have made it clear, their use of deferential tones in their relationship with superiors can be seen as part of a strategy of "pragmatic resignation," one which allows them to achieve specific and (usually) limited goals without challenging the very bases of power and authority. Prevalent ideas about the "appropriate" way of addressing an authority undoubtedly shaped the way prisoners worded their appeals.

Closely related to this strategy, but within the framework of a collective effort — which, of course, reveals a certain degree of organization difficult to find in previous periods — was the use of clientelistic forms of relationship with political authorities. Prisoners were certainly very much aware of the ways in which regimes such as the *oncenio* depended on the establishment of such networks of patron-client relationships. They also knew that adulation of President Leguía was a rather profitable investment — to mention one example, the issues of the *Boletín de Criminología,* which were printed at the penitentiary's printing workshop, always included portraits and praises of the president. It comes as no surprise, then, that inmates resorted to this strategy, hoping that higher authorities would not be indifferent to their claims of political loyalty.

But there were cases in which prisoners offered a more assertive, independent, and even subversive attitude. They denounced abuses and mistreatment, emphasized the contradictions between the alleged purposes of prison discipline and the realities of Lima's prisons, and even outlined their own "prison reform" program. They (selectively) appropriated the discourse of prison reform, using it as a vehicle for denouncing the shortcomings of prisons in attending to their needs and, thus, subverting the essentially oppressive nature of the project for reforming carceral institutions. The prisoners' appropriation of words and concepts such as prison reform, rehabilitation, discipline, modern prisons, and the like, was possible thanks to the combination of several factors: the philanthropic campaigns of patronage societies and individuals such as Angela Ramos; the increasing circulation — both in the form of indoctrinating lectures and publications printed at the penitentiary's workshop — of the ideas and goals of criminologists and penal experts advocating prison reform; and the broader efforts among different sectors of Peruvian society toward organization and collective action.

That all these different types of strategic maneuvers on the part of inmates were used simultaneously illustrates both the diversity of the prison population (an issue that is worth emphasizing) and the complexities of the various transitions taking place in Peruvian society at that time. New parties and movements came into the political arena to represent the urban and rural masses (Aprismo, socialism, labor unions and federations), but they could not overcome the legacy of authoritarianism and clientelism that had permeated Peruvian political culture since the nineteenth century.[70] If prisoners' strategies of coping and resistance are always shaped, at least partially, by the overall context of the outside political culture, then this mixture of various discourses in the prisoners' letters comes at no surprise. On the other hand, the lack of uniformity within the population of Lima's prisons is also reflected in the different strategies that various individuals and groups chose to use. The study of prisoners' views about prison life through the letters they wrote demonstrates, among other things, their reluctance to conform to the oppressiveness of prison life, a fact also demonstrated in a variety of other forms of coping, accommodation, and resistance. Instead of resourceless victims of regimes of control and surveillance, abusive authorities, and social indifference, prisoners appear as they certainly were: individually and collectively capable of voicing complaints, demanding rights, and denouncing abuses. They sought to reach out for help to the same extent that they asserted their rights as human beings; they manipulated in their favor discourses of compassion and paternalism that were otherwise empty; they tried to take advantage of clientelistic forms of political culture that generally speaking did not include them; and they entered into forms of collective action that, by definition, they were not supposed to use. And even if many of the letters they wrote did not move their addressees to act on their behalf, those writings have given us the opportunity to approach their worldview and get a glimpse of their capacity to confront power, oppression, and mistreatment.

Notes

This essay is part of a larger study on the history of prisons in Lima between 1860 and 1930. Research and writing for this project have been generously supported by the Harry Frank Guggenheim Foundation, the University of Minnesota Graduate School, the American Philosophical Society, and the John Simon Guggenheim Memorial Foundation.

1 The main contours of this prison reform package are outlined, for the European cases, in books such as Michel Foucault, *Discipline and Punish: The Birth of the Prison*, trans. Alan Sheridan (New York: Pantheon Books, 1977); Michael Ignatieff, *A Just Measure of Pain: The Penitentiary and the Industrial Revolution, 1750–1850* (New York: Pantheon Books, 1978); Patricia O'Brien, *The Promise of Punishment: Prisons in Nineteenth-Century France* (Princeton: Princeton University Press, 1980); Michelle Perrot, ed. *L'Impossible Prison: recherches sur le systeme pénitentiaire*

aux XIXe siecle (Paris: Editions du Seuil, 1980); and several chapters in Norval Morris and David J. Rothman, eds. *The Oxford History of the Prison* (New York: Oxford University Press, 1995). For the Latin American cases, see Ricardo Salvatore and Carlos Aguirre, eds. *The Birth of the Penitentiary in Latin America: Essays on Criminology, Prison Reform, and Social Control, 1830–1940* (Austin: University of Texas Press, 1996).

2 The article by Lila Caimari included in this volume demonstrates the possibilities of using criminological histories of inmates for attempting a similar goal: apprehend the prisoners' views about life, society, and the prison world.

3 I do not mean to suggest that collective letters were an entire novelty in the late 1920s. I have found, indeed, a few such letters written several decades before. A notable one was sent to the National Congress in September 1870 by dozens of penitentiary inmates requesting a reduction of their sentences (National Congress, Historical Archive, Legajo 6, September 19, 1870). In 1892, prisoners from both the Lima penitentiary and the Guadalupe jail sent collective letters to the Congress also requesting a reduction in their sentences on the occasion of the quadricentennial of Columbus's arrival in America (National Congress, Historical Archive, Legajo 9, "Memoriales," Doc. 327, September 30, 1892, and Doc. 328, September 28, 1892). My essay does suggest, though, that in the late 1920s collective forms of representation became more common and revealed newly acquired political and doctrinal notions, which were absent in previous periods.

4 Because I did not find letters written and sent by female inmates at the Santo Tomás Women's Prison, this essay deals exclusively with the male population of the following Lima's prisons: the Lima penitentiary, the El Frontón penal island, the Guadalupe jail, and the Cárcel de Varones (men's jail), opened in 1928 to replace Guadalupe.

5 See Luis A. Eguiguren (Multatuli), *Las calles de Lima* (Lima, 1945), p. 66.

6 See J. Carlos García Basalo, "La reforma carcelaria y penológica en el Perú," in his *San Martín y la reforma carcelaria. Aporte a la historia del derecho penal Argentino y Americano* (Buenos Aires: Ediciones Arayú, 1954).

7 Julio Altmann Smythe, *Reseña histórica de la evolución del derecho penal, con conclusiones sobre la futura política criminal del Perú* (Lima: Sanmarti y Cía, 1944), p. 264.

8 *Reglamento de Tribunales y Juzgados* (Lima: Imprenta del Gobierno, 1854).

9 *El Diario Judicial* (hereafter EDJ), I, 448, November 14, 1891.

10 *El Comercio* (hereafter EC), January 15, 1894 (emphasis added).

11 Judicial authorities seem to have taken this ritual very seriously, however. At least that is the impression given by a reprimand that the Council of Ministers gave to the Superior Court of Puno after learning that the weekly visita had not taken place due to the absence of one of the magistrates. See *El Derecho*, I, 22, May 15, 1886.

12 *Memoria que el Ministro de Justicia, Instrucción, Culto y Beneficiencia Doctor don Wenceslao Valera presenta al Congreso ordinario de 1917*, vol. 1 (Lima: Oficina Tipográfica de La Opinión Nacional, 1917), p. 33.

13 For several decades after its inauguration in 1862, the Lima penitentiary used to receive visitors, many of them foreigners, who wanted to tour its facilities and have a glimpse of this quite "modern" building, the very first such modern construction of the city, as Alberto Flores Galindo has noted (in *La Tradición Autoritaria* [Lima: Aprodeh/SUR, 1999]). The director estimated that in the two years between 1897 and 1899, no fewer than 1,200 individuals had signed the visitors' book. See "Memoria del director del Panóptico de Lima, Don Manuel Panizo y Zárate," in *Memoria que presenta el Ministro de Justicia, Instrucción y Culto al Congreso Ordinario de 1899* (Lima: Imp. Torres Aguirre, 1899). We are concerned here, however, with those individuals that visited Lima's prisons not as "tourists," but because of their concern with the welfare of the prisoners.

14 See "Sociedad de Patronato," *La Gaceta Judicial* (hereafter LGJ) II, II, 451 (November 4, 1892).

15 "Sociedad de Patronato," LGJ, III, I, 501 (January 3, 1893).

16 On Heredia's crusade, see "El Panóptico," in LGJ, II, II, 436 (October 17, 1892), and "Defraudación en la penitenciaría," LGJ, IV, 961 (December 4, 1893).

17 "Penitenciaría," LGJ, II, II, 489 (December 20, 1892).

18 In an obituary published in *El Diario Judicial* (September 2, 1899), Heredia was praised for his efforts with the Sociedad de Patronato but was criticized for approaching the issue from a strictly philanthropic point of view, without paying attention to the new criminological doctrine. For instance, the article said, a criminal enjoying the protection of the Sociedad might well be a "born criminal," a recidivist, or an anarchist and, thus, unworthy of help and incapable of regeneration.

19 Ernesto Espejo Palma, *Necesidad de crear en el Perú el patronato de ex-carcelados como medio de evitar en los delincuentes la reincidencia en el delito* (Lima: Empresa Tipográfica Unión, 1918).

20 *Estatutos de la Asociación Humanitaria del Perú, fundada el 24 de Marzo de 1923* (Lima: Imprenta Torres Aguirre, 1923).

21 *Código Penal del Perú* (1924), Official Edition (Lima: Talleres Gráficos de la Penitenciaría Central, 1948), articles 402–407. Its membership included the current director of the penitentiary, Hermilio Higueras, prominent criminologist Dr. Oscar Miró Quesada, and the current director of the "Sociedad de Beneficencia." Archivo General de la Nación (Lima, Perú, hereafter AGN), Ministerio de Justicia (hereafter MJ), 3.20.3.1.11.1 October 1, 1924.

22 See, for example, the case of José Rivas Cervantes, who was granted pardon and hired as doorman at the penitentiary, both thanks to the intermediation of the Consejo. AGN, MJ, 3.20.3.1.4.1, April 12, 1926.

23 "Ayer la Junta del Patronato visitó la penitenciaría. Hay que llevar a cabo fundamentales reformas," EC, January 19, 1926.

24 "El estado de nuestras instituciones carcelarias. Interesante informe del Presidente del Consejo Local del Patronato," EC, April 14, 1926.

25 AGN, MJ, 3.20.3.1.11.1 (May 2, 1929), Director General de Prisiones to Mrs. Ada H. Dulanto.

26 AGN, MJ, 3.20.3.3.1.3.45, May 10, 1930.

27 AGN, MJ, 3.20.3.1.11.1, August 10, 1926.

28 These activities are documented in Angela Ramos, *Una vida sin tregua*, vol. 1 (Lima: Concytec, 1990).

29 A harsh vagrancy law had been enacted by the Leguía government on January 16, 1924.

30 See Ramos, *Una vida sin tregua*, pp. 41–237, and several issues of the *Boletín de Criminología* (official bulletin of the Dirección General de Prisiones) for details on Angela Ramos's campaign. Angela Ramos, we should add, was also a close friend of Marxist writer and Leguía opponent José Carlos Mariátegui.

31 For additional insights into the workings of criminology in Peru during this period, see Carlos Aguirre, "Crime, Race, and Morals: The Development of Criminology in Peru, 1890–1930," *Crime, History, & Societies*, 2, 2, 1998, pp. 73–90.

32 See, for example, Abraham Rodríguez, "Estudios criminológicos: Primera parte, Los caracteres del hombre criminal" (University of San Marcos [hereafter USM] Medical School, B.A. thesis, 1899); Mario C. Alegre y Pacheco, "Los delincuentes tatuados de la Penitenciaría Nacional" (USM Medical School, B.A. thesis, 1917); M. León Soto i Macedo, "Lijero ensayo de psicología criminal o psiquiatría. Lijeras observaciones en el panóptico de Lima i algunos casos de jurisprudencia práctica" (USM Medical School, B.A. thesis, 1923); Eduardo Coz Sarria, "La cárcel de mujeres de Santo Tomás" (USM Law School, B.A. thesis, 1927).

33 For an overview of these developments, see Aguirre, "Criminology and Prison Reform."

34 For example, the National League for Hygiene and Social Prophylactics, presided over by Dr. Leonidas Avendaño, organized a series of lectures for penitentiary inmates in 1925, with subjects such as "Civil Heroes," "Anti-Alcoholism," "Sexual Hygiene," and "The Education of the Character inside the prison." AGN, MJ, 3.20.3.1.11.1, September 9, 1925. A similar series was conducted in 1928 by the Federation of Students of Penal Law. EC, September 18, 1928.

35 Paulino Fuentes Castro published in 1892 in his *El Diario Judicial* a series of portraits of famous criminals, including Manuel Peña Chacaliaza, Lorenzo Machiavello, Juan Patiño, and Tomasa Saavedra. See also the portrait of "Tonguito," a famous juvenile criminal in "Algo sobre sociología local: la baja hampa, un ratero incorregible," EC, December 22, 1905; or press coverage of famous criminals such as Alejandrino Montes, "El Negro" Arzola, or Emilio Willman, "Carita." Numerous foreign articles, biographies, cause célèbres, and short novels were also published.

36 See, for example, "La Penitenciaría," EC, May 19, 1901; "La Cárcel de Guadalupe," EC, June 2, 1901; "En la cárcel de mujeres," EC, December 22, 1901; "Una visita a la

penitenciaría," EC, October 15, 1905; "En la penitenciaría de Lima: Una visita detenida a ese establecimiento," EC, October 28, 1908; "Cómo es la cárcel de Guadalupe," *El Tiempo,* September 21, 1918; "Dos horas en la Cárcel de Guadalupe," EC, November 9, 1919; "Visitando el Panóptico," EC, November 30, 1919; "Una visita a la cárcel de Santo Tomás," EC, November 16, 1919.

37 The reporter for *El Comercio* seemed a bit disappointed, in May 1901, when he could not meet Lorenzo Machiavello—an Italian immigrant accused of triple homicide, whose case was one of the most sensational of the time—at the penitentiary because he had been transferred to Guadalupe.

38 See, for example, "Carta de un preso de Guadalupe," EC, August 12, 1915, where the inmate protested that he got eight months in jail only because a policeman accused him of disrespect.

39 For sordid details on Leguía's repressive methods, see, among others, Abelardo Solís, *Once años* (Lima: Talleres Gráficos Sanmarti y Cia, 1934), pp. 51–59. Solís, like many other sources, points to San Lorenzo Island as the main destination for political prisoners during the Leguía oncenio.

40 Jorge Basadre, *Historia de la República del Perú,* 6th ed. (Lima: Editorial Universitaria, 1968), vol. XIII, p. 379.

41 See the memorandum recounting this episode in AGN, MJ, 3.20.3.1.11.1, November 12, 1930.

42 AGN, MJ, 3.20.3.1.12.5.1, November 12, 1932. See also the testimony offered by Juan Seoane, an Aprista convicted for the assassination of President Luis M. Sánchez Cerro, in his novel *Hombres y Rejas* (Santiago de Chile: Ercilla, 1937). The volume *Cartas de Haya de la Torre a los prisioneros apristas* (Lima: Editorial Nuevo Día, 1946) contains a sample of letters written by Haya de la Torre (some of them while he himself was detained) and smuggled into the penitentiary and other prisons.

43 AGN, MJ, 3.20.3.1.12.1.1, December 30, 1924.

44 Conditions at El Frontón were, according to most testimonies, the worst of all Lima's prisons during this period. Penitentiary inmates were sent there as a way of punishment for offenses committed while serving their sentences.

45 AGN, MJ, 3.20.3.1.11.1, April 26, 1926.

46 AGN, MJ, 3.20.3.1.1.2.51, July 26, 1930. A similar tone pervades a letter written by Guadalupe inmates to Angela Ramos, thanking her for all the activities she was organizing in favor of Lima inmates. See Ramos, *Una vida sin tregua,* pp. 139–140.

47 AGN, MJ, 3.20.3.1.12.1.2, April 11, 1930.

48 AGN, MJ, 3.20.3.3.1.3.45, f. 10, s/f.

49 Indigenismo was a cultural and political current that became fashionable in the early twentieth century. Although they hardly constitute a homogenous school, indigenistas shared some common features: they were non-Indians, wrote in the cities and for an essentially urban audience, and displayed a paternalistic, essentializing, and even racist view of the Indian "race." For recent and illuminating

analyses of this trend, see especially Mirko Lauer, *Andes imaginarios: discursos del indigenismo—2* (Lima: SUR/Centro Bartolomé de las Casas, 1997); Deborah Poole, *Vision, Race, and Modernity: A Visual Economy of the Andean Image World* (Princeton, N.J.: Princeton University Press, 1997); Deborah Poole, "Ciencia, peligrosidad y represión en la criminología indigenista peruana," in Carlos Aguirre and Charles Walker, eds. *Bandoleros, abigeos, y montoneros: criminalidad y violencia en el Perú, siglos XVIII–XX* (Lima: Instituto de Apoyo Agrario, 1990), pp. 335–367; and Marisol de la Cadena, *Indigenous Mestizos: the Politics of Race and Culture in Cuzco, Peru, 1919–1991* (Durham, N.C.: Duke University Press, 2000).

50 Francois Chevalier, "Official Indigenismo in Peru," in Magnus Morner, ed., *Race and Class in Latin America* (New York: Columbia University Press, 1977), pp. 184–196.

51 Quoted in Basadre, *Historia de la República,* vol. XIII, p. 309.

52 Our review of the prisoners' letters reveals that, in many instances, they seem to have been written not by the prisoners themselves, but by other individuals. Who these writers were is difficult to establish: they could have been outside relatives, fellow educated inmates, lawyers, informal legal practitioners (*tinterillos*), or even prison employees paid by the inmates.

53 AGN, MJ, 3.20.3.1.12.1.1, February 25, 1925.

54 AGN, MJ, 3.20.3.1.12.1.1, March 30, 1927.

55 James Scott, *Domination and the Arts of Resistance: Hidden Transcripts* (New Haven: Yale University Press, 1990), p. 4.

56 See, for instance, Steve Stein, *Lima obrera, 1900–1930* (Lima: El Virrey Ediciones, 1986); Manuel Burga and Alberto Flores Galindo, *Apogeo y crisis de la República Aristocrática* (Lima: Ediciones Rikchay, 1979); David Parker, "The Rise of the Peruvian Middle Class: A Social and Political History of White-Collar Employees in Lima, 1900–1950" (Ph.D. dissertation, Stanford University, 1990).

57 AGN, MJ, 3.20.3.1.12.1.2, June 12, 1929.

58 AGN, MJ, 3.20.3.1.12.1.2, May 2, 1930.

59 AGN, MJ, 3.20.3.1.1.2.51, August 28, 1930.

60 AGN, MJ, 3.20.3.1.12.1.3, November 3, 1930.

61 AGN, MJ, 3.20.3.1.1.2.51, September 20, 1930. See also EC, December 9, 1931, for another letter with a very similar content. Prisoners of the Cárcel de Varones, this time, asked President Sánchez Cerro to pay a visit to the prison, where they would let him know personally "our pathetic situation."

62 Ramos, *Una vida sin tregua,* p. 133.

63 AGN, MJ, 3.20.3.1.1.2.51, April 10, 1929.

64 AGN, MJ, 3.20.3.1.1.2.51, May 22, 1930.

65 AGN, MJ, 3.20.3.1.12.1.1, January 3, 1926, emphasis added.

66 AGN, MJ, 3.20.3.1.12.2.2, August 15, 1928.

67 AGN, MJ, 3.20.3.1.1.2.51, December 9, 1931.

68 Villavicencio was one of the most conspicuous criminologists and penologists of

this period. He wrote extensively on a variety of issues regarding penal regimes and served in various posts within the administration of prisons. See, among his numerous publications, *La reforma penitenciaria en el Perú* (Lima: Imprenta A. J. Rivas Berrio, 1927). I have also found evidence that Villavicencio was particularly harsh on prisoners, giving them generally low scores during the "qualification" process, which may explain why inmates wanted to get rid of him. See AGN, MJ, 3.20.3.3.1.5.22.

69 AGN, MJ, 3.20.3.1.12.1.4, December 10, 1931.

70 On this, see especially Steve Stein, *Populism in Peru: The Emergence of the Masses and the Politics of Social Control* (Madison: University of Wisconsin Press, 1980).

Girls in Prison: The Role of the

Buenos Aires Casa Correccional de Mujeres as

an Institution for Child Rescue, 1890–1940

DONNA J. GUY

⎯⎯⎯⎯⎯⎯⎯⎯⎯⎯⎯⎯

In late nineteenth- and early twentieth-century Argentina, children sent to jail were not invited to speak in their own defense, except when they were tried as adults for crimes other than misdemeanors. Often viewed as targets of the police and sometimes of their own parents, decisions were made about their incarceration without their input. Their only voice was acts of defiance such as running away from abusive parents, foster homes, and places of employment. Nevertheless, it is possible to reconstruct how public and private authorities imagined and dealt with them. This essay focuses primarily on their debates about young girls between the ages of five and twenty who were jailed in Buenos Aires between 1892 and 1937 for crimes ranging from being homeless to engaging in petty theft and prostitution.

In 1910 Argentine legal historian Roberto Levillier published an extensive essay on criminality in Buenos Aires. When he broached the topic of female criminality, he noted that children inhabited the women's prison, but he focused on female offenders. He claimed that criminologists had ignored these women and that "female delinquency has not inspired the least interest in Buenos Aires. The specialists consider the percentage of these crimes statistically insignificant, and the causes neither important nor long lasting, and they have worried neither about their evolution, nor their prevention, nor their reincidence rate." Furthermore, the female religious who operated the women's jail in Buenos Aires did not run the facility according to scientific principles. Instead, according to Levillier, the institution operated as a vocational school (*escuela taller*) and lacked orientation.[1] Consequently, Levillier worried about the fate of these women and made various suggestions about prison reform.

If women and girls were incarcerated, how could they be rehabilitated? What was the point of putting them in jail? According to Michel Foucault, "detention may be a mere deprivation of liberty. But the imprisonment that performs this function has always involved a technical project."[2] Foucault defined this technical project by referring to male prisoners and men's prisons. But not all people in Argentine jails between 1890 and 1940 were accused of crimes, and many of these unfortunate individuals were young girls, some as young as five years old. What was the function of depriving minor girls of their liberty? This essay attempts to explore the reasoning and "technical project" underlying the incarceration of girls in the Buenos Aires Women's Correctional Facility (Casa Correccional de Mujeres).

A number of scholars have examined the role of criminology and penal reforms in Latin America.[3] Among them only María Soledad Zárate Campos and Lila Caimari have studied female-focused systems of incarceration, and they have dealt with the treatment of women convicted of crimes in Chile and Argentina. Their pioneering work noted how adult female offenders were placed beyond the gaze and reach of positivistic criminologists and left to the moral influence of the nuns from the Order of the Good Shepherd who operated these prisons. Caimari has also analyzed how the frequent use of parole for women led to short stays that limited efforts to rehabilitate them in Buenos Aires. For these women, rehabilitation meant a return to hearth and home where relatives, presumably male, monitored their behavior.

Rehabilitation and redemption were social and religious ideals that had different meanings for males and females, adults and children, yet incarceration was the initial response of public officials for all. As the Buenos Aires police chief noted in the annual report for 1913–1914,[4]

> Vagrancy, begging, and abandoned children are social plagues that my predecessors have reported on many occasions . . . and yet we still need to work on these issues so that this Capital will be socially cleansed. . . . The legislation regarding guardianship of these children

has already been initiated and along with the measures adopted by the National Government regarding the habilitation and expansion of buildings needed to house them, allow us to hope that this problem of minor children . . . will soon be solved.

Yet the following year police reported 574 girls had been detained by police, "mostly for running away from home or from work." Among these were seventy-three servants.[5]

These problems were not easily resolved by expanding prisons. For adult males, rehabilitation was supposed to reform work habits to enable them to support themselves without committing crimes. In contrast, adult females were to return home where they would perform unpaid labor.

For minors, the issues were quite different. Whether male or female, all had either parents, guardians, or the Defensores de Menores (Defender of Minors) to decide on an appropriate rehabilitation strategy. Custody laws prevented government officials from making important decisions that implied long stays at government facilities. Parents or legal guardians had more legal rights over children and thus could thwart the efforts of state officials. In the case of female minors, when public authorities intervened, state rehabilitation meant returning them to their kin or to some other family; alternatively, nuns educated them in jail, often without much governmental enthusiasm, to be domestic servants. As far as the nuns were concerned, prisons holding young girls either had to be turned into educational institutions or girls had to be transferred to such facilities. Neither policy was popular among government officials until the 1930s because they believed female vocational education, if offered at all, should be carried out under familial rather than governmental supervision. For these reasons, traditional concepts of reform and rehabilitation made little sense for the majority of female minors in the prison population. The debate about vocational training as rehabilitation for young female offenders was not resolved until changing economic and social conditions compelled national leaders to open group homes for the young girls.

Until the opening of the new reformatories, in Buenos Aires suspicious girls were usually sent to jail for a short period of time. Adrift in the streets of the rapidly growing capital city, both boys and girls were perceived to be both dangerous and at risk in public places. City officials wanted girls returned to their parents, many too poor or unwilling to care for them. By law all parents were required to feed, house, educate and clothe their biological children, but this was often impossible. Although some of the girls were sent to jail for engaging in prostitution or committing a variety of crimes ranging from infanticide to petty robbery, the majority were street children, homeless, orphaned, or runaways from exploitative parents or employers. In a society that clearly defined patriarchal rights for fathers or single mothers, one with no legal way to adopt children and few public facilities for children over the age of six, Argentine women's jails — whether in Buenos Aires or in interior cities — were used as temporary shelters for many young girls.

The majority of girls who ended up in the Casa Correccional had been sent by the Defensores de Menores, because they operated no shelters. Abandoned infants could be sent to the orphanage (Casa de Expósitos) of the Society of Beneficence (Sociedad de Beneficencia). Sometimes girls under the age of six would also be accepted by the Sociedad into their Girls' Orphanage (Asilo de Huérfanas), but there were never enough places. The rest of the children they received had to be sent out to work, returned to kin, or languish temporarily in jail.[6]

This process, however, was more than warehousing. Once abandoned infants and street children were jailed, their lack of social protection became evident and was reinforced because the act of leaving jail involved placement in a home of an adult who was not a relative and who had to pay the girls a wage appropriate for their age. The child became a laborer without protection. In this new home they had no parents, only employers. They had no relatives, and they received no inheritance. One might argue that the technical project behind the incarceration of poor young girls on the street was to create a rite of passage that removed them from the streets, and, through the powers of public officials, returned them to private, domestic society with new identities that acknowledged their inferior social status.

Street children, whether male or female, were disturbing to the sense of social order in Buenos Aires. They existed in a liminal state, protected only when in the home, and accused of criminality when in public spaces. This often became a wish-fulfilling prophecy. Their parents, if they had any, were perceived to have abandoned their children morally and materially. Male street children were feared more than girls, because they were believed to be potential recruits as criminals or anarchists. Girls were assumed to be prostitutes.

Argentine national politicians first responded to this problem by viewing male vagrant children as juvenile delinquents. In August 1892 President

Carlos Pellegrini claimed that street urchins, particularly young males, were all potential criminals. He suggested that a jail be constructed and dedicated solely to young male offenders. He noted that the overcrowded penitentiary held adults and children and "the growing number of corrupted children sent there daily by Defensores and judges" could never be contained. What the president failed to tell the deputies was that many of these children were arrested for being homeless.[7]

Although legislators were quick to authorize funding for a special facility for delinquent boys, one that opened in 1903, they hesitated to provide similar facilities for either homeless or delinquent girls. Nor did they challenge the authority of female religious orders in charge of women's jails, although they did not always agree with their plans. The nuns operating the women's prison wanted above all to rehabilitate delinquent girls and women through education and labor. This meant separating the girls from female criminals and keeping girls safely off the street in an institutional setting where they could be educated. Unable to provide this, the nuns settled for offering brief opportunities for elementary education and set up workshops for them. The short stays of both the girls and adult prisoners meant that all hopes of rehabilitation were illusory, and the annual reports of the nuns were quick to indicate this as a justification for transforming the jail into another type of institution that offered long-term facilities for inmates. They also urged, to no avail, that the national government construct separate facilities to house minors, one that would allow them to be better educated before they left.

The history of the early years of the Buenos Aires Casa Correccional de Mujeres, as Caimari has noted, is difficult to trace. From 1873 until 1888 nuns had operated the Asilo del Buen Pastor (Good Shepherd Asylum) a jail, and the Casa de Ejercicios, a convent dedicated to rehabilitating delinquent females. Girls were sent to the Buen Pastor if they were considered "incorrigible," and the others were sent to the Casa de Ejercicios.[8]

By the 1880s the Buenos Aires police did not relish the idea of having children wandering about on the streets, but they also opposed sending children to jail. The rules governing the police made it difficult for them to solve the problem of street children, inasmuch as they were discouraged from interfering with private family matters. Thus they were supposed to investigate the circumstances surrounding the presence of these children in public places, and if the children had parents, to find out whether the children had been forced out of their homes. Even if children were incorrigible, they were supposed to tell parents that public jails and institutions were not *lugares de corrección,* correctional institutions. It must have been ironic for them to send girls to Defensores who in turn placed them in the very institutions police disdained as sites of rehabilitation.[9]

The Buenos Aires Asilo Correccional de Mujeres officially opened in 1892. During the early years basic repairs, painting, and remodeling made the building habitable. Additional wings later provided more space for inmates. Most of the children were sent not by the police but from the Defensores de Menores. Officially, girls' ages ranged from five to twenty, yet there is evidence that babies often accompanied their mothers. There, in accordance with the Argentine Civil Code, children were paid a salary commensurate to their age and labors performed in the jail.[10] By the time the first national prison census was taken in 1906, the facility had the capacity to hold 100 adults and 150 minors at one time, operated first and second grade primary school classes for illiterate women and children, and training in laundry and sewing workshops.[11] Eventually the prison offered classes through the fourth grade.

The number of girls who entered the jail varied tremendously from year to year. In 1889, for example, several years before its official opening, 466 were locked up, and most of them left during the same year. In 1892, 694 spent time there, compared with 317 in 1893. This trend continued as the numbers of minors soared to over 1,138 in 1911, and peaked in 1917 with 1,874 admissions. Until the mid-1920s fewer girls were sent there, although in only one year, 1922, did the numbers decline below 1,400. In contrast, the adult prisoners rarely exceeded 400, and tended to range between 200 and 300.[12]

The defensores, like the police, were not enthusiastic about placing young children in the Casa Correccional de Mujeres. On May 7, 1901, defensor José M. Terrero asked the minister of justice to plead with the minister of foreign relations to force the Sociedad de Beneficencia to accept abandoned children between the ages of six and eight. The Sociedad, however, rarely acceded to demands from Defensores because these matrons insisted on setting their own rules for operating their institutions. Another Buenos Aires group, the Sociedad Patronato de la Infancia, could not help them out, as it only offered daycare facilities in its schools. Thus the Defensores had few alternatives.[13]

The population of Buenos Aires soared during this time period. In 1895 there were 663,854 inhabitants, mostly European immigrants, and by 1914

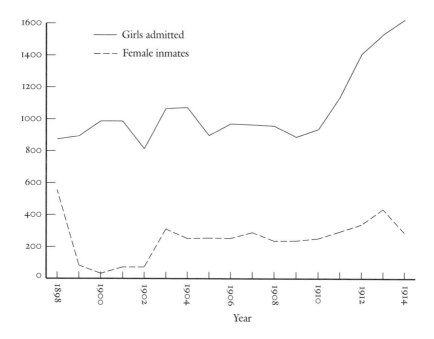

FIGURE I Inmates, Women's Jail (1898–1914). *Source:* Municipalidad de Buenos Aires, Dirección de Estadística Municipal, Anuari estadístico de la ciudad de Buenos Aires, 1896, 1903, 1913, 1914.

the population exceeded 1.4 million. Thereafter waves of migrants from the interior began to replace immigrants as a source of population increase. By 1947 Buenos Aires had more than two million residents. As the city swelled, poor families often found themselves unable to cope with the stresses of adapting to urban life in the capital, despite the new opportunities it offered. For their children, the result was often abandonment, homelessness, and temptations to engage in criminal activities.

In order to deal with this problem, the mother superior of the Casa Correccional de Mujeres wrote to Argentine President Uriburu in 1895 offering to take in more street children. Claiming that there were many poor girls who needed to avail themselves of such shelter, she asked for permission to admit them merely because they were poor, in order to educate them.[14] When informed of this request, the three Defensores de Menores quickly stepped in to complain that such a plan infringed on parental custody rights associated with *patria potestas,* as well as with the powers invested in themselves.[15]

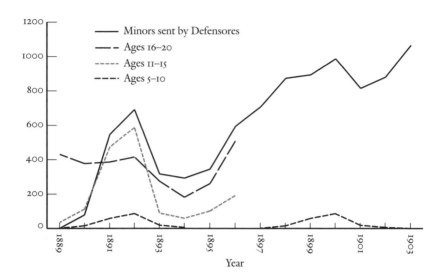

FIGURE 2 Ages of Minor Prisoners (1889–1903). *Source:* Anuario estadístico de la ciudad de Buenos Aires, 1903.

Unwilling to share the task with the nuns, Defensores de Menores had an immense task confronting them. By 1898, 1,878 children of both sexes entered their care, and thereafter the numbers began to taper off.[16] Initially the defensores were quite successful in returning children to their biological families. Parents or relatives took back 30 percent of the children, while another 24 percent were successfully placed under contract in foster homes. This situation began to deteriorate by 1888 when the Asilo del Buen Pastor closed down. At that time Pedro Roberts, defensor for the southern part of the city, received 542 children. Only 172 (33%) were returned to kin, while 210 (51%) were sent to foster families. Among the rest, twenty-five girls ended up in the women's prison (which was supposed to be closed), eleven in the Casa de Ejercicios, and sixty-nine boys (31%) in the penitentiary.[17] Gradually defensores became less able to return their children to their kin.

The records of individual defensores are incomplete, but some demonstrate a greater ability to keep girls out of jail than others. In 1897, for example, defensor Pedro de Elizalde managed to place 342 boys and girls with families (both kin and non kin), while he sent only thirty-one girls to the Casa Correccional and three to the Casa de Ejercicios.[18] For those girls who ended up as servants, their situation was probably not much better, and sometimes worse than being in the Casa Correccional.

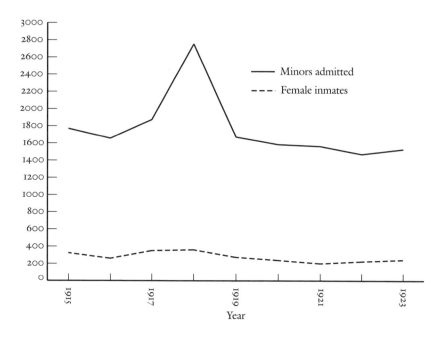

FIGURE 3 Inmates, Women's Jail (1915–1923). *Source:* Anuario estadístico de la ciudad de Buenos Aires, 1923.

The dangers facing employed female minors became clear in 1889 when the physician for the Casa Correccional de Mujeres, Abraham Zenavilla, submitted his report to the mother superior relating conditions between June and December 1899. He noted that the two most common types of ailments were respiratory and gynecological. As he put it: "The latter are most common in the older girls, and the causes are due to abandonment and the lack of considerate treatment of them by people who seek their services." That is, they were sexually abused by their employers or male family members.[19]

This problem was evident to the defensores. In 1908 they penned a joint letter to the Ministry of Justice and claimed that the situation was so bad that when some asked for the services of a female minor, they always asked: "Do you have any sons, Señora?" If she said yes, none of them would allow the girl to work for that family. For that reason they wanted to make sure that girls were not handed out to families directly by the courts or the jails.[20]

Even though Defensores often avoided sending girls to the prison, the building simply did not have the capacity to hold the numbers of minors

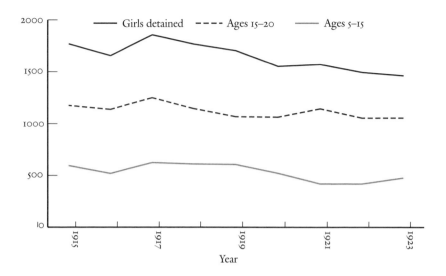

FIGURE 4 Ages of Girls in Prison (1915–1923). *Source:* Anuario estadístico de la ciudad de Buenos Aires, 1923.

sent there. At that time the area devoted to housing minors could only hold 110, but sometimes the nuns were forced to house up to 200 children. In June 1900 the mother superior again suggested that the nuns could provide a more extensive service for vagrant girls. She urged the national government to authorize construction of a completely separate juvenile facility where the children could stay "at least three or four years so they could receive a moderate education and thereby be useful to families by offering services appropriate to their condition, i.e., as cooks, maids, and laundresses."[21] Her request acknowledged the limited usefulness of existing facilities at the same time that its language reaffirmed the technical project of turning homeless girls into servants.

The mother superior's views were occasionally supported by some of the Defensores. In 1903 a new defensor, B. Lainez, suggested a series of reforms. Among them included the transformation of the Casa Correccional de Mujeres into a trade school for the adult women, with sections that would separate delinquent minors from those merely being warehoused. He also argued that a school for juvenile mothers be a part of the trade school. His suggestions fell on deaf ears and he did not remain long in his post.[22]

Parents occasionally voiced their approval of the prison system as a site of rehabilitation. They could request that the state incarcerate their daughters for up to one month because they could no longer discipline them. Luisa Gigena de Saldaño made this request in 1920. She was so poor that she could only offer the address of the Defender of the Poor as her legal residence. Luisa claimed that her daughter, Juana Isabel, was taking advantage of the fact that her father was in Tucumán province to engage in prostitution. Luisa was so enraged that she had the police lock up her daughter, and lacking other resources, she petitioned the court to incarcerate her daughter for the amount of time stipulated by the law. After several witnesses confirmed Luisa's story, the judge ordered that Juana be jailed.[23]

Like the judges, defensores incarcerated very young girls along with adolescents. In 1907, for example, forty-two girls under the age of ten were locked up, while 320 between the ages of ten and fifteen also found themselves behind bars. In total, the number of girls between six and fifteen equaled more than 38 percent of incarcerated juveniles. By 1912, this proportion had decreased to only 33 percent.[24]

Defenders were highly displeased by the number of children languishing in jail, but they had no other alternatives. One defender suggested a new policy. In 1910 Dr. Agustín Cabal, frustrated by the numbers of girls who refused to remain in the home of their employers, began to insist that all girls under his care be fingerprinted by the police. This not only made it easier to capture them, he reasoned, it also offered an incentive to these waifs. According to him, by the time the girl reached legal adulthood, if she had no files with the police other than her fingerprints, she could use that fact to demonstrate "proof of her honesty" (patente de honestidad).[25] Those who could not, ended up in jail and subsequently reentered society with a new, questionable identity.

Within the jail increased numbers of inmates and insufficient funding led to poor conditions. According to a report of the mother superior on April 12, 1910, there was a shortage of warm clothing, bedding, and underwear for both adult and child inmates, and their shoes were in bad condition. Within the section for girls from fifteen to twenty years of age, there were 140 inmates, but only 118 beds. The rest of the girls slept on the floor. On cold nights each only had one blanket. The nuns requested more than four thousand pesos to provide basic elements for the children. They were granted the request, but these and other documents indicate that funding was provided on an ad hoc basis.[26]

Sometimes girls with physical and mental disabilities were housed with able-bodied children. In 1911 Gregoria Gutiérrez was sent by Defensor Cabal to the Casa Correccional. Her only crime was the fact that she was a deaf-mute. Two years later a bureaucrat found out and inquired about her. He was informed that the child had been admitted at the age of fifteen and the physician in charge determined that she was deaf and mute, and had a mental age of three or four. Although the Institute for the Deaf and Mute was notified, no action was taken and the girl continued at the Casa Correccional. In this case, the child was already stigmatized, and therefore she did not need to reenter society in order to be identified.[27]

During the short stay in the women's jail, young girls were expected to work. Yearly more than one thousand girls labored in shops sewing and doing laundry work. Their pay was meager at best, partly because most did not stay long, but also because they had to pay for all the materials they used. An example of this comes from the 1913 annual report of earnings by minors at the Women's Jail. The many girls who passed through the doors of that institution together earned less than 2,500 pesos. Only 417.48 pesos were actually turned over to them as they left. Girls spent 279.77, mostly on clothing and shoes; their expenses far exceeded what they actually received. The costs of thread, fabric, and other articles of production equaled $612.72, and they were also charged almost the same amount for the cost of repairing and use of facilities. In other years reports of child income were quite similar.[28]

The outbreak of World War I affected the poor of Buenos Aires with shortages of fuel and articles of consumption. According to the Defensores de Menores, it also made their task of placing young girls in foster care as paid laborers more difficult. Their 1914 annual report stated, "The current crisis has affected these prospects. Families have begun to cut back on their budgets. Not only have they decreased the number of people working for them, they have also cut salaries." The defensores argued that this resulted in increased numbers of girls in the Casa Correccional, although the statistics do not support the claim. Nevertheless, they proposed reducing the mandatory wages paid to their wards in order to make them more attractive to foster parents. Furthermore, they suggested that incorrigible girls be sent to work on ranches in the territories, a practice that had been used to remove juvenile boys from the city.[29] There are no records of any girls being sent to the country to work.

In contrast to the defensores' view of young girls as burdens that needed to be excised from the body politic, the nuns continued to believe that they could rehabilitate even the most difficult ones through education and work. In an extract of the 1919 annual report for the Women's Jail, the mother superior noted that the girls in her care were worthy of compassion "because the majority of them cannot aspire to the well-being that comes from knowledge of the arts and sciences for the simple reason that they lack the means to obtain them [i.e., family and status]. They inevitably will have to fend for themselves and thus will have to learn to labor as working-class women and servants." For this reason the nuns wanted to educate them to live "honest lives and to practice their duties as Christians."[30] Once again the language of the mother superior acknowledged that girls who entered the jail had insufficient social connections to offer them anything other than work for the uneducated and unprotected. Once again, her words went unheeded.

That same year the problem of juvenile delinquency was discussed extensively in the Argentine Congress. For many years child rights advocates had been arguing for reforms of the penal code that would distinguish the crimes of minors from those of adults, and create special juvenile courts patterned after the U.S. model pioneered in Chicago in 1899. Early efforts included attempts by conservative deputy Luis Agote to empower the national government to assume legal guardianship over all juvenile delinquents and abandoned children under the age of seventeen. To justify his proposal, Agote argued that from 1905 to 1910 1,312 boys had entered national prisons for crimes they committed, and among them 520 were repeat offenders. In addition to these delinquent children, more than a thousand worked as newspaper boys, and even more lived on the streets only to become part of "anarchist bands." He opposed treating juveniles as criminals and suggested that street children be scooped up from the streets and placed in an expanded boys reform school (Marcos Paz), or in a branch of it that might be located at the former lepers' colony on Martín García Island. Agote estimated that ten thousand boys could be rehabilitated in such places.[31] His unsuccessful attempt was followed by others, equally unsuccessful. In 1916 Eduardo Bullrich and Dr. Roberto Gache presented to the Ministers of Justice and Public Instruction a plan to have juvenile courts and mandatory education, rather than work, rehabilitate abandoned and delinquent juveniles.[32]

After Luis Agote's efforts to resubmit his proposal failed in June 1918, the following January Argentine President Hipólito Yrigoyen made child rights reforms a high priority. He sent a message to congress on January 20,

1919, supporting congressional efforts to form a new Association for the Protection of Minors (Patronato de Menores). That year a revised version of Agote's bill was enacted, but no funds were allocated to finance the new institution.[33] During all these debates the plight of incarcerated poor children who had not committed crimes, as well as the special circumstances of girls, were never mentioned.

In 1921 a reformed penal code revised notions of juvenile delinquency that had been operating since the 1880s. For the first time the new law mandated that all children under the age of fourteen not receive punishment, although under certain conditions, offenders could be committed to institutions until they turned eighteen. Many of these cases, however, were dismissed after 1921, and the offenders were never sent to jail. These provisions, however, once again did not account for those juveniles in jail for being homeless.[34]

Although legislators glossed over the plight of the homeless, a 1910 article specifically dealt with this issue. It noted that throughout the province of Buenos Aires, including the city of Buenos Aires, municipal defensores dealt with abandoned and homeless children by placing them as servants in families and argued that this "system operates with doubtful efficiency since few patrons fulfill their responsibilities in a conscientious manner, and the result is that children are left in misery and hunger." This report saw the protection of the state for both boys and girls as the only salvation for them, but it neglected to ask where the children would be housed.[35] Although efforts were made through the national Departamento de Menores Abandonados y Encausados (National Department of Abandoned and Accused Children) — an early bureaucratic effort created in 1913 to place both accused and nonaccused jailed minors in reformatories or school environments — boys were the beneficiaries of these efforts. The Departamento's successor, the Instituto Tutelar de Menores (Supervisory Institute of Minors), founded in 1918, continued this laudable, but gendered effort and focused entirely on boys convicted of crimes.[36] As a result, girls continued to pass through the portals of the Casa Correccional de Mujeres.

There were several alternatives to warehousing these children. The most expensive solution was to construct special facilities for homeless and delinquent children such as those suggested by the nuns of the Good Shepherd. Another, less expensive option was legal adoption. Until 1948 the only way to adopt a child so that he or she could enjoy the same legal rights as a legitimate child was to falsify the public records — a common occurrence.

This method, however, was used principally to integrate infants into the family. By the 1920s a group of legal specialists, in alliance with the Sociedad de Beneficencia and the Museo Social Argentino (Argentine Social Museum), a group of reform-minded elites, began to examine a series of questions regarding street children. Heartened by the organization of national and international child rights congresses held in Buenos Aires in 1913 and 1916, as well as subsequent international meetings in Montevideo in 1919, Rio de Janeiro in 1922, and Santiago de Chile in 1924, child-rights advocates published articles and gave talks on the subject. Adoption was suggested as a solution. By the time adoption became legal in Argentina in the 1940s, it was evident that infants, rather than juveniles, would benefit most from this legal reform.[37]

As part of efforts to deal with this and other issues, Buenos Aires hosted the first Latin American conference of specialists in psychiatry and legal medicine in 1929. Under the guidance of Dr. Gregorio Bermann, participants broached the topic of delinquent and abandoned children and argued that they should be aided rather than punished, and that the state should undertake this responsibility. Yet when he analyzed the situation of abandoned girls, all he could do was reiterate what was already known — that the only place for such girls, particularly those accused of any crime, was the women's jails, whereas boys had more state facilities available to them.[38] Nothing could be done until public officials decided to construct institutions for homeless girls.

The coalition of political parties that supported the election of General Agustín P. Justo in 1931 included many people who strongly endorsed authorizing new state entities to promote child welfare. Aware of the impact of the depression on Buenos Aires, they understood how it affected children and used it as a justification to change state policy toward abandoned children. On January 24, 1931, a decree finally authorized the creation of the Patronato Nacional de Menores, operated by juvenile delinquency specialists and empowered to reorganize the juvenile justice system. The people named to the Patronato included prominent specialists in child-rights issues, and with the support of Justo, they convened a major conference to bring together national and provincial authorities interested in reforming juvenile law.

Held in September 1933, the First National Conference on Abandoned and Delinquent Children attracted the attention of the public at large not only because of the topic, but also due to the presence of the president and his cabinet, and even supreme court judges. There was also a significant female presence owing to the attendance of members of the Sociedad de Beneficencia and the ladies of the Society of St. Vincent de Paul.

At the third conference session on September 28, specialists began to discuss the rehabilitation of girls. The perceived difference between the genders emerged when discussion began to focus on whether vocational education should be different for boys and girls. Some argued that girls should not be given professional training *(enseñanza profesional),* but rather one preparing them for domestic life *(para el hogar).* This was not refuted by anyone.[39] Furthermore, a representative of the ladies of the Society of St. Vincent de Paul commented on the special challenge of helping girls in prison and offered their services, much like the nuns of the Good Shepherd had many years before, to attend to these girls. Noting that they had been accepting girls recommended by the juvenile courts created in 1919, they pointed out that the few they could accept lived in family settings of thirty girls where they learned how to dedicate themselves to keeping house, caring for children, and basic education.[40] Given the number of girls still incarcerated each year at the Casa Correccional de Mujeres, Buenos Aires needed more than a few model homes to deal with young girls forced onto the streets. Nevertheless, the alliance between the Patronato de Menores and the charitable institutions led to the formation of girls' homes under the watchful eyes of penologists and sociologists rather than the nuns of the Good Shepherd, residences that trained them for their own homes, not for domestic service.

Until this transformation was effected in the 1940s, the Casa Correccional de Mujeres continued to serve as an auxiliary to the Defenders of Minors. By 1914 the nuns were finally able to segregate the girls sent to them by the Defenders in a separate wing. This partially alleviated the anxiety of the Defenders who were loath to mix their charges with the general prison population, although they made no effort to change their class-bound views toward their wards.[41] By 1921 the nuns felt that everything was operating well at the jail, and that their constant preoccupation was training both girls and women in basic domestic skills. As they put it, "Experience has shown that indolence and luxury are the principal causes of delinquency among women, as in minor girls . . . and it is necessary to make them love their work: the majority of them depend solely on manual labor to reward them with a decorous life." None were encouraged to transcend the class and gendered nature of their existence.[42]

By 1932, however, economic conditions made it very difficult to place young girls in homes as domestic servants, and a higher than usual number of homeless girls were sent to the women's jail. For those reasons President Justo decreed that the Patronato Nacional de Menores establish an institution for the girls in the Casa Correccional, "so that they can get work in industry or commerce." To that end, a government property was donated to the Patronato.[43] When the mother superior submitted her report to the Ministry of Justice that year, she noted that the prison was overcrowded with an average daily population of 331 women and children, which at times reached 371. The need to reduce the prison population was imperative if workshops were to be expanded to meet national laws. Furthermore, she reiterated that the educational classes did little for inmates because they stayed for too short a time; once again she requested the construction of a separate boarding school.[44] The following year the mother superior complained that the adult prison population had expanded even more, and asked for funds to bring in more female religious to help run the institution.[45] There was no mention of minor girls in the jail, nor was there any direct mention thereafter, although references were made concerning the habitations for *las presas madres,* or prisoners who were caring for their infants.[46] The era of incarcerating young girls had ended.

The demise of this system also presaged the weakening of the institution of the Defensores de Menores. Superseded by the Patronato de Menores as well as by the system of institutional homes for young girls adrift in society, there was now much less need for these elite men to intercede for young children. By now the beginnings of a national welfare state had emerged, one that not only treated juvenile criminals differently from adult offenders, but also no longer sought to place minors in the homes of strangers. This stigmatization of children continued on an informal level through kin and potential employers seeking young children in service, but it was no longer part of an official institutional framework. The nuns of the Good Shepherd had been correct about the need to treat these children differently and ensure their education, but they played no part in that transformation. From then on state-operated group homes and other types of institutions, some still run by other female religious orders, became the safety net for street children. In recent years homes operated by nongovernmental organizations (NGOs) have also been founded.

This chapter in Argentine prison history is important in a number of ways. First of all, it points to the different ways that criminality and poten-

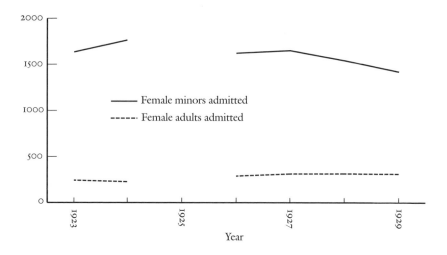

FIGURE 5 Inmates, Women's Jail (1923–1929). *Source:* República Argentina, Ministerio de Justicia e Instrucción Pública, Memorias, 1923–24, 1926, 1928–29.

tial criminality of women and girls were perceived in Buenos Aires. They were potential criminals if visible in the urban landscape, and particularly at risk if they worked in the public sphere. Unlike the men, their site of regeneration was in the home, not the workplace. It was not until the presidential decree of 1932 that public officials indicated that it was appropriate and honest for women to work in commerce and industry. Not insignificantly, that message coincided with a tremendous growth of the Argentine textile industry in the 1920s, one that sought the services of large numbers of female employees. In fact, during this period women entered industry with greater facility than their male counterparts, and even though intellectuals like economist Alejandro E. Bunge worried about the reproductivity of women workers and Argentine women more generally, government officials still recognized the demand for female industrial workers.[47] Educated, poor, single girls could serve the national interests at work, as well as in the home.

The plight of orphaned and street children continued to haunt public officials. The tragic 1944 earthquake in San Juan led to renewed demands for adoption laws to be enacted. It also brought Juan and Eva Perón together. By the time Eva married Juan, she had already begun her quest for informal power as a broker between poor children and the state. The renewed importance of groups like the Sociedad de Beneficencia and the ladies of St. Vincent de Paul as operators of institutions for poor children presaged a great clash of class and power between the upper classes and Evita. By then the image of poor children had became a political pawn in a class-based war that led to the official elimination of public stigmas related to class, parental status, and degree of legitimacy.

Unfortunately, such political efforts did not end the presence of street children in Argentine cities. Their visibility has ebbed and flowed with changing economic and social conditions. The dismantlement of Peronism in the 1950s eliminated many state-supported institutions for poor children without replacing them with other alternatives, and nongovernmental organizations have emerged to fill in the gap. The history of carceral techniques to solve this problem between 1880 and 1940 forms an important segment of the larger history of street children in Argentina.

Notes

Research for this essay was sponsored by a grant from the National Endowment for the Humanities, a University of Arizona Social and Behavioral Sciences Research Professorship, and a SBSRI Summer Research Grant.

1 Alberto Martínez, *Censo general de la población, edificación, comercio e industrias de la ciudad de Buenos Aires,* 3 vols. (Buenos Aires: Compañía Sudamericana de Billetes de Banco, 1910), vol. 3, pp. 418–419.

2 Michel Foucault, *Discipline and Punish: The Birth of the Prison,* trans. Alan Sheridan (New York: Vintage, 1979), p. 257.

3 See Ricardo D. Salvatore and Carlos Aguirre, eds. *The Birth of the Penitentiary in Latin America: Essays on Criminology, Prison Reform, and Social Control, 1830–1940* (Austin: Institute of Latin American Studies, 1996); see also Lila M. Caimari, "Whose Criminals are These? Church, State, and *Patronatos* and the Rehabilitation of Female Convicts, Buenos Aires, 1890–1940," *The Americas* 54, no. 2 (Oct. 1997): 184–208.

4 Buenos Aires Police, *Memoria, 1913–1914,* pp. 13–14.

5 Ibid., 1915–16, p. 18.

6 There were other charitable orphanages in Buenos Aires, but they often charged for the services of their schools, and most were for boys. According to the 1887 Buenos Aires census, the Damas de Caridad operated two day schools for children of working parents, but it is unclear whether they accepted girls. The French Orphanage (Orfelinato Francés), took in only fifty-eight boys, and the Sociedad Protectora de Niños Huérfanos y Abandonados, an organization subsidized by the Club Industrial Argentino, also accepted only boys.

7   Argentine Republic, Cámara de Diputados, *Diario de Sesiones,* August 1, 1892, p. 524. The presence of orphans among these children was recognized in a later discussion on September 16, although no suggestions were discussed that would ameliorate this issue. Ibid., p. 918.

8   Argentine Republic, Ministerio de Justicia e Instrucción Pública, *Memorias,* Report of the Defensores de Menores, 1886, 1:65.

9   "Protección de la Infancia," *Revista de la Policía de la Capital* 14 (July 15, 1888): 37–39.

10 Argentine Republic, Ministerio de Justicia e Instrucción Pública, *Memorias,* 1903. According to the Annual Report of the Defensor de la Sección Sud, pregnant minor girls were often sent to the Casa Correcciónal. After they gave birth at a given hospital, the girls were then returned to prison with their infants. Yet there is no mention of any infants ever housed in the Women's Jail. In the 1909 annual report of Defensor Carlos Miranda Naon, he claimed that there were twenty-four boys and thirty-one girls under his care in the Casa Correcciónal.

11 Argentine Republic, Ministerio de Justicia e Instrucción Pública, *Resultados generales del Primero Censo Carcelario de la República Argentina* (Buenos Aires: Talleres Gráficos de la Penitenciaría Nacional, 1909), pp. 94–95.

12 Buenos Aires Municipality, *Anuario estadístico de la ciudad de Buenos Aires,* 1897, pp. 265, 509; 1903, p. 275; 1915–1923, p. 250.

13 Archivo General de la Nación, [hereinafter referred to as AGN] Fondo Ministerio de Justicia e Instrucción Pública [hereinafter referred to as MJIP], Expedientes Generales, Letra D, Legajo 106, Letter from Defensor José M. Terrero, May 7, 1901. The Patronato de la Infancia was established by Intendente Bollini of Buenos Aires in 1892. It often received funding from public sources, but perceived itself to be a private organization operated by elite men.

14 AGN, MJIP, Letra C., División Expedientes Generales, Legajo 38, 1895, Expediente 308, foja 1, May 21, 1895, Mother Superior to President J. E. Uriburu.

15 AGN, MJIP, Letra C., División Expedientes Generales, Legajo 38, 1895, Expediente 308, foja 2, response of Defensores through the Departamento de Justicia, February 4, 1896.

16 Argentine Republic, Ministerio de Justicia e Instrucción Pública, *Memoria,* Reports of Defensores de Menores, 1886, I:69, 72; 1889, I:131, 136; 1899, pp. 120, 141.

17 Ibid., 1888, 1:81–82. The Defender for the northern area did not hand in a report in time to be included.

18 AGN, MJIP, División Expedientes Generales, Letra D, Legajo 106, April 2, 1898, Annual Report of Defensor de Menores Pedro de Elizalde.

19 AGN, MJIP, División Expedientes Generales, Letra C, 1900, Legajo 46, Letter from Dr. Abraham Zenavilla to Madre Superiora, March 29, 1900.

20 AGN, MJIP, División Expedientes Generales, Letra D, 1908, Legajo 110, Letter of Defensores Figueroa, de Elizalde and Cabal, February 25, 1908.

21 AGN, MJIP, División Expedientes Generales, Letra C., Legajo 47, Exped. 314, Letter of Mother Superior, June 4, 1900. The following day the mother superior wrote to Minister of Justice Osvaldo Magnasco that after writing the first letter she received notice that the prison had been given 24,000 pesos to expand the existing building, a sum that was insufficient to construct the new building she had suggested.

22 Argentine Republic, Ministerio de Justicia, Culto e Instrucción Pública, *Memoria,* 1904, T. 1, pp. 134–135.

23 AGN, División Poder Judicial, Fondo Tribunales Civiles, Letra G., 1920, Gigena de Saldaño, sobre reclusión de su hija menor Juana Isabel, fojas 1–5, August 23, 1920 to Sept. 1, 1920. The judge ordered Juana admitted to the Asilo del Buen Pastor.

24 Buenos Aires Municipality, *Statistical Annuary of the City of Buenos Aires,* 1906; 1907; 1912.

25 Argentine Republic, Ministerio de Justicia e Instrucción Pública, *Memoria,* 1911, p. 130.

26 AGN, MJIP, División Expedientes Generales, Letra A, 1910, Legajo 11, Expediente 46, Asilo Corrección de Mujeres, April 12, 1910.

27 AGN, MJIP, División Expedientes Generales, Letra A, Legajo 14, Expediente 194, Response of Casa Correccional de Mujeres to inquiry of Sub-Secretary, September 9, 1913.

28 AGN, MJIP, División Expedientes Generales, Letra A, 1915, Legajo 16, Expediente 40. Asilo de Corrección de Mujeres. Cuadros demostrativos del movimiento habido . . . durante 1913.

29 Argentine Republic, Ministerio de Justicia e Instrucción Pública, *Memoria,* 1914, t. 1, p. 365. The practice of sending boys to work on ranches dated from 1906. There is no evidence, however, that girls were ever sent there.

30 Argentine Republic, Ministerio de Justicia, Culto e Instrucción Pública, *Memoria,* 1920, p. 413.

31 Argentine Republic, Congreso Nacional, Cámara de Diputados, *Diario de Sesiones,* 1910, T. 1, August 8, 1910, pp. 909–910.

32 Eduardo J. Bullrich, *Asistencia social de menores* (Buenos Aires: Jesús Méndez, 1919), pp. 399–407.

33 Agote's main speech can be found in Argentine Republic, Congreso Nacional, Cámara de Diputados, *Diario de Sesiones,* 1918, T. 1, June 3, 1918, pp. 262–266; President Yrigoyen's message, Ibid. 1919, T. 5, January 20, 1919, p. 214.

34 Argentine Republic, Ministry of Justice and Public Instruction, *The Prevention of Juvenile Delinquency in the Field of Legislation and Social Work in Argentina: A Survey Ordered by Dr. Antonio Sagarna, Secretary of Justice and Public Instruction on the Occasion of the First International Child's Congress at Geneva, August 24–28, 1925* (Buenos Aires: Cía. General de Fósforos, 1925), p. 4.

35 *La Prensa,* August 10, 1910, p. 12.

36 See the reports of these institutions in Argentine Republic, Ministerio de Justicia,

Culto e Instrucción Pública, *Memoria,* 1916, I:35–37, 279–282; 1918, 1:154–159; 1920, 1:267–275; 1923: 1:299–305; 1926, I:232–235. According to César Viale, a noted Argentine specialist in juvenile delinquency, minor female offenders began to be sent to facilities operated by the Instituto Tutelar de Menores from 1923 onward. The total number of girls who entered such facilities between 1923 and 1927 was 130. The other girls were sent to the Asilo Correcional de Mujeres (78), two institutions operated by the Damas Católicas (209), and various institutions of the Sociedad de Beneficencia (80). The girls sent out in later years went to similar institutions. These numbers pale in comparison to the total number of girls who passed through the Asilo or Casa Correcional de Mujeres. César Viale, *Estadística de los menores de que 'dispuso' el Juzgado Correccional entre los años 1923 a 1928 y 1928 a 1932* (Buenos Aires, 1932), passim.

37 Donna J. Guy, "The Pan Am Child Congresses 1916–1942: Pan Americanism, Child Reform and the Welfare State in Latin America," *Journal of Family History* 23, no. 3 (July 1998): 272–292.

38 Dr. Gregorio Bermann, "Direcciones para el estudio de menores abandonados y delincuentes," *Actas de la Primera Conferencia Latino-Americana de Neurología, Psiquiatría y Medicina Legal,* 3 vols. (Buenos Aires: Imprenta de la Universidad, 1929), vol. 3, pp. 317–323, 334–335.

39 Patronato Nacional de Menores, *Primera Conferencia Nacional sobre Infancia Abandonada y Delincuente* (Buenos Aires: Imprenta Colonia Hogar "Ricardo Gutiérrez," 1933), pp. 138–139.

40 Ibid., pp. 140–142.

41 Argentine Republic, Ministerio de Justicia e Instrucción Pública, *Memoria,* 1914, t. 1, p. 365.

42 Ibid., 1921, Report of the Mother Superior, 1:500–501.

43 Decree of December 28, 1932, ibid., 1932, 1:333.

44 Report of the Mother Superior to Minister of Justice and Public Instruction Dr. Manuel M. de Yriondo, March 13, 1933, ibid., 1:334–335.

45 Report of the Mother Superior, February 7, 1934, ibid., 1:464–465.

46 Report of the Mother Superior, no date, ibid., 1937, 1:530.

47 Alejandro E. Bunge, *Una nueva Argentina* (Buenos Aires: Editorial Kraft, 1940), chap. 17, Nuevas normas sociales, pp. 410–417.

Remembering Freedom:

Life as Seen From the Prison Cell,

Buenos Aires Province, 1930–1950

LILA M. CAIMARI

L ike many turn-of-the-century Latin American societies, Argentina witnessed the emergence of positivist paradigms that reshaped the scientific field. Besides introducing certain methodological assumptions that modified disciplines such as medicine and law, new sciences were born from the confluence of positivist theories and the social concerns of contemporary state leaders. Such was the case of criminology, a discipline that both influenced and was influenced by the prevailing ideological and political atmosphere. Following up on recent findings about the role of medicine and law in the formation of the modern Argentine state, new studies have developed critical analyses of the emergence of criminology, its growing power in the scientific arena, and its main postulates, as well as its legitimization as an "official" science by dominant professional and political elites.[1] Little has been said, however, about the concrete use of criminological prescriptions by this state in rapid change, or about the impact of the new science on the population that constituted the object of so many studies. We know, for example, that positivist criminology developed a new range of state interventions designed to control the life of the poor and to turn offenders into disciplined workers. But we know almost nothing about the nature and use of these new instruments as they were adopted in prisons — the laboratories of criminological science par excellence—the police, or the criminal justice system. These areas can hardly remain overlooked in the current debate on science and the construction of modern Argentina, because besides producing politically convenient metaphors and narrative representations, criminology was the source of prescriptions and techniques that "modernized" the punitive system in a way that changed the state, redefined the rights of the working classes, and altered the relationship between both. How were scientific ideas about the causes of crime used to control and reform criminals and their families? What was the place of theories about alcoholism, biological heritage, and environmental factors when it came to defining the causes of crimes already committed, the nature of given criminals, and their ultimate fate? The other end of the change remains similarly obscure: how did the inmates investigated react to—and resist—the relentless inquiries about their lives unleashed by criminologists? This article attempts to approach these issues by examining the use of modern criminological techniques on a specific population of inmates of the Buenos Aires prison system.

Although Lombrosian, theories about the biological roots of crime were influential in the early development of Argentina's new criminology, their most deterministic aspects were soon dismissed. Mirroring the evolution of the European debate about the ultimate cause of crime—biology vs. environment—leading Argentine criminologists such as José Ingenieros developed hybrid explanations. In 1908, he argued that criminal personalities were formed by a complex combination of biological and environmental factors. Criminals were "spirits that carry the fatality of a sickly heritage or suffer the inexorable undermining of environmental miseries."[2] The growing consensus about the complex causes of criminal behavior led to the emergence of new approaches to the study of criminals: understanding the reasons why people turned into offenders, as well as their chances of rehabilitation, required extensive knowledge of their biological, psychological, and socioeconomic backgrounds.

This aspect of criminological theory was particularly important when national and provincial governments undertook the task of reforming prisons according to the new scientific trends. In "modern" reformed institutions, these theories were tested empirically and used as tools to diagnose the "adaptability" or "nonadaptability" of past offenders to outside society.[3] The enormous importance that positivist criminology attached to the individual study and treatment of criminals, coupled with the increasing institutional use of scientific reports to support decisions about the length and nature of the sentences served by inmates, brought about the creation of departments ad hoc within the modern penitentiary bureaucracy. The Institute of Criminology of Buenos Aires, founded in 1907 and directed by Ingenieros himself, represents the first and most visible effort to institutionalize such studies, first applied to the population of the National Penitentiary.[4]

The earliest studies performed on the inmates reflected the strong influence of "hard" positivist categories — their main purpose was to classify offenders according to the theoretical models of prestigious (mostly Italian) criminologists.[5] By the 1930s, such studies were conducted by an important Institute of Classification, composed of psychiatrists, legal specialists, and representatives of the Patronato de Liberados (ex-convict patronage society), all of whom had personal interviews with the inmate in question and participated in the writing of the reports. The institute also had a team of informadores sociales (social investigators), who gathered information on the social and family environment where the inmate had lived and worked prior to committing the crime.

Criminological histories served three institutional purposes: they informed and made suggestions about technical aspects of the sentence (i.e., type of therapy to be prescribed, classification of the inmate, work and instruction schedules); they provided information on the rehabilitation of the inmates, all of whom had an individual file detailing their progress toward moral reform and reintegration into social life; and they supported judges' decisions about applications for parole and probation.[6] The regulations of the Province of Buenos Aires — which followed a very similar path, using almost identical teams and studies — added yet another element to the definitions of the goals of such reports: "To provide insight into aspects of the social environment of the criminal population of the Province of Buenos Aires."[7] Thus, the reports developed by their Institute of Classification [IC] between the 1930s and 1950s devoted large amounts of space to the detailed socioeconomic backgrounds and family histories of prisoners.[8]

These documents present interesting methodological challenges, challenges well known to historians who use the "archives of repression" for their chief primary sources.[9] In our case, the fact that inmates talked about their families and childhood as they remembered them many years later poses a problem common to any autobiographical testimony — that is, we are limited to hearing the past as edited by an individual, a complex construct with a very problematic relationship with historical "truth."[10] In addition, interviews took place after several years of confinement, when perceptions of the past had been colored by this experience. As we shall see, some of these distortions can tell us about the impact of prison on the representation of that past and the long-term context of their life stories.

The most crucial factor in this exchange, however, concerns the circumstances surrounding these "conversations." The audience for these chronicles gave inmates an obvious reason to distort (consciously or unconsciously) their testimony: they answered questions about their lives in a brutally asymmetrical power relationship, fully aware that those who listened would influence decisions about their future. These life stories embedded in criminological histories were born of an exchange that seems to justify, in a rather extreme fashion, Pierre Bourdieu's view that the whole social structure is embedded in each linguistic interaction. Indeed, it would be hard to find a more dramatic example of unequal symbolic power between two parties in a conversation. These interviews provide us with an excellent instance of Bourdieu's idea that the more "institutional" the context of an exchange, the more disparity there is in the relative power of its participants.[11] The choice of subjects discussed, the purpose of the conversation, the institutional mise-en-scène: all of these elements reinforced the power of those who asked over those who answered. Of course, institutional context was further exacerbated by class subordination. The (mostly middle-class) professionals of the penitentiary system were interrogating poor rural workers, who accounted for the majority of the "classified" prisoners. As we shall see, the gap in the class-defined assumptions that both participants brought to this dialogue is in itself an eloquent source of information.

These inmates' representation of themselves and their past was the only means by which they could attempt to influence decisions. However, the terms of these exchanges were not ones with which they were familiar: acceptability was defined by interviewers according to their own scientific, institutional, and class criteria. Thus inmates were describing their lives in a way they *thought* would be acceptable to the doctors, psychiatrists, and lawyers of the penitentiary system. The high degree of symbolic power of the audience, combined with the inmates' anxiety over the outcome of their performance — both determined by this social context — give these stories the character of "façades," as defined by Erving Goffman — that is, the symbolic apparatus used by a social actor during a self-representation in a given social situation.[12] In this case, the elements of this façade and the use of symbolic strategies of representation on the part of the "actor-inmate" were largely limited by the highly structured nature of the conversation. Criminological histories, then, tell the story of the inmates' attempts to build "legitimate" façades in a context of extreme social subordination. They are also the story of the assessment of these representations by a particularly dominant audience.

Distinguishing these two points of view is made possible by the format of these reports. Each section was composed of a summary of the information provided by each prisoner during an interview. This summary, in which excerpts of the inmate's own words were transcribed literally, was followed by a preliminary assessment of this data, compared with information the institute had obtained from other sources. Finally, the report closed with a section in which the inmates could write, in free prose, an autobiographical text of any length. How they chose to use this opportunity varied according to their writing skills, their fears about the potential use of this text by the IC, and the perception of their past after years of confinement. These variations, along with the use made of these autobiographies by the staff of the penitentiary system, will provide yet another window into this first inquiry on the role of Argentine modern criminology as a tool of social control.[13]

Remembering Family and Work

Owing to the importance that positivist criminology attached to the biological heritage and social environment as a source of explanations for criminal behavior, the reports opened with a detailed set of questions about an inmates' family.[14]

Prisoners' descriptions of childhood experiences included detailed profiles of parents and siblings, as well as some insight into family relationships. The strong idealization of the family in these testimonies reflects one of the obvious influences of the years of confinement on these memories, as well as the consistent desire of inmates to legitimize their origins. Fathers had been good, and mothers were one of the main reasons to return to free life. Eventual references to miserable material conditions or to the lack of formal education did not preclude frequent references to the "almost perfect" memory of these same families. In a typical report, one inmate described the poor *rancho de barro* ("dirt shack") where he had spent his childhood, the single room where the parents and seven children lived and slept, the tiny bed that he shared with his brother, the rationing of food, and a childhood devoid of any school experience. He then summarized this characterization of his family and childhood in extremely positive terms.[15] As we shall see, if alcohol abuse on the part of a parent was mentioned, it was usually as the result of persistent questions by interviewers. By contrast, inmates were quite spontaneous in providing details about the poverty of the environment in which they had grown up. Most likely supposing that such a picture would be perceived as a mitigating factor in the assessment of their crime, they could not know that poverty was often mentioned in the report as an important crime-producing influence, or as a source of permanent moral — or even biological — debilitation.

The Institute's questions about family history overlooked one important aspect of many of these recollections: the role of grandparents. Several of the interviews spontaneously digressed to include a grandmother as the most crucial figure in the family: raising two or three of the children, assuming parental responsibilities when fathers disappeared and mothers had to work, or becoming the substitute mother when the actual mother had been sent to prison, the role of grandmothers in these recollections often surpassed the assumptions about family roles implied in the questionnaire.

Family relations certainly appear to be strong in these pictures. Still, the strength of these ties was very often represented in the assessment of interviewers as unsatisfactory. This interpretation provides a glimpse of their view of this reality as a source of good or bad influences for the working poor. The pervasive reference to illegitimate unions and illegitimate children, a first-hand reflection of the historically high rates of illegitimacy in rural areas of Buenos Aires, is one clear reason for this assessment.[16] The gap in the assumptions at either end of this exchange is here at its clearest. Interviewers systematically gathered information about the legal status of marital unions, and routinely mentioned illegitimacy as a negative factor in the final report on the home environment of the criminal in question. Inmates who made obvious efforts to show their family in a positive light, on the other hand, made no secret of their parent's (or their own) *concubinato,* and many did not even know whether their parents had ever married. This does not mean that they refused to pass moral judgment on parental behavior before such an audience — reports could be full of critical comments on various family members. Rather, it seems clear that they did not regard legitimate marriage as an important element in their moral façade.

This tenuous attachment to the institution of marriage does not appear to be linked to a general indifference toward religious values or the prescriptions of the church. It does, however, point to a rather selective appropriation of these prescriptions. Whenever given the opportunity, inmates made a point of providing details about their Catholic beliefs and practices, or those of their parents. Besides showing an awareness of the usefulness of this information in such a situation, these descriptions prove that they did not see any conflict between these (most likely exaggerated) religious convictions and illegitimate unions in their families. The same mothers who were "saints" and "devoted Catholics" were openly referred to as *concubinas*.

By contrast, church attendance was considered by most inmates to be the main indicator of one's standing as a "good Catholic." Several went out of their way to explain that irregular attendance at mass had been the result of their living a great distance from the closest town. In these cases, they appealed to other ways of proving religious faith. "My mother had many saints to whom she lit candles and prayed constantly," stated an inmate when explaining her mother's absence from church. In his free-subject autobiography, another stated: "Day and night, and even more when it rained, my poor *madrecita* made us all kneel to contemplate the image of Jesus, to pray to him a *Padrenuestro*."[17] This practice seems quite independent from the control of the clergy: isolation and distance from urban churches were in fact obstacles to relations with priests and nuns.[18]

The impact of the highly insecure labor market—typical of turn-of-the-century Argentina—figures prominently in these interviews.[19] The average father of these inmates had been a rural *peón*, a label that covered an enormous variety of jobs. Job insecurity had left an indelible mark on the childhood recollections of many. Several inmates mentioned lack of work as the cause of poverty in their families, and often this was the only negative aspect of an otherwise idealized family picture. Because most of these rural jobs were seasonal, temporary, and dependent on weather conditions, income could fluctuate wildly between months of heavy work and long periods of transition to another contract. The transient nature of these jobs also appears as a pervasive theme in these childhood memories: it was not uncommon for a family to follow the father from *estancia* to *estancia* in the high seasons, or from town to town during the winter.

The job history of sons could start at age seven or eight, often interrupting an already irregular school experience.[20] When they grew up, or left the family home (as early as age twelve), they would often embark upon equally irregular job histories: they describe themselves moving from one job to another in different areas of the province, leaving (or complementing) rural jobs with stints as unskilled *jornaleros* — port stevedores, shoemakers, railway workers, truck drivers, masons, waiters, and so on. A representative example, taken from the summary of the labor history of an inmate born in 1913, goes as follows: "He started working at the age of ten as the errand boy at a grocery store in Las Flores. He kept this job until he was sixteen. In 1932 he became an aid to bricklayers in several towns. Between 1934 and 1936 he performed various rural jobs, always as an employee. In 1941 he started working as a car mechanic, until 1947. In 1949 he worked as truck driver, and finally in 1950 he worked at the port of Buenos Aires as stevedore."[21]

Early entrance into the job market, as well as constant movement from one occupation to another, occupied such a prominent place in the memories of inmates that some would turn their free autobiographical text into a list of the jobs held prior to being sent to prison. This is the full autobiography of an inmate born in 1906: "I left school when I was twelve to do rural work, harvesting corn and producing vegetables. When I was twenty I became a construction worker, which I can prove. I was hired by the following people. . . . Then I was hired by Mr. Marina, for whom I baled grass for the animals. This is how I made a living all those years, until I was sent to prison."[22]

As in the case of the exchange about economic conditions at home, the abundant details inmates provided about job fluctuation also indicate that they did not know that this information was likely to be construed by listeners either as a negative environmental influence or as proof of their own lack of work discipline.

As has been demonstrated in recent scholarship, the concern of the authorities with the potential for criminal behavior within this "disorganized" working class had been reflected in criminological theory, and had been the basis of the drive to reform male correctional institutions. According to leading turn-of-the-century criminologists, the main purpose of prisons was to turn offenders into industrious workers by teaching them skills that would be useful in their life after confinement. This would keep them from committing new crimes.[23] A closer look at the experience of inmates who had been subjected to this project provides new insight into the meaning of "work therapy" once it had traveled from scientific journals to the state apparatus. Three of the twenty men interviewed had had previous experience in the correctional system, each had returned to the labor market and mentioned being hired as a result of skills acquired in correctional institutions. Their failure to turn into disciplined workers may be partially explained by looking at their experience of work therapy in the main prison the inmates interviewed were housed: the high-security facility of Sierra Chica.

Originally built to house 536 male inmates, in 1930 Sierra Chica held a population of nearly 1,000. Despite being one of the main prisons in the province, bad organization and poor financing had limited the "work therapy" program to half of these inmates, usually those with the better behavior records. A lack of actual work opportunities was paired with a rather literal enforcement of criminological prescriptions. Positivist criminology had represented the "criminal man" as an urban species, and prescriptions to fight criminality followed this diagnosis.[24] So, the prison population of Sierra Chica (consisting of 75% rural peones) was sent to workshops designed for urban workers, where they acquired skills that they would rarely have the chance to use once they returned to the labor market. In 1938, repeated reports of idleness among these inmates finally pushed Governor Fresco to invest in a major refurbishment of the workshops in all provincial prisons. This time, however, the work added to the prison regime was not chosen based on its future usefulness to inmates (as was called for by the very criminological principles behind the reform), but rather on the amount of money that the state would save by employing inmates in the production of cheap goods for the penitentiary system itself.[25] Work therapy, one of the best-developed concepts of criminology had been adopted by the state from the scientific field, but its meaning had been fundamentally transformed by the very logic of the state.

Criminological histories do not tell much about female work, a result of assumptions about gender, crime and work underlying the questions posed. "Criminal man" was urban, and also male. Although the interviewers did ask whether both the father and mother of the inmate had worked, in the first case this question was followed by more detailed and morally loaded questions about the father's behavior, all of which concerned his labor history: whether he had worked regularly, whether he had supported the family, and so on. The only question about any paying work done by mothers (which was very often answered affirmatively) was followed by inquiries that dealt exclusively with her behavior as it pertained to the quality of her dedication to the home and the education of children.

To some extent, both participants in the dialogue shared certain assumptions about gender roles in the family and the working world. In a few exceptional cases inmates were able to influence the IC's assessment of their family members in the way they intended to either by describing fathers who had failed to support the family (forcing mothers to leave the home and work outside), or mothers and wives who had neglected the home and the children (forcing fathers to assume these responsibilities).[26] The underlying consensus about a mother's duty toward her children provides us with a glimpse at the reception of the state-approved model of motherhood.[27] Born at the turn of the twentieth century out of concerns about infant mortality among the urban poor, the dominant discourse about the "good mother" consisted of a convergence of messages emanating from various social arenas, such as the medical profession, the Sociedad de Beneficencia de la Capital, and the Catholic church. Primarily conceived in relation to poor families, it was fully elaborated by 1930. Although it still involved a definition of womanhood entirely identified with the role of mother, the ideal *madre cariñosa* (loving mother) of modern times was expected to go beyond the passive sainthood of the Catholic model, devoting herself to her children in more practical ways as well. For example, mothers were expected to exhibit knowledge about their children's hygienic and emotional needs.

The highly idealized, and not particularly modern image of mothers as depicted by inmates points to a very limited integration of this model. Certainly, women were above all perceived as either real or potential mothers: trying to prove his moral innocence, an inmate who had murdered a woman argued that the episode had been an accident because "one can never have the intention to kill a woman who is, or can become, another mother." It seems that the argument was not devoid of relevance to the interviewers, in that this was the only statement they bothered to transcribe literally in their final summary.[28] Although inmates and state bureaucrats seemed to agree on the importance of a mother's presence—to clean the house, take care of the children, and so on—prisoner descriptions of their own mothers diverged from the official discourse of the madre cariñosa in two ways. When discussing the rampant infant mortality in their families, they did not link it in any way to their mother's behavior. There are neither visible attempts to downplay infant mortality as a negative indicator of family environment, nor to justify (or blame) mothers for the fate of those children: the centerpiece of the state-medical discourse about a mother's duties is missing from that of the inmates. Furthermore, as we have seen for the representation of religious beliefs, these recollections also reflected the strong presence of the old-fashioned model of the mother, the *pobre madrecita* who prays and suffers in silence, described with a pervasive use of analogies with saints and martyrs.

The impact of prison experience on the labor history of women was limited to making it harder to find work once they left prison. Because the female prison of Olmos was controlled by a religious order that ignored positivist theories about work therapy as a tool for rehabilitation, the work inmates did in prison was limited to cleaning and other manual tasks that could prepare them only for being sent back into the market of low-paying domestic service. Although some inmates expressed long-standing ambitions (one wanted to be a pharmacist, another a pianist), the secular bureaucracy of the penitentiary system did not seem to regard them any differently than did the nuns who ran the prison. When the much-publicized reform of prison work regulations was launched by the state in 1937, the long lists of workshops conceived for male institutions contrasted sharply with the relatively few tasks the government expected from the female inmates in Olmos. Keeping the emphasis on prison work as a cheap source of labor rather than a source of rehabilitation, women were expected to produce goods (sheets, underwear, etc.) for the penitentiary system itself.[29]

Bodies Interrogated, Bodies Justified

The childhood memories of inmates included references to disease and death that were both pervasive and vague. When asked about their siblings, they very often mentioned having lost several at a young age. Interestingly, most ignored basic details about these deaths — one could not recall what it was that had taken the lives of his seven brothers and sisters, and another was not even sure of how many siblings had been killed by disease. Typical answers to questions about the cause of death of relatives were "I am not sure," "She died of a disease," "She was sick from pains," or, in the case of someone referring to his nine dead siblings, "Weak blood ran in the family."[30] Indeed, there is a maddening lack of precision for those looking for data to support decisive conclusions. Digestive disorders, by far the main cause of infant mortality at that time, are not mentioned at all.

One might conclude that information about health conditions was being concealed from interviewers for fear of stigma, or to hide incriminating information about biological heritage.[31] Although concealment was a helpful tool to build an acceptable façade, in the rare instances where inmates mentioned specific symptoms and diseases, they were precisely those most closely associated with poverty in state-led campaigns: tuberculosis and infant mortality. By contrast, venereal diseases and alcoholism were rightly identified as damaging information, and data was obtained only after systematic interrogation.[32]

Inmates consistently attempted to downplay the role of alcohol in their lives — a strategy reflecting both an idealization of family memories, the attempt to paint a more favorable picture of their origins, and an acute awareness of the damage that this information could produce in the outcome of the interview. Of course, this consciousness was linked to their negative personal experiences with alcohol or alcoholics, as many stated in the process of blaming spouses or friends for their having ended up in jail. But the way in which the subject was handled before prison authorities is also an eloquent sign of the extent to which inmates had internalized the moral message of the vigorous state-led antialcohol campaigns.[33]

Indeed, alcohol played an important role in the final decision regarding inmates' chances of rehabilitation, as it did in the corpus of criminological theory. It was viewed as a major consideration in the assessment of their environment, and also as an essential piece of information about biological heritage. Once again, this information emerges through the filter of prevailing assumptions of the IC about alcoholism among the poor: mirroring the gender distinctions of the antialcohol campaigns, the forms inquired about the father's, but not the mother's, alcohol consumption. Although inmates and criminologists shared a basic awareness of the negative moral connotations of alcoholism, the former could not see the importance of this factor in the criminological diagnosis that was being elaborated. Hence the gap between the answers provided and the answers "heard": no matter how much inmates trivialized their parent's consumption of alcohol, the mere mention of wine at family meals almost automatically introduced parental alcoholism into the assessment of the family environment. This "fact" was then assumed as evidence in subsequent sections of the report and was included in the final evaluation of environmental influences, as well as in the medical report on the biological heritage of the inmate in question. In some cases, even the casual mention by an inmate of a father's taste for wine changed the whole outcome of the assessment of that inmate's chances for future adaptability.[34]

The discussion of the sexual life of inmates before prison also seemed to be based on an agreement about certain accepted sexual practices for men and women, a consensus all the more eloquent because some of these practices went beyond explicit norms. For example, when asked about the circumstances of the beginning of their sexual lives, male prisoners did not hesitate to provide information about their relations with prostitutes, at a time when prostitution had been officially banned throughout the country.[35] Far from shocking criminologists, these answers were clearly expected: they were summarized as "normal sexual initiation with prostitutes," and they did not introduce any stigma into the moral profile of the prisoner. Information about venereal diseases rather than moral judgment seemed to be the driving concern behind these questions. Indeed, syphilis did appear in several reports, yet the circumstances of its contraction and treatment were still transcribed in a matter-of-fact style, without further comment.

Not surprisingly, this detached attitude was in striking contrast with the handling of women's sexual history. Traditional moral assessment prevailed over health concerns so completely that it could turn a morally unacceptable sexual history into the main cause of criminality. Although extracted from the same questions, information was scrutinized and handled in very different terms. None of the women interviewed had contracted diseases, but any reference to an active sexual life before marriage (or concubinato) or to children introduced an irreversible stigma that was bound to follow her throughout the report to form the center of the explanations of the moral failures that had driven her to commit crimes.

One woman who was serving a sentence for infanticide, acknowledged early relations with men, including her mother's concubino. Even if she argued that she had had to accept this man's harassment in order to avoid being kicked out of the house, interviewers chose to dismiss such an argument and to develop their own explanation:

> We accept, instead, the hypothesis that her primary instincts, and even a certain depravation, prevailed in her spirit, because she had

sexual intercourse with her step-father only occasionally, and she still saw other men. . . . In the case of a woman with such weak development of feelings, where instincts dominate, we are faced with the question of her future life in society. This question makes us think carefully and assess all the episodes of her life, where modesty and decency were removed to give way to subaltern sexual appetites, such as having sexual relations with her mother's *concubino*.[36]

Her final classification was "nonadaptable."

As they spoke about their medical histories and their sex lives, inmates were simultaneously providing another type of information about themselves. Assessment of their "body-narratives" was complemented by an evaluation of their demeanor: gestures, regard, ways of speaking — an aspect of the inquiry that points to the state having embraced the psychological turn of Argentine criminological theory.[37] If inmates made any attempt to improve their performance through body language — an improbable scenario in any case — these documents do not tell this story. They do tell quite a bit, however, about the way in which the state scrutinized the "manners" of the working classes. Body language and speech skills were tersely summarized in one or two words, which were chosen from the predefined categories listed on the form. Attitudes could be "defensive," "obscene," "reticent," "distrusting." The nature of the inmate's look and demeanor could fall under categories such as "normal," "unpleasant," or "insincere." Of the many ill-defined and subjective categories available to the interviewer, the most commonly chosen bore the heaviest class connotations: the language of inmates was "vulgar."

School and Politics as Recalled from Confinement

As was the case for information on family, work and religion, questions on school experience reflected the state's strong interest in attaching the working class to institutions and symbolic structures that would provide order and organization in their lives.

Most of the inmates and their siblings had attended school for one or two years, at which point they had been removed by their families to go to work. Some had never attended school, either because of the great distance between the estancia and the nearest school or because of a lack of proper clothing. The low literacy levels of many inmates became apparent when they were asked to write their autobiographies in free prose as part of the report. About half of them flatly refused to do so, and many others wrote short paragraphs that conveyed an unmistakable feeling of discomfort.

These portions of the prisoners' memories — which I analyze only partially in this essay — represent good examples of the theory put forward in Michel de Certeau's sociology of popular culture. Based on the premise that culture is not solely defined by the products and symbols received by a subordinate group from dominant groups, but also by the *ways of using* the possibilities imposed by a dominant economic order, Certeau focuses his analysis on the creative strategies of reception of cultural artifacts and symbols, an almost invisible process that he calls "arts of doing."[38] In the dialogue between inmates and professionals of the penitentiary system, the former reflected an approach to cultural products and institutions that was quite diverse, and certainly not as passive as was expected from a poor, semiliterate population. Understanding that great importance was attached to their cultural environment as a source of long-lasting influences, inmates obviously hoped to display intellectual skills that would impress their audience. From this point of view, these sources talk not so much about literacy among the rural poor, but rather about how inmates represented their school experience and the use of what little literacy they had acquired.

Even if the inmate's experience of the school had been short, many depicted it in strikingly bright terms: affinity with the school environment, and intellectual success were not uncommon themes of these memories. A surprising number even volunteered the names of their teachers, some of whom were discussed as crucial childhood figures: a woman who had completed third grade told quite spontaneously of her emotional ties with certain teachers; an inmate who had only attended school to the fourth grade still kept contact with his teacher, who wrote to him regularly at the prison; another, who was exceptional in having completed primary school, devoted half of his two-page autobiography to praising his sixth grade teacher, "whose finesse and high culture have left in me this beautiful memory."[39]

Nevertheless, strong connection with teachers did not change a picture that consistently pointed to a very brief school experience. Obviously, this fact had conditioned their choices in many ways: not only had it limited access to better jobs and more economic security, but descriptions of entertainment and favorite distractions unmistakably pointed to lives spent in a nonwritten culture. When asked about favorite pastimes, the answers were horse races and soccer for men, visits and Sunday walks in the town square for women. Although many attempted to downplay their taste for popular dances (where they would have been exposed to alcohol), insistent questioning showed that these were a popular form of entertainment. Despite its positive connotations, reading was not often mentioned as a regular activity.

Illiteracy or semiliteracy did not mean unfamiliarity with the printed press. Women who could barely read and could not write at all expressed how much they missed looking at the pictures of *fotonovelas* and fashion magazines. Illiteracy had affected the enjoyment of films, another activity mentioned as a favorite pastime, by limiting the experience to Argentine movies with no subtitles.

In some cases, there was a striking gap between descriptions of a brief school experience and the importance attributed to reading. This gap could be so great that interviewers were suspicious about the accuracy of certain answers—as it happened with an inmate who had not finished second grade yet talked enthusiastically about the novels of Alexander Dumas.[40] In other cases, however, the display of the skills learned at school forced interviewers to believe them. Indeed, the approach to written culture of several inmates who had spent little time at school was aggressive and far from fearful. Not only did they refer to their regular exposure to newspapers and sports magazines, but they produced autobiographies that reflected a good command of writing skills. Those who appear to have made such efficient use of their school instruction could also approach the instructional opportunities of the prison in creative ways, and then use them as proof of their "adaptability."

The impact of the instructional/cultural possibilities of the prison experience on this population appears to have been very uneven. Variations seem to correspond primarily to differences in the infrastructure of each institution, the length of sentences and the age of inmates. With the exception of the facilities of Azul and Sierra Chica—both of which had libraries of about 2,500 volumes in 1936—most provincial prisons had meager collections, if they had any books at all. Furthermore, instructional opportunities were limited to first and second grade reading and writing for the illiterate population. In prisons where school instruction and a library were available, attendance in class and the use of books were not mandatory. This gave inmates a certain leeway in how they chose to make use of these opportunities. Reports show an almost direct correlation between perceptions of education, early school experience, and long-term approach to cultural products. Inmates who had attended school and mentioned being successful, or those who had never attended but provided a positive image of the school environment, made a point of using prison time (often the only "free" time they had had in their lives) to develop their reading and writing skills. And these skills could be used as an argument for their cause. One inmate, who was illiterate on entering prison, wrote a long and unusually sophisticated autobiography in which the main subject was precisely the fact that he was able to write such a text. Another one greatly impressed his audience by reporting how the use of the library and regular access to the medical staff of the prison had allowed him to become a surgeon's aide.

Of course, this unexpected use of prison possibilities and the active approach of certain inmates to the writing of their criminological histories should not lead to a naïve overrepresentation of subaltern agency in this process. These stories appear in the context of more numerous testimonies reflecting great passivity—and as in other aspects of prison experience, women were at a further disadvantage insofar as they received mixed messages about the importance of acquiring intellectual skills.[41] Nonetheless, evidence shows that it was possible (if not common) for an inmate to influence the outcome of his report through a skillful use of the opportunities to introduce his own version of the problems of the past and his potential for the future.

It may seem curious that the forms of the IC did not include any questions about the political allegiances and activities of inmates—a striking contrast with the earlier studies of the Institute of Criminology, where the great concern about the influence of anarchism on the working classes appeared reflected in several questions. Nevertheless, the political changes of the 1940s and 1950s seem to have influenced the inmates' perceptions of their potential opportunities after prison strongly enough to appear as spontaneous digressions from the questions asked.

Most of these men and women had been incarcerated in the 1930s or early 1940s, and had followed the emergence of Peronism from within prison. When asked about families, some reported that the material situations of siblings and other relatives had improved due to this change. But Peronism appeared as more than simply a way out of the poverty they remembered: it was also represented as a weapon with which inmates could defend themselves from the penitentiary bureaucracy itself. An *informadora social* who visited a former inmate to gather information about the home environment reported feeling openly unwelcome by the inmate's family. The report included the following digression: "Although we were talking about something else, an aunt (of the inmate) went out of her way to inform me, in a threatening tone, that she was engaged to a high and mysterious leader of the Peronist Party, who is now in the United States, and whose name she refused to say."[42]

For those who were still behind bars, Peronism could appear as an important incentive to return to life outside of prison, because this time that life would be much better than before: "More than ever, I feel today like going out to work to help my old mother, because today things are different. Today we have a President who takes into consideration the life of the worker, not a tyrant like in those past 'times of hell' and little justice."[43]

Criminological histories provide a striking example of the huge expansion of state-sponsored studies of the nature and circumstances of criminals and the poor. The sample analyzed here shows that the portraits of the "criminal man" were framed by questionnaires whose underlying purpose was not to produce accurate biographies but to find elements that would support institutional decisions. The questions driving these stories were based on certain premises about the causes of crime, the profile of the typical criminal, and the best solutions to criminality. These examinations, which occurred as a result of a crime's being committed, seem particularly vulnerable to causal manipulation, because likely causes had been defined beforehand. In criminological histories, casual references or isolated elements were easily transformed into "causes" in interrogations that were structured toward identifying them, and to prescribing reforming treatments based upon their existence. These reports, in turn, validated scientific premises about crime and punishment: case studies like the ones analyzed here represented a great proportion of the articles published in leading criminological journals.

The most fundamental premises behind these studies, such as the importance of the individual study and classification of inmates, had been adopted by the state from the original positivist agenda, as was the emphasis on the biological heritage and past environmental influences of inmates. The conclusions drawn from the data obtained, however, were a complex mix of criminological premises, personal perceptions, and socially defined conceptions about gender, morality, and proper social behavior for the working classes. Ideas that had been well-developed in scientific criminological journals — work discipline, hygiene, alcoholism — appear side by side with less conscious conceptions brought to the exchange by interviewers — positive or negative family roles, proper sexual habits, acceptable ways of speaking, and so on. "Hard" criminological theory could also be used in highly versatile ways. "Work discipline" could serve to evaluate negatively an inmate's labor history displaying an erratic pattern of employment. But it could turn into a more flexible concept when prisons used it for institutional needs rather than social rehabilitation. Similarly, the category of "environmental influences" was vague enough as to allow interviewers a great degree of latitude in their assessments: male syphilis was reported in a neutral fashion according to scientific prescriptions, but female sexual promiscuity carried more weight in the evaluations than did the worst venereal disease.

On the other side of the exchange, those who answered questions developed their own strategies — built their façades — for the purpose of representing the past and the present according to their own suppositions about what officials expected of them, and what it would take to appear "adaptable." The limitations of any individual's symbolic resources, as well as their particular social and institutional subordination, led inmates to make unfortunate decisions about how they should represent the past, as is clear from their attempts to withhold information considered damaging, while at the same time providing generous details about aspects of their lives that would hurt them even more in the final report. These "strategic" mistakes provide a rare glimpse into the prison population's understanding of state policies and dominant messages, as shown in their representations of family, work, and health. There were exceptions, of course. In certain cases, inmates were able to impose their version of the story, and to influence the outcome of the report in their favor. Although it is impossible from these sources to draw conclusive information about subjective changes in the construction of the past, it is clear that memories had been heavily influenced by the experience of prison: mothers were never so missed, teachers never so valued, and political changes never so full of promise.

Notes

1   On the role of doctors and *higienistas* in the process of building of the modern Argentine state, see Jorde Salessi, *Médicos, maleantes y maricas* (Buenos Aires:

B. Viterbo, 1995); M. Zaida Lobato, ed., *Política, médicos y enfermedades: lecturas de historia de la salud en la Argentina* (Buenos Aires: Biblos/Universidad Nacional de Mar del Plata, 1996); Donna J. Guy, *Sex and Danger in Buenos Aires: Prostitution, Family, and Nation in Argentina* (Lincoln: University of Nebraska Press, 1991). On criminology, see Julia Rodríguez, "Encoding the Criminal. Criminology and the Science of 'Social Defense' in Modernizing Argentina (1880–1921)" (Ph.D. dissertation, Columbia University, 1999); Beatriz Ruibal, *Ideología del control social* (Buenos Aires: Centro Editor de América Latina, 1995); Eduardo Zimermann, *Los liberales reformistas: la cuestión social en la Argentina 1890–1916* (Buenos Aires: Sudamericana/Universidad de San Andrés, 1995), chap. 6; Ricardo Salvatore and Carlos Aguirre, eds., *The Birth of the Penitentiary in Latin America: Essays on Criminology, Prison Reform, and Social Control, 1830–1940* (Austin: University of Texas Press, 1996); Ricardo Salvatore, "Criminology, Prison Reform, and the Buenos Aires Working Class," *Journal of Interdisciplinary History* 23, no. 2 (autumn 1992): 279–299; Salessi, *Médicos, maleantes y maricas,* part II.

2 Ingenieros developed this position in his famous preface to the work of Eusebio Gómez, *La mala vida en Buenos Aires* (Buenos Aires: Juan Roldán, 1908), pp. 5–15. For other expressions of the growing emphasis on the environment, see M. A. Lancelotti, "El factor económico en la producción del delito," *Criminología Moderna* (Feb. 1900): 495–500; C. Moyano Gacitúa, "Las influencias mesológicas en la criminalidad argentina," *Archivos de Criminología y Psiquiatría* (1906): 487–499.

3 According to positivist criminology, the moral foundation of the confinement of prisoners resided in the principle of social defense, that is, in the right of societies to defend themselves.

4 An early description of the goals of the first Institute of Criminology in "El Instituto de Criminología de la República Argentina," *Archivos de Psiquiatría, Criminología y Ciencias Afines* 7 (1908): 224.

5 Forms were quite detailed (between twenty and twenty-five pages each), and consisted mainly of a series of tables and charts containing predefined responses on the part of the inmate or the partial conclusions of the interviewers. In an obvious effort to adapt the information to the models provided by science, the interviewers limited themselves to simply underlining one or another of the alternatives provided on the form, keeping digressions to a minimum.

6 "Nuevo Reglamento del Instituto de Clasificación y de los Anexos Psiquiátricos," *Revista Penal y Penitenciaria* 5, no. 17 (July–Sept. 1940): 398.

7 "Reglamento de la Dirección General de Establecimientos Penales en la Provincia de Buenos Aires," *Revista Penal y Penitenciaria* (hereafter, *RPP*) V18 (Oct.–Dec. 1940): 715.

8 This change may be a sign of the decline of "hard" positivist criminology, which placed the emphasis on anthropometric data and biological determination, and the already mentioned consensus about the complexity of causes of crime. Examples of

the critical distance with which academics regarded these old positivist criminological categories in the 1930s can be found in the articles of the Patronato de Recluídas y Liberadas, published between 1933 and 1955.

9   The "discovery" of criminal and judicial archives has generated a wealth of creative literature on their potentiality for social historians. A passionate description of the appeal of these sources in Arlette Farge, *Le goût de l'archive* (Paris: Seuil, 1989). Carlo Ginzburg, *The Cheese and the Worms. The Cosmos of a Sixteenth-Century Miller* (Baltimore: Johns Hopkins University Press, 1992), p. xxi; Ginzburg, "Sorcellerie et piété populaire: notes sur un procès," in *Mythes, emblèmes, traces: morphologie et histoire* (Paris: Flammarion, 1989), p. 17. An example of the creative use of judicial archival testimonies in Natalie Zemon Davis, *Fiction in the Archives: Pardon Tales and Their Tellers in Sixteenth-Century France* (Stanford: Stanford University Press, 1987).

10 An interesting assessment of the value of oral autobiographical narratives as a historical source in Daniel James, "Tales Told Out on the Borderlands: Doña Maria's Story, Oral History and Issues of Gender," in Daniel James and John French, eds., *The Gendered Worlds of Latin American Women Workers: From Household and Factory to the Union Hall and the Ballot Box* (Durham, N.C.: Duke University Press, 1997), p. 35.

11 Pierre Bourdieu, *Language and Symbolic Power* (Cambridge, Mass.: Harvard University Press, 1991), p. 67.

12 Erving Goffman, *The Presentation of Self in Everyday Life* (Hardmondsworth: Penguin, 1971), chap. 1.

13 Most of the information discussed in the following sections was extracted from thirty reports — ten women and twenty men — elaborated by the Penitentiary System of the Province of Buenos Aires between the late 1930s and 1955. I have selected these forms at the expense of those produced by the Institute of Criminology, whose format left too little margin to perceive the voice of any inmate. As it often happens with primary sources in Argentina, the criterion of selection has been mere availability: these reports are the only ones preserved in the archive of the Institute of Classification for these dates. The inmates interviewed between 1930 and 1950 had been born between 1893 and 1925. Such is the rough chronological frame of their recollections about childhood and early experiences. They were serving long-term prison sentences in the main correctional institutions of the Province of Buenos Aires, for major offenses against persons (murder, corruption, or infanticide) or property. Most of the interviews transcribed in the reports had been performed several years after the inmate had entered the prison, and most of them were followed by updates on his/her evolution in the prison environment.

14 Unless otherwise specified, all the information is extracted from Provincia de Buenos Aires, Ministerio de Gobierno, Instituto de Clasificación, Historias criminológicas # 16, 19, 27, 59, 72, 93, 116, 118, 136, 149, 150, 172, 174, 194, 196, 200,

205, 206, 232, 235, 240, 322, 327, 341, 397, 426, 427, 587, 1373, 3598. To keep the anonymity required by the institution, the names of the inmates interviewed will not be mentioned.

15 Historia Criminológica # 93, p. 3.

16 For a good discussion on the interpretations of rural illegitimacy in nineteenth-century Buenos Aires, see Juan Mateo, "Bastardos y concubinas. La ilegitimidad conyugal y filial en la frontera pampeana bonaerense (Lobos 1810–1869)," *Boletín del Instituto de Historia Argentina y Americana "Dr. Emilio Ravignani"* 3, no. 13 (1996): 7.

17 Historia Criminológica # 194, p. 12.

18 Interestingly, the only hint of an evolution into a more institutional approach to Catholicism before prison is provided by a former maid who recalled reading books from the Catholic Action provided to her by her patrona, who had also become her godmother. The weak presence of the clergy in early twentieth-century popular rural life is hardly surprising. It can be linked to the low amounts of lower clergy in the ranks of the Catholic church, a fact that limited its impact to highly populated areas, and that sorely worried the institution's leadership; see Enrique Amato, *La iglesia en Argentina* (Madrid: FERES, 1965).

19 On the strong "casualization" and intermittence of work opportunities for rural workers between 1890 and 1914, see Jeremy Adelman, *Frontier Development. Land, Labour, and Development on the Wheatlands of Argentina and Canada 1890–1914* (New York: Oxford University Press, 1994), p. 116; Hilda Sábato and Luis Alberto Romero, *Los trabajadores de Buenos Aires: la experiencia del mercado, 1850–1880* (Buenos Aires: Sudamericana, 1992), chap. IV; Salvatore, "Criminology," pp. 281–286.

20 There were two main reasons for this change: either the weak economic situation of the family required them to earn a small wage to supplement the general budget, or the father had disappeared, leaving the children and mother in an extremely precarious situation. In the first case, a boy would often start helping his father in rural tasks during the high season, and the pay was given directly to the latter. If the father was absent, or the cause of economic problems was lack of work in the estancia, boys were hired by local stores to deliver milk, meat, bread or the newspaper. They could also find work in the construction business as aids to bricklayers.

21 Historia Criminológica # 72, p. 4.

22 Historia Criminológica # 327, p. 12.

23 In his well-known book *Estudios Penitenciarios* (Buenos Aires: Talleres Gráficos de la Penitenciaría Nacional, 1906), p. 34, Eusebio Gómez stated that "by regulating the psychological and organic life of inmates, work represents the most important moralizing agent that can be used in the struggle of society against crime." See also his article "Trabajo carcelario," *Boletín del Patronato de Recluidas y Liberadas* 1, no. 3. (1936): 11. A discussion on this aspect of criminological theory can be found in Salvatore, "Criminology."

24 A representative discussion on the contrasting influence of rural and urban areas on the development of criminality in Cornelio Moyano Gacitúa, *La delincuencia argentina ante algunas cifras y teorías* (Córdoba: Casa Editora F Domenici, 1905), p. 271.

25 "Régimen e Instituciones Carcelarias de la Provincia de Buenos Aires. Informe de la Comisión de estudios presidida por el Dr. José M. Paz Anchorena," *RPP* I2 (Oct.–Dec. 1936): 337; "Decreto del 10 de Junio de 1937 del Poder Ejecutivo de la Provincia de Buenos Aires, sobre reorganización de talleres carcelarios," *RPP* III9 (July–Sept. 1938): 496.

26 The capacity of inmates to convince a usually skeptical audience is all the more interesting inasmuch as their assessment could be directly linked to the crimes they had committed. Historias Criminológicas # 59 and # 174 concerned the murder of a wife and a stepmother respectively.

27 Donna J. Guy, "Mothers Alive and Dead: Multiple Concepts of Mothering in Buenos Aires," in Donna J. Guy and Daniel Balderston, eds., *Sex and Sexuality in Latin America* (New York: New York University Press, 1997), chap. 10; Marcela Nari, "Las prácticas anticonceptivas, la disminución de la natalidad y el debate médico, 1890–1940," in M. Z. Lobato, ed., *Médicos*, p. 153.

28 Historia Criminológica # 150.

29 "Decreto del 10 de Junio de 1937 del Poder Ejecutivo de la Provincia de Buenos Aires," *RPP*, p. 496. On the enforcement of work therapy in the female prison of the city of Buenos Aires, see Lila Caimari, "Whose Criminals Are These? Church, State and Patronatos and the Rehabilitation of Female Convicts (Buenos Aires, 1890–1940)," *The Americas* 542 (October 1997): 191.

30 Instituto de Clasificación, Historia Criminológica # 232.

31 On the social perception of tuberculosis in turn-of-the-century Buenos Aires, see Karen Mead, "Oligarchs, Doctors and Nuns" (Ph.D. dissertation, University of California at Santa Barbara, 1994), p. 219. The only two cases where inmates were caught omitting data about health history of their families concerned epilepsy and mental disturbance. Although never as deadly as in the capital, figures for the province of Buenos Aires show that between 1911 and 1930, tuberculosis, pneumonia, and broncopneumonia accounted for about 23 percent of diagnosed deaths. Héctor Recalde, *Vida popular y salud en Buenos Aires (1900–1930)* (Buenos Aires: Centro Editor de América Latina), table in vol. 2, p. 245.

32 It is surprising that the representations of disease found in these testimonies are coupled with a complete absence of references to hospitals or medical treatment. The 1940s followed the *higienista* era of influence, where tuberculosis and infant mortality had mobilized both the medical and charitable systems of the city of Buenos Aires, producing a long-term and perceptible decline in mortality rates. There is barely a hint of these efforts in these testimonies. Although isolated, the only two references do not paint an encouraging picture of the popular perception of the health system: in one case, a female inmate blamed her mother's chronic health problems on bad medical treatment: "They had damaged her."

In another case, medical expenses were recalled as the main cause of a family's poverty.

33 On the underlying assumptions of antialcohol campaigns in Brazil, Argentina, and Mexico, see Nancy Leys Stepan, *The Hour of Eugenics: Race, Gender, and Nation in Latin America* (Ithaca, N.Y.: Cornell University Press, 1991), p. 92. On early turn-of-the-century antialcohol campaigns in Buenos Aires, see Recalde, *Vida popular,* vol. 2, p. 176.

34 Historia Criminológica # 235.

35 Brothels were banned by federal law in 1936, and most interviews took place after this date.

36 Historia Criminológica # 427.

37 The Argentine psychological bent of criminological theory is described in Rodrí-guez, "Encoding," chap. 3.

38 Michel de Certeau, *L'invention du quotidien* (Paris: Gallimard, 1990), introduction.

39 Historia Criminológica # 1373, p. 4; # 174, p. 4; # 341, p. 12.

40 Historia Criminológica # 235.

41 Some reports of the Institute of Classification concluded that it was useless to even try to teach reading and writing to inmates who (as the authorities saw it) were obviously incapable of doing anything other than domestic work.

42 Historia Criminológica # 200.

43 Historia Criminológica # 194.

Afterword

Law and Society in Comparative Perspective

DOUGLAS HAY

═══════════

The excellence of the essays in this volume and my own almost absolute ignorance of the wider literatures familiar to Latin Americanists means that what I have to say must be comparative, suggestive, and tentative. I am familiar only with the legal and social histories of England and of English and French Canada; I know something of the labor law of some other parts of the British Empire. What follows therefore is an outsider's view. It is a view mostly (although not entirely) from the common law side of the great divide between western European legal systems; Latin America lies on the other. But it may be useful to say what, from an outsider's position, seemed familiar but different, or unfamiliar and very different, or virtually identical to the legal structures, and political and social significance of law in Britain and its empire.[1] I shall do so under four rather arbitrary headings: legal cultures, inequality, markets, and personality.

Legal Cultures

One of the great strengths of this collection is the attention given to the intersection, exchanges, and conflicts of state legal cultures and popular legal cultures.[2] At the most sharply defined end of the first, we have appellate courts, legislation, and treatises: the creations of the great state-building bureaucracies of medieval and early modern Europe. At the other extreme, we have the compulsive social power of what we increasingly hesitate to call custom: recurrent patterns of social ordering, including legitimized compulsion, that is largely untouched by state law. Central to this volume is the problematic terrain where state law and folk law (however defined) meet. Many of the essays explore this territory, as one of contestation, in fascinating detail.

The conflicts of elite and popular judgements delineated in the sensitive accounts by Piccato and Aguirre are only two instances. Sometimes the fluidity of adaptations, inversions is striking. But when we can see and understand the popular assumptions of legality in particular groups, we also may be surprised at their ability to resist elite discourse and to preserve their own definitions in the heart of the carceral archipelago. The issue, then, of what it means for populist movements and poor individuals to abandon folk law and actually to use state law is central to our inquiry. But before raising a few questions about such attempts, I want to point to the fact that the boundary between elite (state) and popular (folk) legalities is blurred by borrowings and invoked resonances. There are, for example, adaptations by popular legal culture in imitation of state law. Particular courts and bodies of law generate particular kinds of processes, kinds of solutions: and therefore expectations of what "justice" is and how it is done, among their users, among even those who suffer their attentions, and often in broadly held popular belief.

We see many instances of this in England. Prisoners, soldiers, and also some bodies of workers adapt, caricature, but also substantially adopt the forms of the English criminal court: jury trial, the judge, the formal sentence. Larger social groups, sometimes crossing class divides, also developed "folk law," often in the absence of state law, that nonetheless borrowed its elements. Thus the wife "sale," a form of popular divorce in the eighteenth and nineteenth centuries, was explicitly modeled on the sale of horses and cattle in open market in part because state legislation and case law made such transactions with animals the most binding kinds of contracts. A feigned "sale" of a wife (for these were collusive proceedings), watched in public, entered in the market books, and sealed with the passing of consideration in the form of a drink, was popularly held to be equally legal and determinative, at a time when the state refused to provide divorce in its own courts except for the rich.[3]

In other instances the complex, overlapping, multiple mappings of different levels of state law, of different codes, edicts, statutes, and traditions, mean that popular legal culture comes to diverge from that of the state, but by calling on older state law as a critique of the new. The extensive literature we now have on the food riot shows just how persistent popular insistence on old law could be. Rioters demanded that the still extant medieval and early modern laws against forestalling, regrating, and engrossing be enforced, in the face of the state's withdrawal, between the 1750s and 1800, from market regulation; food rioters continued to demand implementation of the laws for more than a quarter of a century after Parliament thought it had repealed them.[4] The persistence of popular trials of witches well into the eighteenth century is another instance. Judges and elite groups had abandoned the cosmology and evidentiary doctrines of witchcraft by the late seventeenth century, and Parliament repealed the Tudor and Stuart statutes in 1736. But mobs continued not only to identify witches, but to "try" them by the methods used by the courts in the seventeenth century, including dragging them through ponds to see whether the waters would reject them. Two centuries of statutes, judicial, and royal declarations against the crime of witchcraft were not easily displaced; popular justice continued to act when the state would not.

A popular legal culture, then, is a persistent formation. It survives legislative change; it may even survive a deliberate attempt by the state to change the entire basis of legal ordering, as in a liberal revolution. For state legal orders are also remarkably persistent, as a great many papers in this collection illustrate, even through such political crises. There are great continuities in personnel; the social assumptions lying at the center of legal ordering may change very little; the need to continue to repress subaltern groups (particularly those with newly aroused hopes) is often manifest to legal elites. It is rare that a political or social revolution is so complete that judges, elite lawyers, and other legal functionaries are displaced entirely, in part because it is so difficult to replace them. They are the enduring personnel of state structures.[5]

Both state legal traditions and popular legal traditions not only have temporal depth, but they are also multifarious. By that I mean, first, that we must be alert to the coexistence of many state legal orders. There are not only civil and criminal jurisdictions, but the particular contributions of ecclesiastical, military, mercantile, occupational courts, and distinctive bodies of law within them. These multiple jurisdictions shift over time — ecclesiastical courts finally disappear in England in 1857, equity and common law courts of different kinds compete for centuries and then fuse by the 1870s. In the essays in this book, police work and executive decision encroach on judicial prerogative, resisted by the lawyers in some jurisdictions much more effectively than others. We must pay attention to the working nature and ideological construction of judiciaries and the lawyers who work with them, take them seriously as durable generators of values and attitudes, as well as the shapers of our records.

But the multiplicity of courts also work, and are worked by lawyers and lay people, as systems. Thus for England Martin Ingram showed in an early article the immensely resourceful exploitation of several courts simultaneously in early modern lawsuits by those with money; we can point to the poor using specific collusive lawsuits to block real ones by wealthier enemies; and in the nineteenth century in England in the highest court, King's Bench, litigants were constantly filing wholly spurious forgery charges (and everyone knew they were spurious) in order to delay litigation and hence increase costs for the opponent in the other common-law courts.[6] So I found myself wondering how much we know for Latin America about such resourceful, multiple, and spurious uses of courts and legal procedures simultaneously by the same protagonists.

But there is also the question of whether some kinds of courts so dominate a society, at least for a time, that they set a particularly powerful stamp on both state law and popular justice. An example is military law. In the case of England it was extremely important, particularly during the period of the French revolutionary and Napoleonic wars, twenty years of almost continuous warfare. A significant proportion of the male population was mobilized. In British colonial settings, often garrison towns, military justice was crucial; it might even be imposed (as in Quebec in 1760–64) on civilian populations.[7] The account Ricardo Salvatore gives us of justice under Rosas recalls many elements of what was probably common military practice in the European states and their colonies. The lavish use of ad hoc corporal punishment; the absence of due process; the identification of the officer class with judge, jury, and counsel; all these are common. Even the use of the lottery to choose a proportion of offenders to suffer capital punishment in Buenos Aires, was a custom practiced throughout the British army, throughout at least the eighteenth century. In short, here we have a common culture of military law extending across centuries, and across the boundaries of civilian legal systems. And to return to my earlier point:

when this is the most common form of state law (as under Rosas) popular legal traditions cannot fail to be formed by some of the same assumptions.

As a final instance of relationships between popular legal culture and that of the state, we might ask about the relationship of ideas of marriage, in the codes and among the people. In Canada, state law initially recognized marriages between Europeans and aboriginal peoples according to "the custom of the country"; that is, aboriginal law. In the nineteenth century that original accommodation was ended: such marriages were first not recognized, then criminalized.[8] As we see in many of the Latin American instances, where marriage laws and the legal status of women change over time, we ask both how popular legal tradition is affected (Arlene Díaz's point) but also where, and why, and by whom, state law is changed, and with what expectations.

Inequality

My favorite appalling statistic is from a British government study which showed, a few years ago, that in three random samples of young men born in the 1950s and 1960s, 31 percent had serious criminal convictions by the age of twenty-eight. Not warnings, not arrests, but convictions.[9] We know that such men come from the least prosperous parts of the population, however we choose to argue the causal connections. I have argued elsewhere that the connections between state violence, private violence, and social inequality are reciprocal and reinforcing.[10] But there is another aspect to social inequality — differential access and experience of state courts — that may be relevant to a number of the papers.

Where social inequality is less, it is easier for courts to serve as resolvers (and prolongers) of disputes. This may be (rarely) possible for a whole society: dispute resolution in some village communities in Africa, among aboriginal peoples, in small religious groups in our own society in the past, are instances. But where social inequality is great or growing quickly (as in most of our countries at the present time), or is already a vast gulf (as in many of the jurisdictions the contributors to this volume study), particular ecclesiastical, civil, but even criminal courts can still find acceptance and use, but only among a fraction of the population. The people appearing before a particular court become highly unrepresentative of the whole population. They may be all of rather similar social class or a limited range or with patronage or kin connections that make them feel safer in that court than would other people. I wonder, therefore, whether those who appeared before Juan Manuel Palacio's justices of the peace, for instance, were distinguished in just such ways. Where patronage and kin connections are strong, apparent social class may not be the only determinant of why some people are willing to use courts while others are not. Moreover, work in England and Europe shows clearly that some litigants, sometimes many, are in fact representatives of much more powerful interests, and that individual cases are often part of much longer, and wider, networks of litigation where the interests of power become manifest.[11]

We must not assume, therefore, that the social or class significance of a court can be read off simply from the social profile of individual complainants and defendants. Charles Walker's essay, though nuanced in its appreciation of multiple, crossing interests, perhaps leads somewhat in this direction. In all the jurisdictions we study, we need to create connected histories of litigation, not just positivist counts (even though we will all, of course, go on counting). And even after we have written those histories (and done that counting) of adjudication and dispute resolution in the courts, we must ask what other people are being simultaneously dealt with by different state agencies, including agencies of repression — the army, the police — and hence hardly appear at all in the courts whose records survive for us to study.

It is useful, then, to ask what other legal activities, state activities, and private repression are coincidentally occurring, irregularly occurring, in the society outside the courtrooms in which "our cases" are occurring, and causing ebbs and flows in the numbers of those cases. An instructive instance from East Africa appears in work by David Anderson.[12] Studying the incidence of penal sanctions for breach of contract in Kenya in the early twentieth century, he was struck by periodic increases, brief blips, in the use of imprisonment, from a generally low level of enforcement. The explanation turned out to be that white Kenyan planters used much more direct means than the law for daily discipline of their African workers: they whipped them. (The Dunlop Rubber Company manufactured the whips when rhinoceros-hide whips were deemed dangerous to rhinoceros preservation.) But every few years a worker was whipped to death in particularly scandalous circumstances. The colonial government prosecuted for murder, and the planters, as a consequence, turned to the courts and imprisonment to discipline their workers for a short while until the furor died down.

In short, the greater number of official punishments in the court records at such periods was an indicator of less punishment for workers, not more.

To mention that instance takes me to the commonplace that a great deal of law, in the past as today, creates social inequality, and indeed is *designed* to do so. It is perhaps useful to conceptualize this process largely as its role in the creation of particular markets.

Markets

There are labor markets in which most people are slaves. The state and state-sanctioned violence necessary to accomplish that feat fills a large literature, and also some of the literature on Latin America — notably, Tom Holloway's sweeping survey of Rio policing.[13] But there are also all those other markets of differing degrees of unfree labor (and indeed, increasingly studies of slavery in the British Empire show how slaves too could bargain, even for wages, within the boundaries of their legal status).[14] The degrees of labor's unfreedom are created by law, bounded by law, and ultimately enforced by the legal violence of the state, whether by forced immigration, or forced emigration, or enforcement of contracts by imprisonment, whipping, loss of wages, coercion by caciques or other means.[15] Donna Guy's account of the incarceration of homeless (that is, unemployed) young girls in Buenos Aires continually counterposes the social hygiene and social welfare discourse with the fact that the system constantly sacrificed education or welfare to the function of supplying poorly paid labor, first for domestic service, then for industry, when it was not exploiting the children for profit in the manufacture of goods for sale within the prison itself. In the continuum between labor law and criminal law that informs many of these essays there are frequent, sometimes very close, parallels to British imperial evidence. The crucial issue of the degree of racial division in constructing elite ideas of criminal identity (whether aboriginal or imported slave) is perhaps the most important organizing distinction within both the English and Spanish-Portuguese imperial legacies. Diane Paton's chapter, an explicit comparative case from the British Empire, demonstrates both the role of imprisonment in recruiting and distributing very cheap labor to higher social classes, and the way in which the penal policy of the elites constructed independence from wage labor, in a black population, as criminal proclivity. But a host of more general laws and regulations also can be found in both sets of jurisdictions to control movement, repress resistance, and to deal with the successful imposition of great inequality. To take only one instance of many: vagrancy laws to arrest anyone suspected of possibly being about to commit a crime. The English 1824 Vagrancy Act closely resembles in intent, structure, and effect the Brazilian acts of 1825 and 1866 described by Holloway.[16]

By these means lawmakers constantly expand, contract, define, and shape markets. The process never stops, and it includes the creation of lesser, specific markets of the most coercive kinds in particular locales. On the micro scale even today, we create special markets (in special conditions of unfreedom) for prisoners in penitentiaries, where the inmates are happy to risk trading their health, in a very limited market with limited goods, through consenting to experimental drug trials, at costs to experimenters that could never be attained in wider labor markets in the general society. Something similar, one suspects, went on in the prison hospital described by Cristina Rivera-Garza — extreme coercion, but also boundary coercion in which the power of inmates to negotiate their lives with their doctor/jailers was dominated by resistance and coercion. But negotiation, exchange, to survive nonetheless also took place.

Many of the essays in this book can be read as the use of law to expand labor or materials markets, curb "illicit" markets, restrict land markets to particular groups, and expropriate from populations the possibility of participating in any other than the most degraded and desperate exchanges of labor for survival. When the state much more rarely intervenes on the side of the poor, of labor, it is often in a period of a crisis of legitimacy. So enforcement of wages, of smallowners' property rights in land were supported by the central state and its courts at specific times over the centuries to attach them to the regime. But over the longer term many of the legal issues we are considering here can be conceptualized as the coercive legal restructuring of markets — almost always in ways that accentuate the accumulation of great wealth and great poverty, until economic crisis, war, rebellion, or revolution ensue, and a new agenda begins.

How such restructuring was accomplished, and what part legal personnel, doctrines, and violence played in it are crucial questions. These issues are at the center of some of the essays of this book: González and Palacio for the twentieth century, for example, and for many of the others the context is no doubt clear to those familiar with the wider literature. Tying the details of how law worked (not necessarily how it was conceptualized or expressed by legal elites) to specific economic interests or changes — to political economy, broadly and socially conceived — is crucial to full explanation. One crucial market is of course the market for legal services itself: law as extractor of surplus, the court as a machine for generating fees, for state-building and revenue generation. And also the issue of professional qualification — whether it restricts the market for legal services. Sometimes that market is much wider, or is a series of concentric circles of expertise: thus Juan Manuel Palacio's pettifoggers have a close parallel in eighteenth-century England, where even in King's Bench, the very highest criminal court, poor people were able to use the law because of unqualified pettifoggers working on contingency fees.[17] But of course contingency fee system still means that only some litigants — those with cases likely to convince judges (or jurors, in the English case) — are able to proceed without money of their own.

A historian of English or American law will also wonder to what extent Latin American law in the nineteenth century, including the criminal law, was influenced by classical political economy as an intellectual system. Although there is much debate about the exact nature of the relationships between legal doctrine and economic theory in common-law jurisprudence of the period, it is clear that classical political economy inflected much legal discourse, and helped shape legal doctrine, between the late eighteenth and the late nineteenth centuries. A vulgarized theory of free markets was often invoked off and on the bench. It was implicitly but also explicitly used by lawyers and by judges, at critical points, to justify cutting back older equitable remedies, and to limit contractual liability in ways that assisted large companies against small business interests, and employers against workers. And as it reshaped doctrine, free market theory was also a thundering rhetoric in politics and intellectual debate (as it has been, again, in the last twenty years).[18]

Now this was, of course, central to the classic liberal project. In these chapters the principal focus is on the political and constitutional reforms promoted by liberals in Latin America. I wondered about the other, economic interests of all those lawyers and politicians, and how explicit or concealed their sense was of creating new economies, and how much resistance was expressed as resistance to the legal changes necessary to classical political economy.

In mid-nineteenth century Canada, for example, the same lawyers, businessmen, and politicians (often an individual filled all three roles) achieved self-government from Britain, reformed the penal code, built the new prisons, and amplified fear of crime through the press. But they also replaced seigneurial tenure in Quebec with more absolute property in land, accumulated large quantities of land through changes in the law that favored large owners, cut back traditional rights of dower for women in order to facilitate land sales, subsidized their railways with taxes targeted at the poorer part of the population, assisted processes of proletarianization in these and other ways, and incarcerated vagrants, recalcitrant workers, and political agitators who somehow appeared. The legal and political elites thought of all those acts as critically necessary to the free market, to economic growth, and (how fortunate the congruence) to their own accumulation of wealth.[19] The Chief Justice of Manitoba, who built his fortune in buying up land scrip from impoverished aboriginals and Métis while as a judge making rulings that fostered such processes, is one instance of many.[20] Meanwhile Manitoba, like other western Canadian provinces, was filling its prisons disproportionately with aboriginal men.

To discuss the criminal law and criminological theory without asking the classic question, "who benefits and how," is I think impossible or misleading — it is to accept the premises of an ideological structure of markets as a description of social reality, even if we recognize the politics as ideology. So, as Emilia Viotta da Costa put it in her comments during the conference, we must unpack liberalism, liberalisms, in all their interrelatedness. Most important, we must not forget that classic liberalism was, above all else, and above all the rhetoric, an economic doctrine that said that free markets had to be ruthless (without sentiment) to fit the logic of the theory.

What do these liberalisms imply for issues of gender? In England nineteenth-century liberals — committed to markets, contractual equality, and even eventually equal political rights (or at least the franchise) for people of all social classes — nonetheless resisted the notion that women are people. England was the most advanced liberal economy and at the same time one of the least democratic countries of the Atlantic region for much of the nineteenth century. The franchise was very restricted until late in the century, and women were denied equality in constitutional law, family law, contractual capacity, and even criminal responsibility. As the male franchise widened in the second half of the century (1867, 1884), women attempted to argue for equal treatment under the law from liberal principles. Parliament and the courts and most male ideologues of market liberalism (with the exception of John Stuart Mill) sternly opposed them. It was not until the twentieth century that women gained the vote, and not until the late 1920s that a Canadian appeal to the Judicial Committee of the Privy Council overturned former doctrine at the highest level, finally establishing (in the "Persons Case") that women were people with respect to political rights (of course, differential treatment of women in other areas, including criminal law, continued, often using a medical model of female personality as the excuse).

Whether the outcome would have been different in England had the argument taken place in a new republic, as in Peru or Venezuela, rather than in a slowly evolving constitutional monarchy, is probably a meaningless question. But the English story suggests, again, that liberalism is a congeries of doctrines, in which the formal equality used to justify the abandonment of policy to market forces need not imply the extension of even formal political rights to large sections of the population. The evidence in Sarah Chambers's work,[21] and in the essays by Arlene Díaz, Ricardo Salvatore, and other contributors to this volume, point specifically to its indifference to the place of women in Latin America. Much work suggests its indifference to the poor. It is not surprising, then, that even where formal political rights were extended, actual political participation and respect for civil liberties might be forcibly foreclosed by what (borrowing an old term) we might call the *effective* as opposed to the *formal* constitution.

Personality

During the period in which freedom of contract was a preeminent organizing idea of discourse in England (the mid-to-late nineteenth century), it helped shape expectations of male personality structure in important ways, as had earlier social and intellectual beliefs. Like them, it did so in large measure in law. Yet female personality was often constructed on quite different premises.

In an earlier period, in the sixteenth to eighteenth centuries, English judges moved from legal doctrines that excused violent reprisals by a man of honor to an ideal of gentlemanly social behavior that condemned interpersonal violence and demanded restraint. I have been tracing some of its further decline in the courts, in such cases. A further evolution took place in the notion of the ideal man by the nineteenth century. The restrained gentleman of the mid-eighteenth century had also been a man freed by his social class from greed and from trade. Now, from being a gentleman who was above base pecuniary motive, the ideal man-at-law becomes a market-wise risk-taker, a man who is not dishonored by seeking to take advantage of those with whom he bargains, but is instead celebrated.[22] The law rewrites the doctrine on expectation profits, contracts for future performance; it discards doctrines that formerly stigmatized unfair practices, usurious interest, unmerited enrichment.

I found myself wondering, as the fascinating salience of medical discourse was discussed in these essays (much rarer, I think, in social discourse in England), whether there was any counterpart in Latin American liberal programs to the Niagara roar of legal rhetoric in England and the United States that celebrated market-wise individualism. In those societies it permeated criminal law too. In England, for example, the intense interest of the judges in contract and other private law cases on emphasizing individual responsibility (the courts would not save you from your mistakes; the population had to be educated into risk-taking, entrepreneurial individualism) meant that similar issues of free will permeated the discourse and administration of criminal law. Two examples: the insanity defense was radically cut back in the 1840s (the McNaughton Rules emphasized free volition); fixed sentencing, serving your time, became conceptualized as a contract with the state (thus indeterminate sentences, executive decisions on executions, or other aspects of administrative discretion, were unacceptable). Only in the early twentieth century was there that reconstruction of the criminal as degenerate, inspired in part by eugenics but very little by Lombroso in England, that brought attitudes to the criminal closer again to views that had preceded classical contractarian doctrines. Only then is there the replacement of a doctrine of the individual over whom the state had strictly limited power, to the idea that the state should be given great legal power to reform, rehabilitate, and mold, by force if necessary.[23]

The idea of a passionate, dangerous, brutalized personality among a residuum, those wholly unable to survive in the market, coexisted in England with early political economy in the early nineteenth century. Here the parallels with some essays in this volume are clear. The critique of punishment developed by Salvatore is immensely evocative for students of English criminal law. He stressed the curbed, limited expression of state violence of the post-Rosas regime's public executions, as part of democracy. There is a huge resonance with the Whig critique of capital punishment in England in the 1820s to 1840s, and later, regimes that in fact fought and feared democracy. As Randy McGowen, Vic Gatrell, and others have shown for England in that period, the propertied fear of amplifying a degenerate working-class violence in the great cities, through the corrupting spectacle of public executions, echoes in almost every respect the post-Rosas fear of amplifying the violence innate in the blood-drenched rural slaughterers of Argentina.[24] We see that argument reprised again in Kristin Ruggiero's account of the fear that public executions would derange the passions of that population.

Ruggiero's emphasis on honor, however, reminds us also of important differences. I have already remarked on the erosion of older ideas of honor by the celebration of risk-taking in the market in English and American law, a very different valuation of human conduct. It seems likely that there are important older roots of such differences, not found only in political economy. Donna Guy pointed out at the Yale conference that the construction of personality may have been very different in Catholic countries with undeveloped industrial capitalism, in Latin America, from countries like England and the northern states with strong dissenting Protestant religious traditions. The specific nature of Latin American catholicisms may be very important: it would be interesting if the role of the hierarchy and religious orders, considered in the chapters by Dain Borges and Guy, and a few others, mediated legal ideologies and penologies and also the consequences of criminal conviction in other ways. As early as the eighteenth century, European visitors remarked on the apparent indifference in England to notions of honor and dishonor in much of the criminal law, notably with respect to conviction, compared to their striking salience elsewhere in Europe. Clearly religious identity is not alone the determinant, although different forms of Protestantism, as well as the mores of local aristocracies, are important. But I assume it to be true that both in popular beliefs and in state law, honor was still central to much of European criminal law (and I assume Latin American) in a way it no longer was in England. Yet it is clear at the same time that honor and its middle-class homologue, respectability, is sharply class-inflected, as Lila Caimari's account of prisoners' encounters with criminologists, and their discordant understanding of reputable behaviors, shows.

Honor becomes dangerous to a governing class seeing in it sources of interpersonal violence; or honor can be used to excuse that violence, as Ruggiero points out; or honor can be associated with republicanism by those anxious to strengthen the claims of the latter, as Sarah Chambers has suggested. And honor is also very interesting to us as the circuit through which interclass and intraclass relations are connected with gender. Honor regulated through male institutions such as the duel, and in a host of lesser ways, is strongly connected with notions of the protected, dependent, idealized woman: a man's honor is most vulnerable, most in need of assertion, when that construction of womanhood, and his woman, is contested. Although, as I have argued, consideration of honor even in this sense was much less salient in England, it is interesting that the personal and political dependency of women, already discussed, opened the way in England to the medicalization of female deviance.

The evidence suggests that the great medicalization of criminological discourse in Latin America did not take place in England to nearly the same extent, with this one exception, a large exception, of women. The construction of the female personality as weak, dependent, prone to aberration, meant in effect that women were not credited with even the possibility of acquiring the strong, brave, individualist, risk-taking personalities that men were expected to show. A corollary was that the state did not need to respect the individual rights of women in the way that a contractarian state was prepared, to a degree, to respect the individuality of even male criminals. Here, the failure of the state to grant liberalism's rights to women feeds back into a criminological discourse that justifies drastic state intervention (including indeterminate sentencing) for late-nineteenth century women.[25]

Perhaps there is a contrast to be drawn between the apparent supremacy of medicalized discourse in Latin America, strikingly illustrated in the papers by Dain Borges, Cristina Rivera-Garza, and a number of others, and the apparent supremacy of liberal market discourse in England and the United States in this period. The liberal state that believes in, celebrates, and seeks to strengthen free markets will create a body of law more resistant to medical and other explanations for human failing, with the notable exception of the failings of women. To oversimplify greatly, the legal elites will resist the pretensions of medical elites to subvert legal categories of responsibility, categories that also appear to guarantee individualist freedoms. The state that has less competitive markets, greater clientage, greater social and gender inequality, and a slave and racist heritage and that continues to celebrate honor will not create so strong a body of individualist law. The way will then be open for a different group of intellectuals, the doctors eager to prescribe for whole societies, to create a criminology and social theory based on nineteenth-century sciences of atavism, evolution, and degeneracy, and to realize its aims, to some extent, in the judicial institutions of the state.

Notes

1 The work of all the contributors raised questions in my mind about comparisons with issues in my own work, some of it cited in the notes that follow.

2 The concept of legal culture, although useful as shorthand in the way used here, is not unproblematic if pressed too far. See David Nelken, ed., *Comparing Legal Cultures* (Aldershot: Dartmouth, 1997).

3 Some of these borrowings, although not all, can be seen in E. P. Thompson, "The sale of wives," in his *Customs in Common* (London: Merlin Press, 1991), and in Samuel Pyeatt Menefee, *Wives for Sale: An Ethnographic Study of British Popular Divorce* (New York: St. Martin's Press, 1981).

4 Thompson, *Customs in Common*, chaps. 4, 5; Douglas Hay, "The State and the Market: Lord Kenyon and Mr Waddington," in *Past & Present* 162 (February 1999): 101–162, and "Moral Economy, Political Economy, and Law," in Adrian Randall and Andrew Charlesworth, eds., *Moral Economy and Popular Protest: Crowds, Conflict and Authority* (Manchester: Manchester University Press, 1999), pp. 93–122.

5 See, for instance, Ingo Müller, *Hitler's Justice: The Courts of the Third Reich* (Cambridge, Mass: Harvard University Press, 1991).

6 M. J. Ingram, "Communities and Courts: Law and Disorder in Early-Seventeenth-Century Wiltshire," in J. S. Cockburn, ed., *Crime in England 1550–1800* (London: Methuen, 1977), pp. 110–134; the other instances will appear in my own work on the court of King's Bench.

7 Jean-Marie Fecteau and Douglas Hay, " 'Government by will and pleasure instead of law': military justice and the legal system in Quebec, 1775–1783," in Murray Greenwood and Barry Wright, eds., *Canadian State Trials* (Toronto: The Osgoode Society, 1996), pp. 129–171; Douglas Hay, "Civilians tried in military courts: Quebec, 1759–1764," in Greenwood and Wright, pp. 114–128.

8 Constance Backhouse, *Petticoats and Prejudice: Women and the Law in Nineteenth-Century Canada* (Toronto: The Osgoode Society, 1991), pp. 9–28.

9 Home Office Statistical Bulletin 7/85, *Criminal Careers of Those Born in 1953, 1958, and 1963* (issued 3 April 1985), table 1 and p. 13.

10 Douglas Hay, "Time, Inequality, and Law's Violence," in Austin Sarat, ed., *Law's Violence* (Ann Arbor: University of Michigan Press, 1992), pp. 141–173.

11 Some English evidence is presented in Douglas Hay, "Dread of the Crown Office: The Magistracy and King's Bench 1740–1800," in Norma Landau, ed., *Law, Crime and English Society 1660–1840* (New York: Oxford University Press, forthcoming).

12 David Anderson, "Master and servant legislation and labour in colonial Kenya, 1895–1939" (unpublished manuscript).

13 Thomas Holloway, *Policing Rio de Janeiro: Resistance and Repression in a 19th-Century City* (Stanford: Stanford University Press, 1993).

14 Mary Turner, ed., *From Chattel Slaves to Wage Slaves: the Dynamics of Labor Bargaining in the Americas* (Bloomington: Indiana University Press, 1995).

15 Paul Craven and I are preparing a volume of studies of the role of coercion and adjudication in the contract of employment in the British empire from the seventeenth to twentieth centuries.

16 5 Geo IV c.83 (1824).

17 C. W. Brooks, *Pettyfoggers and Vipers of the Commonwealth: The "Lower Branch" of the Legal Profession in Early Modern England* (New York: Cambridge University Press, 1986); and forthcoming work on eighteenth-century London courts by Ruth Paley.

18 The principal original studies are Patrick Atiyah, *Rise and Fall of Freedom of Contract* (Oxford: Oxford University Press, 1979), and Morton Horwitz, *The Transformation of American Law* (Cambridge, Mass.: Harvard University Press, 1977); there is now a large critical literature.

19 For some of these themes see Jean-Marie Fecteau, *Un Nouvel Ordre des Chose: La Pauvreté, Le crime, L'État au Québec* (Outremont: VLB, 1989).

20 Paul L. A. H. Chartrand, "Aboriginal rights: the dispossession of the Metis," *Osgoode Hall Law Journal* 29 (1991): 457.

21 See Sarah Chambers, "Crime and Citizenship: Judicial Practice in Arequipa, Peru during the Transition from Colony to Republic," in Carlos Aguirre and Robert Buffington, eds., *Reconstructing Criminality in Latin America* (Wilmington, Del.: Scholarly Resources, 2000).

22 See Atiyah and the other sources cited in note 18.

23 For the argument, see David Garland, *Punishment and Welfare: A History of Penal Strategies* (Aldershot, Gower, 1985), and Martin Wiener, *Reconstructing the Criminal: Culture, Law, and Policy in England, 1830–1914* (New York: Cambridge University Press, 1990). For a critique, see Victor Bailey, "The Fabrication of Deviance: 'Dangerous Classes' and 'Criminal Classes' in Victorian England," in John Rule and Robert Malcolmson, eds., *Protest and Survival: Essays for E. P. Thompson* (New York: The New Press, 1993), pp. 221–256.

24 McGowen, Randall, "The Image of Justice and Reform of the Criminal Law in Early Nineteenth-Century England," *Buffalo Law Review* 35 (1983): 89–125, and other work; V. A. C. Gatrell, *The Hanging Tree: Execution and the English People, 1770–1868* (New York: Oxford University Press, 1994).

25 See Lucia Zedner, *Women, Crime, and Custody in Victorian England* (Oxford: Clarendon Press, 1991).

Contributors

CARLOS AGUIRRE is Assistant Professor of History at the University of Oregon. He is the author of *Agentes de su propia libertad: los esclavos de Lima y la desintegración de la esclavitud, 1821–1854* (1993), and has coedited, with Charles Walker, *Bandoleros, abigeos, y montoneros: Criminalidad y violencia en el Perú, siglos XVIII–XX* (1990), with Ricardo Salvatore, *The Birth of the Penitentiary in Latin America: Essays on Criminology, Prison Reform, and Social Control, 1830–1940* (1996), and with Robert Buffington, *Reconstructing Criminality in Latin America* (2000). He has recently completed a book manuscript on the history of prisons in Lima, Peru.

DAIN BORGES is Associate Professor of History at the University of Chicago. He is the author of *The Family in Bahia, Brazil, 1870–1945* (1992) and several articles on Brazilian social thought, including "A Mirror of Progress," in *The Brazil Reader* (Duke University Press, 1999), "Intellectuals and the Forgetting of Slavery in Brazil," *Annals of Scholarship* (1996), and "The Recognition of Afro-Brazilian Symbols and Ideas, 1890–1940," *Luso-Brazilian Review* (1995). His research on the repression of witchcraft and popular healing is part of a book in progress on intellectuals, scientific psychology, and Brazilian religions from 1880 to 1922.

LILA CAIMARI is a researcher at Consejo Nacional de Investigaciones Científicas y Técnicas, and Professor of Modern Argentine History at the University of San Andrés in Buenos Aires. She is the author of *Perón y la Iglesia Católica* (1995), as well as several articles, including "Whose Prisoners are These? Church, State, and Patronatos, and the Rehabilitation of Female Criminals (Buenos Aires, 1890–1970)," in *The Americas* (1997), winner of the Conference on Latin American History Tibesar Award. Her current project explores the modernization of punishment in Argentina between the late nineteenth century and 1960.

ARLENE J. DÍAZ is Assistant Professor of History at Indiana University, Bloomington. She is the author of "Gender Conflicts in the Courts of the Early Venezuelan Republic, Caracas, 1811–1840," in *Crime, History, and Societies* (1998), as well as other articles on the history of gender and family in Latin America. She is currently working on a book manuscript tentatively titled "'To Not Hide My Face': Female Citizens and Paterfamilias in Caracas, Venezuela, 1786–1904."

LUIS A. GONZÁLEZ received a doctorate in history from the University of Minnesota in 1998, with a concentration in modern Brazil, and has published on social, agrarian, political, and socio-legal history. His research has focused on the processes that underlie grassroots political mobilization and the impact of law on the lives of ordinary people in modern Brazil. During 1999–2000 he held an Andrew F. Mellon Post-Doctoral Fellowship in Latin American Research Librarianship at Duke University. He is currently the head of the Journalism Library at Indiana University.

DONNA J. GUY is Professor of History at Ohio State University. She is the author of *Sex and Danger in Buenos Aires: Prostitution, Family, and Nation in Argentina* (1991) and *White Slavery and Mothers Alive and Dead: The Troubled Meeting of Sex, Gender, Public Health, and Progress in Latin America* (2000), and is coeditor with Daniel Balderston of *Sex and Sexuality in Latin America* (1997), and with Thomas Sheridan of *Contested Ground: Comparative Frontiers on the Northern and Southern Edges of the Spanish Empire* (1998). She is currently researching the history of street children and the rise of the welfare state in Argentina from 1880 to 1955.

DOUGLAS HAY is Associate Professor of Law and of History in Osgoode Hall Law School and in the Department of History, York University, Toronto. He is the coauthor, with Nicholas Rogers, of *Eighteenth-Century English Society: Shuttles and Swords* (1997) and with E. P. Thompson and others, *Albion's Fatal Tree: Crime and Society in Eighteenth-Century England* (1975). He is also the coeditor of *Policing and Prosecution in Britain, 1750–1850* (1989) and *Labour, Law, and Crime: An Historical Perspective* (1987), both with Francis Snyder. He is currently working on two projects, a comparative and collaborative study of the law of master and servant in the British Empire, and a study of the role of the court of King's Bench in English politics and society, 1750–1820.

GILBERT M. JOSEPH is Farman Professor of History and Director of Latin American and Iberian Studies at Yale University, as well as Editor of the *Hispanic American Historical Review*. He is the author of *Revolution from Without: Yucatán,*

Mexico, and the United States, 1880–1924 (rev. ed. 1988), and *Rediscovering the Past at Mexico's Periphery* (1986), and coauthor, with Allen Wells, of *Summer of Discontent, Seasons of Upheaval: Elite Politics and Rural Insurgency in Yucatán, 1876–1915* (1996). He is also the editor of *Reclaiming the Political in Latin American History: Essays from the North* (Duke University Press, 2001) and the coeditor, with Daniel Nugent, of *Everyday Forms of State Formation: Revolution and the Negotiation of Rule in Modern Mexico* (Duke University Press, 1994) and, with Catherine LeGrand and Ricardo Salvatore, of *Close Encounters of Empire: Writing the Cultural History of U.S.–Latin American Relations* (Duke University Press, 1998).

JUAN MANUEL PALACIO is Professor of Latin American History and Co-Chair of the Department of Political Science at the Universidad Nacional de San Martín in Buenos Aires. He completed his doctorate at the University of California, Berkeley, in 2000 and is currently researching on the workings of law and justice and the development of local legal cultures in the rural districts of the Pampas region of Argentina from the end of the nineteenth century to the arrival of Peronism. He is also the author of several articles on the rural and economic history of Argentina in the twentieth century.

DIANA PATON teaches history at the University of Newcastle, England. She received her doctorate from Yale University in 1999. Her edition of *A Narrative of Events, since the First of August, 1834, by James Williams, an Apprenticed Labourer in Jamaica* (Duke University Press, 2001) is one of the few autobiographical narratives by former Caribbean slaves. She is currently working on a book, based on her doctoral research, on punishment and the penal system in Jamaica in the era of slave emancipation (1780–1870), and is coediting with Pamela Scully a volume of essays, *Gender and Slave Emancipation in the Atlantic World*. Her articles have been published in journals such as *Slavery and Abolition* and the *Journal of Social History*.

PABLO PICCATO is Assistant Professor of History at Columbia University. He is the author of *City of Suspects: Crime in Mexico City, 1900–1931* (Duke University Press, 2001) and *Congreso y Revolución: El parlamentarismo en la XXVI Legislatura* (1992), as well as several articles, including "Politics and the Technology of Honor: Dueling in Turn of the Century Mexico," which appeared in the *Journal of Social History* (December 1999).

CRISTINA RIVERA-GARZA is Assistant Professor of Mexican History at San Diego State University. Her publications include "Dangerous Minds: Changing Psychiatric Views of the Mentally Ill in Porfirian Mexico," *Journal of the History of Medicine and Allied Sciences* (2001), a novel based on asylum records, *Nadie me verá llorar* (1999), a book of poetry, *La más mía* (1998), and the forthcoming *Mad*

Narratives: Psychiatrists and Inmates Debate Gender, Class, and Nation at the General Insane Asylum, Mexico 1910–1930.

KRISTIN RUGGIERO is Associate Professor of History and Director of the Center for Latin American and Caribbean Studies at the University of Wisconsin-Milwaukee. She is the author of *And Here the World Ends: The Life of an Argentine Village* (1988) and has recently completed a book manuscript titled In Hostage to the Body: Medicine, Law, and Society in Argentina, 1850–1920, the research for which was funded by grants from the National Endowment for the Humanities and the National Science Foundation.

RICARDO D. SALVATORE is Professor of Modern History at the Universidad Torcuato di Tella in Buenos Aires. He has coedited, with Gilbert Joseph and Catherine Legrand, *Close Encounters of Empire: Writing the Cultural History of U.S.–Latin American Relations* (Duke University Press, 1998), with Carlos Aguirre, *The Birth of the Penitentiary in Latin America: Essays on Criminology, Prison Reform, and Social Control* (1996), and with Noemí Goldman, *Caudillismos Rioplatenses: nuevas miradas a un viejo problema* (1998). His book about the social and cultural history of itinerant workers in nineteenth-century Buenos Aires province is forthcoming from Duke University Press. His most recent essays have been published in the *Hispanic American Historical Review*, the *International Review of Social History*, and the *Journal of Latin American Cultural Studies*.

CHARLES F. WALKER is Associate Professor of History at the University of California, Davis. He is the author of *Smoldering Ashes: Cuzco and the Creation of Republican Peru, 1780–1840* (Duke University Press, 1999), and editor of *Entre la retórica y la insurgencia: las ideas y los movimientos sociales en los Andes, siglo XVIII* (1996). He has published numerous articles on the social and political history of nineteenth-century Peru and is currently working on a project on the social and cultural history of earthquakes in colonial Peru.

Index

Abuse: domestic, 66–68; legal, 38–40, 49; sexual, 71, 161–62, 377. *See also* Sex crimes

Acción Social de la Juventud (Lima), 348

Adelman, Jeremy, 15

Adultery, 40, 66, 213, 216–17, 226. *See also* Divorce; Marriage

Africa, 11, 121, 182, 188, 193–94, 289, 419–20

Agrarian credit, 105–6; and economic instability, 88–89; and judges, 91; and merchants, 87–88. *See also* Land tenancy

Albion's Fatal Tree, 6

Altamira, Rafael, 6

Anarcho-syndicalism, xiii

Anderson, David, 420

Anglican Church, 279. *See also* Christianity; Protestantism; Religion

Annales School, 12

Anticlericalism, xiii

Arequipa, 37

Argentina, xiii–xiv, xvi–xvii, 4–6, 19, 83–84, 308–334, 391–409, 427; 1810 revolutionary junta, 310; 1811 triumvirate, 310; 1853 constitution, 311; 1854 provincial constitution, 309; 1886 penal code, 213–14, 216–17, 219; 1921 land tenancy law, 89–91; 1932 land tenancy law, 91; 1937 agricultural census, 85; Civil Code, 374; and law and passion, 211–29; and penal institutions, 369–87; and public health, 151

Argentine Church, 226

Arica, 356

Arrecifes, 317

Asilo Correccional de Mujeres (Buenos Aires), 374

Asilo de Huérfanas (Buenos Aires), 372

Asilo del Buen Pastor (Buenos Aires), 373, 376

Asociación Humanitaria del Perú, 347

"Assassins of 1840," 315, 320, 326, 328.
See also Mazorca
Atlantic region, 424
Australia, 85
Ayarragaray, Lucas, 211, 213
Azángaro, Puno, 354
Azul, 317, 406

Bahía Blanca, 87, 92, 98–99, 104
Bahia Medical School, 192
Bambarén, Carlos, 350
Banco Hipotecario Nacional, 87
Banda del Automóvil Gris, 253, 255–58
Banditry, 7–8
Bandos de buen gobierno, 4
Bank of Brazil, 116
Barão de São Fidélis, 122
Basadre, Jorge, 351
Bastidas, Micaela, 36
Battle of Ayacucho, 353
Belem Prison (Mexico City), 242, 252–53, 257
Belle Epoque, 194, 196
Bentham, Jeremy, 287
Bermann, Gregorio, 383
Bernhardt, Sarah, 221
Birth of the Penitentiary in Latin America,
The, 9
Blanco, Guzmán, 56–58, 73
Boletín de Criminología (Lima), 350, 361
Bolívar, Simón, 57
Bomfim, Martiniano do, 194
Borah, Woodrow, 6
Bourbon: reforms, 49; state, 36–37, 39,
42, 47
Bourdieu, Pierre, 394
Braithwaite, John, 234, 250
Bravo Lira, Bernardino, 6
Brazil, xiv, 6–7, 12, 18, 113, 121, 188,
224; 1824 constitution, 183; 1825
vagrancy act, 422; 1826 vagrancy act,
422; 1830 criminal code, 183; 1850

Land Law, 117; 1890 penal code, 181–82, 187–88, 192, 203; 1916 civil code,
119; 1930 revolution, 117; 1934 consti-
tution, 117; and agrarian legislation,
114; and civil law, 117; and criminal
law, 183; Decree-Law 6.969, 120, 126;
and Dutra, 124; historiography, 184;
and literature, 194–204; polity, 122;
society, 185; and spiritism, 190. *See also*
Estado Novo; First Republic; Vargas,
Getúlio
Brazilian Rural Confederation, 120
Brazilian Spiritist Federation (FEB),
186, 188–91. *See also* Kardec, Allan;
Religion; Spiritism
Britain: *See* Great Britain
Buenos Aires; 7, 103–4, 217–18, 221,
226, 323; and Baring Brothers, 308;
and crime panic, 309; and criminal
courts, 19; and death sentences, 317;
and girls in prison, 369–87, 421; and
judges, 311; legislature of, 333; politics
of, 332; Province of, 83–84, 86, 91–93,
106, 391–93, 396, 398; and research
seminars, xii; rural power in, 18; siege
of, 319; urban society, 7
Bunge, Alejandro E., 386
Bunge, Carlos Octavio, 229

Cabildos, 21, 37, 92
Caimari, Lila, 370, 373
Calles, Plutarco Elías, 172, 257
Campos dos Goitacases, 113–15, 120–23, 125, 127–28, 130–32, 134–35
Canada, 85, 415, 418–19, 423–24
Cana obrigada, 117
Canas y Canchis (Cuzco), 37, 44
Candido, Antonio, 203
Candomblé, 182–83, 185, 187, 190–91,
193–94, 196–99, 204. *See also* Religion
Capitalism, 184, 217; anticapitalism, xiii
Capital punishment, 9, 19, 36, 201, 216,

218–20, 256, 308, 316, 418, 426; as public spectacle, 309, 317–18, 331, 334, 426–27; history of, 310–13; and politics, 313–15, 326–30; and the press, 319–26; and gender, 332–33. *See also* Punishment; Torture

Caracas, 18, 61, 73

Cárcel Central de Varones (Lima), 352–356–57

Cárcel Pública (Buenos Aires), 330

Caribbean, 121, 277

Carranza, Venustiano, 248–49, 256–57

Casa Correccional de Mujeres (Buenos Aires), 369–70, 372–78, 380, 382, 384

Casa de Ejercicios (Buenos Aires), 373, 376

Casa de Expósitos (Buenos Aires), 372

Caseros, 309–10, 325, 327, 331–32

Castilianization, 36

Catholicism, xv, 39, 42, 160, 183–84, 186–87, 397, 400, 427; and republican discourse, 58; and witchcraft, 181–82, 185, 195–96, 203. *See also* Christianity; Religion

Caudillismo, 4, 17, 308, 326, 327

Causas criminales, 37

Cédulas, 4

Centeno, Miguel Ángel, 15

Central Board of Public Hygiene (Brazil), 186

Chamber of Justice (Buenos Aires), 323

Chicago, 381

Chile, 6, 356, 370, 383

Christianity, 281, 322, 355, 381. *See also* Catholicism; Protestantism; Religion

Chumbivilcas, 37

Citizenship, 2, 246, 309, 342; and class, x; and gender, 57–59; and identity, 12; and liberalism, xii; and prostitution, 167–173; republican, 184; and rights, ix

Civil War: United States, 288

Class, xi, 17–18, 21, 35, 43, 113, 186, 195, 391, 416, 419–21, 427; and access to legal system, 22–23, 67, 96–97, 100; and arrest bias, xviii; and capital punishment, 310, 313, 317, 331; and childbirth, 63, 156–57; and crime, x, 38, 242–44, 256, 258, 276, 299–300, 314, 322, 324–25, 396, 398, 404; and discrimination, ix, 72; and domination, ix, 57, 184; and gender, 61–62, 201, 372, 381, 384–86; and indigenous peasantry, 50–51; and law, 1, 8, 16, 17, 36, 41, 93; and liberalism, 329; and literacy, 203; and marriage, 65–66; and national identity, xv; and patria potestas, 60–61; and penal institutions, 345, 347, 351; and Peronism, 107, 387; and politics, 19; and popular culture, 204; and prostitution, 152–55; and race, 196; and sex, 161; and social control, 408–9; and sugar industry, 135; traditions and rituals, 12; and urbanization, 234, 241; and vigilantes, 38; and World War I, 380

Codes. *See* Argentina; Brazil; Great Britain; Jamaica; Peru; Venezuela

Colonial Office (Jamaica), 275, 280, 283, 290, 295

Colonialism, xii, xviii; and Brazil 182, 193; and Jamaica, 275–77, 280; and justice, 24; and law, 3–4, 6, 11–12, 20, 16, 35–36, 38, 59, 61; and Mexico, 246; and Peru, 7, 47–49; and women, 65, 70

Comité Central Pro-Indígena Tahuantinsuyo (Peru), 348

Common Law, 23

Communist Party (Brazil), 120

Comte, Auguste, 58

Comunero Rebels, 49

Concubinage, 64–66, 396–97, 403–4

Condorcanqui, José Gabriel, 35

Consejo Local del Patronato (Peru), 347–48

"Conservative Liberalism," xiv

Conservative Party, 200

Conservatism, xii, xiv

Coronel Dorrego, 83–87, 89–97, 99–100, 104–5, 107

Corporate privilege, xvii, 4, 20–21

Corporatism, xiii, 117

Correctional Tribunal (Lima), 347

Corruption, 16, 46–47, 49, 66, 356

Corte de Casación (Venezuela), 68

Council of Public Health (Mexico City), 147

Courts of Appeals (Buenos Aires), 92

Crime, ix, xi, 1–3, 18–36; and class, 242–43, 256, 258, 309–10, 314, 325, 421; and collective identity, 257; and criminology, 250; as cultural construct, 259; and degeneracy, 226–28; and economics, 237; and Foucault, 9; and gender, 369, 373, 386, 419; health, 147–50, 164–71; history of, 8, 12; images of, 24; interclass, 38; and legislation, 246; and liberalism, xiii; and passion, 211–29; perceptions of, 233–34; and the press, 312, 315–16, 321–25, 327, 330, 334, 423; protection from, 241; and punishment, 245; and technology, 255; in urban societies, 7, 37. *See also* Criminality; Criminology; Sex crimes

Criminality, 7, 228; and collective identity, 233; criminalization of, 255; explanations of, xv; images and discourses of, xviii; State definitions of, 297–98; and theft, 233–34, 239–41, 243–46, 256; and women, 369, 386. *See also* Crime; Criminology

Criminology, 1, 5, 343, 347, 349–50, 352, 361, 424, 427–28; in Brazil, 192–93; and crime, 234, 243–45, 250, 259; and liberalism, xvi; positivist, xiv–xvi,

23, 213–15, 222, 233, 344, 346, 370, 391–93, 395, 398–99, 402, 404, 407–9; and sex, 161. *See also* Crime; Criminality

Cuba, 7

Cuentas: *See* Agrarian credit

Culture, 357; and arrest bias, xviii; and crime, 233; judicial, 83, 105; and law, 1, 24; legal, xvii, 16, 20–21, 24, 415–19; and medico-legal discourse, 24; political, 355, 362; popular, 405; popular rural, 330; and poststructuralism, 10; and sex, 161; subaltern, 8

Curandeiro, 181, 184, 189, 202, 223. *See also* Folk healing; Medicine

Cutter, Charles, 12

Cuzco, 18, 35–37, 39, 45, 48–50

Daughtrey, John, 277–82, 285, 289, 292, 297

Death penalty. *See* Capital punishment

Decena Trágica, 253

de Certeau, Michel, 405

Defender of the Poor, 23, 379

Defensores de Menores (Buenos Aires), 371–72, 374, 376, 378, 380, 384–85

Delito de contagio sexual y nutricio, 148, 169. *See also* Crime; Sex crimes

Delito de contaminación intersexual, 148, 169. *See also* Crime; Sex crimes

Democracy, x, 15–16, 123–24, 246, 310, 323, 326–29, 331–33

Departamento de Menores Abandonados y Encausados (Buenos Aires), 382

Department of Public Health (Mexico City), 147–48, 164, 167, 170

Department of Reformation (Mexico City), 157

Derecho indiano, xi, 5–6, 20, 24

Derecho patrio, 20, 24

Descuret, J. B. F., 213, 220

Díaz, Félix, 247

Díaz, Porfirio. *See* Porfiriato

Dictionary of Crime, 252

Direction General of Prisons (Lima), 350, 352, 354, 358

Dirty War, ix

Disappeared, ix

Discipline and Punish, 9

Divorce, 59, 65, 67–69, 71–72. *See also* Marriage; Separation of Bed and Board

Don Quixote, 200

Drago, Agustín J., 226

Dumas, Alexander, 406

Dunlop Rubber Company, 420

Ecclesiastical Court, 217–28

El Diario Judicial, 346

El Frontón penal island (Peru), 349, 353, 358

El Hijo del Ahuizote, 236

El Imparcial, 244–45, 247

El Judicial, 4, 322, 324, 329

El Matadero, 331

England. *See* Great Britain

Enlightenment, x, xvi, 49

Escalante, José Ángel, 353

Escriche, Joaquín, 216, 219

Estado Novo, 18, 114, 117, 119, 121–23, 130, 135; 1937 Charter, 121

Estatuto de Lavoura Canaviera, 116, 118–22, 124–25, 129, 131–32, 134

Estupro: *See* Sex crimes

Ethnicity, x–xi, 17, 38

Europe, 278, 280, 294, 297, 315, 347, 350, 374, 392, 416, 418–20; and culture, 199, 217, 255; and historians, 8; and legal history, xviii; and legal tradition, 4; and medico-legal discourse, 24; and positivist criminology, xiv, xv; and poststructuralism, 9; and sexual science, 155–56, 158, 161; and social

history, 7; and sugarbeet industry, 125; and witch-hunts, 182, 189

Execution: *See* Capital punishment

Faculty of Medicine (Mexico City), 158, 160

Facundo, 316, 329

Fazenda Santa Maria, 122

Federales, 311, 314–15, 319, 329

First National Conference on Abandoned and Delinquent Children, 383

First Republic, 113

Flores Galindo, Alberto, 12

Flory, Thomas, 6

Folk healing, 181–82, 185–86, 188, 191, 194–95, 200, 202–3. *See also* Curandeiro; Medicine

Foucault, Michel, x, 8–9, 12, 17, 174, 281, 297, 370. See also *Discipline and Punish*

France, xiv, 4, 9–10, 121, 187, 191, 212–13; French Revolution, xiv, 418

Fuentes Castro, Paulino, 346

Fueros. *See* Corporate privilege

Gaceta de Policía (Mexico City), 247

Gamboa, Federico, 154

Garavaglia, Emilio, 97

García Gallo, Alfonso, 6

Garland, David, 9

Garrotter's Act, 294

Gatrell, V. A. C., 426

Geertz, Clifford, 1, 14

Gender, x, xi, 12, 17–18, 56, 211; and arrest bias, xviii; and class, 72; classification, 153; conflict, 2; and crime, 419, 421, 424–25, 427–28; and equality, 59; and honor, 428; identity, 65; images, 61; and modernization, 149; and nationalism, 57; and penal institutions, 347, 369–87; and penal policy, 276, 278–79, 281–82, 285–86, 290,

Gender, (*continued*)
345, 348, 359; and personality structure, 425; and prostitution, 173; and war, 418. *See also* Sex; Sexuality; Women

General Insane Asylum (Mexico City), 161

General Penitentiary (Kingston), 278, 282, 291

Genet, Jean, 174

Genovese, Eugene, 8

Germany, 147; 1919 Weimar constitution, 117

Gibson, Mary, xv

Goffman, Erving, 394

Gómez, Eusebio, 211, 215, 217, 221

Gramsci, Antonio, 8

Great Britain, 4, 6–8, 121, 155, 275–77, 280, 282, 285, 293–97, 299–301, 309–10, 415–18, 420–21, 423–28; 1824 Vagrancy Act, 422; 1865 Corporal Punishment Act, 295; 1877 Prisons Act, 281

Great Depression, 85, 95, 114, 239, 383

"Great Fear" (Peru), 35, 37, 48

Grito de Alcorta, 90

Grossberg, Michael, 61

Guadalupe Jail (Lima), 349

Guayaquil, 37

Guerrero, Julio, 161, 244, 246

Habermas, Jürgen, x, 17

Hapsburg: notion of state and society, 49

Havana, 246

Hay, Douglas, 7–8

Haya de la Torre, Víctor Raúl, 352

Hegemony, 8, 15–16, 25, 47, 49, 56, 134, 172, 358

Heredia, Ricardo, 347–48

Hidalgo, Miguel, xiii

Historia del derecho, xi, 2, 4–6, 11

Hobsbawm, Eric, 7, 13

Holloway, Thomas, 421

Hospital de Maternidad e Infancia (Mexico City), 156

Hospital Divino Salvador (Mexico City), 161

Hospital San Andrés (Mexico City), 157

Hospital San Hipólito (Mexico City), 161

Hospital San Juan de Dios (Mexico City), 157

House of Maternity (Mexico City), 157

Huamanga, 37

Huerta, Victoriano, 256

Identity: civic and social, 15, 172; collective, 233, 236, 252–53, 257–58; and culture, 1; formation, 2, 11; and gender, 65, 69; of judges, 99; national, xv–xvi, 228–29; and prostitution, 155, 168; and race, 12, 43; and spiritism, 190

Ignatieff, Michael, 9

Imperial Academy of Medicine (Brazil), 191

Inca Empire, 49

Independence: Latin American, xi–xiii, 3, 20–21, 23–24, 36, 57, 310, 345, 353; War of, 36, 49, 51

India, 8, 289

Indian. *See* Indigenous

Indigenismo, 5, 354

Indigenous, 347–48, 353–54, 360; in Argentina, 309, 316, 318, 322, 329, 331; and discrimination, x, 234; and identity, 12; law, 5, 11, 16, 18, 20, 419, 424; and legal discourse, 45–46; legal systems, 2, 11–12, 35–51; litigiousness, 7, 35–51; and obstetrics, 156; religion, 12, 191. *See also* Race

Ingenieros, José, 392–93

Ingram, Martin, 418

Inhibición, 102
Inquisition, 182–83
Inspección de Sanidad, 152
Inspector General de Policía (Mexico City), 248–49
Institute of Classification (Buenos Aires), 393, 395–96, 400, 402, 407
Institute of Criminology (Peru), 350
Institute of Criminology of Buenos Aires, 393, 407
Institute of Medical Sciences (Mexico City), 156
Instituto do Açucar e do Alcool (IAA) (Brazil), 116, 118–20, 122, 125–26, 128–35
Instituto Tutelar de Menores (Buenos Aires), 382
Intendencia, 37, 39, 41, 46
Intendencia-Provincias, 37, 39
International Fair of Paris, 161
Islas Marías penal island, 246–50
Italy, xiv–xv, 117, 220, 393

Jamaica: postemancipation, xviii, 19, 275–300; Penal Servitude Act, 288–89
Jamaican Assembly, 286
Jamaican General Inspector of Prisons, 277, 280, 285
Janet, Pierre, 193
Juárez, Benito, xiii
Judicial Committee of the Privy Council (Canada), 424–25
Justice of the Peace, 92, 96
Justo, Agustín P., 383, 385

Kardec, Allan, 186–87, 190–91, 195. See also Brazilian Spiritist Federation (FEB); Religion; Spiritism
Kellogg, Susan, 12
Kenya, 420
King's Bench, 418, 423
Kingston, 278, 282

Kingston and St. Andrews Girls' Reformatory, 290

La Paz, 37
La Plata, 225, 227
Labor, xi, 40; activists, 351; child, 372, 374, 377–78, 380–85; and class, 391, 397–99; and criminology, 409; discipline, 59; forced, 40, 43–44, 49, 246–50, 277, 279, 281, 288–91, 293–94, 348–49, 360; and gender, 371, 386, 400–401; history, 7; law, 415; markets, 9, 342, 421–22; and mechanization, 86, 105; and property rights, 118–20, 126–29; and protest, 120–26; and racism, 292; relations, 118–26, 129–34; rights, 18, 97, 124; and State intervention, 124–25; and sugar industry, 115–16; unions, 120, 122–23, 344, 355
Labor Ministry, 120–21
Ladies' Reformatory Association (Kingston), 290
Lampa Province, 43
Lancashire, 295
Land tenancy, 83, 89–91; in Brazil, 117, 126–29, 134; and eviction, 97–99, 102–3, 107, 120. See also Agrarian credit
Latin American Studies Association (LASA), xii
Law, ix, 1–3, 17; and access to legal system, 22; and anthropology, xv, 8; and class conflict, 8; and colonialism, 11; civil, 117; criminal, 183; and culture, 425–28; and discourse, 45; Spanish colonial, xii, 3–4, 23, 59, 66, 345; family, xviii, 59; history of, 3, 12, 20; and ideology, 24–25, 48; and indigenismo, 5; and legal cultures, 415–19; and legal institutions, 22; and medicine, 391; and morality, 64; and new social and cultural history, 17–19; and passion,

Law, (*continued*)
211–29; and patriarchy, 72; and popular culture, 24; postindependence, 4; and prostitution, 173; and rule, 14–17, 38; and social contestation, 13, 16, 18; and social inequality, 419–25; and witchcraft, 181, 188–91; and women, xvii. *See also* Crime; Historia del derecho; Legal system; Punishment

Law of Proceedings for the Justice of the Peace of 1887 (Argentina), 92

Lawyers, 13, 20, 22, 106, 194; and corporate privileges, 4; and credit disputes, 101–2; education of, xviii, 99–100; and judicial culture, 105; and land tenancy, 102; and reputation, 104; and witchcraft, 181, 188. *See also* Law; Legal system

Lazareto quarantine hospital (Buenos Aires), 223

League of Defense of Fallen Women (Mexico City), 172

Legal History. *See* Historia del derecho; New Legal History; Poststructuralist Legal Studies

Legal system, 161; of Brazil, 135; of Peru, 346; and social movements, 50; of colonial Spanish America, 35–36. *See also* Law; Lawyers

Leguía, Augusto B., 344, 349–52, 354–58, 361

León y León, Bernardino, 350, 357

Levene, Ricardo, 5–6

Levillier, Roberto, 369–70

Liberal Party, 200. *See also* Liberalism

Liberalism, xi–xiii, 17, 24, 189, 308–9, 312–13, 318, 424–25, 428; classic, 423; and conservatism, xiv; and criminology, xvi; and democracy, x; and gender, 72; as ideology, 57; and individualism, 60; "liberal republicanism," 313; and penal policy, 310–11, 315, 317,

333–34; and the press, 319–26, 334; and reform, 59; and Rosas, 332; and state violence, 327–30

Lima, 51, 342, 344–49, 353, 357, 360–61

Lima Barreto, Henriques, 195, 200–202, 204

Linebaugh, Peter, 8–9

Lohmann Villena, Guillermo, 6

Lombroso, Cesare, xiv–xvi, 192, 214, 243, 346, 392, 426

London, xii, 286, 301, 323

Macedo, Miguel, 243, 245

Macías, Ramón, 158

MacLachlan, Colin, 6

Macumba, 182. *See also* Religion

Madero, Francisco I., 242

Magic, 181, 183, 191, 194, 204

Magonistas, xiii

Manchioneal women's prison (Jamaica), 279

Marcos Paz Boy's Reform School (Buenos Aires), 381

Marianismo, 58–59

Marques, Xavier, 195–200, 202, 204

Marriage, 23, 58–59, 61–65, 73, 186, 201, 216, 220–21, 396–97, 419; abandonment, 66, 68; annulment of, 66; bigamy, 66; Breach of Promise, 59, 61, 63, 65, 67; polygamy, 40; secularization of, 66, 69, 72, 185; shotgun wedding (matrimonio a palos), 61, 63. *See also* Divorce; Separation of Bed and Board

Martín García Island, 223–24, 381

Marxism, 7, 11

Mata Linares, Benito de la, 51

Mazorca, 312–13, 319–20, 324–26, 331–32. *See also* "Assassins of 1840"

McGowen, Randall, 426

McNaughton Rules, 426

Medicine, 12, 18, 24–25, 181, 204, 344; abortion, 63, 161; and criminology, xvi, 426, 428; gynecology, 155–56, 158–60, 162, 171, 377; illegal practice of, 184; and law, xv, 383, 391; medical-legal state, xiv, 17, 24–25; obstetrics, 156–57, 159, 162, 171; and passion, 212–13, 215, 217, 222–23, 225, 228; and politics, xvi; and religion, 185–87; of sex, 171; social, 148, 165, 169; and witchcraft, 195, 202–3; and women, 156, 400. *See also* Curandeiro; Folk healing

Medina y Ormaechea, Antonio, 243–45

Mendes de Almeida, Cândido, 183

Mestizo, 16, 43, 156. *See also* Race

Methodist Church, 226. *See also* Christianity; Protestantism; Religion

Mexican Revolution, 159–60, 163, 165, 169, 173, 248, 256

Mexico, xiii–xvi, 6–7, 38, 147, 149, 151, 153, 155–56, 161, 164–65, 171, 174; 1871 penal code, 244, 248; 1894 penal code reform, 246; 1917 constitution, 148, 169, 245; 1929 penal code, 169, 249; and crime, 233–59. *See also* Mexico City; Mexican Revolution

Mexico City, 7, 18, 147, 150, 152–54, 163–64, 166–68; and rateros, 233–59

Mill, John Stuart, 424

Ministry of Justice: Mexico, 245–46; Peru, 343, 353, 357; Argentina, 377, 385

Ministry of Public Instruction (Buenos Aires), 381

Modernity, x, 17, 229, 252, 343, 358–59

Modernization, x–xiii, xvi–xvii, 7, 149, 194, 255–56, 258, 349, 392

Monkkonen, Eric, 7

Monte de Piedad, 237

Montevideo, 383

Moral regeneration, 56, 58, 72

Morant Bay Rebellion, 286, 296, 299, 301

Morelos hospital, 149–50, 152, 157–60, 168, 172–73

Murilo de Carvalho, José, 184

Museo Social Argentino, 383

Nader, Laura, 12

Napoleonic wars, 418

National Archives (Argentina), 215

National Congress (Argentina), 105

National Department of Hygiene (Argentina), 211, 223, 225

National Guard (Argentina), 324, 331

Nationalism, 11, 121, 124, 173

National Penitentiary (Buenos Aires), 211, 393

Neoliberalism, ix

New Cultural History, 10, 17

New Granada, 49

New Historicism, 10

New Legal History, xi, xviii

New Social History, 6–7, 17

Nina Rodrigues, Raimundo, 192–94, 196–97, 204

North America, 278, 280, 285, 297, 300, 349; historians, 6–8; and positivist criminology, xv; and poststructuralism, 9–10

O'Brian, Patricia, 9

Obregón, Alvaro, 257

Office of Administrative Control of the National Department of Hygiene (Argentina), 223

O'Gorman, Camila, 324, 334

Olmos Prison (Buenos Aires), 401

Ordenanzas, 4

Order of the Good Shepherd, 370, 384–85

Ortiz Rubio, Pascual, 253

Ots y Capdequí, José María, 6

Pacheco, Joaquín Francisco, 212, 222
Palacio, Juan Manuel, 420, 423
Pampas, 83–87, 89–90, 95, 97, 105–7
Paris, 213, 323
Partido Social Democrático (Brazil), 136
Passion, 211, 228–29, 285; and crime, 316; and criminal responsibility, 221–23; and honor, 215–20; and law, 213–14; and nervous disorders, 223–25; and women, 212
Patagonia, 90
Paternity, 63–65, 67–68
Patria potestas, 59–61, 64, 375
Patriarchy, xi, xiii, 68, 72, 217; and civil code, 57; and family morality, 61; and nationalism, 58–59; and patria potestas, 60
Patriotic Battalions, 201
Patronato de la Raza Indígena (Peru), 354
Patronato de Liberados (Buenos Aires), 393
Patronato de Menores (Buenos Aires), 382, 384
Patronato Nacional de Menores (Argentina), 383, 385
Pax Rosista, 327
"Peace of Wheat," 91, 106–7
Peixoto, Floriano, 201–2
Pellegrini, Carlos, 373
Penal institutions, x, 1, 6, 8, 17, 19, 183, 217, 219, 237, 416; and capital punishment, 312, 330; and children, 369–87, 421; and criminology, 391–94; and gender, 401, 403, 409; and impact on populations, xviii, 24–25; and labor, 398–99; and literacy, 405–7; and markets, 422; penal colonies, 245–50; policy and reform, 275–79, 281–82, 284, 287, 289–91, 293–95, 300, 342, 344–62; and prostitution, 173; and sex offenders, 72. See also Prison reform; Punishment
Penitenciaría de Buenos Aires, 330
Pereira, Baptista, 187–88
Pernambuco, 120, 135
Perón, Eva, 386–87. See also Peronism
Perón, Juan Domingo, 107, 386, 407. See also Peronism
Peronism, 106–7, 387, 407–8
Peru, xiii–xiv, 6–7, 12, 18, 35–51, 296, 342–62, 425; 1924 penal code, 347
Philadelphia penitentiary, 278
Philippine Code, 183
Police, x, 7, 14, 130, 240, 247, 259, 275, 317, 373–74, 420–21; in Brazil, 190–92, 194, 196, 200, 202; institutions, 257–58; and Morelos hospital, 158; persecution, 131, 254; and prostitution, 152–53, 167–68; and slave rebellions, 183; and violence, ix
Populism, xvi, 17, 416
Porfiriato, xv, 148, 153–54, 160, 164, 171, 234, 237, 244, 256–57, 259
Portugal, 117, 182, 421
Positivism, xi–xii, xiv–xvii, 17, 21, 23, 58, 189, 194, 196, 213–14, 249, 344, 370, 391–93, 395, 408. See also Criminology
Poststructuralism, 9–12
Poststructuralist legal studies, 8
Prison Commission (Great Britain), 281
Prison reform: Argentina, 330–31, 370–71, 392, 398, 409; Canada, 423; Peru, 342, 344–52, 357–61; postemancipation Jamaica, 275–82, 287, 300. See also Penal institutions
Prisons. See Penal institutions
Progress, 23, 229; and Argentina, xvii, 85, 329; and order, 56–57, 59; and women, 72
Prophylaxis of Syphilis in the Depart-

ment of Public Health, 147, 164. *See also* Sexually transmitted diseases

Prostitution, 12, 18, 66, 148, 157, 174, 257, 369, 372, 403; and discrimination, ix; and hospital riots, 159, 162–63; regulation of, 149–55, 165–69, 173; and sexual science, 161; and sexually transmitted diseases, xvi, 147, 149, 170–72; and subjectivity, 173

Protector de Indios, 6, 35, 39, 45

Protestantism, 427. *See also* Anglican Church; Christianity; Methodist Church; Religion

Public health: and sex, 148, 154; and sexually transmitted diseases, 151, 158, 163, 165–66, 169–71; and the state, 149, 174, 184, 187, 189–91

Public Welfare System (Mexico), 156–57

Puerto Rico, 296

Pumacahua Rebellion, 50

Punishment, ix, xviii, 1–3, 9, 19, 25, 46, 211, 213, 217, 275; corporal, 276, 281–88, 290–91, 293–96, 299–301, 323, 350, 418, 421; for estupro, 71–72; and indigenous communities, 12; history of, 12; modern and premodern, xvii; and passion, 219, 222; and thieves, 245–50, 253–59. *See also* Capital punishment; Penal institutions

Quechua, 36–37, 39, 43

Quincey, Thomas de, 255

Race, x–xi, 2, 16, 46, 211, 276–77, 288, 295–97, 421, 428; and access to legal system, 23; and class, 196; and criminal anthropology, xv; and discrimination, ix; and identity, 12; and legal systems, 36; and racism, 46, 196, 202, 284–85, 291–92, 295–97, 299, 428; and sexually transmitted disease, 151;

and women, 197. *See also* Indigenous; Mestizo

Ramón civil law, 117

Ramos, Angélica, 348–49, 357, 361

Ramos Mejía, José María, 225–26

Ramos Pedrueza, Antonio, 249

Rape: *See* Sex crimes

Real Audiencia, 37, 39, 46

Reglamento de Cárceles (Peru), 345

Reglamento de Tribunales y Juzgados (Peru), 346

Republicanism, 324, 326–27, 329, 345, 354

Rateros, 18; and class, 244; definitions of, 233–34, 248, 250–52, 258–59; and identity, 252–53; perceptions of, 236, 239, 241–43; and police campaigns, 247, 254–56; and street commerce, 237

Real Tribunal del Protomedicato (Mexico), 156

Recopilación de las Leyes de Indias, 3

Reglamento de Prostitución en México, 150

Reis, João, J., 12

Religion, 25, 40, 188–90, 193–95; and healing, 182, 185–87, 191, 200, 203; and penal institutions, 279–81. *See also* Candomblé; Catholicism; Christianity; Macumba; Protestantism; Spiritism; Umbanda

Reparto, 40

Republicanism, 17, 36, 51, 59, 73, 184–85, 191, 196, 200

Reyes, Antonio, 314, 320, 325

Ribeiro, Leonídio, 190

Riera Aguinagalde, Andrés Manuel, 58–59, 68, 73

Rio, João do, 195

Rio de Janeiro, 182, 188, 195; and Barreto, Lima, 200–202; and engineering school, 196; and factory workers, 133;

Rio de Janeiro, (*continued*)
and IAA, 126, 131–32; and international child rights congress, 383; and physicians, 184, 192; and policing, 421; and popular Catholicism, 185; and public health, 189–90; and spiritism, 187, 191; state, 113–14, 120, 135–36

Rivera Indarte, José, 325

Rodríguez, José María, 156

Roll, Jordan, Roll, 6

Rosas, Juan Manuel de, 308–21, 324–34, 418–19, 426–27

Rothman, David, 9

Roumagnac, Carlos, 161, 252

Royal Commentaries of the Incas and General History of Peru, 36

Ruelas, José, 154

Sáenz Quesada, María, 320, 323

Salvador de Bahia, 120, 182, 185, 190–91, 193, 196–97, 199–200, 204

Salvarsan, 159, 165, 170, 173. *See also* Sexually transmitted diseases

Sánchez Cerro, Luis M., 356

Sánchez Santos, Trinidad, 244

Sanitary Police (Mexico), 149–50, 153–54, 157, 160, 165–66, 168–70, 173

San Lázaro penitentiary (Mexico), 245

San Lorenzo Penal Island (Peru), 356

San Martín, José de, 345

Santa, 154

Santiago de Chile, 383

Santiago-Valles, Kelvin, 296

Santos Lugares, 315, 325

Sarmiento, Domingo Faustino, 316, 325, 329

School of Medicine (Mexico City), 156, 160

Schwartz, Stuart, 6

Scott, James, 355

Separation of Bed and Board, 66–69. *See also* Divorce; Marriage

Sesmarias, 117

Sex, 62, 161, 186; behavior, 149–50, 161, 170–71, 283, 285, 403, 409; and commerce, 152, 155, 166–68; medicine of, 169, 171; and public health, 148, 174; sexuality, xi, 12, 149, 151, 154, 157, 160, 162, 164–65, 168, 170–72, 278, 284, 286, 349–50; sexual science, 149–50, 155–64, 171; and technology, 157. *See also* Abuse; Sex crimes; Sexually transmitted disease

Sex crimes, 59, 69, 72, 170, 354; estupro and rape, 70–71, 161–62, 283, 285–86, 316. *See also* Abuse; Sex; Sexually transmitted disease

Sexually transmitted disease, 147, 153–54, 157–58, 163, 170, 172–73, 402, 409; syphilis, 71, 147–51, 155, 158–59, 162–67, 169–72, 403, 409. *See also* Crime; Sex

Shaw, H. B., 285, 287, 293–94, 297

Sierra Chica Prison (Argentina), 399, 406

Siete Partidas, 3, 57, 66, 224

Sindicato dos Empregados Rurais, 120

Sindicato dos Trabalhadores Agrícolas e Pecuários de Campos, 120

Slavery, x, xvii, 7, 11, 13, 23, 120, 183–84, 193, 201, 275–78, 280–81, 284, 287, 289, 311, 348, 354, 421, 428

Social hygiene, 23

Sociedad de Beneficencia (Buenos Aires), 372, 374, 383–84, 387

Sociedad de Beneficencia de la Capital (Buenos Aires), 400

Sociedad de Patronato (Lima), 347

Sociedade Cooperativa Açucareira Fluminense, 122

Sociedad los Amigos del Preso (Lima), 348

Sociedad Patronato de la Infancia (Buenos Aires), 374

Sociedad Popular Restauradora. *See* Mazorca

Society of St. Vincent de Paul, 384, 387

Soldaderas, 165

Spain, xiv, 5–6, 20, 50, 225–26, 228, 311, 421; 1820 constitution, 345

Spierenburg, Pieter, 9

Spiritism, 181–82, 186–92, 194–95, 203. *See also* Brazilian Spiritist Federation (FEB); Kardec, Allan; Religion

St. George's Home and Reformatory for Boys (Jamaica), 289–90

Stern, Steve, 7

Stuart Statutes, 417

Structuralism, 11

Subaltern, 310, 329, 342, 358, 360, 402, 407; and access to legal system, 22–23, 36; alterity, 12; and law, 16–17, 21; politics, xi; resistance, xi, 14, 25, 49; and popular justice, 20; studies, 8, 11

Sucre, Juan Antonio, 64

Sugar industry: and class, 135; and foreign capital, 121; and labor, 113, 115, 120–26; and legislation, 116, 121, 124, 129–30, 132–34; and property rights, 118–20, 126–29; and protest, 122–23, 134; and state intervention, 114, 128

Superior Court of Justice (Venezuela), 67

Superior Sanitation Council (Mexico), 148, 152–53

Superior Tribunal of Justice (Argentina), 313, 330, 333

Supreme Court (Venezuela), 61, 68

Taussig, Michael, 174

Taylor, William, 7, 38

Tejedor, Carlos, 213

Tepito, 236, 241, 254

Thompson, E. P., 7–8

Tinterillos, 22

Tlatelolco, 241

Torture, ix, 357, 359

Tribunal de la Acordada (Mexico), 6

Tudor Statutes, 417

Tupac Amaru II, 35–36, 42, 44

Tupac Amaru Rebellion, 35–37, 39, 41–43, 48–50

Umbanda, 191. *See also* Religion

United States, 277–78, 280, 315, 381, 408, 426–28; and culture, 255; and historiography, 6; and legal history, xviii; and medio-legal discourse, 24; and New Deal, 117; and positivist criminology, xiv

Unitarios, 311, 318–19, 326–29, 333

University of San Marcos (Lima), 347

Urbanization, 7, 234, 241

Urquiza, Justo J. de, 308–9, 320

Utilitarianism, xvii, 229

Valle Nacional Labor Colony (Mexico), 245–46

Vanderwood, Paul, 7

Van Young, Eric, 10

Vargas, Getúlio, 113–14, 116–17, 120, 122–23, 129–31, 134–36

Vega, Inca Garcilaso de la, 36

Venezuela, xiii, 18, 68, 73, 425; 1871 liberal civil code, 59; 1873 civil code, 56–57, 60–61, 72; 1873 civil marriage law, 66; 1873 penal code, 56–57, 70, 72; 1911 constitution, 57; Code of Criminal Procedure, 71; late colonial period, 65

Villavicencio, Víctor M., 350, 359

Violación. *See* Sex crimes

Viotti da Costa, Emilia, xiv, 424

Virgin Mary, 58–59, 73

Viveiros de Castro, José Francisco, 189

Warwick School, 6

West India Prisons Act, 277

West Indies, 275, 277

Witchcraft, 181–85, 188–91, 194, 196–97, 199–204

Wolf, Eric, xii

Women, 298; and abuse, 71; and access to legal system, 23; and citizenship, 58; and class, 201–2; and crime, 250, 312, 316–17, 322, 324, 333–34; discourse on, 162, 174, 198; and discrimination, ix, 61; and divorce, 68; and gender ideology, 73, 160; and honor, 428; and hospital riots, 159, 162–63; and labor, 399; and law, xvii, 11; legal status of, 57, 59, 65, 69, 72, 419, 424–25; and literacy, 406–7; and morality, 64–65; and "moral regeneration," 56; and motherhood, 400–401; and passion, 212, 217–18, 220–22, 225–27; and patria potestas, 60; and penal institutions, 348, 359, 369–87; and penal policy, 278–79, 286–87, 290; and pregnancy, 62–64; and prostitution, 150–55, 172–73; and race, 197; and Sanitary Police, 166; and science, 155–56, 171; and sex crimes, 70–72; sexual control of, 73, 150, 168; and sexually transmitted disease, 157, 161, 172; and sexual practices, 403–4; and Zapatistas, 257. *See also* Gender

Women Without Homes, 173

World War I, 288, 380

Xangô, 182

Yoruba, 182, 199

Yrigoyen, Hipólito, 381

Yucatán, 246, 248

Zapatistas, 256–57

Zárate Campos, María Soledad, 370

Zavala, Silvio, 6

Zeballos, Estanislao Severo, 4, 229

Zorraquín Becú, Ricardo, 6

Library of Congress Cataloging-in-Publication Data
Crime and punishment in Latin America : law and society
since late colonial times / edited by Ricardo D. Salvatore,
Carlos Aguirre, and Gilbert M. Joseph.
p. cm.
Includes index.
ISBN 0-8223-2734-1 (cloth : alk. paper)
ISBN 0-8223-2744-9 (pbk. : alk. paper)
1. Crime — Latin America — History.
2. Justice, Administration of — Latin America — History.
3. Punishment — Latin America — History.
I. Salvatore, Ricardo D.   II. Aguirre, Carlos.
III. Joseph, G. M. (Gilbert Michael).
HV6810.5 .C745 2001
364.98–dc21   2001023935